THE RUGG SOCIAL SCIENCE COURSE

THE READING BOOKS

VOLUME I · An Introduction to American Civilization
VOLUME II · Changing Civilizations in the Modern World
VOLUME III · A History of American Civilization: Economic and Social
VOLUME IV · A History of American Government and Culture
VOLUME V · An Introduction to Problems of American Culture
VOLUME VI · Changing Governments and Changing Cultures

THE WORKBOOKS

VOLUME I · Pupil's Workbook of Directed Study to accompany *An Introduction to American Civilization*
VOLUME II · Pupil's Workbook of Directed Study to accompany *Changing Civilizations in the Modern World*
VOLUME III · Pupil's Workbook of Directed Study to accompany *A History of American Civilization: Economic and Social*
VOLUME IV · Pupil's Workbook of Directed Study to accompany *A History of American Government and Culture*
VOLUME V · Pupil's Workbook of Directed Study to accompany *An Introduction to Problems of American Culture*
VOLUME VI · Pupil's Workbook of Directed Study to accompany *Changing Governments and Changing Cultures*

THE TEACHER'S GUIDES

VOLUME I · Teacher's Guide for *An Introduction to American Civilization*
VOLUME II · Teacher's Guide for *Changing Civilizations in the Modern World*
VOLUME III · Teacher's Guide for *A History of American Civilization: Economic and Social*
VOLUME IV · Teacher's Guide for *A History of American Government and Culture*
VOLUME V · Teacher's Guide for *An Introduction to Problems of American Culture*
VOLUME VI · Teacher's Guide for *Changing Governments and Changing Cultures*

A HISTORY OF AMERICAN GOVERNMENT AND CULTURE

America's March toward Democracy

BY

HAROLD RUGG

PROFESSOR OF EDUCATION, TEACHERS COLLEGE
COLUMBIA UNIVERSITY

GINN AND COMPANY
BOSTON · NEW YORK · CHICAGO · LONDON
ATLANTA · DALLAS · COLUMBUS · SAN FRANCISCO

COPYRIGHT, 1931, BY HAROLD RUGG
ALL RIGHTS RESERVED
PRINTED IN THE UNITED STATES OF AMERICA
431.12

The Athenæum Press
GINN AND COMPANY · PRO-
PRIETORS · BOSTON · U.S.A.

PREFACE

A History of American Government and Culture is the fourth volume of the Rugg Social-Science Course. It should also be regarded as the second of a two-volume history of American civilization, the first of which was the third book of the series, *A History of American Civilization: Economic and Social*. Together the two volumes comprise a comprehensive history of the United States in its geographic setting. Whereas the preceding volume dealt with the land, and with industrial and commercial history and their effect upon American society, this present one deals with government and other aspects of cultural history.

The two volumes have been prepared to help young Americans understand the chief modes of living in their own country. The problems arising from these modes of living are presented, in their historical and geographic setting, in the form of thought-provoking activities in the *Pupil's Workbooks of Directed Study*. To be most effective the *Reading Books* and the *Workbooks* should be used in conjunction with each other.

What is this Course in Social Science?

These textbooks with their accompanying *Workbooks* will introduce young Americans to world civilizations and their historical development. The first volume, *An Introduction to American Civilization*, is devoted chiefly to a study of economic life in the United States today. The second volume, *Changing Civilizations in the Modern World*, introduces the pupil to life in other lands. It considers especially the great industrial nations, the changing agricultural countries, and the interrelation of the two. The third and fourth volumes, as stated, present the historical development and geographic setting of the United States. Accompanying each is a corresponding *Pupil's Workbook of Directed Study*.

The fifth volume, *An Introduction to Problems of American Culture*, will deal with the life of the individual in the communities of our changing American civilization. The sixth volume, *Changing Governments and Changing Cultures*, will deal with the life of the individual in other civilizations. Thus Volume V rounds out the material of Volume I, and Volume VI of Volume II. The six volumes taken together attempt a comprehensive introduction to modes of living in the modern world.

The Importance of introducing Youth to an Understanding of Contemporary Civilization

The author firmly believes that young Americans can be given an appreciation of the significant contemporary problems of living together. Current conditions in America throw into sharp relief the critical need of teaching our youth to understand American life and its relation to the modern world. Our schools are confronted with the difficult task of educating pupils to become informed, thinking citizens. During the past 150 years the rapid development of industrial civilization has produced problems of living together that baffle even the keenest adult minds.

It is of the utmost importance that schools bend every effort to introduce our young people to the chief conditions and problems which will confront them as citizens of the world. That is the essential purpose of this new unified course in the social studies.

The Materials are based upon the Findings of Specialists

The foundation of this new course is a series of studies of the basic modes of living and the problems of modern life, the great movements through which institutions and problems have evolved, and the chief concepts and principles which, as history has proved, lie at the roots of living together.

Who knows best what these great institutions, problems, and trends are? Specialists on the frontier of thought who see society from a height, who detect its trends and the long-time movement of its affairs. From the mature thought of established students of modern life and its historical development, therefore, instead of from the single judgments of the textbook-maker, the skeleton of this course has been designed. It is based upon nine years of investigational work. In that time thirteen research studies of what to teach have been made.¹

A Unified Course in Social Science

Why one general course rather than the separate subjects of history, geography, and civics? Because the chief aim is to understand modern life and how it came to be. To understand any institution or condition of life today the mind must utilize facts, meanings, generalizations, and historical movements that in the past have been set up in separate school subjects. For example, to understand the westward movement of the American people one must see in close relationship the tide of immigration across the continent; the blazing of trails; the evolution of new land and waterways; the rapid development of new types of transportation; constantly changing forms of social life; the rise of cities behind the advancing frontier; the influence of mountains, deserts, climate, rivers, and soil upon travel, transportation, and communication; and where and how people live. All these factors must be tied closely together in their natural relationships. Hence the necessity of combining them into one general course instead of teaching them as separate subjects. In constructing this course one question has constantly been in the foreground: What facts, historical movements, meanings, and principles do young people need to study together to understand the modern world?

In *A History of American Government and Culture* and the other volumes of this series, historical, geographic, economic, and other materials are studied *in close relationship*. Whenever history is needed to understand the present, history is presented. If geographic relationships are needed to throw light upon contemporary problems, those geographic relationships are incorporated. The same thing has been done with economic and social facts and principles.

[1] See Harold Rugg's *American Civilization and the Curriculum of the Social Sciences* (Bureau of Publications, Teachers College, Columbia University), John A. Hockett's *The Determination of the Major Social Problems of American Life* (Bureau of Publications, Teachers College, Columbia University), and Harold Rugg and John A. Hockett's *Objective Studies in Map Location* (Bureau of Publications, Teachers College, Columbia University).

This has *not* caused a reduction in the amount of history or of geography included in the course. Rather, it has produced a sharp increase in the amount of these subjects in the curriculum, and in addition has added to the curriculum a wealth of new material. Comparisons of the amount of history and geography in these six *Reading Books* with that of conventional textbooks in these subjects *should be based on a study of the total series and not on any one book.*

The Use of the Dramatic Episode

The readers of this book will encounter a second novel characteristic: *the frequent use of dramatic episodes.* If young people are to be brought to an understanding of our complicated civilization, it must be chiefly through the medium of words. Hence the imperative need of dramatizing the past and present story of the important modern civilizations and their relations to one another. In this course each topic is illustrated by vivid episodes and by a wealth of maps, graphs, and pictorial material far in excess of their present use in textbooks. The substitution of this vivid episodical treatment for the encyclopedic one which characterizes many of our current school histories and geographies has necessitated a marked increase in the volume of reading material.

"Learning by Doing": the *Pupil's Workbook* of *Directed Study*

The very center of this course in the social studies is the *Workbook*. The chief goal of the social studies is active and intelligent participation in American civilization and tolerant understanding of other civilizations. To guarantee the attainment of this goal the school must organize its work around a core of dynamic pupil activities. *Young people grow in understanding only by participating actively in the study of the society around them.* Even to the present day the work in the social studies has consisted too much of memoriter recitation from the contents of encyclopedic textbooks in history, geography, and civics.

The essence of this new course in social studies is a succession of pupil activities, dynamic and thought-provoking. Many optional suggestions for these activities have been incorporated in the *Workbook* and presented as a series of problems. Each problem of this course is an organized scheme of things for the pupil to do. Each unit compels him to find the answer to one or more important questions. The course, as presented in the *Workbook*, therefore, constantly confronts the pupil with stimulating problems, insight into each of which is important for an adequate understanding of the problems of the modern world. Hence the *Workbook* is the very core of the course, and the *Reading Book* has been constructed, unit by unit, in close conjunction with it.

PLANNED REPETITION

The fourth characteristic of this course is the carefully planned recurrence of important concepts, generalizations, and historical themes in varied settings. One of the weaknesses of current school courses in history, geography, and civics is lack of planned repetition. In the present course this defect has been remedied by designing a carefully planned scheme of repetition. In preparing each topic the outstanding concepts, generalizations, and themes that an educated mind should understand have been charted in advance. Episodes, narratives, statistical and graphic exhibits, pictures, and maps have been selected with the need for the illustration of these items clearly in mind. Hence the student will encounter the important meanings, principles, and movements over and over again, but constantly presented in new and varied settings.

HUNDREDS OF SCHOOLS HAVE COÖPERATED IN THE PREPARATION OF THIS COURSE, 1922–1929

How can one feel sure that this course is within the comprehension and ability of the pupil?

It has passed through three experimental editions — the first was used in mimeographed form, 1921–1922; the second consisted of printed books used in 1922–1923 in more than 100 school systems; the third consisted of completely reconstructed printed books (known as the *Social Science Pamphlets*) used in more than 300 school systems, 1923–1929.

This series of books could not have been developed successfully without the coöperation of a large number of public and private schools. In more than 40 states, hundreds of schools have purchased and tried out under our direction copies of the experimental editions. Over 600,000 copies of the pamphlets were used by pupils from 1922 to 1929.

Furthermore, this present book has been written with a much simpler vocabulary than was used even in the third experimental edition.

Every kind of community in the United States — small towns, medium-sized cities, large cities — has made experimental use of these books. More than 50,000 tests taken by pupils have been returned to us for examination. The judgments of more than 1000 teachers have been obtained, concerning needed revisions. Many round-table conferences have been held with small groups of teachers using the experimental editions. The theory of the course has been discussed with hundreds of audiences in the past seven years. Debates have been held with specialists in history and geography. Furthermore, careful measurements have proved that several thousand pupils studying the experimental edition achieved a markedly superior understanding of modern life and a distinctly higher ability in thinking about it than a group of 1500 pupils who had studied under similar conditions the conventional history-geography-civics courses.

The Course is based upon an Elaborate Program of Research [1]

Twenty-two thorough investigations have been made dealing with the following topics:
1. Thirteen studies of what to teach of the problems of contemporary life, of the chief trends of civilization, and of the central concepts and principles which educated minds use in thinking about them.

[1] The entire nine years' investigational work is reported in a monograph entitled *American Civilization and the Curriculum of the Social Sciences* (Bureau of Publications, Teachers College, Columbia University). It will also be summarized in *The Psychology and Teaching of the Social Studies* (in preparation). Of the studies upon which this course is based the following have already been published: C. O. Matthews, *Grade Placement of Curriculum Materials in the Social Studies* (Bureau of Publications, Teachers College,

PREFACE   xi

2. Three scientific studies of grade placement of curriculum materials and of the development of pupil's abilities.
3. Six studies of learning and of the organization of curriculum materials. These have also contributed to the arrangement of the material in this course.

The Need for a Large Allotment of Time for the Social Studies

Finally, no adequate course in the social studies can be developed successfully in the time now allotted to it in most public and private schools. Our elaborate program of research and our seven years of work with experimental editions prove conclusively that *more* than 60 minutes of daily class time must be devoted to the social studies in order that young people may obtain even a partial understanding of modern civilization. The social-studies course should be the intellectual core of the school curriculum. It is earnestly hoped that schools will provide adequately for this central core by allotting to it a large amount of time.

An Important Caution about Accuracy in using Facts

In this book there are many statements of fact which are necessary for an understanding of the history of our country and its relations to other nations. We have tried to make sure that the facts are stated accurately. One difficulty has been encountered, however: that even the most reliable sources from which the statistics and other facts have been selected do not always agree. It was necessary, therefore, to choose among them those statements which appear to us to be most accurate.

The reader will note the frequent use of round numbers in statements of number of inhabitants, distances, areas, etc. In

Columbia University); Harold Rugg and John A. Hockett, *Objective Studies in Map Location* (Bureau of Publications, Teachers College, Columbia University); Hyman Meltzer, *Children's Social Concepts* (Bureau of Publications, Teachers College, Columbia University); Earle Rugg, *Studies in Curriculum Construction in the Social Studies* (State Teachers College, Greeley, Colorado); "The Social Studies in the Elementary and Secondary School," Part II of the Twenty-second Yearbook of the National Society for the Study of Education (Public School Publishing Company); Neal Billings, *A Determination of Generalizations Basic to the Social Science Curriculum* (Bureau of Publications, Teachers College, Columbia University).

most cases it is not important to remember the exact figures; it *is* important, however, to obtain a correct impression from the use of the facts. Hence approximate numbers and estimates have been frequently used. The student should constantly ask himself, How reliable are these facts? He should learn that in the past 100 years the scientific way of doing things has made our records more and more accurate. Nevertheless, much improvement in this matter is still needed. In spite of great care in checking the facts that have been given, the reader may find instances in which correction should be made.

In Acknowledgment

This enterprise could not have been developed without the coöperative support and friendly and critical advice of many persons. First, there are several thousand progressive administrators and teachers who contributed criticisms and suggestions. From 1922 to 1929 inclusive these educational leaders gave unsparingly of their energy to the experimental trial of the tentative editions of these books. By their courage and vision in utilizing novel materials in the social sciences, they have put the children of American schools as well as myself in their debt.

Second, there is the administration of Teachers College, Columbia University, and of the Lincoln School. The American children who will use these materials owe a debt of gratitude to the deans of Teachers College and the directors of the Lincoln School for permitting and encouraging the development of this course by experimental methods.

I have acknowledged with pleasure in the body of the text many instances of coöperation from publishers who permitted quotations from their publications and the reproduction of illustrative materials. Almost without exception requests for coöperation of this character have been cordially granted.

Without the unfailing encouragement of my friends John R. Clark, Marshall Dunn, George Nugent, R. P. Nugent, Jr., and Jesse H. Newlon, it would often have been difficult to carry on.

I have listed on a following page the names of the members of the research and editorial staff who contributed studies and materials to the various editions of these books. In the preparation of this edition, however, several of my associates have given such conspicuous and loyal assistance that I wish to acknowledge their contribution more specifically. First, Gertrude M. White, who has carried the burden of office management during the past five years; second, Joan Walker Coyne, who gave unsparingly of her time and energy to the reconstruction of *A History of American Civilization* and *A History of American Government and Culture*; third, my colleague James E. Mendenhall, collaborator in the preparation of the *Pupil's Workbooks of Directed Study* and *Teacher's Guides*; fourth, to Frances M. Foster special acknowledgment is due for valuable editorial services from 1923 to 1927 inclusive and from 1928 to date. The present form of *Reading Books*, *Workbooks*, and *Teacher's Guides* owes more than I can measure to her editorial insight and constant labor. Finally, I wish to acknowledge Louise Krueger's special service in the editing of Volumes III and IV.

This statement of my indebtedness should not be permitted to close without referring to the unsparing efforts of the staff of Ginn and Company to produce a practicable, attractive, and teachable body of materials. But especially I wish to express my appreciation for the encouragement and support given by Messrs. Charles H. Thurber, Henry H. Hilton, and Burdette R. Buckingham.

HAROLD RUGG

NEW YORK

The following research and editorial staff contributed studies or materials utilized in the various editions of this series of books.

THE FIRST EXPERIMENTAL EDITION
1921–1923

PREPARED BY

HAROLD RUGG

WITH THE ASSISTANCE OF

EARLE RUGG
EMMA SCHWEPPE
MARIE GULBRANSEN

THE SECOND EXPERIMENTAL EDITION
1923–1926

PREPARED BY THE COLLABORATION OF

HAROLD RUGG
ELIZABETH G. WOODS
EMMA SCHWEPPE
JOHN A. HOCKETT

RESEARCH ASSOCIATES

JAMES E. MENDENHALL, 1926–1931
EARLE RUGG, 1921–1923
JOHN A. HOCKETT, 1924–1927
JOHN N. WASHBURNE, 1923–1926
H. MELTZER, 1924–1925
C. O. MATHEWS, 1925–1927
B. R. SHOWALTER, 1924–1925
NEAL BILLINGS, 1924–1927, 1928
HELEN M. LYND, 1926–1927
LAURANCE F. SHAFFER, 1926–1928, 1928–1929

EDITORIAL AND RESEARCH ASSISTANTS

FRANCES M. FOSTER, 1923–1927, 1928–1931
ETHELWYN M. MENDENHALL, 1926–1928
FRANCES YOUTZ, 1927–1929
ELIZABETH MOREY, 1927–1928
JOAN WALKER COYNE, 1929–1930
LOUISE KRUEGER, 1929–1931

CONTENTS

UNIT I

AMERICA'S FIRST STEPS TOWARD DEMOCRACY

CHAPTER	PAGE
I. Introducing the Study of Government	3
II. How the Early Colonies were Governed	16
III. The Later Struggle within the Colonies for Democratic Government	30

UNIT II

THE STRUGGLE FOR SELF-GOVERNMENT, 1660–1783

IV. The Beginning of the Struggle with England for Independent Government, 1660–1760	51
V. The Climax of the Struggle, 1760–1776	64
VI. The War for American Independence, 1776–1783	93

UNIT III

THE MAKING OF THE AMERICAN CONSTITUTION

VII. The Making of the American Constitution, 1783–1787	121

UNIT IV

THE FIRST YEARS OF NATIONAL GOVERNMENT

VIII. The National Government under Hamilton and the Federalists	151
IX. Did Democracy March Forward under the Republicans?	176
X. Manners and Customs during the First 40 Years of the Republic	203

UNIT V

JACKSONIAN DEMOCRACY AND ITS EFFECT UPON AMERICAN CULTURE

CHAPTER	PAGE
XI. The "Reign of Andrew Jackson"	223
XII. The Culture of the Middle West and of the Northern Seaboard, 1830–1860	244
XIII. Life in the Cotton Kingdom, 1830–1860	268

UNIT VI

THE GREAT CONFLICT: ONE UNITED NATION OR TWO

XIV. The Controversy over Slavery	283
XV. Political Parties and Presidents, 1837–1861	307
XVI. The Civil War	322
XVII. The Reconstruction Period of the South	357

UNIT VII

THE STRUGGLE OVER GOVERNMENT IN THE AGE OF BIG BUSINESS, 1865–1914

XVIII. Government by Professional Politicians	373
XIX. The Rise of Government by Business	387
XX. The Political Revolt of Farmers and City Workers	397
XXI. The Common People March toward Democracy	416
XXII. American Government Extends Abroad	432

UNIT VIII

THE RED MAN AND THE WHITE MAN'S GOVERNMENT

XXIII. The Red Man and the White Man's Government	449

UNIT IX

THE CHANGING CULTURE OF THE AMERICAN PEOPLE

CHAPTER		PAGE
XXIV.	POPULAR EDUCATION AND THE MARCH TOWARD DEMOCRACY	473
XXV.	THE SOCIAL LIFE OF HOMESTEAD, VILLAGE, AND CITY, 1865–1900	493
XXVI.	AMERICAN SPORTS	516
XXVII.	THE "LIVELY ARTS"	531

UNIT X

THE UNITED STATES AFTER 1914: CURRENT PROBLEMS

XXVIII.	AMERICA AND THE WORLD WAR	549
XXIX.	THE UNITED STATES SINCE THE WORLD WAR: FACING THE PROBLEMS OF DEMOCRACY	569
APPENDIX		597
INDEX		619

A HISTORY OF AMERICAN GOVERNMENT
AND CULTURE

UNIT I

AMERICA'S FIRST STEPS TOWARD DEMOCRACY

CHAPTER I

INTRODUCING THE STUDY OF GOVERNMENT

"What do you think is the best way to learn the meaning of democracy and self-government?" The Social Science Club of the George Washington Junior High School was holding its weekly meeting. Mr. Harris, the teacher, had opened the discussion with this question.

"Government! Democracy!" cried Henry Tildsley, the star debater of the club. "If we are really going to learn the meaning of these things we have got to see them work. In fact, fellow members,"—Henry liked to put on the airs of the public speaker, —"in fact, what we ought to do is to practice democracy and government right here in this school. We ought to take a hand in running the George Washington Junior High School!"

When Henry talked like that everybody listened, even if he disagreed with him. Betty Warwick was one of the doubters. "Government!" she exclaimed. "What do we know about government or about running our school? We haven't even studied about the government of Middletown yet — or at least not much. How could we govern our school? Why —"

"How?" interrupted Henry. "Why, by just running it, with the advice of the principal and teachers, of course. How did Washington and Jefferson —" Henry was again putting on his best public-speaking airs — "How did Washington and Jefferson learn to run the government of the United States? By running it! The English government didn't think the Americans knew enough to run their affairs in 1789, but they did. Practice democracy right here, that's what I say. Then we'll be ready to study democratic government in America."

"Democratic government?" asked Ben Pillsbury, the president of the club, quietly. "What do you mean by democratic government?"

"I mean government in which everybody has a share. Abraham Lincoln said it all in his Gettysburg Address: 'Government of the people, by the people, for the people.' He really meant *all* the people, not just a few. I'm asking for self-government in this school exactly as Patrick Henry and Thomas Jefferson asked for it for the thirteen colonies in 1775."

There was a lull in the club's discussion. Mr. Harris, sitting on the outside of the circle, nodded approvingly, thinking that Henry's remarks had started the club's study of American government very well indeed.

Just then John Rogers rose and raised a question which turned everybody's attention in a new direction. "Aren't we taking it for granted," he asked, "that we must have a government? Why do we need a government, either in this school or in this town or for that matter in the country as a whole?"

"No government at all?" exclaimed Elizabeth Staunton. "Why isn't that what we call anarchy? Without a government it seems to me that everyone would try to do as he pleased. Nothing at all could be done without a government. Everything would be all mixed up."

The president of the club looked at the teacher. "How about that, Mr. Harris?" he asked.

Mr. Harris said he would like to ask John a few questions. "Let us suppose, John, that we had no government in Middletown — no mayor, no policemen, firemen, water department, or health officers. Suppose that while your family was away over the week-end a fire broke out in your house. Who would put it out?"

"Why, the neighbors, of course," answered John.

"Well, what would they use to put the fire out? Would they have a steam engine, hose, and ladders all ready in their basements?"

"Why, no, they would use the city apparatus."

"Yes," cried Henry Tildsley quickly. "But now you've answered your own question. There wouldn't be any city apparatus if there were no city government to buy it."

There was a chorus of assent from the club.

"Do you mean that it is the city government that buys the fire apparatus, and —"

INTRODUCING THE STUDY OF GOVERNMENT 5

"Yes, and it hires the firemen. It also hires the policemen, the judges of the police court, the street-cleaners, the health officers, and all the other public officials who keep the town running smoothly."

Mary Reed timidly offered another illustration. "Don't you remember the awful jam we got into down in the square the other night when John Nolan, the traffic policeman, was helping that old man into the ambulance? There must have been fifteen automobiles tangled up. Everybody wanted the right of way. Nobody would give way to the others. When the officer came back everybody did as he said, and in less than a minute the traffic jam was all straightened out."

"Yes," said Mr. Harris. "That's an excellent illustration of the way 'government' keeps things running smoothly in a community. It works the same way in the state or in the nation as a whole."

"Here's a fine example of it," added George Thomas, holding up the morning newspaper, which he had taken from the table. There, blazing across the top in tall headlines, the club read:

> ## Strikers Riot in Franklin
> GOVERNOR TO CALL OUT STATE TROOPS TO ESTABLISH ORDER
>
> Martial Law to be Declared

"Yes, and don't forget the headlines we have in last year's scrapbook about the Mississippi flood." Helen soon had it out and held it up for the club to see:

> ## GREAT DISASTER
> Mississippi Floods Country
>
> DISORDER REIGNS AS LEVEES BREAK
>
> Government sends Troops to aid in Rescuing Marooned People

"Excellent," said Mr. Harris. "Whenever a disaster sweeps over a community, a state, or a country, then the government steps in. But don't think that the government carries on its work merely in times of disaster or emergency. Continually, behind the scenes, the government of the community or of the country is managing *group affairs*. And because we depend so much upon one another, its task is especially important. Don't you think a complicated civilization like ours should have an orderly way of keeping things going? It is the government that does that."

Just to illustrate his point about the many things which the government does, Mr. Harris now held up a copy of a weekly magazine. "These cartoons," said he, pointing to a page of the magazine, "illustrate some of the problems which the local, state, or national government has to handle for all of us. This one [figure 1] reminds us that there is a problem of providing for good schools as well as the problems of providing warships and soldiers for the defense of the country. Here is one [figure 2] which suggests a difficulty faced by the national government when it passes a high tariff law. This one [figure 3] deals with an old, old problem — the conflict between the rights of state governments and the rights of national government. Of course these are only a few of the many problems of government."

FIG. 1. In the picture Uncle Sam is building battleships. The child is asking, "What about schools, Uncle Sam?" Education is one of the problems of government. (Courtesy of the *New York Evening Post*)

The club gathered around and studied the cartoons. "I understand that one about schools," said John Rogers, "but the other two mean nothing to me."

"Exactly," said Mr. Harris. "They may be puzzles to you now. But they will not be at the end of this year, when we finish our study of the history of government. In your discussion this morning you have already brought out many topics which the Social Science Club is to study this year. Let us see if you can name the chief ones. Ben, will you write the topics on the board?"

The club eagerly entered into the work of making this list, and the members, as well as Mr. Harris, were pleased and not a little surprised at the length of it.

In the study of American government in which you are about to engage, your class may be thought of as a Social Science Club like the one at the George Washington Junior High School. You will have your discussions and your differences of opinion. You will, no doubt, debate with each other just as, you may be sure, Henry and Betty, John and Elizabeth, often argued their points of view. At the close of your discussions it is to be hoped that you will summarize what has been said in your class even as these boys and girls did in the account you have just read.

FIG. 2. This picture represents the results which some people think are brought about by high tariffs. Tariffs present one of the problems of government. (Courtesy of the Dallas *News*)

Moreover, since you have just been following their discussion, you can begin now by making, just as they did, a list of important problems of government.

In the three preceding books of this series [1] we centered our attention upon the economic and social life of people in the modern world. We studied how they produced food, shelter, and clothing,

---

[1] Harold Rugg, *An Introduction to American Civilization, Changing Civilizations in the Modern World*, and *A History of American Civilization: Economic and Social*. Ginn and Company, Boston, 1929–1930.

and how they provided means of transportation, communication, and exchange. We also had brief glimpses of the social life of the people on the frontier, in early colonial homes, in the manufacturing towns and cities of the North, on the cotton plantations of the South, and on the cattle ranges and in the mines of the West.

FIG. 3. This picture shows that the states still control child labor. Shall the Federal government make the laws for child workers? (Courtesy of the St. Louis *Star*)

Now we must study the government under which all these things went on.

As American civilization developed, a new American government evolved with it. In the first settlements, because the settlers were British, the government was British in plan. As life on the continent of North America changed the British emigrants into Americans, their government changed, too. It became a new thing, partly British but essentially American. Decade by decade it changed, especially after the formation of the Constitution of the United States in 1787. Because it changed and is still changing, perhaps more rapidly than ever, we may call it an *experiment* in government.

The unusual setting which North America provided for the American experiment in government

In the three centuries between 1600 and 1900 the Americans were much freer than the people of Europe and Asia to *experiment* with government. The setting in which they developed their civilization and worked out their government was not duplicated anywhere else in the world. It was unique in at least three respects:

First, North America was isolated, remote from the wars and political quarrels of the European countries. During the first 200 years there were no steamships, telegraphs, or other means of rapid communication between Europe and America. Thus for the greater part of the time the Americans were left alone to work out their problems.

Second, for at least two centuries and a half there was a more widespread spirit of individual liberty in America than in the Old World of Europe and Asia. The chief factor in producing this spirit was the *frontier*. Until almost 1900 Americans always had a frontier — free land "out West" — ready for the taking. On this frontier men and women were forced to depend upon themselves. Thus a spirit of self-reliance, of initiative, of democracy, was preserved among the people. This frontier spirit of individual liberty played a most important part in changing the American government to fit the needs of the changing American civilization.

Third, the American colonists possessed another important advantage. They were largely British, and for several centuries vigorous leaders of the British people had been practicing self-government. Intelligent and rebellious leaders among the rising middle class had been steadily demanding and obtaining an increasing share in their government. Thus the colonial emigrants to North America brought with them not only courage and the spirit of independence but also some knowledge of government.

Therefore as we study the story of America's march toward democracy keep in mind the three unique conditions which made it possible: first, the remoteness of the vast virgin continent from European interference; second, the existence of the free frontier with its spirit of self-reliance and individual initiative; third, the tradition of increasing democracy inherited from British ancestors.

Thus the history of the American experiment in government is unlike that of any other country in the world. Some people think that the government that has grown out of that history is better than the governments of other countries. On the other hand, many leaders in other countries think that their governments are better than ours. That problem, however, is not one which we shall need to consider in this volume. Later you will be ready to draw your own conclusions concerning various plans of government.

First we must understand American government.

Government: National, State, and Local

Figure 4 tells you that the American people have found it necessary to set up three kinds of government:

I. A national government, which manages such things as
   1. Issuing money and establishing national banks.
   2. Maintaining postal service.
   3. Conducting affairs of state with foreign countries.
   4. Arranging matters of industry and trade *among* states and with foreign countries.
   5. Defending the country against foreign or native disturbers.
   6. Raising money for all these *national* things.
   7. Deciding who can vote in national elections and hold Federal offices.
II. A state government in each of the 48 states, which manages such things within each state as
   1. Education.
   2. All questions of property, industry, and trade.
   3. Decisions as to who can vote and hold office within the state.
   4. Legislation, that is, the making of criminal and civil laws.
III. Local governments in towns, cities, and counties. These vary greatly in different states, but in general they have charge, *within the local territory only and under the laws of the state*, of such things as
   1. Protecting lives and property through their departments of police, fire, health, streets, and the like.
   2. Education.
   3. Regulating trade, transportation, and other public utilities.

Government is simply the machinery by which people try to carry on their collective affairs. Without government it would be impossible for millions of interdependent people to live together. Everyone wants certain things. Since the wants of some people frequently conflict with the wants of others, there must be a government to arrange matters among them. Indeed, we shall

INTRODUCING THE STUDY OF GOVERNMENT

find that the history of government is really the history of the struggle of different groups to get some of the things they want.

Thus to keep collective affairs going smoothly in our vast and complicated country, the people have developed a vast and complicated government. Several million people are at work for it. This number includes a million teachers in elementary and secondary schools and colleges; more than 800,000 clerks, supervisors, and the like in the national, state, and local governments;

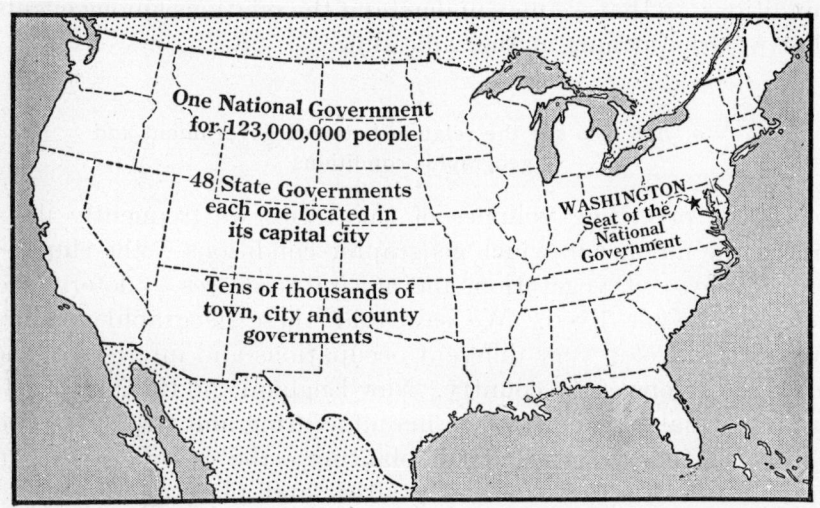

FIG. 4

hundreds of thousands of policemen, firemen, and health officers; hundreds of thousands of soldiers, sailors, airmen, engineers, and foresters; tens of thousands of mayors and councilmen; thousands of representatives, senators, judges, and their staffs.

Since the whole problem is too complicated for a single book, we shall study in this volume only the growth of government.

We must study government in close relation to ways of living in America

One important caution: Government did not develop in America apart from trade, from farming, from manufacturing, or from the recreations of the people. *These all developed together.* Really to understand how the American people lived in any one period of their history *we must see how all their activities were related* — the economic activities, the political activities, and the recreational activities.

It was impossible to deal with all phases of life at the same moment; so we took up the economic phase first. Now that we have studied that phase, we are ready to use our knowledge in studying political and cultural history. But in studying political and cultural history we shall review frequently the chief economic conditions, so that we may understand the relations among events that were happening at the same time.

We shall also see the relation between government and geographic conditions

In the preceding volumes of this series we frequently illustrated the manner in which geographic conditions — the climate, topography, soil, vegetation, and natural resources — determined how the people lived. We saw that these geographic factors helped to develop very different occupations and interests in the various sections of the country. New England and the Northeastern industrial zone engaged in manufacturing and trade; the Old South, in tobacco and cotton planting; the Middle West, in grain farming; the Western prairies and plateaus, in cattle-raising; and the mountain sections, in mining, lumbering, and the like. Thus "geography" and economic and social life were closely bound together.

In the present volume we shall see the same close relationship between geographic conditions and government. We shall learn that the people of the manufacturing northern section wanted certain things from government and that they tried to control the government to satisfy their needs. The Southern cotton states wanted different things, and they tried to control the government to satisfy *their* desires. Frequently the needs of the various geographic sections conflicted. Hence many times there was a struggle between the leaders of the different sections to control the national government, so that laws would be passed which would favor their sections. Many illustrations will be used to show this close relation between "geography" and government.

We shall also sum up all the modes of living in what we shall call American culture

In this volume we shall also attempt to bring together in close relationship all the threads of American history — the economic, the political, the social, and the recreational. The American people were developing their farms, factories, mines, and stores; providing schools for their children; governing themselves; and providing for their recreations and social life all at the same time. The history of any epoch is *all* these things seen together.

We shall frequently use the single word *culture* to sum up all these ways of living. At first, no doubt that word will seem strange and meaningless to you, but as we continue to meet examples of the many ways the people lived the meaning of the term will become clearer. Try to acquire the habit of using it. Remember that culture simply means *all the ways of living, thinking, and feeling* of the people. Therefore the culture of the people of any region or nation is, in brief, what they do and what they are. It is their work life, their play life, their political (governing) life. It is what they think and talk most about, what they enjoy and what they fear, what they appreciate, what they dislike, what they approve and what they disapprove, what they love and what they hate. It is what they want most and what they will sacrifice anything to get. Hence the discussion of the culture of the people really brings together all the aspects of their group lives.

In this volume we shall study this problem historically. We shall try to see the culture of the American people as it developed, period by period.

IMPORTANT TOPICS AND QUESTIONS WHICH WILL GUIDE OUR STUDY

1. *The constant struggle of the mass of the people for a larger share of the government.* In considering each period of history we shall ask: How democratic was the government? Who had the privilege and responsibility of voting? Who were excluded from voting or holding office? Why?

Thus America's march toward democracy will be viewed as a three-century-long struggle to bring about in the United States what Abraham Lincoln so well phrased: "Government of the people, by the people, for the people." This important theme leads us to regard political history, therefore, as

2. *The continual conflict between groups of people desiring to control the government.* Hence in studying each period we shall be guided by the questions: What class or group of citizens is in control of the government? What classes and groups are opposing them and trying to get control of the government?

3. *Changing civilization and changing government.* One fundamental theme has appeared again and again in our studies — namely, that we live in a rapidly changing civilization. Hence we shall ask such important questions as: Did the government change to keep pace with the changing needs of the people? Were the laws amended to meet these needs? In this process have all classes and groups of citizens worked together, or have some advocated and others opposed changes in government?

4. *The power of the people to change their government to fit their changing needs.* The Preamble of the American Constitution states that it was established to "secure the blessings of liberty to ourselves and our posterity." In studying certain periods of history, therefore, we shall ask: Did government in this period probably do that? Were the people free to change their government to fit their changing civilization? These questions will lead us to the important problem of freedom of speech. Were the rank and file of the people permitted to criticize their government and, as Jefferson once said, to change it when it did not meet their needs?

5. *The political parties through which the people have set up and carried on their government.* Differences in the thinking and in the interests of the American people brought about political parties. In each period we shall ask: What are the chief parties? How and why did they come into being? What groups, classes, and interests did they represent? Which ones controlled the government? What were the real issues among them?

6. *The extension of the services carried on by the government.* What were some of the responsibilities of the national government at various periods? What were some of the responsibilities that

INTRODUCING THE STUDY OF GOVERNMENT

were left to the governments of the states? Has there been an increase in the control of the national government over our lives? What increases came in the various periods?

7. *The increasing extension of American government over larger territories.* This is the problem of the expansion of the United States. We shall ask how each new territory added to the country was obtained — by purchase, by friendly arbitration, or by conquest?

8. *The increasing leadership of the United States in world affairs.* For the later periods we shall ask: To what extent did the country participate in European affairs? To what extent did it coöperate with other nations in bringing about world unity and peace?

9. *Education and democracy.* We shall inquire: To what extent were the masses of the people educated in each period? Was there a constant, onward march of the people toward universal education, and did this parallel their advance toward universal suffrage?

10. *The amusements, recreation, and social life of the people.* Finally, we shall ask: What were the principal interests of the people? Were they in making money, in accumulating property, or what? Were their wants few and simple, or many and extravagant? Were they interested in studying how to provide better government? In general, what was the mood of the people?

Summing up: What, in short, was the state of culture in America?

Although our Approach is Historical our Real Purpose is to understand Government today

To understand American government we must see it growing and changing as civilization changed. Only by seeing it in long-time historical perspective can we form wise conclusions about the needs of government today and about the changes that may be necessary tomorrow.

Remember constantly that we study history chiefly to understand our lives today. Hence in studying each period ask yourself one fundamental question:

What lesson does this period teach us that will help to solve our problems today?

CHAPTER II

HOW THE EARLY COLONIES WERE GOVERNED

The necessity for government has always been understood by the American people, and government has always played a most important part in their lives. Often the colonists tried first one plan and then another, but there was always some kind of government.

In the early colonies this government controlled a great many of the people's affairs. For example, it determined who received the grants of land, who paid taxes, and who was allowed to vote and to hold office, that is, which people were to share in the government itself. It passed laws regulating the conduct of men, women, and children. Sometimes the government even fixed the wages that a laborer could charge for his services, and the prices that merchants could charge for their goods.

We cannot understand our history unless we see the development of our government. Let us consider first the kind of government which the English colonists had left behind.

THE GOVERNMENT OF GREAT BRITAIN AT THE TIME OF THE EARLY AMERICAN SETTLEMENTS

In the early 1600's there were some people in Great Britain who still believed in the divine right of kings. They believed that a king was a representative of God on earth and hence could do no wrong. The kings themselves believed this to be so. James I, who reigned when the first permanent English colonies were founded in America, once said, "Kings are not only God's lieutenants upon earth and sit upon God's throne, but even by God himself they are called gods."

James I and Charles I, his successor, both felt it to be their right to levy taxes, declare war, and raise armies as they chose, and to force new forms of religion upon their people — in short, to govern as suited them.

HOW THE EARLY COLONIES WERE GOVERNED 17

There was, to be sure, a governing and lawmaking body in England, called Parliament. Its members belonged to one of two groups — to the House of Lords or the House of Commons. The House of Lords was easily managed by the king, for it was made up of nobles many of whom benefited from the king's friendship. They inherited their membership and passed it to their descendants. About all the House of Lords could do (and retain the king's friendship) was to approve the king's acts and pass such laws as he desired.

Members of the House of Commons were small property-owners, well-to-do merchants, and manufacturers. They were not members by birth but by election. In the 1500's the House of Commons had little power. Upon one occasion when an English king wished to have a law passed and the House of Commons opposed it, the king summoned its members to the palace and said, "I will have either my bill or your heads!" In the early 1600's, however, the House

FIG. 5. Charles I. (From a painting by Van der Heist)

of Commons was questioning the divine right of kings and beginning to oppose some of the royal acts. The king could no longer demand "my bill or your heads," but when Parliament went too far in opposing his wishes he could dismiss Parliament. For eleven successive years, during the first half of the 1600's, England was governed directly by the king and was without a Parliament.

Whether or not the king dismissed his Parliament made little difference in the condition of the majority of the English people. Few of them owned property and only property-owners were

18   AMERICAN GOVERNMENT AND CULTURE

permitted to vote for members of the House of Commons. Thus it is seen that while the nobles and the property-owners sometimes had a voice in the management of the government, by far

FIG. 6. A session in the English House of Lords. (From an engraving by John Pine)

the greater number of the English people had no one whose duty it was to protect their rights. Even when there was a Parliament the government was in the hands of the few and was carried on in the interests of the few.

The inclosure of the commons, about which you read in

HOW THE EARLY COLONIES WERE GOVERNED

Changing Civilizations in the Modern World and in *A History of American Civilization*, had made life harder for the poor people of the countryside. The wealthy middle class were dissatisfied with the autocratic manner in which the king dismissed their representatives in the House of Commons. And the nobles were fearful for their own power because of the increasing influence of the wealthy middle class.

Heavy taxes were making many people of all classes discontented, and the persecution of those who did not belong to the Church of England was arousing both Catholics and Dissenters alike. So all England was in a state of unrest and dissatisfaction.

Because of these and other conditions many of the English people looked toward America as a haven — a place in which they could live in independence and peace, and where they might worship as they chose.

So, as you already know, in 1607 a band of Englishmen established a colony at Jamestown, Virginia. In 1620 a little group of Dissenters against the autocratic Church of England settled in Plymouth. In the decade following 1629, thousands of Puritans established the Massachusetts Bay Colony — a group of towns around Boston Harbor. And no sooner had each of these bands of colonists embarked on their expedition than they established a government.

Were these first colonial governments any more democratic than the autocratic ones from which they had fled in England? Let us see.

THE FIRST COLONIES WERE "OWNED" BY TRADING COMPANIES

In *A History of American Civilization* you learned that the Virginia and Massachusetts colonies were business ventures. Wealthy British merchants organized the London Company (later the Virginia Company), the Plymouth Company, and the Massachusetts Bay Company, and sold shares of stock in these companies in order to raise money. With the money thus secured the necessary ships and provisions for the colonists were purchased. Those who owned the stock regarded the colonies as business organizations from which they hoped to make money.

Who, therefore, would govern such a business enterprise as a colony — the settlers in America or the stockholders in England? The stockholders, of course. The stockholders appointed the officers for the colony — the governor, the deputies, and the assistants to the governor. They owned the lands which were to be settled, and later they apportioned these lands to the individual colonists.

From whom had the stockholders obtained the title to the lands? They had received it from the King. And how had the King received the land? According to the law of those times new lands found by an explorer belonged to the king under whose flag the explorer sailed. Thus when the Cabots found the north Atlantic coast of North America they claimed it in the name of the King of England.

The English kings, therefore, "granted" strips on the Atlantic seaboard either to various trading companies or to individuals who were called proprietors. Of course the King himself was to have a profit from those colonies. It was understood that the Virginia Company and the Plymouth Company could mine gold, silver, and copper, but one fifth of the gold and silver and one fifteenth of the copper obtained were to go to the King.

Charters were granted and colonies governed in three different ways. These three ways are illustrated by the cases of Virginia, Massachusetts, and Maryland. Let us study them briefly.

1. *Virginia*. In the charter which the London Company received from the King, the chief stockholders were mentioned by name and were made members of the governing council of the company. To them was given the power to appoint officers.

Thus the stockholders of the company, not the settlers themselves, were to be the real rulers. It happened that most of these company members did not actually emigrate to Virginia. They governed the colony from England through their representative, the governor. Most of the first colonists, therefore, were not stockholders and had no voice whatever in the government of the colony.

2. *Massachusetts Bay*. There was an important difference between the government of Massachusetts and that of Virginia. Many of the leading Puritan stockholders themselves emigrated

HOW THE EARLY COLONIES WERE GOVERNED 21

to the New World and took charge of the building of the colony. Thus Massachusetts was governed directly by stock-holding colonists and not through a representative from London.

3. *Maryland.* Maryland provides an example of the third type of colonial government. The colony was governed by a proprietor, who had been granted the land. This proprietor was Lord Baltimore, a very good friend of Charles I. In return for the grant Baltimore was to send to King Charles every year a portion of the gold found in the colony and two Indian arrowheads. These gifts indicated that the King was the supreme ruler. But the proprietor himself really governed the colony.

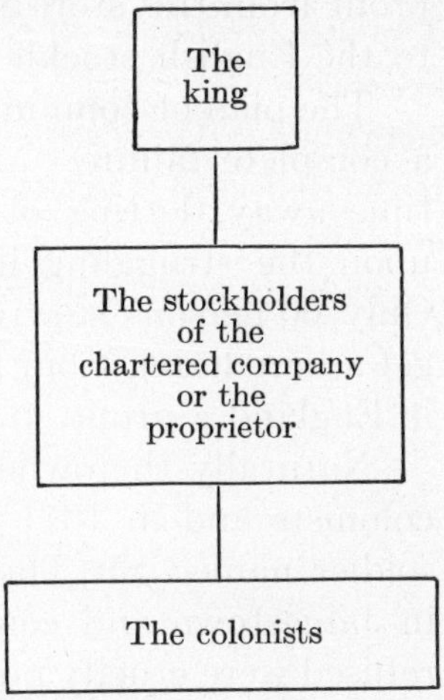

Here is a chart which shows how the people of the colonies were governed.

FIG. 7. The king held supreme control over the colonies. The stockholders or the proprietor of each colony ruled the colonists

So much, then, for the early form of government in Virginia, Massachusetts, and Maryland. The governments of these three colonies illustrate the chief kinds of government in the other colonies.

THE GOVERNMENT OF THE VIRGINIA COLONY

The first government in Virginia was undemocratic

The stockholders of the London Company were not in business for the pleasure of seeing their colony grow into a fine, self-governing body of freemen. They were in business for profit, and their governors were ordered to make the colony pay a profit.

During the first four years after the arrival at Jamestown in 1607, the land of the colony belonged to the London Company (later the Virginia Company). It was not divided among the settlers. Therefore no man could own a piece of land, plant and harvest his own crops, and feel that he was working for himself. Instead the land was worked by a kind of community system,—

a kind of "communism," to use a term employed today. The fruit of every man's labor went into a common store, and the profit from this store after the colonists received their living went to the English stockholders.

The plan of community ownership, as tried at Jamestown, was a complete failure. Many men refused to work and idled their time away, letting others support them. In 1609 famine fell upon the struggling little colony and lasted for nearly a year. Only 60 persons survived. These colonists were scarcely able to get a bare living from the land, much less to pay the stockholders in England a profit.

Naturally the owners of the company were annoyed with the colonists and in 1611 sent over as governor a harsh, autocratic soldier named Sir Thomas Dale. Dale established military rule in Jamestown and compelled the colonists to work. Those who refused were cruelly punished. Some were flogged, some had their tongues bored with a hot iron. A few were shot, and others were hanged. Some fled into the woods, and Indians were sent to fetch them back.

The beginnings of the system of private property in America

Dale did one thing which helped to make the colonists self-supporting. He changed the system of land ownership. First, he divided the land among the settlers and gave to each white freeman — but only to a freeman — a small farm. The freemen who had money were also permitted to buy additional lands in tracts of 100 acres. Then each purchaser was to be given an additional 100 acres as soon as the first lot was under cultivation. If a landowner brought in from England another laborer at his own expense, he received another 100 acres of land. For every additional servant brought in, he received 50 additional acres. Thus those freemen who had money — capital — had a decided advantage over those who were poor.

By this system the well-to-do were enabled to build up big estates, or plantations, while the poorer freemen barely got a living.

Whether it was due to Dale's division of the land among the settlers, to his autocratic rule which compelled all people to work, or to the fact that the colonists ceased looking for gold and began to raise tobacco — whatever the cause, the colony began to prosper. Not many years had passed before they were able to pay the stockholders in England a profit on their investment and to make a profit for themselves.

Slight beginnings of democratic government in Virginia, 1619

In 1619 Sir George Yeardley, a more gently mannered noble than Dale, came to Virginia as governor, and another change was made in the government. Yeardley brought permission from the London Company to have an Assembly of two governing houses. The upper house was to consist of the governor and a group of councilors chosen by the company in England. The lower house was to be called the House of Burgesses, and its members were to be elected by the colonists. In the same year the first representative legislature in America met in Jamestown.

The House of Burgesses was not really *representative* of the entire colony. It consisted of 22 landowners, that is, of two delegates sent from each of eleven large plantations scattered along the rivers. These plantations had a total population of about a thousand persons. The delegates were the well-to-do planters. Thus the government of Virginia was not thoroughly democratic. The House of Burgesses was, nevertheless, the beginning of self-government and of representative government in America. With the election of the Assembly, a *little* of the power to make laws passed from the company stockholders into the hands of the planters.

That first step toward democracy seems very slight to us. Yet it set an example which the other colonies later followed, and was the beginning of a march toward democracy which has continued for more than 300 years.

In Virginia the march was very slow at first. At times it seemed that no progress was being made. The King and some of his councilors were dissatisfied with the government of the Virginia Company since it provided for an assembly which was, in their opinion, too "democratical." Therefore in 1624 they decided to take away the company's old charter and make Virginia a royal colony. Although the House of Burgesses was not dissolved, it did not meet for several years.

The colonists were still required to pay whatever taxes the governor and council saw fit to levy. The King appointed the governor and council for Virginia who, except in purely local matters, were to take orders from England. In purely local affairs the governor and the council were to decide what to do.

FIG. 8. Governor Yeardley presiding over the Assembly, the first governing body in Virginia

The Virginia colonists, however, were independent in spirit. They did not like the new state of affairs and protested in a Bill of Rights containing the following historic resolution:

That the Governor shall not lay any taxes . . . upon the colony, their lands, or comodities other way than by the authority of the General Assembly, to be levyed and ymployed as the said Assembly shall appoynt.

This meant in brief "no taxation without representation" in the government, and was to be the rallying cry of the colonists during the Revolution (1775).

Their protest was not heeded by the council or the King. The planters continued to ask for a meeting of the House of Burgesses, but for four years there were no general assemblies. Then in 1629 after several changes in governors, there came an announcement from the King that His Majesty was "pleased graciously to extend his favor to the planters" and would grant the holding of a general assembly. Still the planters were far from satisfied, for the government was very autocratic. The King required that any laws passed by the Assembly must be approved by him. Thus the House of Burgesses was really almost without power.

Again the planters protested. For twenty-five years they sent petitions to the British rulers, asking for more representative government in the colony. They also asked to be allowed to send representatives to the British Parliament.

Then for eleven years England was without a king. From 1649 to 1658 Oliver Cromwell, a Puritan, ruled England, and the Virginia House of Burgesses obtained more and more power. Indeed, from 1652 to 1660 it was permitted to choose its governor and the governor's council. This was the highest point of representative government in the early Virginia colony.

The Government of the Massachusetts Bay Colony

While the Virginia planters were working out their colonial government, a somewhat different experiment in representative government was going on in the northern colony of the Company of Massachusetts Bay. Here the stockholders themselves settled in America and governed the colony. They were to have control over the admission of new stockholders. They were to "correct, punish, and rule" all who might settle in the land and resist "by all fitting ways and means whatever" any person who might attempt to destroy, invade, or annoy the settlers.

The voting stockholders, who must be freemen, were to hold four general assemblies, known as the General Court, each year. These courts were to make laws and elect those who were to govern the colony.

Eight aristocratic stockholders ruled 2000 colonists

Of the 2000 colonists who came in 1630 only twelve men were both freemen and stockholders in the company. Before leaving England John Winthrop had been chosen governor. The other eleven stockholders were made assistants. Governor and assistants together were known as the magistrates. Before the first General Court meeting in October, 1630, however, the number of assistants had been reduced to seven. Thus eight men alone were making and enforcing laws for 2000 settlers.

What manner of men were these eight? They were first of all well-to-do owners of property. Every one of them had saved a fairly large amount of capital, some of which he had invested in the Massachusetts Bay Company.

Most of them came from the influential middle class in England. They were respectable, God-fearing Puritans. Sudden and far-reaching changes were most distasteful to them. They had very little patience with such extreme doctrines as those which the Quakers or other radical churchmen believed and taught. Some of these Puritans had been members of Parliament in England.

Thus government in the Massachusetts Bay Colony started as a kind of oligarchy, or government by a small group of men who held the reins of power tightly in their hands. Eight men ruled the colony exactly as controlling stockholders manage a corporation today.

Soon rumblings of discontent began to come from the common people. One hundred and nine heads of families — sturdy, independent-minded English settlers — came to the General Court with the demand that they be made freemen.

A short time later the assistants yielded somewhat to the demands of the people by admitting 116 new freemen. Before this happened, however, the governor and the assistants had passed two laws which were contrary to their charter and which prevented the newly made freemen from having much control. The first law gave the assistants the right to hold office " during good behavior " instead of for one year. The second allowed the assistants to choose the governor. It was also decided that thereafter only members of the Puritan Church could be made freemen.

HOW THE EARLY COLONIES WERE GOVERNED

Gradually more power in the government was extended to a slightly larger number of settlers

In 1632 the colonists were again dissatisfied with the government of Governor Winthrop and the assistants. The little settlement of Watertown was the first to protest. The assistants had levied a tax upon the town to build fortifications. The freemen of Watertown refused to pay it. They were then called before the Governor, when the representatives of the town decidedly softened their tone. After discussion the citizens yielded and agreed to pay taxes. The other towns, however, were not satisfied. Resentment was growing among the settlers. In the same year the freemen insisted upon the annual election of governor and assistants and also upon their right to help choose these officers. New laws were enacted which did not help the situation. Many of them benefited the wealthy class and worked hardship on the poorer people of Massachusetts. For example, in 1633, the assistants had gone far in dictating how people should live. They passed laws which stated the wages that artisans could charge for their labor.

It is ordered, that maister carpenters, sawers, masons, clapboard ryvers, brickelayers, tylars, joyners, wheelwrights, mowers, etc., shall not take above 2s. a day [about 50 cents], findeing themselves dyett [that is, if they provide their own food], and not above 14d. [28 cents] a day if they have dyett found them.

The Bloodless Revolution of 1634

Such laws drove the freemen to demand a larger share in the government. Shortly before the day on which the next court was to meet, two representatives of the people of each town met Governor Winthrop in Boston and demanded to see the company charter which they had never been permitted to read. Winthrop could not refuse. After they had read the charter, the freemen pointed out to the Governor and his assistants that provision was made for *all the freemen of the colony,* not the assistants alone, *to make laws.* Winthrop then declared that there were not enough freemen who were "qualified for such business." In spite of opposition, however, the freemen insisted upon their rights. This incident, resulted in a somewhat more representative form of government. Eight towns of the Massachusetts Bay Colony gained the right to elect representatives to the General Court.

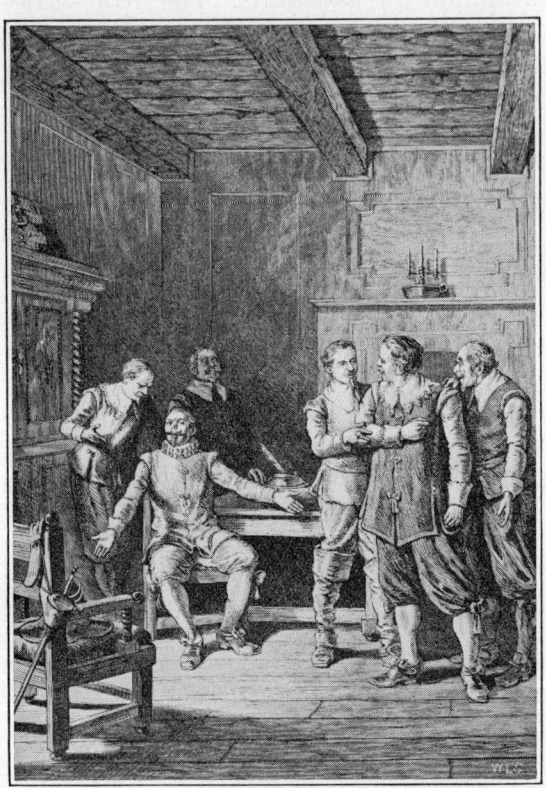

FIG. 9. There were quarrels not only between the rulers and the colonists but among the rulers themselves. In this picture Winthrop and Dudley are quarreling, and the other members of the governing body are trying to restore peace

The newly elected freemen helped to change the state of affairs. They elected as governor Thomas Dudley instead of Winthrop, who had served for four years. They also decided that members of the General Court should vote by secret ballot instead of openly by show of hands. The show-of-hands method put the voters under the control of influential men in the colony. The poorer men who were dependent upon them for a living found it difficult to vote against them in open ballot; so secret voting was now used. Other rights which the assistants had taken away were restored. One of these was "trial by jury," which had been one of the inalienable rights of Englishmen since the days of Henry II, in the middle of the 12th century.

The worst days of autocratic rule in the little colony had passed. The magistrates had lost absolute control of the government. More colonists had been made freemen. But Massachu-

HOW THE EARLY COLONIES WERE GOVERNED 29

setts was still far from *a real democracy*, although it had gained a representative form of government. To qualify as a voter a colonist had to be a freeman, a man of property, and in good standing in the Church. Anyone who was not able to fulfill those conditions had no rights whatsoever in government.

Another step toward more democratic government: the local town meeting

The freemen not only improved the central government of the colony; they also worked out a kind of democratic government for the small towns. In 1633 provision was made for regular general town meetings. Twelve selectmen were chosen by the people to serve as a governing town council.

The town meetings were not really more democratic, however, than the General Court. Only "gentlemen" and "industrious artisans and freeholders," that is, property-owners, could vote or hold office, though every person in the town had the right to speak his opinion at the town meeting. Nevertheless, Massachusetts had begun to build a democratic government. The ruling power had been extended from eight charter members of the company to a small group of well-to-do freemen who were property-owners and church members. Gradually it spread to include more and more of the population.

INTERESTING READINGS FROM WHICH YOU CAN GET ADDITIONAL INFORMATION

AUSTIN, JANE G. David Alden's Daughter and Other Stories of Colonial Times. Houghton Mifflin Company, Boston.
AUSTIN, JANE G. Standish of Standish. Houghton Mifflin Company, Boston.
DIX, BEULAH M. Hugh Gwyeth: a Roundhead Cavalier. The Macmillan Company, New York.
JOHNSTON, MARY. Prisoners of Hope. Houghton Mifflin Company, Boston.
JOHNSTON, MARY. To Have and to Hold. Houghton Mifflin Company, Boston.
MARBLE, ANNIE R. Standish of Standish (a dramatization of the story by Jane G. Austin). Houghton Mifflin Company, Boston.
SCOTT, SIR WALTER. Fortunes of Nigel. The Macmillan Company, New York. A picture of life in London and at the court during the 1600's.
WEST, WILLIS M. A Source Book in American History to 1787. Allyn and Bacon, Boston. Excellent source material.
Old South Leaflets. Directors of the Old South Work, Old South Meeting House, Boston. These leaflets are excellent source material; 5 cents each.

CHAPTER III

THE LATER STRUGGLE WITHIN THE COLONIES FOR DEMOCRATIC GOVERNMENT

The next period of American history reveals two great conflicts over the control of the government. The first was the struggle within the colonies between the ruling class and the common people. The second was between the colonies and the British government. In this chapter we shall study the first of these conflicts.

Think of the colonists as divided into three social classes

As we have seen, all men were not equal in the early years of the colonies. There was a small group of wealthy "gentlemen" — owners of large estates, plantations, mansions, stores, or ships. There was a second group consisting in the main of small property-owners and craftsmen. In the third group were the indentured servants and Negro slaves.

Of course the second group greatly outnumbered the owners of the large estates. In any one colony there were no more than a few hundred wealthy landlords. For example, it is estimated that in Virginia in 1671 there were about 45,000 settlers. A few hundred of these were owners of very large plantations, ranging from several hundred to several thousand acres. Approximately 20,000 people were craftsmen and small farmers, owners of, say, 50 to 600 acres each. The rest were indentured servants and Negro slaves. Thus in 1670 more than half of the population owned property, but the majority of these were poor planters who could barely eke out a scanty living from their little tracts of land.

In Massachusetts, New York, Pennsylvania, and other Northern colonies the situation was somewhat like that in Virginia.

STRUGGLE FOR DEMOCRATIC GOVERNMENT 31

A few men of wealth owned great estates; a large group owned small amounts of property or were craftsmen; and a third smaller group were indentured servants and slaves.

In each colony, therefore, the greater part of the wealth was in the hands of not more than a few hundred men. The rest was divided into small amounts among the majority of the colonists, who might be called the common people.

You have seen how the stockholders in the first trading companies governed the colonies of Virginia and Massachusetts Bay. As time went on other intelligent and ambitious men acquired wealth and obtained a larger share in the government. But the situation continued much the same. A small group of well-to-do landowners, merchants, and shipowners ruled in each colony.

FIG. 10. A shipowner of the Massachusetts Bay Colony and a member of the wealthy class

The attitude of the well-to-do ruling class toward the common people

Throughout the colonies the "gentlemen" had a real contempt for the rank and file of the people. Again and again in the records of that day are shown the rigid class lines which were drawn between "gentlemen" and "people of mean condition." Consider one example from the *Records of the Governor and Company of the Massachusetts Colony*, 1651:

Wee cannot but account it our duty . . . to declare our utter detestation . . . that men or weomen *of meane condition* should take upon them the garb of *gentlemen,* by wearing gold or silver lace or buttons, or points at their knees, or to walk in great bootes, or weomen of the same rancke to weare silk or tiffany hoodes or scarfes . . . allowable to persons of greater estates or more liberall education . . . it is therefore ordered by this Courte . . . that no person . . . whose visible estates shall not exceed . . . two hundred pounds, shall wear any gold or silver lace [etc.], upon the penaltie of ten shillings *for every such offence.*

FIG. 11. It had been the custom of the English people to erect a pole on an open space every May Day. The pole was wreathed with flowers, and around it the people held dances and played games. In the Massachusetts colonies the May poles were cut down. One reason was that dancing and games were frowned upon by the Puritans

Since the upper class believed that they had a right to interfere in matters of dress, is it any wonder that they insisted upon deciding who should vote and hold office?

Thus while America was taking her first faltering steps toward democracy, there was a sharp division of the people into classes. The wealthy upper class was governing; the poorer lower class was governed. From the very first, however, the people of the lower class protested against this arrangement. Unceasingly they demanded for themselves more power in the government.

STRUGGLE FOR DEMOCRATIC GOVERNMENT

How the Church Members governed Massachusetts

The Congregational, or Independent, Church was the established Puritan church in Massachusetts. Everyone was obliged to attend that church and that church only. For a very long time no man who was not in good standing in the church could even vote; and to be in good standing one had to pass rather

Fig. 12. Endicott, governor of the Plymouth Colony, was intolerant of religions other than the Puritan. Offended by what he considered the emblem of Roman Catholicism, he cut the cross from the king's ensign. Even the assistants were shocked at this action and openly declared their disapproval

severe religious tests. No member of the Church of England or of the Quaker, the Roman Catholic, or the Baptist Church could become a voter.

Very influential among the "gentlemen" of Massachusetts were the ministers of the Congregational Church. Hand in hand the ministers and the magistrates governed the colony. The ministers supported the magistrates, who made and enforced the laws, and the magistrates forced the people to worship in the established church. In this way the well-to-do church members and the church leaders so arranged that the governing power should be kept in their hands.

The church had such great power over the government that

the officers of the colony punished, even tortured, men and women for not believing exactly as the church instructed. Robert Winthrop, son of Governor Winthrop, tells in one of his letters of a poor woman in Salem who demanded openly in the church her right to worship in accordance with her own creed:

> This woman was brought to the Court for disturbing the peace in the church . . . and there she gave such peremptory answers, as she was committed [to prison] till she should find sureties for her good behavior. After she had been in prison three or four days, she acknowledged her fault in disturbing the church. . . . But . . . she still held her former opinions, which were very dangerous. . . .
> About five years after, this woman was adjudged to be whipped for reproaching the magistrates. She stood without tying, and bare her punishment with a masculine spirit, glorying in her suffering. But after . . . she was much dejected about it. She had a cleft stick put on her tongue half an hour, for reproaching the elders.[1]

The Quakers were also the object of political and church persecution in Massachusetts Bay. Shortly after the founding of the colony these people came there in large numbers. They refused, however, to attend the established church and preached openly the doctrines of their Society of Friends. For this they were whipped or thrown into prison, some were hanged, and many were banished from the colony.

This Puritan attitude toward freedom of thought was a curious contradiction. One of the reasons for which the Puritans had left England was to establish a church which should be free and independent of the Church of England. Nevertheless, they would not tolerate any religious beliefs which differed from their own. They did not intend to admit people outside their church. They even disapproved of the Pilgrims, who formed the Plymouth Colony.

Governor Winthrop had been in America only a few months when Captain Miles Standish of the Plymouth Colony introduced to him two "gentlemen" from England. These people of the upper class had gone first to Plymouth but decided that they wanted to settle in Massachusetts Bay. Since they had no "testi-

---

[1] Robert C. Winthrop, *Life and Letters of John Winthrop*, pp. 232, 233. Little, Brown & Company, Boston, 1895.

mony," or certificate, to show that they were in good church standing, Winthrop would not receive them. "Gentlemen" of another faith might prove a dangerous influence in the colony!

At another time six men were shipped back to England without trial simply because the magistrates and the ministers decided that they were "unmeete to inhabit here."

RHODE ISLAND AND CONNECTICUT WERE REALLY FOUNDED BECAUSE OF THE INTOLERANCE OF THE MASSACHUSETTS PURITAN RULING CLASS

Even in those early days, however, when people had less liberty than we have today, there was much discontent and sometimes even rebellion against such oppressive acts. Even then the desire for democracy and religious tolerance in America was growing. Three episodes are important in New England history. They prove that even then some people would not submit unquestioningly to an absolute church and political control. The first episode concerns Roger Williams and the founding of the new colony of Rhode Island. The second is the story of the rebellion of the minister Thomas Hooker, who led the people of several Massachusetts townships into the wilderness and founded Connecticut. The third is the story of the banishment of Mistress Anne Hutchinson and the building of another colony in Rhode Island.

1. Roger Williams founded Rhode Island, 1635–1636

Roger Williams was an English minister, a believer in justice to all mankind, and in the rights of all people whether of high or low estate. He also believed and publicly declared his belief that the Indians were the true owners of the land which King Charles was so generously granting to Englishmen. Driven from England for his liberal views, he had come to Massachusetts Bay Colony and had been made pastor of a church in Salem. Williams's conscience led him to question openly the government of Winthrop, the magistrates, and the ministers. He preached that the government and the church should be kept entirely separate, that political officers should have no authority over what people thought or did on Sunday, and that they should have the power to arrest only such persons as were committing crimes or damaging other people's property. The leaders of the colony desired to seize Williams and send him to England for punishment. He was warned in time, however, and escaped to the woods, where he spent the winter of 1635 with his friends, the Narraganset Indians. In the spring four colonists from Plymouth joined Williams in the wilderness. Together they bought land from the Indians and founded a settlement which they called Providence, in what is now Rhode Island.

Williams and his friends practiced what they preached. They allowed people of any religious faith to come to live among them, and people were allowed to think as they would, provided they did not break laws regarding life and property. By the other colonies the new colony was regarded with dislike and suspicion because of its laxity in religious matters and its tolerant spirit. The Massachusetts Bay Colony at one time even thought of absorbing it and driving out the settlers; they tried also to persuade England to interfere in the affairs of Rhode Island, but with no success. In spite of all, the colony prospered and was for many years a haven for people cast out of other colonies because of differing beliefs.

2. Thomas Hooker and the Connecticut Colony, 1635–1636

The second instance was that of Thomas Hooker, who had been the pastor of the church at Newtowne (Cambridge). A man of education but born of common stock, Hooker was a true spokesman for the common people. Some of his beliefs were that a general council, chosen by all, should transact business in all that concerned the common good; that the consent of the people governed should be the basis for government; that the choice of magistrates belongs to the people; and that therefore the people have also the right to limit the power of those appointed. Whole townships in Massachusetts Bay packed up their belongings and joined him when he announced his intention of founding a new colony. Tempted by the fertile land in what

STRUGGLE FOR DEMOCRATIC GOVERNMENT 37

is now Connecticut, they chose a site at the mouth of the Fresh River for their new settlement. In this new colony they put into practice their belief in a more democratic government than that in Massachusetts Bay. They gave to every Christian freeman the right to vote without first passing a religious test, retaining only a property requirement. The General Court made the laws

FIG. 13. Thomas Hooker leading his followers into Connecticut. (From a painting by Frederic Edwin Church. Courtesy of the Wadsworth Athenæum, Hartford)

and held the governing power, being able to overrule the governor, who was elected for one year only. At the end of his term the governor could not be reëlected immediately, but could hold office again at the end of the next governor's term.

3. The banishment of Anne Hutchinson from Massachusetts Bay, 1638

The third incident shows that there were in the Massachusetts Bay Colony women as well as men of independent spirit and courage. Among these was Mistress Anne Hutchinson, a "gentlewoman." When she had first arrived in the colony with her husband and her large family, in a kind and neighborly way Mistress Hutchinson had begun to visit and to help women who were ill or in sorrow. She observed that, while the men were engaged in occupations which provided more or less opportunity for the exchange of ideas, the lives of the women were drab and monotonous beyond all endurance — so much so that some of the women were becoming insane because of loneliness and the conditions under which they had to live. To provide relief for this situation, Mistress Hutchinson began inviting the women to tea at her house; and at first, merely as a way of entertaining her guests, she began to repeat the Sunday sermons and to give occasional comments of her own. Some of the women often questioned her as to meanings and interpretations. In giving these she at times differed from the ministers' teachings. The teas became more and more popular because of the wit of the hostess and her qualities as a speaker, so that men also began to attend in large numbers.

As time went by Mistress Hutchinson became more outspoken, and an open quarrel broke out in Boston over her criticism of the ministers. At first a powerful party, including John Wheelwright (her brother-in-law), John Cotton, and Governor Vane, favored Mistress Hutchinson's side of the controversy; but many prominent men, including Governor Winthrop, were bitterly opposed to her. She was brought to trial, and though she defended herself with the full power of her "voluble" tongue and brilliant mind, she was convicted, was expelled from the church, and was ordered to leave the colony. It was in 1638 that she and a number of her friends made the difficult overland journey to Rhode Island, and there founded a settlement on the island of Aquidneck.

These three episodes illustrate the first struggles of the colonists against the autocratic rule of the few wealthy church members in Massachusetts. They were but the first of a long series of attempts to break down the control of government by the few. Gradually more people under democratic leaders succeeded in gaining the right to govern themselves. The fight for democracy went on. But throughout the colonial history of New England, property continued to govern.

What was happening in Virginia?

We have already learned that the wealthy planters controlled the business and government of Virginia. By 1670 these men owned a vast share of the land of the colony which lay along the rivers and Chesapeake Bay. They had built up considerable fortunes. On the other hand, many of the small farmers and planters of the frontier, who had been pushed back from the

FIG. 14. By 1670 large and flourishing plantations had grown up near the seacoast of Virginia, and already ships were carrying the produce to Europe. As the wealth of the planters grew, their influence in the government of Virginia increased

coast nearly to the foothills of the Appalachians, were growing very discontented with their lot. They felt that they were being taxed unjustly, ignored in the government, and that in many other ways their rights as Englishmen were being disregarded.

Bacon's Rebellion, 1676: the short-lived era of democracy in Virginia

It was during the administration of Governor Berkeley that the conflict between the small planters and the wealthy landowners finally broke out in open warfare.

The occasion of the outbreak was an Indian attack in 1676 on the outlying frontier plantations. In the border country between the wilderness and the settlements white men's farms were being burned. They and their families were being killed or driven from their land. Frantic appeals for men and munitions to protect them were sent to the governor. Berkeley, however, refused to send militia to help the distressed frontiersmen. The governor's refusal angered the westerners. They knew only too well that he had been taxing them unfairly, wasting the money raised by taxes, and that he was granting special privileges to his friends with magnificent generosity.

Nathaniel Bacon, a popular young planter of the borderland, came to the rescue of the frontiersmen. Although he was a member of the House of Burgesses, he understood and sympathized with the grievances of the poorer people. The Indians killed the overseer of his plantation and Bacon asked Berkeley for a commission in the colonial army, so that he might have the support of the government to lead an army of volunteers against them. Berkeley refused his request.

Thereupon the colonists took matters into their own hands. With great enthusiasm 300 frontiersmen followed Bacon, attacked the Indians, and completely routed them.

Bacon became a democratic hero. He was now determined to bring about reform in the government of Virginia. Governor Berkeley feared that the people would rally to Bacon's support and remove him (Berkeley) from office. The people of the colony lined up on two sides — the wealthy and the poor. However, many of the owners of large estates deserted Berkeley. In order to regain his position Berkeley pretended to become a friend to Bacon. He called for a new election of Burgesses. In the election there was much more democratic representation. Indentured servants who had just gained their freedom were given the vote, and some were elected as Burgesses.

In the new House of Burgesses, known as "Bacon's Assembly," unjust laws, long on the statute books, were reformed. All white freemen were given the vote regardless of whether or not they owned property. Short terms for government officials were agreed upon. Assemblies were to meet frequently. The common people were to be allowed to examine the public financial records. The tax laws and the land laws were changed. The wealthy planters were denied special privileges. Finally, the governor was forced to promise that he would grant Bacon a commission as commander in chief of the militia.

STRUGGLE FOR DEMOCRATIC GOVERNMENT

Berkeley hated this group and their leader, who were taking away his power. As soon as he safely could, he broke his promise to Bacon. Instead of granting the latter's commission, he plotted the death of the popular hero. But Bacon did not wait for Berkeley to act. With 400 foot soldiers and 120 horsemen he prepared to get his commission by force. While the Burgesses were sitting comfortably in their chairs, Bacon and his cavalcade stopped before the building.

Panic broke loose in the town. The white-haired old Governor Berkeley alone remained calm. He arose from his chair on the dais and, followed by his councilors, marched out to where Bacon stood at the head of his men. To his face the governor called Bacon a "rebel and a traitor." Then, wrenching open his fine cavalier coat and baring his chest, he cried: "Here! Shoot me! 'Fore God, a fair mark — a fair mark! Shoot!"

FIG. 15. Governor Berkeley facing Bacon and his men

Bacon did not move. Then Berkeley drew his sword and challenged Bacon to single combat. But Bacon wanted a commission, not a duel.

Finally, after a long and fruitless argument, Bacon lost patience. Then he shouted, "I'll kill governor, council, assembly and all, and I'll sheathe my sword in my own heart's blood!"

He wheeled about and ordered his guard to "Make ready, and present!"

The volunteers shouted, "We *will* have it! We *will* have it!" and pointed their muskets at the little group of rulers. At that moment a frightened Burgess waved his handkerchief from a window as a flag of truce. Immediately Bacon's guard grounded their weapons. Then they shouldered arms and marched quietly back to where the volunteer army waited. A truce had been made.

Even with the truce, however, trouble was not over. Civil war broke out. Bacon and his volunteers defeated Berkeley and burned Jamestown. The people thought that they were at last to be considered. But the success of the rebellion was short-lived. Bacon died within a month, whether of malaria or of poison administered by his enemies, no one knows.

With the death of the young leader, the spirit of the people was broken. Soon Berkeley began to wreak terrible vengeance upon the rebels. He executed so many people that when Charles II heard of it he exclaimed, "The old fool has taken more lives in that naked country than I for the murder of my father!" Berkeley was called to England to account for his cruelty and misgovernment.

All of Bacon's work was speedily undone. The laws were changed and the whole government turned back to an aristocracy. The poorer people were reduced to their former lowly position, where they remained for nearly a century. Except for a meeting of Burgesses every year or two they were unrepresented. To be sure, the small farmer took some part in *local* politics, for he was allowed to attend the annual county elections. But the government was still controlled by the larger planters.

But we see that in the two oldest colonies — Virginia and Massachusetts — the poorer people early began to struggle for a larger share in the government.

In Pennsylvania the Scotch-Irish revolted against the Quaker Aristocracy

In time the same kind of struggle went on in the younger colonies as more people demanded a share in the government.

Pennsylvania, for example, was established in 1682, and by the middle of the 1700's three groups of people were settled there in three districts. The Quakers were in the eastern part and in Philadelphia. To the west beyond the Quaker settlements lay a broad band of farms of the German colonists. Still farther west, in the mountain wilderness, were the small farms and backwoods homes of the Scotch-Irish.

Thus we have in this one small colony three distinctly different types of people — three nationalities with three different outlooks on life. Most of the Quakers were peace-loving and thrifty Englishmen and Welshmen. They had prospered and were well in control of affairs long before the Germans or the Scotch-Irish had come. The Germans were hard-working folk, and soon they too gained some wealth and influence. But the Scotch-Irish were very unlike either Quakers or Germans. They were energetic and adventurous. They lived in more isolated homes on the edge of the wilderness near the Indians. The chief equipment in many of their households consisted of rifles, axes, a few tools, and rough furnishings.

By 1760, three quarters of a century after the founding of Pennsylvania, the differences among the three groups had brought about intense dislike of one another. The wealthy Quakers on the eastern coastal plain were in control of the government. They had passed laws limiting the number of representatives from the western frontier and in this way were able to hold the reins of colonial government in their own hands.

In 1762 and 1763, during the French and Indian War, the Scotch-Irish on the border were frequently in danger from Indian raids. Warlike though the frontiersmen were, they were so few in number that they could not protect their homes. They appealed to the Pennsylvania assembly for troops to help them. The Quakers turned a deaf ear to the petition. They had always tried to keep peace with the Indians, and they disliked now to attack them. So the Quaker rulers let the frontiersmen look out for themselves.

The frontiersmen began to organize

When help did not come from the government, the Scotch-Irish decided to take matters into their own hands. They formed a troop of able-bodied men known as the Rangers, to patrol the Indian border. The Quaker rulers in the east were angered by this move of the frontiersmen and denounced the Rangers.

The frontiersmen declared war upon the red-skinned natives, — all of them, enemies and friends,— and their wrath found many innocent and harmless victims.

Then heated messages began to fly back and forth across the colony of Pennsylvania. In pamphlets and articles the eastern Quakers sharply criticized the frontiersmen. The frontiersmen replied even more vigorously. One pamphlet issued by the frontiersmen accused the Quakers of having more sympathy with the Indians than with the members of their own race.

In a petition to the government they asked again for protection of their borders and also representation in the assembly. Both were refused them.

Scenes in North Carolina: the Struggle of Frontiersmen against the Seaboard Aristocracy

In the year 1765 the drama of the struggle for government control shifted to North Carolina. For a century the people of the colony had been dissatisfied with their government. The charter granted to the colony by King Charles had expired, and the government was now under royal control. In 1765 the King's representative, Governor Tryon, and his friends ruled the colony. The people of the western hills had almost no part in making or enforcing laws. They were under the heels of "clerks" and other officials sent out from the seaboard to collect taxes and manage affairs. Officials were profiting mercilessly at the expense of the back-country people. Naturally, the westerners hated bitterly the dishonest officers of the crown.

STRUGGLE FOR DEMOCRATIC GOVERNMENT 45

Can you not imagine these words shouted to a rollicking tune by a group of children clad in homespun?

> When Fanning[1] first to Orange came
>   He looked both pale and wan,
> An old patched coat upon his back,
>   An old blind mare he rode on.
> Both man and mare wa'n't worth five pounds
>   As I've been often told,
> But by his thieving robberies
>   He's lined his coat with gold.[2]

We can picture their tall, lean father teaching them what the words meant. Perhaps as he did so he looked sadly down at his own aged hunting jacket. Perhaps neither he nor his children were able to contrast it with the hat and jacket which Fanning had just ordered with "some double gold lace for a hat and some gold lace for a jacket, plain, narrow, and good." But it did not help the frontiersman's opinion of Fanning to remember that poor men were being ruined while the officer was lining his coat with gold.

The back-country men organized to protect their rights

Thus the frontiersmen of North Carolina were driven to protect themselves against the government. They formed an organization which they called the Regulators. Meetings were held at which petitions were drawn up and sent to the governor. In the petitions the westerners protested against high taxes, dishonest officials, and unreasonable fees for public services. Their pleas were in vain. The governor refused to do anything.

Then open resistance took the place of petitioning. The pioneers began to resist forcibly the collection of taxes. They would not permit the courts to sit. They attacked some of the most detested officers. Fanning was one of those who received a sound beating.

---

[1] A Recorder of Deeds for Orange County under the royal government, who was so unpopular that he was virtually driven from the colony by an uprising of the "Regulators," an organization largely composed of frontiersmen.

[2] Quoted in Willis Edwards Fitch's *Some Neglected History of North Carolina*, p. 181. The Neale Publishing Company, New York, 1905.

The governor, a trained soldier, determined to crush the uprising. In 1771 he led an army against the Regulators. The frontiersmen went out to meet him. Messages were exchanged, but neither side would yield. The Regulators sent the governor's messenger back with the word that "they had defied him and battle was all they wanted." Then they advanced against the trained soldiers. The governor sent another message to the rebels, saying that unless they would give up their leaders and return to their homes he would fire upon them.

"Fire away!" was the reply of the Regulators.

The governor gave the order to fire. The troops did not obey at once. Then the governor cried, "Fire on them or fire on me!" The troops fired, and the Regulators dropped behind trees and bushes for protection. They were no match for the soldiers, however, and in two hours they were routed. Thus the resistance of the frontiersmen was ended. The government remained in the hands of the aristocrats of the seaboard, and dissatisfied frontiersmen crossed the mountains into what is now Tennessee.

These Scenes are Typical of the Conflict which was going on between Aristocracy and Democracy in the Colonies

From one colony to another we have seen conflict along the Atlantic coast during 150 years of settlement. In Virginia there were many more episodes in the struggle. In Massachusetts the poorer men protested constantly against the rule of aristocracy. In Pennsylvania the Scotch-Irish were a constant source of irritation to the Quakers. In the Carolinas the governors were almost in despair over the refusal of the hardy backwoodsmen to submit to their rule. There were also conflicts in the other colonies, always with the same theme — the determination of the "aristocrats" to govern the colony and the determination of the "common men" to govern themselves.

These conflicts are all part of America's three-century-long march toward democracy. As the colonial period went on, the bitter feeling between classes deepened.

INTERESTING READINGS FROM WHICH YOU CAN GET ADDITIONAL INFORMATION

DIX, B. M. The Making of Christopher Ferringham. The Macmillan Company, New York. Massachusetts in the 1650's, giving a vivid picture of Quaker persecutions.

HALSEY, FRANCIS W. (Editor). Great Epochs in American History. Funk & Wagnalls Company, New York. See Volume II, pp. 164–172 (Bacon's Rebellion).

HART, ALBERT B. American History told by Contemporaries. The Macmillan Company, New York. See Volume I, pp. 242–246 (Bacon's Rebellion).

JOHNSTON, MARY. Audrey. Houghton Mifflin Company, Boston. Audrey, the heroine of this story, is the daughter of a poor backwoodsman.

UNIT II

THE STRUGGLE FOR SELF-GOVERNMENT,
1660–1783

THE STRUGGLE FOR SELF-GOVERNMENT, 1660–1783

Our first unit introduced the story of the conflict within the colonies for control of the government. At the same time there was another conflict — between the colonists and the mother country. That struggle finally culminated in a war — the American Revolution. In that war the British armies were defeated; the colonies declared themselves an independent nation; and the United States of America came into being.

To understand our country today, therefore, it is necessary to understand this second conflict in the colonies. In Unit II we shall study it carefully. In Chapter IV we shall witness the chief conditions which led to the conflict between the colonies and the mother country. In Chapter V we shall study the events which sharpened it and brought about a crisis. In Chapter VI we shall discuss the conflict itself.

There are widely differing points of view as to the real underlying causes of the American Revolution. Today, a century and a half since the events took place, even with the help of countless records, it is very difficult to unravel the tangle of contributing causes. Many forces acted together. To name only outstanding ones, there were the desires of people for a better living, the determination to decide one's own course of action, rivalries of business leaders, ambitions of political leaders, the subtle effects of 150 years of residence in a new land in changing Englishmen into Americans, and the difference in view about the purpose of the colonies.

CHAPTER IV

THE BEGINNING OF THE STRUGGLE WITH ENGLAND FOR INDEPENDENT GOVERNMENT, 1660–1760

We have witnessed the conflict in the colonies between the ruling classes and the mass of the people. That conflict continued throughout the years of colonial history.

During the same years another conflict was taking place — the conflict between the colonists and the ruling powers in England. No series of events in American history is more important than this one.

As you have learned, most of the original colonies were founded by trading companies or by well-to-do proprietors. From the very first, therefore, the leading British people regarded the colonies as a money-making venture. The stockholders of the companies, the proprietors, the king, the members of Parliament, and most British business men held that view. To these people in England the colonists were merely their employees, making a profit for them.

The colonies were important so long as they benefited English trade and England's power in Europe. The colonists were in America to grow tobacco or otherwise to make profits for the British investors. Education, schools, self-government — these ideals did not interest them. Governor Berkeley once remarked that he thanked God there were no free schools or printing in the colony of Virginia.

The colonists, on the other hand, although loyal subjects of the king of England, were essentially interested in their own welfare. They had dared the dangers and hardships of a wild continent mainly to improve their own conditions. They had come there to *live*, to educate their children and make it possible for them to live even fuller lives in their own time. Naturally they were not primarily interested in the profits made by British rulers and investors in their colonies.

There was a second factor that increased the differences between the two peoples. That was the attitude toward the British Empire and toward government. Although most of the colonists were little aware of it, they were changing from Englishmen into Americans. As generations passed they came to regard America as home exactly as the English, Scotch, Welsh, and Irish had long regarded England, Scotland, Wales, and Ireland as home. But it was to a different climate, a different kind of soil and topography, in short, to a different "geography" that the colonists had come. For the mass of the people, occupations were carried on somewhat differently, houses were built in other ways, clothing was not the same, as in the country from which they had come. Even speech gradually became different. Then as children were born and grew to manhood and womanhood, they became more American than English.

Furthermore, the colonists were more than 3000 miles from the mother country. The fact that it took months sometimes to get advice or help from England forced the people to become independent and self-sufficient. *They had to think more and more for themselves.* They had to solve their personal problems of living — how to provide food, shelter, and clothing, and how to worship. At the same time, also, they began to solve their problems of *government*. Gradually they built up ideas of self-government. Without knowing how they had changed, they were becoming Americans in this respect too.

Thus, after several generations the two groups — Englishmen and colonists — had grown farther and farther apart. Each had its own point of view. Each wanted to satisfy its own desires and needs.

Of course the leaders among the Americans would not admit that they were not Englishmen — even in the middle 1700's. They were still loyal to the king of England. They still regarded themselves as his subjects. The well-to-do planters, merchants, and shipowners were proud of their British blood. Since they had plenty of money, many of them ordered their clothes from London, made in the latest English styles. Many built their new manor houses and town residences on English lines. At home and in public places they drank toasts to the king and the empire.

STRUGGLE FOR INDEPENDENT GOVERNMENT

But gradually, as important events developed, the leaders in America began to differ from the leaders in Great Britain. There was rivalry between the groups of business men on both sides of the sea, and soon the interests of the planters and merchants of America clashed with those of the manufacturers and merchants of England. The stanch vessels of the New England shipmasters were sailing the seven seas, taking trade away from British merchantmen. The manufacturers of the Northern colonies were not only making their own people's wares, but were also selling their products to England's customers in other countries. Before 1700 the infant colonies were becoming competitors of the mother country. As that took place trouble began to brew between the two peoples.

A SMALL GROUP OF WEALTHY LANDOWNERS AND MERCHANTS WERE GAINING CONTROL OF PARLIAMENT, 1660–1760

In England during the latter 1600's the House of Commons was becoming a rather powerful governing body. It had even succeeded for a short time in dethroning kings and replacing them with rulers chosen by Parliament. To be sure, the House of Commons was not a truly representative body as yet. Of the population of approximately five million people only about 160,000 prosperous property-owners had the right to vote, and of these a still smaller group played the most important part in the government.

Thus a tiny group of wealthy men passed the laws and ran the government. It was this group that slowly but surely came to clash with the small group of merchants, planters, shipowners, and manufacturers of the colonies. Throughout the struggle the common people were more or less indifferent.

THESE BRITISH BUSINESS MEN PASSED MANY LAWS WHICH RESTRICTED THE TRADE OF THE AMERICANS

Thus we find that by the time the first colonies became well established, conflict between these two groups had already begun. The British merchants asked that Parliament pass laws which

54 AMERICAN GOVERNMENT AND CULTURE

would favor them in the growing rivalry for trade. Parliament responded to their demands and laws were passed, some of which were a decided disadvantage to the planters, craftsmen, and shippers of America. Soon the colonies began to resent the grip which the mother country held upon them, and a century-long struggle for freedom developed.

You already know in outline the story of the struggle over the laws restricting trade and manufacturing in the colonies. Recall

FIG. 16. The port of Philadelphia during colonial days. (From an old engraving)

from your reading of *A History of American Civilization* the two types of laws passed in the century between 1660 and 1760:

1. The navigation and trade laws.
2. Laws restricting colonial manufactures and forbidding the issue of colonial money.

The Navigation Acts provided that all goods shipped to and from British colonies could be carried only in ships owned and manned by the *British*, which of course, at that time, included the ships of the colonists. This law met with no objection from the colonial shippers. It really protected their shipping as well as that of England and enabled them to extend the shipbuilding industry. By 1680 the Northern colonies were building large numbers of ships and selling many of them to English companies. Such great strides were being made that in the year 1720 Massachusetts alone launched 120 vessels.

By that time the shipbuilding companies of England began to protest. They even petitioned Parliament to make laws which would hold their lusty young competitor overseas within reasonable bounds. Forty years later (1760), however, more than 30 per cent of all the ships in the English merchant marine were vessels which had been launched from New England shipyards.

Then came the various trade laws. Some of these laws provided that if the colonists shipped their tobacco, tar, pitch, turpentine, masts, and other articles to any country but England, they must pay an export duty. In this way English merchants could obtain a profit for handling the goods. After a cargo had arrived in London, they could resell it elsewhere. Other laws placed heavy duties upon rum, molasses, and sugar carried into the American colonies from the West Indies. If these laws were enforced, it would mean that the triangular trade of the New Englanders would be ruined.

In addition, the colonists were not allowed to buy goods from other countries than England. If Americans wanted to buy from countries on the continent of Europe, they must have the goods sent first to England and from there to America. Thus British merchants could handle these goods and make a profit on them.

Colonial Resistance to the New Laws

1. In Virginia

The Southern planters, as well as the Northern merchants, were seriously affected by the laws, and they resented bitterly the interference of England in their growing trade. By 1667, shortly after the passage of the first trade laws, the price of tobacco had dropped to a cent a pound. Strong protests were soon heard. The small farmers were openly discussing rebellion, for their profits were cut to almost nothing. One of the Virginia leaders declared in a letter to a London official that there were but three influences restraining the smaller landowners in Virginia; namely, faith in the mercy of God, loyalty to the King, and affection for the government.

In 1671 Governor Berkeley warned the British government that there was great dissatisfaction in Virginia about the trade laws. Even in England the colonial planters found friends to plead their cause. Many Englishmen understood the plight of the Virginians and objected to the new laws. One London merchant wrote:

If the Hollanders must not trade to Virginia, how shall the planters dispose of their tobacco? The English will not buy it [all] . . . will it not then perish on the planter's hands?

2. The conflict between the colonists and the King in Massachusetts

On a hot day in July, 1664, Boston was tense with excitement. It was time for the town meeting to begin. Outside the Town House citizens were gathered in little groups, talking about the English frigate that lay out in Boston harbor. Breath-taking news had come.

Goodman Dull, a prosperous merchant, hurried with the news to Master Sewell of the Puritan council. "They're here for to meddle in our private affairs, Master," panted Goodman Dull. "'Tis said they are coming to take New Netherland from the Dutch, but the master of the frigate says 'tis rumored in England that they have business for King Charles in Boston. What can this be, think you?"

"'Twill be talked of in the meeting," replied Master Sewell curtly.

He and the other Puritan leaders already knew the purpose of the commission which the King was sending but had not yet decided what they would do; so it was just as well for simple, ignorant folk like Goodman Dull to hear nothing of the matter.

King Charles was really calling the Massachusetts colonists to account. They were disobeying his laws. First, they manufactured what they wished and sent ships wherever they pleased. They also purchased European wares in foreign ports more cheaply than could Englishmen themselves. In fact, the government of New England under the control of the prosperous merchants was becoming powerful enough to break laws as well as to make them; so King Charles was looking into the matter.

There were other violations to be investigated. The Puritans were defying the English government in religious matters. The staid Congregationalists yielded to no one on religious issues and allowed only members of the established church of Massachusetts to vote or to hold office. Even members of King Charles's Church of England, as well as Quakers and other Protestants, were denied the privilege of citizenship. The Quakers had already written to the King, protesting against this discrimination. The Puritans had replied that the Quakers were "open and capital blasphemers . . . open enemies to the government itself." Now King Charles did not object to the persecution of the Quakers; he felt about them very much as did the Puritan elders.

FIG. 17. Unlike Massachusetts, Virginia had accepted the religion of the Church of England. The Reverend James Blair, who was appointed in 1689 to represent the church in the colony, founded William and Mary College four years later

But the barring of Church of England members was quite another matter. That must be looked into!

Then, too, the Puritans were issuing their own money, and that was against the law. They were also taking land in New Hampshire without lawful authority from the home government, and they even bought the title to the territory without consulting the King. They had created their own courts, and they were preventing the people of Massachusetts from appealing to the higher courts in England.

Such acts of independence astonished and angered the English authorities. They insisted that the King send a commission to the colony to bring the disobedient colonists to their senses. Hence the frigate in Boston Harbor! The commissioners arrived, held many meetings, made many investigations, and returned to England — with nothing accomplished.

The colonists and their leaders were not easily managed. They continued to go on as they had before, trading with whatever country they wished. They coined their own money; they moved westward into the interior of New England and took land where they found it good. They continued to prevent persons who were not members of their own church holding office or even voting.

As time went on, the British government became more and more annoyed with Massachusetts. More agents were sent to the colony, but the Puritans could not be threatened or coaxed into obedience.

FIG. 18. Reading the document which announced to the citizens of Boston that Sir Edmund Andros was no longer governor. (From an old engraving)

Finally, in 1684, the British government decided to take away the colonial charter, and Sir Edmund Andros was sent to Massachusetts in 1686 to act as royal governor of all New England in addition to New York and New Jersey. He appointed his own council and made the laws, levying taxes and granting lands. He demanded a church with the English service. Worst of all he

STRUGGLE FOR INDEPENDENT GOVERNMENT 59

prohibited town meetings except once a year. An absolute royal government replaced the rule of the Puritans.

The people sent Increase Mather to England in the spring of 1688 to plead for a new charter which would again give the colonists their old liberties. Then one day new rumors spread in Boston. Parliament had placed William, a more liberal king, on the English throne. Soon the Puritans seized Governor Andros and put him and his assistants into prison. They proclaimed themselves the government of Massachusetts. In 1691 the new charter was granted, and the Plymouth Colony, Massachusetts, and Maine were all united under a fairly liberal government. Nevertheless, the old freedom in Massachusetts was sharply limited.

The government, for example, was a royal and a British government. A governor was appointed and sent over by the King. The Massachusetts assembly was allowed to choose the governor's council but only with the approval of the governor. The governor proclaimed that there must be religious freedom in the colony. All men who owned a certain amount of land were allowed to vote and hold office regardless of whether they were members of the Congregational Church or not. The Puritans might make the best of it! Of course they were not at all pleased.

3. In New York the Zenger trial illustrated the fight of the colonists for freedom of speech

The colonists still thought of themselves as loyal Englishmen and insisted upon their rights as British subjects. No one of these rights was prized more highly than that of freedom of speech, especially when criticism of their government was involved.

Between 1733 and 1735 events occurred in New York which illustrate clearly that the colonists insisted upon their right to criticize the government. A tyrannical royal governor, William Cosby, became involved in a dispute with colonial leaders. It was discovered that he was changing titles to land and in various illegal ways was building up a fortune. In the course of the disagreement Cosby removed from office the colonial chief justice of the supreme court of New York. The newspapers of the time

60 AMERICAN GOVERNMENT AND CULTURE

took sides in the controversy. *The New York Weekly Journal*, published by John Peter Zenger, severely criticized Governor Cosby's actions. The governor and his council angrily demanded that the colonial assembly punish Zenger. The assembly refused to do this.

Zenger was arrested, thrown into jail, and denied communication with his friends. The colonial grand jury, however, refused to bring action against him. Zenger was kept in prison illegally

FIG. 19. The trial of Peter Zenger. (From an old engraving)

for months and finally tried by a colonial jury called by the attorney-general, a man whom Cosby had appointed. Zenger was accused of a "false, scandalous, malicious, and seditious libel."

The trial became a center of interest throughout the colonies. Colonial leaders regarded Zenger as *their* representative and believed that the decision in the case would be a momentous one in American history. In the trial itself Andrew Hamilton, one of the ablest and most noted lawyers in all the colonies, made a remarkable speech defending the right of individual citizens to criticize the government and insisting upon free speech. The royal governor, his attorneys, and judges disagreed and tried to restrict the rights of the jury. Nevertheless, after a few minutes

STRUGGLE FOR INDEPENDENT GOVERNMENT   61

of discussion, the colonial jury declared Zenger not guilty. The decision was greeted with cheers, speeches, and dinners in honor of Hamilton and Zenger. The event was hailed as a great step in the march of democracy in the colonies.

The Zenger trial is a striking illustration of the manner in which the American colonists, while remaining loyal subjects of England, were demanding the protection of their inalienable rights as Englishmen.

4. The quarrel with the Northern colonies over paper money

England also disputed the right of her young colonies to issue money. This disagreement is somewhat difficult to understand. We shall outline it as simply as possible.

1. Business was carried on in the colonies with English money. All money was supposed to be coined in England.

2. Banking for the colonies was done in England, especially in London in the Bank of England. This made profits for English bankers.

3. British officials and men who studied carefully the business conditions of England and her colonies believed at that time that as much gold as possible should be kept in England.

4. The colonists were compelled to send their gold and silver to England in order to pay for goods purchased from British merchants. After the imports had been paid for there was often very little gold or silver in the colonies by which the colonists could trade with one another. The Northern colonial assemblies thought of a way out of the difficulty. They decided to issue paper money. Several colonies issued large amounts of this paper currency, and it was used widely among the colonies for purchases within the colonies.

5. The Southern merchants and planters complained to England about the Northern paper money. They objected to accepting it in exchange for their products, for it was not worth much outside the colony by which it was issued.

6. The British Parliament passed a law (1751) which forbade the colonies to issue paper money.

The assemblies of New England were much annoyed at this act and took steps against it. When the royal governors were ordered by Parliament to veto bills for paper money, the assemblies refused to pay the salary of the governor and his officials. In this way the assemblies kept control of the purse strings of the colony and tied the hands of the governor.

The fight between the royal government and the colonies went on. In 1686 New York, New Jersey, New Hampshire, Maine, Massachusetts, Rhode Island, and Connecticut were all united and for three years were ruled by one governor. By the middle of the 1700's nearly all the colonies had lost their charters and become "royal provinces," ruled by governors sent over from England by the king. In some cases the original charter expired. In others the charter was withdrawn by the king. Pennsylvania alone had more self-government than the rest.

Thus the conflict between the colonies and the mother country went on

So the years went by from 1700 until after the middle of the century. The colonies tolerated the English laws so long as they were not enforced. They were a source of friction, nevertheless. Leading citizens, respectable merchants, and assemblymen smuggled goods in and out of the colonies in open defiance of the law. All along the seaboard the leaders ignored the laws whenever they saw fit. Most of the leading people felt the same way on the subject. They believed that the laws were wrong, for they were passed without their consent. The colonists had had no representatives in Parliament to vote on the laws; therefore they set them aside.

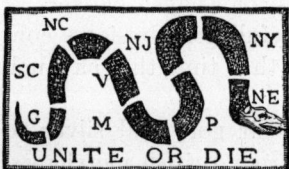

FIG. 20. In 1754 this cartoon appeared in print. It was the first to suggest that the colonies might unite for mutual protection

In the meantime, the colonies grew prosperous, powerful, and able to support themselves without help. In and out of the ports of Philadelphia, New York, and Boston, as well as smaller ports, went ships in greater numbers each year. To and from England, France, Spain, Portugal, and the West Indies they carried goods. Out of the Northern ports went timber, fish, and rum. Into the Northern ports came molasses from the West Indies; clothes,

STRUGGLE FOR INDEPENDENT GOVERNMENT

furniture, and manufactured goods from England; fruit and salt from Spain and Portugal. The shrewd New England traders were growing rich. From the South tobacco was shipped to England, and in return the colonists imported European luxuries for the homes of the planters. Remember that much of this trade was opposed to the Navigation Acts and was thus against the law.

Industries were also growing in the colonies, as you have learned in *A History of American Civilization*. Long before 1700 there were many spinning and weaving shops, factories, and iron forges. Tools, implements, and weapons were being made in the colonies instead of being purchased in England.

Then, after 1760, came events that sharpened the conflict.

INTERESTING READINGS FROM WHICH YOU CAN GET ADDITIONAL INFORMATION

ANDREWS, CHARLES M. The Fathers of New England, Vol. VI of The Chronicles of America, pp. 147–193. Yale University Press, New Haven.

COFFIN, C. C. Old Times in the Colonies. Harper & Brothers, New York.

FARIS, JOHN T. Makers of our History. Ginn and Company, Boston.

FARIS, JOHN T. Real Stories from our History. Ginn and Company, Boston.

FISHER, S. G. The Quaker Colonies, Vol. VIII of The Chronicles of America. Yale University Press, New Haven.

HART, ALBERT B. American History told by Contemporaries. The Macmillan Company, New York. See Volume I, pp. 463–466 (The Revolution against Andros (1689)). For the best readers.

HAWTHORNE, NATHANIEL. Twice-Told Tales. "The Gray Champion" is a beautiful story which tells of the revolt against Governor Andros.

LAMPREY, L. Days of the Colonists. Frederick A. Stokes Company, New York.

TAPPAN, EVA M. Letters from Colonial Children. Houghton Mifflin Company, Boston.

WEST, WILLIS M. A Source Book in American History to 1787. Allyn and Bacon, Boston.

Old South Leaflets. Directors of the Old South Work, Old South Meeting House, Boston. Sold at 5 cents a leaflet.

CHAPTER V

THE CLIMAX OF THE STRUGGLE, 1760–1776

In 1760 a new king, George III, ascended the throne of England, and three years later the French and Indian War came to an end (1763). England had defeated her old enemy, France, both in Europe and America, and now the British government was free to attend more completely to the colonies.

How the Close of the French and Indian War brought on the Climax of the Struggle

The French and Indian War did two things which affected the relations between the colonies and England:

1. It broke the French power in North America. The colonists were now no longer afraid that French traders would take the land to the west, and they were safe against attack by French soldiers. England had helped to protect them against an enemy. Now that the fear of the French was gone, the colonies had less need of England.

2. The war united the colonies. They had always quarreled so much among themselves that many people thought that they disliked one another more than they disliked England. They had rarely been able to act together in anything. During the war, however, they had united and had shown that they could work together.

England was also seriously affected by the war. Her debt had been doubled, and the cost of maintaining the American colonies had risen during the years 1748 to 1763 from £70,000 to £350,000.

Now England's ministers remembered that the colonies had profited by the war which drove the French from North America. Moreover, troops had still to be sent to the colonies for their continued protection. Why should not the colonists pay for these troops? Why should they not house and feed the soldiers in their own homes? English people were heavily taxed to pay for the wars with France. Why shouldn't the colonies also bear their share? In 1776 they still argued thus:

> On what principle therefore of policy, equity, or humanity, ought the English artificers to be oppressed with taxes and the Americans exempt? Why should the ship builder or sailor of Boston or New York be put in better condition than the ship builder or sailor of Whitby or Port Glasgow? These in Britain are at least as useful members of the empire as those in America.[1]

In 1763, therefore, when the French and Indian War ended, Parliament decided to make the colonies pay part of the costs. Within two years laws were passed which gave British officials much greater control over the American colonies. To obtain this control four steps were taken.

How England tried to make the Colonies pay

1. Enforcement of the navigation and trade laws

The navigation and trade laws began to be strictly enforced after 1763. Larger numbers of British vessels patrolled American shores to prevent smugglers from carrying on their trade.

2. Restrictions on fur-trading

Acts were passed in the same year (1763) forbidding the colonists to carry on fur-trading in western lands without permission of the king's officials.

3. The new Sugar Act, 1764

An earlier tax on sugar was revised by the act of 1764, by being somewhat reduced, but new articles were added to the tax list. The lowered tax on sugar was provided in order that there should be less temptation for colonial shippers to smuggle it into the country. Under the Navigation Acts officers of the navy were

---

[1] J. Roebuck, *An Enquiry, Whether the Guilt of the Present Civil War in America ought to be imputed to Great Britain or America*, pp. 54, 55. Printed for John Donaldson, London, 1776.

given the power to stop and seize ships carrying forbidden goods. Every vessel was to be suspected. Furthermore, any citizen might awake any night from a sound sleep to find a British officer at his door armed with a document called a Writ of Assistance. This document gave the officer and his men the right to search the citizen's house for smuggled goods. Since smugglers were to be tried in admiralty courts, they were thereby denied trial by jury.

The New Englanders were aroused by the Sugar Act. Merchants who were growing rich from the triangular trade suddenly ceased to do business. Shipowners fumed while their vessels lay idle at the dock. Distillery-owners saw their buildings empty and quiet. Many people found themselves without work.

4. In 1765 followed the Stamp Act

It had been a quiet day in the British Parliament. The members had discussed casually the bill proposed by Grenville, the minister, to levy a stamp tax upon the North American colonies. The bill provided that stamped paper, sold by the government, should be used in the colonies for all legal documents and other printed matter such as newspapers, calendars, playing cards, and college diplomas. This stamp tax would bring in a rather good sum to be used in payment for the defense of the colonies.

Most of the members accepted the idea as a good one. Townshend asked whether "these American children, planted by our care, nourished by our indulgence to a degree of strength and opulence, and protected by our arms" would now be so ungrateful as to "grudge to contribute their mite to relieve us from the heavy burden under which we lie."

Perhaps the members of Parliament were a little bored by the discussion. Nothing could be clearer to them than that the colonists should help to pay for their own defense. What could be better, then, than the Stamp Act? Furthermore, the colonists had been given a year's warning of the act. They had been told that if they could offer better suggestions for raising money, their plans would be considered. No suggestions had been received.

The bill was passed by a large majority.

THE CLIMAX OF THE STRUGGLE, 1760–1776

THE COLONISTS RESISTED THE NEW LAWS VIGOROUSLY

James Otis defends the Boston merchants against the Writs of Assistance

The colonists, especially those who were smuggling goods into the colonies, objected strenuously to the Writs of Assistance. They began to oppose the writs everywhere, both in court and out. Lawyers were engaged to fight every case in which they were used.

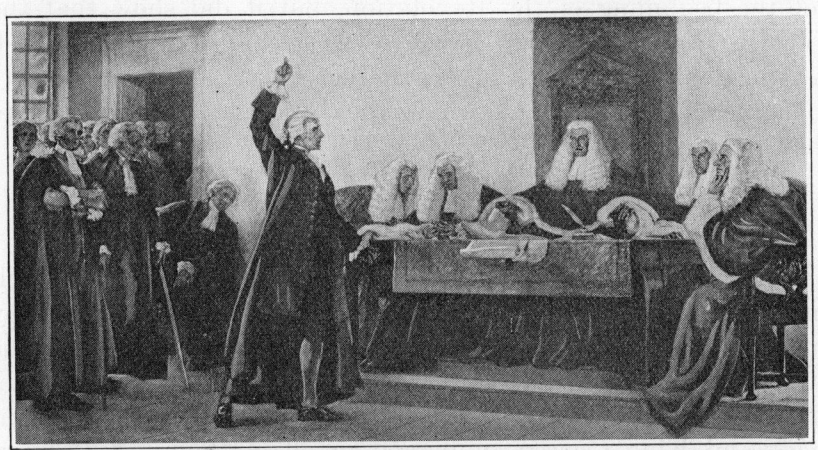

FIG. 21. James Otis defending the Boston merchants and protesting against the Writs of Assistance. (From a painting by Robert Reid)

One such case is famous in American history. It was the trial held in the council chamber of the Town House in Boston, in February, 1761. A young colonial lawyer, James Otis, defended some of the Boston merchants.

For five long hours the eagle-eyed young politician spoke against the Writs of Assistance. He was fiery and passionate, and the people in the chamber listened to him intently.

In the court room that day there was another young man, John Adams, who was to play a leading part in the drama of the Revolution and in the later history of our country. Long years afterward, when Adams was an old man, he wrote of Otis and his speech as follows:

Otis was a flame of fire. With . . . a prophetic glance of his eye into futurity, and a torrent of impetuous eloquence, he hurried away everything before him. American independence was then and there born; the seeds of patriots and heroes were then and there sown. . . . Every man of a crowded audience appeared to me to go away, as I did, ready to take arms against Writs of Assistance. Then and there was the first scene of the first act of opposition to the arbitrary claims of Great Britain. Then and there the child Independence was born.[1]

Probably the speech of James Otis was less important than the young John Adams thought it had been. It was probably not the beginning of the Revolution, but it did show that the colonists were becoming more unwilling to submit to British laws made in the interest of British merchants. They were ready to fight against anything which they believed was opposed to their own interests.

The passage of the Stamp Act gives the colonies a common grievance

The news of the passage of the Stamp Act reached the colonies in April of 1765. Each of the colonies had been affected by one or another of the trade laws, but until the passage of the Stamp Act no one law had affected all sections. Now all the colonies had one common grievance, and resentment against Parliament and King George smoldered in all of them. They were united in their protest for the first time.

The flames burst out in the Virginia assembly when Patrick Henry presented his resolutions, 1765

It was the 29th of May. The session of the Virginia assembly was almost over. Two thirds of the representatives had gone home, believing that all the important business had been transacted.

Patrick Henry, a young lawyer from the back country of Virginia, stood with a copy of an old law book in his hand. On the fly leaf he had written a number of resolutions which he was reading to the assembly.

A bold young man, indeed, this Patrick Henry. The assembly contained many polished and brilliant men, members of the aristocracy who for years had been active in the government of

[1] James K. Hosmer, *Samuel Adams*, p. 44. Houghton Mifflin Company, Boston, 1885.

THE CLIMAX OF THE STRUGGLE, 1760–1776

Virginia. Young Henry had just been sent down from one of the poorer frontier counties. To be sure, he had previously gained a reputation for his fiery eloquence and for his defense of the common people, but who was he to stand in this assembly and propose resolutions to these older and more experienced men?

After a long debate, five of Henry's resolutions were passed. They stated in brief (1) that the first settlers in Virginia brought

FIG. 22. Bostonians were filled with indignation and resentment when they learned of the passage of the Stamp Act

with them all the liberties and privileges of Englishmen; (2) that the early royal charters granted to the colonists the same liberties as those enjoyed by native-born British subjects; (3) that the Virginians had always been governed and taxed by their own representatives in the assemblies; (4) that the people of Virginia had never given up or been denied the rights of British subjects; (5) that the general assembly should have the exclusive right of taxation.

Little did Patrick Henry realize that after he was gone from the assembly some of the older members removed from the record that last resolution. But Henry had won his point. Before the fifth article was canceled, all the resolutions had been sent out by post. Soon they were broadcast throughout the colonies.

The Patrick Henry resolutions started a fire which would burn long

Many leading men considered the Virginia Resolutions treasonable; but most of the colonists approved them. The British governor of Massachusetts wrote that "nothing extravagant appeared in the papers till an account was received of the Virginia resolves." Then the *Boston Gazette* declared:

The people of Virginia have spoken very sensibly, and the frozen politicians of a more northern government say they have spoken treason.[1]

In 1765 the Massachusetts assemblymen called a Stamp Act Congress, to which all the colonies were invited to send representatives. The congress met and passed a declaration of rights and grievances. These were not very strong, but they showed that there was a growing spirit of united opposition in the colonies.

Riots and demonstrations: The common people began to take matters into their own hands

The mechanics and laborers who were out of work were not satisfied with the opposition shown by many of the colonial leaders, including those at the Stamp Act Congress. All through the colonies anti-Stamp Act riots broke out. The streets of cities were bright with torches and noisy with mob cries.

Soon a secret organization called the Sons of Liberty was formed to resist the Stamp Act. Most of the members came from the laboring class, although there were some business and professional men among them. At that time, as well as later, we find that the upper classes were cautious and slow to act.

The Sons of Liberty knew that English merchants depended upon the colonies to buy large quantities of goods from England; so they brought about the nonimportation agreements.

[1] "Letter from Virginia," June 14, 1765, in *London Gazeteer* of August 13, 1765; quoted from William W. Henry's *Patrick Henry*, Vol. I, p. 94. Charles Scribner's Sons, New York, 1891.

THE CLIMAX OF THE STRUGGLE, 1760–1776

By these acts the merchants agreed that they would not import English goods until the Stamp Act was repealed.

Not all the merchants, of course, were willing to destroy their own profitable trade by refusing to import English goods. But

FIG. 23. The coffeehouse where the New York Sons of Liberty met. (From Valentine's *Manual*, 1838)

the Sons of Liberty knew how to bring pressure upon those merchants who loved their own profits better than they did the cause of liberty. Notice the wording of the handbill[1] which was posted in the streets of Boston:

WILLIAM JACKSON
an Importer at the
BRAZEN HEAD

North Side of the TOWN HOUSE, and Opposite the Town-Pump, in Corn-hill, Boston.

It is desired that the Sons and Daughters of LIBERTY would not buy any one thing of him, for in so doing they will bring Disgrace upon themselves and their Posterity, for ever and ever, Amen.

---

[1] Adapted from an original handbill, in Justin Winsor's *Narrative and Critical History of America*, Vol. VI, p. 80. Houghton Mifflin Company, Boston, 1888.

The New York Gazette carried in large type the legend "It is better to wear a homespun coat than lose our liberty."

The Massachusetts Gazette of October 31, 1765, contained the following verse:

> With us of the woods
> Lay aside your fine goods,
> Contentment depends not on clothes;
> We hear, smell, and see,
> Taste and feel, with high glee,
> And in winter have huts to repose.

The Stamp Act repealed, 1766

The Stamp Act, which had been passed so quietly, was the center of controversy in England as well as in America. Some of the greatest statesmen in England were decidedly opposed to it. William Pitt believed it was unfair. Lord Rockingham thought it was fair but not wise. Soon English business men began to complain to members of the British government:

> Our trade is hurt; what ... have you been doing? For our part, we don't pretend to understand your politics and American matters, but our trade is hurt; pray remedy it, and a plague on you if you don't.

Benjamin Franklin, who had been sent to England to represent the colonists, protested in the House of Commons. Franklin is reported to have described the unfair acts in these words:

> I have some little property in America. I will freely spend nineteen shillings in the pound to defend my right of giving or refusing the other shilling. And, after all, if I cannot defend that right, I can retire cheerfully with my family into the boundless woods of America which are sure to afford freedom and subsistence to any man who can bait a hook or pull a trigger.

In March, 1766, the Stamp Act was repealed. There was great rejoicing in America. The taverns echoed with the songs of the jubilant Sons of Liberty. Gentlemen drank toasts to the King. In New York an ox was roasted, and twenty kegs of beer were opened. It was a great day for the colonies.

But the rejoicing was not to last. During the next year other acts were passed.

The Townshend Acts

The majority in Parliament believed that England should assert the right to tax the colonists. Charles Townshend, Chancellor of the Exchequer, spoke in Parliament in January, 1767.

"I do not expect to have my statue created in America. England is undone if this taxation is given up," he said. And

FIG. 24. A street scene in Boston. The building at the right is Faneuil Hall. It has often been called "the cradle of American liberty," for here the patriots of Massachusetts met and here many of the important resolutions of the American colonists were passed. (From an old print)

most of the members agreed with him. There were others who did not agree, but they were not enough to prevent the passage of the Townshend Acts. These acts suspended the New York assembly and provided for enforcement of the trade laws. They also placed duties on glass, paper, lead, painters' colors, and tea imported into the colonies. If the colonists bought these things abroad they must pay a tax on them at their ports.

When reports of the new taxes reached the colonies, there was great anger. The Sons of Liberty soon became active and once more there were riots in the streets of the cities. The spirit of rebellion again walked abroad. Samuel Adams wrote to the colonial assemblies, asking them to unite. Almost the whole population was opposed to the measures, since the ordinary people would have to pay extra for what they bought and the merchants would find their trade hampered by the duties.

Once more the British merchants found their trade endangered, and the British politicians found themselves facing rebellion in the colonies. So in 1770 the Townshend duties also were repealed, *with the exception of the duty on tea.*

Parliament left this duty on tea as a proof of the right to tax colonists. There was no real trouble until three years later, when the British East India Company, which had a large amount of surplus tea, received from Parliament the right to sell tea in America subject to a small tax. The East India Company could sell tea to the colonists which even with the tax cost them less than they could buy it from the colonial importers. Thus the colonial tea merchants were angered by the British competition. Other Americans began to fear lest powerful English companies, like the East India Company, might gain direct control of business; so they also objected strongly to the tea tax. Among the patriots there was a widespread feeling that no matter how small a tax was imposed it was unjust, since they had no part in deciding it themselves.

The "Boston Massacre"

British troops had begun to appear in the colonies. Their bright red coats did not please the eyes of the Americans. Here and there riots broke out between soldiers and populace. In Boston real trouble occurred. Two British regiments had arrived there. The men had been careful to try to give as little cause for complaint as possible. They had been instructed not to annoy the colonists, nor to interfere with their liberties.

Trouble came, however, on the evening of March 5, 1770, when the British troops, angered by the taunts of a group of men and boys, fired upon them, killing five.

The resentment of the people of Boston was again stirred. Distrust and anger became more intense.

© National Portrait Gallery, London

FIG. 25. George III, ruler of Great Britain from 1760 to 1820, was incapable of dealing with the colonial problem

© Detroit Publishing Company

FIG. 26. William Pitt, who understood and sympathized with the spirit of the American people

FIG. 27. Edmund Burke, who urged compromise with the colonists. (Courtesy of the New York Public Library)

Fig. 28. Charles Townshend, author of the Townshend Acts. (Courtesy of the New York Public Library)

THE BRITISH KING AND THREE MEMBERS OF PARLIAMENT WHO INFLUENCED AMERICAN HISTORY

The Revolutionary movement in the colonies was growing; Committees of Correspondence were being formed

About the year 1770 one might have seen in Boston a very busy man by the name of Samuel Adams. Mr. Adams's whole life lay in politics, and he was a master politician.

For some time his attention, so long centered upon local politics, had been turning toward fighting the cause of the colonies as a whole. The question was how to go about it. He believed that the colonies should be brought together, so that there should be some way of exchanging ideas on the difficulties with England.

© Detroit Publishing Company
FIG. 29. Samuel Adams

In 1768 the Massachusetts assembly, inspired by Adams, had sent a letter of appeal to all the colonies. Adams was careful to write with great tact, but English officers scented rebellion beneath his carefully chosen phrases. The royal governor ordered the assembly to retract what Adams had written. The assembly refused.

The movement to unite the leaders of various colonies went on, however. Samuel Adams was working out an idea of how to form "associations and combinations." Later in December of the same year we find this note in the town records of Boston:

It was then moved by Mr. Samuel Adams that a Committee of Correspondence be appointed, to consist of twenty-one persons, to state the rights of the colonists and of this Province in particular as men and Christians and as subjects; and to communicate and publish the same to the several towns and to the world as the sense of this town.[1]

The plan for Committees of Correspondence was enthusiastically received throughout the colonies. Soon these appeared in

[1] James K. Hosmer, *Samuel Adams*, p. 199. Houghton Mifflin Company, Boston. 1885.

many towns and villages. In five colonies members of the committees were chosen by the assemblies. This plan brought together leading men in the colonies, who were living so many hundred miles apart.

The common people began to take part in the Revolutionary movement

On flowed the Revolutionary movement, but it was changing as it flowed.

When, with the exception of the tax on tea, the Townshend duties were repealed, most of the well-to-do people — that is, the "gentlemen," the merchants, the professional men — were satisfied. Their business was safe. After all, they had no idea of breaking away from the mother country. They had great sympathy with the ruling classes in England — more, indeed, than with the lower classes in the colonies. They felt that these lower classes were looking for trouble, that they were pushing the matter too far. For the most part the upper classes wanted to keep peace with England.

But a movement had started which they could not stop. The artisans and workers of the cities, the frontiersmen and the small farmers, and a few intelligent leaders were actively bringing about a revolution. They frequently forced hesitating merchants to act. From that time on, the rebellion proceeded largely against the wishes of the upper classes. There was increasing opposition from many well-to-do people who sympathized with England.

All who favored England's point of view were called Tories. Of course there were Tories among the common people, and here and there were members of the upper classes who were active in the Revolutionary movement. On the whole, however, the aristocrats were more anxious for peace with England than were the common people.

The Boston Tea Party, 1773

During the late autumn of 1773 news traveled back and forth among the colonies. The Committees of Correspondence were busy exchanging opinions on new grievances. Samuel Adams was unusually busy on his committees. A crisis was at hand.

News had come that a number of ships were bound for the chief colonial ports. These ships were loaded with tea — the tea which still bore a tax and which was being forced upon the colonists.

The Committees of Correspondence agreed to resist the landing of the tea. From Philadelphia, from Charleston, from New York, word came to Boston that the patriots would not allow the tea to be taken off the ships and sold.

FIG. 30. This is a caricature of the Sons of Liberty forcing a government officer to drink tea. Notice that the officer has already received a coat of feathers. (From a lithograph copied from an engraving of 1774)

In Philadelphia the Liberty Boys said that when the expected ship came in they would put a halter round the captain's neck, pour ten gallons of liquid tea over him, and then put the feathers of a dozen wild geese over that.

In Boston the feeling against the landing of the tea was even more violent. A number of town meetings had stirred excitement to fever pitch. In the Old South Church and crowded into the streets round it 7000 people, massed at a meeting on December 16, were unanimously determined against allowing the tea to be landed. Although darkness fell and candles had to be lighted before the meeting had reached a decision as to what course to pursue, the people still waited. At last, when a messenger arrived from the governor with word that he could not allow the tea to be returned to England, Samuel Adams exclaimed, "This meeting can do nothing more to save the country." It was as if a prearranged signal had been given. War whoops rang out, and 40 or 50 "Mohawks" rushed past the church and toward Grifflin's Wharf, the crowd following close behind. On board the ships anchored there the "Indians" worked quietly and swiftly. Three hundred and forty-two chests of tea were ripped open, and the tea was cast into the waters of the harbor.

The Intolerable Acts and the First Continental Congress, 1774

"The die is now cast," wrote King George III to his prime minister. "The colonists must either submit or triumph." The British government knew that the critical moment had come. Parliament passed a number of measures which were meant to punish the rebellious Bostonians. These measures were called in America the Intolerable Acts. One of them forbade that town meetings be held unless allowed by the governor. Also all judges and other port officials were to be appointed by him. Another, the Quartering Act, required the colonists to provide shelter for British soldiers and officers. Persons accused of crime were to be taken to England for trial in British courts. Worst of all, however, was the Port Bill, which closed the port of Boston so that no ships could go in or out with food. By this act the inhabitants were threatened with starvation.

The Massachusetts charter was taken away. West of the colonies the boundary of the distant Canadian province of Quebec was extended southward to the Ohio River. This was a severe blow to Massachusetts, Connecticut, and Virginia, for each of those colonies had planned to settle this western country which England had recently won from France.

From Virginia came the suggestion that a congress be held to which all the colonies should send representatives. From the Committees of Correspondence of all the colonies, except Georgia, representatives to the congress were chosen.

On September 5, 1774, the First Continental Congress met. Patrick Henry and George Washington were there, as well as John and Samuel Adams. John Adams described the convention as "one third Tories, one third Whigs (patriots), and the rest

Mongrels." True it was that the two sides — one wanting to avoid trouble with England and the other anxious to maintain colonial rights at all costs — were rather evenly balanced. For seven weeks the two sides struggled to decide what action should be taken. In the end the patriots won.

The Congress recommended an association of all the colonies which should agree to boycott all British goods. They also agreed to discontinue the slave trade. A date was set after which the signers of the association would import no goods from the mother country. Another date was set after which they would export no goods to Great Britain. Note that the Congress did not mention independence from the mother country. The boycott was only an attempt to make the English government repeal the unfair acts.

Preparations were being made in each colony for resisting England

Assemblies and congresses were meeting in the various colonies, preparing for active resistance. Patriotic and historic speeches were being made. None is more thrilling and historic than that of Patrick Henry before the Virginia convention in 1775. The question before the meeting was Should Virginia join the association of colonies? Should she support the Continental Congress? Henry spoke these passionate words in favor of the united colonies:

> Gentlemen may cry peace, peace,— but there is no peace. The war is actually begun. The next gale that sweeps from the north will bring to our ears the clash of resounding arms. Our brethren are already in the field. Why stand we here idle? What is it that gentlemen wish? What would they have? Is life so dear, or peace so sweet, as to be purchased at the price of chains and slavery? Forbid it, Almighty God! I know not what course others may take, but as for me, give me liberty, or give me death!

The answer of Patrick Henry and the Virginia convention was, "Yes! Sign the association! Unite with the Northern colonies!"

At the same time Patrick Henry was helping to organize the Virginia militia. Fired by his enthusiasm, many young men enlisted in a volunteer company.

In the other colonies this story was being repeated. Conventions and congresses were also held. Preparations for war were

FIG. 31. Patrick Henry speaking before the First Continental Congress. (From a painting by Clyde O. De Land. Courtesy of the American Telephone and Telegraph Company)

made. Within six months after the first meeting of the First Continental Congress, all but two of the colonies had signed the pact of association.

WAR BEGINS

The battles at Lexington and Concord, April 19, 1775

"Stand your ground. Don't fire unless fired upon; but if they mean to have war, let it begin here."

These were the words of Captain Parker, who led the first band of Americans in the Revolutionary War. They were uttered on the village green of Lexington, Massachusetts, on the morning of April 19, 1775, as a regiment of British soldiers, nearly 1000 strong, marched through the town. "If they mean to have war, let it begin here!" And there it began.

What had happened to bring on war? General Gage, governor of Massachusetts, had determined to arrest the patriots John

Hancock and Samuel Adams and to destroy stores of ammunition held by the colonists at Concord, a town about eighteen miles from Boston. To Concord, therefore, marched 800 red-coated British soldiers. In the meantime an American had learned of the plan and, on the night of April 18, had signaled to two daring riders, Paul Revere and William Dawes, to dash toward Concord by separate routes and warn the citizens along the way.

FIG. 32. Spreading the news of the battle of Lexington throughout the countryside. (From a painting by John Ward Dunsmore)

Revere was stopped at Lexington by British soldiers and compelled to go back. Dawes was successful, however, and aroused the farmers over a broad countryside.

When the British troops reached Lexington the next morning, they found Parker and 60-odd colonial "minutemen" drawn up in military form on the village green. The British rushed forward. Their officer, Major Pitcairn, cried, "Disperse, ye rebels!" A shot was fired, whether by a British soldier or by an American, no one knows. At any rate, this shot was followed by a volley from the redcoats, and eight of the militiamen fell dead.

On to Concord marched the British soldiers. When they arrived, they destroyed what stores they could find (Hancock and

Adams had escaped) and started back toward Cambridge. Then they met disaster. As they marched along the roads in their bright red coats, they were suddenly attacked. From behind trees, bushes, and fences came the deadly fire of the farmers who had gathered to meet them. Their foe could seldom be seen. The British soldiers could only march on. By the time they reached Cambridge, 247 of their men had been killed. War had indeed begun.

The next days were filled with fearful suspense. Groups of villagers were gathered everywhere, talking excitedly over their grievances and the possibility of winning a war against England.

The Second Continental Congress meets and becomes the Body which is to carry on the War

On the 10th of May, 1775, the Second Continental Congress met in Philadelphia. What tremendous problems confronted this body of men, so small in number and so inexperienced! War had started and it must be carried on. Armies must be organized; funds must be raised; government must go on. How could these problems be solved?

Congress forms a Continental Army and George Washington becomes commander in chief

It was near the end of June, 1775. In the villages that dotted the road from Boston to Philadelphia there was bustling activity. Breathless excitement had seized the people. Little bands of men paraded daily on village commons. These patriots, as they called themselves, were training to carry guns and fight. The thirteen colonies, and particularly the town of Boston, must be defended against the British soldiers. One by one the colonies were ordering that militias be raised and trained.

Suddenly there came another startling bit of news. It passed rapidly from house to house, from village to village, raising enthusiasm among the patriots and gloom among those still loyal to Great Britain. The Continental Congress had acted. The delegates had decided that there must be one army to defend all the colonies and a commander in chief to direct the war.

This commander was George Washington. He was even then on the way to Boston to take over the army that had been quickly gathered near Cambridge, Massachusetts. The people poured out of their houses along the roadsides to await him and give him welcome.

There were some people, however, who did not join in the welcome. They were the loyalists, or Tories — those who still

FIG. 33. The retreat of the British from Concord. (From an engraving after a painting by Alonzo Chappel)

believed that the colonies should not fight against England. They heard the news with misgivings and even scorn. What could this untrained colonial "general" do against the army of one of the greatest nations of the world?

Meanwhile there was much excitement in Cambridge. Great preparations were being made for the proper reception of General Washington. A house for his use must be made ready, the army put in its best order, and escorts sent out to meet him.

John Adams wrote:

I hope the utmost politeness and respect will be shown. . . . The whole army, I think, should be drawn up upon the occasion, and all the pride, pomp, and circumstance of glorious war displayed.

THE CLIMAX OF THE STRUGGLE, 1760–1776

This, indeed, was done. On July 3, in the presence of a vast crowd of volunteers, which was now to be called the American army, Washington took command. He sat on horseback under an elm tree, and an observer noted that his appearance was "truly noble and majestic."

Until 1924 the famous elm tree under which Washington took control of the army stood and was cherished as a monument to that great occasion. It was called the Washington Elm.

Why George Washington was chosen

Who was this man to whom such honors were paid and upon whom the hopes of all the patriots were centered — to whom presently the eyes of all Europe would turn?

Do you remember the story in *A History of American Civilization* of the young surveyor from Virginia who went to help General Braddock early in the French and Indian War, and who, when General Braddock was defeated by the Indians, stepped in and saved from massacre all that remained of the English army by leading them in retreat?

The people of the colonies had not forgotten this incident. They remembered, too, other experiences which Washington had had in warfare. Since the time of Braddock's defeat he had often served Virginia in her battles, and even now was commander of her troops.

Washington was also a man of wealth and owned a large estate in Virginia. He had long been a member of the Virginia assembly and was among the first to resent the acts of the English ministry. He had recently represented Virginia at the Continental Congress.

Were his wealth and experience the only reasons for the confidence people gave him? No, indeed. He had other qualities for which even his enemies honored him — the qualities of a great and generous character.

This, then, was the man into whose hands fell the task of winning the war against England — a man known and respected throughout the colonies as one of America's gentlemen of ability.

Is it surprising, then, that, for the moment, enthusiasm and hopes mounted high among the patriots?

General Washington found himself facing great handicaps

Was this army, which had so enthusiastically received the commander in chief under the Cambridge elm, like the army which General Howe, the British commander, held in Boston? Were they a band of well-clothed, well-trained men who had long understood the methods of battle? Far, far from it! They were, instead, as one historian described them, "a motley crowd, clad in every variety of rustic attire, armed with trusty muskets and rifles . . . but destitute of almost everything else that belongs to a soldier's outfit."[1]

You see, these men had rushed together suddenly to defend Boston in her hour of need. They had not thought that they were entering upon a long war. When affairs in the colonies were settled, they would return to their homes and continue tilling their farms or carrying on their trades. As yet there was really no great common purpose to bind Washington's army together. That is why one of the first great problems which he faced was that simply of holding his men together.

Then, too, neither were the people from whom the troops were drawn united in one great, common purpose. There were still large numbers of Tories who believed it was wrong to take up arms against the British troops and who did everything they could to hinder the cause of the patriots. As their anger against England grew, the patriots became more intolerant of the Tories. Soon no Tory's life or property was safe. Sometimes just for holding opinions that were contrary to those of the patriots, even when they did nothing deliberately to provoke anger, they suffered outrages. They were tarred and feathered, their houses were destroyed, and sometimes they themselves were hanged.

This feeling against Tories was strong throughout the war, and many of these unhappy people had no recourse but to try to escape to England or to Canada.

Thus, in truth, a condition of "civil war," with lack of a common purpose, made Washington's task a very difficult one.

---

[1] John Fiske, *The American Revolution*, pp. 155-156. Houghton Mifflin Company, Boston, 1891.

Some people were beginning to hope for complete independence from England

As we said before, there was at first no mention of independence. Washington and nearly every other leader of colonial life had hoped that the trouble with England would quickly end, and that friendly relations would again be established between King George III and his colonies. People did not blame the King for the trouble as much as they blamed his ministers in Parliament. Even after war had actually begun, expressions of loyalty to King George were common in the mouths of the patriots.

However, in order to raise their armies, carry on war against the British troops, and resist the acts of the English government which the troops were trying to enforce, the colonies had been forced to form governments of their own. Thus in one sense they were already independent of the King and his ministers.

Some of the most radical men in the Continental Congress, such as Samuel Adams, began to urge the Congress to look this fact in the face and declare America independent, but most of the delegates were distressed at the thought of separating from England. They sent a polite and carefully written petition demanding that the oppressive acts be repealed and that they be represented in Parliament.

Torrents of protests against the attitude of Parliament poured forth everywhere in the colonies. Those leaders of public life who desired complete independence from England seized the opportunity to inflame people with their own passion.

Pamphlets, newspapers, and earnest leaders roused the people to action

In January, 1776, a pamphlet called *Common Sense* was circulated widely throughout the colonies. More than 100,000 copies were sold! Its phrases were, it seemed, on the tip of everybody's tongue.

The pamphlet was anonymous, that is, published without the author's name. Great curiosity was aroused as to who wrote it. Some guessed Jefferson, others Adams, and nearly all the aggressive leaders were accredited with it.

88   AMERICAN GOVERNMENT AND CULTURE

Thomas Paine, an Englishman who had been in the colonies only about a year, proved to be the author. He had been discharged from a government post in England, and after a year

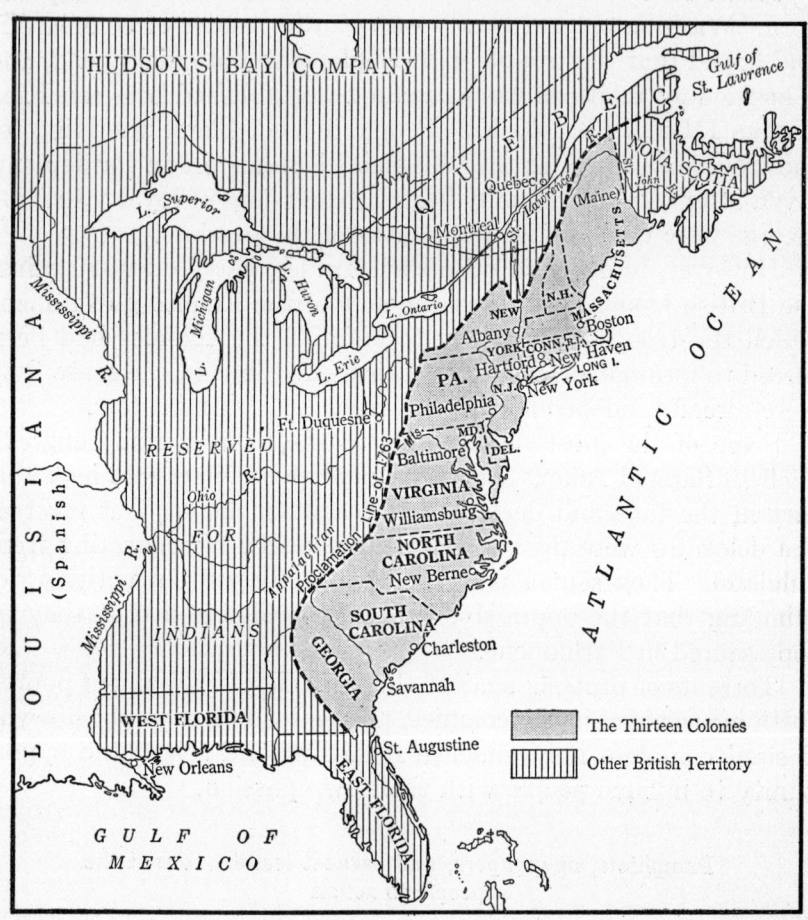

FIG. 34. In 1775 Great Britain owned all the land east of the Mississippi River. Thirteen flourishing colonies bordered the Atlantic Ocean. West of the colonies lay land reserved for the Indians. North and south lay land owned but not settled by the British. In the struggle that was to follow the thirteen colonies could expect little help outside their own boundaries

here burst forth in his fervent denunciations of kings and tyrants. Kings were "crowned ruffians," and George III in particular was a "sceptered savage," a "royal brute," and other evil things.

Paine's *Common Sense* was indeed fiery in spirit, and people have thought since that it was that little 50-page pamphlet more than any other single thing which brought people's minds to accept the idea of complete independence. Here are some extracts from it:

> The period of debate is closed. Arms ... must decide. ... By referring the matter from argument to arms, a new era in politics is struck. ... All plans ... prior to the nineteenth of April are like the almanacs of last year. ...
>
> Where, say some, is the king of America? I'll tell you, friend. He reigns above, and doth not make havoc of mankind, like the royal brute of Britain. ... A government of our own is our natural right. ... Freedom has been hunted round the globe. Asia and Africa have long expelled her. Europe regards her like a stranger; and England has given her warning to depart. O receive the fugitive and prepare in time an asylum for mankind.

There were, indeed, many people who deplored such violent language and argued against what seemed to them the result of frenzy. Nevertheless, Paine's pamphlet exerted a far-reaching influence. Newspapers of the day reflected the great debate. Ministers discussed it in the pulpits. In the colonial assemblies and town meetings there were passionate speeches on both sides of the matter. People everywhere were thinking over the question of separating from England.

Independence would bring America foreign help, which she needed

One of the very first problems which the colonies faced when they went to war was that of scarcity of powder and shot for the army muskets. From the beginning of war Frenchmen (without, however, the open support of their government) had been secretly sending arms to America. As time went on and Washington's army suffered a number of defeats by the British, many people began to hope for the aid of foreign soldiers and battleships and money. France was the source to whom they turned for help, because they knew France hated England. But France would not *yet* send help. In April, 1776, this item appeared in the *Pennsylvania Journal*: "France declares she will not assist the American colonies until they dissolve their connection with Great Britain."

It was clear that France would not openly help America until she broke her relations with England. This was one more very influential factor that urged Americans to consider independence.

A Great Decision is made

The American Declaration of Independence is signed, July 4, 1776

Thus, by the first days of 1776, independence had become a burning question. It was felt that Congress could not act without definite expressions of opinion from the colonial assemblies. The question was warmly debated in nearly all of them. In the end Virginia "instructed its delegates [to the Continental Congress] to urge a declaration by Congress of independence." On June 7, 1776, Richard Henry Lee of Virginia rose in Congress and moved that "these united Colonies are, and of right ought to be, free and independent states."

For nearly a month following, the great question was undecided. There were fervent speeches in Congress by the conservative delegates and by the more radical ones. Among the latter was Washington's friend John Adams, who had fought long and hard for this action, even to the point of making himself unpopular. Under the stirring influence of Revolutionary pamphlets, of assembly resolutions favoring independence, and of such speeches as John and Samuel Adams and Patrick Henry had made, the Continental Congress swayed toward separation from Great Britain.

At last the moment came when decision could no longer be postponed. On July 4, 1776, a committee of Congress passed the great resolutions which separated America from England. This document is the famous Declaration of Independence.

Thomas Jefferson of Virginia, that same young law student who eleven years before had stood in the doorway of the Virginia assembly and heard the "bloody debate" led by Patrick Henry, was the author of it. Jefferson and John Adams with several

THE CLIMAX OF THE STRUGGLE, 1760–1776

other leaders had been appointed to draw up the formal declaration. Forty-six years later John Adams told how it happened.

Jefferson proposed to me to make the draught. I said, "I will not." "You should do it." "Oh! no." "Why will you not? You ought to do it." "I will not." "Why?" "Reasons enough." "What can be your reasons?" "Reason first — You are a Virginian, and a Virginian ought to appear at the head of this business. Reason second — I am

Fig. 35. The Second Continental Congress voting for independence. (From a painting by Robert Edge Pine. Courtesy of the Pennsylvania Historical Society)

obnoxious, suspected, and unpopular. You are very much otherwise. Reason third — You can write ten times better than I can." "Well," said Jefferson, "if you are decided, I will do as well as I can."

By July 4, 1776, twelve of the colonies had voted to support the Declaration. Soon afterward New York, the thirteenth colony, consented to support it.

Thus the Fourth of July is our greatest national holiday. It was the birthday of the United States.

Meanwhile in many parts of the country the Declaration was being received with "pomp and parade." There were bonfires, the ringing of bells, the firing of guns, and torchlight processions.

The Declaration drew the people of the colonies closer together. For "weal or woe" they had together taken a bold step from which they could not draw back. For the moment their enthusiasm filled them with a new feeling of power and loyalty to America.

INTERESTING READINGS FROM WHICH YOU CAN GET ADDITIONAL INFORMATION

BECKER, CARL. The Eve of the Revolution, Vol. XI of The Chronicles of America. Yale University Press, New Haven. The best readers will find this book of great interest.

ELSON, HENRY W. Sidelights on American History. The Macmillan Company, New York. See Volume I, pp. 1–23 (Declaration of Independence).

HART, ALBERT B. (Editor). American History told by Contemporaries. The Macmillan Company, New York. See Volume II.

STEVENSON, BURTON EGBERT (Editor). Poems of American History. Houghton Mifflin Company, Boston. The page numbers given after the following titles refer to this collection. You will find many poems which deal with events of the Revolution. Select one such poem, whether in this list or not, and read it to the class during your English period.

FRANKLIN, BENJAMIN. "The Mother's Country," p. 142. A very humorous ballad, written at the beginning of the trouble.

HOLMES, OLIVER WENDELL. "A Ballad of the Boston Tea Party," pp. 136–137.

LONGFELLOW, HENRY WADSWORTH. "Paul Revere's Ride," pp. 144–146. A familiar old ballad everybody loves.

MORE, HELEN F. "What's in a Name?" p. 146. William Dawes was sent by way of Roxbury to give the alarm at the same time that Paul Revere was sent by way of Charlestown to Lexington.

CHAPTER VI

THE WAR FOR AMERICAN INDEPENDENCE, 1776–1783

The die was cast! Independence had been declared! Revolution had begun!

Between Lexington, April 19, 1775, and Independence Day, July 4, 1776, the war had been merely armed resistance against the mother country's oppressive acts. Since the declaration that America was to be free, it had become revolution. Nothing would satisfy the patriot leaders now but complete self-government.

How the Strength of Great Britain and the New States compared

Great Britain was regarded as the richest and most powerful of the world's nations. What could the American states — if one could call them that — do against such an antagonist? What chance of victory did the colonies have? Let us see.

How did the opponents compare with each other?

1. Estimated populations in 1776

It is difficult to compare the populations of Great Britain and of the American colonies because the statistics are unreliable. No accurate census had ever been made in the colonies. Even in Great Britain only estimates were available. These estimates, however, give us 11,000,000 for Great Britain and 2,750,000 for the colonies, in 1776. Various estimates agree closely enough, however, so that we can be fairly sure of one general conclusion. Great Britain had probably four times as many people as the American states. Among the states themselves the population of the southern section exceeded that of each of the other sections by about 400,000. That is important to remember because the early campaigns were carried on in the northern and middle sections.

Let us not forget that neither the people in the American colonies nor the people in Great Britain were united in feeling toward the war. We have already seen that many Tory colonists sympathized with Great Britain. It is estimated that not less than 100,000 Tories finally left America — went to Canada or back to England to live. In England many leaders strove for years to avoid war with the colonies and, after it had begun, tried repeatedly to end it. Other leaders, who had formed England's policy toward the colonies, defended the war. The British people were no more united in their attitude toward the war than were the leaders.

2. Wealth and available money

By 1776 England had already built up a powerful empire which commanded the trade of the Orient and of America. The story of how that was done was told in *Changing Civilizations in the Modern World*. Britain's armies and navies had defeated her chief enemies in Europe — France, Spain, and Holland. Her rising middle class was rapidly building up wealth through manufacturing and shipping. The new machines of James Watt and Hargreaves and Arkwright were being put to work and production was being increased through their use. Capital was accumulating and considerable amounts of money were available for taxation.

In the states, on the other hand, there was little wealth which could be put to the service of the Revolution. America's wealth was *potential*; that is, although it was there, it was not yet available. For example, there were millions of acres of virgin farm land, vast stretches of forests, deep rich mines of coal, and lakes of oil. The great potential wealth lay almost untouched. This was a great disadvantage, since it might have bought millions of dollars' worth of guns, ammunition, food, and clothing, which were needed for the new army. America's *available* wealth in 1776 lay in the colonists' farms and plantations, in their merchant ships and stores.

There was no national money. Practically all gold and silver money had previously been coined in England, and much of it had been sent back to England to pay the colonists' debts. The

Fig. 36. Robert Morris

Fig. 37. John Adams

Fig. 38. Benjamin Franklin

Fig. 39. John Jay

Four Men by whose Efforts the American Revolution was financed

little gold that was left in the states was hidden away by those who had it. Banks were few and far between, and most people had little confidence in them; so people hid their gold.

In the emergency the Second Continental Congress tried to obtain loans from France, Holland, and England's other European rivals. During the first two years of the war, however, it could get little from the Europeans. Then the Congress began to issue paper money.

Today paper money is accepted without question everywhere in America — indeed, in European countries also. The people know that the governments which issue the paper bills are sound financially, that is, that they will exchange the paper money for gold. People have confidence in gold.

In 1776, as you know, there was no strong central government in America. The weak Continental Congress was the government, and the Congress had no gold. Between 1775 and 1779 the Congress issued paper money to the face value of $240,000,000. It was called Continental money and was issued to pay the soldiers, and to buy food and clothing, guns, ammunition, and other war supplies. In addition, the separate independent states also issued paper money totaling over $200,000,000. Thus more than $450,000,000 of paper money was issued with almost no gold in existence to support it.

What happened to the Continental paper money? It lost its value rapidly. By 1778 a Continental dollar would buy scarcely twelve cents' worth of goods; by 1779, not three cents' worth! More millions of paper dollars were printed. The value dropped and dropped until finally a Continental dollar was worthless. People fell into the habit of speaking of things as "not worth a Continental."

It was clear that Continental money would never win the war. Congress begged the colonies to give money, but the gold which was sent in response was but a trifling amount. Most of the colonies responded with quantities of their own worthless paper money. Then Congress issued war bonds, asking the people to buy them and pay for them in gold. But the people had only paper money. The financial situation was bad, indeed.

As we said before, the Congress had turned for aid to Great

THE WAR FOR AMERICAN INDEPENDENCE 97

Britain's rivals as early as 1776. Silas Deane of Connecticut, "the first American diplomat," was sent to France to see if loans could be arranged. The French would say no more than that France will "not assist the American colonies until they dissolve their connection with Great Britain."

Then came the Declaration of Independence, and immediately diplomatic agents were sent by Congress to all the chief European countries: Benjamin Franklin and Arthur Lee joined Deane in

FIG. 40. Independence Hall in Philadelphia about the time when within its walls the Declaration of Independence was read to the Second Continental Congress

France, John Jay went to Spain, and John Adams to Holland. England's lesser rivals were also visited by other ambassadors. The French government alone gave much help, after victory began to seem possible. Franklin's great skill as a diplomat, combined with the hatred of the French for the British, finally unlocked the French coffers, and money, ships, supplies, and men were lent to the Americans. Altogether France spent about $60,000,000 and sent about 8500 soldiers and a fleet.

Another condition was a decided handicap to the colonies. There was no Treasurer of the United States because there was no national Treasury, not even a National Bank. Lacking real power, Congress tried one scheme after another. In 1775 it had, first, two treasurers, then a Congressional committee of thirteen delegates. In 1776 it tried a finance board of five members. But in spite of all attempts to establish national control of finance the situation grew worse and worse.

Finally, when the war was nearly over, the Congress appointed a prominent landowner and business man of Philadelphia, Robert Morris, as superintendent of finance and gave him great power. For three years Morris did the best he could to raise money in the thirteen states, to stop the depreciation of the paper money, to get loans from abroad, and to establish the credit of Congress. But even he was powerless to solve the real financial problems of the country.

Thus we see that in wealth and available money, as well as in other respects, the thirteen colonies were weak compared with Great Britain.

3. Military strength

In 1776 Great Britain already boasted that she was Mistress of the Seas. She might well claim that title, with her powerful navy and great merchant marine. But the holding of that position made serious demands upon her. The empire was scattered all over the world from the Far East to North America, and her ships were needed to patrol those great distances. Then, too, her rivals — France, Holland, and Spain especially — were watching eagerly for a chance to attack her. Great Britain's whole attention, therefore, could not be given to the revolting American colonies.

The great distance from the colonies also complicated Great Britain's task of sending armies to America. She dared not send her regular forces from other parts of the empire, and it was difficult to get voluntary enlistments because so many of the British people had close relatives in the colonies and others sympathized with the Americans. In those days men were not drafted for the armies, that is, forced to serve. Since few enlisted Great Britain was compelled to hire soldiers from other countries. During the course of the war George III hired about 30,000 soldiers. Most of these came from the German state of Hesse and

Fig. 41. Major General Nathanael Greene

Fig. 42. General Anthony Wayne

Two American Commanders

Fig. 43. Lord Charles Cornwallis. (Courtesy of the National Portrait Gallery, London)

Fig. 44. General John Burgoyne. (Courtesy of the New York Historical Society)

Two British Commanders

were known as Hessians. You see, therefore, that although Great Britain had difficulty in finding among her own people those who were willing to fight the colonists, because of her wealth she could hire soldiers when her own people would not enlist.

In America, on the other hand, there was no money with which to hire large numbers of soldiers. Until France sent troops in 1778, the united colonies had to depend entirely upon voluntary enlistments.

The situation was indeed difficult. During the spring and summer of 1775 thousands of untrained militia had rushed to the defense of Boston. Raw recruits they were, merely enthusiastic merchants, farmers, and mechanics defending their liberties. They were untrained for the art of warfare.

When General Washington took command in 1775 he had about 16,000 men. This seems to be about as many as the American army ever numbered at one time. There are no accurate records to tell us how many men were actually engaged at various times.

Washington and his generals never once had the compact army of 30,000 well-disciplined men which Washington wanted and with which it is believed he could have ended the war in six months. The men enlisted for six months or a year, and as hardships became severe they deserted by the hundreds. In 1776 Washington stated that the soldiers

> come in, you cannot tell how; go, you cannot tell when; and act, you cannot tell where; consume your provisions, exhaust your stores, and leave you at last at a critical moment.

Even in the sixth year of the war half of Washington's troops were untrained volunteers. Some states even hired deserters from the British armies.

The officers of the army were equally untrained. Few had ever heard the whistle of enemies' bullets. General Benedict Arnold was a merchant, Wayne a surveyor and farmer, Marion a Southern planter, and Greene a Rhode Island blacksmith. Generals Gates and Schuyler had had some experience because of service in the French and Indian War. The commanders of regiments and companies were almost altogether ignorant of warfare.

THE WAR FOR AMERICAN INDEPENDENCE

While the British army increased, in spite of the number of men killed or lost as prisoners, the American army became smaller and smaller.

On the sea the situation was much the same — Britain's large experienced navy against a few American privately owned vessels commissioned by Congress.

Thus we have compared the colonies and Great Britain in population, wealth, and military strength. Did not the balance of probable victory seem to rest with Great Britain? So thought many people in Europe as well as in America.

In the meantime, however, Congress was struggling with its problems of money, credit, supplies, and food for the army, and the war was going on.

A Brief Story of the War itself

Let us return to the spring of 1775. The war had begun in the New England states, but was later to be concentrated chiefly in the middle and Southern states. For that reason we shall study it in the order in which it took place: first, the campaigns in New England and Canada, 1775–1776; second, the campaigns in the middle states, 1775–1777; third, the campaigns in the Southern states, 1776–1781.

1. The campaigns in New England and Canada, 1775–1776

General Gage and about 10,000 British troops were assembled in Boston, surrounded by colonial militiamen. In the remaining colonies of New York and Pennsylvania and in the South were an additional few thousand British. Another force was stationed in Canada.

The battle of Bunker Hill and the evacuation of Boston

On the night of June 16 the Americans under Putnam and Prescott occupied and fortified Breed's Hill, which commanded Boston. The British knew that as long as the Americans held that hill they were in danger. So on June 17, 1775, General Gage launched 3000 troops against Colonel Prescott's 1200 militiamen on Breed's Hill. Twice the redcoats advanced, were mowed down like grain, and had to fall back. But the Americans were now out of ammunition. A third time the British charged up the hill and the Americans were driven from their fortifications.

FIG. 45. Colonel Prescott and his militiamen at the fortifications during the battle of Bunker Hill. (From a painting by F. C. Yohn. Courtesy of the Continental Insurance Company)

For some reason this battle has been known ever since by the name of Bunker Hill, a hill just west of Breed's Hill. The British had won the first important battle of the war, but with terrible losses. A thousand men lay dead on the field.

On July 3 General Washington took command of the militiamen and tried to discipline them. For months the raw recruits were drilled, and cannon and supplies were assembled around Boston.

The Capture of Forts Crown Point and Ticonderoga

In the meantime (May, 1775) the "Green Mountain Boys" (Vermont militiamen) had taken two British forts on Lake Champlain. One of them, Crown Point, was captured by a detachment of these militiamen under Seth Warner. The other, Ticonderoga, was taken by another force of Vermont militiamen

THE WAR FOR AMERICAN INDEPENDENCE 103

under Ethan Allen. At these two forts the Americans had captured many cannon and large quantities of war supplies. Some of these were sent to Washington to help him in his siege of Boston.

In March, 1776, Washington established batteries of cannon on Dorchester Heights, and so commanded the town of Boston. General Gage had been replaced by General Sir William Howe. When General Howe saw that his fleet in the harbor as well as the town itself was at the mercy of the Americans, he decided to leave. The entire army and hundreds of American Tories embarked on his ships and sailed to Halifax, Nova Scotia. From that day Boston was never again occupied by the British. The scene of warfare changed to other sections.

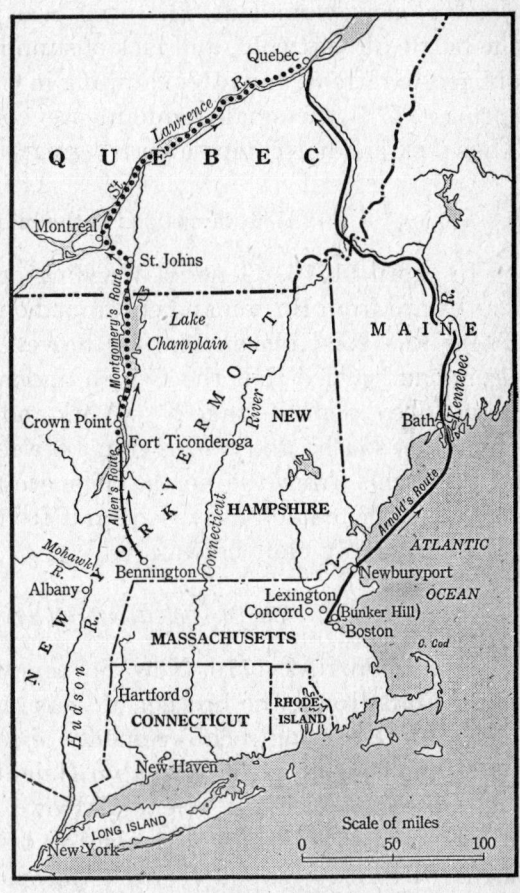

FIG. 46. The Campaigns in New England and Canada

The Americans attempt to take Canada, 1775–1776

At first the Americans hoped to arouse the French inhabitants of Canada to join them in throwing off the British rule. To do this, two armies were fitted out and sent northward. One of them, led by General Benedict Arnold, made its way under severe winter hardships through the Maine wilderness to Quebec. The other, under General Richard Montgomery, went through the valleys of New York State, across Lake Champlain, and thence to

Montreal. After capturing the city the army proceeded down the St. Lawrence River toward Quebec. The two armies finally met outside the city, where they attacked the British. In a blinding blizzard the battle raged. Montgomery was killed and Arnold was seriously wounded. The army was practically destroyed by the battle, illness, cold, and lack of supplies. The Americans were obliged to retreat, and after camping in Canada until the following spring (1776) the small remnant was compelled to return home. Thus the Canadian campaign was a great disaster for the Americans.

2. The campaigns in the middle states

In April, 1776, General Washington and his army hurried southward from Boston and encamped on Long Island, New York. There was good reason for this move. Washington and his officers had learned that the British under Howe had an important plan. They meant to take New York and the Hudson River valley from the south, and the region between the Hudson and the St. Lawrence from the north. If successful in this strategy, the British could cut off New England from the other states. This would probably end the war.

The struggle for the Hudson River

Late in August, 1776, New Yorkers were greatly stirred. Admiral Lord Howe, the brother of General Howe, had just arrived with a fleet bearing reënforcements of soldiers. Washington had placed half his army on Brooklyn Heights, Long Island, opposite the city of New York. General Howe defeated him there in a terrible battle in which Washington lost about one fifth of his men. Washington then realized that he could not stay in that position. Both the English fleet and land forces threatened to capture his entire army. So he retreated northward through the city of New York at night without arousing the British fleet in the harbor, or the army which lay only 600 yards from the American camp.

The defeat was a cruel blow to Washington. For the first time the people in the colonies began to realize the danger of losing the war. England's powerful army, her excellent navy, and her

THE WAR FOR AMERICAN INDEPENDENCE 105

money made British victory seem near. Admiral Lord Howe decided that it was a good time to make peace. The King had instructed him to offer to withdraw if the colonies would yield.

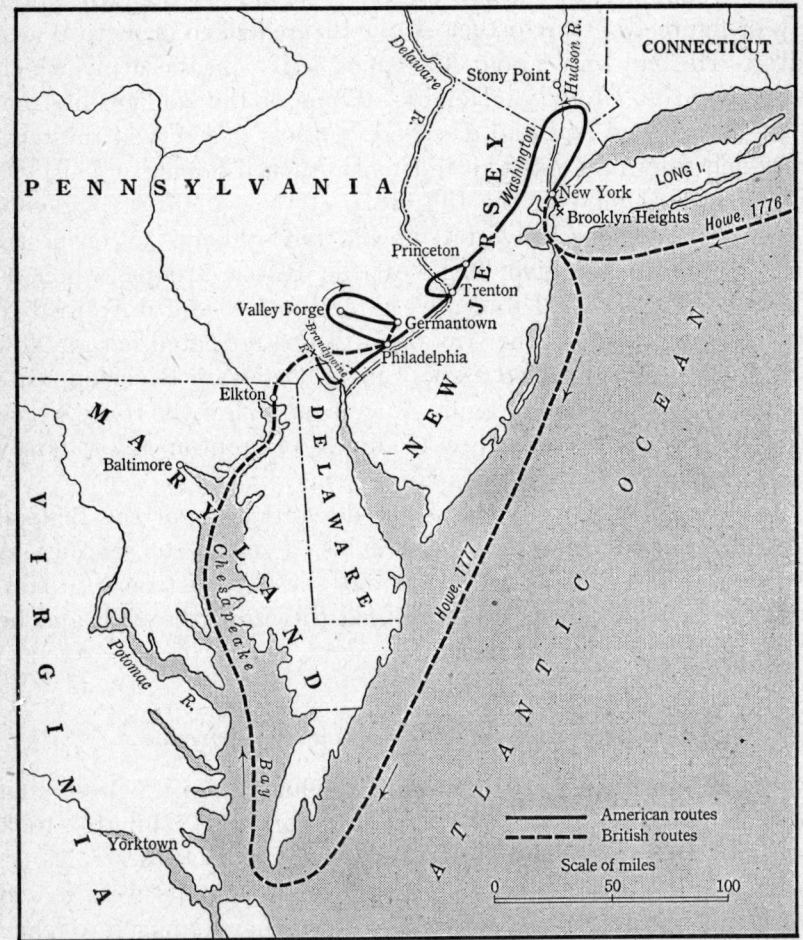

FIG. 47. The Campaigns in southern New York and in New Jersey

Congress sent John Adams and Benjamin Franklin to confer with Howe. They demanded that England recognize the independence of the colonies. Lord Howe was obliged to refuse, of course, and the war went on.

Washington had succeeded in winning one important stronghold from the British. This was a narrow, fortified spot on the Hudson River, called Stony Point. As long as the Continental Army held that spot the British army could not move reënforcements or supplies up or down the river. (Find Stony Point on the map of figure 47.) Nevertheless, the future looked grim to Washington. He had only about 4000 men left from the army which had camped at Brooklyn Heights. Some of the soldiers had become discouraged and had deserted. Others had served the term for which they had enlisted and had returned home.

We cannot tell you the full story of the gallant struggles of Washington and his brave but bewildered soldiers. Often he refused to stand and give battle to the British troops, when he knew that the colonial forces were far too few and untrained to win decisive battles. The American troops retreated across New Jersey, until they reached a spot on the Delaware River opposite Trenton. (On the map of figure 47 you can follow the route which they took.) Howe followed and camped at Trenton. New Jersey also seemed lost to the Continental Army.

Yet the colonial army had some advantages over the British. Washington had learned to fight a losing battle, to sacrifice as few men as possible, and to wear out the British troops in constant movement. He was determined to win in the end, and he never considered surrendering.

The Americans win at Trenton and at Princeton

On Christmas Day, 1776, when the gallant and pleasure-loving Howe had gone to New York City to celebrate, Washington took 2300 men from his small force and crossed the Delaware River. The water was filled with floating ice, and the boats were tossed by a biting storm of sleet and snow, but the men managed to reach the New Jersey shore at Trenton. They surprised the Hessian troops, who had been left to guard the city, and captured them.

The British general sent an army from New York to recapture Trenton. When they arrived, they found that Washington had gone. He had cleverly slipped into Princeton, New Jersey, and captured it. Fearing that they might be cut off from their main base of supplies in New York, the British retreated northward.

THE WAR FOR AMERICAN INDEPENDENCE

At the end of the year 1776, the British had won almost every battle. In only three months they had captured more than 4000 prisoners, including three generals, and had taken an enormous quantity of ammunition and equipment, including flour, baggage, and tents. Nevertheless, the patriots once more took heart, since the larger part of New Jersey had been reclaimed by the Continental Army.

The British capture Philadelphia, the capital, 1777

Although Washington had blocked Howe's advance on the American capital at Philadelphia by controlling New Jersey, Howe circumvented him. He put his army on board ship, sailed around to Chesapeake Bay (see figure 47), landed his men at Elkton, and marched on Philadelphia from the south. Washington learned of his plan, hurried southward, and met him twice. In both battles, — of Brandywine and of Germantown, — however, the Americans were defeated, and on September 26, 1777, Howe and his men took Philadelphia. Things looked dark, indeed, for the colonists.

The capture of Burgoyne at Saratoga: the turning point of the Revolution

Then came a great American victory.

In the summer of 1777 the British had begun their campaign to separate New England from the other sections. General Burgoyne was to march south from Montreal by way of Lake Champlain and Lake George to Albany on the Hudson River. Colonel St. Leger was to come down the St. Lawrence and east through the Mohawk valley to Albany. Howe was to move north, capture and hold all points on the Hudson River, and meet Burgoyne and St. Leger at Albany. If successful, New England would be cut off, and New York, New Jersey, and Pennsylvania would be in British hands. That would undoubtedly end the war.

But the British plans went askew! One of their forces, that under Colonel St. Leger, was defeated at Oriskany and had to retreat to its base at Montreal. A part of Burgoyne's force was defeated at Bennington, Vermont, by General Stark and his

"Green Mountain Boys." Burgoyne, however, *was* successful in recapturing Fort Ticonderoga, which Ethan Allen had taken two years before. But General Howe did not move up the Hudson River to meet Burgoyne at Albany. Never having received the instructions to join Burgoyne, Howe moved south, as you have just learned, and took Philadelphia. So Burgoyne was left alone in the northern Hudson valley.

Washington saw that the Continental Army had a rare opportunity. "Now let all New England turn out and crush Burgoyne," he wrote. At once the New England troops rallied. Burgoyne's Indian allies left him. His supplies gave out. He was surrounded by Americans and was getting farther and farther away from his source of supplies in the north. He could not find horses to pull his heavy guns and supply wagons, nor food for his men. Finally, realizing that his position was hopeless, he was forced to surrender to General Gates at Saratoga on October 17, 1777.

FIG. 48. The campaign which had as its object the cutting off of the New England states from the middle Atlantic states

Five thousand men and a vast army of supplies were taken by the Americans. The country rejoiced.

Washington felt that a real turning point in the war had come. If the British plans had not miscarried, no doubt the whole course of the war would have been changed.

How the Continental Congress and the People nearly defeated their Own Army

The terrible suffering at Valley Forge

General Washington had taken his army to Valley Forge near Philadelphia for the winter (1777–1778). He could not attack General Howe; he had too small an army. Day after day more and more of his soldiers either deserted or fell ill. On more than one of their recent marches over snowy roads their tracks could be followed by blood stains left by their bare feet. Some of the men actually lay in camp without clothes. Often there had not been enough powder or enough guns. For all these reasons there had been horrible suffering among the men of the Continental Army. Now they were facing yet more terrible days, days when starvation stalked through the camp and maddened and weakened the bravest of them.

Most of their horses starved to death, and the men who had strength enough to stand took the places of horses and oxen to drag whatever wood and food could be found to their shivering and starving companions. Meat, which the sick soldiers cried for constantly, was not to be had.

One officer wrote in his diary: "It snows ... I'm sick ... eat nothing ... No Whiskey ... No Forage ... Lord ... Lord ... Cold & uncomfortable."

Washington wrote of his condition:

My situation is inexpressibly distressing, to see the winter fast approaching upon a naked army, the time of their service within a few weeks of expiring.... The military chest is totally exhausted; the paymaster has not a single dollar in hand; the commissary-general assures me that he has strained his credit, for the subsistence of the army, to the utmost. The quartermaster-general is in precisely the same situation; and the greater part of the troops are in a state not far from mutiny, upon the deduction from their stated allowance. Without immediate remedy the army must absolutely break up.

Meanwhile the army of General Howe in Philadelphia had all the food and clothing it needed, bought often enough from the colonists themselves.

Why was the American army so badly provided for? Why did Washington's men have to suffer so terribly?

There were many reasons, of course, some of which you already know. One Tory said when he tried to explain the large number of desertions in Washington's army: "The [American] soldier had thirteen kings and no bread." That was partly true, but the principal reason was that the Continental Congress was often inefficient and sometimes unable to enforce its decisions. When there were enough supplies, often there were no means found for moving them to the army camps. The men Congress put in charge of these affairs were often unreliable, or were only interested in making money for themselves out of their country's misfortunes.

Then, too, Congress was struggling to carry on a war without the power that comes from a united government. Money was needed for war, and taxation was necessary to secure that money. But the colonies were fighting England for imposing taxes on them to support her government. Would they permit Congress to do the same thing? Not without protest. At every turn the state assemblies opposed the suggestions of the Congress. These assemblies could draft men, raise money, and pay soldiers for service within the states; but the Continental Congress could only *ask* for contributions to carry on the war.

How it happened that in spite of the Great Difficulties the United Colonies won the War

With the return of spring, 1778, hope once more began to live in the army of Washington. News had come that the French were actually sending a great fleet of warships to fight the British fleet in New York. General Howe had been recalled to England and General Clinton was now in charge of the English army. He too had heard the news of the French fleet and knew that he must get his army back into New York. One part of it was put on the boats waiting in Delaware Bay, and the other he led back across New Jersey. The Continental Army pursued him, making things as unpleasant as they could.

The Americans felt, joyously enough, that with the coming of the French their cause would be saved. But as yet that was not to be true. The French fleet did come, but its commander took no decisive action, disappointing the Americans time after time by refusing to attack when he might have done so successfully. Washington's army, meanwhile, took up its position near New York to guard the surrounding country.

France comes to the aid of America

Congress had tried for some time through its messengers to France to persuade that country to take up arms openly against her old enemy England. At first France hesitated, and it was not until the surrender of Burgoyne's army that she was persuaded to help America in this way. Early in 1778 a treaty of friendship between France and the new nation was signed.

For two years, however, France did little. Then her aid — in men, in ships, in loans of money, and in munitions of war rapidly increased. But, unfortunately, as the French increased their aid, the Americans reduced their own contributions.

At the same time many of the Americans seemed to lose much of their interest in fighting too.

FIG. 49. The Marquis de Lafayette used his influence and his money to further the American cause. He also fought with the American troops during the war

Once the young French leader Lafayette was forced to beg his friend Washington to take action, so that the French allies might not lose their enthusiasm for the American cause.

It is estimated that France spent in and for America about $11,000,000 a year for five years. Between 1778 and 1781 about half the total of the American army was made up of our French allies. The Americans, on the other hand, raised in 1780 just 1000 fewer men than in 1779 and 8000 fewer than in 1778.

George Rogers Clark captures the Northwest Territory, 1778-1779

While these stirring events were taking place on the seaboard, the frontier was witnessing fighting also. In *A History of American Civilization* you read the story of George Rogers Clark and his heroic backwoodsmen. Under the most difficult circumstances, and with great daring, Clark and a few hundred men captured the British outposts in Illinois and Indiana. One by one they fell — Kaskaskia, Cahokia, Vincennes. Finally, in February, 1779, even the British leader General Hamilton was captured, and the Ohio valley was under American control.

3. The campaigns in the South

While patriots in New England and the middle states were opposing the British in the North, their comrades in the far Southland were helping the American cause. As early as April, 1775, Patrick Henry called for volunteers in Virginia. In North Carolina people had been imprisoned and even hanged for opposing British rule. The South was more torn by struggles between Tories and patriots than were other sections. It was not until 1778, however, that important military engagements took place there. In that year the British captured Savannah, Georgia. Soon afterwards Atlanta was taken and, in 1779, Charleston, South Carolina. American troops under Gates were defeated at Camden, South Carolina.

Then the tide turned. Late in 1780 American frontiersmen destroyed a detachment of Lord Cornwallis's British army at King's Mountain. Another group of backwoodsmen under Morgan defeated the British leader Tarleton at Cowpens.

Slowly, however, the British under Lord Cornwallis worked their way northward toward Virginia. They were marching to Yorktown. From Yorktown, which lay about halfway between New York and Charleston, a fleet could easily bring armed men from either point. After a campaign through the Southern colonies, Cornwallis took up his position there as a safe place.

THE WAR FOR AMERICAN INDEPENDENCE 113

The young French nobleman Lafayette, who had fought beside Washington since 1776, was ordered to command the American troops at Richmond, Virginia. Immediately he followed

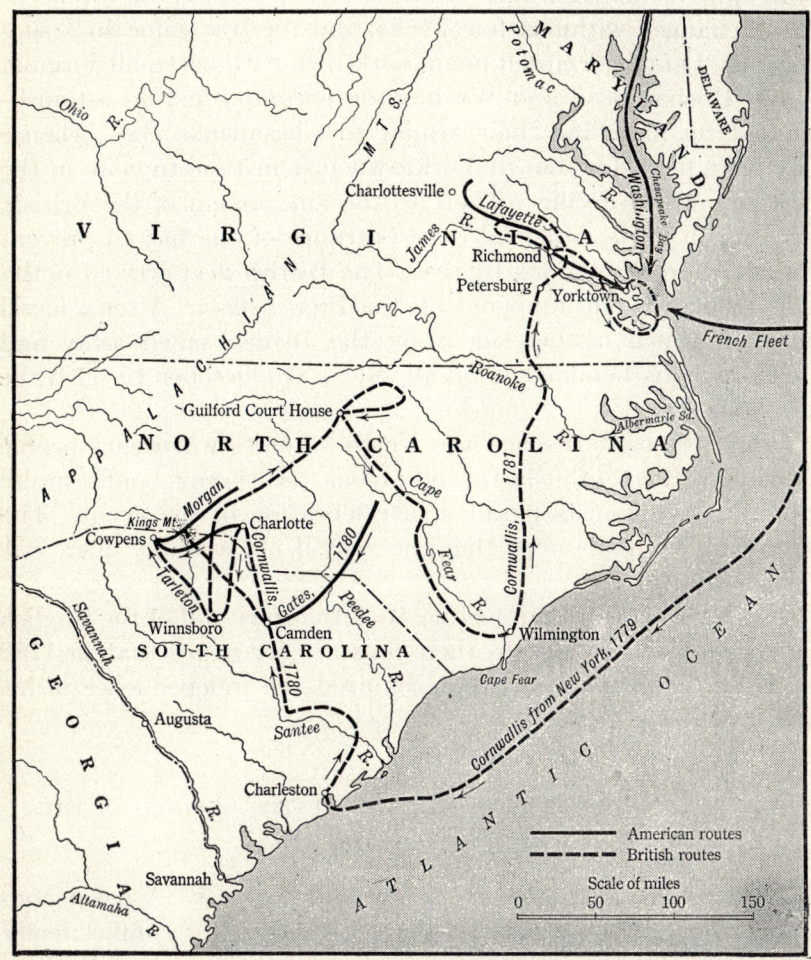

FIG. 50. The campaigns in the South

Cornwallis to Yorktown and shut off his way of retreat by land. Cornwallis saw no real danger in this. He referred to Lafayette as a "mere boy" and not as a military man to be feared. General Washington was far north on the Hudson, watching Clinton, who was in New York; the American generals Greene and

Morgan were fighting inland in Georgia and the Carolinas; most of the French troops were at Newport, Rhode Island, under General Rochambeau. What was there to fear?

In spite of the assurance of Cornwallis, however, the whole situation changed within a few weeks, and the war came to a sudden end. Lafayette closed in on Yorktown with his small Virginia army. Rochambeau and Washington accomplished an astonishing feat by marching their armies to Chesapeake Bay, whence they were ferried across to Yorktown just in time to close in the gaps around Cornwallis. Then, to the amazement of the British, two French fleets sailed into the entrance of the bay to prevent Cornwallis from escaping by sea. The British fleet arrived in the harbor but was outnumbered by the French fleet. After a naval battle in which neither side won, the British sailed away and left Cornwallis hemmed in on all sides. On October 19, 1781, he surrendered.

When the news reached the Northern cities war-weary people suddenly turned enthusiastic and joyous. Bells rang, bonfires were lighted, and colonists paraded in celebration of the event. The victory inspired the hope that the war, if not actually over, was soon to end.

Indeed, this American victory took the spirit out of the English leaders, and it was due to their pressure for peace that in 1782 the King finally yielded and recognized the independence of his former colonies.

What England and the United States decided in the Treaty of Paris, 1783

The war was not officially at an end, however. A peace conference was held in Paris, and there for a time the conflict really continued. To be sure, there were no battles with musket and bayonet, but great battles of words and ideas were fought by the men whom England had sent to discuss peace with the ambassadors of France and America.

Just what was this independence claimed by America? That was one of the problems which they had to decide; and until it was decided more or less as America wished, she would not lay down her arms. In fact, General Washington did not resign his command of the army, nor did Congress dismiss the men who had fought so long, until nearly four months after peace was signed.

The most perplexing problem was that of territory. What were the new United States of America to include? How far west was her boundary to extend? Benjamin Franklin, John Adams, and the clever John Jay represented the interests of our country. They wanted to bring about a settlement which would give the United States the western territory beyond the Appalachians. By 1782 this western district had been settled to a small extent and some of it was claimed by nearly all the states. On this basis the American ambassadors asked for all land west to the Mississippi River. They asked, also, for certain fishing rights off the shores of Nova Scotia

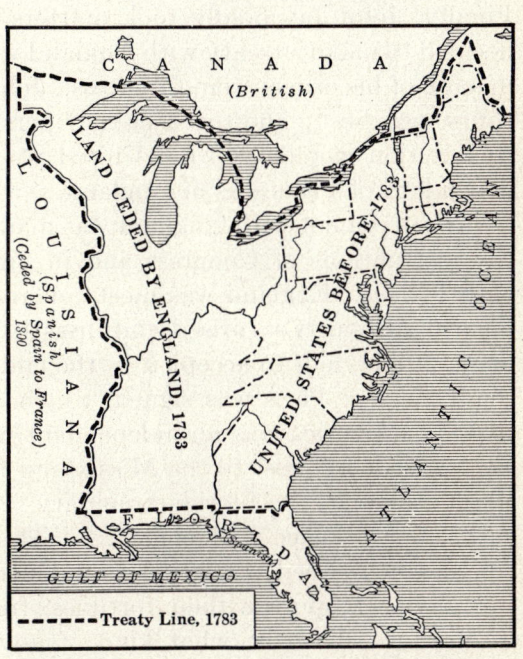

FIG. 51. The treaty line marks off the territory which belonged to the United States in 1783

and the right of navigating the full length of the Mississippi River.

The French representatives at the conference were using the opportunity to better their country's position in world affairs. France was trying to help Spain, who was her ally, and who was afraid that an independent, growing nation in America would threaten Spanish interests in Florida and around the mouth of the Mississippi. In the meantime Congress had sent instructions to the American ambassadors to allow France to guide them in their decisions. This really made America dependent on France for what she was to get through the treaty, and put the three commissioners in a most embarrassing position. John Adams indignantly wrote in his diary, February 18, 1783: "Congress surrendered their own sovereignty into the hands of a French minister. Blush! blush! ye guilty records! Blush and perish!"

Of course France and Spain delayed final decision and opposed America's desire for the territory west to the Mississippi. Finally, John Jay boldly took matters into his own hands. He decided to make a treaty with England without the help of France, in spite of his orders from Congress. John Adams agreed that this course was best; and together they persuaded Franklin that only such action would keep the United States independent — as independent of France as of England.

An agreement with England was made in great secrecy against the instructions of Congress and in violation of the agreement with France. England was most generous to her recent colonies. France, although surprised and dissatisfied when this treaty was made public, had to accept it in the end. On September 3, 1783, the Treaty of Paris was signed, which declared that the United States of America was an independent nation, and that it owned all the territory west to the Mississippi River and south from the Great Lakes to the Florida boundary.

1783 ... Peace had come.... Thirteen of Great Britain's colonies now faced the world as independent states. They were free — free to pursue their fortunes, free to govern themselves.

Now we shall see what kind of government they set up to carry on their affairs.

INTERESTING READINGS FROM WHICH YOU CAN GET ADDITIONAL INFORMATION

ALTSHELER, J. A. My Captive. D. Appleton and Company, New York. The Revolution in South Carolina.

BARNES, JAMES. With the Flag in the Channel, or The Adventures of Captain Gustavus Conyngham. D. Appleton and Company, New York.

BARNES, JAMES. For King or Country. Harper & Brothers, New York.

BROOKS, ELBRIDGE S. The True Story of Benjamin Franklin. Lothrop, Lee & Shepard Co., Boston.

BROOKS, ELBRIDGE S. The True Story of Lafayette. Lothrop, Lee & Shepard Co., Boston.

BROOKS, ELBRIDGE S. The True Story of George Washington. Lothrop, Lee & Shepard Co., Boston.

THE WAR FOR AMERICAN INDEPENDENCE 117

Coffin, C. C. The Boys of '76. Harper & Brothers, New York. If you like accounts of battles, this reference will interest you.

Cooper, J. F. The Pilot, a Tale of the Sea. G. P. Putnam's Sons, New York. The daring work of John Paul Jones, the naval hero of the Revolution.

Cooper, J. F. The Spy. G. P. Putnam's Sons, New York. Thrilling story; pictures the work of rebel spies among the Tories.

Faris, John T. Makers of our History. Ginn and Company, Boston. Short biographies of Benjamin Franklin, George Washington, and Robert Morris.

Kaler, J. O. At the Siege of Quebec. Penn Publishing Company, Philadelphia. Benedict Arnold and Montgomery's failure before Quebec.

Lisle, Clifton. Diamond Rock, a Tale of the Pailo Massacre. Harcourt, Brace and Company, New York. Full of adventure and interest.

Mason, Alfred B. Tom Strong, Washington's Scout. Henry Holt and Company, New York. The boys will like this.

Roosevelt, Theodore, and Lodge, H. C. Hero Tales from American History. The Century Co., New York. "George Washington," pp. 1–16; "George Rogers Clark and the Conquest of the Northwest," pp. 29–42; "The Battle of Trenton," pp. 43–56; "Battle of Bennington," pp. 57–58; "Battle of King's Mountain," pp. 69–78; "The Storming of Stony Point," pp. 79–80.

Root, Jean Christie. Nathan Hale, in the True Stories of Great Americans series. The Macmillan Company, New York.

Stevenson, Burton E. Poems of American History. Houghton Mifflin Company, Boston. The page numbers given after the following titles refer to this collection. You will find many poems which deal with events of the Revolution.

  Bryant, William Cullen. "The Green Mountain Boys," p. 157.

  Bryant, William Cullen. "The Song of Marion's Men," p. 248. The war in the South.

  Cloud, Virginia W. "The Ballad of Sweet P," p. 31. How a girl disarmed a group of English soldiers.

  Holmes, Oliver Wendell. "Grandmother's Story of Bunker Hill Battle."

  Holmes, Oliver Wendell. "Lexington," pp. 147–148. Read the three poems you like best.

  Lanier, Sidney. "Lexington," pp. 146–147.

  Whittier, John Greenleaf. "Lexington," pp. 153–154.

Stoddard, W. O. Guert Ten Eyck. Lothrop, Lee & Shepard Co., Boston. The Revolution in and about New York.

Stoddard, W. O. Two Cadets with Washington. Lothrop, Lee & Shepard Co., Boston. Siege of Boston, and Washington and his work.

Tomlinson, E. T. The Camp-Fire of Mad Anthony. Houghton Mifflin Company, Boston.

UNIT III

THE MAKING OF THE AMERICAN CONSTITUTION

INTRODUCTION TO THE MAKING OF THE AMERICAN CONSTITUTION

Was there a central government during the Revolution? In the autumn of 1777 the Second Continental Congress proposed a plan called the Articles of Confederation, and sent it to the states for approval. Some of the states approved it at once; in others it was debated at great length. By 1781, however, all thirteen states had ratified the Articles, which became thereby the central government. Among other provisions it was agreed that the new nation be known as the United States of America, that there should be a central Congress to which delegates were to be chosen each year and in which each state was to have but one vote, and that the vote of nine of the thirteen states should be necessary to pass any law. The Confederation was to be a firm league of friendship among the states for their common defense, the security of their liberties, and their mutual and general welfare.

What kind of government did the new states which formed this league of friendship have in 1783? Was the government of the colonies adequate for the new states? Were many changes necessary?

In most of the states the change had been a relatively simple matter. For a century and a half the colonies had been governed under charters granted by the king, in some of which a large amount of self-government had been permitted. The former colonies now had constitutions, that is, written plans of government. In all the thirteen states the new forms of state governments included a governor, a legislature, and a system of courts. In making their new state constitutions the people gave the legislatures much more power than the lawmaking bodies had been given under the colonial charters. Having long feared the power held by the royal governors, they made sure that the legislature would have more control over the government than the governor would.

Little change had been made except in the **form** *of government. British control had been discarded, but the government continued to be aristocratic, not democratic. Although the individual states did not offer a democratic government, still there was a beginning of democracy in their union, where each had one vote.*

In spite of its limitations, the league of friendship under the Articles of Confederation created, even during the Revolution, the beginnings of national, or federal, government. This in itself was a real gain. Whether the Articles were satisfactory for the new states, we shall see in the next chapter.

CHAPTER VII

THE MAKING OF THE AMERICAN CONSTITUTION, 1783–1787

It is difficult to say just how well or how badly off the Americans were in the first years following the treaty of peace. People of the time differed so widely in their opinions that accurate statements are not available. One traveler in these years wrote:

Population is increasing, new houses building, new lands clearing, new settlements forming, and new manufactures establishing . . . and what is more, the people are well clad, well fed, and well housed. Yet, I will not say that all are contented. The merchants are complaining that trade is dull, the farmers that wheat and other produce are falling, the landlords that rent is lowering, the speculators and extravagant that they are compelled to pay their debts, and the idle and the vain that they cannot live at others' cost and gratify their pride with articles of luxury.

These conditions were probably only partially true, but let us study the matter more carefully.

I. The Poor and Debtor Classes

It seems clear that many of the poorer people in the cities, on the small farms, and out on the frontier were having a hard time. A writer of that time said that men who had been in the army "went home without even a ceremonious 'thank you' from the nation. To this day, most of them are unpaid and will be." Those who were given a small part of their back pay, received it in worthless paper money or in almost equally worthless government bonds. Many of them were in debt for the money which they had to borrow during the war to keep their families alive. In those days a man who could not pay back the money he had borrowed was thrown into the debtors' prison. Even as late as 1827, a record shows that one man was imprisoned for *six months* for a debt of three dollars.

Is it any wonder, then, that the men who were thrown into the filthy debtors' prisons and the men who feared that they would go there said, "If only there were more money, our troubles would be over." These debtors began to say to the state legislatures, "Issue paper money. Then we shall have more money with which to pay our debts."

The story of paper money in Rhode Island

It was January, 1785. The people of Rhode Island were holding town meetings. From one town to another went petitions to the legislature, asking that more paper money be issued. Everywhere they were signed eagerly. But the legislature was not composed of farmers and workingmen; most of its members came from among the more well-to-do citizens. These people did not want paper money.

Nevertheless, the common people arose to action. In the spring of 1786 they elected a new legislature, and in place of many well-to-do men were chosen men who wanted to issue paper money. Immediately the great question was raised, and there was disagreement. Representatives from the country districts favored paper money; those from the more prosperous cities opposed it. The bill was passed, however, and the paper money was issued.

Immediately it began to lose value. Down and down it went. Less and less did it buy. Then the prosperous men of the cities had their revenge. They would not accept the paper money at its face value, that is, at the value that was printed on its face. Merchants who sold goods, business men who lent money — none of them would give, for example, five dollars' worth of goods for a five-dollar bill.

Again the paper-money men acted. They passed in the legislature an act which required that people accept the paper money *at its face value*. Then the merchants refused to accept it at all.

The farmers said that if the merchants would not sell goods to them and take paper money, then the merchants should receive no more farm goods, and the town people would starve.

In Newport riots broke out. The hungry people demanded grain from the merchants, who refused to give it to them. Threats were also made to break open the cribs and barns of the farmers.

But the rich merchants and business men on one side, and the farmers on the other, still held out.

The people were especially angry at the courts, the judges, and the lawyers. The courts gave orders that farms be sold to pay the debts of the owners, and when their debts exceeded the

Fig. 52. Continental paper money

selling price of their farms the courts threw the debtors into prison. Now the debtors were demanding more time in which to pay their debts, but their demands were little heeded.

Such were conditions in Rhode Island in 1786.

In Massachusetts Shays's Rebellion broke out

There were similar troubles in Vermont and New Hampshire, and in the year 1786 the people of Massachusetts were on the verge of rebellion. Driven to desperation by poverty and debts they demanded that the government of Massachusetts do something for them. Like the poor people of Rhode Island, they wanted paper money and also more time in which to pay their debts. They wanted anything that would help them out of their troubles.

Finally rebellion broke out in 1786. Men armed with swords and muskets were determined to stop the sitting of courts of law that no more debtors might be sent to prison.

All Massachusetts was in a ferment. Men who had more power were entering the conflict. Luke Day, who had been a captain in the Continental Army, gathered a large following in West Springfield. At the same time Daniel Shays, who was also a captain in the Continental Army, was drilling men. Meanwhile independent mobs continued to prevent the lower courts from sitting and Shays's and Day's men combined to check the proceedings of the supreme court.

FIG. 53. Shays and his men take possession of a courthouse [1]

Massachusetts raised an army to put down the "rebels," and the Continental Congress sent aid. Governor Bowdoin of Massachusetts sent General Shepard with a small body of militia to Springfield, to protect the government arsenal which was located there. Shays's men marched on the arsenal. In the attempt to capture it several men were killed and many wounded. The "rebellion" was soon put down, but it created great anxiety among the leaders. General Washington, on hearing of Shays's Rebellion, burst out:

[1] From a drawing by Howard Pyle in *A Larger History of the United States*, by Thomas Wentworth Higginson, Harper & Brothers, 1885.

What, gracious God, is Man that there should be such inconsistency and perfidiousness in his conduct! It is but the other day that we were shedding our blood to obtain the constitutions under which we now live — constitutions of our own choice and making — and now we are unsheathing our sword to overturn them!

In other states conditions were little better.

Thus we have seen what the poor and debtor classes were striving for in several of the states — for money which would be worth its full value and for more time in which to pay their debts. What kind of government could bring about these things? No one seemed to know.

II. THE BUSINESS MEN AND OTHER WELL-TO-DO PEOPLE

What was the condition of the well-to-do?

Some of the people seem to have been doing quite well. A Boston merchant speaks of the demand for such luxuries as French silks and cambrics. He says in one letter:

I would observe that people dress as much and as extravagantly as ever. The ladies lay out much on their heads in flowers and white gauze, and hoop petticoats seem crawling in.

A Virginia writer who remembered these years wrote of them:

Immense quantities of British and French goods were soon imported; our people imbibed a taste for foreign fashions and luxury. . . . Fine ruffles, powdered heads, silks and scarlets, decorated the men, while the most costly silks, satins, chintzes, calicoes, muslins, etc., etc., decorated our females.[1]

Thus it is certain that in some of the states business men, farmers, and mechanics alike were fairly prosperous. In 1787 Benjamin Franklin said that the prosperity of the country was so great as to call for Thanksgiving. He said:

Market reports then showed that the farmers were never better paid for their produce, that farm lands were continually rising in value, and that in no part of Europe were the laboring poor in such a fortunate state.

[1] Samuel Kercheval, *History of the Valley of Virginia* (1833), pp. 199–200.

He also said that there were some bad conditions, but in general things were going well. Some historians also maintain that in only seven of the thirteen states was business bad and the paper money situation serious.

In several states, however, the well-to-do people were hoarding their money, and industry was at a standstill

Money could have been available for industry and trade, but accounts written by historians of those years prove clearly that, in many parts of the country, the wealthy people were refusing to invest their money.

Men who had made money placed it in safe hiding places. They were waiting until a strong central government should be set up — a government in which the people could have confidence. If they invested their money before that time, however, they could not be sure of profits, and they might even lose all they had.

Each year after 1785 groups of prominent merchants and business men sent petitions to the Continental Congress, asking that greater powers to develop industry and shipping be given to the national government. One of the reasons was that English manufactured goods were being sold at low prices all over the American states. Indeed, American manufacturers were finding it impossible to make and sell their goods even in their home markets at as low prices as the English manufacturers were selling them in the United States. So they too wanted to see a stronger national government established.

It is fairly certain, therefore, that practically all the business people of the states wanted a strong central government to be set up. They wanted new laws which would protect their industries and shipping, their businesses and their banks. They did not want more paper money issued.

Wealthy Speculators in Public Land and Paper Money also wanted a Strong Central Government

During the Revolution many shrewd business men had invented ways of making large sums of money by means of speculation. One of these ways was to buy vast quantities of cheap

THE MAKING OF THE CONSTITUTION 127

public lands in the West, hold them until they increased many times in value, and then sell to the incoming settlers.

These lands were valueless, of course, unless they could be sold to persons who would move West and settle upon them. At this time, however, more and more people were moving into Kentucky and the Northwest Territory, and the lands were steadily rising in value.

We know on the authority of eminent historians that many men, including some prominent in public life, were speculating in Western lands. Timothy Pickering, who was one of the members of the Pennsylvania convention which ratified the Constitution, wrote in 1796: "All I am now worth was gained by speculations in land." Many other prominent people could have said the same, for land speculation later involved many leaders. Among them were Franklin, Gallatin, Patrick Henry, Robert Morris, James Wilson, and many less widely known men.

The speculators soon saw that to protect their ownership they must have the help of a recognized central government which would establish land offices, make accurate surveys, and establish army posts to protect the settlers.

There was a second group of speculators who also wanted a central government. They were gamblers who were buying up the depreciated paper money of the Continental Congress and the states, intending to hold it until a strong central government should be established which would buy it back at its full value.

Shrewd speculators paid $2, $3, even $10 or $15 in some cases, for a $100 note because they believed that a strong national government would be established which would redeem these notes at a value much higher than the price which they paid for them.

These two classes of speculators were gambling in public lands and public money. They added in no way to the country's wealth; they produced nothing from the earth, manufactured no new goods, originated no new ideas to benefit the people. They were simply profiteering. To make their speculations profitable a strong central government was necessary. It is easy to understand, therefore, that they would be among those who worked hardest to establish such a government.

The Articles of Confederation had Grave Weaknesses

Some of the conditions which we have described were no doubt due to the fact that the Articles of Confederation were not strong enough to hold the colonies together. There were many defects, but the following were the most important:

1. There was no central executive department to enforce the laws passed by the Congress, nor a system of courts to pass upon them; that is, there was no president to carry out the laws and no Federal courts to interpret them. Congress served as the supreme court of the land.

2. The Continental Congress was merely a government of thirteen separate states. Each state had only one vote in the Congress. Thus little Delaware with 60,000 people had as much power as great Virginia with three quarters of a million.

3. The Congress had no real power to raise money or to provide for an army or navy. It could only *request contributions* from the thirteen states to pay the bills of the national government. Since it had no president or officials to enforce laws, it could neither tax people directly nor draft them into the national army or navy.

4. The Congress had no power to institute a national system of money without the consent of nine states.

5. The Congress had no power to control business between states. Thus each state could charge a tax on goods of other states sold within its boundaries. This harmed business.

In short, the Articles of Confederation gave almost all the responsibilities to the national government and allowed it few of the powers.

In 1786 Washington and Other American Leaders acted to strengthen the Central Government

The many weaknesses in the government of the states, the poor condition of manufacturing and business, and other important factors led the thinking men of America to see the necessity of improving their affairs. Rebellions like that of Daniel Shays, the riots in Rhode Island, and the frequent petitions of business men for a stronger national government forced the leaders to realize that far-reaching changes must be made.

THE MAKING OF THE CONSTITUTION 129

By the summer of 1786 George Washington, James Madison, Alexander Hamilton, John Jay, and other leaders were determined to bring about a closer union among the states. Representatives from the thirteen states were invited to meet at Annapolis, Maryland, in September, 1786, for the purpose of discussing commercial relations among the states.

When the Annapolis convention met it was found that only five states had sent representatives. This number was not enough to insure a satisfactory discussion. Three of those present determined to find a way to form a new national government. The first was George Washington; the other two were James Madison and Alexander Hamilton. These three men were to play a most important part in the history of our country during the next few years. It was their decision that a real national convention should be called for the purpose of revising the Articles of Confederation and establishing a strong central government.

The Constitutional Convention, May–September, 1787

Through the influence of these men the Continental Congress, in February, 1787, requested the states to appoint representatives to a national convention which was to be held in Philadelphia in May. All the states, except Rhode Island, responded to the request and selected delegates. Among the most prominent of these were men whose names we know well: General Washington, as dignified as ever; Benjamin Franklin, now an old man and but recently returned from Europe, where he had so long served the colonists and the United States; and the young Alexander Hamilton of New York, a brilliant student of national government and finance.

Another young man, destined to become of great renown in America's history, was present. That was James Madison, who had come up to the convention early with the Virginia delegation. How this little man had slaved to work out a plan for a Federal government! A delegate from Georgia wrote of him:

> In the management of every great question, he evidently took the lead in the Convention. . . . From a spirit of industry and application which he possesses in a most eminent degree, he always came forward the best informed man on any point in debate.

Because of his great efforts James Madison could truly be called "the Father of the Constitution."

The two Morrises of Pennsylvania — Robert and Gouverneur — were there. The two Pinckneys — Charles and Charles Cotesworth—from South Carolina were there; likewise Edmund Randolph, who was a member of the Virginia delegation. Business leaders like Rufus King and Roger Sherman were there.

Fig. 54. George Washington, after completing seven years of service as commander in chief of the Continental Army, was again drawn back into public work and persuaded to preside over the Constitutional Convention. (From a painting made at Mount Vernon in 1785 by Robert Edge Pine)

Some of the leaders were conspicuously absent from the convention

But what of John and Samuel Adams? What of Patrick Henry? What of Thomas Jefferson? Were these prominent leaders of Revolutionary days at the Constitutional Convention? Not one. John Adams and Jefferson were in Europe, attending to the affairs of the new country. Samuel Adams had not been elected. Sam Adams, as he was known about Boston, had been regarded as a "fiery radical," even a crank on politics. Patrick Henry had been elected, but refused to attend because he said he "smelt a rat." Thomas Paine, the author of the famous Revolutionary pamphlet, *Common Sense*, was absent in Europe.

What manner of men, then, made up the convention?

The convention was made up chiefly of prominent leaders from the more well-to-do and prosperous classes. It was a convention of intelligent, even brilliant, Americans. The records of the convention as well as the histories of the careers of the individual delegates show clearly that many of them were exceedingly conservative men. Rufus King, a substantial man of business, wrote to a friend concerning the election of delegates: "If Massachusetts should send deputies, for God's sake be careful who are the men; the times are critical; a movement of this nature ought to be carefully observed by every member of the community."

This injunction was observed throughout the states. The delegates, almost without exception, were lawyers, business men, owners of great plantations, merchants, and manufacturers.

Toward the end of May a sufficient number of the delegates had arrived to permit the convention to organize. General Washington was elected president of the convention, and so began the meetings which were to continue through a long hot summer.

The sessions of the convention were secret

For four months the debates of the delegates went on behind closed doors. At the beginning the members decided that the proceedings should be kept secret. No outsiders were admitted. It was agreed that no official record should be made of happenings in the convention except a statement of the matters actually presented for vote and the number of votes cast. The members were pledged not to disclose information concerning the discussions.

Were it not for the work of James Madison, we should now know little of what took place in the historic Constitutional Convention. Madison alone of the entire group went home from the meetings each day and wrote voluminous notes of what had taken place. More than 50 years later Madison's *Journal* was made available to historians. From their careful studies of the *Journal* and other autobiographies and reminiscences of members of the convention, scholars have pieced together a fairly complete account of the great convention.

The convention made an almost entirely new body of laws

The delegates to the convention had been given the power merely to revise the Articles of Confederation. In no instance were they authorized to make a new national constitution. But we must remember that these men were determined to strengthen the central government, especially in its control over industry, commerce, and finance. They soon found that it was impossible to establish a strong or satisfactory form of government by merely revising the Articles of Confederation. A few of the Articles were retained but most of them were thrown aside, and a new plan of national government was made. This plan has since been known as the *Constitution of the United States of America*. Upon its principles the people of the United States have been governed for almost 150 years.

In making the Constitution the delegates exceeded their authority, but history has proved that the serious condition of affairs in the various states justified them in deciding for themselves how far they should go.

Nearly all the delegates agreed upon some things

More than anything else the representatives wanted a strong central government.

They agreed that a powerful central government should be set up which could do the following things:

1. Pay the national foreign debt.
2. Protect property owned by individuals.
3. Protect the owners of slaves and the masters of servants.
4. Maintain an army and a navy sufficiently powerful to defend the country against foreign enemies and to maintain order within it.

In addition the new national government must be given the power to tax the people in all the states, to manage commerce among the states and with other countries, and to do all other things which were necessary to carry these things out. Similarly, all claims against the Continental Congress and against the states must be paid — all were agreed on that.

Fig. 55. Gouverneur Morris. (Courtesy of the New York Historical Society)

Fig. 56. Roger Sherman. (Courtesy of the Gallery of Fine Arts, Yale University)

Fig. 57. Edmund Randolph

Fig. 58. Charles Pinckney

SOME OF THE MEN WHO HELPED TO FRAME THE CONSTITUTION

There were Two Important Conflicts over the Form of Government

1. The conflict between large and small states

Throughout the discussions of the convention one important problem confronted the delegates; namely, how many members to the national Congress should each state have? Under the Articles of Confederation each state had one vote irrespective of the number of inhabitants. Small states like New Jersey, Delaware, and Rhode Island, for example, had as much power as larger states like Massachusetts, Pennsylvania, and Virginia.

The large states now insisted that Representatives to the Congress should be elected according to number of inhabitants or according to wealth. They themselves were rich and their inhabitants were numerous. Hence they knew that their votes would decide important issues in the Congress.

"No!" said the small states. "If Representatives are elected according to number of inhabitants or wealth, our representation in Congress will be so small that we shall have little power. We have few people and little wealth. Let each state send the same number of Representatives."

Through the hot days of June and early July the argument continued. At times it seemed as though the convention would break up without reaching a decision. During this period Washington, the president of the convention, wrote:

> I almost despair of seeing a favorable issue to the proceedings of our convention, and do therefore repent having had any agency in the business.

Finally a compromise was reached which pointed a way out of the difficulties between the large and small states and made it possible for the work of the convention to go on:

1. The national Congress was to be made up of an upper house, called the Senate, and a lower house, called the House of Representatives.
2. In the Senate each state was to have two members chosen by the state legislature.
3. In the House of Representatives the number of members was to be determined according to the population; that is, one Representative

THE MAKING OF THE CONSTITUTION 135

was to be chosen for each certain number of people in the state. Thus the large states were to have more Representatives than the small ones.

4. Bills for raising money were to originate in the House of Representatives.

2. The conflict between the planting South and the commercial and industrial North

The South at that time consisted of six agricultural states: Virginia, Maryland, Delaware, North Carolina, South Carolina, and Georgia. The North consisted of seven states, whose chief interest was manufacturing and trade: Massachusetts, New Hampshire, Rhode Island, Connecticut, New York, Pennsylvania, and New Jersey. (Maine was still a part of Massachusetts.)

Geographic conditions — that is, differences in climate, in soil, and in natural resources — had produced very different interests in these two groups of states. James Madison himself recognized these differences and pointed out that they were causing many states to work against each other in the government. Speaking of two large Northern states — Massachusetts and Pennsylvania — and one large Southern state — Virginia — he said:

> They are far apart. Their trade is different. Their religions are unlike. Massachusetts is engaged in the fisheries and the carrying trade. The staple of Pennsylvania is wheat and flour. Virginia cultivates tobacco. Can such states ever form a combination?

The Northern states wanted one thing more than all else. They wanted to give the national Congress power to control trade — trade among states and trade between foreign countries and the United States. This was the very power which the Southern states feared to grant to the national government. They feared that laws would be passed by Congress favoring the Northern commercial states and opposed to the interests of the Southern agricultural states. For example, Congress might charge a high tariff on manufactured goods brought in from other countries. This would force the Southern states to buy goods in America when, without a tariff, they could buy them more cheaply abroad. The Northern states, of course, wanted this high tariff to protect their business and trade while they were developing their mills and factories. So the conflict between the two sections developed.

On their side the Southern planting states also wanted one thing especially, namely, to count Negroes as citizens in determining the number of Representatives each state could have in Congress. But they wanted the national taxes to be laid according to the number of white people. This demand of the Southern states raised an important question. On all other issues Southerners regarded slaves as property, not as people. They were not citizens; they could not vote or hold office. Was it fair, then, to claim them as citizens when it came to national representation?

There was a long, sharp debate over this question. For a long time neither the Northern nor the Southern delegates would give way.

The Northern and Southern states arranged a compromise

At last some decisions were made. The Northern states were granted their demand that the Federal Congress should regulate trade among states and between the United States and all foreign countries. The Southern states were permitted to count three fifths of the slaves in determining the number of Representatives that they should have in the Congress; that is, five slaves were to be counted as three citizens. Importation of slaves was to be permitted until the year 1808, and runaway slaves were to be returned to their masters wherever they might be found.

Thus by making compromises both North and South won certain demands. In this way the convention successfully passed another very rough place on its road.

In addition, other problems arising out of the conflict over the powers of state government and Federal government were finally solved. In certain matters the states were to be supreme. In others the national government was to be supreme.

Such powers as the following were granted to the states:

1. The decision as to who can vote.
2. The control of education.
3. The making of criminal and civil laws.
4. The determination of the powers that counties, cities, towns, and other districts shall have.

5. The settling of all questions of property, industry, transportation, and communication *within the state.*

6. The control of certain aspects of family life, such as marriage and divorce.

On the other hand, the Federal government held such powers as the following:

1. The management of foreign affairs for all the states.
2. The issuance of money.
3. The levying and regulation of taxes necessary to carry on the government.
4. The organization of the postal service.

The Convention set up a Government by which Changes were made Difficult

The Fathers of the Constitution feared "too much democracy." They were afraid of what the majority of people, who did not possess property, would do to the minority, who did. They were afraid of what they regarded as the ignorance and rashness of the lower classes.

The spoken and written words of the men in the convention show very clearly that they regarded democracy as a dangerous thing. Gerry, for example, said that the unsettled condition of the country "came from the excess of democracy."

Randolph used almost the same words, pointing out that the bad times were due to "the turbulence and follies of democracy." Another delegate, during the debate over the qualifications for Senator, maintained that the Senate should be made up of wealthy men "to keep down the turbulence of democracy."

Even Madison wanted to protect the small class of well-to-do people against the majority, that is, against the common people. In one of his writings he said:

> It is of great importance in a Republic not only to guard the society against the oppression of its rulers, but to guard one part of society against the injustice of the other part. Different interests necessarily exist in different classes of citizens. If a majority be united by a common interest the rights of the minority will be insecure.

138 AMERICAN GOVERNMENT AND CULTURE

Alexander Hamilton wanted Senators to serve for life. He said:

All communities divide themselves into the few and the many. The first are the rich and the well-born, the other, the mass of the people . . . are turbulent and changing; they seldom judge or determine right.

Fig. 59. A meeting of the Constitutional Convention. What faces do you recognize in this group? (Courtesy of Clarence Dillon, New York City)

Give, therefore, to the first class a distinct permanent share in the government. They will check the unsteadiness of the second, and as they cannot receive any advantage by change, they, therefore, will ever maintain good government.

Thus it was that the Fathers wished to guard against the dangers of too much democracy. How did they do it?

1. They established a government of checks and balances

The members of the convention divided the government into three parts: first, the executive body, which consisted of the president and other executive officials; second, Congress, the legislative body, consisting of the House of Representatives and the Senate; third, the judicial department, or the courts, at the head of which would be the Supreme Court of the United States.

Then, not wanting alterations to be made easily in the form of government, the Fathers of the Constitution worked out a plan by which these three parts of the government should act as checks upon one another. If the people of the country became restless and dissatisfied, and wanted certain new and, perhaps, dangerous laws passed, this form of government would prevent such laws from being made too rapidly or too easily. In other words, they made it difficult for the mass of the people to get new laws passed. This is how they did it.

1. The Congress, as you know, was to be composed of two Houses — the House of Representatives and the Senate. These two bodies were to make the laws of the country. The convention provided that in order to become a law, a bill, or proposed law, must pass *both* Houses. A majority in the House of Representatives might vote for a certain bill, but if the majority of the Senate did not also approve the bill, it could not become a law. Thus the two Houses were to act as a check upon each other, *and so they have acted from that day to this.*

2. Furthermore, as the Constitution was written in 1787, the House of Representatives was the only part of the government to be *elected directly by the people*. The two Senators from each state were to be *chosen by the state legislature*. Thus the people themselves might elect a new House when they wanted a change made, but they could not themselves elect a new Senate. Only the state legislatures could do that.

3. There was another check on changing government in the Senate. Each Senator was to hold office for six years, and only one third of the Senators was to be chosen every two years. For example, in 1801, one third of the Senators would be new; in 1803, another third was to be new; in 1805, another third, and so on. You see, then, that it would take some years to change completely the membership of the Senate, since many former members would remain in office for two or four years longer. They might also serve a second term. In the meantime the people might have to wait many years to get the new laws passed. And so matters have worked out from that day to this. The Senate has been very reluctant to approve changes in the Constitution or to pass laws which would bring sharp changes in the govern-

ment. Many students of American government, therefore, have concluded that those who control the Senate really play a controlling part in the United States government.

4. The president also was to have a check upon changes in government. If he did not approve of a bill which Congress passed, he could veto it. Then it could not become law *unless two thirds of the Senate and the House should pass it again*. Frequently this check has worked out as the Fathers of the Constitution planned.

5. The convention also provided that the people should not elect the president directly. They were to vote for electors, who in turn should elect the president. The delegates believed that most of these electors, like members of legislatures, would probably be conservative people who would not elect a rash president.

6. Still another check lay in the Supreme Court of the United States. That body of judges, like the Senate and the president, was not to be elected by the people. Here again the "danger of democracy" was feared and avoided by the convention. Supreme Court justices were to be appointed by the president, *with the consent of the Senate*. Thus again the Senate checked the president. Whether the Fathers of the Constitution intended it or not, the Supreme Court came to have great power over lawmaking.

By such provisions as these the Constitutional Convention made of the American government a government of checks and balances. Each department — executive, legislative, judicial — was to act as a check upon the others. Thus the Fathers of the Constitution provided for a *strong*, stable government, one that would not change rapidly, one that would protect property, and one that would not respond too quickly to sudden desires of the mass of the people.

2. The convention also made it difficult to amend the Constitution

Provision had to be made, of course, for changing the Constitution when necessary, but the members of the convention wanted to make this difficult to do. They provided, first, that an amendment would have to be passed by a two-thirds vote of both

Houses; second, that it must be ratified (approved) by the legislatures in three fourths of the states. An amendment might also be proposed at a special convention called by Congress on the application of the legislatures of two thirds of the states. In that case also three fourths of the states would have to approve the amendment. From that day to this it has proved to be fairly difficult to change the Constitution. Only nineteen amendments have been made to it in more than 140 years. Ten of these were passed within two years after the ratification of the Constitution.

When the Constitution was finally completed, in September, 1787, the purpose of the brilliant, conservative leaders who called the convention was achieved. A plan had been agreed upon which, if ratified by the states, would create a powerful national government. The merchants, the landowners, the manufacturers, the shippers, and the bankers were given what they wanted, namely, a government which would stabilize money and trade, keep order within the country, and defend the nation against foreign enemies.

Were the makers of the Constitution satisfied with it? Not completely, but they knew it was the best compromise that could be worked out under the difficult conditions of 1787.

Only one question remained now to be answered: Would the people of the country ratify the Constitution? That question weighed heavily on the minds of the Fathers of the Constitution as they departed for their respective homes.

Were the People of the Country Friendly to the New Constitution?

Within three weeks after the close of the convention a New York friend of Washington wrote to him:

> The new Constitution is received with great joy by all the commercial part of the community. The people of Boston are in raptures with it as it is, but would have liked it still better had it been higher toned . . . but, notwithstanding my strong persuasion that it will be adopted generally, and in a much shorter time than I sometime ago believed, yet it will be opposed, more or less, in most of the states.

As Washington's friend said, "the commercial part of the community" — the merchants, shippers, manufacturers, and bankers — were greatly in favor of it. Here was the plan for a strong central government, a government that would see to it that debts were paid, that commerce was protected, that uprisings would be put down, that the country would be defended against foreign enemies, and that the common people would not make radical changes.

Those who opposed the Constitution were principally the small farmers, the frontiersmen, the artisans, the poorer people, many of whom were in debt. Another correspondent of General Washington's wrote to him:

> The opposition, here, as has generally been the case, was composed of men who were involved in debt and, of consequence, would be averse to any government which was likely to . . . cut off every hope of accomplishing their favorite plan of introducing a paper currency.

Generally speaking, then, the well-to-do classes were in favor of ratifying the Constitution, and the poorer debtor classes were opposed to ratification.

Very soon those who were in favor of the Constitution came to be called Federalists. Those who were opposed to the Constitution were called Anti-Federalists. The difference lay even deeper than simply a difference in opinion regarding the constitution. Generally speaking, the Federalists approved a strong central government while the Anti-Federalists believed that more power should be vested in the states. Although the Anti-Federalists largely outnumbered the Federalists, they were scattered principally on the farms and in the back country. They were not rich, they were not so well educated, and they were not well organized.

State Conventions were called which ratified the Constitution

It had been decided in the convention — although the delegates had no legal authority to do so — that the Constitution should go into effect as soon as nine of the thirteen states ratified it. Now the Federalists knew that they were better organized than the Anti-Federalists. They were eager to call state conventions at once to approve the Constitution. This would give their opponents less time to organize against it. Almost at once, therefore, they began a political campaign to persuade the states to accept it.

The struggle for and against the Constitution became bitter. Leaders on both sides made speeches and wrote articles in the newspapers. Hamilton, Madison, and Jay published through newspapers a series of brilliant defenses of the Constitution, which

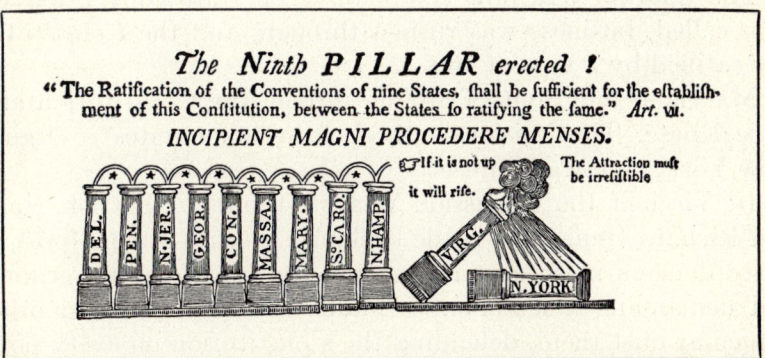

FIG. 60. A cartoon published in 1788, showing the nine states which first ratified the Constitution. These states are represented as pillars which support the arches of government. The pillars Virginia and New York have not yet been erected, since these two states had not yet ratified

were afterwards issued in book form and called *The Federalist*. These essays are regarded as among the most brilliant studies on government ever produced in the United States. Fighting against the Constitution were such important patriots of the Revolution as Patrick Henry and Richard Henry Lee of Virginia, and Samuel Adams and John Hancock of Massachusetts.

It was soon believed, however, that the Constitution would be ratified. In December, 1787, Delaware approved it. Within a month Pennsylvania, New Jersey, Georgia, and Connecticut had done likewise.

In Pennsylvania questionable tactics were employed to get the Constitution ratified quickly. In order to prevent hasty ratification the Anti-Federalists in the legislature stayed away from the meeting of the legislature. They wanted to give the people sufficient time to discuss the Constitution before voting on it. The Federalists, however, forced them to come to the assembly room, so that there would be enough representatives present to take action. The officers and a Federalist mob went to the lodgings of the Anti-Federalists,

broke open the doors, laid hold upon them, dragged them . . . through the streets to the State House. There they were forced into their places . . . with clothes . . . torn and faces white with rage.[1]

The quorum was now complete. The state convention was then called, business was rushed through, and the Constitution was ratified by a vote of 46 to 23.

Maryland and South Carolina ratified the Constitution after some debate. The decisions in three of the larger states—Virginia, New York, and Massachusetts—were very close.

In Virginia the discussion was most bitter. Patrick Henry and Richard Henry Lee made brilliant speeches setting forth the grave dangers in so centralizing the control of the government and demanding amendments. Madison, Randolph, and others argued against them, defending the Constitution on every point. Finally, on June 25, 1788, a bare majority of the Virginia convention approved it.

In the meantime the New Hampshire convention had met on June 21, 1788, and had accepted the Constitution, thus making the necessary nine ratifications. The new national government of the United States of America was at last a fact.

On July 4, 1788, celebrations were held all over the country. There were torchlight processions, pageants, and parades. Speeches were made and the people in the cities and towns generally rejoiced.

The remaining states were slower to decide in favor of the Constitution. In New York the Anti-Federalist delegates were in the majority, but in the discussion later Alexander Hamilton won over enough members so that, on July 26, 1788, there was a vote of 30 for the Constitution and of 27 against it. The New York ratification brought the total of ratifying states to eleven.

[1] John Bach McMaster, *History of the People of the United States*, Vol. I, pp. 456, 457. D. Appleton and Company, New York, 1930.

These ratifications were achieved, however, only with the definite promise to some of the states that a new national convention would be called at once to adopt certain amendments to the Constitution.

North Carolina and Rhode Island still remained outside as independent states. Not until November, 1789, did North Carolina

Fig. 61. The procession in New York in honor of the ratification of the Federal Constitution by that state. The good ship *Constitution* is represented sailing into port. (Courtesy of the Century History Company)

accept the Constitution and join the new republic, and then only when her leaders realized that North Carolina could not exist as an independent state in the midst of the Union.

In only one state of the thirteen — Rhode Island — were the people themselves permitted to vote directly upon the Constitution and not merely to elect delegates to a state convention. The popular vote in Rhode Island was overwhelmingly *against* accepting the Constitution: 232 people voted for the Constitution; 2708 people voted against it. Two years later, however, after the new national government was actually established, the voters of Rhode Island elected delegates to a state convention.

They too realized the danger of remaining outside the Union. A long debate ensued, and finally the vote was taken: 34 voted to accept; 32 voted to reject.

Thus even after two years of discussion the little state of Rhode Island — since the days of Roger Williams a center of democracy — decided only by a narrow margin to accept the Constitution.

An Important Problem: Was the Constitution Adapted to a Rapidly Changing Civilization?

One fact is clear from the foregoing discussion — the American Constitution was planned to provide for a stable, conservative, slowly changing government. Practically every provision prevented rapid change. As we study the development of the national government, therefore, keep constantly in mind one important question: *As American civilization changed did the Constitution, the laws, and the government change with it?* No question of government is more worth your study than this one.

In the preceding volumes of this series one characteristic of American life has been constantly illustrated — namely, change, ever more rapid change. Every aspect of American life has changed radically since 1787. The Industrial Revolution developed in America after that time. Even before 1900 a totally new civilization had been produced. This civilization is new in the ways in which food, shelter, and clothing are provided; new in transportation and communication; new in ways of conducting business; new in the ways in which people live. In this new civilization change is the most important characteristic.

Did the Constitution of the United States and the business of government change to keep pace with the new manner of living? This is a question which we must ask ourselves as we witness each scene in the drama of American government.

INTERESTING READINGS FROM WHICH YOU CAN GET ADDITIONAL INFORMATION

ELSON, HENRY W. Sidelights on American History. The Macmillan Company, New York. See Volume I.

FARRAND, MAX. The Fathers of the Constitution, Vol. XIII of The Chronicles of America. Yale University Press, New Haven. "The Federal Convention," pp. 108–142; "Ratification of the Constitution," pp. 143–166.

FISKE, JOHN. The Critical Period of American History, 1783–1789. Houghton Mifflin Company, Boston. "Trading Difficulties between the States," pp. 142–147; "Money Troubles and Shays's Rebellion," pp. 165–183; "Federal Convention," pp. 216–305; "Ratification of the Constitution," pp. 306–345.

HALSEY, FRANCIS W. (Editor). Great Epochs in American History. Funk & Wagnalls Company, New York. See Volume IV, pp. 31–37 (The Convention which framed the Constitution).

HART, ALBERT B. (Editor). American History told by Contemporaries. The Macmillan Company, New York. Vol. III: pp. 45–48 (An Underground Prison); pp. 185–187 (The Annapolis Convention); pp. 191–194 (Shays's Rebellion); pp. 205–211, 221–228 (Characters in the Convention); pp. 221–228 (The Closing Scene of the Convention). The class will find it interesting to use "The Closing Scene of the Convention" as the basis for a dramatization.

STEVENSON, BURTON E. Poems of American History. Houghton Mifflin Company, Boston. There is a radical song of 1786 on page 271. "Convention Song," pp. 271–272, is a jolly ballad on the difficulty of getting ratification of the Constitution in Massachusetts.

UNIT IV

THE FIRST YEARS OF NATIONAL GOVERNMENT

THE FIRST YEARS OF NATIONAL GOVERNMENT

At last the Constitution was adopted. The new republic had a plan for a strong central government.

*How would it work? That was one question in the minds of most thinking people in 1789. Would it serve **all** the people, that is, would it be a democratic government? Or would it serve only privileged classes, that is, would it be an aristocratic government?*

There was another important question in the minds of many Americans. Who would put the new Constitution to work? What group would carry on the national government of the United States? There were no well-organized political parties at that time — no Democrats, no Republicans, no Socialists. Who would take charge of affairs? Who would be president? What manner of men would make up the first Congress? What kinds of laws would they pass?

As we study the first years of American government in Chapters VIII and IX ask yourself, "What were the real needs of the people and how far were these needs satisfied?"

In Chapter X we shall take up the manners and customs during these first years of American government.

CHAPTER VIII

THE NATIONAL GOVERNMENT UNDER HAMILTON AND THE FEDERALISTS

We, the people of the United States, in order to form a more perfect union, establish justice, insure domestic tranquillity, provide for the common defense, promote the general welfare, and secure the blessings of liberty to ourselves and our posterity, do ordain and establish this CONSTITUTION for the United States of America.

In this historic Preamble to the American Constitution the purposes of government in America were stated: (1) to form a more perfect union, (2) to establish justice, (3) to insure domestic tranquillity, (4) to provide for the common defense, (5) to promote the general welfare and secure the blessings of liberty. These purposes are the same today as they were in 1789. How closely did they agree with the true needs of the people in 1789?

What did the American people need that government could provide?

First, they needed peace and "domestic tranquillity," so that they could make better homes for themselves, settle the new land of the West, develop their trade, build factories, improve roads and other means of transportation and communication — in short, make possible a healthier and happier living for all the people.

Second, they needed a system of money in which they could have confidence, so that without difficulty they could trade with their neighbors in different states and with the business men of other countries.

Third, they needed to have trade among states regulated so that they could exchange goods with their countrymen without unjust tariffs. They needed laws which would protect their infant industries, businesses, and farms from being ruined by people of other countries who could produce and sell things in the United States more cheaply than the Americans could.

Fourth, they needed a government which would carefully conserve and distribute among *all the people* the returns from the enormous natural resources of the country. The American people now owned all the land from the Atlantic to the Mississippi. This was a gigantic possession of natural wealth. There were millions of acres of fertile soil, valuable forests, underground lakes of oil, and huge deposits of iron and coal and other minerals. In 1789 most of this wealth was owned jointly by "the people of the United States." The soil, the forests, and the minerals could become the property of individuals only by the government of all the people legally transferring them to the individuals. Hence the need for a government which would wisely control and distribute this public wealth among all the people.

Fifth, to "secure the blessings of liberty" the people themselves needed really to control their government. They needed power to elect true representatives, to check them up, to remove them from office if inefficient, and, as the needs of the people changed, to make corresponding changes in the government.

In the famous Declaration of Independence, written by Jefferson, the delegates had said:

We hold these truths to be self-evident: — That all men are created equal; that they are endowed by their Creator with certain unalienable rights; that among these are life, liberty, and the pursuit of happiness.

And in the very next sentence they gave the *true purpose of government*, namely,

to secure these rights, governments are instituted among men, deriving their just powers from the consent of the governed.

They needed, therefore, a national government which would endow them with their rights of "life, liberty, and the pursuit of happiness," and which would pass no laws that did not really have *the consent of the people.*

Sixth, to "promote the general welfare," they needed a national government which would discover ways of raising the standard of living for all the people, of making towns and cities

GOVERNMENT UNDER THE FEDERALISTS

more healthful, of improving farming, of encouraging the more efficient use of natural resources, of developing industry and business — in general, a government which would help to make life easier for the rank and file of the people.

These, then, were the great needs of the American people in 1789.

ON APRIL 30, 1789, GEORGE WASHINGTON WAS INAUGURATED AS THE FIRST PRESIDENT

After the Constitution had been adopted early in 1789, electors were chosen by the legislatures of the states to elect a

FIG. 62. Washington was ferried from the New Jersey shore across New York Bay to the new capital. Everywhere he was received with the same enthusiasm as that displayed by the people in the picture

president and a vice president. There was no doubt in the minds of the leaders as to who would be the choice of the people for president. When the ballots of the electors were opened in March, 1789, it was discovered that every one of them had cast a vote for George Washington, and he was declared to be the first president of the United States of America. The next largest number of votes was given to John Adams of Massachusetts, and he became the first vice president. At the same time Representatives and Senators were also elected by the various states to comprise the first Federal Congress.

On the twenty-third of April, 1789, after a triumphal journey northward from his home at Mount Vernon, Virginia, President-elect Washington reached the capital, then New York City.

FIG. 63. The first inauguration of George Washington

He had been received everywhere with acclaim. The towns through which he passed made his coming an occasion for celebration. His inauguration[1] one week later was made a holiday; church bells were rung, and the people assembled in churches

[1] March 4 was the day which had been set for Washington's inauguration, but owing to the fact that the majority in Congress did not arrive until later the ceremony was postponed until April 30. Today citizens vote for presidential electors on the Tuesday following the first Monday in November of each fourth year. The electors cast their votes for president and vice president on the second Monday in January. The new president is inaugurated on the following 4th of March. We speak of the day when citizens cast their votes as election day, although the president is not legally elected until the votes of the electors are counted before Congress in the following February. The important thing to remember is that although citizens cast their votes in November the president does not take office until March of the following year, when the term of the preceding president expires.

and town halls. The ceremony of inauguration took place in the city hall of New York.

Finally the shouts of the multitude told of the approach of Washington. A moment later he entered the chamber. His tall, solemn figure was clad in a suit of deep brown, with white stockings; a sword was at his side, and his hair was dressed in a big-wig. In his face there was a slight trace of embarrassment, but he walked firmly down the room, bowing to the right and the left, and took a seat by the side of the Vice-President. In a moment Adams arose and said to Washington that the oath of office should now be administered. Out to the balcony which overlooked the street passed the parties concerned, and there Livingston, chancellor of the State of New York, administered the prescribed oath. A second later he turned to the crowd and shouted, "Long live George Washington, President of the United States!" and the vast throng re-echoed his words.[1]

Establishing the New Government

Congress soon provided for three Federal departments to carry on the work of the national government: the Department of State, in charge of foreign affairs, the Department of the Treasury, and the Department of War. As president, Washington had the power to choose the secretaries who were to direct the work of these departments. He named Thomas Jefferson as Secretary of State, Alexander Hamilton as Secretary of the Treasury, and General Henry Knox of Massachusetts as Secretary of War. In 1789 Jefferson, who then was a man of 46, had just returned from France, where he had made many friends among the most intelligent men of Europe. He was an idealist, much more in love with "democracy" than were the Federalists.

Alexander Hamilton, Secretary of the Treasury, was a quite different man — small, dapper, and aristocratic. He was to have charge of the Department of the Treasury of the new government, a position for which he had been chosen because of his extended knowledge of finance. Moreover, he could be relied upon to support the Constitution, since he was one of the men

[1] John Spencer Bassett, *The Federalist System*, pp. 11-12. Harper & Brothers, New York, 1906.

who had helped to make it. William Pierce, a delegate from Georgia to the Constitutional Convention, said of him:

> Colonel Hamilton requires time to think — he inquires into every part of his subject with the searchings of philosophy, and when he comes forward, he comes highly charged with interesting matter; there is no skimming over the surface of a subject with him, he must sink to the bottom to see what foundation it rests on. ... He is about 33 years old, of small stature and lean. His manners are tinctured with stiffness and sometimes with a degree of vanity that is highly disagreeable.[1]

FIG. 64. The secretaries of the new national departments. These men — Knox, Jefferson, Randolph, and Hamilton — formed the first presidential cabinet

You can see from this that even those people who did not admire Hamilton entirely believed that he was a man who could and did think well.

Other offices were created and appointments made. Edmund Randolph was chosen as Attorney-General, although there was no recognized Department of Justice until 1870. A Supreme Court was organized, and Washington appointed John Jay as Chief Justice. Other Federal courts were established in the various circuits and districts of the country, and judges were appointed by the President. The postal system was continued under Benjamin Franklin.

[1] A. B. Hart, *American History told by Contemporaries*, Vol. III, p. 206. By permission of the Macmillan Company, New York.

GOVERNMENT UNDER THE FEDERALISTS

Postmasters, customs officers, army officers, and surveyors were appointed to carry on the business of the national government in the various states. Soon the machinery of national government was in working order. One of the important tasks before Congress was the consideration of the amendments promised to the states at the time of ratification. By 1791 ten new amendments had been ratified by the states. These amendments, known as the Bill of Rights, guaranteed to the people such rights as freedom of speech and of the press, protection against unjust arrest and punishments, privilege of jury trial by one's peers, and peaceable assembly.

The same men who made the Constitution carried on the Federal government during the first years

Washington had been the chairman of the Constitutional Convention and exercised throughout an influence upon its deliberations. Eleven of the first 24 Senators had served in the convention and helped to frame the Constitution. In the House of Representatives was a large body of men who had taken part in the making and ratifying of the Constitution. Washington's cabinet of close personal advisers included two of the leading men in the Constitutional Convention: Alexander Hamilton and Edmund Randolph.

Jefferson, the first Secretary of State, was the only outstanding leader who had not actually helped to make the Constitution.

THE NEW GOVERNMENT PROVIDED A SOUND MONEY SYSTEM AND PROTECTED TRADE AND INDUSTRY

Hamilton knew that the government must have good credit

There was only one way in which the new government could gain the confidence of the American people and of foreign nations, namely, by arranging to pay its debts. These amounted to nearly $75,000,000, a vast debt for the new nation.

The government owed this money to three different groups.

First, France, and other European countries had lent to the colonies during the Revolution approximately $11,000,000.

The second debt was money which the United States owed its own people for depreciated paper money which the Continental Congress had printed and also for loans to the government during and after the Revolution. Most of these loans had been secured by bonds or notes, that is, promises to pay. Also, toward the end of the war, when the soldiers would not accept paper money in payment of their wages, Congress had given them interest-bearing securities which were to be paid by the new national government. This debt amounted to over $42,000,000.

Third, there were the state debts, which amounted to about $20,000,000.

In order to pay this vast national debt Hamilton evolved four plans.

FIG. 65. To the ardent Federalist, Alexander Hamilton, belongs much of the credit for evolving the plans by which the new government could be financed

1. The Funding Bill

Hamilton proposed to pay the national debt by a method called funding. By this plan new government bonds were to be issued in exchange for the old Continental bonds, and interest at 6 per cent was to be paid over a long term of years. In addition to the interest, a small part of the debt itself was to be paid off each year.

Hamilton sent his plan to Congress in January, 1790, stating that if it were adopted the national credit would become good. Those who favored the plan argued that as soon as the people saw that they would receive interest on their money, they would be glad to lend more to the government in the form of gold and silver. Also, as people gained more confidence in their government more goods would be bought and sold, gold and silver would start to circulate among the people again, and business would become prosperous.

There was one real danger, *the danger of speculation.* Most of the securities were in the hands of people in the distant back country who regarded them as so much worthless paper. There were no telegraphs to tell the owners of these securities that Congress was about to exchange them for bonds at full value; so many of them did not know of the opportunity. Hamilton's

FIG. 66. The backwoodsmen were often too far from the larger communities to know what was happening in governmental affairs. Therefore when people offered to buy from them the Continental bonds, which were believed to be almost worthless, the backwoodsmen were glad to sell them

plan had scarcely been revealed to Congress when members of the Senate and House of Representatives and well-to-do friends who were in the secret sent agents all over the country to buy up the old Congressional securities at far less than their full value.

Four days after [Hamilton's report] was read, expresses with very large sums of money were on their way to North Carolina for purposes of speculation in certificates! . . . Two fast sailing vessels chartered by a member of Congress who had been an officer in the war, were plying the waters southward on a similar mission.[1]

[1] C. G. Bowers, *Jefferson and Hamilton*, pp. 46, 47. Houghton Mifflin Company, Boston, 1925.

About half of the members of Congress were enthusiastic in support of Hamilton's plan, but the other half were opposed to it. As the debate over the Funding Bill went on, speculators crowded into the galleries and even onto the floor of the House of Representatives, where they mingled with the members of the House. Even those Representatives who favored the bill were divided into two groups. One was made up of some of those who were speculating themselves and the other of those who honestly believed that this was the only way to sustain public credit. Both these groups were in favor of paying full value for all government securities. Those who opposed the bill condemned ruthlessly the speculation that was going on and maintained that the brave soldiers of the Revolution were being robbed.

Outside the Congress ugly rumors went about. Men met in the taverns and coffeehouses, on the docks, and in the streets, and discussed the reports of the latest happenings. The newspapers, some controlled by one side, some by the other, reported many stories.

Opposition to Hamilton's plan grew steadily. Thomas Jefferson and James Madison took the lead in the argument. On the floor of the House Madison made powerful and honest pleas against the Funding Bill. Madison wanted the speculators to receive for their securities only what they had paid the original owners. This he said was fair and all that they should have. However, the wealthy members of Congress and their friends denounced him as a dreamer and as "an enemy of public faith."

So the fight went on under the threats of the speculators in the galleries. Madison, Jefferson, and their group did their best, but to no avail. Hamilton's Funding Bill was passed.

2. The Assumption Bill

Hamilton next proposed the Assumption Bill. This was a plan to assume and pay the state debts (about $20,000,000) out of the Treasury of the national government instead of having the separate states pay their own debts. This bill produced even greater division among the members of the Congress than the Funding Bill. Representatives of some states, like Virginia, which had paid most of its debts, could not see why their people should pay taxes to help the states like Massachusetts and Connecticut, which had not paid their debts. Other states which had never gone very deeply into debt because little of the war had been fought within their boundaries, felt likewise.

The battle over the bill was hard fought. In the course of the debate bargains were arranged between delegations of the different states. For example, Pennsylvania wanted the national capital, the location of which was not yet settled, to be within her boundaries. Hamilton, having great power in the government, promised Robert Morris of Pennsylvania that if he and the other Representatives from Pennsylvania would vote for the Assumption Bill, he would arrange it so that the residence of the capital would be located in Pennsylvania, *at least for a term of years.* Later Hamilton promised Jefferson that the *permanent residence* of the capital would be located south of the Potomac River. Thomas Jefferson helped Hamilton to get a majority of votes in favor of the bill, and it passed. Years later, however, Jefferson said that he would not have helped Hamilton if he had thoroughly understood the bill. He said he never forgave Hamilton for coming to him to get his aid for the Assumption Bill.

3. The laws taxing the people

Hamilton also proposed to raise money to run the government and help pay off the national debt by levying a tax on goods brought into the country from other countries and on what he called luxuries. Among other things, he selected whisky as a luxury and had Congress pass a law taxing its manufacture.

Now, among the farmers in the western sections of Pennsylvania, Virginia, and North Carolina, the distilling of whisky from corn and rye had become a profitable business, since poor roads made it impossible to carry crops to market and the whisky made from the grain could be transported much more easily and exchanged for other goods. With great indignation, therefore, they refused to pay Hamilton's tax. Government officers soon arrested them; but the farmers resisted, and in the skirmish some of them were wounded and a few were killed. In

162   AMERICAN GOVERNMENT AND CULTURE

Pennsylvania, where it was estimated that there were 5000 distilleries, farmers organized in groups and burned the homes of the men who accepted positions as government tax-collectors.

FIG. 67. When the whisky tax went into effect, those who tried to evade the payment of the tax moved their distilleries far into the woods so that the government agents might not find them and demand a payment. (From *Harper's Weekly*, December, 1867)

Then President Washington called out 15,000 government troops, which Hamilton himself led into the Pennsylvania region. The whole affair was soon at an end, but in the meantime much criticism of Hamilton's ideas and even of Washington began to spread up and down the frontier.

4. Establishing the first National Bank

Hamilton's fourth financial plan provided for the establishment of a National Bank. Long before the Constitutional Convention Hamilton had worked out a brilliant plan, one which was now received with admiration by a majority of the members of the Senate and the House of Representatives. Most of the leaders agreed that there should be a central coinage unit which alone should have the power to make coins and paper money.

As to the need for a National Bank, most Northern business men were agreed. They believed that it was necessary not only to guarantee a sound system of money but also to make credit available to industry and trade. In later years this argument became a most important one.

Within the House and the Senate charges were freely made that a group of Northern business men under the leadership of Hamilton were building up control over the national government.

In the debate on the National Bank great opposition came from the South. The group which opposed the National Bank was made up of the most famous men in the Southern states. It was led by Thomas Jefferson and included such brilliant and respected men as Madison and Randolph. It was at this time that the agricultural South began definitely to line up against the manufacturing and merchant North in Congress. The Southerners,— mostly planters and small farmers,— having no banks in their region, saw that the National Bank would help primarily the business men and manufacturers of the North. Also there was no specific authority in the Constitution for such a bank.

The National Bank bill finally passed Congress. Twenty votes were cast against it, nineteen of which were Southern votes.

As a Result of the Autocratic Policies of those in Control of the Government, the First Organized Political Parties came into Existence

Hamilton had succeeded in putting through this financial system. Under his leadership the central government was strengthened. The national, state, and foreign debts had been cared for. A National Bank had been established and a sound system of money inaugurated. A system of taxes and tariffs on foreign goods had been set up, and money was coming into the government's Treasury. All these things had taken place in George Washington's first administration, 1789–1793.

Confidence in the new government was being established among certain classes. The well-to-do Northern town and city people — the merchants, manufacturers, bankers, and shippers — were hearty supporters of the government. But Hamilton and his supporters had made many political enemies. Some of the most important leaders, such as James Madison and Thomas Jefferson, who had originally believed in the necessity of a strong central government, were among them.

After serving the four-year term to which he had been elected, Washington was reëlected. By the beginning of his second administration, in 1793, the leaders had split into two groups, or two political parties, called the *Federalists,* headed by Hamilton, and the Republicans (the former *Antifederalists*), led by Jefferson.[1]

Who were Federalists and who were Republicans?

Belonging to the Federalist group, of course, were the business men, the manufacturers, the owners of ships, and the men who had money to invest. For 25 years these people were the backbone of the Federalist party. Hence the great centers of that party were the towns and cities of the North, where business, commerce, and banking thrived.

The Republicans, on the other hand, were the people whose interests were opposed to those of the Northern business men. They were Southern plantation-owners, workingmen of the Northern cities, small farmers in all the states, and most of the frontiersmen. In other words, the Republicans included two groups of people: first, the well-to-do plantation-owners, whose interests were not the same as those of the Federalists; second, the rank and file of the people themselves — small farmers, clerks, mechanics, and most of the frontiersmen of the West.

Do you see somewhat the same division between the well-to-do aristocrats and the poorer democrats in the first years of American government that we found throughout the century and a half of colonial government?

---

[1] Do not confuse this first "Republican party" with the present Republican party. The latter was not founded until 1854. Furthermore, do not confuse the name *Democrats,* which was sometimes applied by the Federalists to Jefferson's party, with the Democratic party of today. The present Democratic party did not start until about the time of Andrew Jackson, president from 1829 to 1837.

The influence of the French Revolution (1789–1793) on American politics

During the same years that Hamilton and the Federalists were setting up their powerful business government, stirring events were happening in Europe which were to have an important influence on America.

The French Revolution was taking place. You have already read a brief story of it in *Changing Civilizations in the Modern World*. You know how the people of the towns and cities joined hands with the peasants, overthrew the royal government, and established a republic in its place.

The Revolution broke out in 1789, in the same year that our own national government was established. At the time even such conservative American leaders as Washington and John Marshall received news of the events with great satisfaction. Thomas Paine, who was then in Europe, hailed the uprising of the French common people with the words "The principles of America have opened the Bastille." The Bastille was the worst of the Paris prisons. The revolutionists had burned it after releasing its prisoners, who had been sent there for political offenses. General Lafayette sent the key of the Bastille to President Washington, who received it as a "token of the victory gained by liberty." Thus even the more aristocratic leaders in the United States congratulated the French people upon overthrowing their king and the nobles.

The leaders of the French Revolution became more and more intolerant, however. They ruthlessly killed the nobles and went from one excess to another. It was then that the conservative leaders in the United States turned away from them. John Adams, Hamilton, Morris, and their associates openly denounced the "murderous" practices. Federalist newspapers were outspoken against the murder of the King and his court.

The rank and file of the American people, however, seemed more enthusiastic about the success of the French common man. Liberty poles "surmounted by French liberty caps" were erected in the public squares of many towns. Republican clubs sprang up in many places. One New York Republican Club announced its organization by saying: "We take pleasure in avowing that we are lovers of the French nation; that we esteem their cause as our own." In some places men and women called each other "citizen" and "citizeness" after the general practice in France,

FIG. 68. In 1789, when the French Revolution began, many of the American people remembered the days when they too had struggled for liberty. Enthusiasm for the French cause ran high, and on many public squares the people gathered to voice their approval. Notice the French liberty cap atop the pole

cut their hair in French style, and adopted extreme French fashions in dress. French songs, the "Marseillaise" and "Ça Ira," were often sung in place of the native "Yankee Doodle."

Soon many aristocrats who had escaped from France with their lives, and often with little more, were welcomed by the members of the more aristocratic group in the United States. Here they were entertained royally and often helped to establish themselves on plantations of their own or in business of one sort or another.

Thus the democratic uprising in France helped to make still sharper the division between the aristocratic Federalists and the democratic Republicans.

Foreign Affairs

During these early years America found it difficult to stay out of war with England and France

After the first years of the French Revolution, Napoleon Bonaparte, a young Corsican officer of great military ability, seized control of the army and, with it, control of the government of France. From 1799 to 1815 the political history of Europe centered largely around Napoleon's attempts to conquer the whole continent. Not until 1815 was the turmoil quieted. Then England decisively defeated Napoleon's army, and Napoleon himself was exiled to the island of St. Helena, west of southern Africa.

The great desire of Washington and the Federalists had been to stay out of this French-English war. This was exceedingly difficult.

Party strife kept the European war before the American public. Most of the Republicans, under the leadership of Thomas Jefferson, sympathized with the French. They remembered the important part the French had played in lending money to the states and in sending soldiers and ships to help them throw off the control of England. Most of the Federalists, however, favored the cause of England. They were keenly interested in the business and financial welfare of the country, and many British merchants had established businesses in the United States since 1783. Much British capital was also being invested in public land as well as in factories and trade.

There was another reason why it was difficult to prevent conflict with either one or both of the European countries. French and English ships were preying upon American merchant vessels plying between the United States and Europe. Almost daily, outrages were being committed, for there was no strong American navy to protect our merchant marine. American seamen were seized and forced to work on British ships, the American flag was insulted, and cargoes were confiscated. When the American minister in London protested against the situation, he was received "with a courteous smile and contemptuous indifference." England was too busy with France to pay attention to America. Of course these acts aroused the rank and file of the

American people against England. In most states demonstrations were made, and Washington's problem became increasingly acute.

About this time the French Republic sent a revolutionary by the name of Genêt to act as the French minister in the United States. Early in 1793 he landed at Charleston, South Carolina, and was received with great enthusiasm by the people. His journey northward to the national capital was one of triumphal acclaim. Washington, Hamilton, Adams, and the Federalists in general received him coldly and warned him that he must be careful not to stir the Americans still further. Genêt disregarded the warning, however. He committed some very unwise acts, and was finally recalled by France at the demand of Washington.

The Neutrality Proclamation and the Jay Treaty

On April 22, 1793, a few days after Genêt's arrival, Washington issued his now famous Neutrality Proclamation declaring that it was the policy of the United States to remain neutral in European wars. A year later he sent John Jay, the first Chief Justice of the United States Supreme Court, to England to settle the differences between England and America. Jay was closely associated with Hamilton, Washington, and those Federalists who wished to maintain friendly relations with England. After months of discussion with the British leaders, Jay arranged a treaty which secured very little for the United States. The British agreed to fix the boundary line between Maine and Canada, to withdraw their troops from Detroit and other Western forts, and to pay damages for ships unlawfully seized. They did not agree, however, to stop seizing American merchant ships and sailors.

When the treaty arrived in the United States in March, 1795, it was received with a storm of protest from the Republicans. In several cities John Jay was burned in effigy. Hamilton was even stoned in one demonstration, and President Washington himself had to stand violent abuse through the press. However, after prolonged debate Congress approved the treaty, and Washington signed it. It had served one important purpose, namely, it had kept the little American republic out of a European war. But the treaty had also produced other difficult situations; it estranged the French, and it created a wider division than ever between the Federalists and the Republicans.

WASHINGTON'S SECOND TERM ENDED AND JOHN ADAMS WAS CHOSEN SECOND PRESIDENT OF THE UNITED STATES

Toward the end of Washington's second term, Jefferson, Madison, and the other more democratic leaders had succeeded in binding together the local leaders of the rank and file of the people into the Republican party. They had established several newspapers and written many pamphlets and articles which were widely distributed throughout both Northern and Southern states. Steadily the people became aware that they had leaders who were interested in bringing about a more democratic kind of government.

In 1796 there was a bitter campaign for the presidency. The Republicans chose Thomas Jefferson as their leader; the Federalists chose John Adams. The rival newspapers of the two parties — the *United States Gazette* of the Federalists and the *National Gazette* of the Republicans — attacked each other ruthlessly. But the time was not yet ripe for the Republicans. The race was very close, but Adams won by a majority of three electoral votes. Jefferson received the next highest number and was made vice president.

Notice that at that time the candidate receiving the second largest number of votes, irrespective of the party to which he belonged, was made vice president. By an amendment to the Constitution in 1804 this condition was made impossible of recurrence.

In the administration of John Adams (1797-1801) the Federalists steadily lost power and became more severe in their government

Although Adams succeeded in keeping his popularity for a few months, it was not long before the conflict between the Federalists and the Republicans became intense. On the floors of Congress and in the rival newspapers the battle of words went on. On every occasion the Federalists ridiculed and attacked the Republican leaders. Jefferson was openly called "Slanderer of Washington!" "Assassin!" "Anarchist!" At Federalist dinner parties Adams was toasted and Jefferson openly insulted.

On their side the Republican newspapers retorted, using much the same tactics. On the floor of the House two members of Congress even came to blows. Matthew Lyon of Vermont, hot-tempered and uncouth, but an honest Democrat, constantly provoked the Federalists, and at one time engaged in physical combat with Roger Griswold, a Federalist leader.

The Alien and Sedition Acts

As the Federalists saw the rising popular movement against them, their rule became more and more harsh. In 1798 they passed two laws aimed directly at preventing criticism of their administration. The first of these — the *Alien Act* — gave the president of the United States power for two years to send out of the country any foreigner regarded as "undesirable."

For some time past the Federal newspapers had opposed the migration of Irish to America. Irish refugees were entering the country, most of them seething with rebellion against England. Naturally Americans who were in sympathy with the Irish cause joined the Republicans. At many Republican dinners toasts were offered to the success of the rebellion of the Irish against their English masters. Then England suppressed the open rebellion of the Irish people, and Rufus King, the Federalist minister in London, wrote a note of rejoicing to Hamilton. At this very time French Republicans were being sent out of the United States, but French Royalists were being welcomed into the country by Hamilton and the Federalists.

Many people thought that the Alien Act was aimed especially at Albert Gallatin, the brilliant son of a wealthy Swiss, who had emigrated to America. Gallatin had settled in Pennsylvania, where he had become an influential member of the Republican party. Before the end of the 1790's he was regarded as the outstanding rival of Alexander Hamilton because of his knowledge

GOVERNMENT UNDER THE FEDERALISTS

of finance. We shall hear later of his great success in public finance. Hamilton and the Federalists feared Gallatin; so many thought that the Alien Act was passed in the hope that he might be expelled from the country as "an undesirable citizen." But the Alien Act was never enforced.

The *Sedition Act*, passed soon after the Alien Act, was an even more vicious attack upon the liberties of the common people. It provided, among other things, that *any person who criticized the government or its officials could be arrested and, if convicted, thrown into jail and compelled to pay a fine.* When Hamilton heard of the "monstrous measure" he was amazed at the brutality of his own associates. He warned them that they were going too far, that they would "endanger civil war," and that what they were doing would "establish a tyranny."

The scenes that took place in the House of Representatives were little short of disgraceful. For his speech on the Alien Bill a Republican leader, Edward Livingston, was denounced by the Federalists as guilty of sedition. Livingston warned the Federalists that the people would rise against any government which tyrannized over them in such high-handed fashion. He said that if such a bill were passed "the country . . . [would] swarm with informers, spies . . . and all the odious reptile tribe that breed in the sunshine of despotic power." The First Amendment to the Constitution had definitely stated that

Congress shall make no law . . . abridging the freedom of speech, or of the press; or the right of the people peaceably to assemble and to petition the government for redress of grievances.

In spite of all that the Republican leaders could do, the Sedition Act passed with a vote of 44 to 41. And then began the "Reign of Terror," as the next few years were called.

The "Reign of Terror": free speech prohibited

Men on both sides now armed themselves for defense. Crowds of Federalist supporters pulled down the Democrats' liberty poles. Attacks were made upon Republican newspaper offices. Matthew Lyon, member of Congress from Vermont, published an attack upon the Sedition Act. Immediately he was arrested, taken before a Federal judge, and found guilty of sedition. He was thrown into a foul, unheated, disease-breeding jail for four months and fined $1000. To his friends and neighbors he became a martyr and a hero, and they petitioned President Adams for a pardon. Adams refused even to receive the petition. As a result, the Revolutionary soldiers of Vermont, who had fought with Matthew Lyon, rose in their anger against the Federalists, and through their efforts Lyon was unanimously reëlected to the House of Representatives at the next election.

Other incidents of the kind were numerous. The Reverend John Ogden was thrown into jail on the pretext of being in debt, but really because he defended Lyon. Others in various states were added to the growing list of victims of the vicious laws. Anthony Haswell was arrested, declared guilty of sedition for defending Lyon in his paper, the *Vermont Gazette*, and thrown into jail for two months. In Massachusetts "an illiterate and irresponsible soldier of the Revolution," David Brown, was seized as a "seditious person," fined $400, and sent to jail for a year and a half.

A study of the records of these and other instances clearly shows that the trials were farces, "brazen attempts to suppress free speech and freedom of the press," that the presiding judges were unfair, and that in no instance were the Republicans given justice. On the other hand, each one of these trials strengthened the Republican party.

The Kentucky and Virginia Resolutions

The Republican leaders in Virginia and Kentucky took official legislative action against the obnoxious laws. Jefferson issued public printed statements vigorously condemning the action of the Federalists. For such a stand he himself could have been jailed under the Sedition Act, but the Federalists did not dare go that far. Jefferson drew up a set of resolutions which were passed by the Kentucky legislature. About the same time the Virginia legislature passed other resolutions against the laws. In these a most important stand was taken. The resolutions declared that *whenever Congress passed laws which violated the Constitution such laws were not binding upon the people.*

Bear in mind these Kentucky and Virginia Resolutions. They are the first of several instances in which state legislatures have declared that certain laws passed by the Federal Congress have no force. This action of state legislatures has become known as *nullification*. You will read of important instances in which national laws were nullified by other states before 1860.

At the Next Presidential Election the People turned the Federalists out of Office

In the midst of the excitement caused by the "Reign of Terror," a new presidential election occurred (1800). The Federalists renominated John Adams. The Republicans nominated Thomas Jefferson for president and Aaron Burr for vice president. The campaign went on with increased bitterness on both sides.

By the winter of 1799 public opinion against the Federalists had risen all over the country. One of their most turbulent and irresponsible newspaper men —"Porcupine"— was driven out of Philadelphia, and another, the younger Fenno, editor of the *United States Gazette*, had to close his office and leave the capital. One of the Federalist members of the House had resigned.

By this time Hamilton had lost his hold on the government. John Adams had deserted the young leader and associated himself with John Marshall, his sane, clear-thinking Secretary of State. Although Marshall was himself a stanch Federalist, he had honestly and courageously opposed the Alien and Sedition Acts. Almost alone among the Federalist leaders, the Republicans admired and respected Marshall.

So the campaign went on. The larger cities — New York City, especially — played a most important part. Here it was that the workingmen and small business men were centered. Here they met, and politics was the constant theme of conversation. Under the leadership of Colonel Aaron Burr they organized the *Tammany Society*, a social and political organization which has been most influential in New York politics from that day to this.

Election day came. The vote was close, but Adams was defeated. When the electoral votes were counted, it was found that each of the two Republican candidates, Thomas Jefferson and Aaron Burr, had 73 electoral votes.

The Constitution provided that in such an event the House of Representatives, voting by states, should decide the election. Which would they take, Jefferson or Burr? Hamilton, who disliked Burr more than he did Jefferson, led a sufficient number of Federalists to vote for the latter. Twenty-nine times during the first 24 hours of the election in the House, the members balloted. For four more days the contest went on. At last on the 36th ballot Vermont and Maryland cast their votes for Jefferson. He had ten states and thus was elected president of the United States.

The rule of the Federalists was at an end. No one could then foresee that they would never again come back into power, but so it was. All over the country they and their newspapers warned the people of the dark days coming under the administration of the Republicans. But the Republicans exulted. They were soon to be in power.

The Federalists' last attempt to control the government: Adams appointed many new Federal judges

Although Adams was defeated for reëlection in November, 1800, the new administration was not to go into effect until March, 1801. In the meantime Adams and the Federalists still held office and made one last attempt to intrench themselves in the national government. Adams appointed several new Federal [1] judges. Now, Federal judges serve for life; once appointed, it is exceedingly difficult to remove them. They have always had tremendous power, for they interpret the law, that is, they decide what the laws mean that are passed by Congress. We shall see many instances in which the United States Supreme Court has exerted tremendous power over the national government.

[1] The word *Federal* as used here has no connection with the political party. The Federalists have long ceased to exist as a party, but today we still use the title *Federal judge* of a judge of the United States court. Indeed, we often use the word *Federal* today instead of *national* — Federal government, Federal office, etc.

GOVERNMENT UNDER THE FEDERALISTS

In the last days of Adams's administration a new Judiciary Act was rushed through Congress. The number of Federal courts was increased, and near midnight of his last day as president, Adams announced his appointments to the new judgeships. These judges were afterwards called "the midnight judges," for Adams was signing appointments far into the last night of his presidency.

This closing act of Adams, however, was to exert a great influence on American national government for years to come. He appointed the ablest of the Federalists — John Marshall — to be Chief Justice of the United States Supreme Court. For 34 years Marshall decided momentous issues. In the succeeding chapters we shall hear his name many times. More than any other one man, he upheld the power of the Federal government over that of the state governments.

FIG. 69. John Marshall, Secretary of State under John Adams and Chief Justice of the Supreme Court for 34 years

INTERESTING READINGS FROM WHICH YOU CAN GET ADDITIONAL INFORMATION

ATHERTON, GERTRUDE. The Conqueror. The Macmillan Company, New York. The biography of Alexander Hamilton.

FORD, H. J. Washington and his Colleagues, Vol. XIV of The Chronicles of America. Yale University Press, New Haven. The best readers will enjoy this book.

HALSEY, FRANCIS W. (Editor). Great Epochs in American History. Funk & Wagnalls Company, New York. Vol. IV: pp. 51–61 (The Election and Inauguration of Washington); pp. 62–64 (Washington's Inaugural Address, the State Dinner, and the Levee).

JOHNSTON, MARY. Lewis Rand. Houghton Mifflin Company, Boston. The fierce fight between the Federalists and Republicans. Rand becomes implicated in Burr's conspiracy.

MITCHELL, S. WEIR. The Red City, a Novel of the Second Administration of President Washington. The Century Co., New York. The sequel to *Hugh Wynne, Free Quaker*. Many historical characters are introduced.

SPARKS, EDWIN E. The Men who made the Nation. The Macmillan Company, New York. Hamilton, pp. 151–180; Washington, pp. 181–217.

CHAPTER IX

DID DEMOCRACY MARCH FORWARD UNDER THE REPUBLICANS?

Jefferson and the Republicans were now in control. Would they bring more democracy into the government? Would the voice of the common people be heard more often in government affairs? We shall see.

What manner of man was the new president?

Thomas Jefferson, like Washington, Randolph, and other Virginia leaders, was a man of property. Two large estates were among his possessions. At one time these were valued at $200,000 but near the end of his life they became worth very little and Jefferson died almost in poverty. He was brought up as the son of a well-to-do Virginia farmer, owner of over a thousand acres. This land was located on the frontier, where the courage necessary to fight the Indians and wring a fortune from the wilderness bred a general spirit of democracy.

As a young man he went to William and Mary College in Virginia, where he compared the aristocratic society of the seaboard with the growing democratic movement of the frontier. After his graduation he was influenced by the democratic opinions of Patrick Henry and the other Revolutionary patriots. Then had followed years of residence in France as the representative of his country. There he lived in an atmosphere of revolution. Thus Jefferson's earlier connections developed in him democratic inclinations. As you remember, because of his brilliant and accomplished style of writing, the great task of wording the Declaration of Independence was given to him.

Now in 1801 he was president, the recognized head of the more democratic party, the Republicans.

Jefferson introduced more democratic customs into Washington society

Jefferson's inauguration was to take place in the little town of Washington, the new national capital. Washington had only recently been established in the forests which bordered the Potomac River.

As vice president under Adams, Jefferson had been living in Conrad's boarding house near the Capitol building. Here he lived very simply, eating at the common table. Except that he used a private drawing room for the reception of his visitors, he lived much as did the other boarders.

The freedom and lack of formality which Jefferson wanted to bring into government circles was not by any means pleasing to everyone. Among the people outraged by it was Anthony Merry, the rather pompous British minister.

He wrote home in deep disgust of his reception on the occasion when he went by appointment to meet the President of the United States. He complained that he was kept waiting in an ante-room, and finally presented, in a most undignified manner.... Merry himself was in the most correct of ambassadorial costume, and, not unnaturally, was aghast to see Jefferson, his tall, shambling form clad in garments arranged with studied negligence, his shoes somewhat down at the heel and fastened with a shoe-string in place of bow or buckle, and his whole appearance indicative of utter indifference to the dignity of a British Minister's visit.[1]

FIG. 70. Thomas Jefferson. (Courtesy of the New York Historical Society)

To the people of that day Jefferson's lack of formality and the social democracy which he introduced into Washington seemed to prove that he was also an ardent believer in political

---

[1] Maude Goodwin, *Dolly Madison*, pp. 87-88. Charles Scribner's Sons, New York, 1896.

democracy. Such changes alone, however, did not mean that the people played a greater part in the government.

This quotation from Jefferson's inaugural address shows how he tried to rub out the old bitterness between Republicans and Federalists:

> Let us ... fellow citizens, unite with one heart and one mind, let us restore to social intercourse that harmony and affection without which liberty, and even life itself, are but dreary things.... We have called by different names brethren of the same principle. We are all republicans; we are all federalists.

Was Jefferson right? After all the bitterness of the struggle between the two parties, could it be that the Republicans were really no more democratic than the Federalists? To be sure, Jefferson did try to get rid of much of the formality of the Federalist administrations, but he himself made few radical changes in government. After all, he was a Virginia "gentleman." In spite of his carelessness in dress and informality in manner, he held many of the views of the Southern aristocracy. For example, he distrusted the common people of the cities — the artisans and workers generally. He believed that *upon the farmers rested the happiness and welfare of the country.*

To a large extent also the Republican party stood for the farming interests, particularly for the interests of the large plantation-owners of the South. Thus *the change that was made in 1801 was not so much from less to greater democracy, as from the party representing the business and commercial interests of the North to the party representing chiefly the Southern plantation interests.*

The Republicans did make certain reforms

Much of the strength of the Republican party came out of the opposition to Hamilton's financial system. Let us see what changes the Republicans made when they came into power.

Under the Federalists, only land and slaves were directly taxed. To this plan the Republican landowners objected because it exempted those merchants, manufacturers, and bankers who did not own land or slaves from paying taxes to the government. As

DEMOCRACY AND THE REPUBLICANS

one Republican wrote, in the Charleston *City Gazetteer and Daily Advertiser,* October 3, 1800, the government had arranged its system so that

Mr. Adams, owning as he probably does, a large estate in stock, shall not pay for his stock a shilling, while Mr. Jefferson, *whose whole estate is in land and negroes,* will have to pay a heavy tax.

Recognizing that the heavy taxation bore especially hard upon the farmers, Jefferson's Secretary of the Treasury, Albert Gallatin, worked out a plan by which these taxes might be decreased and the national debt paid off more rapidly. Rigid economy should be practiced in government expenses, and the army and the navy should be reduced. Thus the people would be relieved of much of the burden of taxation.

FIG. 71. Albert Gallatin. (Courtesy of the Metropolitan Museum of Art)

A new principle — namely, that war might perhaps be avoided by cutting down military preparations — was also announced. "Sound principles," said Jefferson, "would not justify our taxing the *industry* of our fellow-citizens to accumulate treasure for wars to happen, we know not when, and which might not, perhaps, happen but from temptations offered by that treasure."

Thus the Republicans were bidding for the support of the bankers, the business men, and the merchants just as the Federalists had done.

Jefferson also feared "too much democracy"

Though the will of the majority is in all cases to prevail, that will, to be rightful must be reasonable; ... the minority [must] possess their equal rights, which equal laws must protect ... to violate ... [this] would be oppression.

Is this a Federalist who speaks of the rights of the small class of propertied men against the rights of the majority of the people? No, indeed. It is Jefferson, the Republican, speaking at his second inauguration as president in 1805.

As a young man, Jefferson had believed that the power to vote should be limited to men who owned a certain amount of property. When he grew older, he began to believe that more people ought to have the power to vote. As president, however, he did little about it. Some of his writings indicate that he feared what the majority would do to the minority.

There was one time in particular when Jefferson might have used his influence to make the election of the president more democratic. That was when the *Twelfth Amendment to the Constitution was passed in 1804*. This amendment (see Appendix) merely provided for certain minor changes in the method of electing the president and the vice president. Students of government have asked: Could not the Republicans, while making changes in the method of election, have made the needed change of permitting the people to vote directly for these offices? Thus would democracy have marched forward. But the Republican administration failed to do so, and neither has any other administration done so even to the present day.

The power of the central government continued to increase

It had always been the desire of the Federalists to give as much power to the Federal government as the Constitution would permit. To this principle the Republicans had always seemed to be opposed. At one time they had said: "You want to make the central government autocratic; to take away the powers of the states and give them to the Federal government." Now what did they do when they got into power? Let us study two examples.

1. *By the purchase of Louisiana, 1803, the Republicans exceeded the power given them by the Constitution*

In *A History of American Civilization* you read the story of how Louisiana was bought from France. Recall that Jefferson sent James Monroe, who, with the American minister, was to arrange a treaty with Napoleon and his ministers whereby the Mississippi would be kept open to American traders. Napoleon proposed that the United States government purchase outright the whole territory of Louisiana, covering approximately what was later to become thirteen states, west of the Mississippi River. In April, 1803, the agreement was signed by the United States and France. When the news came to President Jefferson he was puzzled. He had wanted to gain control of the Mississippi, and this vast domain which he was offered opened up even greater possibilities for his people. But, under the Constitution, did the government have the power to make the purchase?

In the meantime the Western people were clamoring for Louisiana. There would be trouble if France held it; so Jefferson simply took the power which he did not believe the Constitution gave him. At first he planned to ask Congress to pass an amendment which would legally give him the power he sought, but his followers thought the amendment was not necessary. It was never passed. The purchase was made, and Louisiana became a part of the United States.

Thus Jefferson and the Republicans were willing to extend the power of the central government and stretch the Constitution just as the Federalists had done.

2. *The national government assumed the power to make internal improvements*

In 1800 the region between the Appalachians and the Mississippi was rapidly being settled. Communities were springing up in the wilderness. Trade was growing along the Ohio and the Mississippi. Crude trails and paths were gradually changing into better roads. More than all else the Western communities wanted means of transportation and communication with the towns and seaports of the East. Years before, George Washington had foreseen clearly the need for a nation-wide system of land and water transportation, but relatively little had been done during his and Adams's administrations.

Under Jefferson and the Republicans, however, came the first great movement for the building of roads, canals, and harbors.

Jefferson's brilliant Secretary of the Treasury, Gallatin, had stated that roads built by the central government between the East and the West would contribute "toward cementing the bonds of the Union between those parts of the United States whose local interests have been considered as most dissimilar." Indeed, in 1806, one of Jefferson's Western correspondents had written him that a

> sentiment of disunion . . . pervades many of our western citizens. . . . Could not this sentiment be counteracted . . . by commencing the grand national undertaking of opening avenues for commerce. . . . This would convince our western citizens that their interest would be to remain with us. . . . This I think ought to be under the control of the general government.

Evidently Jefferson agreed with this sentiment, for although the Constitution gave the central government no clear right to do so, the Republicans lent their support to a movement for making improvements in transportation. Shortly after the close of Jefferson's administration, the Cumberland, or National, Road, built by the Federal government, was begun. This road joined the East with the Middle West, starting in Maryland and finally reaching central Illinois.

Thus we see that the powers of the Federal government were beginning to increase. Note how they expanded as time went on.

Jefferson continued the custom of declining a third term as president

Washington had served only two terms, although he was urged to accept a third term. In 1809 Jefferson's second term would expire. The legislatures of five states asked him to run for a third term. He too refused, saying that if a president held office more than two terms in succession it would be "dangerous to republican institutions."

The example set by Washington and Jefferson was in sharp contrast to the life tenure of office that Alexander Hamilton and John Adams had originally proposed for the presidency and the Senate. We must bear in mind, of course, that both Washington and Jefferson were old and in ill health at the end of their second terms. Both men were frankly "sick of the job." They had been abused ruthlessly by their political opponents, and both of them left office with great relief at the opportunity to retire to the quiet life of private citizens.

No president of the United States since that day has ever been nominated for a third full term.

In the Meantime Foreign Troubles were brewing

As we learned in the last chapter, France and England were at war in the early 1800's. Each was trying to cut off the other's trade with neutral countries. Orders were issued by both countries, closing the ports of the enemy country to the ships of the rest of the world. Warning was given that ships carrying goods to the enemy's ports would be captured. Now American ships laden with rich cargoes for all parts of the world were in danger.

At the same time Great Britain was having a difficult time to get sailors into the British navy. In those days the conditions of the ordinary sailor were intolerable and few were eager to enlist. The British resorted to harsh practices to secure men. They "impressed," that is, forced, men to serve against their will. The "press gangs" of the navy forced men from prisons, from river boats, and from the streets of the cities to serve as sailors. On the high seas, too, private British merchant vessels were stopped and their sailors seized.

Many a British seaman had sought escape from his hard life by deserting and later signing up on American merchant ships. As a result British vessels began to stop merchant vessels from the United States and search them for deserters. Those whom they found were forced back into the British service, whether or not they had taken out citizenship papers in the United States. "Once an Englishman always an Englishman," said the officers in charge. Such procedure would soon lead to war.

The Embargo Act and the Nonintercourse Act

By the year 1808 the great shipping towns of the United States were strangely quiet. Wharves were deserted; ships rotted in their docks; sailors wandered around the towns.

What had happened? In December of 1807 President Jeffer-

184 AMERICAN GOVERNMENT AND CULTURE

son had signed the Embargo Act, prohibiting any American vessel from sailing for a foreign port. It was made illegal to exchange goods with foreign countries. Jefferson hoped by this measure to avoid war with both England and France, and to bring them to terms by cutting off their trade entirely.

FIG. 72. This is the way the cartoonists of the time regarded Jefferson's policy toward France and England. The United States (represented by the figure of Jefferson) is shown badly in need of foreign goods (note Jefferson's tattered garments), but Jefferson is saying: "I have stripped myself rather than submit to London or Paris fashion!" (From Bancker's Collection, 1898)

All throughout 1808 and into the year 1809, the New England shipowners and merchants were bitter against the Republicans for taking away their profitable business. So, too, were the sailors and the other people who earned their living in the shipping and shipbuilding business. The Federalists violently opposed this Republican policy. One of the Federalist embargo songs ran thus:

> Oh, dear, what can the matter be?
> Dear, dear, what can the matter be?
> Oh, dear, what can the matter be?
> The Embargo's so long coming off.

> It promised to make the great Bonaparte humble,
> It promised John Bull from his woolsack to tumble,
> And not to leave either a mouthful to mumble,
> At our nod to make their caps doff.

Finally, on March 1, 1809, just before Jefferson ceased to be president, he signed the bill which removed the embargo. Soon after Madison became president Congress passed the Nonintercourse Act, which allowed American ships to trade with any country except France and Great Britain. If either of these countries should change its attitude toward American shipping and allow American ships to pass into the enemy ports, the president might order trade resumed with that country also. England at once offered to withdraw her orders on certain conditions, but the British Minister to the United States, too anxious for peace, withheld the conditions from the president. Madison, being equally anxious for peace, did not ask to see the terms, and announced that trade would be resumed with Great Britain. American ships again began to ply between Europe and the United States. Trade revived, but only for about three months.

JAMES MADISON, "THE FATHER OF THE CONSTITUTION," BECAME THE FOURTH PRESIDENT, 1809–1813

Since the early 1780's James Madison of Virginia had played a conspicuous part in forming the new government. He, more than any other one man, was "the Father of the Constitution." At first he too was a Federalist, but as the Federalists became increasingly autocratic Madison left them and joined Jefferson in organizing the Republican party. In 1808 he was elected president by a large majority.

Madison's administration is remembered chiefly for the War of 1812

It was twenty years since George Washington had taken office as the first president. During all that time, in spite of insults from England and France, in spite of the seizure of merchant ships, the impressment of American sailors, and serious damage to American trade, the United States had remained out of war. Madison, himself a believer in peace, wanted to continue the policy of not engaging in Europe's quarrels. For three years he maintained neutrality.

In the meantime, however, the war spirit, especially in the South and West, began to flame high against England. A new group of younger men had begun to take over the control of Congress, long held by the older Federalists and Republicans. This group, known as the War Hawks and led by John C. Calhoun of South Carolina and Henry Clay of Kentucky, took an active part in bringing about the conflict. In spite of the Embargo Act and the Nonintercourse Act, many ship-owners continued to send their ships to France and England. Cargoes destined for England were seized by French ships, and others destined for France were taken by the British. In 1812 the *Weekly Register* of Baltimore reported the following incident, which clearly shows the odds against those ship-owners who attempted to maintain their trade:

FIG. 73. James Madison

What next? — the Schooner *Pert*, Captain Jenkins, laden with hides and fish, from Baltimore, for Bordeaux [France], was captured on the 29th of March ... about 20 miles from the Capes of Virginia — by the *Belvidere* frigate! The *Pert* received two shots ... and had her sails and rigging much cut; the frigate having fired (it is said) 25 shots at her. The valiant British captors took out the mate and crew, and put 15 men aboard, and ordered the prize to the Bermudas.

The captain of the *Belvidere* had received intelligence of every American sailing or intended to sail for France — from British spies, consuls, doubtless in our sea ports.[1]

[1] From the *Weekly Register*, Baltimore, April 4, 1812.

The desire for trade affected the decisions of the people

The three sections of the country did not agree over the question of war with England. The Southern planters and the Western frontiersmen wanted it; the New England business men were opposed to it. Clay tried to stir the Eastern men in Congress by pointing out that England was ruining American commerce. He said: "We have complete proof that England would do everything to destroy us. Resolution and spirit is our only security. . . . War we shall have in sixty days." Calhoun also stated the reasons for war: "the control of our commerce by Great Britain . . . seizing and confiscating . . . our vessels with their cargoes . . . the impressment of our citizens." In the West, too, the British were *competitors* for the fur trade; hence the Westerners *opposed the British*. The War Hawks aroused the Western Congressmen by showing them that if war came the Indians would be conquered and the British fur-trading companies would be driven out of the Northwest Territory, with the result that the West could be settled in peace. The South also wanted to expand its trade and therefore advocated war. So those Northern ship-owners whose boats lay rotting in the docks, the Southern cotton-growers whose product was piling higher each month on the Southern wharves, and the Western fur-traders whose chief competitors were the British, felt that only through war could their interests be secured.

The merchants and business men of the Northern states, however, were opposed to war. Their commercial interests were closely tied up with the commercial interests of English business men. They feared that the great British navy would sweep American commerce from the seas and that their trade would be wiped out.

Is it not an interesting fact that the desire for personal profit determined exactly opposite views which the people took about the war? Thus we see again that the occupations of the people are bound up closely with problems of government.

But we have learned repeatedly in this series of books that occupations are determined in part by the "geography" of the regions where the people are living. In New England, as you already know, the occupations, and hence the desires, of the people with respect to government, were largely determined by such factors as the cold climate, the arid soil, the many fine harbors, and the water power of the rivers.

On the Western frontier the geographic conditions of agriculture made farming and fur-trading with the Indians the chief occupations of the people.

In the South the rainfall, climate, and soil made cotton-raising the most profitable occupation.

Thus "geography" had helped to bring about differences in economic life and to develop different views about government. Again and again *American history illustrates the close relation between geographic factors, ways of living, and government.*

We can see now how the war spirit developed in the country. As we said, Madison did not want war (although his enemies called it "Mr. Madison's war"), but he saw that it could not be prevented. On June 18, 1812, he signed the resolution declaring war on Great Britain. The War of 1812 had begun.

The War of 1812: an Outline

When war was declared the United States was almost completely unprepared. The entire army, untrained and badly equipped, numbered only about 4000 men in January, 1812. It was clear that the ranks must be filled by volunteers.

The campaigns on the Canadian border

The American military leaders planned three campaigns against Canada: first, by way of Niagara; second, through Detroit; third, by way of the route up the Hudson River, Lake Champlain, and the St. Lawrence River. This plan provided for a combined attack on Canada all the way from Quebec to Detroit.

The entire plan failed. At Detroit General Hull's army of about 2000 men was basely surrendered to a contingent of about 1000 British, Canadians, and Indians. The Niagara plan proved equally unsuccessful because of incompetent leadership. The campaign from Lake Champlain failed both because of incompetency of its leaders and because the state militias which were used refused to cross into Canada, where they would be on foreign soil.

American victories in 1813

The humiliation of these defeats was offset a year later, however, by American victories at Chippewa and Lundy's Lane. The town of York (now the city of Toronto) was captured and

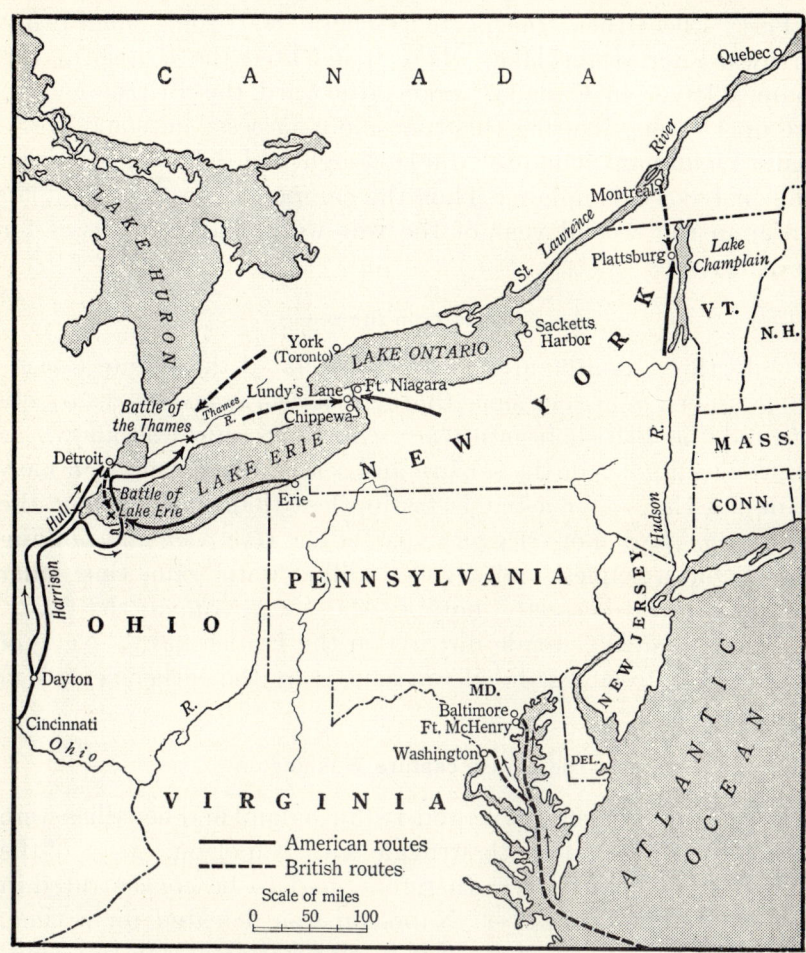

FIG. 74. Campaigns in the War of 1812

burned. In the meantime, on September 12, 1813, Commodore Oliver Hazard Perry, with a little rough-hewn fleet, decisively defeated a British fleet at the western end of Lake Erie. This is regarded as one of the outstanding exploits of the American navy.

Perry and his men had built their nine little vessels from timber cut on the shores of the lake. At the close of the battle Commodore Perry sent his historic message to General Harrison, who was in command: "*We have met the enemy, and they are ours. Two ships, two brigs, one schooner and one sloop.*"

Perry's fleet then transported General Harrison's small army northward across the lake, where it defeated the British at the Thames River in Canada. Soon afterward the British had to give up Detroit. During this time more success had come in the East. Lieutenant Thomas MacDonough had defeated a British fleet on Lake Champlain. Thus the campaigns on the Canadian border in the second year of the war were chiefly successes for the Americans.

Warfare on the sea

Only three months after war was declared the frigate *Constitution*, known in history since that date as *Old Ironsides*, decisively defeated the British frigate *Guerrière*. This ship was known as the worst offender in the seizure and searching of American merchant vessels. After a battle lasting less than half an hour the *Constitution* had shot off every spar of the *Guerrière* and nothing was left but a helpless and wrecked hulk. At the same time other American naval vessels — notably the *United States*, the *Essex*, and the *President* — made inroads on the British navy. News of these exploits relieved the gloom caused by the earlier defeats in Canada.

The British capture Washington

Recall that between 1799 and 1815 England and her allies were engaged in a life-and-death struggle with Napoleon. Most of the military and naval forces, therefore, had to be concentrated in Europe. In 1813, however, Napoleon was defeated for a time, and Great Britain was more free to give her attention to a campaign against the United States. Ship after ship of the American fleet was defeated until at last there was hardly a vessel left.

During that year also a British army was landed on the shores of Chesapeake Bay. The capital, Washington, was unprotected. Almost unmolested the British troops marched on the city, captured it, and set fire to the Capitol and the White House. Many incidents are recorded of the evacuation of the city. Dolly Madison, the wife of President Madison, is remembered for her forethought in saving a valuable portrait of George Washington. Among the treasures removed from the capital before the attack of the British soldiers was the original copy of the *Declaration of Independence*.

The British fleet had sailed up Chesapeake Bay, where it had attacked Fort McHenry just below Baltimore. Although the fort was severely bombarded the American flag continued to fly. It was that inspiring sight which caused Francis Scott Key, a young American lawyer, to write "The Star-Spangled Banner."

FIG. 75. At the battle of Lake Erie, Perry's flagship was wrecked. Under fire from the British ships, Perry made a dangerous trip from his sinking flagship to another. He bore his battle flag, which read "Don't give up the ship"

By the autumn of 1814 both sides wanted peace. Greater opposition to the war had developed in New England. In other parts of the country also there was a growing desire that peace be arranged with Great Britain. The British too, having lost scores of ships and seeing the cost of war mounting constantly, were glad to consider overtures for peace. Representatives of the two governments met at Ghent, Belgium, in the late summer of 1814, and on Christmas Eve the treaty of peace was signed.

When the terms of the treaty were made known in America there was great astonishment. Not one of the important questions for which the United States had gone to war was really settled. The seizure of American ships and the impressment of sailors were not mentioned. In June, 1815, however, the problems settled themselves when Napoleon was defeated forever by the allies at Waterloo. Peace came to Europe, and Great Britain stopped interfering with American trade and citizens.

Thus ended *the only European war in which the United States was to engage during the first 100 years of her national life.*

General Andrew Jackson decisively defeated the British at the battle of New Orleans, January 8, 1815

Two weeks *after* the treaty of peace had been signed another battle was fought. This may seem strange to you, but in those days transportation and communication were so slow that news of the making of peace reached the country long after it had happened.

Late in 1814 the British, under General Pakenham, were landing troops at New Orleans and threatening control of the Mississippi. General Andrew Jackson was ordered South from Tennessee with a force of frontier sharpshooters. Near New Orleans the Americans intrenched themselves behind cypress logs and cotton bales. Pakenham unwisely ordered an open attack. Protected as the Americans were, these sharpshooters mowed down the oncoming British, and in twenty-five minutes the British army was in retreat, leaving a third of their number dead or dying on the field. The Americans lost only 71 men.

During the war threats to break up the Union had come from New England

We have already seen how difficult it was to keep the states together as one Union. Under Adams's administration the Alien and Sedition Acts had brought open threats of nullification. Kentucky and Virginia had defended the right of any state to ignore any national law with which the people of that state did not agree. In 1807 and 1809, during Jefferson's and Madison's administrations, it was the New England shippers and merchants who resisted the Embargo and Nonintercourse acts. Conservative Massachusetts communities held town meetings, and even appointed "committees of safety," as in Revolutionary days, to keep in touch with other towns and to resist jointly Federal officers who tried to enforce the Embargo Act.

Fig. 76. The battle of New Orleans, which was fought after peace had been declared

The storm of protest that arose was so great that Congress finally had to yield to public opinion and repeal the Embargo Act.

When the War of 1812 began, the New Englanders foresaw the ruin of their trade on the high seas. Soon they began to resist the efforts of the Federal officers to enlist troops and to raise money. Newspapers defended the right of a state to nullify the declaration of war, maintaining that each state was sovereign and independent and could decide whether or not it would stay in the Union. In 1812 the Massachusetts legislature resolved that "Mr. Madison's war" had been declared without cause. Some of the New England states refused to call out their militias. New England business men even sold food to the British army in Canada.

Early in December, 1814, affairs were in such a bad state that representatives from Massachusetts, Rhode Island, and Connecticut held a meeting to discuss whether or not they should secede from the Union. This meeting was held at Hartford, Connecticut, and has since been known as the Hartford Convention. During the session, delegates from Vermont and New Hampshire arrived. Prominent New England leaders who had fought to form the Union were there. For three weeks there was heated debate.

The South and West were startled. What could all this talk in New England mean? Was New England going to break up the Union? Were the Federalists, who had been so active in making the Constitution and in forming the Union, now going to destroy both?

Finally, amendments to the Constitution were proposed, the object of which was to make it impossible for Congress to pass laws and to declare war without the consent of all the states. The Hartford Convention came very close to proposing secession from the Union. Arrangements were made to hold another convention if their demands were not met by Congress.

Before another convention could be held, however, peace had come. So ended this particular movement toward secession.

Important outcomes of the war

Albert Gallatin, the Secretary of the Treasury, later pointed out one of the important outcomes of the War of 1812. He said it had

renewed and reinstated the national feeling and character which the Revolution had given and which were daily lessening. The people . . . are now more Americans; they feel and act more as a nation; and I hope that the permanency of the Union is thereby better secured.

This was very significant in the light of what had happened at the Hartford Convention.

There was another important outcome of the war — the complete break-up of the Federalist party. The unpatriotic acts of the Federalists during the war had injured the party so much that after 1816 it never nominated candidates for national offices.

There were two other indirect results. In 1811, under Madison, the Republicans had defeated the attempts of the Northern business men to renew the charter of the first National Bank, which had been established under Hamilton. Within two years after the close of the war, however, they were convinced of the need of establishing another National Bank. Similarly, they were now ready for the development of a protective tariff. Thus we see another example of the manner in which the Republicans, who originally had opposed giving certain powers to the central government, now advocated two of the chief measures of the Federalists.

The Growth of Nationalistic Spirit

We are great, and rapidly — I was about to say fearfully — growing. This is our pride and our danger, our weakness and our strength. . . . We are under the most imperious obligation to counteract every tendency to disunion.

John Calhoun, the young leader from South Carolina, spoke those words in Congress in December, 1816. Remember them well, for Calhoun was later to become an advocate of state rights and disunion. In 1816 most leaders agreed with him. The War of 1812 had largely wiped out party lines. Many Federalists had become Republicans; only the extreme Federalists remained aloof. On the other hand, the Republicans had taken over the two central ideas of the Federalists: (1) that the powers of the central government should be increased; (2) that the financial and industrial interests should be helped and protected. *So do the principles of political parties change as time goes on.*

The country was indeed growing with tremendous rapidity. Pioneers were pushing on and filling up the Western country. New states were being admitted to the Union. Men of all sections believed that in order to hold the widening regions together the government would have to take over greater powers. At the same time, business was flourishing and industries were growing. It was a day of expansion and growth.

James Monroe (1817–1825) the Fifth President

The "era of good feeling"

In 1817 James Monroe became president. Like Washington, Jefferson, and Madison, he was a Virginian, an aristocrat trained in the old school of politics. Under him the period of comparative peace in politics, which began under Madison, reached its height.

Fig. 77. James Monroe. (From a painting by Rembrandt Peale. The original is in the possession of John Frederick Lewis of Philadelphia)

Tranquillity pervaded the country like the placid calm of an Indian summer.

There was a pause in politics. ... The great achievement of Mr. Monroe's administration was to keep everything quiet, to please everybody and to secure a second term of office. We were all Federalists then, and all Republicans.

It is true that storms were brewing. A keen observer might have heard ominous, though distant, rumblings, but for the present all was quiet.

At the same time a new group of young leaders were appearing in Congress. Some of them we have known before as the War Hawks. From the South came John C. Calhoun, of whom John Quincy Adams of Massachusetts once said, "[He] thinks for himself, independently of all the rest, with sound judgment, quick discrimination, and keen observation. He supports his opinions, too, with powerful eloquence." From New England there was the able but unpopular John Quincy Adams, who was Monroe's Secretary of State and a Republican. He was the son of John Adams, the second president. Trained by his father in foreign diplomacy from his boyhood, he was an able political leader. Gallatin called him "a virtuous man, whose temper is not of the best." From the West came Henry Clay, Speaker of the House of Representatives. He was quite the opposite of Adams — very popular, witty, and clever, and a lover of sport.

Different as these three men were, they agreed for a few years on a national policy, that is, a policy which aimed to unite the country and to strengthen the national government.

The power of the government was increased and finance and industry were helped and protected

1. *The second National Bank was established*

In January, 1816, Calhoun reported a bill to the House of Representatives providing that a Bank of the United States be chartered for twenty years. The Bank he proposed was much like the one which Hamilton had established. Notice how the viewpoints of these parties had changed. Clay, the Republican, now spoke in this way: "The Constitution, it is true, never changes; it is always the same; but the force of circumstances and the lights of experience may evolve." This meant that times had changed and other policies were necessary.

The change of the Federalists was as strange as that of the Republicans. The few Federalists who were left, led by Daniel Webster, now opposed the Bank!

In 1816 the second National Bank was chartered to operate for twenty years. Note carefully the term — twenty years. The charter would expire in 1836. In the meantime stirring events were to take place, and the Bank was to play an important rôle.

2. *The growing industries were protected by a tariff*

You remember that during the embargo and the War of 1812, shipping and trade had suffered. After peace had been declared, however, commerce began to resume its pre-war condition. British ships sailed in and out of the harbors of the United States. British merchants sold their goods in our cities. But the goods were being sold at prices less than those at which our own manufacturers could afford to sell theirs.

During three days in August [1815] sixty-five vessels came into the port [of New York] from foreign countries laden with cargoes worth in several instances fifty thousand pounds sterling [$250,000]. On November fourteenth the value of property entered at the Custom House was more than twice as great as had ever before been entered in one day. . . .

What took place at New York took place in every importing city. On one occasion the *Charleston Courier* was so crowded with advertisements of British goods for sale in packages, and of auctions soon to come off, that of the sixteen columns the journal contained, but two and a half were given to news.[1]

American business men were greatly disturbed. This flood of cheap English goods will destroy American industries, they said. There is reason to believe that the English merchants are selling their goods cheaply, so that they may destroy the young American industries. Indeed, it was said in Parliament during one of the debates on the question that

it was well worth while to incur a loss upon the first exportation, in order, by a glut, to stifle in the cradle those rising manufactures in the United States.

It was then that some of the manufacturers in the United States hired and sent to Washington a "lobby"— that is, a group of private citizens who represented their interests — to demand that Congress pass a tariff law. They wished a tariff law that would oblige merchants buying cotton, iron, and other goods from foreign countries to pay a duty when these goods entered United States ports. This was an old custom in other countries and in the states, but what the manufacturers of 1815 and 1816 demanded was a *protective* tariff — that is, a tariff so high that foreign goods of certain kinds would either have to be sold at a very high price, or would be kept out entirely.

In arguing the question of a protective tariff, Calhoun said:

It is the duty of this country, as a means of defense, to encourage its domestic industry, more especially that part of it which provides the necessary materials for clothing and defense. . . . A certain encouragement should be extended, at least, to our woolen and cotton manufacturers.[2]

[1] John B. McMaster, *History of the People of the United States*, Vol. IV, pp. 323–324. D. Appleton and Company, New York, 1895.
[2] Edward Stanwood, *American Tariff Controversies in the Nineteenth Century*, Vol. I, p. 148. Houghton Mifflin Company, 1903.

Remember this defense of the tariff by Calhoun, for later he was to be its most bitter opponent.

The bill was opposed by a small group of shipowners, of whom Daniel Webster of New England was a representative in Congress. Shippers did not want a tariff, because it cut down trade between countries, and so cut down their business. In April, 1816, however, the bill became a law. The duties charged were not high enough to please most manufacturers, and from that time to the present day they have clamored for increasingly higher duties.

The Supreme Court, under John Marshall, also added to the power of the national government

John Marshall, as you remember, had been appointed Chief Justice of the Supreme Court by John Adams in 1801. He was a peculiar-looking man, very tall and thin. Good humor and jollity sparkled in his black eyes. This black-eyed, dark-faced man was to be the ruling spirit of the Supreme Court for 34 years.

Marshall was a stanch Federalist. He believed that the Federal government should be a powerful government, and during his years as Chief Justice he made many decisions defending that point of view. In the year 1819, in a suit between the United States and the state of Maryland, he announced an important decision, namely, that a state had no right to tax a branch of the United States Bank. The national government, according to Marshall, had the power to establish the National Bank, and the states could not interfere with it. Thus the Federal government, not the states, was the supreme power of the land. In many later cases he applied this principle in court decisions.

Marshall's decisions affected the development of government in America in another very important way. He started the practice of having the Supreme Court decide whether laws passed by Congress agreed or conflicted with the Constitution. If they conflicted, then the laws were declared *null and void*, and citizens need not obey them.

This *power to interpret the laws of Congress had not been given to the Supreme Court by the Constitution.* Under Marshall the Supreme Court simply assumed the power during those early years when the government was forming. It thus became one of the most powerful branches of our national government. For example, a law which people wanted might pass the House; it might pass the Senate, and it might be signed by the President. Yet it might still be declared unconstitutional by the Supreme Court. In this way the court could even defeat the will of the people themselves. Sometimes in the past 100 years it has appeared to do so. Search for examples as you study the political developments of the next century.

You can now see how this power assumed by the Supreme Court, of deciding whether a law was constitutional or not, also helped to centralize power in the Federal government.

The Monroe Doctrine, 1823

President Monroe's administration is remembered especially for the establishment of another important policy of government. It was during his presidency that the Monroe Doctrine was announced to the world. To understand what this means we must know several facts. In *Changing Civilizations in the Modern World* you read the story of the revolt of the Latin American people against their Spanish and Portuguese rulers. Between 1810 and 1826 eight new independent states arose in Latin America — Paraguay, the provinces which later became Argentina, Chile, Great Colombia (later divided into Ecuador and Colombia), Peru, Bolivia, Mexico, and the Central American federation.

During the same years, the rulers of Austria, Russia, and Prussia formed a protective union known as the Holy Alliance. In 1822 representatives of these countries together with those of France met to discuss how they could help the Spanish king to recover his American possessions and how they could establish themselves on the North and South American continents. England had been asked to join them, but refused. She already controlled Canada and various islands off the coast of the two Americas, and was carrying on a prosperous trade with Latin America, whose enmity she did not wish to incur. The other leading European governments, however, emphatically opposed the rebellion of the Spanish colonies.

This threatening move of the European powers against Latin

America aroused the American government into action. The leaders feared that the Russians, holding Alaska, would establish themselves farther south on the western coast of North America and that other European nations would intrench themselves in Central and South America. Thus the United States would be surrounded on all sides by powerful enemies.

Recognizing that England would probably act as an ally of the United States against the encroachment of other Old World countries, President Monroe sounded out some of the American leaders as to the best way in which to tell European monarchs to keep out of the two continents of America. Madison and Jefferson, both of whom were still living, advised Monroe to join with England in opposing European interference in the New World. This important foreign problem was vigorously discussed in the United States. Finally, on December 2, 1823, Monroe sent a famous message to Congress, which has since become known over the entire earth as the *Monroe Doctrine*. Today we are not sure how much of it was written by Monroe and how much by John Quincy Adams or by other advisers. Probably it was the joint work of several men.

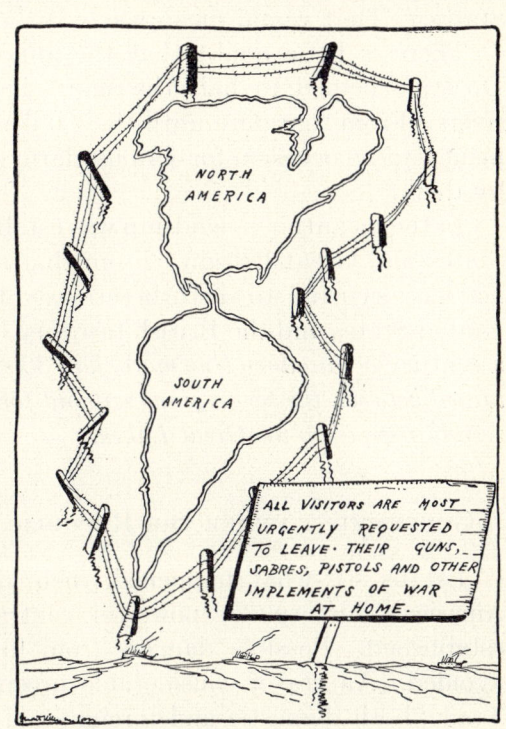

FIG. 78. This cartoon is a picture interpretation of the Monroe Doctrine. What does the fence mean? What does the lettering on the signboard mean? (Courtesy of Hendrik Willem Van Loon)

The Monroe Doctrine declared that the United States government would regard "any attempt on their [European governments'] part to extend their system to any portion of this hemisphere as dangerous to our peace and safety." It warned all European countries that any attempt to extend control over territory in North or South America would be regarded as "the manifestation of an unfriendly disposition toward the United States." That would mean war!

There is little doubt that the announcement of the Monroe Doctrine helped to halt the aggressive moves of the European rulers. From that date until the Civil War the American government had no occasion for serious alarm over proposed interference by them.

In the meantime friendship was established between the United States and Great Britain. From that day to this, no unfriendly act has occurred to disturb seriously the relations between the United States and the British territory of Canada. For more than a century *a boundary line more than 3000 miles long has been maintained between the two regions without fortifications and without war vessels patrolling the Great Lakes.*

Government under the Republicans was near its End

Let us see what happened, then, during the first period of America's history. A powerful central government had been established. Possible dangers from foreign countries had been avoided. An era of considerable prosperity had been launched. Trade, both domestic and foreign, had developed rapidly. Government and business were working hand in hand. Thus the initial difficulties of founding a new national government in North America had been weathered.

But the bothersome question still confronts us: Was it a period of much democracy in government? As you read further, watch for answers to this important question.

In the meantime let us turn back the hands of the history clock and witness a little more intimately the life of the people during this first period of American national life. While the government was forming, what was the social life of the people? Were they still divided into classes? How were these classes living?

CHAPTER X

MANNERS AND CUSTOMS DURING THE FIRST 40 YEARS OF THE REPUBLIC

The United States Senate met in New York in 1789 to welcome Washington as the first president of the Republic. The Senators were busy "collecting flowers and sweets . . . to amuse and delight the President . . . on his arrival," while Roger Sherman was trying "to devise some style of address more novel and dignified than 'Excellency.'"

The short, usually dignified, vice president, John Adams, was in a flurry of indecision. He noticed that the President's chair was made wide enough for two. Now Adams was both vice president of the United States and president of the Senate. Was he to share the chair with Washington? How was he to be addressed? What would be his real position? Was the vice-presidency of the United States or the presidency of the Senate the more influential position?

Many other Americans were asking themselves much the same questions. They had fought a war on the principle that "all men are created equal." But the war was over, and many of the leaders of the colonies were no longer quite sure that these words were true. In fact, there were many patriots who had begun to think seriously of adopting the titles and the customs of Europe. They wanted to keep the power which they had won. They were people of wealth and, for the most part, of good families, and they firmly believed that it was their duty and privilege to rule those who, less fortunate than themselves, had neither property nor family tradition. Yes, the classes which had formed throughout colonial times were again dividing the people as sharply as ever. There seems to have been as little real democracy in the social life of the larger cities during these years as there was in the political life.

Social life in New York, the national capital from 1789 until 1790

In the largest cities of the colonies — Philadelphia, New York, Boston, Charleston — the wealthy, aristocratic people had formed a compact social group of a few hundred families. They were the social leaders. Immediately after the adoption of the Constitution the aristocracy of the cities flocked to New York, the temporary capital. Their numbers were swelled by certain large plantation-owners from the South. At once these people from

Fig. 79. This scene from the Peace Ball shows the formality of social gatherings conducted by the aristocratic group in the new republic. George Washington is shown introducing one of the guests to his wife, Martha

city and plantation set about building a brilliant society modeled as closely as possible upon European court manners and customs.

If we glance into old, yellowed newspapers, into letters upon which the ink has faded, into the intimate pages of diaries, we shall be able to read in the words of the members of that society how they lived and what they thought. We shall piece together fragments which will produce a fairly accurate picture of the social life of the brilliant personages whose names we find in American history.

The figure which stands above all others, of course, is that of the president, George Washington. His Excellency's countenance is almost always grave now. He is in poor health and looks pale and thin. Surrounding him are a host of advisers, who are striving to maintain the office of president with all possible pomp and ceremony. Hamilton and Adams are trying to set the president apart from the common people. Adams, especially, is determined to introduce the manners of the European courts in which he spent so many years. How he sneers when the simple title of president is given the chief executive! "What will the common people of foreign countries . . . say . . . to George Washington, president of the United States? They will despise him to all eternity."

Public entertainments are frowned upon. The President is urged to limit his social life to small, select dinners, teas, or receptions. He should make calls with "few attendants," and formal visits are to be reserved only for a visiting king or emperor. On state occasions the President rides forth in regal style. Well attended, he passes through the city in the most decorative coach ever seen in America. It is an imported, cream-colored conveyance adorned with garlands of flowers and with cupids, and is drawn by at least four horses.

Martha Washington had her own imported conveyance which, like the President's, was cream-colored and richly ornamented. When she arrived at the capital in New York City, bringing with her many luxuries from Mount Vernon, a royal welcome awaited her. She was "conducted over the bay in the President's barge, rowed by thirteen eminent pilots in handsome white dress." Many ladies gathered on the landing to pay their respects.

President and Mrs. Washington then moved into a simple, colonial brick house on Cherry Street, where they took up their duties as host and hostess to the nation, or rather to the little group of social and political leaders of the nation.

During the short period that New York was the nation's capital other famous personages of the day made their home in the vicinity. Alexander Hamilton and his lovely, dark-eyed wife lived comfortably at Broad and Wall Streets. Aaron Burr's beautiful home, famous for its garden and grape arbor and for the brilliant wit of the guests who assembled there, was just around the corner. Thomas Jefferson, a widower, lived simply but comfortably with his two daughters on Broadway. John Adams was holding court on a splendid estate near the capitol. The fashionable manner in which Adams's mansion was kept led his coachman to put on airs which offended the farm people of the countryside. General Knox of Revolutionary fame and his wife were living in grand style in the city. Within a few blocks we might have found the lodgings of Robert Morris, Caleb Strong, Fisher Ames, James Madison, and others.

FIG. 80. Martha Washington. (Courtesy of the Museum of Fine Arts, Boston)

Wall Street was then the center of fashion, not of banking as it is today. Very few shops intruded upon the privacy of the brick residences along that narrow, poorly paved street. There leisurely gentlemen and ladies strolled in the late afternoon, returning from tea. Sedan chairs passed now and then, each carried by two uniformed Negro slaves. Through the drawn curtains one might catch glimpses of fair faces crowned with powdered hair. The lady within might be guarding her nose from the unpleasant odors of the town with a dainty lace handkerchief.

In the taverns of the fashionable section gentlemen were seated playing cards, smoking, or drinking ale. Some were chatting, others were scanning the *United States Gazette*. "The Court Journal," as that newspaper was called, edited by John Fenno, echoed faithfully the aristocratic tone of the day.

The theater had formerly been considered vulgar and immoral. Now fashionable society was attending the performances, and the drama was rapidly becoming a fine art in the capital city.

"It is whispered that *The School for Scandal* and *The Poor Soldier* will be acted on Monday night for the entertainment of the President," wrote the *Daily Advertiser*, another aristocratic paper. "Mrs. Henry [a famous actress of the day] ought, on this occasion, to give passion and tenderness to [her rôle]. . . . Mrs. Henry ought to take no offense at the suggestion."

Dressing, dining, theatergoing, card-playing, calling, gossiping, and tea-drinking occupied the idle hours of the social leaders. They must be fashionable at any price, although some fortunes

FIG. 81. The first presidential mansion in the United States. This was situated in Cherry Street, New York, and was occupied between 1789 and 1790, while New York was the capital. (From Vallentine's *Manual*, 1853)

were strained to the utmost. No wonder, then, that Thomas Jefferson was shocked to notice "a preference for kingly over republican government."

Although polite society was leading a gay and fashionable life and New York shopkeepers were growing rich, life for the common man in the new capital had not changed much since the Revolution. Negroes were still being sold in the slave market in New York City. People were still thrown into prison for debt, and Revolutionary soldiers continued to petition Congress for back pay. A whipping post for punishing lawbreakers could still be seen in one of the public squares. The common people rubbed elbows with Federalists and Anti-Federalists at cockfights and horse races. There were 131 taverns in New York City, where men of all classes met to quaff ale. In the taverns near the water front sailors, pirates, and laborers congregated.

Up the Hudson River country gentlemen were running their large estates, and farther inland small farmers were toiling to get a living from the soil, more interested in the weather and the crops, upon which their livelihood depended, than in political doctrines.

FIG. 82. A scene from a performance of *The School for Scandal* given in the early days of the republic. (Courtesy of the Harvard Theater Collection)

The mass of the people throughout the United States were still questioning whether the new government had the right to tax them as England had done. A Baltimore paper printed the following imaginary conversation between a friend and an enemy of taxation:

"An outrage," cried the enemy of taxation. "Did we not go to war with England on a tax?"

"Ah, but," said the defender, "then we were taxed by another country and without representation, while here we tax ourselves through our chosen representatives."

MANNERS AND CUSTOMS, 1789-1829

The difference was no doubt too difficult for the frontiersmen, farmers, and artisans to understand. The common soldier was not convinced that he had profited through the war. The farmer and the tradesman were sure that they were no richer, although they suspected increased fortunes among the aristocracy. There were grumblings, but the Hamiltonians were in power.

Fashionable society in New York, however, was more disturbed by another important question: Where would the national capital be located? In New York, Philadelphia, or somewhere in the South? After months of argument and political maneuvering, Congress settled the matter. For ten years, from 1790 to 1800, Philadelphia was to have the honor. Thereafter the seat of government was to be removed to Conogocheague on the Potomac River,

> Where the houses and kitchens are yet to be framed,
> The trees to be felled, and the streets to be named.

It was rumored in social circles that this wild spot was to be named Washington after the first president.

In 1790 the aristocracy moved to Philadelphia, the new capital.

Social Life in Philadelphia, the National Capital, 1790-1800

When Congress met in Philadelphia the young Alexander Hamilton was at the height of his power. He had established the nation's credit and was hailed by the aristocracy as the savior of his country. Philadelphia society was a faithful mirror of his aristocratic principles. Young, handsome, and ambitious, he regarded himself as the prime minister of the United States and George Washington as the ruler of a limited monarchy. Meanwhile his more gentle-mannered opponent, Thomas Jefferson, was writing that "more attention should be paid to the general opinion," and that he hoped for "a more agricultural representation in the House."

Of all the charming and brilliant ladies of Philadelphia none could outshine "the dazzling Mrs. Bingham," who was the wife of William Bingham, the director of The Bank of the United

States. In her drawing-room she entertained the cleverest men of the Federalist party "with only a sprinkling of Jeffersonians." She always served the best of food, and her costumes and manners were of the latest European mode. She was also the first to adopt the foreign custom of having her arriving guests announced by a servant. More than one awkward Senator was dismayed by his first experience with the new custom.

FIG. 83. Mrs. William Bingham was one of the fashionable hostesses of Philadelphia society

Like the theater in New York, the theater in Philadelphia was patronized by the fashionable, and even according to European standards it was very good. An Englishman commented: "To judge by the dress and appearance of the company around me, and the actors and scenery, I should have thought I had still been in England." The performance began at a very early hour, for the entertainment was long and varied. After the drama followed farces, dances, songs, pantomimes, and acrobatics. There was a favorite skit called "The Federal Bow-wow," in which a singer imitated "the surly dog, the knowing dog, the kind dog ... the barking dog, to the delight of the gallery and the pit."

No sooner had polite society changed its residence from New York to Philadelphia than the cost of living in the latter city leaped upward. Mrs. Abigail Adams, wife of John Adams, wrote to her daughter:

If New York wanted any revenge for the removal [of the capital] the citizens might be glutted if they could come here, where every article is almost doubled in price and where it isn't possible for Congress ... to be half as well accommodated for a long time.

Indeed, Congressmen found difficulty in renting clean and decent lodgings within reach of their pocketbooks. We can imagine, then, the condition of the workmen of Philadelphia, who earned but a dollar a day and board. Houses, even on the fringe of the city, rented for $300 a year, a goodly sum in those days. Board cost from eight to twelve dollars a week, and this did not include wine, candles, or fire, which must be bought as "extras."

FIG. 84. Fourth of July in Philadelphia in the early 1800's

In spite of the handicap of a low salary and a high cost of living, however, the mechanics and laborers of Philadelphia refused to be humble. They seemed ready to practice Jefferson's democratic principles and to fight for real equality. Many of them were so convinced of this equality that they imitated the manner of living of the rich. Even servants entertained their friends with balls.

So with politics and gay society as the central interests of life in the cities, the years of the 1790's wore on.

How the Country Gentlemen were Living

Meantime, away from the cities, the large landholders were cultivating the rather leisurely life of the country squire. Jefferson was the leader of a considerable group of such people in the days following the Revolution. His Virginia plantation, Monticello, consisted of several thousand acres of forest and farm land. The mansion house stood on a rise of ground, surrounded by tall trees. Jefferson himself had designed the house. He was greatly interested in architecture and was often called upon to help in the designing of other country homes. He had submitted a plan for the president's house in the new capital, Washington, and was planning the buildings for the University of Virginia.

Besides the responsibilities of running large plantations, country gentlemen of that day had many interests, many hobbies, to occupy their spare time. For one thing they interested themselves in botany and zoölogy (which were just beginning to be known as sciences) and in philosophy. Washington was fond of experimenting with plants and animals, and Madison and Jefferson were both much interested in a certain scientific toy which it was rumored was a practical success in English factories,— the steam engine! Rumsey and Fitch were trying to make boats go with it. Robert Livingston predicted to Madison and Jefferson that soon the "steamboat" would be carrying their goods on the rivers.

Jefferson was interested in almost every subject: science, philosophy, music, and invention, as well as architecture and politics. He was fond of the violin and played it very well until an injury to his right arm made his wrist too weak to handle the bow. Another of his interests was experimenting with growing Spanish olives in America. He and most of the other gentlemen of the day experimented with the raising of merino sheep.

The American country gentleman and gentlewoman enjoyed hunting. Almost any day, on the outskirts of Philadelphia, New York, Baltimore, Charleston, or New Orleans, one might have seen men and women dressed in brightly colored hunting jackets, riding across country to hounds. Cockfighting, which had once been a very popular country sport, had fallen into disuse, but horse racing continued to be a very popular sport, especially "quarter racing," which consisted in matching two horses to run a straight quarter of a mile.

Nearly all the country gentlemen of the day owned Negro slaves. Washington is reported in one of the newspapers of the day to have owned 500 slaves, while Jefferson, the democrat,

FIG. 85. Riding to hounds was always a favorite amusement of American country gentlemen

owned 150. Nevertheless, he (and Washington too in his later life) disapproved of the system and favored freeing the slaves.

John Bernard, a famous English actor who toured the United States in 1799, remarked regarding the manners of the planters:

> As to the planters . . . in their manners they have ever been austere to their inferiors, and when abroad, reserved with their equals; but all frost vanished the moment you crossed their threshold. . . . Their favorite topics [of conversation] were European, and I found men leading secluded lives in the woods of Virginia, perfectly . . . [familiar] with the literary, dramatic, and personal gossip of London and Paris. But the mystery was soon explained; they had all been educated in France or England [a practice which gradually ceased after the Revolution].

Thus the country gentlemen, from New York to Georgia, reflected the same aristocratic views as the social leaders in the cities.

The National Capital Removed to Washington, 1800

During the last days of the administration of John Adams, his wife, Abigail, made the uncomfortable trip over the rough roads from Philadelphia to Washington.[1] She had a bad journey and was lost for a time in the woods which extended almost from Baltimore to Washington. What a discouraging sight met her eyes when she arrived at the new capital!

In his diary Gouverneur Morris has left us a description of the "town."

We only need here houses, cellars, kitchens, scholarly men, amiable women, and a few other such trifles to possess a perfect city. I hasten to assure you that building stone is plentiful, that excellent bricks are baked here, that we are not wanting in sites for magnificent mansions ... in a word, that this is the best city in the world to live in — in the future.

The tactful Abigail could find nothing more flattering to say of Washington than that "the situation *is* beautiful." It is true that except for the Capitol and the one finished wing of the White House, no one would ever have suspected that there was a "city" in the midst of the woods. The bridges, the canals, the parks, and the fine residences were still on paper. There were only some 20 or 30 houses near the Capitol. Most of the Congressmen and foreign ministers lived in crude boarding houses. There was no business, no society, no industry. If a Congressman wished to live comfortably, he was obliged to have his home in Georgetown, several miles away, and to drive over terrible roads to the Capitol.

Mrs. Adams entered the White House under great difficulties. There was not a single bell in the house by which one of the

---

[1] An area ten miles square on the north bank of the Potomac was given to the government by the state of Maryland. It is now known as the District of Columbia. Here the city of Washington grew, and here were erected the buildings in which the work of the various national departments has been carried on since 1800.

30 servants who were needed to run the large establishment could be summoned. She could hire no one to cut and haul the wood necessary to feed the fireplaces. Later Mrs. Adams wrote that there was not "fence, yard, or other convenience without; and the great unfinished audience room I make a drying room of, to hang the clothes in." In spite of the disadvantages, however, this cheerful, elderly New England lady proceeded to hold a "levee" in the oval drawing-room shortly after her arrival.

FIG. 86. The new "city" of Washington in 1800 as seen from the southern bank of the Potomac River. Notice how few buildings had been erected when Washington became the center of government. (From an old engraving in the Library of Congress)

How dismal her brave attempt must have seemed to the elegant people who for years had enjoyed the best of everything at Mrs. Bingham's in Philadelphia!

But Abigail Adams was to be hostess in the scattered little town of Washington for only a few months. On March 4, 1801, she and John returned to New England to spend the remainder of their days in the quiet of private life. On the same day, Thomas Jefferson, simply dressed, and accompanied by a crowd of citizens and a troop of militia, amid the beating of drums and the firing of cannon, left his boarding house and climbed the hill to the White House. "The Mammoth of Democracy," as the "democrats" called him, "the President by no Votes," as the

Federalists called him, was the hero of the hour. He was the first president to enter the new Capitol for a full term of office. He was also the first Republican president, and the people expected great things from him.

In Washington society it soon became clear that the formalities of Mrs. Washington and Mrs. Adams were ended. The regular weekly "court" levees were discontinued. Guests were no

FIG. 87. Abigail Adams   FIG. 88. Dolly Madison

TWO OF THE HOSTESSES AT THE WHITE HOUSE IN THE EARLY 1800's

longer seated at table according to their "social rank." Jefferson proclaimed equality in the White House. Someone spitefully remarked, however, that "the President and his family take precedence everywhere, in public or private."

Since Jefferson was a widower, there was no "First Lady of the Land." Mrs. James Madison, wife of Jefferson's best friend and Secretary of State, acted as hostess. Dolly Madison tried her best to calm the tempest in the Washington teacups which Jefferson had caused by his informality. Polite American society, and foreign ministers and their wives especially, were deeply shocked to behold a president who was eccentric, careless in his dress, and without becoming dignity in receiving guests.

But whether they liked it or not, for eight years Washington society had to accept Jeffersonian democracy. In March, 1809, Jefferson returned to Monticello, and his good friend Madison became the next president. "Drawing-rooms" and "levees" promptly came back into vogue. The White House — now called the Castle — was a center of the aristocratic social life of the capital.

The ceremonial life of the White House no longer had the cold formality of the day of Martha Washington, however. Ease, freedom, and equality — always restricted to the aristocratic circle, of course — were to distinguish their social gatherings. Beautiful Elizabeth Monroe and pretty, scholarly Louisa Adams were to uphold the aristocracy of Dolly Madison during their years in the White House. This period was to last until the triumph of the "people" during the "reign of Andrew Jackson," beginning in 1829.

How the Middle Class lived

While this new republican society was forming in the United States, how were the shopkeepers, master workmen, and professional people living? Had democracy or aristocracy got hold of them?

In the towns the houses of the poorer people were built on fairly uniform lines. The home of the small tradesman was not greatly unlike that of the professional man. There were two connecting rooms on the ground floor, the front room used either as an office or as a shop, the rear room for the use of the family or for the informal meetings of friends. On the second floor the front room usually was a drawing-room, where the family entertained most of their guests. The hostess would sit at the table to pour tea or serve refreshments. The guests walked about and chatted together. After food was served everyone sang or played a musical instrument. The flute and the guitar were the favorite instruments, but the fiddle (violin) was considered vulgar. Ballads, hunting songs, and hymns were the favorite songs of the unfashionable people.

Among the more snobbish members of the common people, however, it was considered smart to scoff a little at the old-fashioned tunes. After 1793 truly up-to-date people affected a fondness for French opera and for French popular songs.

The French vogue had swept all over the country. People wore French clothes instead of English clothes. The men wore their hair cut short and brushed from the crown over the forehead in a sort of bang. They wore longer breeches, tight-fitting, and coming up almost to the wearer's armpits. The few who still wore knee breeches, silk stockings, powdered hair, or square-toed boots were marked as aristocrats — Federalists. Almost every man wore a spotted neckerchief and a "cutaway" coat. The women wore long, high-waisted, short-sleeved gowns, small hats of straw, and flowing curls.

The theater, of course, was too expensive for most workers. A dollar a day would barely keep life together. But amusements they must have. Consequently they flocked to see the strolling players and musicians, traveling museums, and waxworks. Sometimes gay skits were performed by the use of puppets with a cast of characters including Mr. Democrat, Citizen Moderate, Mr. Aristocrat, and Miss Modern. The favorite performance was that showing the execution of Louis XVI and Marie Antoinette of France.

A real and even more exciting spectacle to the people was the balloon ascension of Jean Blanchard,[1] the daring Frenchman who brought the first balloon to America. Before the eyes of Washington and his friends and a great horde of people, Blanchard ascended in a green taffeta balloon and made a successful flight near Philadelphia.

Meanwhile Another Civilization was growing up on the Western Frontiers

While social life was forming in the cities and towns, the hunters and trappers on the frontier were moving westward in advance of settlement. Here and there lone cabins dotted the wilderness. Isolated, far from village or town, the frontiersmen trapped, hunted, and traded with the Indians. Very little social life broke the monotony of their days.

[1] See *An Introduction to American Civilization*, pp. 286–287.

Behind them came the settlers with their few belongings, crossing the Appalachians under terrible hardship. They also had little time or opportunity for social affairs. Their waking hours were devoted to the struggle for existence. Uneducated for the most part, they took little interest in the witty sallies of the multiplying newspapers of the county seats. They may have

FIG. 89. A frontier scene of the early 1800's

felt longings for power, for wealth, and for equality with all men, but they were very busy toiling and fighting the overpowering wilderness.

Behind the westward-moving settlers a frontier civilization was building. By 1803 Ohio, Kentucky, and Tennessee were already states. Life was still crude and hard; homes were poor and rough. There was still danger from the Indians on the edge of this civilization. There was little time for education. Superstition rather than science governed many of the ways of the farmer. According to one old superstition, vegetables which grew under the ground, such as potatoes, onions, turnips, or beets, were planted in the "dark of the moon"; those which grew aboveground, as peas, beans, etc., were planted in the "light of the moon."

Was there any social life in the villages of the growing West? Yes; occasionally people relaxed from the hard labor to join in community corn-huskings, sugar bees, roof-raisings, weddings, or christenings. The coming of visitors from beyond the mountains was always a welcome occasion to the pioneers, for they brought news of the Eastern cities and the fashionable outside world. News traveled slowly and was eagerly received. It is interesting to note that the people on some of the frontiers did not learn of the Declaration of Independence until after it was known in Europe!

More of the changing social life of the United States will be discussed in later chapters. We must return now to the story of government after 1829.

INTERESTING READINGS FROM WHICH YOU CAN GET ADDITIONAL INFORMATION

HART, A. B., and CHAPMAN, A. B. How our Grandfathers Lived. The Macmillan Company, New York. Stories for young students concerning people of our country before and after the Revolution.

LAUT, AGNES C. The Blazed Trail of the Old Frontier. Robert M. McBride & Company, New York. Interesting stories of the westward movement after the Revolutionary War.

LODGE, HENRY CABOT. Alexander Hamilton. Houghton Mifflin Company, Boston. The story of Hamilton's boyhood and youth are particularly interesting.

MINNIGERODE, MEADE. Lives and Times. G. P. Putnam's Sons, New York. Brief biographies of prominent Americans.

MINNIGERODE, MEADE. Some American Ladies. G. P. Putnam's Sons, New York. Very entertaining biographical sketches of American women prominent in society.

SEAWELL, M. ELLIOT. Decatur and Somers. D. Appleton and Company, New York. The stories of two young naval officers during the war with the Tripoli pirates.

SKINNER, CONSTANCE LINDSAY. Silent Scot, Frontier Scout. The Macmillan Company, New York. A vivid picture of frontier life; historic incidents relating to John Sevier and Andrew Jackson.

UNIT V

JACKSONIAN DEMOCRACY AND ITS EFFECT
UPON AMERICAN CULTURE

JACKSONIAN DEMOCRACY AND ITS EFFECT UPON AMERICAN CULTURE

In the early years of the new republic government had been carried on by a small well-to-do group of merchants, manufacturers, bankers, and landholders. A small proportion of the people — certainly not more than 10 per cent — governed the great mass. Five presidents had held office and passed on — Washington, John Adams, Jefferson, Madison, and Monroe.

Then came a radical change in the politics of the new nation and in 1829 a political combination of the common people defeated the older parties and took control of the government.

In Chapter XI the rise of the common man into political power will be discussed. We shall see how the frontier spirit of freedom and independence led to the more active participation of the people in their government. We shall see how the new states led the way in the march toward democracy. We shall discover new leaders preparing to guide the people. You will see the passing of the Fathers of American government and the appearance of a new and powerful political group.

In Chapter XII we shall see the emerging social life of the frontier and the industrial towns of the East. Democracy was showing itself from the Atlantic to the Mississippi. Slowly a new order of life was being produced. The American people were forming.

In Chapter XIII we shall consider corresponding changes in the life of the South.

CHAPTER XI

THE "REIGN OF ANDREW JACKSON"

Two factors in American life must be recalled to understand the astonishing changes which took place in American government in the early decades of the nineteenth century: first, the settlement of the West; second, the industrial development in the cities and towns of the East. Let us consider first some of the factors which produced the changes.

THE FIRST FACTOR: THE SPIRIT OF INDIVIDUAL LIBERTY AND THE FREE LAND IN THE WEST

In 1800 the West contained not more than one tenth of the population of the entire country. In 1830 it comprised one third!

By 1830 eleven new states had been added to the original thirteen. Nine of the new states were west of the Appalachians. Jefferson had long since bought Louisiana from Napoleon, and the Mississippi River was alive with flatboats and traders. Lewis and Clark had explored the Far West even beyond the Pacific mountain ranges, and traders and settlers had moved the frontier many miles beyond the Mississippi.

The West was also drawing many of the youngest, most energetic youth of the East. A new section and a new society were growing up west of the mountains. One fact which distinguished this section from those of the older East was the widespread spirit of democracy and individual freedom.

Now the very basis of this spirit of freedom was free land. Millions of acres of free, fertile land! Every man and woman in the new West knew that if conditions grew intolerable where he was, there lay just to the west a great empire of level, fertile agricultural land. This was public land, that is, *it belonged to all the people*. At any moment any man could move "out West" and stake out a new homestead.

Bear constantly in mind as you study American history that the frontier spirit of individual freedom played an important part until nearly 1900.

The Second Factor: the Rising Democracy of the Laboring Men of Eastern Towns and Cities

The demand for individual freedom — better conditions for *each individual* — was being heard in the East as well as in the West. Recall that between 1810 and 1830 the machine era was beginning. With the adoption of new inventions factories were springing up throughout the northeast section. Immigrants were arriving from Ireland, England, and other parts of Europe. They began to work in factories. They helped to dig canals and to make the much needed roads that were spreading throughout the land. The country was getting into its stride for rapid industrial growth.

The growth of factories and other industrial enterprises brought laboring men closer together. They began to discuss their mutual problems, not only of wages and hours of work, but also of government. They began to organize unions to regain their bargaining power and to protect themselves against employers.

Everywhere the People were demanding a Larger Share in Government

The Declaration of Independence had declared that all men were free and equal and that government was established to secure *for all men* the " unalienable rights . . . [of] life, liberty, and the pursuit of happiness.", To secure the blessings of liberty the people as a whole needed to control their own government, to vote, to elect their own representatives, and to remove them from office if they were inefficient.

The people revived the old question: Who can vote?

At Washington's election no man could vote unless he had a certain amount of money or land. In some states more property was required than in other states, but there was no state in which

THE "REIGN OF ANDREW JACKSON"   225

all the adult population could vote. In other words, the people were not considered equal. In those days scarcely anyone even suggested that women and Negroes should be allowed to vote, but many people believed in *manhood suffrage*, which they interpreted to mean that every white man who was 21 years old and was a citizen of the United States should be allowed to vote, no matter how poor he was and no matter what religion he held.

This belief in manhood suffrage spread rapidly. At Jefferson's election (1800), few states permitted manhood suffrage. By 1824 more than half of the states had removed most of the restrictions. In the West a man was a man if he could survive the struggle for existence with the wilderness. Hence there was a more general belief in democracy. Almost without exception the new Western states came into the Union with constitutions calling for manhood suffrage, and the influence of the West increased as the population grew.

An example of the struggle for the right to vote

In the East, however, there was much opposition to manhood suffrage. Rhode Island, for example, which Roger Williams had established in the name of individual liberty, did not extend complete suffrage to all white men. The state still clung to the old property restrictions which had been in force from 1663, when Rhode Island received its charter. During the early 1840's Rhode Island was torn by civil war because those who were in control of the government would not extend the right to vote to all those who paid taxes. In 1842 the mass of the people held a convention and, under the leadership of Thomas Dorr, a courageous and intelligent young lawyer, drew up a new constitution giving all white men the right to vote. This was done without the approval of the legislature. The constitution was then ratified by *popular vote*, and Thomas Dorr was himself elected governor of the state, although illegally. Thus for a while there were two state governments.

Civil war within the state followed. The president of the United States, at that time John Tyler, supported the property government, which was the only legal one. Dorr's government was soon defeated. He himself was arrested, convicted of treason, and sentenced to life imprisonment. Hundreds of Dorr's associates were also thrown into jail. Then the legal government called a constitutional convention and drew up a constitution which granted to all men of American birth the right to vote, provided they paid a small personal property tax. It was many years later before this property qualification was wholly removed through amendments to the constitution.

After the convention a new legislature was elected. This legislature was much more representative of all the people. It released Dorr from prison, but he died a few years later.

This example shows us, however, one of the ways in which government is changed in a democracy. These are the steps: (1) Leaders appear who demand changes in the government. (2) At first these are refused by the group in power. (3) Protests and discussion grow among the people, during which the merits of the proposed changes are debated. (4) Sooner or later new representatives are elected to office. (5) Then, if the discussion has shown the value of the measure, these representatives pass laws which are more in accord with the desires of the people. Sometimes, when the group in power is too strong, civil war comes. Shays's Rebellion in Massachusetts and Dorr's Rebellion in Rhode Island are examples.

The people raised another question: How should the president be elected?

How "King Caucus" died

From the days of Washington the candidates for president and vice president had really been chosen by little groups of people. No law or constitution provided for this, but gradually there had grown up the "caucus" method of choosing the candidate. Congressmen would get together and hold a "caucus"—that is, they would talk over the situation and decide who ought to be president.

Later, as parties began to form, the Congressmen of *each party* held a caucus and chose their nominee. Then the qualified voters of the country were permitted their choice among the va-

THE "REIGN OF ANDREW JACKSON" 227

rious nominees. The citizen voted for the electors of his party. The electors then came together and voted for the president.

By that method the people had little to do with choosing the president. Before 1824 there was a strong protest, especially from the West, against the caucus nomination of a president. The caucus was considered undemocratic. Many people thought that this method of nominating presidents made the latter feel responsible to Congress rather than to the people. Newspapers published articles against it; legislatures passed resolutions against it; meetings were held to "resolve" against it. No change came, however, until after Monroe's administration.

By 1824 the opposition to the caucus was so great that less than one third of the Republicans entitled to admission to the caucus were present. William Crawford was nominated for the presidency; but that was the last Congressional caucus to nominate a candidate for that office.

It was during this campaign that the states first held a convention and nominated other candidates. The villages, towns, and cities all over the country chose delegates to attend this convention. It is true that members of Congress and of state legislatures, cabinet members, and other persons prominent in the national, state, and local governments still managed to keep most of the control of elections in their hands. Nevertheless the abolition of the Congressional caucus was a little step in advance. The officeholders were compelled to listen to the demands of delegates who in many instances were sent, as Andrew Jackson used to say, "fresh from the people."

The Election of 1824

At the nominating convention to which we have just referred three candidates were chosen to contest the election with Crawford — Andrew Jackson, Henry Clay, and John Quincy Adams. The campaign was very exciting, and no one could predict how it would come out. Before the electors met it was known that General Jackson led in the *popular* vote. But in order to be elected a candidate must have a *majority*, that is, more than half, *of all the electoral votes.*

The final vote gave Jackson 99 electoral votes, Adams 84, Crawford 41, and Clay 37. Jackson was clearly the *popular* choice, but the makers of the Constitution had arranged things so that he could not get the election unless he received more than half of the electoral votes. If more than two candidates were nominated and none of them was supported by more than half of the electoral votes then the members of the House of Representatives were empowered to choose a president from among the three who had received the largest electoral vote.

On this occasion John Quincy Adams was chosen president by the House of Representatives. Before the vote took place, however, there was much talk of bargaining between candidates. Bitter charges and countercharges went back and forth. It was said, for example, that Clay had promised his votes to Adams in exchange for the position of Secretary of State. To this day we do not know the truth about this matter; but we *do* know that Clay's adherents voted for Adams and that Clay *was* made Secretary of State.

How the 1824 election affected democratic sentiment: the landslide of 1828

The action of the House in electing Adams against the expressed will of a majority of the people aroused the country to a high pitch of excitement. By 1826 party machinery had been set up in every state by Jackson's supporters in preparation for the election of 1828. A vigorous campaign was made to interest the voters. The farmers of the West and the workers of the East rose in support of their hero. When the votes were counted in 1828, Andrew Jackson, the Democratic standard bearer, had received more than twice as many electoral votes as John Quincy Adams.

The passing of the Fathers of American government

For nearly 40 years the national government had been in the hands of the men who made the Constitution. Now practically all of this group had passed on. Washington, chairman of the Constitutional Convention, had died in 1799. Alexander Hamilton, Thomas Jefferson, and John and Samuel Adams were also dead.

Fig. 90. John Quincy Adams

Fig. 91. Andrew Jackson

Fig. 92. John C. Calhoun

Fig. 93. Henry Clay

Two Presidents of the United States, and Two Southern Statesmen who helped to mold Popular Opinion from the Early 1800's until the Middle of the Nineteenth Century now nearly 80 years of age, took no part in the government, but occasionally spoke out against all attempts to break down the power of the central government.

A New Leader of the People

At last the people, especially those of the West, had their leader — General Andrew Jackson. He was in no sense an aristocrat. He came of people poor both in money, land, and family tradition. Yet he had struggled upward from a poverty-stricken youth, had fought the Indians, had defeated the British at New Orleans, and had served a term in the Senate. He was called "Old Hickory."

Now the inauguration of Andrew Jackson was taking place. Let a Washington woman of the day describe it.

We stood on the south steps of the terrace; when the appointed hour came [we] saw the General and his company advancing. . . . The south side of the Capitol hill was literally alive with the multitude who attended him. . . . At the moment the General entered the portico and advanced to the table, the shout that rent the air still resounds in my ears. When the speech was over, and the President made his parting bow, the barrier that had separated the people from him was broken down and they rushed up the steps all eager to shake hands with him. It was with difficulty he made his way through the Capitol and down the hill to the gateway that opens on the avenue.[1]

The same lady says of the reception at the White House:

The President, after having been *literally* nearly pressed to death . . . by the people in their eagerness to shake hands with "Old Hickory," had retreated through the back way and had escaped to his lodgings at Gadsby's. Cut glass and china to the amount of several thousand dollars had been broken in the struggle to get the refreshments. Punch and other articles had been carried out in tubs and buckets, but had it been hogsheads it would have been insufficient, [as were the] ice-creams, and cake and lemonade, for 20,000 people. Ladies fainted, men were seen with bloody noses and such a scene of confusion took place as is impossible to describe.[2]

[1] Mrs. Samuel H. Smith, *The First Forty Years of Washington Society*, p. 292. Charles Scribner's Sons, New York, 1906.   [2] Ibid. pp. 295–296.

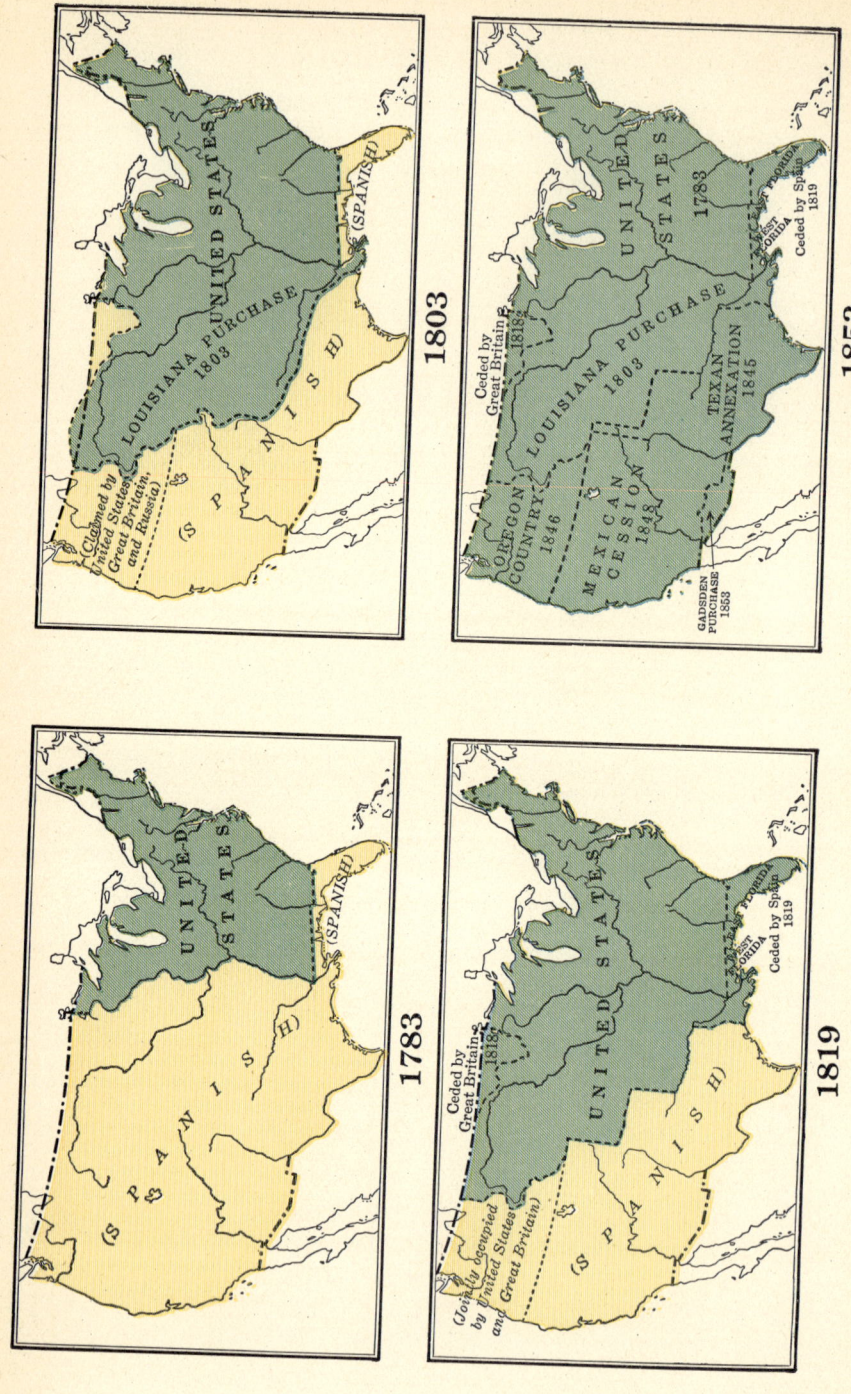

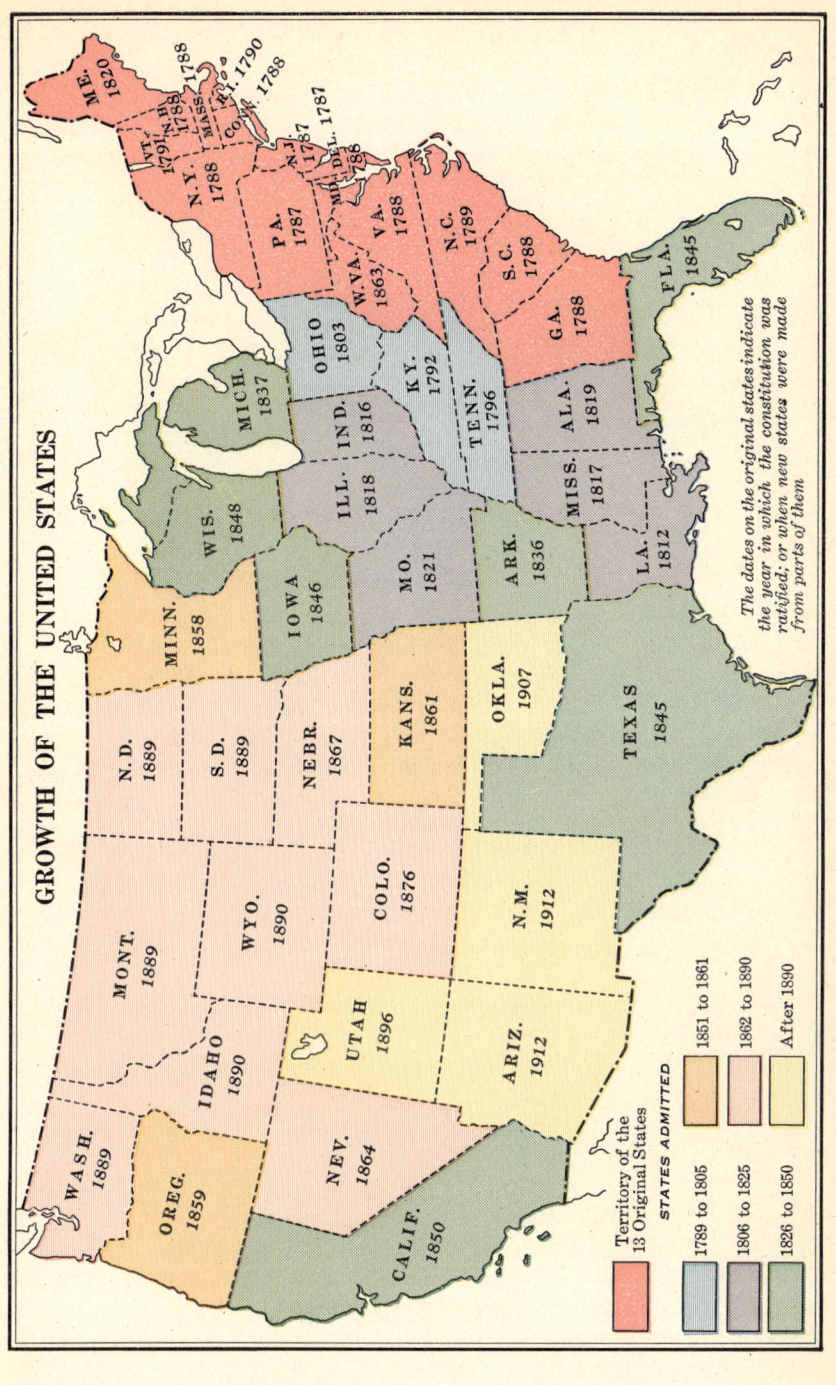

THE "REIGN OF ANDREW JACKSON" 231

The White House episode was, indeed, a rough and disorderly affair. It was certainly not what a truly democratic and intelligent people would be proud of, but it was typical of the times and the people's way of welcoming the new administration. The "Adamsites" sneered at the rowdyism of the people. What was going to become of their fine plan of checks and balances with *mobocracy* in power? Looking on at a reception to "the People's President," these aristocrats felt nothing but alarm for the security of government. To them the day's performance at the White House proved that the people had not the intelligence to govern themselves properly. Government should be *of* the people, *for* the people, but — by the *best* of the people! Not by *all* the people, thought they.

What do *you* think? Were the "Adamsites" right? Standing on damask-covered chairs with muddy boots, breaking china, and ruining rugs did show that the *people* had not the manners of the aristocracy. *Did it also prove that they did not have enough intelligence to learn to govern themselves?*

How Jackson tried to make the Government more Democratic

The stern, hot-tempered democrat who had become president believed that the common people should have more power in the government. Every one of his eight annual messages to Congress contained the recommendation that the people elect the president and the vice president directly. This recommendation has never been carried out. Other policies of his administration also showed his eagerness to make the government more democratic.

The spoils system in government

"To the victor belong the spoils." This slogan, which implied that men in office should appoint those who had been loyal to them, had long been the principle of politicians. With the reign of Andrew Jackson it became a national slogan.

For 100 years most historians have given Andrew Jackson the credit or discredit for applying this principle to the selection of officeholders in the national government. Yet he really was not responsible for it. The British rulers of colonial America had rewarded their supporters by giving them land or offices in the colonies. Washington himself had appointed to office men who believed mainly as he did about the national government. Later, when the Republicans elected Jefferson, even that democratic person used great care in appointing to office men of his own general turn of mind. So also John Adams, Madison, Monroe, and John Quincy Adams — each had filled the offices of the government with loyal supporters.

During Jackson's administration, however, the practice reached its height. In the summer of 1829 hundreds of office-seekers, with their wives and daughters, descended upon Jackson and his advisers, demanding jobs in the government, until many of the cabinet officers freely confessed that life had become a burden as a result of being harassed and followed from their offices to their homes and from homes to offices again by these people. It became such a nuisance that the only way in which they could accomplish any of their public business was to close their doors to all applicants except for a brief period in the late afternoon.

When Jackson became president he put out of office many men who had served in Adams's administration or earlier administrations and installed others of his choice. Careful historians have proved, however, that the proportion of removals was not so great as people generally supposed, being only from 5 to 30 per cent in the various departments.

No president can know personally all the candidates who are applying for such minor positions as those of postmasters, collectors of revenue, marshals, and the like. He depends, therefore, on Congressmen or local and state politicians within his own party to choose men for him. This tremendous personal power of "patronage" enables the president, Congressmen, and other officeholders to build up "political machines." Of course they will choose those people who are loyal supporters.

At any rate, the principle "To the victor belong the spoils" began to be used in local, state, and national government and by all political parties. As a result there developed in American

THE "REIGN OF ANDREW JACKSON"

politics the power of patronage which enabled the victorious political party to appoint officeholders to government positions.

Thus politicians came to control the government.

Jackson's associates found examples of fraud on the part of officeholders of the previous administrations

Although it has been estimated that Jackson turned out of office nearly 1000 officeholders during his first year in office, it must also be said that his new officials found many examples of evil practices on the part of their predecessors. For example, it was found that Tobias Watkins, a friend and appointee of John Quincy Adams, had defrauded the government to the extent of more than $7000. He was arrested and convicted and served a term in prison. Historians have established from the records that several collectors of public money had misused public funds. Eighteen months after Jackson's inauguration his men had uncovered instances of defrauding the government out of public money amounting to $280,000.

Jackson had made many enemies in Congress, both in his bitter election campaign and in his use of the spoils system. No sooner was the Congress organized in December, 1829, than brilliant orators in the House and the Senate — John Tyler, John C. Calhoun, and Daniel Webster — began a campaign against Jackson that was to last during his presidency. They opposed practically every suggestion of his and, having a majority in the Congress, they succeeded in defeating many of his proposed changes in government. Jackson nominated as heads of departments in the government, as foreign ministers and consuls, and as less prominent officials, many personal friends and advisers. Among these were a number of newspaper editors who had played an active part in the support of his campaign. Now the Constitution provided that all presidential appointments must be confirmed by the Senate. So Calhoun, Tyler, Webster, and their associates denounced Jackson's nominations and succeeded in having some of them repudiated by the Senate.

In Jackson's Administration the Conflict between the Separate States and the National Government became more Serious

Although Jackson had to face many difficult problems in his administration as president, none was more difficult than that of the great issue Shall the United States be one country with the national government supreme over all the states, or shall it be regarded as merely a confederation of independent, "sovereign" states? Several times this problem had become acute in the first 40 years of American history. Now in Jackson's time it became alarmingly serious.

The question had been raised even before the Constitutional Convention. Madison, Hamilton, Jefferson, and their associates constantly discussed it. What kind of government shall we make which shall be sufficiently strong and centralized to bind us closely together for our protection, and which shall also leave sufficient power to the several states? The Tenth Amendment to the Constitution stated that all the powers not definitely given to the Federal government by the Constitution should be *reserved* to the state governments or to the people.

Each section of the country interpreted the Constitution according to its needs

You remember how different were the needs of the various sections of the country. It was to be expected that their interpretations of the Constitution would be equally different. Let us see how this was true by giving five examples. You have already read of three of them.

Three examples of "nullification" before Jackson's administration

First, Virginia and Kentucky "nullified" the Alien and Sedition Acts in 1798 and 1799 (see page 172). Second, the New England Federalists nullified the Republican Embargo Act and opposed the War of 1812 (see page 192). Third, Maryland and other states nullified the National Bank acts, declaring that they were unconstitutional.

THE "REIGN OF ANDREW JACKSON" 235

These three examples show that even *before* Jackson's administration individual states had asserted a right to nullify Federal laws which they felt were hurtful to them. The following examples show that *during* Jackson's administration not only was this repeated but, as the interests of the sections became more sharply divergent, the feeling regarding the rights of states began to spread. Whole sections of the country now began to take sides.

Fourth example: Georgia nullifies a Federal treaty with the Indians

Before 1827 the United States government had made a treaty with the Southern Indians, reserving certain lands for their use. Georgia had passed laws which ran counter to this treaty, and the Georgia legislature threatened to use force against the government of the United States unless the Indians were removed from the state. Several missionaries to the Indians were thrown into prison by Georgia for violating her state laws, and the case went to the United States Supreme Court. Chief Justice Marshall declared that the Georgia law was *void* and ordered that the missionaries be released. President Jackson, however, did not enforce the decision of the Supreme Court because he disliked both Marshall and the Indians.

Interestingly enough, by the time the case of Georgia came up the New England states, whose Indian problems had long since been settled, believed thoroughly in the power of the Federal court to decide the meaning of the Constitution. Pennsylvania, Massachusetts, and Connecticut asserted their belief in the power of the Constitution and of the Supreme Court! How does that correspond with what they did in earlier times?

Fifth example: The South carried on a campaign of nullification

A very different issue arose at last, however, to split the country into two sections, and that issue was the tariff.

One thing is certain, by 1824 the South as a whole did not want the tariff. It had practically no manufactures to protect; all its energies were centered on cotton-raising. At the time when the tariff of 1816 was passed, Calhoun and, indeed, South Carolina had been in favor of it, for it was then believed that in the future the South would turn to manufacturing. But the views of Southern people had changed since the South had found that because of its reliance upon cotton-growing its economic life was being injured by the tariff.

New England, on the other hand, was mainly interested in protecting its growing manufactures. Our Northern manufacturers *must* have protection for their industries, said the Congressmen from that section, since English manufactured goods could be sold in the United States as cheaply as — and sometimes more cheaply than — the products of the North.

Thus were the two sections divided. The South, opposed to the tariff, soon fought it by the well-tried method of nullification. As early as 1824 the South Carolina legislature resolved that a protective tariff was "an unconstitutional exercise of power." The states of Virginia, Georgia, Alabama, and Mississippi joined with South Carolina in protesting against the tariff as *unconstitutional*.

The debate between Daniel Webster and Robert Y. Hayne

In 1830, during Jackson's administration, Senator Hayne of South Carolina launched into a defense of state rights and attacked the position of the Federal government with special reference to the sale of public lands. Daniel Webster, Senator from Massachusetts, probably the greatest orator of his day, stepped into the Senate Chamber just in time to hear him; instantly he realized that he must take up the cudgels against Hayne.

Webster was a fitting representative of the best of New England; Hayne, an equally fitting representative of the finest of the South. Each passionately believed in the right of the position he maintained. The ensuing debate, one of the most famous ever held in the United States Senate, has aptly been called "a battle of the giants." Webster's part in the battle was a defense of the Union against the right of any individual state to nullify a Federal law.

We cannot give here the details of the debate. Suffice to say that it centered the attention of the whole country on the problem of *the power of the "Federal Union" versus the power of the states*. Webster argued that the states were then a nation, no matter what they were in 1787, and that in 1830 the needs of a great people could be satisfied only by one complete union. Hayne, on the other hand, wanted the powers taken by the Federal government to be restricted to those which the states had granted it in the Constitution. He believed that any state, on

FIG. 94. Daniel Webster   FIG. 95. Robert Y. Hayne

provocation, might justly withdraw from the Union. No legislation came from the debate at once. It simply set the people thinking about all sides of the problem, and made clearer the difference between the interests of the North and the South.

Then in 1832 Congress passed another high protective tariff, and South Carolina, alone of the Southern states, passed an *Ordinance of Nullification*. Furthermore, she elected Hayne as governor of the state and prepared to arm herself to prevent the Federal government from carrying out the tariff law there. That Jackson resolved to assert the power of the government is shown by what he said to a Southern Congressman about to go home:

> Tell them [the nullifiers] for me that they can talk and write resolutions and print threats to their heart's content. But if one drop of blood

be shed there in defiance of the laws of the United States, I will hang the first man of them I can get my hands on to the first tree I can find.

In 1833, however, Congress repealed some of the objectionable parts of the tariff, and the South Carolina convention repealed its Ordinance of Nullification. The issue — national rights versus state rights — was laid for the time being. It was to flare

FIG. 96. Webster, in the Senate Chamber, replying to Hayne's defense of state rights

up again shortly over still another issue — slavery — and finally to sweep the whole country into a horrible Civil War.

These are five examples of how states nullified Federal laws. Through all this trouble the sections *stayed in the Union. Force was not used and civil war did not come.* Nevertheless, the relations between North and South were being severely strained.

Jackson Abolished the National Bank as a Monopoly

Let us return to a series of events in Jackson's two administrations that illustrates the General's attempts to govern in the interest of the mass of the people.

THE "REIGN OF ANDREW JACKSON"

Recall that Hamilton and the Federalists had established the first National Bank in 1791; also that the Republicans had chartered the second National Bank in 1816. Its charter was to expire in 1836. Now Jackson had scarcely come into office when he served notice on the owners that he regarded the Bank as a monopoly which benefited only the financial classes and that he was determined to destroy it.

During the years in which the second National Bank had operated, it had established branches all over the country and virtually controlled the gold and silver in circulation. That was regarded as a dangerous power in the hands of a few private citizens.

Now the first half of the 1800's was a period of very rapid development in both farming and industry. Millions of dollars were being spent by state governments in roads, canals, and other public works. Added millions were being spent in industries and farms by private citizens. Most of these enterprises were being run on credit,— that is, on borrowed money,— and private and public debts were mounting rapidly. From 1820 to 1840 state debts rose from $13,000,000 to over $170,000,000. In interest alone $12,000,000 had been paid to capitalists, mostly European financiers, who had lent the money.

Throughout the West people were doing most of their business on *credit*, and the state banks, which had been established as branches of the National Bank, were reckless in their granting of credit. The individual consumer ran accounts, the local storekeeper ran accounts, the wholesaler ran accounts. Thus many people were living on borrowed money and conducting their businesses by the same means. It was a *new* country, and little gold and silver were in circulation. State banks were printing paper money but no more than their supply of *hard* money would permit. If the National Bank should withdraw its gold and silver from the state banks there would be grave danger of a bad financial panic. Thus the second National Bank *did* have great power over business and over the lives of private citizens everywhere. In this sense it was a monopoly, and its officers did have the power to injure the country seriously.

At the same time, however, the Bank had helped to build up

American business, and it tried, through its president, Nicholas Biddle, to restrain the "wild cat" recklessness of the state banks. In some instances it had refused to coöperate with the Southern and Western banks. The latter resented this treatment and maintained that the National Bank was an Eastern monopoly, that it controlled the money and the credit of the country.

President Jackson believed that, too, and so determined to abolish the National Bank when its charter ran out. That was not until 1836, however, and it was then only 1829! Jackson's first term would expire in 1833, and no one could predict whether or not he would be reëlected.

The issue was clear: Jackson versus the National Bank. The farmers of the West and South and the workingmen of the Eastern cities knew Jackson and believed that he was working for *all* the people. Jackson said the Bank was a dangerous monopoly. The people believed it, and they hated monopolies. The Bank fought back, appealing to the people through Congressmen and newspapers and orators. It secured the aid of about 30 Congressmen, using whatever methods were thought necessary. Jackson was attacked in every conceivable way.

But the rank and file of the people supported Jackson, and in the campaign of 1832 Jackson was swept back into office by a larger popular vote than any since Washington's time. As candidate of the Democrats he received 219 electoral votes. Henry Clay, the candidate of the "Whigs," received 49.

Jackson now felt that he was vindicated; so he decided to start the abolition of the Bank without waiting for its charter to expire in 1836. He straightway refused to let the Secretary of the Treasury deposit any more of the government money in the National Bank, and ordered that it be sent instead to certain state banks which he favored.

Immediately there followed a real financial and political war between the president of the Bank and Jackson. In the end Jackson destroyed the Bank. For several years the country had seemed to be in a prosperous condition. In 1835, for the first time, the entire national debt was paid and the national Treasury was actually accumulating a surplus of money.

Jackson believed that this money should be lent to the states

THE "REIGN OF ANDREW JACKSON"

instead of being allowed to accumulate at one center. He therefore divided the surplus among the states as a loan subject to recall by Congress. (It has never been recalled.) This only made financial matters worse. The money thus distributed was lent to farmers and small business men. There was, as you know, a tremendous wave of speculation in land. People were buying government land at low prices — $1.25 an acre was the standard price — and holding it for a rise in value so as to sell it at a profit.

Now if the land had been paid for in gold and if no more money had been lent than could be backed up by crops or goods of some kind, all would have been well. But, as you have already learned, nearly everything in the West in those days was being bought on credit, and an enormous amount of paper money was being issued — *paper without gold behind it.*

Jackson himself realized that the country was engaging in dangerous speculating practices, and, in 1836, fearing for the consequences, he ordered government land offices to take *only gold or silver in payment for land.*

The financial panic of 1837

This order was all that was needed to bring on a panic all over the country. The people became frightened. They hid their gold and silver. Why should those who had gold and silver hide it and refuse to exchange it for paper money? Principally because the people got panicky. They feared that business would not go on as usual. They had confidence only in gold and silver, and so they held on to it. Those who held the paper currency took it to banks and asked for gold and silver in exchange. The supply at the banks soon ran out, of course. Then the banks had to close their doors. The paper currency they had printed "promised to pay" the amount stated on the bill in *gold or silver.* But the banks had no gold or silver; so 600 of them failed.

In 1837 *every bank in the United States* stopped paying out specie (gold or silver). Then the people grew more frightened. They stopped buying goods. When they stopped buying, factories had to stop manufacturing. That threw tens of thousands out of work. Merchants could not meet their debts. They too

242 AMERICAN GOVERNMENT AND CULTURE

failed. In 1835 there had been a crop failure, and there was another in 1837, the year of the panic. Farmers had no money

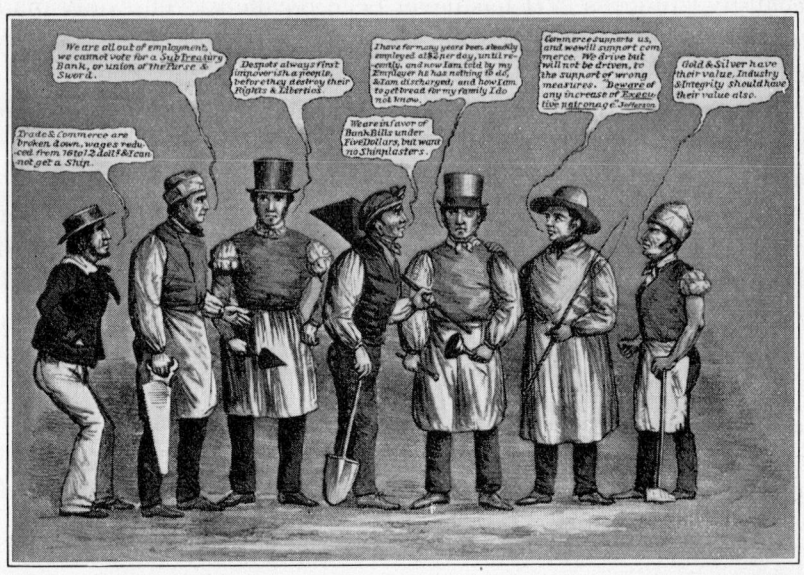

FIG. 97. In this cartoon, each man represents one of the occupations. In each of these occupations there was much unemployment following the panic. The words which have been put into the mouths of these men show you what people thought about the business depression of the time

with which to meet their debts. It was a terrible nation-wide business crash and its effect was felt for many years afterward.

Do you begin to understand what a financial panic is and what it does to a country?

The panic of 1837 led to the establishment of the National Treasury in 1840

Martin Van Buren, Jackson's Secretary of State, became president in 1837 just as the panic occurred. He saw that the government must have *independent treasuries* in various large centers of the country in which to store government gold for security.

In 1840 Congress passed the Independent Treasury Act, adopting Van Buren's plan. This plan gave the government control over the country's gold supply *without using private banks.* The plan of 1840 helped matters a great deal, but it could not avert several bad panics which came later.

Let us ask again the very important question How much had democracy marched forward in the "reign of Andrew Jackson"? He had carried the spoils system further than any other president. He had consistently fought financial and business monopolies. He had abolished the National Bank and indirectly brought about the establishment of the National Treasury. He had held together the country in one union in spite of nullification and threats of secession. So much for acts of government under Jackson.

Meanwhile how were the people living? We have had glimpses of the manners and customs in the social life of the upper classes. How were Jackson's people — the common men — faring? Was the experiment in democracy producing "life, liberty, and happiness" for the individual American citizen? To this we shall turn in Chapter XII.

INTERESTING READINGS FROM WHICH YOU CAN GET ADDITIONAL INFORMATION

BOWERS, CLAUDE G. Jefferson and Hamilton. Houghton Mifflin Company, Boston. For the best readers.

HART, ALBERT B. (Editor). American History told by Contemporaries. The Macmillan Company, New York. Volume III: pp. 540–544 (a humorous paper on Jackson's Political Spectacles); pp. 531–535 (The Spoils System).

MACDONALD, WILLIAM. From Jefferson to Lincoln. Henry Holt and Company, New York. "Jeffersonian Democracy," pp. 44–62.

OGG, FREDERIC A. The Reign of Andrew Jackson, Vol. XX of The Chronicles of America. Yale University Press, New Haven. Very interesting. Read the chapters on Jackson's youth, his life as a planter, and his campaigns against Indians and English.

RICHARDSON, C. F. (Editor). Daniel Webster for Young Americans. Little, Brown and Company, Boston. Contains speeches of Daniel Webster. See especially "Reply to Hayne," pp. 115–173; "The Constitution and the Union," pp. 194–199.

CHAPTER XII

THE CULTURE OF THE MIDDLE WEST AND OF THE NORTHERN SEABOARD, 1830–1860

When Andrew Jackson entered the White House after John Quincy Adams, a new epoch in American life began. That it was new in politics we have already seen. But it was more than that; it was new in every phase of living. The event marked the passing of the graceful dignity of the aristocrats and the appearance of a boisterous, hustling, democratic way of life.

The American was really forming. Not only had the British government long since been cast off; British customs, speech, modes of living, and standards of taste were also being discarded.

By 1860 the United States embraced a large part of the continent — 33 states spread from the Atlantic to the Pacific and from Mexico to Canada, a domain nearly as large as the continent of Europe. By 1860 the Americans had transformed nearly half of the country into civilized settlements. The frontier lay far west of the Mississippi River. Only the eastern slopes of the Rocky Mountains and the Western plateau country still remained to be settled. Furthermore, the Mississippi Valley had been tied to the Atlantic seaboard by a growing network of improved roads, canals, and railroads. Steamboats plied the Western rivers, and telegraph lines gave the Middle West the same news of the world as came to Boston and New York City.

Not only had the settlers transformed the continent; the continent had transformed them. Already a new civilization was developing a new kind of man with characteristic *American* modes of living and special *American* ways of thinking. The frontier was still doing its work! If we look more closely into the life of the American in various sections of the country, we shall see what had been happening.

Let us try to know this American. Let us go into his farms and villages, his towns and booming cities, and see him as he

CULTURE OF MIDDLE WEST AND NORTHEAST   245

was between the years 1830 and 1860. In order to understand him, we must first recall the physical setting in which he was developing his new civilization.

THE MIDDLE WESTERN FARMER OF THE 1830'S AND 1840'S

The Middle Western farmer lives on a 100-acre farm. His house is astonishingly large and comfortable. It contains a living

FIG. 98. From 1830 to 1860, comfortable farmhouses, like that shown in the picture, replaced many of the log cabins of frontier days in the Middle West. More land was being cleared, and each year larger amounts of land were being sown to wheat, corn, and other farm products

room, a kitchen, and several bedrooms, for the family is large. The "best room" is well furnished with mahogany Windsor chairs and a rocking-chair, the latest thing in furniture. The walls are white, without paintings, pictures, or other decorations. The window shades are of green paper, and trim white curtains are looped back from the windows. On the floor is a rag carpet, which has been woven by the farmer's wife and his daughters.

The farmer is also a craftsman. By means of shoemaking, harness-making, or brick-making he earns a little extra money.

No doubt he has learned his trade, as one shoemaker said of himself, "just as a cow learns kicking — out of my own head." The odd craft jobs provide fairly well for the family needs. There is even enough money to buy Sunday clothes for everyone. The men wear dark Sunday suits, gay flowered waistcoats, ruffled shirts, and top hats. The women have heavy silk dresses to wear at church, but these are always expected to last for several years.

FIG. 99. Wrestling was a favorite amusement in the Middle Western communities. There were few if any rules. The object was to get your man down and keep him down by any means possible

At table the family, the hired man, and the hired girl all eat together. No napkins are provided, for everyone is expected to use his own pocket handkerchief. Most people eat with their knives because the two-tined forks in use are more awkward to handle than the knife blade. New "balanced" knife-handles, made to keep the knife from soiling the tablecloth, have recently been invented.

In the farming community singing is one of the favorite amusements of the young people. The boys and girls gather together several evenings a week at the singing school. Part songs are learned, the teacher using a tuning fork to guide the singers. The favorites are hunting ballads, sentimental songs, and hymns. Country dances are sometimes held in farming communities, but the older people do not quite approve of dancing.

An exciting event in the life of the Western farming family is the arrival of the freighters' wagons from the Eastern cities. The wagons are huge, clumsy covered vehicles pulled by six horses. One of them stops at the general store. Immediately everybody rushes there to watch the storekeeper break open the crates and pull out rolls of muslin and silk, boxes of tinware, tea, and coffee, and other Eastern luxuries.

No less exciting to the farm people is an occasional trip down the Ohio River to trade. The farmers are also beginning to think about selling their crops in the East and of buying cloth and other articles which formerly they made in their homes. Village craftsmen will soon begin to drift farther West where Eastern goods cannot so easily be obtained and where craftsmen can find more work.

You can see that the farming life of the country from New England to Ohio is becoming fairly well settled during the 1830's and 1840's.

Other settlements of the Middle West

Beyond Ohio new settlements are opening. The level land of Michigan and Wisconsin, which can be reached easily from the new steamboats on the Great Lakes, is being cleared for houses and farms. The more well-to-do newcomers have set up quite substantial homes. One woman has actually brought her piano with her to the forests of Wisconsin. Others who still have their fortunes to make look forward to replacing their log cabins with more comfortable frame houses.

Land speculators are even now "locating" cities along the shores of the Great Lakes, in the hope of enticing people West. Chicago in the 1830's is a small town growing up around Fort Dearborn. In the 1840's there are still no pavements, and women ride in drays for lack of coaches, but there is hope in the air. Manufacturing is beginning to spring up. The industrial movement of the East is spreading even into Illinois. Soon there will be a fashionable district on the north bank of the Chicago River.

Milwaukee is still a tiny settlement in the wilderness. Detroit, the old French outpost, is growing into a considerable town. In

FIG. 100. Chicago in 1830. (From an old print)

1805 every house but one was destroyed by fire but by 1830 the city has been rebuilt and is the center of the constantly increasing trade with the Northwest and Middle West over the Great Lakes.

FIG. 101. Detroit in the 1850's. (From Ballou's *Pictorial Drawing-Room Companion*, April 12, 1856)

Although Cincinnati is only a little more than 40 years old, it too is a surprisingly well-developed community with neat houses, smooth lawns, and well-kept gardens surrounding a booming business and factory district.

St. Louis has become a thriving river trading town. The more

CULTURE OF MIDDLE WEST AND NORTHEAST

well-to-do have long since built substantial, painted frame houses. "Society" is forming even on the frontier. Receptions and balls are frequent. More than one distinguished British visitor is entertained and astonished at some of the customs.

Thus in the 1830's and 1840's up and down the Mississippi Valley civilization is in the making. The Americans are in a hurry — clearing, settling, building. The West is already a varied patchwork of the many types of community life in America. Occasionally a visitor comes upon a typical New England village. This is to be expected since whole New England communities packed up and moved West in the hope of bettering their fortunes or trying a new experiment in living together. So we have the stern, thrifty atmosphere of New England in some of these Western communities. With this atmosphere is mixed the gayety of the Old South and perhaps the rough and ready courage and daring of the Scotch-Irish and Irish immigrants. In other communities one finds large groups of Germans, steadfastly cultivating the soil or building substantial German towns.

The spirit of democracy in the growing West

Thus it happened that young America was taking Horace Greeley's advice: "Go West, young man, and grow up with the country." The settlers were young and sure of themselves. They were confident of the future, eager to try new things, burning with ambition to succeed. Everyone was hopeful, sure that a fortune was awaiting him even though he might have to go still farther West to find it.

These "Easterners gone West" were hungry for land. They were greedy for wealth, for individual power, for freedom, for equality. They believed that a democracy could be developed in America which would make it possible for each individual to achieve any height that his abilities were capable of achieving. Indeed, they already had proof of this. Had not "Old Hickory," one of the backwoodsmen, become president? Before the middle of the century frontier mothers were wearing themselves out in order to educate their boys, each believing firmly that her son had a chance to be president.

Among the professions, law and politics were the most popular. Law was the open door to the legislature of the state, to Congress, to a cabinet position, a diplomatic post, a judgeship, or even the presidency. It was easy enough to become a frontier lawyer. A few months of study and any bright, hard-working young man could plead before the circuit-riding judges, whose own knowledge of law was none too secure. In the Western courts the reputation of young lawyers was being made overnight. It was during these years that Abraham Lincoln was tending a country store in Illinois and reading law when he found the time.

Social life in the changing towns and cities of the East

Life was also moving rapidly on the Atlantic seaboard. Trade was humming on the rolled roads, the sluggish Eastern canals, and the rough railroads. Immigrants were pouring in from Europe. Not only were young farmers leaving the rocky New England fields for the virgin soil farther west, but some of them were trying their hands at various occupations in the towns and cities. Urban population was growing rapidly, and society was forming along new lines. Boston, New York, and Philadelphia were still the chief cities.

Charles Dickens, the famous English author, visited America in 1842. In his *American Notes* he frankly described what he had seen. Boston, he said, was a fascinating city with handsome public buildings, and an air of refinement which he thought was due to the "quieting influences of the University of Cambridge" (Harvard).

Philadelphia was quite different from Boston. A European visitor remarked: "It is a comfortable city, with no miserable and filthy streets . . . no Dutch town could be cleaner." Charles Dickens, however, found Philadelphia too regular in its arrangement of streets and houses. He would have given the world for a crooked street, and liked Boston because of its resemblance to English cities in this respect. In general the life of Philadelphia revolved around business, the Dorcas Society, formal social calls, politics, and, at intervals, the theater. An art gallery was already in existence there.

New York had now become the metropolis and was thenceforth never to be passed in the urban race for size. Its inhabitants included representatives of almost every European nation. Poverty-stricken Irish and German immigrants rubbed elbows with descendants of the old Knickerbocker aristocracy. Delicate, overdressed ladies dragged their long trains through the same mud that ragged newsboys trod.

City households were undergoing changes no less remarkable than those in the Middle West. Fireplaces were giving way

FIG. 102. Roads leading into the Middle West were busy places during the years between 1830 and 1850. Conestoga wagons were often seen bringing supplies to the "Easterners gone West." (Courtesy of the Philadelphia Commercial Museum)

to iron stoves. New Yorkers could scarcely remember a more important event than the opening of the new reservoir on Forty-second Street. A loud and brilliant celebration was held. Henceforth few people would be required to get their water from the Tea-Water Pump, the wooden mains of the Manhattan Water Company, or from springs. Houses were then equipped with running water from city mains. A few houses even had bathrooms.

Kitchens were quite transformed by the new cookstoves which had taken the place of the hearth. Bright tinware, for use in the kitchen, adorned the windows of the stores and tempted the eye of the housewives. And now that American firms had learned how to imitate the French originals, everybody aspired to wall paper. Carpets, which had begun to replace rag rugs, were patterned with bowers of large, gaudy roses. There was a perfect mania for flowers and nature in interior decoration. Many parlors now boasted rocking-chairs. Coffee was already replacing tea as the national drink, and even the rising middle classes used ice.

Thus the economic standard of living in the Eastern cities was improving, although, according to our standard today, it would not be regarded as high. For the well-to-do and the middle

FIG. 103. Wall Street in New York between 1845 and 1850

classes there was plenty of food and clothing; for the rank and file, a bare subsistence. The day of huge fortunes had not yet arrived; $10,000 was a modest fortune, $20,000 was real wealth.

It is from the accounts of such foreign visitors as Charles Dickens, Captain Marryat, Frances Trollope, and Harriet Martineau that we get word pictures of the changing society of the time. If we can believe their interpretations, that society was marked by a mass of curious contradictions — love of freedom and equality, snobbishness, bad manners, artificial pretensions to morality, and the like. These critics agreed on one point, however — Americans were inclined to brag.

The craze for European knickknacks, dances, dramas, architecture, and dress was sweeping the country. Even in far-off Cincinnati youths affected the long curls of the English poet Byron. By 1840 chin whiskers and even full beards were considered "smart." Fashionable men wore swallow-tailed coats, silk hats, tight waistcoats, and long trousers fastened down by a strap passing under the foot. As for fashions in women's dress, Dickens was forced to exclaim:

Heaven save the ladies, how they dress! We have seen more colors in these ten minutes than we should have seen elsewhere in as many days. What various parasols, what rainbow silks and satins, what pinching of thin shoes, and fluttering of ribbons and silk tassels, and display of rich cloaks with gaudy hoods and linings!

It was said that on any fine day one might see enough velvet at $4 a yard to cover Broadway from one end to the other. It seemed to be quite impossible to tell a woman's social position by her dress. Styles were already becoming standardized. One thing was clear: all were overdressed.

The theater was becoming an American institution. Wandering players were delighting a small public with such plays as *Metamora* and *The Gladiator*. Shakespeare's plays were also given fairly regularly. Already several famous theatrical families attracted and delighted audiences with their productions of *Macbeth*, *Hamlet*, and *Othello*. Opera companies were just beginning to appear on the American stage. In vocal music the period is remembered as the one in which P. T. Barnum, the circus man, introduced so successfully the European singer Jenny Lind. To their dying days the audiences never forgot how "the Swedish Nightingale" sang that new popular song "Home, Sweet Home."

The things which amused the common man were of another order, however. Shrewd showmen like Barnum had learned to appeal to his taste. Barnum's advertisements of his museum invited the public to inspect

industrious fleas, educated dogs, jugglers, automatons, ventriloquists, living statuary, tableaux, gipsies, albinoes, fat boys, giants, dwarfs, rope dancers, caricatures of phrenology, "live Yankees," pantomimes, music, singing and dancing . . . panoramas, models of Dublin, Paris,

Niagara, Jerusalem, mechanical figures, fancy glass blowing, knitting machines and other triumphs of the mechanical art, dissolving views, and American Indians.

Many of the wonders he advertised were humbugs. Among the most popular of these were the mermaid with the head of a monkey and the body of a fish, the mechanical chess-player

FIG. 104. A Scene at Barnum's Museum. So popular was the museum that families used to bring their luncheon and stay all day

(moved by an expert chess-player concealed inside!), and Joyce Heth, advertised to be "161 years old, and the nurse of George Washington." No wonder Mr. Barnum earned the title of "Prince of Humbugs."

Negro minstrels were also very popular amusements of the common man in the 1840's. Most of the "minstrels," however, were white, and the "plantation melodies" were written by white men. Stephen Foster's "Swanee River" and "My Old Kentucky Home" are examples of the white man's Negro songs.

Fads seized the credulous public

The mass of the people, with little education, were led to adopt one fad after another. Many quacks appeared, advocating their remedies for one disease or another and sometimes for all of them. Mesmerism, for example, became a favorite fad, practiced by quack doctors — a kind of "spiritual healing." People afflicted with all kinds of ailments went to mesmerists, who were reported to perform wonders by simply "laying on of hands." The quacks found it much easier to practice mesmerism than any other form of cure which they had tried. Small fortunes were made at it.

Many other forms of "cure" were developed. There were the vegetarians, who refrained from eating flesh, and the hydropaths, who recommended for every kind of disease the drinking of unlimited quantities of water.

Lectures and demonstrations of the new "science" of phrenology were well attended. The phrenologists claimed that by feeling the bumps on a man's head, they could read his character. At the height of the movement a wag wrote in a current newspaper:

> Press the bump . . . of innocent hilarity,
> And just behind the ears
> Are faith, hope, and charity.

Prophesying future events also succeeded in attracting many credulous believers. A "prophet" named William Miller raised a nation-wide commotion by predicting that the end of the world would come between March 21, 1843, and March 21, 1844. Many people who heard of his prophecies hastened to put their affairs in order and prepare for the next world. As the time approached, suicides became frequent. Scores of people were reported to have gone mad. An enterprising New York shopkeeper advertised "muslin for ascension robes." Many ignorant people believed that the widespread use of machines, railroads, and steamboats was clear proof that the world was about to come to an end.

There were many contradictions in this period of American history. There were much comedy, much misery, much persecution, and much intolerance, yet much reform and idealistic democracy. Barnum's traveling circus was a part of American life as well as the philosophical writings of Mr. Ralph Waldo Emerson, the quiet Concord philosopher. Factories where men, women, and little children slaved for a meager wage existed side by side with the extravagances of the luxury-loving newly rich society of New York. In the same country whose leaders were advocating free public education for all, several million Negroes were still bought and sold as property. All these things were a part of the American scene between 1830 and 1860.

Many Reforms were launched

It is true that the average American had extremely bad manners, lacked social grace, and was too fond of displaying his wealth. At the same time he was the world's leading exponent of liberty, equality, and democracy. The American of this period believed in himself; he believed in mankind; he believed in the right of the individual to live reasonably well. Naturally, therefore, he set about to right the injustices of the times, and a great wave of reform swept the country. Campaigns were waged against slavery, against the saloon, against ignorance, against injustice to women, against child labor, against cruelty to animals, to criminals, and to the insane.

The newspapers of the day, controlled by the political and business leaders, viciously attacked and ridiculed the reform movements. These criticisms did not daunt the reformers; their meetings went on just the same.

A social experiment
Brook Farm

Some of the leading thinkers of America — among them Ralph Waldo Emerson, Henry Thoreau, and Margaret Fuller — had formed a little discussion group called the Symposium Club. They were popularly known as the Transcendentalists. For years this small group of cultured men and women met in Concord, Massachusetts, and discussed important problems of American

CULTURE OF MIDDLE WEST AND NORTHEAST

life. They wrote essays, novels, and poetry; they collected and published for Americans large volumes of European literature. In 1840 they launched the *Dial*, a magazine of the highest literary quality. Emerson and others among them corresponded with Carlyle, William Morris, and other thinking men of Europe. Few small groups, indeed, were as renowned as these so-called Transcendentalists. They did much to raise the cultural standard of life in America, and they contributed to the worth-while reform movements of the time.

In 1841 several members of this group decided to experiment with a small community. They had been reading and discussing the communistic plans proposed by Fourier, the French social philosopher. Fourier preached that society must be entirely rebuilt. He urged people to form themselves into small groups, to organize little communities, and to abolish private property. Everything must be owned jointly; all must work and, regardless of the kind of work, all must profit equally.

FIG. 105. Ralph Waldo Emerson, through his lectures and writings, contributed more than any one other person to a criticism of the civilization of his day

George Ripley, Nathaniel Hawthorne, and a number of others established Brook Farm during that same year. Each member took stock in the community; each was to receive a share of the profits from the farm, which was to be self-sustaining. Work was not to be compulsory, but it was believed that the ideals of the individual members would lead them to do their share of work. All workers were to receive equal wages, from which they were to pay their board and to purchase whatever they needed from the community warehouse.

Emerson, the clear-minded philosopher, and Margaret Fuller refused to join them, although they often visited their friends at

Brook Farm. Emerson said that he knew they would fail, and after three years of experiment they did. Various reasons were given for their failure. Some said that the members of the community were skilled conversationalists but poor cooks and farmers. Certainly it was true that if one of the members had not done practically all the plowing, food would have been scarce

FIG. 106. One of the buildings at Brook Farm in Massachusetts. This building, called *The Hive*, was the meeting place of all those who lived in the farm community. Here lectures took place, usually followed by long discussions

even the first year. Finally, in March, 1846, the buildings were destroyed by fire, and the community, which had already failed entirely, disbanded.

EQUAL RIGHTS FOR WOMEN!

During this period of great reforms a host of voices was being raised to demand equal rights for women. Women had no political rights, and married women were still legally unable even to own property.

The women's suffrage movement, however, was getting under way. Frances Wright, a Scotch woman, had come to America, bringing her principles of democracy and equality for women and advocating the abolition of slavery. Fanny Wright societies were formed in many cities. Margaret Fuller, supporter of the Brook Farm experiment and brilliant editor of the *Dial*, whom Horace Greeley called "the loftiest, bravest soul that has yet irradiated the form of an American woman," took an active part. She was soon joined by Lucretia Mott and Elizabeth Cady

FIG. 107. Margaret Fuller   FIG. 108. Susan B. Anthony
TWO LEADERS IN THE MOVEMENT FOR EQUAL RIGHTS FOR WOMEN

Stanton. In the 1830's and 1840's were added a host of historic names — Lucy Stone, Julia Ward Howe, Susan B. Anthony, Mary Walker, Amelia Jenks Bloomer.

It was not merely the vote which these leaders wanted. Most of them were abolitionists — that is, they wanted to abolish Negro slavery. Most of them were also temperance workers. Seeing the evils of extreme drunkenness, they were trying to stamp out the public saloon.

In addition, they wanted girls and boys to be educated to the idea that women should share with men the responsibility of earning their own living. Women, they said, should become lawyers, doctors, bankers, public speakers, aldermen, mayors, superintendents of schools, heads of factories, and members of Congress.

A most interesting illustration of the way in which these leaders would free women was found in their ideas for reform in women's dress. It was the day when women wore many pounds of clothing. A typical dress of the day was described as a "flannel petticoat, an under petticoat three and a half yards wide, a petticoat wadded to the knees, a white starched petticoat, two muslin petticoats, and finally the dress." Is it any wonder that leaders like Amelia Jenks Bloomer and Mary Walker preached reform? Mrs. Bloomer is remembered even to this day for the "sensible costume for females" which she devised. It was known as the "bloomer" and consisted of a skirt reaching only midway between the knee and the ankle over trousers which were gathered at the ankle with an elastic band. Mrs. Stanton and other leaders adopted the bloomer costume and pronounced it comfortable and convenient.

Dr. Mary Walker went even further in her dress reform. During the Civil War she adopted men's clothing for her work as nurse among the wounded. Later, when she appeared thus attired on the streets of Eastern cities, many of her own sex were shocked at her immodesty. It is reported that more than once they set dogs upon her in the street.

Another privilege advocated by these leaders was the right to keep their maiden names after marriage. Lucy Stone, a graduate of Oberlin College in 1847, was the special sponsor of this reform, and to this day married women who do not take their husbands' names are sometimes called "Lucy Stoners."

In 1848 these leaders of the women's suffrage movement called a National Women's Rights Convention. A new kind of Declaration of Independence was drawn up and signed, in which the delegates declared that "all men and women were created equal."

In spite of derisive attacks from the newspapers and the condemnation of their own sex, the leaders went on with their work. Gradually property laws were changed in the various states, and today, in most states, women have been given the right to hold and dispose of their own property. Only comparatively recently, however, was the Nineteenth Amendment to the Constitution passed, granting suffrage to women on equal terms with men.

Public education, the greatest improvement

In the period which we are discussing it was not uncommon for children to work from twelve to fourteen hours a day every day except Sunday. They had no time for schooling. There was, however, much agitation for education and against child labor. For example, the *Mechanics' Free Press* of January 24, 1829, had declared that real liberty and equality have no foundation but in universal and equal instruction, and in 1832 a Boston convention of New England mechanics denounced child labor. Many adults in America were illiterate, that is, they could neither read nor write. From New England to Georgia the people of the hill and mountain sections were almost totally illiterate. In the communities of the West conditions were little better. Throughout many parts of America, for the rank and file there was little education, even of the most rudimentary kind.

On the frontier whatever education there was, was crude indeed. Little log schoolhouses housed tiny classes. Three months each year the teachers, chiefly young men preparing for another profession, gave lessons from readers and spellers, arithmetics and language books. One woman teacher received $1.25 a week, "often uncollectable." Teachers "boarded around" from family to family. In these Western communities there were few books and no magazines or newspapers. Abraham Lincoln and other ambitious youths had to walk many miles to borrow books from those who owned them.

In the growing cities of the West as well as in the East, however, colleges and universities were being founded. Some were set up by religious denominations such as the Methodists, the Baptists, and the Presbyterians. State universities were coming into existence. They were modeled on Eastern colleges, and only men were admitted.

In Chapter XXIV you will learn that during this period the idea of popular education at public expense began to take a firm hold in the United States.

There was a vague recognition that both earning a living and participation in democracy depended in some way upon education. Parents began to think that their children could earn a better living and rise to a higher social position through education. Throughout the United States there grew the conviction that education was the ladder to "success." A few leaders saw that government would be really democratic in America only to the extent that education was universal and highly developed.

Other improvements and reforms

In the meantime improvements were being brought about in the conditions of criminals, paupers, and the insane. It was well known that all these classes of people were cruelly treated and neglected.

Prominent among the reform crusades was the anti-gallows movement, the purpose of which was to end capital punishment (punishment by death) and also to put a stop to such treatment as flogging, branding, and the use of the stocks. Even in the 1830's and 1840's the opponents of capital punishment won some victories. Maine abolished capital punishment in 1837, and Vermont did likewise in 1842, though it was reintroduced there later. In several other states the debate over the question was prolonged, but few actually abolished it.

Other leaders devoted themselves to persuading state legislatures to improve the conditions of insane asylums, prisons, and poor farms. Much was accomplished, and the care of the incompetents in these institutions was made much more humane. Institutes for the deaf, the blind, and the crippled were established in many states, some through private funds, others through state funds.

So it is that a people living under democratic forms of government bring about change in public affairs. Leaders appear, generally brilliant and courageous men and women who see clearly the evils of their time. They form organizations of men and women who believe in the same principles and who will support publicly a demand for change. Then other people, including more conservative leaders, oppose these demands. Lectures and public meetings are held in which various aspects of the matter are presented. Groups of citizens then become interested and demand that new laws be passed. Little by little the interest grows and the reforms win. Slowly but surely ways of living become more humane. The period from 1830 to 1860 is especially remembered for the growth of the reform spirit.

What was the literary and artistic life of the North?

In the preceding pages we have had glimpses of Northern society in the first half of the nineteenth century. Noisy, boisterous, money-mad, active, and full of commotion the age certainly was. There was, however, a growing group of thinkers and writers who worked for the building up of American culture.

In literature there were three men of unusual originality — Ralph Waldo Emerson, Henry Thoreau, and Walt Whitman.

Ralph Waldo Emerson, known as the Sage of Concord, stood aloof from the mad rushing current of American life. He had been a Unitarian preacher in Boston, but had resigned the position and retired to his little white cottage in Concord, where he meditated upon the movements and problems of American civilization.

Emerson was a central figure in the Symposium Club. He applauded the social experiments which were going on, but he held aloof from what he regarded as misguided enthusiasms.

In the quiet of his home he wrote essays which were read around the world. He discussed the evils and the difficulties of American society and the movements for reform. In 1840 he wrote: "We are all a little wild here, with numberless projects of social reform. Not a reading man but has a draft of a new Community in his waistcoat pocket." Shortly after he looked on at some of the reform conventions and described them: "Madmen and madwomen, men with beards, Dunkers, Muggletonians, Come-outers, Groaners . . . Abolitionists, and Philosophers." Yet he saw a meaning in these movements. He said in the *Dial* in 1841 that the trumpet of reform was sounding throughout the world for a revolution of all human affairs. Many students regard Emerson as one of the greatest minds America ever produced.

In the little Concord group of philosophers and writers was an odd genius, Henry Thoreau. He was Emerson's closest friend.

Believing that the world was full of injustice and that men worked harder than they needed to, he decided to withdraw from society and live independently with the wild life of nature. On the shores of Walden Pond, near Concord, he built a hut. There he tilled a few acres, read considerably, wrote much, and came to know wild life with a beautiful intimacy. His book *Walden*, now known in many lands, was written during his two years' experiment with nature.

One day in 1855 Emerson laid down a little volume of poems called *Leaves of Grass* and wrote a letter to the author. In this he said that the book was "the most extraordinary piece of wit and wisdom that America has yet contributed." The little volume was the work of an unknown writer, Walt Whitman, who lived in Brooklyn and spent most of his time carpentering, building, and selling small houses. From time to time he contributed poems and prose writings to magazines and reviews. Later his poems were revised and issued again and again under the original title of *Leaves of Grass*. Today it is a large volume of several hundred pages, one of the world's renowned books. In Whitman's lifetime, however, it was not understood even by the writers of the day. Only Emerson and a small group recognized its importance.

Minor poets, novelists, and essayists

Perhaps not so original as the three men whom we have just described, but generally more popular, was a group of poets, novelists, and essayists which may be roughly described as belonging to the New England school. The most famous of these were Oliver Wendell Holmes, James Russell Lowell, John Greenleaf Whittier, Nathaniel Hawthorne, and Henry Wadsworth Longfellow. They were men of education and refinement. Most of them were sons of old American families and were connected with universities. No attempt will be made here to list their writings. They are familiar in every household.

On the whole, the New England writers gave to the young nation its most highly prized literary tradition.

In New York another group of writers was developing during this period — William Cullen Bryant, poet, and editor of the

Fig. 109. Oliver Wendell Holmes

Fig. 110. James Russell Lowell

Fig. 111. Henry Thoreau

Fig. 112. Walt Whitman

FOUR AMERICAN AUTHORS WHOSE WRITINGS HELPED TO INFLUENCE AMERICAN THOUGHT

New York Evening Post, Washington Irving, who wrote many charming essays and sketches, James Fenimore Cooper, whose novels of the frontier and the sea have perhaps been more widely read than the writings of any other American, and Edgar Allan Poe, who was undoubtedly the leading poet and short-story writer in the latter part of this period.

The Fine Arts in the Changing America

The literary development of Americans was far superior to their development in the other arts. Artists received little encouragement, for most Americans had had little time to cultivate a taste for the arts. The chief encouragement that the painter received had its source in the desire of people to see themselves in portraits, and after the camera was invented even portrait-painters had the greatest difficulty in making a living. The great fondness for nature which developed toward the end of the period found its expression in a group of painters called the Hudson River School, which pictured the beauties of sylvan scenes.

In sculpture the chief works were statues of statesmen and other prominent Americans clad in the ancient Greek style or in Roman togas. These were ordered as adornments for parks, squares, and public buildings.

In music there was little real development. Folk music and dancing had almost disappeared. Only among the Dutch and Germans was there some remembrance of old peasant tunes. Scotch and English songs survived in the mountain regions, and frontier events sometimes found expression in ballads. On the Great Lakes and the Northwestern rivers, French Canadian boatmen and lumberjacks sang ballads at their work which recorded in song the life of the woods. But words meant more to most Americans than music. Sentimental, humorous, and religious songs were great favorites because of their romantic feeling.

We have now described in some detail the social and cultural life of the North in the years between 1830 and 1860. In the next chapter you will learn how the people of the South were living during the same period.

CULTURE OF MIDDLE WEST AND NORTHEAST

INTERESTING READINGS FROM WHICH YOU CAN GET ADDITIONAL INFORMATION

ALLEN, CHARLES FLETCHER. David Crockett, Scout. J. B. Lippincott Company, Philadelphia. A frontiersman of the South writes his adventures from 1830 to 1860.

BARNUM, P. T. Struggles and Triumphs. Alfred A. Knopf, New York. The autobiography of a great American humbug.

COOPER, JAMES FENIMORE. The Deerslayer; The Pathfinder; The Prairie; The Wept of Wish-ton-wish. Houghton Mifflin Company, Boston. The first American novels of the frontier written by a contemporary; most interesting and dramatic.

DICKENS, CHARLES. American Notes; Martin Chuzzlewit. Two books about American life by a leading English writer of the time.

GARLAND, HAMLIN. A Son of the Middle Border. The Macmillan Company, New York. The autobiography of a frontier boy.

HAWTHORNE, NATHANIEL. Mosses from an Old Manse; The Marble Faun; Twice-Told Tales; The Blithedale Romance; The Scarlet Letter. Novels by one of the best of the New England school of writers; many of them are written about the time which we are studying.

HOLMES, OLIVER WENDELL. Poems; The Autocrat at the Breakfast-Table. The collected poems and one of the best-known prose works of a typical New England writer.

IRVING, WASHINGTON. Knickerbocker's History of New York. A. L. Burt Company, New York. Droll tales of Diedrich Knickerbocker and his friends and neighbors.

LAMPREY, L. Days of the Pioneers. Frederick A. Stokes Company, New York. Interesting stories of great American pioneers.

MINNIGERODE, MEADE. The Fabulous Forties. G. P. Putnam's Sons, New York. Entertaining sketches of the uproarious life of American cities during the 1840's.

POE, EDGAR ALLAN. Short stories and poems.

STODDARD, WILLIAM O. The Boy Lincoln. D. Appleton and Company, New York. Stories of the frontier life of the boy Lincoln up to about 1830.

THOREAU, HENRY. Walden. Houghton Mifflin Company, Boston. Thoreau's experiences among the animals and birds of Walden Pond.

TICKNOR, CAROLINE. May Alcott: a Memoir. Little, Brown and Company, Boston. Rich in the social background of the New England reform group.

WILKINS, MARY E. A New England Nun. Harper & Brothers, New York. Rich in the background of New England social customs of 1830 and 1860.

CHAPTER XIII

LIFE IN THE COTTON KINGDOM, 1830–1860

Was the same spirit of hurried building and settlement pervading the South as well as the North during the period from 1830 to 1860? Was democracy in the air in Southern towns and cities as it was in the North? Were there communistic experiments? Were women demanding equal rights? Was education spreading? Were there cultured leaders? Let us see.

In *A History of American Civilization* you have read the story of the growth of the cotton kingdom in the South after 1800. You have seen how the plantation-owners of Virginia and the Carolinas moved southwestward. By 1860 there stretched from Virginia to Texas a great agricultural section given over chiefly to raising cotton.

THE CHIEF SOCIAL CLASSES OF THE SOUTH

In the South in 1860, as in the North, society was divided into property classes. There were four chief groups: first, a small group of very wealthy planters, each the owner of twenty or more slaves and of hundreds, if not thousands, of acres; second, a much larger group of small planters, owners of from five to twenty slaves and of small plantations; third, a great mass of very poor white people,— fully half of all the people of the South,— each possessing not more than a small cabin and a few acres of land; fourth, between three and four million Negroes, nearly all slaves. The adjoining table sums up the estimated numbers of people in 1860 in each of the four groups.

Estimated Number of People in the Chief Economic Groups of the South, 1860 [1]	
Wealthy planters .	125,000
Small planters . .	750,000
Poor farmers . . .	6,000,000 to 8,000,000
Negro slaves . . .	3,000,000 to 4,000,000

[1] Estimates from U. B. Phillips's *Life and Labor in the Old South*, Little, Brown and Company, Boston.

LIFE IN THE COTTON KINGDOM, 1830–1860

Careful students estimate that in 1850, out of a total of 667,000 *families* in the South, about 1000 of them received practically half of the income of the entire South and the other 666,000 received the other half.

I. SOCIAL LIFE AMONG THE WEALTHY PLANTERS

Between 1830 and 1860 the Southern planting aristocracy was in its Golden Age, its period of chivalry and gracious charm. The "mellow, bland, and sunny luxuriousness of her old time society" shed a soft glamour over plantation life. In contrast to the hustling, bustling North, there was much leisure in which to enjoy good fellowship and hospitality. The wealthy planters of the cotton-growing South "lived" and enjoyed the days as they passed.

In the house the planter's wife ruled supreme. She was an interesting combination of busy housewife and gracious hostess, entertaining an almost ever present group of guests. As mistress of the plantation she was responsible for a large establishment. In it were usually many children of her own and a score or more of Negro servants. The Negro servants kept the house, served the table, grew the vegetables and fruit, and made the clothing for the Negro field hands. In addition to the superintendence of this work, the lady of the plantation could never be sure when she would have to turn nurse and doctor either in her great house or in the slave quarters. If the "missus" failed to attend to the hurts of pickaninnies or grown-ups there was sure to be whining and crying in the "quarters."

In the fields, as you have already learned, work was done mainly by Negro slaves, often under the supervision of white overseers. Except for the household the general direction of affairs was the planter's own.

When the market for cotton was good, his crops large, and his slaves free from sickness, the planter had leisure in which to enjoy his guests and such amusements as the country afforded. His chief amusements were hunting, fishing, and politics. It was rare indeed to find a Southern gentleman indifferent either to local or national politics.

As the cultural leader, he was almost sure to be a well-read man. Almost every planter's home boasted a considerable library of law books, histories, English novels, and Greek and Roman classics. The *Southern Review* of Charleston, the *Southern Literary Messenger* of Richmond, and *De Bow's Review* of New Orleans were usually to be found in the Southern home of this type. Southern literary taste favored European literature — such as Sir Walter Scott's novels and Lord Byron's poetry — rather than the literature produced in the Northern states. News of the world was brought to the plantations regularly through the Southern newspapers — the *Mercury*, the *Daily News*, and the *Courier*, of Charleston, the *New Orleans Pickayune*, and the *Richmond Enquirer*. Political debates between the champions of oratory — Robert Hayne and John C. Calhoun of South Carolina, Daniel Webster of Massachusetts, and Henry Clay of Kentucky — were widely read and discussed.

The mansion, which was the name given to the finest of these plantation homes, generally consisted of ten or twelve rooms. The lower floor was given over to the parlors, the library, and the dining rooms. These were large, high-ceilinged rooms, with tall windows opening onto generous porches. Walls were paneled and adorned with portraits of ancestors, political paintings, and perhaps English hunting scenes.

As visitors were frequent the houses were built with several guest rooms on the upper floors. In cooler seasons guests would be greeted on awakening by a cheery fire crackling in the fireplace. Black household servants were at hand to provide for every need. At eight o'clock breakfast was served on the polished mahogany table — cold ham, hot breads, chicken and waffles, fruit, and the newly introduced and fashionable coffee as well as the old-fashioned tea. After breakfast there were casual conversation, writing, reading, or card-playing. The planter went through his mail and rode about the plantation. Indeed, everyone rode. One was almost sure to see fine saddle horses hitched close to the porch. In a corner might be discovered a confusion of saddles, riding boots, whips, and horse blankets. Planters' sons were brought up in the saddle. Even boys of ten were superb riders.

LIFE IN THE COTTON KINGDOM, 1830–1860

In the early afternoon one took a siesta; then more guests — usually from neighboring plantations — arrived for dinner, which was at three o'clock. Planter and mistress were the centers of interesting circles of vivacious neighborhood society. The host carved the enormous roast, while his wife played the double rôle of gracious hostess and deft leader in the conversation. Strangers

FIG. 113. For a few of the Southern people life held many comforts. They had time in which to read and to entertain their friends. They built up a culture which was different from that of the wealthy people of the North and from that of most other Southerners

to the Southland would not have dreamed that this delicate and cultured lady was the efficient manager of the great household.

In the evening there was probably a light supper, served in the soft glow of candles. After supper perhaps a game of whist, more conversation and reading, and then the guests who were to remain were guided to their rooms by servants bearing tall candlesticks. Through the windows warm breezes rustled, nightingales sang plaintively, and katydids called. Finally sleep descended, and another day had passed.

Then would come a day in spring when, with great excitement, the family went to Charleston. Boxes and bags would be loaded into massive wagons and sent on ahead. The planter and his family would follow in an elegant coach, richly upholstered and ornamented. Perhaps for days the carriage would rock and roll on to Charleston, where there were many amusements — racing, bathing, the theater, the music of the St. Cecilia Society, teas, levees, and balls. Here the planter could talk with friends from other parts of the South and exchange his views on the cotton crop,

FIG. 114. The balls given in Charleston were brilliant social events, and invitations to them were eagerly awaited

cotton markets, and politics. Here he could talk over his worries and his troubles when he had them, and perhaps find help in the opinions and advice of his friends. Here the younger daughters of the family could attend dancing school and the sons could continue their studies in preparation for their entrance into the university.

Charleston was a gay city with its elegant belles and beaux, its dancing, its horse racing, its theater, and its music — indeed, a city to capture the imagination. It was also justly proud of its distinguished society, and it still guarded the social standards of Old England. Hugh Legaré, the Charleston literary leader, proudly wrote: "We are decidedly more English than any other city in the United States." Social lines were clearly marked; one *did* or *did not* belong to "society."

Charleston was not all social gayety, however. A serious life lay beneath its surface, in many respects as serious as that of Boston. As on the frontier of the West and the North, the lawyer assumed the leadership of the South. One writer of the day said that law books were as highly regarded in the South as the Bible in old New England. Here too, as in the West, law was the open door to a career in politics; and the men of Charleston were the head and front of the political power of the South in Congress. Here was the home of John C. Calhoun, of Robert Young Hayne, and of the Pinckneys.

In Charleston, also, the best writers, the literary leaders of the South, were gathered. There lived the Rutledges, Robert James Turnbull, and the Petigrus. There Hugh Legaré edited the *Southern Review*, a magazine which played much the same part in the South that the *North American Literary Review* played in the North. There the best newspapers — the *Daily News* and the *Courier* — reported the latest debates in Congress.

In the autumn the social season ended, and society returned to the plantations. Then there was much hunting in the forests and lowlands. Finally, the cotton-picking season having come and gone, many planters went to New Orleans to sell their crops.

New Orleans! Was there a more interesting city in the country than this large cosmopolitan community? It was a strange half-foreign city — partly French, partly Spanish, partly American. An air of romance hovered over its streets. In some of them one was transported to Paris; in others, to Seville or Madrid. Along one street the visitors looked into the windows of Swiss clock shops with their tiny carved wooden figures. In others the latest French styles were offered for inspection. Through an open doorway one might see a Spanish leather worker at work upon a saddle; perhaps next door, a Negro barber. At the end of the street perhaps there was a boarding house for sailors of every nationality. At the wharves Ohio flatboats lay side by side with rafts, dugouts, and river steamboats. Not far away ocean-going clipper ships rode at anchor. Along the levees strolled sailors and merchants of every color, and occasionally red-shirted Ohio flatboat men strode by.

New Orleans was also a social center for the South, but how different in atmosphere from Charleston! It was truly a world city, boasting its carnivals, its theater, its French opera, of which the people were so proud. And there, at least once a year, all kinds of world society met to amuse themselves at the carnival. The carnival took place a few days before Lent, ending on Shrove Tuesday. On Mardi gras, as the French-speaking people of New Orleans call the day before the beginning of Lent, the celebration reached its height. A British traveler of 1846 has left us a description of the celebration:

It was quite a novelty and a refreshing sight to see a whole population giving up their minds for a short season to amusement. There was a grand procession of parading the streets, almost every one dressed in the most grotesque attire, troops of them on horseback, some in open carriages, with bands of music, and a variety of costumes — some as Indians, with feathers in their heads, and one, a jolly fat man, as Mardi Gras himself.[1]

There were other interesting cities, but few had the glamour of New Orleans and Charleston.

II. How the Small Planters and Poorer Farmers Lived

After all, the very wealthy planters were few. The small planter and the poorer farmer formed the great mass of the white population of the South.

With them too life was leisurely, but there was little opportunity for culture. The great mass of Southern whites lived upon small, isolated farms, their lives as meager as those of the Northern and Western frontiersmen.

The small planter usually owned one or more slave families, who lived in shanties near his house. The planter's own dwelling would vary in size and attractiveness according to his fortune. He might boast of a miniature mansion, or he might own but a

[1] From Charles Lyell's *New Orleans* (1846); quoted in *American Social History as recorded by British Travellers* (compiled and edited by Allan Nevins), pp. 333-334. Published by Henry Holt and Company, 1923.

two-room or three-room log cabin. The mistress of the house would probably attend to the youngest of the Negro children as well as her own large brood while the Negro mother toiled in the fields with the men.

In the next class, that of the poor farmer, there were no slaves. The total belongings of the family often consisted of a small rough house of two or three rooms, a barn, a kitchen garden, and a few poor acres. Once or twice a year the farmer took his cotton crop to market and bought the few necessities which his small farm did not provide. Family life centered around the great open fire. Inside the fireplace swung a large iron crane, from which were hung various pots and kettles. From the ceiling hung bags of seed corn and strings of dried fruit and peppers. Above the door perhaps could be seen the long rifle and the powderhorn. Greens, bacon, porridge, and of course sweet potatoes and corn bread, constituted the staple foods. Very likely the windows were closed with a wooden shutter only. There were no claims to beauty in such a home and, indeed, little claim to comfort.

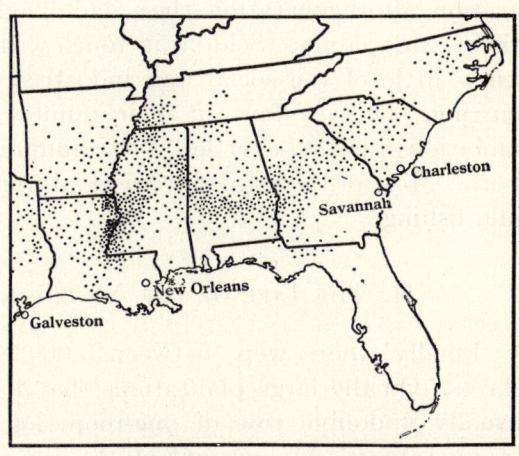

Fig. 115. The dots on the map indicate the localities in which cotton was being grown in 1860. Cotton had been the chief agricultural product of the South for many years. Most of the Southern people depended for their livelihood upon its growth

There was not much opportunity for education in the small-farmer population. There was likely to be little if any reading matter in the home. The Bible and Bunyan's *Pilgrim's Progress* might rest upon the table, but there was little time or inclination for reading and writing. Hence it is difficult for us today to build up from their own written words pictures of the lives of these people which would be as accurate and clear as those of the lives of the large planters. It was difficult for any of these poor farmers ever to become Southern leaders. A few of them did, however; for example, President Andrew Jackson and President Andrew Johnson. Johnson was a poor Southern boy, unable to read or write until his wife taught him while he was serving an apprenticeship to a tailor.

These farmers had changed their customs little since the late 1700's, when Daniel Boone had led the pioneers westward. Generation after generation they had lived on their tiny farms in their crude cabins. Seldom in touch with the outside world, they knew little of the social and industrial changes which were occurring. Only a few of their number, occasional bright and ambitious youths, ever left the communities in which they were born. Most of them lived from hand to mouth, farming, hunting, and fishing.

III. The Life of the Negro in the Old South

Finally, there were between 3,000,000 and 4,000,000 Negro slaves. On the large plantations they lived in the "quarters"— usually a double row of one-room log cabins or whitewashed frame cabins. At one end of the row might be the overseer's house; at the other, the tool sheds, gristmill, and various outbuildings. Inside the cabins family life centered about the fireplace. Cabins were almost sure to be crowded, for Negro families were large. All slept in the single room or in the garret on beds, mats, or quilts. All the activities of the household were carried on in the single cabin room.

For the field hands work was almost sure to be hard, and because of the lack of such knowledge of sanitation as we have today there was much needless illness and misery. Then, too, it was almost impossible to keep the quarters clean, for those who lived in them worked long hours in the fields and were too tired at night to do much cleaning up. On the better plantations the quarters were moved every two years to prevent too great filth from accumulating. Once a month the ground under the cabins was cleaned, and perhaps twice a year the cabins themselves were whitewashed, inside and out.

On some plantations the slaves cooked their own meals and

tended their little gardens in such spare time as they had. On other plantations a cook prepared the meals for the field hands in order that the workers might have more rest and better food. Clothing, of course, was very crude — in summer, cotton jackets and trousers for the men and calico gowns for the women. In winter woolen jackets, hats, and shoes were usually added.

FIG. 116. A scene in the quarters for the household servants on a Southern plantation. When the day's work was over, there might still be time for the Negroes to play with the children, to strum the banjo, or to amuse themselves in other ways. (From a painting by E. Johnson)

Among the slaves as among the whites there were social distinctions. A lady's maid, a "mammy," a butler, a coachman, and a cook held the highest positions. They had better meals, better clothing, less work, and, on the whole, better treatment than the field hands. Often they were endeared to the family and held positions of confidence.

Many stories have been told of the harsh treatment of Negroes on Southern plantations. No doubt some of these were true. Often unintelligent and severe overseers were employed. Slave-owners sometimes found great difficulty in hiring good men to oversee their fields.

The records of the overseers themselves, however, reveal that many of them were intelligent and conscientious in their duties. Note, for example, a letter from one overseer to his employer:

> I killed 28 head of beef for the people's Christmas dinner. I can do more with them this way than if all the hides of the cattle were made into lashes.

Accounts of visitors to the Old South vary so much that it is difficult to know the extent of ill treatment of the Negroes. We are inclined to think today that it was much exaggerated by Northern advocates of abolition. We know that some overseers were tyrannical and brutal. We know that there were runaway slaves. Probably, however, the treatment of the slaves in the South was no worse than that frequently accorded to employees in the mills and factories in the North. In the two sections the conditions of the poor — either white or black — were much alike.

We know, furthermore, that on many plantations masters and servants lived in close touch and with warm friendliness.

The wiser slave-owners — and there were many such — were considerate of the family relations of slaves. There are many records of planters who refused to sell the members of a family separately; there are other records of those who refused to buy slaves because the slaves had expressed a dislike for them as owners. One planter, for example, wrote in his diary that he had refused to purchase a slave because "entirely contrary to what I expected, Henry objected to belonging to me."

When the "old massa" or the "old missus" died, there was sure to be wailing in the quarters. The mourning was due partly to real affection and partly to the fear that the plantation would be divided and that slave families might be separated through a public sale of property. When slaves died, owners regretted their loss, not only because they were valuable property but also because many had been loved by the planter's family. One planter wrote after the death of a slave child: "He was a remarkable child of his age, a pet of us all. I feel as if I had lost some dear relative."

Culture in the Old South

We have now had brief glimpses of the social life of the South before 1860. Under the conditions we have described would you expect a high development of education and the arts? Among some classes, yes; among others, no. The great rank and file of the Southern people, like their fellows in the North, were illiterate. Among the poor white farmers, especially, schools of any description were rare and books and magazines were almost never found.

Among the wealthy planters, however, culture had reached an advanced state. Both on the plantations and in the cities elementary-school instruction was given, for the most part, by tutors. The public high school was almost unknown. Virginia and South Carolina had private military academies which prepared young men for college, but both secondary and elementary instruction was given largely by tutors. There were a few "female academies," well developed on the side of the "accomplishments"—"embroidery, wax work, and hair flowers"— but weak on the side of learning. The young ladies on the plantation learned the practical necessities from their mothers and from their "mammies."

By 1860 it was estimated that there were more young men from the lower South in college than from any other section of the country, but the greater part of these were enrolled in Northern colleges or European universities. One investigation showed that at the moment that Massachusetts had 1733 students enrolled in college the Southern states, with approximately twice the white population, had 11,000.

At the University of Virginia a thousand young men gathered from every state of the South with their servants, their horses, and their hounds. The professors of Southern universities, under the leadership of Thomas R. Dew, were writing a new philosophy of life for the cotton planter. In the 1840's and 1850's this philosophy was stimulating a love for the Southland and a loyalty to her.

In the leading centers of culture and social life — Charleston, Richmond, and New Orleans — there was a considerable development of literature. A novelist and poet of no mean ability was William Gilmore Simms. He sprang from the humbler class, but while he was yet young his ability in picturing the life of the Southern farmers and frontiersmen and of the laborers on the levees attracted much attention. Some of his characters — Supple Jack Bannister, Thumb-Screw, and Isaac Muggs — suggest similar characters in the writings of Mark Twain. Simms also wrote poetry, issuing before his death twenty volumes of verse. Toward the end of his life he achieved a rather large income from his writing, and acquired a few slaves and a fine home.

Simms was only one of an important group of writers who portrayed life in the Old South. Joseph Baldwin, for example, pictured the characteristic social types in Virginia. A. B. Longstreet, William Tappan Thompson, and Johnson Jones Hooper did likewise for other parts of the South. Thus we see that in the South as in the North a literary tradition was developing.

You have now had glimpses of the social and cultural life of the South. Our next chapter will introduce you to the conflict which arose between this section and the North.

INTERESTING READINGS FROM WHICH YOU CAN GET ADDITIONAL INFORMATION

CABLE, GEORGE W. The Grandissimes. Charles Scribner's Sons, New York. A charming background of old New Orleans.

CABLE, GEORGE W. Old Creole Days. Charles Scribner's Sons, New York. A story of old New Orleans before the Civil War.

HARRIS, JOEL CHANDLER. Uncle Remus, his Songs and his Sayings. D. Appleton and Company, New York.

PAGE, THOMAS NELSON. In Ole Virginia. Charles Scribner's Sons, New York. Tales of Negroes and white people on an old Virginia plantation.

PAGE, THOMAS NELSON. Two Little Confederates. Charles Scribner's Sons, New York. A story of the Civil War and its effect upon two little Southerners and their family.

SAXON, LYLE. Old Louisiana. The Century Co., New York. Interesting, accurate stories of old Louisiana and its people.

STOWE, HARRIET BEECHER. Uncle Tom's Cabin. Houghton Mifflin Company, Boston.

UNIT VI

THE GREAT CONFLICT: ONE UNITED
NATION OR TWO?

THE GREAT CONFLICT: ONE UNITED NATION OR TWO?

At this point we must turn to one of the most important conflicts in American history — the conflict between the North and the South over slavery and the Union.

The conflict between sections was not new. From the very beginning of the colonies political history had been chiefly the story of conflict between groups and between sections which differed in climate, soil, and natural resources, as well as in cultural traditions.

After 1825 the differences which had long existed between the North and the South steadily became more acute. A vital issue had arisen: Should human beings be held in slavery? The same issue was even then being debated in Europe and other parts of the world.

In Chapters XIV to XVII we shall study the manner in which this conflict engaged the American people for several decades. In Chapter XIV we shall watch the scenes of the developing slavery controversy itself. In Chapter XV will be continued the story of political parties and presidents from Jackson's administration until the Civil War. In Chapter XVI we shall study the Civil War and how it brought about a new social and economic revolution. Finally, in Chapter XVII, we shall see the distressing period of reconstruction in the South.

CHAPTER XIV

THE CONTROVERSY OVER SLAVERY

In every race and nation there has been slavery

Slavery! The buying and selling of human beings! Throughout the history of man this practice has existed. It was prevalent among the early Hebrews. In ancient Greece most of the population were slaves. The Romans, in conquering the peoples of Europe, the Near East, and northern Africa, enslaved tens of thousands of people, both white and black. Then, throughout the 1000-year period of the Middle Ages, the mass of the population lived enslaved as serfs on the land. Like houses, implements, and tools, they were part of the lord's property. Indeed, not until 1863 did slavery entirely disappear from Europe.

In considering the difficult problem of slavery in America we must remember that for thousands of years the right of people to hold others in slavery was scarcely ever questioned. Moreover, whenever it was questioned, there were many who believed in it sincerely and brought arguments in defense of it. What did Americans believe in regard to slavery?

THE ATTITUDE OF AMERICANS TOWARD SLAVERY BEFORE 1800

In *A History of American Civilization* you have already read the story of the growth of slavery during the first 200 years of American history. You know that during the 1600's and 1700's the New Englanders made fortunes from their "triangular trade." When the Constitution of the United States was signed, there were slaves in every state in the Union.

Meanwhile, however, feeling was growing against the buying and selling of human beings. In the *original* draft of the Declaration of Independence the King of England was definitely charged with encouraging the slave trade. The King had violated human nature's "most sacred rights of life and liberty in the persons of distant people who never offended him, captivating and carrying them into slavery in another hemisphere."

This passage was omitted from the final draft of the Declaration, but it shows us the general point of view of many prominent citizens. Most of the leaders were opposed to slavery. Even the Southerners, among whom were Washington, Jefferson, and Randolph, openly spoke their regret at carrying on the system. Some of them found a way gradually to free their slaves.[1]

Then came the cotton gin and textile machines, and slavery increased in the South

As you know, the work of ridding the cotton of its seeds was a hand process in 1792. Only a small amount could be prepared in a day. Since the demand for cotton was not great and the profits were small, it did not pay to keep large numbers of slaves.

Had the age of invention been postponed and had the cotton gin not been devised, it is quite possible that slavery would have died out in the South in much the same way as it was dying out in the North. But the cotton gin *was* invented; spinning and weaving machines *were* devised; and a great demand for large amounts of cotton sprang up, both in old England and in New England. The South had the appropriate climate and soil in which to grow the plant. It also had plenty of cheap labor to cultivate, pick, and gin the cotton. The Southerners began to move out from the Atlantic plain to the more fertile lands of the lower South — to Mississippi, Alabama, and Louisiana — and there to build up their powerful cotton kingdom.

Thus by the time Andrew Jackson was put into the White House on the rising tide of democracy, many Southern families had large cotton plantations and had become owners of numbers of Negro slaves. Their homes, their livelihood, and the continuance of their ways of living depended upon slavery. They were becoming determined to keep it at all costs.

[1] By 1860 there were half a million free Negroes in the South. These Negroes did not enjoy the full rights of American citizens, however, but they could own land and work for wages as did white people. Some of them also owned slaves.

The "Geography" of Slavery

By 1800 the "geography" of slavery was beginning to be clearly marked out. The South was depending largely on slave labor, the North largely on free labor. Free labor meant that each person either worked for himself, as in the case of the small farmers, storekeepers, and factory-owners, or worked for somebody else for wages. Throughout the North, therefore, each man was considered free to work for whom he pleased and for the best wages he could get. In those days if he were not satisfied with his lot, he could always move West and establish a homestead on the frontier — if he knew a little about farming and had saved a small amount of money.

Mason and Dixon's line and its western continuation

In 1760 Mason and Dixon, two surveyors employed by Pennsylvania and Maryland, had surveyed the line marking the boundary between those two colonies. (See figure 117.) When the line was surveyed there were six Southern colonies and seven Northern colonies.

The Second Continental Congress passed the Ordinance of the Northwest Territory in 1787. The ordinance prohibited slavery forever in this new territory north of the Ohio River. In the meantime, as the Western lands were settled, the latitude of 36° 30', just south of the junction of the Mississippi and Ohio rivers, had come to be regarded as the continuation of Mason and Dixon's line, although no provision had been made to forbid slavery in lands west of the Mississippi. It was generally understood in the North, however, that 36° 30' marked the limit north of which slavery would be forever prohibited.

How new states were admitted after 1789

In 1791 Vermont joined the Union as a *free* state; in 1792 Kentucky, which had been a part of Virginia, joined as a *slave* state. Then, in 1796, Tennessee, formerly a part of North Carolina, joined the Union as a *slave* state. In 1803 Ohio entered as a *free* state. Nine years later (1812) Louisiana was admitted as a *slave* state. At that time there were *eighteen states evenly divided* — *nine slave and nine free*.

For a long time this even division was maintained. In 1816 Indiana was admitted as a *free* state and, in 1817, Mississippi as a *slave* state. In 1818 Illinois joined as a *free* state and, in 1819, Alabama as a *slave* state. Thirty years after Washington's inauguration the Union had grown from thirteen states to twenty-two states, evenly divided — eleven free and eleven slave.

Thus by 1819 two important sections had grown up, one of which favored slavery, while the other frowned upon it. All leaders in the two sections of the country, including editors of newspapers and Congressmen, were giving serious attention to the issue. As each new Western territory applied for admission to the Union during the next 40 years, members of Congress either favored or opposed its entrance largely on the basis of whether it would become a slave state or a free state. One reason for maintaining a balance between slave and free states was that each new state added two new members to the Senate. As long as the number of free and slave states was the same, neither side could outvote the other in the Senate on a sectional issue.

The Missouri Compromise, 1820

In 1819, when Missouri applied for admission to the Union as a slave state, there was a heated debate on the floor of Congress. Missouri was not within the Northwest Territory, but it lay north of 36° 30′. In many communities lecturers on the platform, editors in their newspapers, and preachers in their pulpits argued the matter. Naturally, the South wished the territories beyond the Mississippi River to enter the Union as slave states, and, just as naturally, the North wished them to be free states. In 1820 the two sections came to an agreement and passed a law called the Missouri Compromise. This provided that the latitude 36° 30′ should serve as the dividing line through the Louisiana territory; that all territory north of this line, except Missouri, should come in as free states; that Missouri should enter as a *slave* state; and that Maine, for a long time a part of Massachusetts, should be admitted as a *free* state.

THE CONTROVERSY OVER SLAVERY 287

So the matter stood for sixteen years. In 1836 Arkansas was admitted to the Union as a *slave* state and, in 1837, Michigan as a *free* state. In that year the 26 states were still evenly divided, 13 against 13. Although slavery was not by any means a dead

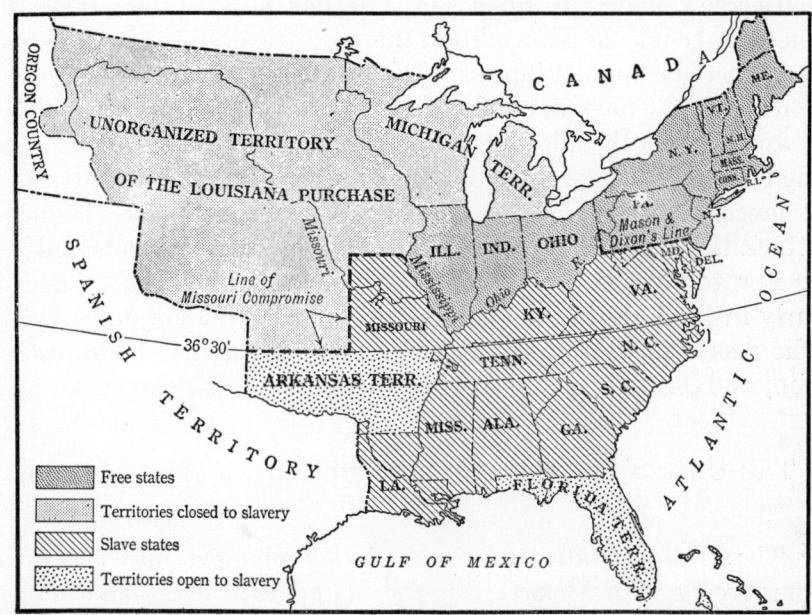

FIG. 117. The map shows how the United States in 1820 was divided over the slavery issue. East of the Mississippi River, Mason and Dixon's line and the Ohio River form the dividing line; west of the Mississippi, with the exception of Missouri, the latitude 36° 30' separates the slave territory from the free

issue, no other states were admitted to the Union between 1837 and 1845. Other events were taking place, however, which were to strain the relations of the North and the South.

The Admission of Texas and the Mexican War

You have already read in *A History of American Civilization* the story of the settlement of the Mexican province of Texas by Americans. You learned that after 1821 this Mexican territory was overrun by colonists from the United States. These settlers finally set up their own government, organized an army under General Sam Houston, decisively defeated the Mexicans, and declared their independence. In 1837 the Republic of Texas was recognized not only by the United States but also by Great Britain and several of the other European countries.

Some months before recognition was given, however, the Texans had asked Congress to annex Texas to the United States. If the request had come 25 years earlier, there is little doubt that Congress would have complied immediately. But in 1837 Northern Representatives in Congress opposed the annexation for the reason that it would mean the addition of a huge amount of slave territory to the Union. So vigorously did John Quincy Adams (at the time a Representative in Congress) and his Northern associates lead the attack that in 1838 a resolution to annex Texas was defeated.

For ten years the struggle over Texas continued. Finally, early in 1845, during the administration of President John Tyler, who was sympathetic to slavery, Congress approved the resolution, and Texas was admitted to the Union as a slave state.

The United States conquers More Land from Mexico, 1846–1848

The United States was immediately plunged into a serious controversy with Mexico over the boundaries of the land which had been annexed to the United States. Mexico had never officially admitted the loss of Texas itself and had notified the American government that she would regard the annexation of Texas as a sufficient cause for war. Yet when the United States annexed Texas, it was not the *annexation* which was protested by Mexico, but the boundary. The Mexicans insisted that their powerful northern neighbor was annexing *too much* territory, for the United States government claimed all the land (see the map of figure 118) as far south as the Rio Grande, while the Mexicans maintained that the boundary was the Nueces River. (Notice on the map the strip of territory which was in dispute.)

In January, 1846, President James K. Polk ordered General Zachary Taylor and 10,000 soldiers to hold the Rio Grande as the boundary line. It is said that Mexican soldiers fired upon them, maintaining that they were upon Mexican soil. . Several Americans were killed and others were wounded.

THE CONTROVERSY OVER SLAVERY

Polk and his advisers now had a reason for military conquest. Mexico, they could maintain, had committed an act of aggression. War could be declared — and it was. Congress appropriated $10,000,000 and authorized the raising of an army of 50,000 men.

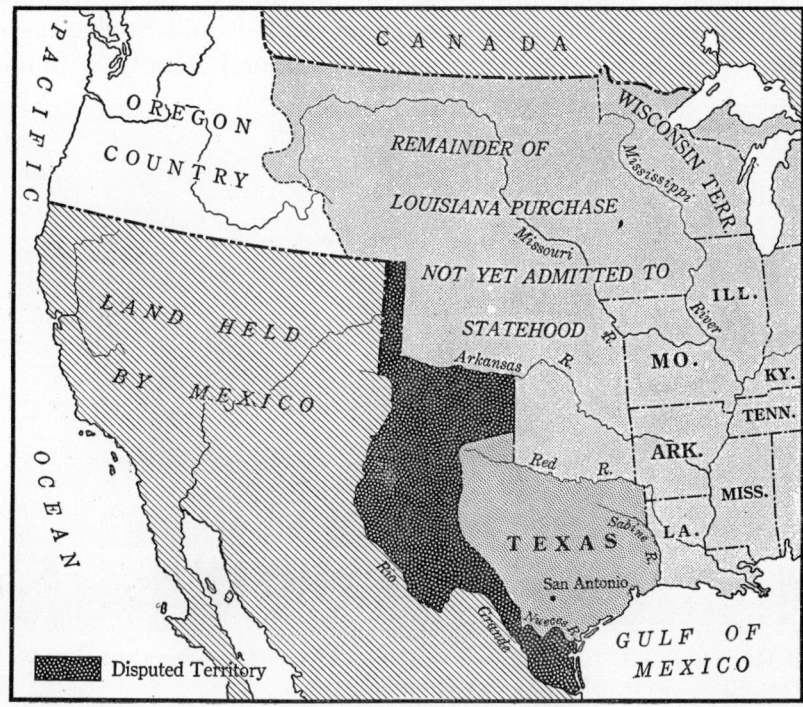

Fig. 118. The map shows the lands in western North America which belonged to the United States and those which belonged to Mexico in 1845. It also shows the land whose ownership was disputed by both countries. The newly admitted state of Texas claimed the land between the Rio Grande and the Nueces River, and the United States upheld the claim

Three campaigns were launched against the Mexicans:

1. An army under General Taylor crossed the Rio Grande and defeated the weak Mexican troops at Monterrey and at Buena Vista.

At these successes feverish enthusiasm for the war spread all over the United States — throughout the North as well as the South. Volunteers were recruited and hurried off to the southern boundary.

2. A second army of American soldiers, under General Winfield Scott, crossed the Gulf of Mexico and landed at Vera Cruz. From there they marched inland and, after a campaign of several months, captured the capital, Mexico City.

3. Another campaign was launched in the extreme Southwest. A naval contingent under Commanders Sloat and Stockton coöperated with the well-known explorer General John C. Frémont

Fig. 119. General Scott's army landing at Vera Cruz. (Courtesy of the New York Historical Society)

and soon made themselves masters of the coastal region of California. In the meantime a small army under Colonel Stephen W. Kearny had marched southwestward from Fort Leavenworth across the disputed territory. (See the map of figure 120.) Had the Mexican opposition been at all powerful this expedition would have been a most foolhardy military campaign. The American forces were small, the troops were badly equipped, and they lacked adequate food and water supplies. Throughout the long march, however, they met with little resistance. At Santa Fe the Mexicans surrendered almost at once. From there Kearny continued his march southwestward and finally joined Frémont's forces in southern California.

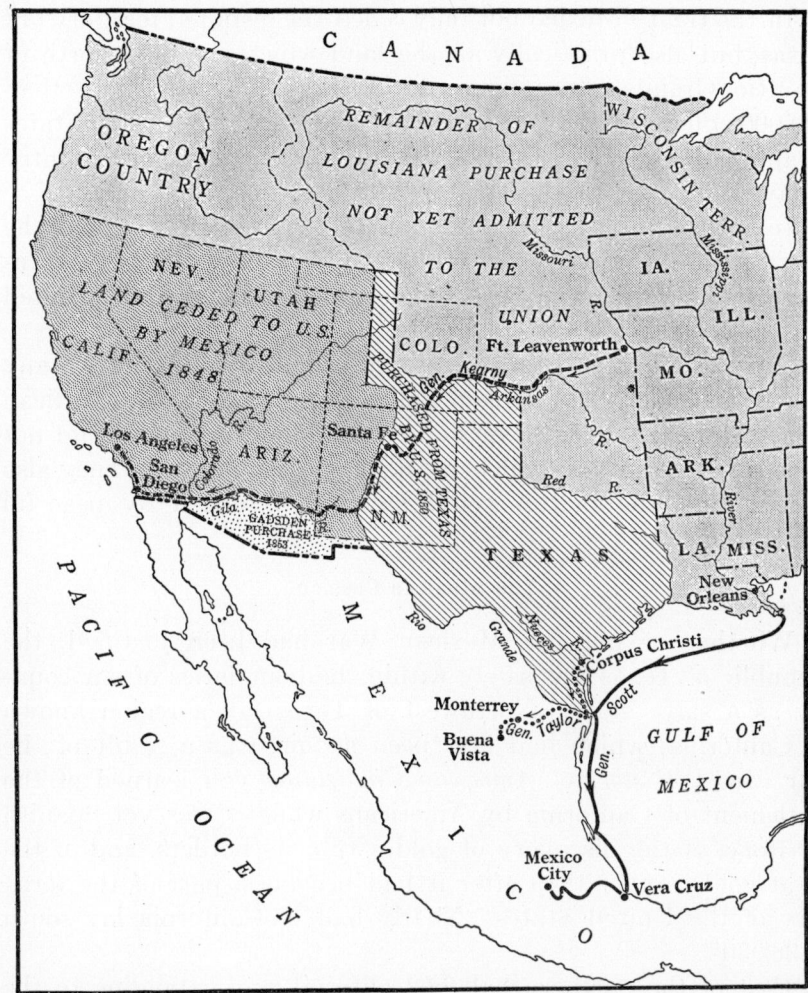

Fig. 120. The routes of Generals Scott, Taylor, and Kearny during the Mexican War. The war resulted in the Mexican surrender of the disputed territory shown in figure 118. Through the war also all the territory held by Mexico from the present boundary of Mexico northward to the Oregon country was ceded to the United States except for the small strip marked "Gadsden Purchase." The Gadsden Purchase was added to the United States in 1853

On every side and in every battle the powerless Mexican troops were defeated. On February 2, 1848, their government made a treaty of peace with the United States and ended an unfortunate if not a dishonorable war.

In the treaty Mexico not only ceded the disputed territory [1] of Texas, but also practically all the land which she held north of the Rio Grande. (See figure 120.) Besides Texas more than 500,000 square miles of territory were added to the United States — approximately one sixth of the total land area of our country today.

In return for this vast domain the United States paid the Mexican government $15,000,000.[2] The United States government also agreed to pay the claims which citizens of the United States held against Mexico.

Thus the United States again spread its boundaries. Many Northern leaders had spoken and written against the Mexican War. Many students have since maintained that we would not have entered into this war had Mexico been powerful. They also believe that the matter could have been settled by peaceful arbitration.

The Mexican Cession

Whether or not the Mexican War had been justified, the Republic of Texas was safely within the boundaries of our country as a slave state. Northwest of Texas lay a region known as California, which had also been acquired as a result of the war. In *A History of American Civilization* you learned of the settlement of California by Americans while it was yet Spanish territory, of the discovery of gold within its borders, and of the great gold rush of 1849 after it had become a part of the territory of the United States. Nearly half of California lay south of 36° 30′.

East of the northern half of California and extending to the borders of Nebraska lay the land called Utah. The Mormons had settled here in 1847. They had been driven from one place to another because many Americans disapproved of their religion. Finally, in 1847, they settled outside the borders of the

---

[1] Some of the disputed territory was bought from Texas by the American government and later became parts of five new states.

[2] Five years later another small strip of territory was bought from Mexico for $10,000,000. This is shown on the map of figure 120, along the southern border of New Mexico and Arizona. The purchase was arranged by an American, James Gadsden, and has been known in American history as the Gadsden Purchase.

THE CONTROVERSY OVER SLAVERY 293

United States in order that they might, in the wild, unsettled land, live free from persecution. Then, by the Mexican treaty of 1848, the land in which they had settled was ceded by Mexico, and they found themselves again within the United States. Other settlers came to join them. Soon iron was found near by, which attracted more people to this part of the country. By 1850 so many had come that Utah Territory [1] was organized. Most of this territory, as you can see by the map of figure 122, lay north of Mason and Dixon's line. You will see later how the slavery question was settled in this territory.

Extending south from the border of Utah Territory to the northern border of Mexico lay another part of the cession of 1848. Soon after it was acquired it was given a military government, and the region became known as New Mexico. Territorial organization was set up in 1850, but it was not until 1912 that the two states of Arizona and New Mexico were formed from it and admitted. These two states were the last to enter the Union, and completed the "United States" as we know it today. Almost all New Mexico Territory lay south of 36° 30'; but there was little likelihood that it would become slave territory, for the land was not suited to cotton production.

The peaceful settlement of the Oregon claims

While the Mexican War was in progress another boundary dispute arose.

You know that the United States had northern neighbors as well as southern neighbors. One long strip of land extending from California to Alaska (then owned by Russia) was claimed by the United States. It was also claimed by Great Britain as a part of Canada. This tract was called Oregon. By a treaty in 1818 the United States and Great Britain agreed to hold the land jointly.

You remember, from your study of *A History of American Civilization*, the story of the heroic men and women who dared the Oregon Trail and who were welcomed into Oregon by John

---

[1] From Utah Territory the state of Utah, most of Nevada, and part of Colorado were formed.

McLoughlin, the manager of the English trading post. Americans settled the land in such great numbers that by 1843 they had framed their own territorial constitution for this tract.

A prolonged dispute arose over the ownership of the region. The claim of the United States extended as far north as Alaska, that is, to latitude 54° 40'. So heated did the dispute become that in 1844 it was one of the issues of the American presidential election. Indeed, one of the ringing slogans of the Democrats in that political campaign was "Fifty-four forty or fight!" In 1846, however, an understanding was reached, and a treaty was signed by the two countries. By its terms the United States accepted the land south of the 49th parallel and Great Britain received (as a part of Canada) the land from that parallel to Russian Alaska. The part granted to the United States was organized into a regular territory in 1848,[1] and slavery was forbidden within its boundaries.

What a contrast there is between the stories of these two disputes, the one with Mexico and the other with Great Britain! The first was settled only after war; the second, by peaceful arbitration.

The Louisiana territory

What was happening in the great region called Louisiana, which had been purchased by Jefferson in 1804?

By 1846, as you remember, four states had already been formed from it — Louisiana, Missouri, Arkansas, and Iowa. The first three had been admitted as slave states, although Missouri lay north of 36° 30', while the fourth, Iowa, was a free state.

Almost all the rest of Jefferson's purchase lay to the west of these states, extending as far as the Rocky Mountains. This region was called Missouri until the admission of the state of Missouri, when its name was changed to Nebraska. Its 485,000 square miles were almost uninhabited by white people, and it had no local *white* government. Almost all the land lay north of 36° 30'; so it was to be expected that the states formed from it would be free states.

---

[1] This territory was later divided, and two states were made of it — Oregon (admitted 1859) and Washington (admitted 1889).

THE CONTROVERSY OVER SLAVERY

You will learn later how the slavery controversy raged anew when it was proposed to give Nebraska[1] territorial rights.

From this short résumé of the formation of Western territories and states between 1845 and 1850 you now have a picture of the lands west of the Mississippi. You also have a background which will help you to understand the discussions about slavery that were taking place from the Atlantic to the Pacific, reaching their height in Congress.

During these years the last two areas east of the Mississippi River which had not yet received statehood were admitted. Florida came into the Union in 1845 and Wisconsin in 1848.[2] With the admission of Wisconsin the number of states had grown to 30 — 15 slave and 15 free. The balance had been retained. But what of this great Western area — Nebraska, California, Utah, and New Mexico? Would the latitude 36° 30′ continue to divide the slave states from the free states?

The Compromise of 1850: the North got California and the South got the Fugitive Slave Law

In 1849 California, which was largely populated by Northerners, asked to be admitted to the Union as a free state. Immediately open defiance arose from the South. There were definite threats to secede if California were admitted, just as there had been similar threats on the part of New England Congressmen over the annexation of Texas. Prominent men on both sides openly suggested dividing the nation into two independent countries. Many Northerners cared little if the Southerners did secede. John Quincy Adams, a few years earlier while still a Representative in Congress, had frankly declared his belief that the two sections could not live together as one nation.

Throughout this period of conflict two individuals expended their best efforts to bring the sections to an agreement, namely,

---

[1] From the Nebraska territory the states of North Dakota, South Dakota, Nebraska, Kansas, Oklahoma, and parts of the states of Montana, Wyoming, and Colorado were formed.

[2] West Virginia had been admitted as a part of Virginia, and it was not until 1863 that it became a separate state.

Henry Clay and Daniel Webster. Clay, who had retired from Congress eight years before, now stepped out of this retirement to plead "peace, concord, and harmony." He had made similar pleas before, especially in the case of the Missouri Compromise. For this policy he had earned the name "the Great Pacificator." Webster in his great Seventh-of-March speech also took a conciliatory attitude and asked that a compromise be made. Finally, these two men succeeded in arranging the Compromise of 1850, thereby staving off war for a few years longer.

The Compromise of 1850 had several provisions: first, California was to come in as a free state; second, the slave trade (but not slavery) was prohibited in the District of Columbia; third, the new territories of New Mexico and Utah were themselves to settle whether they would have slavery or not (this was properly known as popular sovereignty, but was usually called squatter sovereignty); fourth, a new and more effective Fugitive Slave Law was to be passed. This law stated that any slave who had escaped might be seized by his owner or his owner's representative and must be returned, no matter in what state or territory the runaway had been found. He was not entitled to a trial by jury.

The Compromise of 1850 disposed of the question of slavery in three of the five areas that we have been discussing (see figure 122).

The Fugitive Slave Law stirred up More Trouble

Neither the North nor the South was really satisfied with the compromise. The Fugitive Slave Law, especially, called forth a blast of protest. Citizens were required to aid officers in their search for runaway slaves. Ralph Waldo Emerson, the gentle philosopher, said of it:

We shall never feel well again until that detestable law is nullified in Massachusetts . . . all I have and all I can do shall be given and done in opposition to the execution of the law.

Something that happened in Boston in 1854 illustrates the revolt of the North against this law.

THE CONTROVERSY OVER SLAVERY

Anthony Burns, a fugitive slave, was arrested in Boston on May 24, 1854; and a futile attempt at rescue, led by Theodore Parker, Wendell Phillips and Thomas Wentworth Higginson, was made on the night of the 26th. On June 2 the slave was marched to the wharf through a crowd of fifty thousand jeering and groaning people, and placed on board a Federal revenue cutter to be taken back to the South. To guard the streets that day the authorities used the Boston police, twenty-two companies of Massachusetts soldiers, a battalion of Federal artillery, four platoons of marines, and a large civil posse. The cost of remanding the prisoner southward was nearly $40,000.[1]

The "underground railroad"

Between 1830 and 1850 many Negroes escaped from their masters and lived in freedom either in the North or in Canada. While fleeing northward many of them were hidden during the day in the homes of friends. By night they passed on to other towns. This scheme was called the "underground railroad." There were "stations" from Kentucky and Virginia across Ohio, and from Maryland across Pennsylvania and New York to New England.

Although it involved some risk, many Northerners, even the leaders in the communities, helped the Negroes to escape and sometimes rescued fugitive slaves from officers or owners even in broad daylight. They wrote signed communications to the newspapers, declaring that they had aided slaves and calling on anybody to "prosecute me if you dare!" Generally nobody did. One couldn't have got together a jury in many Northern towns that would have brought in a verdict of guilty.

You see that the Compromise of 1850 did not solve *all* the difficulties of the situation.

THE KANSAS-NEBRASKA BILL AROUSED THE COUNTRY FURTHER

In 1854 Senator Stephen A. Douglas of Illinois read a report to the Senate which had been prepared by the committee on territories. In the report was proposed the Kansas-Nebraska Bill, which provided that all the territory west of Missouri,

---

[1] Allen Nevins, *American Press Opinion*, p. 198. D. C. Heath & Co., 1928.

known as Nebraska, should be divided into two territories; that these should have territorial governments and should be permitted to enter the Union "with or without slavery" as the separate territories themselves should decide in their constitutions.

This plan sounded well, but immediately the Northern people opposed it bitterly. Why? Because the Missouri Compromise of 1820 had already provided that (except Missouri) all the land north of 36° 30′ through the Louisiana territory should *always be free territory*. The Kansas-Nebraska Bill would make it possible for the region to become slave territory. In the North meetings were held and protests were made. Many people who before had wanted to avoid trouble with the South were angry and ready to fight.

Others thought that the balance would be kept as it had been for so long, Nebraska deciding upon a free government and Kansas voting for a slave government.

FIG. 121. Stephen Douglas

The Missouri Compromise was repealed, and the Kansas-Nebraska Bill became a law (1854). Immediately the South was determined that Kansas and Nebraska should be slave territories; the North, that they should be free. From the Northern states came thousands of emigrants, many of whom were helped by the New England Emigrant Aid Society. They built their shacks and new rambling towns over the flat prairie land which was Kansas.

The Southern people claimed that these Northerners were not real settlers; that they were sent just to keep Kansas from becoming slave territory and that they should be driven out. Across the border from Missouri came bands of slave-owners to settle other new towns.

Then came the effort to set up a government in Kansas. Southerners from Missouri came across the border to vote in the Kansas elections. This practice was illegal, of course, but it went on for several years. Both sides were armed. Both sides carried on warfare. Each burned and ravaged the property of

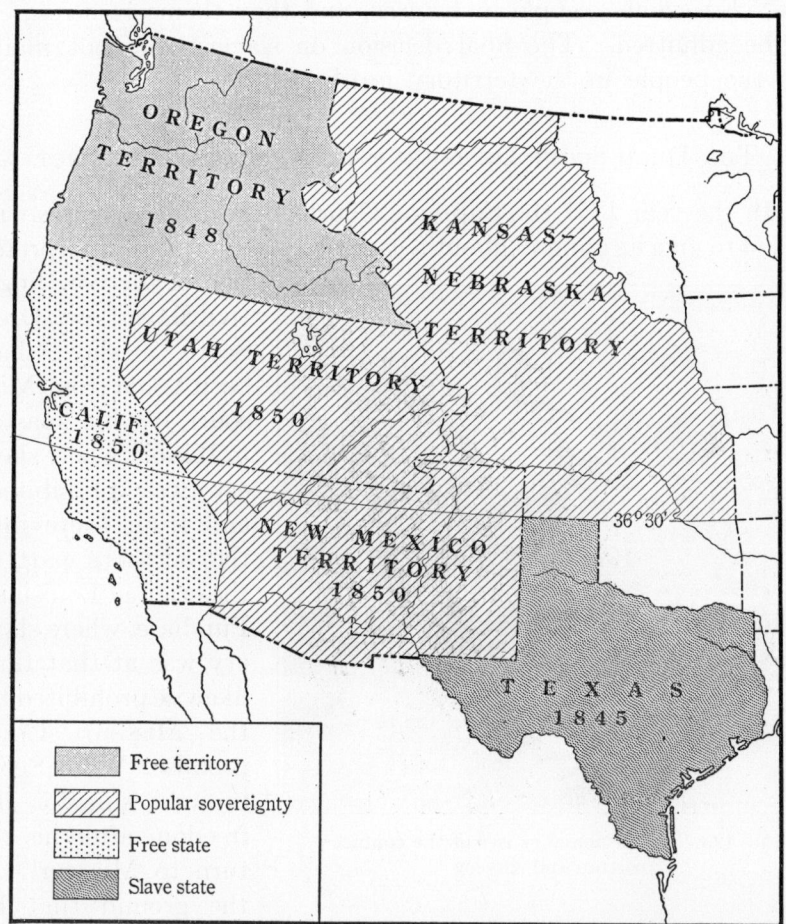

FIG. 122. This map shows how the question of slavery divided the western half of the United States in 1854. Where the territories were allowed "popular sovereignty" they could decide for themselves whether or not they would allow slavery within their borders

the other. At one time *two* governments were actually set up in Kansas — one a slave government and the other a free one. The struggle became increasingly bitter, and "Bleeding Kansas" was the theme of more than one editorial in the 1850's. Three years after the Kansas-Nebraska Bill of 1854 became a law the recommendation was made to Congress by the President that Kansas be admitted as a state. The conditions were not satisfactory to the "Free Soil" people in Kansas, and they themselves refused to be admitted. The final decision on slavery was not made by the people in the territory until 1861.

THE DRED SCOTT DECISION INTENSIFIED THE CONFLICT

In the year 1857 the Supreme Court of the United States was asked to give its opinion about a case which required an interpretation of the new Fugitive Slave Law. Dred Scott, a slave, had been taken from Missouri by his master to Illinois, where slavery was prohibited, and from there into the northern part of the original Louisiana Purchase, where slavery was at that time likewise prohibited by the Missouri Compromise. When Scott brought suit for his freedom after his return to Missouri, on the ground that he had been in free territory, the Supreme Court denied his plea and took occasion to state its views regarding slaves and slavery.

FIG. 123. The principal causes of the conflict — cotton and slavery

"Congress has no right," said the Supreme Court, "to exclude slavery from the territories." This meant that the master of Dred Scott could regard him as a slave in free as well as in slave territory. The Supreme Court also took the position that the Constitution did not give citizenship to slaves and that only citizens had the right to ask aid of the law.

THE CONTROVERSY OVER SLAVERY

The South was pleased. "The nation has achieved a triumph," said the *Richmond Enquirer*. "Sectionalism has been rebuked and abolitionism has been staggered and stunned. Another supporting pillar has been added to our institutions."

The North was enraged. "Alas, that the character of the Supreme Court of the United States as an impartial judicial body has gone!" cried a writer in the *New York Tribune*. "It has abdicated its just functions and descended into the political mire. It has sullied the ermine; it has draggled and polluted its garments in the filth of pro-slavery politics."[1]

The Crusade against Slavery

Early indifference

In the 1820's and 1830's the rank and file of the American people were not much concerned about slavery. In the South the greater number of people were small farmers, owning no slaves at all, and these men paid little heed to the growing national problem. Even more indifferent to it were the mass of Northern farmers, artisans, and clerks. On the other hand, the *Northern manufacturers* of cotton yarns and cloth, who depended on the cotton kingdom for their raw material, favored slavery. Their profits were made possible by it. Similarly, most of the bankers and shippers favored it. All these groups, therefore, stayed outside the movement for its abolition.

A small group of abolitionists led the crusade

In both the North and the South, however, a few bold leaders had demanded that the slaves be freed. Among these leaders several men and several women stood out above all the others. Chief among them were Benjamin Lundy, James G. Birney, William Lloyd Garrison, the Grimké sisters, and Frances Wright. In this movement also the Society of Friends, or Quakers, of whom we have already heard, played a very important part.

Benjamin Lundy, a New Jersey Quaker who had lived for

[1] Theodore C. Smith, *Parties and Slavery*, p. 205. Harper & Brothers, New York, 1906.

some years in the western part of Virginia, began to hate actively the buying and selling of human beings which he saw going on around him. In a little Ohio village he and his neighbors organized the Union Humane Society. Rapidly the society grew until it numbered hundreds of members. Indeed, the greater part of Lundy's life was spent in launching this movement to abolish slavery. He published abolition newspapers, and he repeatedly took his life in his hands in speaking out publicly against slavery. For twenty years he traveled through the North and the South, lecturing as he went.

At the same time James G. Birney, the son of a wealthy slaveholder in Dansville, Kentucky, was carrying on the work. At the age of 24 he was already working against slavery in the Kentucky legislature. Later, although keeping slaves on his plantation, he still believed in providing for the gradual emancipation of the Negroes. In 1834 Birney freed his own slaves and became one of the leaders in the American Antislavery Society. He traveled widely over the country, addressing abolition meetings and state legislatures. In 1836 he established an abolitionist newspaper, the *Philanthropist*, in Cincinnati.

FIG. 124. Angelina Grimké

Liberty-loving women too joined the movement. Among the leaders of these women were Sarah and Angelina Grimké, born in Charleston, South Carolina, "of a slaveholding family noted for learning, refinement, and culture." For years Angelina Grimké proved to be one of the most powerful orators of the abolition cause.

Frances Wright also made a gallant attempt to help the slaves. She founded in Tennessee a colony called Nashoba, where she and her friends bought as many Negroes as they could, freed them, and tried to educate them. The Nashoba colony was so persecuted, however, that Miss Wright was finally obliged to move it to Haiti.

William Lloyd Garrison declares war on slavery

Let Southern Oppressors tremble. I shall strenuously contend for immediate enfranchisement. . . . I will be as harsh as truth and as uncompromising as justice. . . . I do not wish to think, or speak or write with moderation. . . . I am in earnest — I will not equivocate — I will not retreat a single inch — and I *will be heard*.

That is the startling paragraph that appeared in 1831 at the head of a new Boston paper called the *Liberator*. It was printed by a young man named William Lloyd Garrison, who was so poor that he had to buy paper on credit and set up the type himself.

During the same year (1831) Nat Turner, a Negro of Southampton County in Virginia, led an insurrection of slaves against their white masters. In this uprising 61 whites were killed. Terror spread throughout the South, and slave-owners in Congress and out launched attacks upon the abolitionists. Many claimed that Garrison and his associates were directly responsible for the massacre. Garrison denied this, and history has failed to prove that he was responsible.

In 1833 Garrison organized the New England Antislavery Society, and a year later he played an important part in the establishment of the American Antislavery Society. In 1843 he printed at the head of the *Liberator*:

The compact which exists between the North and the South is a covenant with death and agreement with hell — involving both parties in atrocious criminality and should be immediately annulled.

Then he started a country-wide assault on violations of the principles of freedom of speech and freedom of the press. Southern governors sent messages and Southern legislatures passed resolutions demanding that newspaper editors and publishers residing in Northern states be given up to them for trial and conviction. Before a committee of the Massachusetts legislature

Garrison and his friends tried to defend the right of a free press and of free assemblage. Members of the legislature refused to hear them. The abolitionists denounced the Southern resolutions and messages as "fetters for Northern freemen."

In May, 1836, the House of Representatives passed the famous "gag resolution," which said that all petitions to Congress relating to slavery should "without being printed or referred [to a committee] be laid on the table, and that no further action whatever shall be had thereon." Thus the House of Representatives of the United States denied a part of the Bill of Rights that had been written into the First Amendment of the Constitution. It refused to hear petitions from the American people. This resolution was passed again in 1837, 1838, 1839, and 1840. It was repealed only after a long debate in 1844.

Fig. 125. William Lloyd Garrison

An attempt was made to prevent the use of the mails in distributing literature against slavery. Postmasters in various sections of the country illegally opened the mail and refused to deliver anything which they regarded as "incendiary." Against this practice, Amos Kendall, Jackson's Postmaster-General, refused to take action. During Andrew Jackson's second administration, the controversy had become so bitter that the President himself asked Congress to pass a law which would "prohibit, under severe penalties, the circulation in the Southern states, through the mail, of incendiary publications." Congress, however, refused to do this and instead enacted a law which required postmasters to deliver all mails turned over to them.

THE CONTROVERSY OVER SLAVERY

Most Southern leaders defended slavery

Although, as you have seen, there were abolitionists in the South, their number was small. John C. Calhoun and Robert Rhett of South Carolina, Jefferson Davis of Mississippi, and William L. Yancey of Alabama—in fact, practically all the political leaders—came out squarely in defense of slavery. Professor

FIG. 126. Robert Barnwell Rhett. (Courtesy of Robert R. Lewis)

FIG. 127. William L. Yancey. (From an old engraving)

TWO POLITICAL LEADERS IN THE SOUTH WHO FAVORED SLAVERY

Thomas R. Dew, afterward president of William and Mary College, boldly advocated it on *ethical and moral grounds*, while the poet and novelist William G. Simms of South Carolina wrote and spoke in defense of the idea that the Negroes were really happy in slavery.

JOHN BROWN'S RAID

In 1859 the country was startled by the announcement that John Brown and a little force of twenty men had seized the Federal arsenal at Harpers Ferry, Virginia.[1] Brown and his sons had been active in the slavery warfare in Kansas. They were

[1] Now in West Virginia.

now planning to establish "camps of refuge" in the mountains for escaped slaves. Brown hoped for a general uprising of Negroes throughout the South, and with the ammunition from the arsenal he meant to arm those who would rebel. He succeeded in freeing about 30 slaves and retired to the arsenal with them and his men. They were all trapped by United States marines under Colonel Robert E. Lee. Brown was captured, tried for treason, convicted, and hanged.

You have now seen that the conflict between the North and the South was deepening. In the next chapter we shall see how political parties and presidential elections were affected by the struggle.

INTERESTING READINGS FROM WHICH YOU CAN GET ADDITIONAL INFORMATION

CABLE, G. W. Old Creole Days. Charles Scribner's Sons, New York. Seven stories of New Orleans in the 1840's.

ELSON, HENRY W. Sidelights on American History. The Macmillan Company, New York. See Volume I, pp. 265–294, 295–309, 310–332, and Volume II.

HART, ALBERT B. (Editor). American History told by Contemporaries. The Macmillan Company, New York. See Volume III, pp. 574–636, and Volume IV, pp. 59–79, 80–92, 97–144.

HOUGH, EMERSON. The Purchase Price. Grosset and Dunlap, New York. The slavery question before the war.

MACY, JESSE. The Anti-Slavery Crusade, Vol. XXVIII of the Chronicles of America. Yale University Press, New Haven. Excellent reference for the best readers.

PRINGLE, E. W. A. Chronicles of Chicora Wood. Charles Scribner's Sons, New York. Southern life before and after the Civil War.

CHAPTER XV

POLITICAL PARTIES AND PRESIDENTS, 1837–1861

You will remember from preceding chapters that from Washington's election to Monroe's, 1792–1820, political leaders and voters aligned themselves with either the *Federalists* or the *Republicans*. By 1808 these party lines began to weaken, and by 1820 they had disappeared so completely that Monroe was elected to his second administration by an almost unanimous vote.

Before the election of 1824, however, two new parties arose — the *National-Republicans*, under Henry Clay and John Quincy Adams, and the *Democratic-Republicans*, under Andrew Jackson. Each took its name from the original Republican party, led by Jefferson, but the Jackson group soon became known as Democrats. You remember that Jackson, "the people's friend," defeated John Quincy Adams.

The Rise of the Whigs

In 1834, during Jackson's second administration, the National-Republicans, under the leadership of Adams and Clay, began to call themselves *Whigs*. This name was derived from the British party which was opposed to the tyranny of the king and the royalists in the House of Commons. The Whigs stood for

1. Conciliation and compromise in settling disputes between opposing interests in the United States.
2. A protective tariff.
3. A national bank.
4. Internal improvements financed by the *Federal* government.
5. A broad interpretation of the Constitution[1] and a strong central government.

[1] Those who interpret the Constitution *broadly* wish to give the Federal government not only the powers granted according to the actual wording of the Constitution but also the powers implied or suggested by that wording. This means a strong central government.

In the campaign of 1832 the Whigs chose Henry Clay as their candidate. He was defeated, however, by Andrew Jackson, the leader of what was now called the Democratic party.

For four years longer Jackson and his party "reigned." His enemies called his administration "the reign of a tyrant." There was no doubt that he was a stubborn president. One political wit of the day portrayed him as defending his own stubbornness: "It has always bin my way, when I git a notion, to stick to it till it dies a natural death; and the more folks talk agin my notions, the more I stick to 'em." And "stick to 'em" he did — increasing the spoils system, abolishing the Bank, and maintaining the Union against the nullifiers.

Even at the end of his second term of office, Jackson's influence was so powerful that he succeeded in naming his successor. He chose Martin Van Buren, who had been his Secretary of State. "Little Van" or "the Little Magician," as Van Buren was called, was nominated and won the election of 1836 on the strength of the popularity of Jackson and the Democratic party. Van Buren, however, although a close friend of Jackson, was hardly one of the plain people. He had cultivated tastes and soon restored to the White House much of the aristocratic charm and graceful manners of the days of Dolly Madison, Elizabeth Monroe, and Louisa Adams. But "Little Van" reaped the whirlwind sown by Andrew Jackson's policies. After the panic of 1837 his entire administration was marked by hard times.

The noisy campaign of 1840

Twice — in 1824 and in 1832 — Henry Clay had been defeated for the presidency. He was not a man who appealed to the mass of the people. In 1840, instead of choosing Clay or Adams or some other person who might have made public enemies, the Whigs nominated a military hero who had been remarkably successful as an Indian fighter, General William Henry Harrison. Although Harrison was something more than a soldier,— having served as governor of the Northwest Territory and as a Representative and Senator in Congress,— it was his soldierly qualities which captured the imagination of his followers.

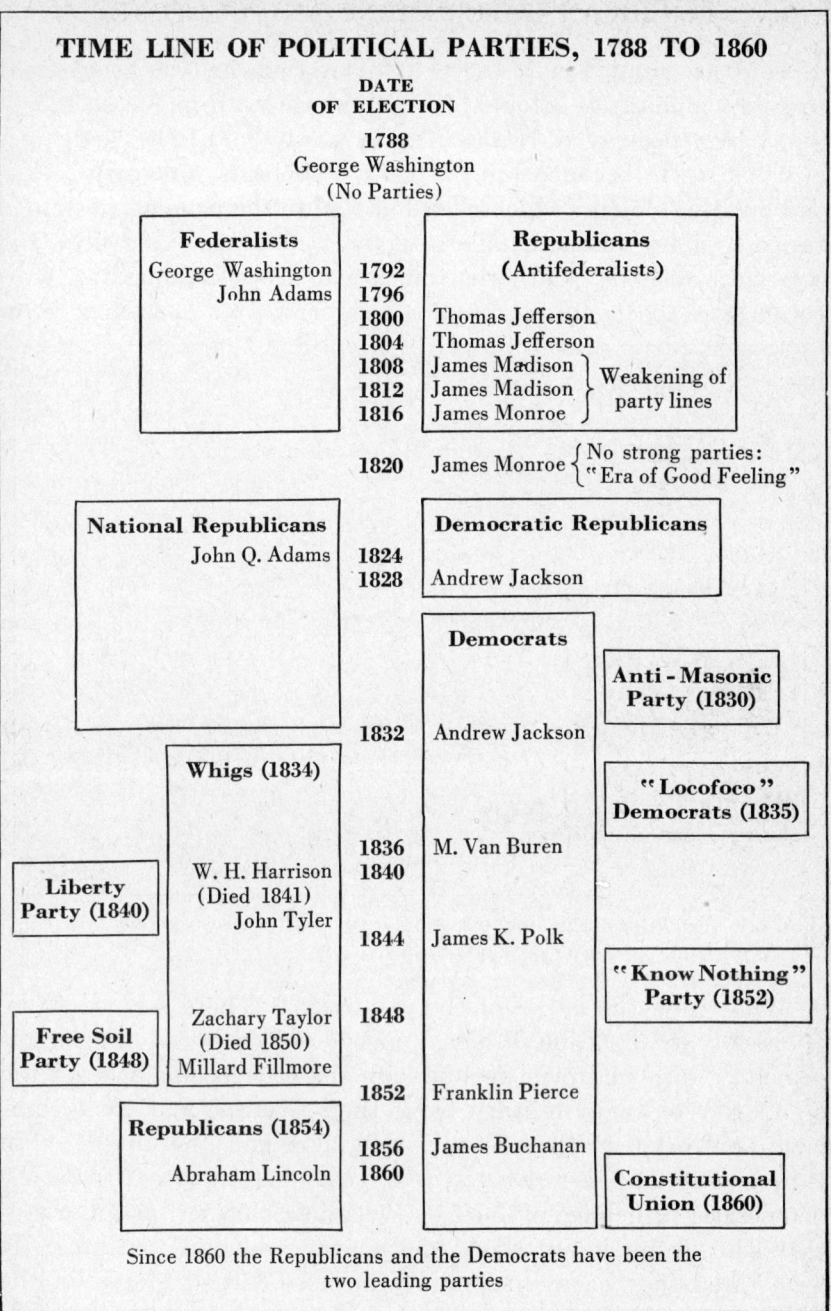

Fig. 128. Time line of political parties, 1788–1860

He was popular with the people; indeed, he was proclaimed to be a "man of the people." To make their campaign a success the Whigs portrayed Harrison as a hardy man who had been brought up in a log cabin. Thus by choosing an army officer and creating slogans which would appeal to the people, the Whigs hoped to unite all the smaller independent parties and both the Northern and the Southern branches of their own party. Van Buren was the candidate of the Democrats for a second term.

FIG. 129. The Whigs beginning to assemble at one of their early conventions held on a race course

What were the issues of the campaign? There seemed to be no issues at all. The Whigs, indeed, neglected to state their principles in a platform, feeling sure that they could win on the popularity of their military hero, their slogans, and their campaign oratory. Each side viciously attacked the other. Van Buren, who had been elected four years before to carry on the democratic principles of Jackson, was now pictured as an aristocrat who drank imported Madeira wine and used perfume. It was stated that he was spending the hard-earned money of the common people "for silk tassels, galloon, gimp, and satin medallions to beautify" the blue elliptical saloon in the White House.

Fig. 130. Martin Van Buren. (Courtesy of the Metropolitan Museum of Art)

Fig. 131. William H. Harrison. (Courtesy of the Ehrich Galleries, New York)

Fig. 132. James K. Polk

Fig. 133. James Buchanan

Four Presidents of the United States who served between 1837 and 1860

So the people of the country had to choose between the blue elliptical saloon and Madeira of Van Buren and the log cabin and hard cider of Harrison. The political leaders aroused great enthusiasm among the people. Thousands paraded the streets of the cities in the 1840 campaign, singing, "Tippecanoe [1] and Tyler too." (Tyler was nominated for vice president.) The people hauled miniature log cabins and hard-cider barrels through the streets, chanting,

> "What though the Hero's hard 'huge paws'
> Were wont to plow and sow,
> Does that disgrace our sacred cause?
> Does that degrade him? No!"

In vain the Democrats pointed out in their newspapers that Harrison was not really a log-cabin or hard-cider man. He was a Virginia gentleman, owner of a 2000-acre estate in Ohio! All in vain! The Whigs sang and paraded their hero into office. The eyes and ears of the common people were closed to anything but processions, slogans, and campaign songs. On election day the plain people, the hard-cider people, the log-cabin people, defeated "the Little Magician" with a majority of 174 electoral votes. The Democrats summed up the matter by announcing after their defeat, "We have been sung down, lied down, drunk down!"

Thus without a platform and without a policy for running the American government, "Tippecanoe" and the Whigs came into power. Their joy was short-lived, however. Within a month after his inauguration Harrison died, and John Tyler, the Virginia vice president, who succeeded him, was really no Whig at all. Now it was the Democrats who rejoiced. Tyler opposed the National Bank, the protective tariff, internal improvements by the government — in short, nearly all the Whig principles.

The campaign of 1844 — the first presidential "dark horse"

In great disappointment and annoyance the Whigs cast off Tyler and, in the campaign of 1844, once more selected Henry

---

[1] Harrison had been so nicknamed because he led the American forces against the Indians in the battle of "Tippecanoe" in the Northwest Territory (1811).

Clay as their party leader. The chief issues before the American people were the annexation of Texas and the Oregon boundary dispute. The question of slavery was a disturbing one. Both the major parties, however, refused to be definite in their campaign platforms. Each preferred to ignore the real issues and tried to elect a president by means of torchlight processions, oratory, campaign slogans, and the like.

This time it was the Democrats who engaged in clever politics. Martin Van Buren was not considered as their nominee for president for the reason that he had opposed the annexation of Texas, saying that he considered it unjustifiable and that it would lead to a war of aggression against Mexico. For a long time the nominating convention could find no candidate who could secure the necessary two thirds of the delegates' votes. Finally they chose James K. Polk, a "dark horse" from Tennessee — that is, a candidate who had not been seriously considered before.

Mr. Polk's nomination was received with "speechless amazement." It is true that he had been in public life a long time — had indeed been Speaker of the House of Representatives and governor of Tennessee. But no one had ever seriously thought of him as a candidate for president. It was the first time that a political party had nominated a "dark horse," but as we shall see it was by no means the last.

Immediately after his nomination Polk came out squarely in favor of annexing Texas and settling the Oregon boundary dispute even at the cost of war with England. Clay had been outspoken in Congress for years. His policies were known. Yet, as it happened, he did not speak loudly enough in favor of either of those issues. At the same time the question of slavery was helping to split the party. Many of the abolitionists who had been Whigs had formed the Liberty party in 1840 and had chosen James Birney, the noted abolitionist, as their candidate for president. Birney was defeated but ran once more in the election of 1844, when he polled a large Whig vote. Birney was not elected, but the support he received weakened Clay.

In the election of 1844 Clay was defeated in his third attempt to become president, and James K. Polk was elected. The Democrats were then free to carry out their policies. Texas was annexed,[1] and the Mexican War took place. The Oregon question was settled by arbitration, and the slogan "Fifty-four forty or fight!" which had been used in the campaign, was forgotten by Polk and his advisers, who, once safely in office, were content to compromise on the 49th parallel.

The campaign of 1848: more generals and parades

Next came the campaign of 1848. This time the Whigs were the cleverer politicians. They remembered the hard-cider campaign and took as their nominee "the people's choice," a hero of the Mexican War — General Zachary Taylor. "Old Rough and Ready," as he was called, was certainly no politician. The Whigs were not even sure that he was a Whig, but they were satisfied that he was a hero and would win votes. General Taylor admitted that he had never voted for the Whigs and that it made no difference to him whether he ran on the Democratic or the Whig ticket. He was not a party candidate, and, if elected, he said he would not be "the president of a party but the president of the whole people." No platform was drawn up by the Whigs. There was no mention of issues.

In the meantime, however, there were other political groups of Americans who had framed their platforms. The Liberty party, as you know, had been organized largely by Whigs to whom the question of slavery in the territories was becoming increasingly important. In the campaign of 1848 the Liberty party and the Workingman's party joined forces under the name *Free Soil party*. The Free Soil platform proclaimed "Free soil, free speech, free labor, free men."

There was another issue and, correspondingly, another new political party — the *Native Americans*, an offshoot of the Democratic party, known generally as the *Know-Nothings*. The Know-Nothings were really a powerful secret organization which had been got together to check the continued immigration of Europeans, especially Roman Catholics. Even as early as the 1840 campaign the society had achieved popularity with its slogan of

[1] The annexation resolution was actually passed by Congress while Tyler was still president, but after Polk had been elected.

"Native Americanism." They had received their nickname *Know-Nothings* from their practice of replying to all questions about themselves with the answer "I know nothing."

Thus the campaign of 1848 was marked by the splitting up of the old parties and the appearance of new ones. However, "Old Rough and Ready" defeated both the new political parties and the Democrats. Once more the Whigs went into office. It was their last success. In 1850 President Taylor died.

The vice president, Millard Fillmore, who now took President Taylor's place, was supposedly an antislavery man. He proved to be a "middle of the road" compromiser. The old leaders, Clay, Calhoun, and Webster, who had felt discouraged, indeed, about the future of the country, now had Fillmore's help and succeeded in passing the Compromise of 1850. They believed that this would end the slavery problem. You remember, however, that neither North nor South seemed to be satisfied with the Compromise of 1850, and slavery became a pressing issue in the following campaign.

The campaign of 1852: still more generals

As the campaign of 1852 approached, popular belief regarding slavery began to determine the membership of the two major parties. Although the Democratic party tried hard to appeal to the whole country on the principle of compromise, it was becoming more and more a proslavery party. Thus the Southern Whigs began to drift into the Democratic ranks, and Northern Democrats were joining the Free Soil party.

Again the politicians were at work. Both Whigs and Democrats chose as their candidates generals who had served in the Mexican War. The Democrats nominated one popular hero, General Franklin Pierce; the Whigs, another, General Winfield Scott.

After another campaign of hurrahs and processions and but little thinking, General Pierce won overwhelmingly over General Scott, carrying all but four of the thirty-one states. The Whig leaders saw clearly that their party could no longer command a majority of the votes of the country. They saw that the vote was increasingly with the Free Soil party and the Know-Nothing party.

The formation of the Republican party and the election of 1856

Before the campaign of 1856 took place the slavery question had forced every other issue into the background. At this time (1854) a new party was formed, made up of the Northern Whigs, the Free Soilers, the Northern antislavery Democrats, the anti-Nebraska men (who were opposing the Kansas-Nebraska Act), and part of the Know-Nothings. They took the name of *Republican*. Southerners called them Black Republicans because they believed they were essentially abolitionists. The new Republican party chose as its candidate in the campaign of 1856 John Frémont, who was known to the people for his explorations in California and his part in the Mexican War. Their political leaders thought that Frémont, "the Pathfinder" and "the Conqueror of California," had a good chance to win.

FIG. 134. President Pierce and three of his "supporters." Pierce is resting on the shoulders of Linn Boyd, the Speaker of the House. Senator Stephen A. Douglas is shown at the left, with the Nebraska Bill in his hand, and W. L. Marcy, Pierce's Secretary of State, stands at the right. (Courtesy of the New York Historical Society.)

The Know-Nothings still continued as a party in spite of a split. They and the remnants of the Whig party nominated as their candidate former President Millard Fillmore.

The Democrats nominated James Buchanan, a man who had

just returned to this country after serving as minister to Great Britain. He was safe; he had no enemies; he had had nothing to do with the Kansas-Nebraska Act. The Democratic platform did, however, support popular sovereignty in the territories.

The campaign of 1856 was a vicious and noisy one. There were cheers for "Bleeding Kansas," for "Free labor, free speech, and Frémont," and denunciation of "Buchanan and his Buchaneers" by those who feared that the Democratic party would expand the domain of slavery. In the meantime the Know-Nothings were urging the people to "Vote as you pray! Pray as you vote." In the end the safe and conservative Mr. Buchanan won by a large majority of electoral votes.

During Buchanan's administration (1857–1861) the turmoil and bitterness of the slavery controversy increased. The Supreme Court rendered its famous Dred Scott decision. The Republicans were intensely opposed to the decision, but the Southern Democrats were delighted.

A new Northern leader

About this time a new leader appeared among the Republicans. This was the young Illinois lawyer Abraham Lincoln. Already he had attracted attention by his masterly skill in public speaking and debating.

In 1858 Lincoln became recognized as a leader in connection with the Senatorial campaign in Illinois. Senator Douglas's term would expire the next year; so the Democrats renominated him for Senator. The Republicans nominated Lincoln. In accepting the nomination Lincoln made clear his views on preserving the Union. He said:

"A house divided against itself cannot stand." I believe this government cannot endure permanently half slave and half free. I do not expect the Union to be dissolved — I do not expect the house to fall — but I do expect it will cease to be divided. It will become all one thing, or all the other.

In the campaign that ensued Lincoln and Douglas toured the state, engaging in a series of notable debates. Throughout these debates Lincoln did not oppose slavery in the established states, only in the new territories. At the same time he insisted upon the preservation of the Union.

The chief issue between the two men was over Douglas's principle of popular sovereignty; that is, the right of a majority of the people of any given territory to decide for themselves whether or not they would have slavery. During the course of the debates Lincoln asked Douglas whether a territory could lawfully deny its people the right to own slaves. The question was very skillfully worded. If Douglas answered "Yes" he would greatly offend the South. If he answered "No" his reply would offend the North. So he hedged and said that slavery could not exist in a territory unless the people made laws to protect it. "Hence," said he, "no matter what the decision of the Supreme Court may be on that abstract question, still the right of the people to make a slave territory or a free territory is perfect and complete under the Nebraska bill." This answer satisfied Illinois, and Douglas won the Senatorship which he and Lincoln were both seeking. But it did not satisfy the South, since it denied an important part of the Dred Scott decision, and it ruined Douglas's chance for the presidency two years later.

FIG. 135. The lawyer, Abe Lincoln, "riding the circuit." Judges used to hold court for a short time in each county. A few lawyers always followed the judge's circuit and often took cases an hour or two before trial. (From a drawing by Rollin Kirby. Courtesy of *Collier's Weekly*)

PARTIES AND PRESIDENTS, 1837-1861   319

These debates served to bring Lincoln prominently before the people. Within the next two years he came to be regarded as an important candidate for the presidency on the Republican ticket.

THEN CAME THE MOMENTOUS ELECTION OF 1860

The problem of slavery and the maintenance of the Union had swung most of the voters into one or the other of the two leading parties — Democrats or Republicans. The ranks of the Democrats, however, were divided. The Northern faction favored popular, or "squatter," sovereignty. In 1860 this group nominated Douglas for president. A Southern faction, the so-called Fire-Eaters, opposed Douglas as a result of his reply to Lincoln's question in the Illinois debates, and in a separate convention chose as their candidate John C. Breckinridge. A third group, mostly Democrats, organized a new party, called the *Constitutional Union party*, and nominated John C. Bell of Tennessee. This group ignored the slavery question and conducted their campaign on the issue of preserving the Union.

FIG. 136. Abraham Lincoln as he appeared directly after his nomination

In the meantime the Republicans met at Chicago and on the third ballot chose Abraham Lincoln as their nominee. Their platform was written so as not to oppose slavery in the established Southern states, but to deny it in the new territories. They also demanded that Kansas be admitted immediately as a free state.

320 AMERICAN GOVERNMENT AND CULTURE

The campaign of 1860 was a dramatic struggle over slavery and Union. It did little good for Lincoln to announce that he would not interfere with slavery. The Southern Democrats believed he would, and warned the country flatly that if Lincoln were elected they would secede from the Union. It was indeed a spectacular

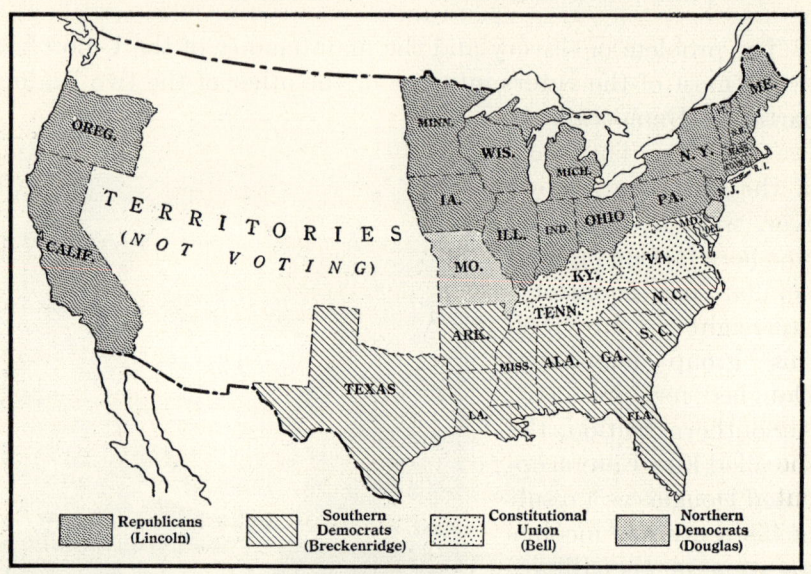

FIG. 137. The election of 1860. Notice that the state of New Jersey is the only one north of the Ohio River whose electors did not vote unanimously for Lincoln. Of the seven electors from New Jersey, four voted for Lincoln and three for Douglas. Notice also the large area of land which had not yet been admitted to statehood and so was entitled to no electoral representation

campaign. In the North the "Wide-awakes" — a picturesque marching club — paraded the streets in glazed hats and oil-cloth capes, singing:

> "Old Abe Lincoln came out of the wilderness,
> Out of the wilderness, out of the wilderness,
> Old Abe Lincoln came out of the wilderness
> Down in Illinois!"

The South resounded with cries of "We want a statesman, not a rail-splitter, as president." The Breckinridge supporters marched with blue nullification cockades on their hats.

Like Lincoln, Douglas believed that at any cost the Union

must be preserved. When Lincoln was elected and secession became a fact, Douglas was one of his strongest supporters, maintaining that secession was a crime and that the Union would be safe under Mr. Lincoln if it could only be held together long enough for his influence to be felt.

Election day came. The country went to the polls — a country sharply divided into factions. As the votes were counted it was seen that the Democrats by dividing into three groups had defeated themselves. Lincoln received less than half of the *popular* vote, but he had 180 *electoral* votes against a total electoral vote of 123 for the other candidates. The map of figure 137 will explain how it was possible for that to happen.

The Popular Vote in 1860	
Lincoln	1,866,452
Douglas	1,376,957
Breckinridge	849,781
Bell	588,879

The news was telegraphed throughout the country. Lincoln had been elected president of the United States. There had been threats before of secession in both the North and the South, but the Union had always been preserved. Would the South carry out its threat? The nation waited.

The answer was not long in coming.

INTERESTING READINGS FROM WHICH YOU CAN GET ADDITIONAL INFORMATION

Minnigerode, Meade. Presidential Years, 1787–1860. G. P. Putnam's Sons, New York. Amusing surveys of the presidential campaigns from Washington to Lincoln, with the campaign songs and the antics of the American people as their candidates were swept into office.

Minnigerode, Meade. The Fabulous Forties. G. P. Putnam's Sons, New York. Such campaigns as that of "Tippecanoe and Tyler too," with all the hurrahing and singing, are given in detail.

CHAPTER XVI

THE CIVIL WAR

Abraham Lincoln was elected in November, 1860, but his inauguration did not, of course, take place until March of the following year. Between his election and the day on which he took office, the South had acted on its threat of withdrawal from the Union.

On December 20, 1860, a convention of delegates from South Carolina met at Charleston and seceded from the Union.[1] By February 1 six more states, all of them from the far South, had joined South Carolina. They were Mississippi, Florida, Alabama, Georgia, Louisiana, and Texas.

The Seceding States established the Confederate States of America

On February 4, 1861, the delegates from the seceding states assembled at Montgomery, Alabama,[2] drafted a new constitution, and inaugurated an independent government — the Confederate States of America. Its constitution was much like that of the United States. The government was to be in the hands of a president, a house of representatives, and a senate.

In two important respects, however, the Confederate constitution was different: first, it emphasized that each state was sovereign and independent; second, it frankly stated that slavery should be protected in all the states and territories.

Jefferson Davis of Mississippi was elected president of the Confederate States of America. He, like Lincoln, was the son of a Kentucky farmer, but a Kentucky farmer who had moved into the far South and made a small fortune as a Mississippi planter.

---

[1] The Ordinance of Secession which they passed declared that "the Union now subsisting between South Carolina and other states under the name of the United States of America is hereby dissolved."

[2] Richmond became the Confederate capital in May, 1861.

THE CIVIL WAR

Davis was a graduate of West Point and had served in the Mexican War. He had been Secretary of War during Pierce's administration and had been a United States Senator for many years. He was a man of distinction and one of the outstanding leaders of the South.

Confederate leaders defended their secession from the Union on various grounds. Jefferson Davis frankly declared that it rested upon the natural right of all peoples to change their government at any time. Other Southerners, however, called the secession an act of revolution. One leader summed up the situation by saying:

"You may call it 'secession,' or you may call it 'revolution'; but there is one big fact standing before you ready to oppose you — that fact is *freemen with arms in their hands.*"

Fig. 138. Jefferson Davis

Now was revealed one of the difficulties of carrying on the "government of checks and balances" which the Fathers of the Constitution had set up in 1789. Buchanan was still in office. As required by the Constitution about four months would pass after the election in November, 1860, before Lincoln and the newly elected Senators and Representatives could take office. During these unhappy months the affairs of the country drifted.

Buchanan himself was bewildered by the problem of secession. At one moment he would give out a statement that the Southern states had no right to secede and, almost in the same breath, another statement that he himself had no legal power to compel them to stay in the Union.

The members of Congress were not able to agree upon a definite course. In Washington the tension increased; passions became violent. Southerners who had homes in the capital closed

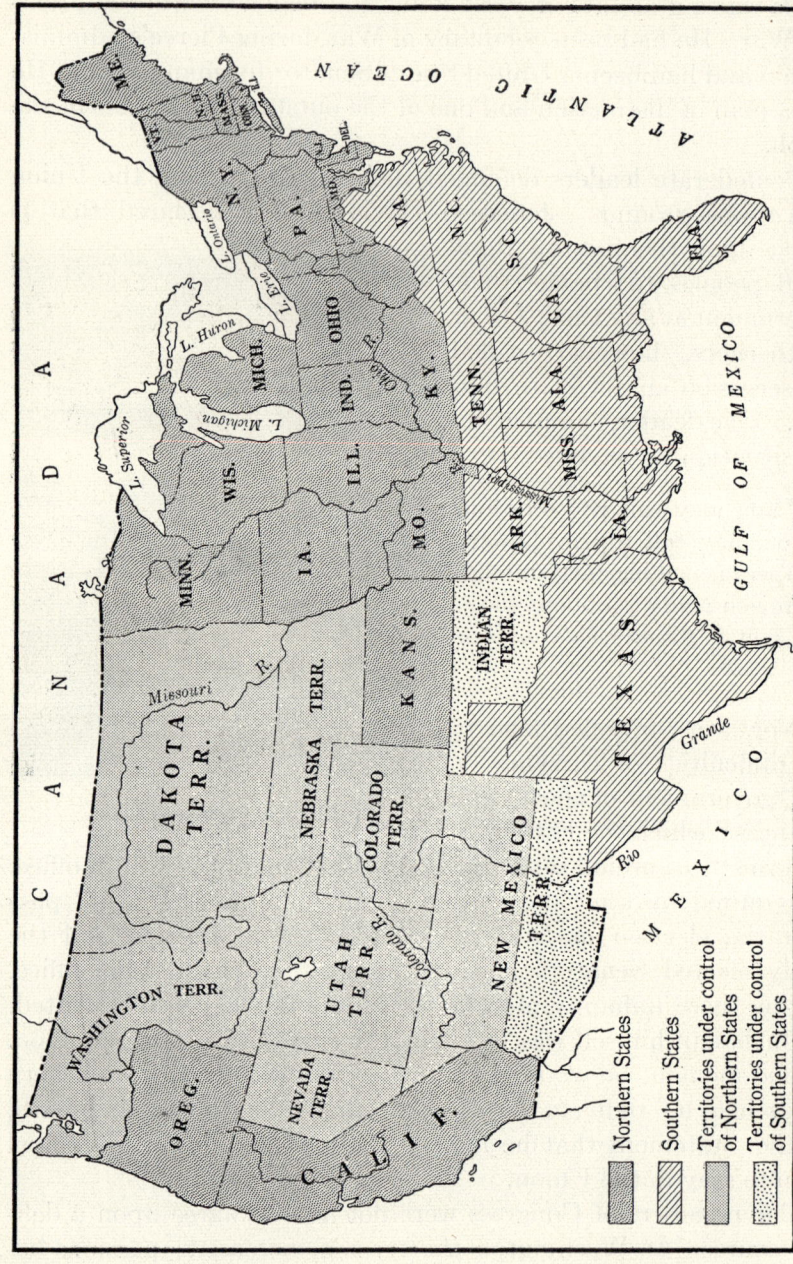

FIG. 139. The division of the United States in 1861 over the question of slavery and states rights

them and went to their homes in the South, many saying that they were moving "to their own country."

The sentiment of the North was divided. The abolitionists and such leaders as Henry Ward Beecher, the minister, and Horace Greeley, editor of the *New York Tribune,* said of the seceding states, "Let them go." Other Northerners wanted the Union to be preserved at all costs and advocated war to preserve it. Northern business men, to whom Southern planters owed the large sum of $200,000,000, did not want war, and neither did they want the Southern states to leave the Union.

Lincoln's attitude

Abraham Lincoln wanted more than all else to preserve the Union. At his election he had announced publicly that he would not disturb slavery in those states in which it then existed. He also made the firm declaration, however, that he would oppose its extension into any new territory.

FIG. 140. Horace Greeley, who said of the seceding states, "Let them go"

Finally March 4 came and with it Lincoln's inauguration. In his inaugural address Lincoln made it perfectly clear that he would use force, if necessary, to maintain the Union.

To the Southerners he said:

In your hands, my dissatisfied fellow countrymen, and not in mine, is the momentous issue of civil war. The government will not assail *you.* . . . *You* have no oath registered in heaven to destroy the government, while *I* shall have the most solemn one to preserve . . . it. . . . We are not enemies, but friends. . . . The mystic chords of memory, stretching from every battlefield and patriot grave to every living heart and hearthstone, all over this broad land, will yet swell the chorus of the Union, when again touched, as surely they will be, by the better angels of our nature.

One thing is clear. Lincoln and a majority of the Congress still hoped to be able to arrange a compromise which would keep the states in the Union and prevent war. On the day Lincoln was inaugurated a resolution was passed and submitted to the states which, if ratified, was to become an amendment to the United States Constitution. This declared that the Federal government should henceforth be denied the power to interfere with slavery in an existing state. Within a month after Lincoln's inauguration two states had actually ratified it. If two thirds of the states had ratified it, this amendment would have protected slavery forever in existing states. But dramatic events intervened to prevent ratification by other states.

FIG. 141. This cartoon was published after Lincoln's election and before he became president. Beneath it were the words, "A job for the new cabinet maker." What do you think this means? (From *Leslie's Illustrated Newspaper*, February 2, 1861.)

The spark which set off the explosion

For weeks Southern army officers had been collecting ammunition and other materials of war, taking over Federal army posts and preparing for armed conflict. The island fortress of Sumter stood in the harbor of Charleston, South Carolina. By April, 1861, the Federal commander, Major Anderson, who had been besieged for nearly four months, lacked food and other necessary supplies. President Lincoln ordered these supplies sent to the fortress. Many Southerners stationed at Charleston thought that not only food but reënforcements of soldiers were being sent. General P. G. T. Beauregard, stationed at Charleston with about 7000 men, was ordered by Jefferson Davis to demand the surrender of the fort.

THE CIVIL WAR

Upon Major Anderson's refusal to surrender, Beauregard's troops opened fire on Fort Sumter at 4:30 on the morning of April 12, 1861. For two days Anderson and his men held out. Then on April 14, 1861, the unexpected news was telegraphed north and south that they had surrendered.

On April 15 President Lincoln called on the states for 75,000 volunteers to deal with disturbances and resistance to the laws of the United States in the Southern states. The Northern states responded generously. Before July 1 more than 300,000 soldiers had enlisted for a term of three months.

In the South there was equal if not greater enthusiasm. Many Southerners had been expecting war. They saw no other way by which to settle their quarrel with the North, and they believed in their cause. By April 29 there were 45,000 men under arms, and volunteers were coming in by hundreds every day. As one of their leaders said, the only question was "not as to who shall go to war but who shall stay at home."

Other Southern states joined the Confederacy

As you have already read, seven states — those lying farthest south — originally formed the Confederate States of America. The question immediately arose: What would the other states south of Ohio do — secede or stay with the Union? What would Missouri do?

Three states somewhat farther north, North Carolina, Tennessee, and Arkansas, cast their lot with the Confederacy. Opinion in these states regarding secession or, indeed, slavery was far from unanimous, however. Many citizens, especially the poorer farmers, cared little about the sovereignty of states. Few of them owned slaves.

In the states on the northern border, however, the division of opinion was particularly strong. In Virginia 48 counties in the northwest mountain section were decidedly against slavery and were, therefore, opposed to seceding from the Union. In 1861 they formed a separate state called Kanawha and were admitted to the Union two years later as West Virginia.

Maryland, Delaware, Kentucky, Missouri, and Kansas (which

had been finally admitted as a state in 1861) were also centers of bitter controversy. These states finally stayed in the Union, although thousands of their citizens enlisted in the Southern armies.

Thus the extreme Southern and the middle Southern states seceded, and the Border States remained in the Union.

Contrast in the Resources of the North and the South

How well prepared were the sections for the great conflict before them? How did they compare in wealth, in industries, in trade, in laborers, in trained soldiers?

Recall from *A History of American Civilization* the contrast in economic resources:

Northern States	Southern States
1. 23 states	1. 11 states (see figure 139)
2. About 22,000,000 people, mostly white	2. About 9,000,000 people, over one third black slaves
3. 1,557,000 enlisted soldiers	3. 1,082,000 enlisted soldiers
4. More than two thirds of the nation's capital	4. Less than one third of the nation's capital
5. The control of nearly all the iron, steel, textile, and munition industries	5. Only a few manufacturing industries, and they in their infancy
6. The control of most of the nation's foreign commerce	6. Few ships and little outside trade
7. Millions of skilled laborers	7. Few skilled laborers
8. About 20,000 miles of railroad	8. About 10,000 miles of railroad (see figure 142)

In two respects the South had advantages over the North. It had — at least at the beginning of the war — a greater number of officers trained in the art of warfare, and it was fighting on its own territory. These were most important assets and helped to account for the superiority of the South during the first two years.

Raising money to finance the war

The Southern states were especially handicapped in raising money for the war. From the beginning the new government faced the insistent question How can we raise money? The Southern planters had land and buildings but little cash.

There were several ways in which the South tried to secure money with which to finance the war:

First, the government levied customs duties on all materials and goods brought into the states from abroad. This, however, failed to produce much income, because after the first year the Federal navy maintained so strict a blockade of the Southern ports that few "blockade runners" succeeded in passing through.

Second, the Confederate officials tried to collect money by taxing property. This brought in little cash, however; so they began to issue bonds, borrowing in Amsterdam, in Paris, and in other European financial centers.

Third, the Confederates began to issue vast amounts of new paper money. Gold money is the standard money of the world. Yet paper money such as you now see every day is perfectly good money too.

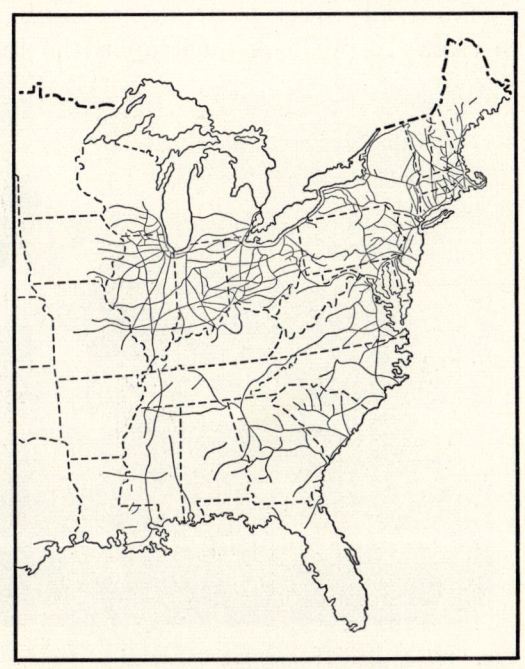

FIG. 142. The railroads of the United States in 1860. Notice how many more railroads there were in the North than in the South. In the South only one short line connected the land west of the Mississippi with the East

This is because our government will exchange it for an equal number of dollars in gold. The Confederate States, however, had very little gold. Nevertheless tons of paper bills of every denomination dropped off the Confederate printing presses. At the same time the state governments printed it, private state banks printed it, and municipal governments printed it. Even business men in local communities — owners of stores, shops, and factories — printed their own paper bills. As the printing increased, the value of the money dropped. By 1863 as much as

$22 in paper money was required to buy one gold dollar. This meant, of course, that the price of everything went up. Food, clothing, materials of all kinds, were high in price and hard to get. In Richmond, in 1863, an ordinary restaurant meal cost $50 in paper money.

From all these sources the South raised only $30,000,000 in cash. As we look back upon the terrific struggle which the

Fig. 143. A patriotic meeting, intended to demonstrate loyalty to the government during the war. (From a contemporary drawing)

Confederate States endured for four years, it appears to be little less than a miracle that they were able to go on as long as they did.

Although the resources of the North were far greater, President Lincoln's government also found it difficult to raise money. At the beginning of the war not one tenth of the money needed for the armies was secured by taxation; over nine tenths came from bond issues. However, the European bankers were more willing to lend money to the government at Washington than to the new, untried government at Richmond. Furthermore, there were more people in the North who had savings to invest in government bonds. Hence the North had a decided advantage over the South in raising money.

THE CIVIL WAR

Early in the war the Northern government turned over to prominent New York bankers the task of organizing a great bond-selling campaign throughout the country. The leader in this work was Jay Cooke. From Massachusetts to California, Cooke put on a nation-wide drive. So successfully did he sell the bonds of the government and accumulate huge amounts of cash that he was known as "the financier of the Civil War."

The Government Debt in 1861 and in 1865	
1861	$74,985,000
1865	2,856,000,000

In the meantime, Congress increased the tariff on imports and levied increased taxes on the people. Whereas in 1862 the revenue obtained from taxes amounted to only $50,000,000, in 1865 it was $300,000,000.

In spite of all these efforts, however, as the war went on the Northern government was also compelled to issue unsecured paper money — that is, paper money which it could not exchange for gold. By the end of 1864 there had been issued more than $400,000,000 in "greenbacks," as these paper bills were called. History repeated itself! The Northern paper money also steadily fell in value. By 1864 a paper dollar bill was worth less than 35 cents.

The Aims of Each Side

At the beginning of the war neither the Northern nor the Southern military leaders had a complete plan for carrying on the war. Both sides were uncertain, but as the months passed their campaigns were better planned.

Briefly stated, the aims of each side were as follows:

War Plans of the North
1. Blockade the entire Southern coast to prevent the South from receiving supplies from Europe
2. Hold the Border States of the South in the Union
3. Dishearten the South by the early capture of Richmond, the capital
4. Split the Confederacy by (1) seizing control of the Mississippi River and by (2) marching through the Confederacy from Kentucky to Georgia

War Plans of the South
1. Keep the ports open for foreign trade
2. Bring the Border States of the South into the Confederacy
3. Dishearten the North by the early capture of Washington, the capital
4. Raid the Northern states on the border whenever possible

1. The war on the sea

The Northern blockade. The earliest plan of the Northern leaders was to prevent the South from receiving help from Europe. If the South were unable to export cotton, there was less chance that foreign governments would offer help. Six days after the fall

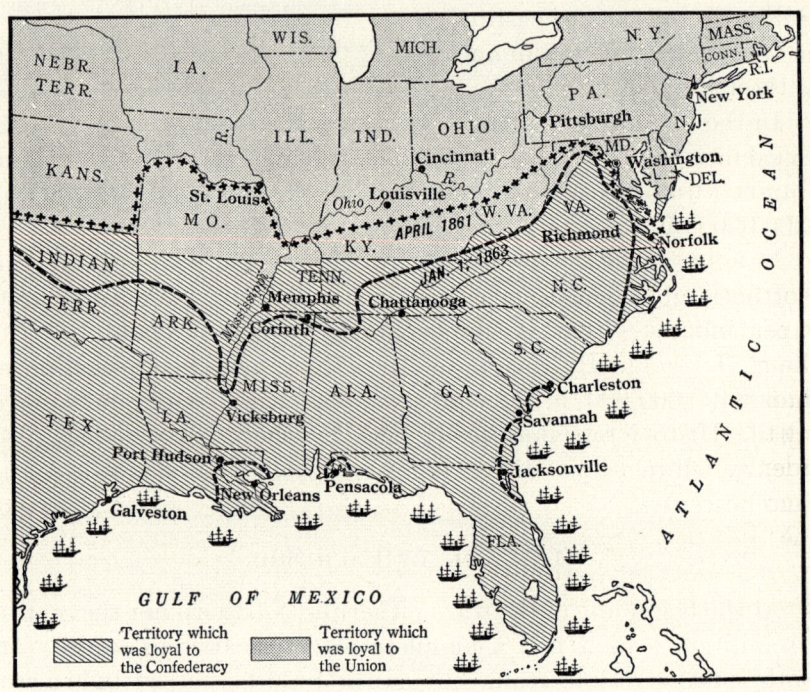

FIG. 144. This map shows the blockade which was thrown about the Southern coast by Union ships. It also shows the territory held by the Union in the first and third years of the war

of Fort Sumter, the Northern government declared a blockade of the Atlantic coast from South Carolina to Florida.[1] Admiral David Glasgow Farragut, a Southerner by birth, who had cast his lot with the Union, was given command of the navy. Not much of a navy! Thirteen wooden vessels,— eight steamships and five sailing ships,— none of which was really well armed. These ships constantly patrolled the coast line of the South.

[1] By the end of the year the blockade had been extended. It reached from Virginia to Florida and westward along the Gulf of Mexico to Texas.

THE CIVIL WAR

Soon Northern shipyards were busy building more naval vessels. By the end of 1861 the navy had grown to 264 vessels. Every sort of vessel that was available was put to service. Tighter and tighter grew the blockade each year. All ships — both Confederate ships and those belonging to other countries — which attempted to enter Southern harbors were ordered to be seized.

Fig. 145. Admiral David Glasgow Farragut. (Courtesy of the Signal Corps)

Shortly after the beginning of the war a few ships were built in Southern harbors, and others were purchased from ship-building companies in England. Long, swift steamships they were, designed especially for running the blockade. And run it they did — stealing in and out of Southern ports in the dark of the night or in the midst of raging storms. During the first year of the war considerable numbers of runners succeeded in getting through the Northern patrol. From that time on, however, the number of Northern ships increased. Steadily the blockade tightened. It has been estimated that during the entire war 15,000 vessels, small and large, were taken by the Northern fleets.

Smaller and smaller grew the exports of cotton from the South. Month by month the imports, or supplies, from Europe decreased.

Cotton exported from the South	
1860	$200,000,000
1862	4,000,000

As to naval craft the South had but a few. Two of these, however, are particularly remembered — the *Alabama*, a privateer, and the *Virginia*, an armored war vessel.

The *Alabama* was built for the Confederate States in a British shipyard. This was not permitted according to international law, but the British government did nothing to prevent it. For two years, from 1862 to 1864, the *Alabama* preyed upon Northern commerce, sank Northern vessels, and succeeded in evading the blockade. Then in June, 1864, near the French port of Cherbourg, the United States ship *Kearsarge* met the *Alabama*. The latter challenged the *Kearsarge*, and the battle began with all Cherbourg watching. For an hour the two vessels shelled each other. Then the *Alabama* began to list and finally was sent to the bottom.

Fig. 146. Battle between the Monitor and Virginia (Merrimac). (From a painting by Henry Reuterdahl. Courtesy of the National Gallery of Art)

The first use of armored ships: the Virginia (Merrimac) *and the* Monitor. The war on the sea between the North and the South is especially remembered as being the scene of the first use of "ironclads" in naval warfare. At the beginning of the war a Federal vessel, the *Merrimac*, had been sunk in Portsmouth Harbor (Virginia). The Confederates raised her, covered her wooden sides with iron rails, and installed cannon, renaming the ship the *Virginia*. On March 8, 1862, she boldly attacked the Northern fleet lying in Hampton Roads, destroying several vessels, among them the *Cumberland* and the *Congress*, two of the fastest ships in the fleet.

THE CIVIL WAR

But the Northern naval leaders had had the same idea of armoring their ships. The following morning a queer-looking vessel, called by some "a tin can on a shingle" and by others "a cheesebox on a raft," sailed into Hampton Roads to attack the *Virginia*. It was the *Monitor*, under the command of Captain John L. Worden. The queer craft consisted of a long, low body with an iron-plated revolving tower equipped with two powerful guns. It had been invented by Captain John Ericsson, a Swedish-American.

The *Virginia* and the *Monitor* shelled each other for three hours in a famous battle between the first ironclads. Finally the *Virginia* steamed off into Norfolk Harbor. A month later she made another raid.

Shortly after that the Confederates were compelled to abandon Norfolk; so they destroyed the *Virginia* to prevent her being taken and used in the Northern fleet. The *Monitor* sank in a storm.

Though both ironclads were so soon afterwards destroyed, the battle between them was decisive in one respect. It proved that ironclads were more effective than wooden ships in withstanding shell fire. England had already been experimenting with armored vessels. From that time on the modern nations began to give up wooden naval vessels and to use armored ones.

2. The campaigns in eastern United States, 1861–1862

At the outbreak of war the people, both in the North and in the South, demanded the immediate capture of the enemy's capital. In the *New York Tribune* Horace Greeley was sounding the battle cry of the North with "On to Richmond!" Answering it was the cry of the Southland, "On to Washington!" Each side hoped — indeed, believed — that it could win within a few weeks or a few months, and each side massed its untrained troops on the line between Washington and Richmond.

The first battle of Bull Run (Manassas Junction). For more than three months after the capture of Sumter, not a single land battle was fought. Both sides lacked experienced soldiers and organization. On the Northern side General Winfield Scott, hero of the Mexican War, was the ranking officer, though illness and age prevented his taking any active part in the war. With him were associated Generals McClellan, McDowell, Burnside, Hooker, and others. Opposing them were some of their former friends and associates — Generals Lee, Jackson, Beauregard, Albert Sidney Johnston, and Joseph E. Johnston.

The leaders on both sides knew that their troops were in no condition to fight. Yet the clamor for action grew louder and louder. At last on July 21, 1861, General Scott ordered McDowell into action against General Beauregard. The two forces met at the muddy little stream called Bull Run, near Manassas Junction. Throughout the day the advantage lay with the Northern troops, who advanced slowly but in amateurish and not too orderly fashion. Then, late in the afternoon, fresh Southern reënforcements, which had eluded the army of General Patterson, turned the advance of the Northern soldiers into a panic. Pell-mell they ran from the field, even throwing away their guns in their anxiety to reach Washington, 35 miles away.[1]

With the defeat of the Union soldiers the road to Washington lay defenseless. But the city itself was not unprotected, and General Beauregard's army was in no condition to pursue its victory further. By the time it was ready, troops had been brought from the North to oppose it.

The most important outcome of the battle was that the North was shaken from its attitude of overconfidence. This was no uprising to be quelled in one battle, as many Northerners had confidently believed.

The Seven Days' Battle. Throughout the summer and autumn of 1861 and the following winter the two armies drilled and prepared for action. The elderly General Scott had been retired and the command of the northeastern armies of the Union given to General George B. McClellan. McClellan had already won popular support in the North by his work in clearing the western

---

[1] One little episode of the first battle of Bull Run has been remembered — the nicknaming of General Jackson. During the battle a Southern colonel, whose men were fleeing from the field, shouted at them, pointing to Jackson's brigade, "See where Jackson stands, like a stone wall." Indeed, like a stone wall he stood, all through the battle. Henceforth, he was known as "Stonewall" Jackson. He became General Lee's right-hand man, one of the most daring, brilliant, and popular of the Confederate generals.

Fig. 147. Robert E. Lee

Fig. 148. "Stonewall" Jackson

Two Confederate Generals

Fig. 149. W. T. Sherman

Fig. 150. P. H. Sheridan

Two Union Generals

counties of Virginia of Confederate troops after these counties had "seceded from secession." He had been nicknamed "the Little Napoleon." He was a splendid drillmaster and a tireless worker, but overcautious.

Finally he was ready to advance upon Richmond. Between him and the Southern capital, however, was Lee's army, and to the west, guarding the Shenandoah valley, Jackson. McClellan's plan was to lay siege to Richmond (see map, figure 151); so he transferred 110,000 men from Washington to Fort Monroe, on the peninsula between the York and the James rivers, where he joined them, April 2, 1862. He advanced across the peninsula to Yorktown, which the Confederates were holding with a very small army. There he besieged the Confederate army for a month, withholding attack because of awesome guns which later proved to be made of wood. Then he discovered that the Confederate army had slipped away. He resumed his march. Closer and closer he approached Richmond. Finally his army was only twenty miles from the Southern capital. The nearest Federal picket stood under a signpost which read "Richmond $4\frac{1}{2}$ miles." The month's delay had enabled the Confederates to reënforce their army, but deep gloom spread over the South. News had just come that a Northern army had taken New Orleans and that Federal gunboats were clearing the Mississippi River.

At length, on June 26, Lee attacked. For seven days the battle continued, and for seven days Lee's forces held their line together and McClellan's army slowly retreated. Finally, on July 2, Jackson joined Lee, and McClellan retreated to the coast, where he found the Northern fleet. Thus the Seven Days' Battle was also won by the Confederates, and this attempt of the North to take Richmond was a failure.

The second battle of Bull Run. About 80,000 soldiers under General John Pope were sent south to "chase Jackson." After the Seven Days' Battle Jackson quickly moved 25,000 of his troops northward, surprising the Union soldiers who were receiving and guarding supplies at Bull Run. He captured the food supplies and burned all of them that his army could not carry away. Time after time the Federal leaders had tried to trap him, but each time Jackson managed to evade them. One of them, under criticism from his superiors, said of Jackson and his men: "I can't catch them. They leap fences and walls like deer." Finally his rapid movements resulted in a confusion of orders on the Union side, and reënforcements which Pope was daily expecting failed to arrive. Three days after he had destroyed the Union

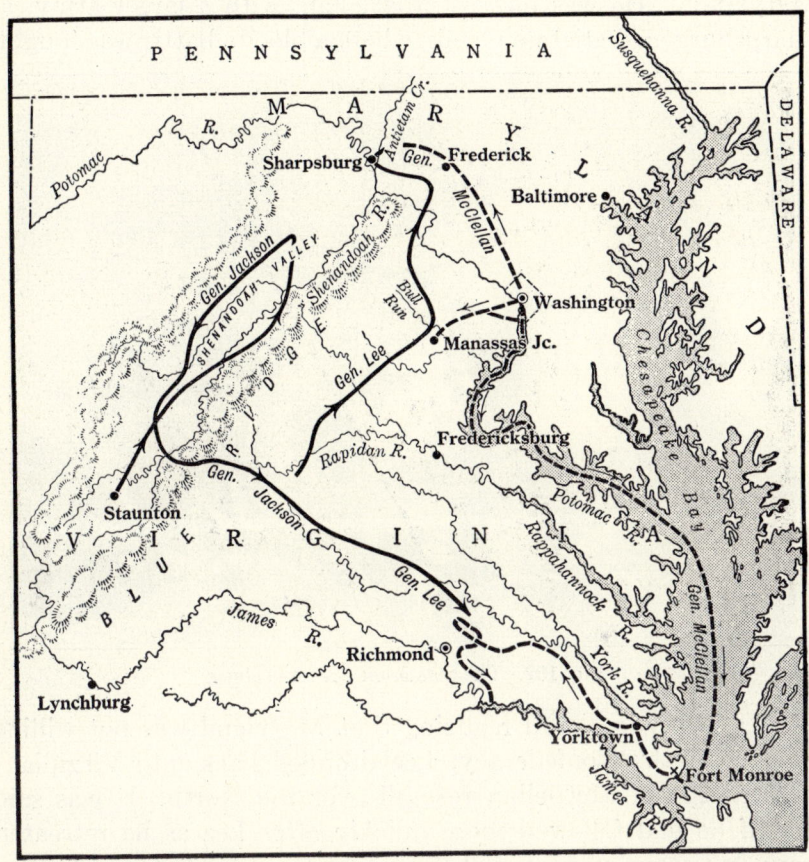

FIG. 151. McClellan's campaign in the South and Lee's first invasion of the North

supply station, Jackson was joined by a large reënforcement, and began a general attack. For two days a second battle raged at Bull Run, and again the defeated Union army sought the protection of Washington.

Lee invaded Maryland. Now it was time for the people of the North to be gloomy, while the Southerners were mad with joy.

A Confederate campaign was launched on the Border States by the Southern army. The Southern leaders believed that the time had come when they could bring Maryland into the Confederacy. Lee's plan was to march through Maryland and invade the North. He and his army crossed the Potomac, singing "Maryland, my Maryland." He was met by McClellan, with a larger army, at Sharpsburg on Antietam Creek, where a bloody battle was fought.

Fig. 152. The attack on Fredericksburg

After a heavy loss, and realizing that Maryland was not willing to support the Confederacy, Lee dropped back into Virginia.

Criticism of McClellan rose all over the North. It was said that if he had followed more quickly after Lee as he retreated from Antietam a great victory would have been won. At any rate, he was removed from the command of the Army of the Potomac and was succeeded by General Ambrose E. Burnside.

In December, 1862, Burnside attacked Lee at *Fredericksburg*. The attack was ill-planned, and the Confederate position was excellent. Thousands of brave men were sacrificed in vain, and Burnside had to withdraw. He soon resigned his command, and General Joseph ("Fighting Joe") Hooker succeeded him.

Thus a year and a half after the beginning of the war neither side had gained much in the campaigns in the east. The Confederate army had won some battles, but had been unable to profit by its victories.

The Union Armies carry on their Plans in the West, 1862–1863

While the eastern campaigns between Richmond and Washington were in progress and the Union blockade was becoming tighter, stirring events were taking place in the western theater of war. The Northern armies were trying to capture the key points in the Mississippi River region. If successful they would split the South into two sections. Texas, Arkansas, and Louisiana would be isolated from the eastern section of the Confederacy. The Northern plans included attacks by naval vessels and river gunboats and by land forces.

Grant's army and Foote's gunboats captured Fort Henry and Fort Donelson. Accompanied by Commodore Andrew H. Foote and his fleet of gunboats, General Grant and 17,000 Union soldiers were transported up the flooded Tennessee to Fort Henry. The Confederate commander, realizing that his small garrison was powerless, sent most of his soldiers to Fort Donelson and surrendered Fort Henry. Fort Donelson was but twelve miles overland on the Cumberland River. Foote was ordered to join Grant at Fort Donelson. Both land and water journeys were difficult because of bad weather and swollen rivers. Foote and Grant were each delayed. By the time they arrived at the fort the Confederate garrison had received reënforcements, but because of disagreement among their officers the Southerners did not attack. When the enemy did not attack, Grant reasoned that they must be in a worse situation than he. He decided to strike the first blow. The gunboats proved useless before the guns of Fort Donelson; but, in spite of this, Grant continued in his plan of besieging the fort. Discovering that the Confederate officers were trying to escape with their troops rather than to fight, the Union forces attacked with restored confidence. Two days later an officer was sent from the garrison to ask for terms. Grant replied that he would consider nothing but "unconditional surrender." Thereafter he was often called "Unconditional Surrender" Grant.

The battle of Shiloh. Victory at Donelson was hailed with great joy in the North. At that time Grant said that a good leader in sole command with trained armies could have marched straight through the Southland, splitting it from Missouri to the Atlantic coast. But the Northern army was handicapped because of sharp disagreements and jealousies among its generals. During all this time there was no single Northern general who had charge of *all* the Union armies.

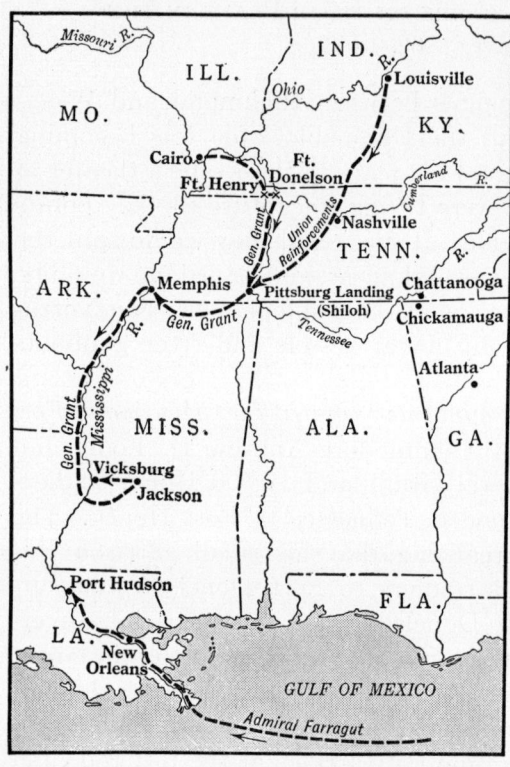

FIG. 153. How the North gained control of the Mississippi River and split the Confederacy into an eastern and a western section

In spite of the confusion at headquarters Grant's army drove its line of battle through Tennessee to the very borders of Mississippi. Then at *Pittsburg Landing* (Shiloh), on the Tennessee River, a terrible battle was fought, in which the Southern general, Albert Sidney Johnston, was killed. Beauregard now took command. On the second day of the battle Union reënforcements arrived, and the Confederates were forced to fall back. It was greatly to the credit of their new commander, Beauregard, that the entire army was moved out of danger before the Northern troops could follow up their success.

Admiral Farragut captured New Orleans, April, 1862. Admiral Farragut took part of the Union fleet into the Gulf of Mexico and steamed up the Mississippi to attack New Orleans. A barricade of the hulks of ships blocked the river at a point where two strong forts were situated. Although under fire from the forts, Farragut broke through the barricade and destroyed a fleet of Southern ships. Then he proceeded to New Orleans, where he found the loaded wharves in flames. From that day until the end of the war New Orleans was in the hands of Union troops.

The North was overjoyed, and the Union leaders saw their plan to gain control of the Mississippi almost realized. It was not, however, until more than a year later that the entire course of the river through the Southern states was in the power of the Union forces.

The fight for Missouri and Arkansas. As early as the summer and autumn of 1861 a struggle had been going on west of the Mississippi. In August of that year a Confederate army under General Price defeated Northern troops under General Lyon at *Wilson's Creek*, Missouri. This was practically the only Confederate victory in this region, however. Month by month Union troops took control of Missouri and advanced into Arkansas, where, in March, 1862, a Union army defeated the Confederate force, at *Pea Ridge*.

Before the close of 1862, although the Northern army had gained little in the east, they held most of Kentucky and Tennessee, Missouri and Arkansas, and controlled the Mississippi north of Memphis as well as from its mouth to New Orleans.

The fall of Vicksburg in 1863 gave the Union armies complete control of the Mississippi. In order to complete their division of the western Confederacy from the eastern, the Union leaders realized that they must take Vicksburg, "the Gibraltar of the Mississippi." Beginning opposite Vicksburg, on the western shore of the Mississippi, was a continuation of the railroad which entered the city from the east. Vicksburg was then the only Southern city south of Missouri connected with the West in this way. It was a key point, and the Southerners had fortified it. They expected attack from the north or east.

Under Grant the Northern armies worked their way down the western bank of the Mississippi, while gunboats ran the gantlet of Vicksburg's fortifications, brought them supplies, and finally ferried them across the river about 60 miles south of Vicksburg. Grant's armies marched north and with the fleet laid siege to the city. The siege lasted about six weeks. The Southern forces under General Pemberton held out in spite of the greatest privations. Week by week the food supply diminished, and finally citizens and soldiers were eating horses, mules, rats — anything

FIG. 154. A scene during the battle of Vicksburg. As a result of this battle the North gained control of the Mississippi River. (From *Harper's Weekly*, March, 1863)

they could find. At length, on July 4, 1863, Pemberton surrendered. A few days later the Union forces captured Port Hudson, in Louisiana, and the Mississippi River was in the control of the Northern armies. At the receipt of the news President Lincoln remarked, "The Father of Waters again goes unvexed to the sea."

With the fall of Vicksburg and Port Hudson one of the Northern aims was realized — the South had been divided. In the meantime the blockade of the seaports had become tighter and tighter. The importation of food and war supplies from Europe had dwindled to almost nothing. The superior resources of the North were beginning to have their effect.

Lincoln issues the Emancipation Proclamation

In 1862 Lincoln took an important step. In the election campaign of 1860 and during the first year of the war, Lincoln had not proposed to abolish slavery. He had merely opposed secession and the introduction of slavery into new territories. Gradually, however, Lincoln came to the decision that slavery must be abolished.

There were several reasons for his change in point of view. One was the humane one of making human beings free.

There were other reasons, however — reasons that had to do with winning the war. First, in the summer of 1862, owing to defeats in the east, the spirits of the North were low. There was much criticism of Lincoln's administration, and he felt that to announce the emancipation of the slaves might unite the Northern people in loyal support of the cause.

Second, Lincoln knew that the service of several million Negroes on the farms of the South was one of the great sources of Southern military strength. The Negroes raised food while the white men were fighting in the armies. If the slaves were declared free, Lincoln believed, many would leave their masters, and a telling blow would be delivered at the resources of the South.

Third, Lincoln believed that emancipation would swing wavering European governments to the support of the Northern cause. Since the outbreak of the war the British government had not concealed its hope that the South would win its independence. Indeed, financial and business leaders who controlled Parliament had urged that the British government recognize the independence of the Confederacy. Such recognition would give the Confederates certain rights which they did not then possess, such as those of building vessels and obtaining war materials in England. Among the mass of the English people, however, and among a few liberal leaders there was definite antislavery feeling, and this fact had so far served to keep the British government from recognizing the independence of the Confederate States.

Furthermore, Lincoln knew that Southern agents were in several European capitals, trying to influence public opinion and to persuade the governments to recognize the independence of the South. Lincoln saw the danger only too well. If England and France should recognize the Confederate States, supplies and money would pour into the South, and the North might even be defeated in the end. It was a difficult situation, indeed. But Lincoln solved that problem in addition to handling all his other terrific burdens. From month to month, through one dangerous incident after another, he succeeded in maintaining friendly relations with European governments.

By the summer of 1862 the various factors in the situation led Lincoln to decide to issue a proclamation of emancipation. He had promised that if McClellan forced Lee back across the Potomac he would "send the proclamation after him." The day after the battle of Antietam had been fought, while Lee, unable to achieve his aims in Maryland, was in retreat, Lincoln issued the *Emancipation Proclamation*. It was given to the country on September 22, 1862, with the announcement that it would become effective January 1, 1863, in any state which was resisting the Union on that date.[1]

At first the news of the proclamation was not received with enthusiasm by the people. It was regarded as too radical, and Lincoln was freely criticized for his stand. Later, in answer to Horace Greeley's criticisms in the *New York Tribune*, Lincoln replied by saying:

My paramount object in this struggle is to save the Union, and is not either to save or destroy slavery. If I could save the Union without freeing any slave, I would do it; and if I could save it by freeing all the slaves, I would do it; and if I could save it by freeing some and leaving others alone, I would also do that.

In Europe the proclamation was so well received that it soon became evident that the South could no longer hope for aid from England or France. When the people of the North saw the effect which the proclamation had on Europe, they were converted to the wisdom of Lincoln's move.

[1] Remember that the Emancipation Proclamation *did not abolish slavery* in America. It simply indicated to the world that it was the intention of the Northern government to free all slaves in any state of the South which had not surrendered by the following January. The legal freeing *of all the slaves* came later with the passing of the Thirteenth Amendment to the Constitution (in force December 18, 1865).

Opposition to the War both in the North and in the South

At the beginning of the war regiments of young men had thrown themselves into the fray enthusiastically. They enlisted for three months only, since each side believed that the war would soon end. You know now how the struggle wore on, month after month, at first with little superiority on either side.

Fig. 155. A scene during the draft riots in New York, when houses were sacked and people were killed. (From the *New York Illustrated News*, July, 1863)

Within a year it was becoming impossible to secure sufficient volunteers to take the places of tens of thousands of youth who were being captured, wounded, or killed. Early in 1862 the South was compelled to resort to the draft, or conscription, by which every able-bodied man between certain ages was *compelled* to serve in the army. In 1863 the North was forced to take the same step.

The draft met with great opposition in both North and South. In New York City a terrible riot broke out, which lasted from July 13 to 16. More than 1000 people were killed or wounded, government offices were wrecked, and homes of Federal leaders were burned. In other parts of the country hostile uprisings also broke out. In the South governors of states denied the right of the Confederate government to draft men for the army. The people of the Southern seaboard states openly resisted the officers, and many men fled into the hills to avoid going to war.

There were many exemptions from military service, which caused great bitterness among those not exempted. In the South any person who owned fifteen slaves was exempted; in the North any person might furnish a substitute or was exempted if he paid $300. Thousands of citizens who could afford to do so hired other people to take their places.

On both sides the enemies of the established governments denounced their governments and opposed them, adding to the grave difficulties of carrying on the war itself.

On both sides a few men were making fortunes for themselves through their contracts to furnish military supplies. The mass of the people, however, who remained at home, were in a worse condition than ever. Although wages rose high, the cost of living rose even higher. One historian asserts that the only persons to profit by the war were those few financial and business leaders who sold war necessities to the governments.

The Eastern Campaign of 1863

Lee again invaded the North. In May, 1863, General Lee, with an army about half the size of the Northern army, defeated General Hooker at *Chancellorsville*, Virginia. But it was a costly victory for the South, for during the battle "Stonewall" Jackson was shot by his own Southern soldiers, who mistook his staff for Federal cavalry. The next day he died, saying, "Let us cross over the river and rest under the shade of the trees." A great leader had been lost to the South. When General Lee heard of Jackson's death, he exclaimed, "I have lost my right arm." It was true. He had lost one of his greatest supporters as well as a loyal friend.

Lee again invaded the North. Up through the Shenandoah valley and across the Potomac his men marched into the state of Pennsylvania. Onward he went, until within a few miles of Harrisburg. Great anxiety reigned throughout the North. In Philadelphia defenses were thrown up. Union regiments were

THE CIVIL WAR

hastily sent into Pennsylvania to hold Lee back. Hooker was severely criticized for his failure at Chancellorsville and was replaced by General George G. Meade.

The battle of Gettysburg. Then followed one of the most decisive battles of the war — the bloody three-day slaughter at Gettysburg, July 1–3, 1863. For the first two days the battle was favorable to the Confederate army. On the third day came a turning point. One of the Southern commanders, General Pickett, with 15,000 chosen men, made a charge across a mile of open valley against the Federal batteries. As confidently and gaily as if they were on dress parade, Pickett's men marched forward. Both Union and Confederate soldiers held their breath

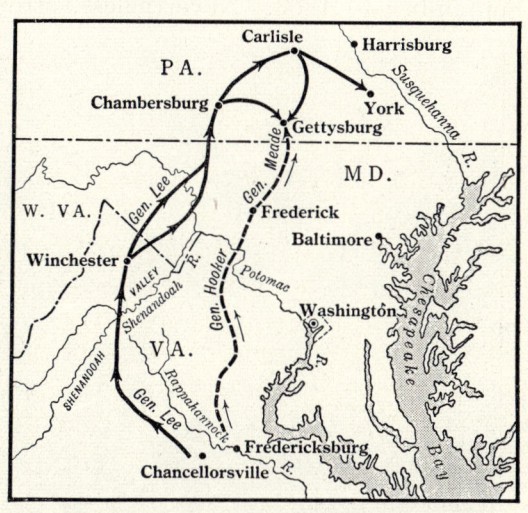

FIG. 156. Lee's final invasion of the North

with admiration. There was little sound, except when the Union officers could be heard saying quietly to their men, "Steady, men, steady! Don't fire yet!"

Pickett's division disappeared in a hollow. Then, as they came within close range, they all appeared as if risen from the ground, running toward the Federal lines. The Federal rifles cracked, cannon roared, and great holes were gouged into the gray ranks. They closed immediately, however, and on went the gallant Southerners. They surged up to the Union ranks, but were forced back under a murderous fire. Not one mounted officer was left uninjured, and three fourths of the soldiers were killed or wounded. The tide of battle had turned. Lee retreated across the Potomac. At the same time came the news that Vicksburg on the Mississippi had fallen.

The Second Partition of the Confederacy

In the meantime, the Union armies in the west were continuing their endeavor to drive another wedge into the Confederacy. *Chattanooga*, near the southern boundary of Tennessee, was captured by the Northern commander General Rosecrans, on September 9, 1863. Nevertheless, strong Southern forces still

Fig. 157. During the battle of Lookout Mountain

blocked the way, and on September 20 Rosecrans was defeated by Bragg at the bloody battle of *Chickamauga*. The Northern army was forced back to Chattanooga, where it was besieged by Bragg's army for two months.

It was at that point in the war that General Ulysses S. Grant was placed in sole command of the western armies. Then followed Union successes at the battles of *Lookout Mountain* and *Missionary Ridge*. The Southern troops were pressed back into Mississippi, Alabama, and Georgia.

General Grant made commander in chief of the Union armies. Early in 1864 Lincoln appointed Grant lieutenant-general in command of all the armies of the United States. A new plan was then worked out by which it was hoped the war would soon be ended. Sherman was to push southeast from Chattanooga, Tennessee, to Savannah, Georgia, in a further effort to split the Confederacy, and Grant, who had gone east to assume his command, was to march south and attempt to take Richmond.

Sherman's march to the sea. Sherman's men drove onward from Chattanooga to Atlanta, raiding as they went. Soon they were cut off from supplies from the North, but they lived off the land which they raided.

After a battle near Atlanta in which the losses to both sides were tremendous, Sherman captured the city. Then he started with 60,000 men on his well-known march "from Atlanta to the sea." A swath 60 miles wide was cut through the heart of the South. Rails were torn up; roads and bridges were destroyed. Supplies which could not be consumed by the army were burned. Raiding, burning, destroying as he went, he finally reached Savannah. The Southern forces withdrew from the city, and Sherman entered it on December 20, 1864.

A month later Sherman started north to join Grant in Virginia. Onward he went, more slowly now because Southern troops were destroying railroads and bridges as they retreated before him.

Grant's Final Campaign

Sherman's march from Chattanooga had begun on the same day that Grant began his final campaign to capture the Southern capital. In order to reach Richmond Grant was obliged, after crossing the Rapidan River, to travel through a desolate region rightly named "the Wilderness." There he encountered the Southern army, and desperate fighting took place. Battles were now fought almost daily, and the losses, especially on the Northern side, were very large.

Lee attempted a last offensive, sending General Early with a large force down the Shenandoah valley to attack Washington. Grant then sent Sheridan with a part of the Union army to reënforce the troops in Washington. Several hard battles were fought, and Early was driven back out of the valley. This was the last attempt of the Confederates to advance on Washington.

During the following winter peace negotiations were considered. President Davis sent representatives to Lincoln to try to arrange terms. Lincoln, however, demanded the return of the seceding states to the Union. To this the Confederates would not agree, and the war went on.

Petersburg and Richmond were under siege the entire winter. In March (1865) Lee, although faced by Grant with more than twice the number of his troops, believed that if he extended his

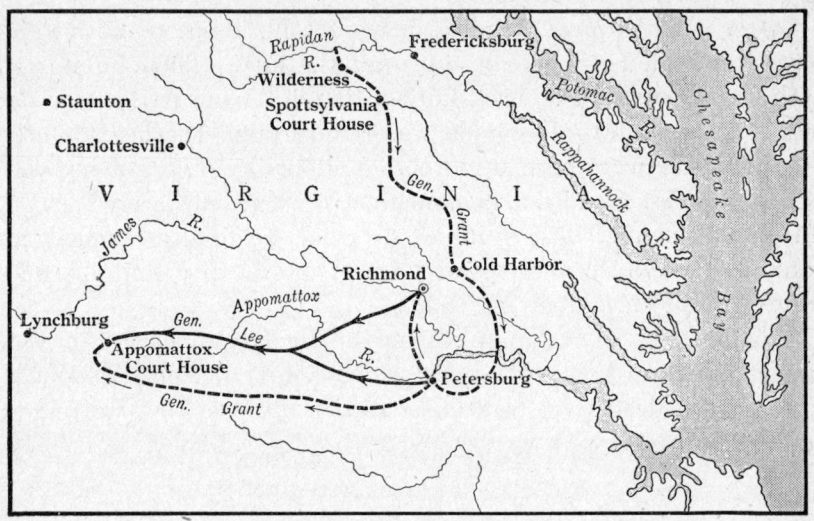

FIG. 158. Grant's final campaign

line to join Johnston at Lynchburg he might postpone the day of surrender. Grant ordered Sheridan to prevent this union. At Five Forks Sheridan won a decisive victory. Lee was obliged to withdraw from both Petersburg and Richmond. With retreat cut off by Sheridan and hotly pursued by Grant, Lee realized the hopelessness of his position. Grant communicated with him, pointing out that he was far outnumbered, that his army lacked supplies, and that it was impossible for the South to win. Lee met Grant at Appomattox Court House on April 9, 1865, to arrange for surrender. Grant held out his hand and said quietly, "I met you once before, General Lee, while we were serving in Mexico. . . . I think I should have recognized you anywhere." Lee was equally courteous and cordial. The terms of surrender were quickly agreed upon. Grant asked only that the men lay down their arms and return to their homes. He allowed those who had horses, to keep them, saying that they would "need them for the spring plowing." Lee thanked him, adding, "It will do much toward conciliating our people." Lee then turned toward the soldiers who crowded around him and said, "We have fought through the war together. I have done the best I could for you. My

FIG. 159. The meeting between Lee and Grant, which resulted in peace between the North and the South. (From a painting by Stanley M. Arthurs)

heart is too full to say more." Grant sent the news of the surrender to Washington and forbade his men to celebrate the victory.

Shortly after the surrender at Appomattox, Johnston, the Confederate general, surrendered to Sherman, and other Southern forces likewise laid down their arms.

After the War

The war was over. The house divided against itself was now united. There was joy and relief throughout the country that at last peace had come.

The joy in the North was short-lived, however. Six days after Lee had surrendered, Lincoln was dead. An actor, John Wilkes

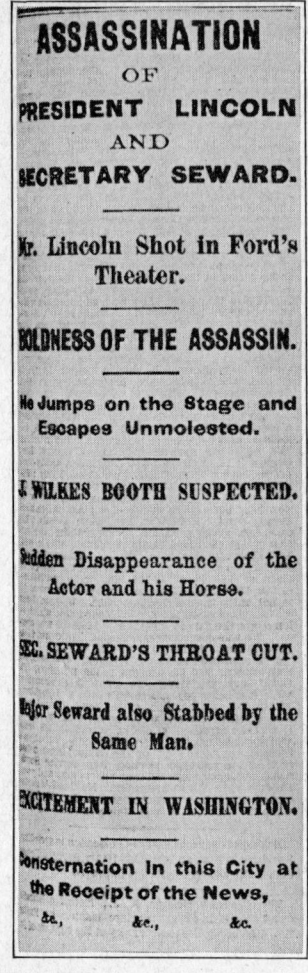

Fig. 160. Headlines announcing the assassination of Lincoln. (From the *New York World*, April 15, 1865. Courtesy of the New York Historical Society)

Booth, believed to have been made insane by the surrender of the South, shot the President while he was sitting in his box at Ford's Theater in Washington, April 14, 1865. Amid great excitement the President was taken to a private house opposite the theater, where he died the next morning. The North had lost its great leader, and the South a true friend.

Many people of the South were desperately poor — those who had been rich as well as those who had always been poor. Property in slaves, each slave worth $1000 or more, was gone. Men who before the war had been wealthy were now forced to plow in the fields. Brave mistresses of what were once great plantations cooked for the returning soldiers. In the diary of one Southern planter's daughter we read:

Good Friday, 1865. This is the saddest Good Friday I ever knew. I have spent the whole day praying for our stricken people, our crushed Southland. . . .

Unless I can get work and make some money, we must stay indoors for decency's sake. [Her shoes had holes in them.] They are but shoes I cobbled out of bits of stout cloth. . . . O God, what can I do! I who have never been taught any work that seems to be needed now! Who is there to pay me for the few things I know how to do? I envy our negroes who have been trained to occupations that bring money; they can hire out to the Yankees, and I can't. Our negroes are leaving us. We had to advise them to go.[1]

[1] Myrta L. Avary, *Dixie after the War*, p. 77. Doubleday, Page & Company, New York, 1906.

What was happening to the Negroes who had been freed?

In December, 1865, the Thirteenth Amendment was added to the Constitution, and the Negroes were free. "Free as a bird" was what the Negroes often said of themselves in the very first days after the war. Free to go where they pleased. But where should they go?

Some of them stayed on living in their old cabins on the plantations. Many of them began to drift to the cities, not knowing for what they were looking. They knew only that they had been given their freedom and that with that freedom they should have "a better life." Some innocently thought that they could live as their masters had done before the war. More often they thought of the "forty acres and a mule" which they firmly believed the Northern government was going to give each freedman.

The Federal government had never had any intention of giving the black man more than his freedom. What more could he ask?

A famous and respected Negro, in writing of the condition of the emancipated slave, said that

he was free from the old plantation, but he had nothing but the dusty road under his feet. He was free from the old quarter that once gave him shelter, but a slave to the rains of summer and to the frosts of winter. He was . . . turned loose, naked, hungry, and destitute to the open sky.

Disappointed, worn out, starving, many of the Negroes who had hoped for so much slipped back to the plantations of their old masters. There at least were work, food, and, with good fortune, wages.

What the War cost

In round numbers, it is highly probable that more than 800,000 men lost their lives in the Civil War. How many more were maimed for life we have no means of knowing, since the records were badly kept.

The actual war expenditures on both sides were estimated to be more than $5,000,000,000. The estimated cost of the first three years of reconstruction work in the South was $3,000,000,000. It is known that the national debt in 1865 had grown to nearly $3,000,000,000 and that most of this enormous amount had been spent on the Civil War. In addition to these expenditures, however, huge amounts of money had to be raised in taxes — national, state, and municipal. Enormous sums were spent for pensions for the soldiers and their dependents. Putting all estimates together, historians are now of the opinion that the Civil War cost not less than $25,000,000,000. How tragic to realize that this war cost many times as much as would have been necessary to purchase the slaves of all the Southern states outright and give them their freedom!

The days of the slave power were over. A new social and economic order was to develop. The control of the national government was to pass into other hands.

INTERESTING READINGS FROM WHICH YOU CAN GET ADDITIONAL INFORMATION

BACHELLER, IRVING. A Man for the Ages. The Bobbs-Merrill Company, Indianapolis. The story of Abraham Lincoln.

BARNES, JAMES. The Son of Light-Horse Harry. Harper & Brothers, New York. The life and adventures of Robert E. Lee.

BULLARD, F. LAURISTON. Tad and his Father. Little, Brown and Company, Boston. Lincoln during the war.

HILL, FREDERICK T. On the Trail of Grant and Lee. D. Appleton and Company, New York. Interesting biography of two great leaders.

NICOLAY, HELEN. The Boys' Life of Abraham Lincoln. The Century Co., New York. Most interesting.

NICOLAY, HELEN. The Boys' Life of Ulysses S. Grant. The Century Co., New York. An interesting biography.

PAXSON, FREDERIC L. The Civil War. Henry Holt and Company, New York.

ROOSEVELT, THEODORE, and LODGE, H. C. Hero Tales from American History. The Century Co., New York.

SPARHAWK, FRANCES C. Life of Lincoln for Boys. Thomas Y. Crowell Company, New York. You will enjoy this reference.

STEPHENSON, NATHANIEL W. Abraham Lincoln and the Union, Vol. XXIX of The Chronicles of America. Yale University Press, New Haven. A reference for the best readers.

STODDARD, W. O. The Battle of New York. D. Appleton and Company, New York. The author was a volunteer with the police in the great draft riot in New York.

STODDARD, W. O. The Boy Lincoln. D. Appleton and Company, New York. Story of Lincoln's life from ten to sixteen, written by a friend who knew him well.

STODDARD, W. O. Long Bridge Boys. Lothrop, Lee & Shepard Co., Boston. An authentic record of what happened in Washington at the beginning of the war.

CHAPTER XVII

THE RECONSTRUCTION PERIOD OF THE SOUTH

As you know, when the Southern states seceded, they set up their own government. Departments were organized to take care of the needs of the Southern people. They were similar to those of the Federal government. Now that the Confederacy was overthrown, all the departments of government throughout the South were in a state of confusion.

On the day following Lee's surrender, Lincoln and the Federal Congress faced the serious problem of establishing a working government throughout the South, which could operate until the regular government could be restored.[1]

Lincoln's plan

Lincoln's desire to deal kindly with the South was shown immediately after the announcement of Lee's surrender. Mobs of overjoyed people besieged the White House, calling on the President for a speech. It was a trying moment for Lincoln. What words should he speak to his people — South as well as North — that would please all of them and not increase the bitterness between the two sections. Lincoln rose to the occasion.

He said in his quaint way that he had no speech ready, and concluded humorously: "I have always thought 'Dixie' was one of the best tunes I ever heard. I insisted yesterday that we had fairly captured it. I presented the question to the Attorney-General and he gave his opinion that it is our lawful prize. I ask the band to give us a good turn upon it." In that little speech, he claimed of the South by right of conquest, a song — and nothing more.[2]

---

[1] There were equally serious problems of restoring agriculture and trade in the South. These difficult and important problems you have already studied in Chapter XXII of *A History of American Civilization*. It is likely that you will wish to re-read that chapter at this point.

[2] Myrta L. Avary, *Dixie after the War*, p. 43. Doubleday, Page & Company, New York, 1906.

Later Lincoln said to a Virginian: "You people will all come back now, and we shall have old Virginia home again." That was what he wanted — to bring the Southern states back into the Union with the least friction, the least hard feeling, and within the shortest time possible.

Before his death Lincoln had also planned to set up governments immediately in all the Southern states. At his last

FIG. 161. A view of Washington today. In the left foreground stands a building called the Lincoln Memorial. It is a national tribute to the president who preserved the Union

cabinet meeting, on April 14, the day he was shot, he said, "If we are wise and discreet, we shall re-animate the states and get their governments in successful operation before Congress meets."

The plan which Lincoln intended to use was a simple one. As soon as 10 per cent of the people of a state who had voted in 1860 took an oath of loyalty to the Constitution and the Union, they could set up a government. Indeed, Arkansas and Louisiana had already done so, and before Lincoln's death reconstruction had been begun in Tennessee and Virginia.

With Lincoln's death the most powerful influence for moderation was gone and there was none to take his place. How did the lesser leaders and the people of the North feel regarding the South?

RECONSTRUCTION PERIOD OF THE SOUTH

Northern leaders were divided as to policy

Sentiment in the North was sharply divided as to how the problems of the South should be met. There were two groups, the moderates and the radicals. The moderates did not wish to punish the states which had seceded. They wished to help the Southern white people to reëstablish their government as easily and quickly as possible. Lincoln himself had been the leader of this group. On the other hand, the radical group believed Lincoln's plan was too lenient. They wanted to punish the South. One way was to give the freed Negroes the right to vote. In this way they could prevent the Southern whites from regaining much of their former power. Moreover, many of the radical Republicans had formerly been abolitionists. They believed that the Negro should be not only free but should have all the rights of a citizen, for example, the right to hold office. Members of the Republican party also saw in these proposed measures a way of obtaining political support from the 3,000,000 or more Negroes in the South.

Then, too, after Lincoln's assassination feeling in the North had become more bitter against the South. Many Northerners believed that Southerners were responsible for the assassination. In the months after that fatal April 14 the North was angry. Many men who would otherwise have accepted a mild policy were no longer willing to do so.

The events of the next twelve years, 1865–1877, known in American history as the Reconstruction Period, revealed the struggle between these two groups and these two policies.

The new president

Andrew Johnson, vice president during Lincoln's second administration, now took the place left vacant by Lincoln's death. What manner of man was it on whom so great a problem rested?

Andrew Johnson came of a poor Southern family. He had received little education; in fact, his wife had taught him to write after their marriage. Before his entrance into political life Johnson had been a tailor. Then he had risen first to a position of local importance in the politics of Tennessee and later to the governorship of that state. He was a member of the United States Senate when Tennessee seceded from the Union. He was the only Southern member of that body who had remained in his seat after his state had seceded. He loved the Union, and he hated slavery. He was known to be industrious, courageous, and intelligent. Yet he was often coarse in manner and totally lacking in tact.

Fig. 162. Andrew Johnson

Whatever the attributes of Johnson were, it is unquestionably true that he faced a situation made doubly difficult by the determination of Congress to regain the power which, during the war, had necessarily fallen into the president's hands. Then, too, Johnson's position was weak, for he lacked the prestige of having been an elected president.

Now that Lincoln was gone, the radicals thought they could carry out their policies. Johnson had expressed himself in strong terms about the way the South should be treated. He apparently believed in a stern policy of repression toward all former "rebels."

Johnson changes his Views

During the first few weeks of his presidency, however, a change came over Johnson. It is difficult to be sure what happened. No doubt two moderate Republicans in his cabinet — Seward and Welles — influenced him somewhat. No doubt also, when he realized the tremendous task of uniting the two sections and of doing it peaceably, he decided that Lincoln's plan was the most satisfactory one. At any rate, we find him reorganizing the remaining Southern states on a plan very much like that which

Lincoln had used. This plan provided that the white voters of a state who would take the oath of loyalty should (1) hold a convention and organize a state government without slavery, (2) repeal the act of secession, (3) repudiate the war debt of the state, and (4) ratify the Thirteenth Amendment to the Constitution, which had been proposed by Congress on February 1, 1865.

During the summer of 1865 Johnson persuaded the white leaders of the South to take these steps. When Congress assembled in December, 1865, he was able to report that nearly all the Confederate states were ready to be readmitted to the Union.

The Thirteenth Amendment had provided nothing whatever for the Negro but his freedom. All the details of his economic, political, and social status were left to the individual states. Under these circumstances the Southern states, confronted by an almost impossible situation, passed laws which were intended to meet the need. In many states they made it difficult or impossible for the Negro to vote. They placed various other restrictions upon him: in some states he could not own property; in others he was required to obtain a license before he could work at certain trades; in still others he was forced to work or be arrested. Congress immediately rejected these laws and began to make plans for reconstruction along lines of its own.

And then began the struggle between President Johnson's moderates and the radicals in Congress. Thaddeus Stevens, the leader of the radicals, demanded that the Negro be given all the political rights which the white man possessed. When the Southern states, having fulfilled the terms laid down by Johnson's plan, applied for recognition of their state governments Congress refused their petitions. President Johnson and the moderates resented this attitude of Congress. Nevertheless the radicals now proceeded with *their* plan of reconstruction, totally disregarding the state governments which had been set up according to Johnson's plan.

THE FOURTEENTH AMENDMENT TO THE CONSTITUTION

In 1866 Congress passed a *Civil Rights Bill,* which protected the person and the property of the freed Negroes in the same manner that the white man was protected. President Johnson vetoed the bill, saying that it was unconstitutional. More than two thirds of the Congress was opposed to Johnson, however, and passed the bill over his veto. Then still further to make sure

FIG. 163. The lobby of the House of Representatives during the passage of the Civil Rights Bill in 1866. (From *Harper's Weekly,* April, 1866)

that the rights of the Negroes would not be taken away from them, Congress proposed the *Fourteenth Amendment* to the Constitution.[1]

This amendment declared that *all* persons (except when disqualified by law), whether born or naturalized in the United States, were to be citizens. The second section of the amendment provided that any state which deprived its citizens of the right to vote (except for certain crimes) should have its number of Representatives in the Federal Congress reduced. The Fourteenth Amendment also excluded from holding office (unless Congress later provided for it by a two-thirds vote) all men who had formerly been national or state officials serving the Confederate

[1] See Appendix. This amendment was not adopted until 1868.

cause. Furthermore, the amendment forbade the Southern states to pay the war debts incurred by the Confederacy; but it held them equally liable with the Northern states for payment of the national debt. Tennessee ratified the Fourteenth Amendment and was readmitted to the Union. The other states of the old Confederacy refused to ratify it, and the radicals in Congress took steps to punish them.

The Reconstruction Act

In March, 1867, Congress passed the *Reconstruction Act*, which provided that all the territory of the seceding states (except Tennessee) should be divided into five districts, each in charge of a military commander supported by Northern troops. These commanders were to register all voters; that is, *all* male citizens, whether white or black, with the exception of the white soldiers and officials of the Confederacy, who were denied citizenship. The voters thus registered were to elect delegates to state conventions. Then the delegates were to set up new state governments, which could apply for readmission to the Union. According to the Reconstruction Act the terms of readmission were hard. Each state must include Negro suffrage in its constitution, and this constitution must be ratified by the people of the state. Finally, the state must secure from Congress the approval of its constitution and permission for its readmission into the Union. Even then readmission was to be delayed until three fourths of all the states had ratified the Fourteenth Amendment. The Reconstruction Act, like other acts of Congress dealing with the reconstruction of the South, was vetoed by President Johnson. Again, however, the radical Congress passed it over his veto.

This act really placed the control of the Southern state governments in the hands of Northerners and ignorant Negroes. There were not more than 600,000 white men who (under the act) could qualify as voters in the entire South. These were far outnumbered by the Negroes, who had been given citizenship. Seven states — Arkansas, North Carolina, South Carolina, Alabama, Louisiana, Georgia, and Florida — formed new governments under the Reconstruction Act, officially gave the Negroes the vote, and ratified the Fourteenth Amendment. They were readmitted to the Union in 1868 and most of the troops were withdrawn. Georgia, however, removed the Negroes in her legislature and replaced them with white men who had served in the

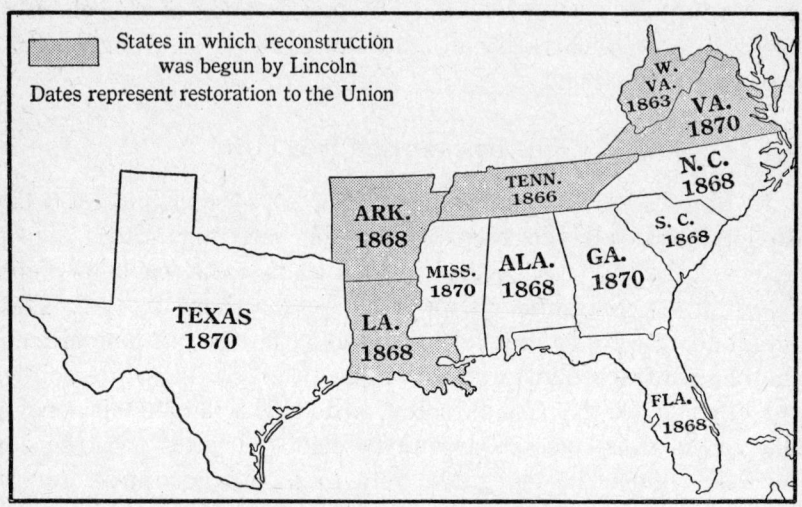

FIG. 164. The Reconstruction of the South

Confederacy. For this act the military government was reinstated. It was not until 1870 that Georgia, Virginia, Mississippi, and Texas were finally brought into the Union.

The impeachment of Johnson

Month by month the bitter quarrel between the radicals and the President increased. Johnson vetoed each new law, only to be overridden by a two-thirds majority of the Congress. Finally an open break came. Among other laws aimed at reducing the power of the President, Congress passed the *Tenure of Office Act*, on March 2, 1867. This forbade the President to remove members of his cabinet from office except with the consent of the Senate. In August of the same year Johnson, who had long been out of sympathy with his Secretary of War, Edwin M. Stanton, removed him from office. Then the radicals brought impeachment proceedings against the President, that is, they accused

Johnson of "high crimes and misdemeanors" and proposed to remove him from office. The trial, conducted before the United States Senate, was bitterly contested on both sides. Finally, on May 26, 1868, the vote was taken. The radicals lacked one vote

FIG. 165. A scene at the trial of Andrew Johnson. This is the first and only time a president of the United States has been impeached. Note the crowded visitors' gallery. (From *Leslie's Illustrated Newspaper*, March, 1868)

of the necessary two thirds to remove the President. Johnson had won by a narrow margin and retained office until the expiration of his term in 1869.

Under the radical plan carpetbaggers, scalawags, and Negroes ruled the South for several years

Although Johnson had won his case and retained the presidency, Congress now ruled supreme.

The Reconstruction Act inaugurated one of the most disgraceful episodes in the history of American government. Many Northern adventurers, known as carpetbaggers because they carried all their worldly goods in the old-fashioned carpetbag, rushed south to get what spoils they could from the new governments.

Assisting them were Negroes and "turncoat Southerners," white men who had deserted their former Southern friends and were now known as scalawags. There were many honest people who took part in the reconstruction movement, but the good they were able to accomplish has been overshadowed by the great damage which came from the disreputable carpetbag rule.

Fig. 166. This is a cartoon of a carpetbagger preparing to take office. The weapons indicate that he is ready to use force if necessary

What part did the Negroes play? They were like bewildered children. They had been long held in slavery and had long been denied education and political rights. It is little wonder if in their ignorance they became the tools of unscrupulous carpetbaggers and scalawags.

During these years the radical Republicans attempted to build up a very strong political organization in the South. The Republicans had freed the Negroes; naturally they expected the Negroes to support them politically. The Republicans did everything in their power to help bring the Negroes into their party. Societies, like the *Union League Club*, organized to help carry on the war, formed branches among the Negroes and drilled them into the belief that the Republicans were their friends and the Democrats their enemies.

The carpetbag governments were both inefficient and corrupt. Whites and Negroes who could neither read nor write were sent as representatives to the state legislatures. Other officials, both high and low, were appointed to positions for which they had not the slightest qualifications.

The white planters retaliated with terrorism: the Ku-Klux Klan

The white planters, who had ruled the country for so long, were determined to recover their lost power and get rid of the corrupt governments which were completing the ruin of their states.

One method they used was that made possible by the Ku-Klux Klan. This was a secret organization of Southern whites which had been formed soon after the war by a group of young ex-Confederate soldiers. At first it was merely a social organization, but as it increased in numbers and new branches were formed it came to be used for other purposes — to frighten Negroes, carpetbaggers, and scalawags, and to force undesirable officials to promise to leave a district or resign their positions.

By night the Klan members would ride forth clothed in long white garments which made them look like ghosts.

Fig. 167. Disguises used by the Ku-Klux Klan

Many people, long bred in superstition, were easily frightened by the sight. If fright did not accomplish their purpose, however, sometimes the Klan resorted to violence. The most important purpose of the Klan was to break down Republican power and to restore the power of the Democratic party.

The Negroes were the chief victims of the Ku-Klux Klan, but whites who sympathized with the Negroes were also attacked. Many incidents could be told of the manner in which the Klan terrorized whole districts of the South. The force used by the Klan was sometimes brutal and wrong, but so were the things the carpetbaggers were doing. The latter were often corrupt, and their Negro tools were, with few exceptions, illiterate and incapable of governing. Thus the white planters, deprived of other means of protection, attempted through a secret organization to "fight fire with fire."

THE FIFTEENTH AMENDMENT WAS PASSED, 1870

Although the *Fourteenth Amendment* had guaranteed "citizenship" to the Negroes, the Southern whites in power had succeeded in preventing most of the Negroes from voting. To protect further the Negro's right to suffrage, Congress proposed the *Fifteenth Amendment* to the Constitution. This provided that the rights of citizens of the United States to vote should not be denied or abridged by the United States or by any state on account of race, color, or previous condition of servitude. This amendment was ratified and made effective in 1870.

Thus between 1865 and 1870 three new amendments were added to the United States Constitution. All of them were intended to guarantee the new status of the Negro. The Thirteenth Amendment declared him free, the Fourteenth declared him a citizen, and the Fifteenth maintained his right to vote. No amendments had been made to the Constitution since the passing of the Twelfth Amendment in 1804. For more than half a century government in the United States had been conducted under legal provisions established before 1804. And not for nearly another half-century was the Constitution to be changed again.

In spite of the Fourteenth and Fifteenth Amendments the former ruling classes gradually regained some of their power in the Southern states. Ways were found to evade the Negro's Constitutional rights. Laws were passed which kept most Negroes from voting. Some states passed laws which required each voter to be able to *read* or to "*understand*" the Constitution. But in each election district white men decided whether the would-be voters could "understand." The records show clearly that these laws, which were used against the Negroes, were not applied to the poor whites who were equally unable to read or to understand the Constitution.

In retaliation the Federal Congress passed laws in 1870 and

RECONSTRUCTION PERIOD OF THE SOUTH 369

1871 which declared that any attempt to prevent Negroes from voting should be regarded as a crime. They also provided that deputy marshals should be present at elections to protect the Negro voter.

Thus by laws and counter-laws, by fear, by force, the struggle went on between the Northern politicians and the Southern ruling class. But gradually the Southern whites regained their

FIG. 168. Negroes voting at the polls in New Orleans. (From *Leslie's Illustrated Newspaper*, November, 1867)

power; gradually the carpetbaggers and scalawags were ousted. By 1875 all the Southern states except South Carolina, Louisiana, and Florida had passed into the control of the Democrats. In these states the results of the election of 1876 were disputed, and only the presence of Federal troops kept the Democrats from taking over these state governments, too. Accordingly, when in 1877 the troops were withdrawn from all the Southern states, Republican rule disappeared in the South.

Several years before this it was evident that radicalism in the North was losing ground. For example, in 1872 Congress passed the *Amnesty Act*. By this act full citizenship was given to all

Southern white men with the exception of about 500 who had been active leaders in the Confederacy. Many of these were later restored to citizenship by special acts, and in 1898 a general amnesty act included all who were still unpardoned.

Thus by 1877 fairly peaceful conditions were restored throughout the South. All the states had been readmitted; practically all white men had been restored to citizenship. Slavery was gone; the black men now worked for wages. But they lived much as they had lived before. Only a few could vote, and these had little power. White men's governments had been reëstablished throughout the South, and the period known in American history as the Reconstruction Period was over.

Then began a half-century of peaceful development in the South. From your reading of *A History of American Civilization* you know how the New South rose from the ashes of the Old South. Agriculture revived; more people came to own and farm land; new crops were introduced. Textile mills sprang up through the Southeast. Iron mines were opened up. Large manufacturing centers grew up. Modern cities rose where many crude villages and towns had stood before. Slowly but surely the breach between the two sections was closed.

INTERESTING READINGS FROM WHICH YOU CAN GET ADDITIONAL INFORMATION

CABLE, G. W. John March, Southerner. Charles Scribner's Sons, New York. Story of the Reconstruction Period.

ELSON, HENRY W. Sidelights on American History. The Macmillan Company, New York. See especially Volume II (on reconstruction), pp. 149–183.

FLEMING, WALTER L. The Sequel of Appomattox, Vol. XXXII of The Chronicles of America. Yale University Press, New Haven. Good general reference for the best readers.

GLASGOW, ELLEN. The Voice of the People. Doubleday, Page & Company, New York. Virginia during the Reconstruction Period.

HALSEY, FRANCIS W. (Editor). Great Epochs in American History. Funk & Wagnalls Company, New York. See Volume IX, pp. 3–15, 59–69, 188–195.

HART, ALBERT B. (Editor). American History told by Contemporaries. The Macmillan Company, New York. See Volume IV, Part VII. For the best readers.

PAGE, THOMAS NELSON. Red Rock. Charles Scribner's Sons, New York. Plantation life during and after the Civil War.

PAXSON, FREDERIC L. The New Nation. Houghton Mifflin Company, Boston. The Restoration of Home Rule in the South, pp. 39–58. For the best readers.

UNIT VII

THE STRUGGLE OVER GOVERNMENT IN THE AGE OF BIG BUSINESS, 1865-1914

THE STRUGGLE OVER GOVERNMENT IN THE AGE OF BIG BUSINESS, 1865–1914

Now we come to the most important conflict of all — the struggle between the rising industrial and business leaders and the farmers, laborers, and civic reformers for the control of government.

In Chapters XVIII–XXII we shall consider the changes in government in the 50 years that stretched between the Civil War and the World War (1865–1914). Remember that this was the period of the great industrial expansion. It was the age of the corporation. It was the period in which the United States extended its boundaries beyond the continent.

In Chapter XVIII we shall set the stage for the discussion of how the political parties built up their machine organizations and took control of the government. In Chapter XIX we shall see how the wealthy captains of industry and their corporations began to play the leading rôle in political affairs.

Against this control of local, state, and national government by industrial and financial leaders there arose the nation-wide revolt of the farmers and the city laborers. In Chapter XX we shall study their attempts from 1865 to 1914 to obtain a larger share in government. In Chapter XXI we shall see the extent to which these groups were able to secure political power and pass laws putting the control of government more directly in the hands of the mass of the people.

Finally, in Chapter XXII we shall study the manner in which our national government extended beyond the borders of the North American continent — how the American flag came to fly over islands thousands of miles from Washington.

CHAPTER XVIII

GOVERNMENT BY PROFESSIONAL POLITICIANS[1]

The problems of the Negro and reconstruction in the South were not the only ones which the government at Washington had to face after the war. The North and the West likewise presented great difficulties.

You have already learned from *A History of American Civilization* how the Civil War brought rapid changes in manufacturing and business; how the demands created by the war for gigantic quantities of goods and supplies taught the Northern manufacturers to accumulate large amounts of capital and to produce manufactured articles in great quantities.[2]

During the period that followed the war the country changed more rapidly than ever before. The West was being settled; transcontinental railroads were being laid down; deposits of iron, gold, and silver were being discovered and mined; great underground lakes of oil were being exploited. At the same time, fortunes totaling millions were rapidly being made by daring and ambitious financiers in the North. The captain of industry was becoming a new figure in American life. In the meantime the great mass of the people was struggling to make a living.

In the first fifteen years after the close of the Civil War most people believed that any individual with intelligence, energy, and the gambling spirit could achieve a fortune or secure an important place in the government, thereby improving his social standing.

---

[1] The term *professional politician* as here used has an unpleasant meaning. It is true that the term may also be used in a good sense. What we mean by the expression is a politician who makes politics a business for personal gain. He is not interested in the science of government except as it may give him personal advantage. He is like the professional in sport. On the other hand, the professional politician in the good sense has spent years in training and perfecting himself with a view to public service. He is a true professional man.

[2] See Chapter XIX of *A History of American Civilization* at this point.

The difficulties the American people faced in trying to carry on democratic government

The American people were trying to carry on democratic government under difficult conditions. Let us see what these conditions were.

1. *People scattered over a tremendous territory.* The nation was spread over a vast area, the geographic features of which had created various ways of living in the different sections. Thus we see that the geographic conditions alone presented problems of government.

2. *Millions of foreign-born to assimilate.* Millions of immigrants were entering the North and the West, bringing to America their customs, languages, and standards of living. To teach them American ways of thinking and living and to make them Americans was indeed a difficult problem for any government.

3. *The lack of education among the masses.* Great numbers of people in the United States were uninformed as to the problems of government. They were spending their energy and time in earning their living and cared little about what was happening in the government.

4. *Wealth in the hands of a few people.* The control of banks, credit, railroads, and of coal, iron, and other key industries was exercised by a few persons. From the earliest days of the Republic there had been a feeling that government had no right to interfere in matters of business. As a few individuals began to build up large fortunes they became powerful in political affairs, and this power presented serious problems to the government. Business was now beginning to interfere in government.

Thus we see that the task of making America a really democratic country was difficult.

Two major political parties struggled for the control of government

Since 1800 the history of government had been the story of the struggle between political parties. First, the Federalists and the Anti-Federalists, or "Republicans," battled for control. Then the Democratic Republicans and the Whigs came into power,

GOVERNMENT BY PROFESSIONAL POLITICIANS 375

and many minor parties emerged. Finally there came the great slavery crisis, and the new Republican party under Abraham Lincoln appeared.

At the close of the Civil War most of the voters of the country belonged to one of the two major parties — the Republican party

FIG. 169. A procession of the Wide Awakes of the Republican party in 1860. This group took its name from the "wide awake" hats which they affected. (From *Harper's Weekly*, October, 1860)

or the Democratic party. And of these the Republican party led. It had "won the war," it said, and had firmly established itself in control.

The Organization of Political Parties

As the years went on each of the two chief parties developed a vast nation-wide organization to deal with its complicated activities.

1. The larger cities and towns all over the country were divided into large areas called districts. These in turn were divided into wards, and the wards into neighborhoods called precincts.

Over each district, precinct, and ward was a political leader, or "boss," who was usually chairman of the local committee.

2. Each city, town, or village also had its committee, presided over by its leader, or boss.

3. Each state was divided into counties, and the party in each county was directed by the county committee. The chairman of each county committee was also the county leader, or boss, of the party. Delegates to county conventions were elected by the towns and the city districts.

4. In each state the voters of the state were organized under a committee known as the state committee. The chairman of this committee was the leader, or boss, of the party in the state.

5. At the head of the whole organization was the central national committee, under the leadership of its chairman. This chairman, elected by the executive committee, was, therefore, one of the most powerful leaders in politics in the entire country.

It was an elaborate organization,— a great machine,— extending from the tiniest hamlet or village and the little neighborhood precincts in towns and cities to the state and national organizations and it has continued in practically the same form to the present day. Little wonder that the men who built up and directed such a political organization began to be known as machine politicians.

Who belonged to the Chief Parties?

The Republican party

Who belonged to the Republican party? Why was it so powerful? Was it because its political machine was better organized? Yes, better organization was partly responsible for its power, but it was also due to the fact that during the years following the Civil War the Republican party brought together many persons of wealth and power and large groups of citizens who had been benefited in one way or another by the party.

First, remember that the Republican party rode into power in 1860 on the slavery issue. It was the Republican party which controlled the government during the Civil War. Hence its members always claimed that the party had won the war, and many of its adherents were to be found among former abolitionists and reformers.

Second, at the close of the war most of the veterans of the Northern armies joined an organization known as the Grand Army of the Republic. This organization, nation-wide and effectively organized, was made up of nearly 1,000,000 men. Most of them were Republicans. Furthermore, in 1862, under the Republican administration, pensions had been provided for disabled Union soldiers and sailors of the Civil War or for their dependents in the event of their death. In later years the pension system, under Republican administration, was greatly expanded.

Third, in the North and West landowners and homesteaders, large and small, were usually Republicans. By the Homestead Act of 1862 thousands of homesteaders had taken up 160 acres of land on the Western plains at a cost of a $10 registry fee. Many, if not most, of these felt that they owed their land and hence their allegiance to the Republican party.

Fourth, in addition there were thousands of manufacturers and merchants who were aided by the maintenance of the high protective tariff for which the Republican party stood. These people were predominantly Republicans.

Fifth, there were the Negroes in the South, who had been freed by the Republican president, Lincoln, and who had been given the vote by a Republican Congress. They naturally voted the Republican ticket.

Thus the Republican party, as it developed after the Civil War, was a powerful partnership of people who had received or were receiving benefits under Republican administrations.

The Democratic party

Who belonged to the Democratic party? Quite naturally those people who felt that they had received no benefits and those who had suffered under the Republican administrations.

First, there was the Solid South. Before the Civil War less than half of the voters of the Southern states were Democrats. After the war, however, the white people of the South lined up unanimously against the Republicans and their carpetbag governments. Steadily, through a quarter of a century, in one national election after another, all the electors from the Confederate states were Democrats.

Second, there was a great mass of working people in the metropolitan centers of the North who had lately arrived as immigrants. Many of them had been discontented with the governments of their home lands. Rather naturally, therefore, when they became naturalized citizens they opposed the party which was in control of the national government. In other words they tended to join the Democratic party. These people were organized into party machines by the rising city bosses.

Third, a considerable group of people throughout the North disliked the high protective tariff which the Republican party sponsored. They were the merchants and the importers who brought in materials and manufactured goods from other countries to sell in this country for a profit. Their livelihood depended upon a low tariff just as the livelihood of many of the manufacturers depended on a high tariff. Hence most of the importers joined the Democratic party because that party sponsored a low tariff. These persons and the machine politicians formed the real leadership of the Democratic party in the North.

Fourth, there was another small but very influential group who were Democrats. These were the bankers who were responsible for selling railroad and other industrial bonds in Europe. Foreign buyers paid for American bonds with goods and not with money. When the tariff was too high these foreign buyers lost money, for they had to pay not only the worth of the bond in goods but also the tariff on the goods.

Thus not all the capitalists of the country belonged to the Republican party. Most of the larger importing merchants, some of the bankers, and some of those interested in railroads, industries, and other public utilities were Democrats. So the ranks of the capitalists were split between the two parties.

Political machinery and not great political statesmen controlled the government during these years. Let us turn to the events following the Civil War and see how this fact was illustrated.

"The Dreadful Decade"

In 1869 General Ulysses S. Grant became president of the United States. What manner of man was he to cope with the difficult problems of the government?

He was an honest, plain soldier, skillful in military strategy and wise in the management of troops, but quite inexperienced in government. He had known poverty in his youth and hardship throughout most of his life. Perhaps because he had never had money, he was overawed by it when confronted with gigantic governmental and financial problems. One man who knew him well, said of his administration: "I think the warmest friends of Grant feel that he has failed terribly as a president, but not from want of honesty."

Grant had not been president for very long when newspapers and reformers throughout the country began to ask blunt questions concerning the unusually large, personal expenditures which Congressmen in Washington were making. *The Cincinnati Enquirer*, for example, wanted to know how Congressmen of comparatively small incomes could build houses in Washington. "Where did they get the money?" was frequently asked, not only about Congressmen, but about the members of many state legislatures and city councils.

FIG. 170. Ulysses S. Grant

From all over the country the answer began to come from honest and outspoken editors, legislators, preachers, and social reformers. Governing officials were being corrupted. Who was responsible for this corruption? Investigations were begun in Congress and in the various states, and startling facts were unearthed which showed dishonest handling of government lands and funds.

The Union Pacific and Crédit Mobilier scandal

As you learned in *A History of American Civilization,* Congress adopted the policy of aiding private corporations to build the transcontinental railroads. At that time it was regarded as lawful and right to use the money in the United States Treasury (which had been raised by taxes, tariffs, etc.) for that purpose.

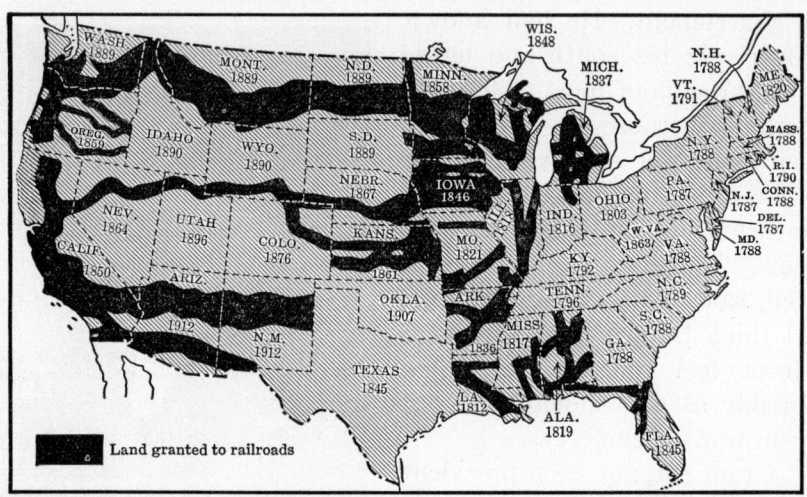

FIG. 171. The immense tracts of land which the government granted the railroads

It was maintained that no private companies could raise sufficient money to carry on such expensive enterprises. So Congress granted millions of dollars and millions of acres of land to the Union Pacific and other railroad companies.

In the three years that followed the war about three times as much land had been granted to the railroads as had been given to homesteaders in the same period. The whole country seemed railroad-mad. In one period of four years nearly 25,000 miles of railroad were built. Meanwhile the promoters of the companies made more than $200,000,000 by dealings in railroad stocks.

For example, in order to build the Union Pacific Railroad, a construction company, known as the *Crédit Mobilier,* was formed. As time passed the operations of this company fell under suspicion. A Congressional investigation was held in 1872 and 1873, when it was learned that the stockholders and directors of the

Union Pacific had themselves organized the Crédit Mobilier and that they were making huge profits not only from the contracts for constructing the railroad but also from government grants and from the purchase and sale of stock. It was also discovered that a number of government officials owned stock in the company, among them the vice president of the United States and several Representatives and Senators. These men were, in substance, granting government money and land to themselves.

Unscrupulous Individuals amassed Great Fortunes

It was during the 1870's also that dishonest speculators openly bribed legislatures and city councils in utter contempt for law and the rights of the public. They disregarded law, public opinion, and the rights of defenseless people, admitting that they were interested only in piling up wealth and accumulating power.

Some of these people bought the control of railroads, that is, they bought in each case more than half of the stock. Then they advanced the price of the stock to the highest possible point, which was often far beyond its real worth, and sold it to the general investing public. Having bought it when the price was low and sold it when it was high, they made millions of dollars. They also "watered" the stock, that is, they issued more stock than the earnings of the companies warranted. In the meantime, most of the railroad financiers let the locomotives, cars, rails, and other equipment of the railroads go to rack and ruin, making the stock of even less worth. They put the surplus income, which ought to have been spent in keeping up the railroads, into their own bank accounts.

Today, of course, such methods are illegal. The government has passed laws prohibiting them. In the 1860's and 1870's, however, they were not illegal, because the financiers bribed legislatures to let them do such things and bribed courts to support the legislatures.

Of all their daring speculations the boldest perhaps was their attempt to corner the gold supply of the country in 1869. In this scandal some of President Grant's relatives and near associates were involved.

"Black Friday," 1869

The manipulator of this scheme was Jay Gould, and with him in the enterprise was James Fisk, Jr. At that time the value of gold varied a great deal and people regularly gambled on its rise and fall. Gould's plan was to buy all the available gold, thus forcing the price up. Then he could sell it at a profit to those who had to have it in conducting their business. The only danger lay in the possibility of the government's selling some of the

FIG. 172. A scene in New York on "Black Friday" during the frantic attempt to buy gold. (From *Leslie's Illustrated Newspaper*, October, 1869)

gold held in reserve in the United States Treasury. This would send the price of gold down and defeat the plan. Through a relative of Grant's Gould succeeded in convincing the President that if gold went up Europe would use it to buy much American wheat and that by this means the farmers would be benefited. Grant accordingly advised his Secretary of the Treasury not to sell gold.

Gold then went up day after day. At last some of those who needed it appealed to the President, and Gould, learning of this and realizing that Grant would probably yield, began selling gold without letting his associate know what he was doing.

GOVERNMENT BY PROFESSIONAL POLITICIANS 383

Fisk continued to buy and to force the price still higher. Then on Friday, September 24, 1869, news came that the government had started to sell gold. Instantly the price fell. "The gigantic gold bubble had burst, and half Wall Street was involved in the ruin." The day has since been known in financial history as "Black Friday." Incidentally, Gould sold all his holdings at a good price.

Other scandals of "the Dreadful Decade"

President Grant's administration was also involved in other national scandals. One was in connection with the improvement of the city of Washington. One man had been given charge of such improvements as paving the streets and building new parks and squares. Investigation proved later that he had stolen thousands of dollars from the government.

Fig. 173. After the investigation of the Whisky Ring was well under way this cartoon appeared. Members of the Whisky Ring are shown on their way to the United States Treasury. The policeman in the picture is saying: "Step up, gentlemen. Don't be bashful." What does the cartoon mean? (From *Harper's Weekly*, November, 1875)

Still another political scandal was that of the "Whisky Ring" of St. Louis. Grant had once lived in that city and on being elected president had rewarded one of his former soldiers, John McDonald, by appointing him collector of revenue for the St. Louis district. At that time a "Whisky Ring" was at work there. McDonald and members of the United States Treasury were connected with it and were making a great deal of money. In 10 months they robbed the government of nearly $1,650,000 by paying it only about half of the tax due on liquor.

Grant's Secretary of War, William W. Belknap, was involved in another nation-wide scandal, in connection with the trade privileges at a government trading post in Indian Territory (Oklahoma). The wife of the Secretary of War had succeeded in securing the position of superintendent of the post for a friend with the understanding that he was to pay her about $6000 a year in return for the favor. More than twenty thousand dollars was collected before an investigation had got under way. Then Belknap was impeached by the House and was tried before the Senate, but resigned before judgment was rendered against him.

The panic of 1873

Too rapid railroad-building, speculation in Western land, inflation of stock, and the wholesale dealings of the financiers were fast driving the finances of the country to ruin. Then, in September, 1873, came the crisis. In two days twenty firms of stockbrokers failed. Jay Cooke and Company, which had helped to finance the Civil War and was then financing the Northern Pacific Railroad, was the first to close its doors. This company was one of the richest and most reliable of the financial houses. Immediately the prices of all kinds of stocks dropped, and a great financial panic began. Many banks failed; business was paralyzed; there was intense excitement. White, terror-stricken men tried to redeem their fortunes on the New York Stock Exchange. Factories closed all over the country. Hundreds of thousands of people were thrown out of work.

CORRUPTION IN THE CITY GOVERNMENTS

The Tweed Ring controlled the government of New York City

Perhaps the most outstanding example of dishonest handling of city government is that furnished by a political boss of Tammany Hall in New York City.

The Society of St. Tammany or Columbian Order was founded in 1789 as a social club. Soon it became a political organization with headquarters at Tammany Hall.

GOVERNMENT BY PROFESSIONAL POLITICIANS 385

In the early 1800's, when New York was growing rapidly, the members of Tammany made friends with the mass of the voting public. Its district, ward, and precinct workers knew the needs and interests of every family. They worked busily among the poorer people, especially the immigrants, building up loyalty to their candidates through charity, through persuasion, and even sometimes through fear. By 1869 it had become a powerful organization.

FIG. 174. This cartoon of the Tammany ring is meant to show how difficult it is to place the blame for political corruption. The people shown in the picture are replying to the question "Who stole the people's money?" Can you tell from the picture what each person is replying? (From *Harper's Weekly*, August, 1871)

During Grant's administration, William Marcy Tweed, the boss of Tammany Hall, was a member of the New York legislature. Tweed was associated with many of the large speculators in public utilities and with officials in the city government. He and his friends robbed the city in almost every one of its departments. For example, a private company, organized under Tweed's management, printed the city stationery at an enormous profit. Another company sold the city worthless water meters. Business men doing work for the city were required to present bills for more than the actual contract price. One contractor holding a claim for $5000 was ordered to present a bill for $55,000. The bill was paid from the city treasury, and Tweed and his group pocketed the additional $50,000.

Taxes were becoming so great and city services so bad that the New York public grew suspicious. Sweeping exposure was finally made of the corrupt work of the ring. The investigation proved that more than $6,000,000 had been stolen from the treasury by means of fraudulent warrants. Finally, in December, 1871, Tweed himself was arrested, found guilty, and with several associates sent to prison.

With the downfall of Tweed other officials of the municipal and state government were found to be involved. They were removed or compelled to resign their offices. It was impossible to tell exactly how much had been stolen, but the total was estimated to be as high as $75,000,000.

In this chapter as well as in Chapter XVII we have seen the many factors which made good government difficult, indeed, almost impossible, during the period following the Civil War. It was not only the South that suffered from corruption. The rise of the political machine in the two major parties was perhaps the most significant factor in the corruption of the North. As a part of this machine came the city and state bosses, who, when favoring the projects of industrial and financial leaders, often wielded a czar-like power in the government of the areas they controlled.

Following this group came another of different character but of equally great power. We shall read about it in the next chapter.

CHAPTER XIX

THE RISE OF GOVERNMENT BY BUSINESS

A brief review of the groups that controlled American government

Throughout this book we have illustrated how government has been carried on amid the conflict of opposing groups of people, each group striving to dominate the others. Bear in mind this one fact: It is inevitable that the most strongly organized group shall control the government. This has been true throughout the history of civilization. In earlier centuries and in other countries and continents *the most powerfully organized group always governed*. Sometimes it was a group of military heroes supported by strong armies. Sometimes it was the Church. Sometimes it was a group of nobles or a king supported by nobles.

In the American colonies, throughout the 1600's and 1700's, the conflict took place between the seaboard planters, the shippers and merchants, and the small farmers and artisans. Later, in making and ratifying the Constitution, the owners of large amounts of property struggled with the great mass of the common people. Then, during the first 30 years of national history, the conflict was waged between the Federalists and the Republicans. In the late 1820's and in the 1830's the struggle shifted, and the settlers and traders of the West joined hands with the laboring people of Eastern towns and cities and took the control of government away from the merchants and manufacturers of the Northeast.

From then until the outbreak of the Civil War the well-to-do planters of the South and the well-to-do merchants and manufacturers and bankers of the North struggled for advantage. As you know, the victory of the North in the Civil War for a time eliminated the South from the contest. The control of government now lay in the hands of the rising manufacturers, business men, and bankers of the North. New political parties were formed to protest this control, but they were weak. Their opponents had the largest amount of wealth; they were concentrated in the Northeastern cities; they were leagued together in business associations; and their interests and aims were similar. The large cotton-planters were ruined. The Western farmers, the skilled laborers, and the professional people were scattered. Naturally, therefore, the business leaders and the professional politicians controlled the government after 1865.

Let us consider three examples of the way in which they exerted their power.

I. The Politicians protected Business by maintaining a High Tariff

Almost from the first years of the republic the question of a high or a low tariff was one of the living issues of politics. As you already know, the majority of those who wanted a high tariff, especially manufacturers and the owners of all industries which competed with foreign goods, were within the Republican party. Most of those who wanted a low tariff were in the Democratic party. Now, from 1860 to 1884 the Republicans were in power and a high tariff was maintained.

Then, in 1884, Grover Cleveland, a Democrat, was elected president. By that time there was a large surplus in the national Treasury, much of which had come from the money received from the tariff. He at once urged a reduction in tariff duties. For three years it seemed that nothing would be done.

Roger Q. Mills, a Democratic Representative in the House, drew up a bill for a low tariff shortly before the end of Cleveland's term. When it was presented to the House, a heated debate took place between Democrats and Republicans. Two of the chief debaters were Mr. Mills himself and a young Republican by the name of William McKinley.

Mr. Mills contended that high tariffs, which protected some industries, increased the price of goods for all the people, and that this increased price went to the manufacturer in the form of profits rather than to the workingman in the form of wages.

THE RISE OF GOVERNMENT BY BUSINESS

After a long debate the Mills Bill passed the House but was defeated by the Republicans in the Senate. In the judgment of many students this meant that the mass of the people, who were represented in the House, wanted a low tariff, but they were defeated by the manufacturers, who controlled the Senate. At any rate, the Democrats had failed to lower the tariff.

The McKinley tariff

At the end of Cleveland's administration (1889) the Republicans came into power again, with the election of Benjamin Harrison. The associations of manufacturers had been striving to get their Republican Congressmen to increase the tariff on foreign products which competed with theirs.

William McKinley of Ohio prepared a tariff bill in 1890 in which the duties were higher than ever before. It was often stated that the iron-and-steel manufacturers, the wool growers and manufacturers, and other business men really decided how much duty should be laid on the different commodities imported from abroad. The duties were made so high that foreign-made goods were practically kept out of the country.

FIG. 175. In the picture each brick in the hod represents some sort of goods which were protected by a tariff in 1889. Another brick is being added to the pile. The hod carrier is trying to stand up under his burden. Whom does the figure of the hod carrier represent, and what is the meaning of the cartoon? (From *Puck*, January, 1889)

Two Republicans, William McKinley in the House and Nelson W. Aldrich in the Senate, carried the bill through.

The Democrats made another attempt to modify the tariff

After the passage of the bill, *retail prices rose all over the country*. Immediately it was certain that the farmers and laboring people of the West were strongly opposed to the high duties. Indeed, the opposition was great enough to defeat the Republicans in the next election. In 1893, Grover Cleveland, the Democrat, again became president. Would the Democrats now succeed in reducing the tariff duties?

In 1894, William L. Wilson, a Democrat in the House, introduced a bill which was intended to lower the tariff. The bill passed the House by a large majority. When it reached the Senate there was much opposition to its provisions. Then Senator Gorman, a Democrat from Maryland, proposed various amendments. Indeed, the changes were so radical that the bill became in reality a high protective tariff. It passed the Senate in this form. When the votes were cast, it was found that Democratic as well as Republican Senators had yielded to the demands of the business men.

The bill, which was now known as the Wilson-Gorman Bill, had to go before the House for another vote. Finally, after much discussion, it was passed. Cleveland would not sign it, but he allowed it to become a law without his signature. Thus the manufacturers had won again.

In 1897 the Republicans again came into power with William McKinley as president

In 1896 Marcus A. Hanna (later a Senator but at that time a wealthy business man of Ohio) was largely instrumental in making William McKinley president of the United States. Although Hanna had no political ambitions for himself, he believed that business and government should work together, and he used his great wealth to help candidates who believed as he did. Hanna succeeded in having McKinley nominated as the Republican candidate, and he managed McKinley's campaign.

Mr. McKinley's support of a high protective tariff was well

known, and from financiers and manufacturers Hanna raised money to bring the campaign to a successful conclusion. McKinley won the election in 1896 and again in 1900.

During the first year of his administration (1897) the Republicans passed the Dingley Tariff Bill. This law provided higher tariffs than ever before. Nor were the rates materially reduced by the Payne-Aldrich Bill of 1909. Then in 1912 the Democrats won again. In 1913 Woodrow Wilson became president, and the Underwood Tariff Bill which followed made real and substantial reductions on many items.

Thus during the 50 years from the Civil War to the World War the industries of the country were protected against foreign competition by a high tariff. In the meantime, farmers, mechanics, clerks, teachers, and professional people complained that *they* did not need the tariff; it did not protect *them*; and it did raise the cost of living.

II. The Decisions of the Supreme Court favored the Well-to-Do

The Supreme Court and the new interpretation of the Fourteenth Amendment

During this period the Supreme Court of the United States became a powerful influence in favor of Big Business. As you have already learned, the Republican party was sympathetic to Big Business. It was natural, therefore, that the long line of Republican presidents from the beginning of the Civil War to the beginning of the World War should have made appointments which on the whole favored the capitalists, just as the long line of Democratic presidents before the Civil War produced a Supreme Court favorable to the Southern planters.

However, the Supreme Court of the United States did not interpret the Fourteenth Amendment so as to protect the property of corporations until nearly twenty years after the close of the Civil War. In several cases the Court ruled that the Amendment applied only to the freed Negroes. Indeed that opinion was general.

Gradually, however, the personnel of the Supreme Court changed. Justices came increasingly from the class associated with business. By the late 1880's the decisions of the Supreme Court definitely favored the interests of corporations and individual owners of property. Minnesota, Texas, and other states were passing laws authorizing state railroad commissions to fix "reasonable" railroad rates. The railroads objected and eventually the United States Supreme Court was asked to decide the matter in various lawsuits. In the Minnesota Rate Case, 1889, the Supreme Court changed from its former position. It ruled that state laws giving railway commissions power to fix rates were unconstitutional. The Justices quoted the Fourteenth Amendment, saying that if states were permitted to do this it would deprive corporations and individuals of their property "without due process of law."

This, then, is one example of the way in which the Supreme Court itself came to favor the interests of owners of private property.

The Supreme Court declared the income tax unconstitutional

At the same time, there was a growing demand among the poorer people that the wealthy people of the country should bear more of the burden of taxation than they had been doing. In the Wilson-Gorman Bill, therefore, provision was made for an income tax on all incomes over $4000 a year.

The well-to-do people of the country were alarmed. A case was taken before the United States Supreme Court, and a decision was given that the income-tax law was unconstitutional. In its written decision the court said:

The present assault upon capital is but the beginning. It will be but the stepping stone to others, larger and more sweeping, till our political contests will become a war of the poor against the rich; a war constantly growing in intensity and bitterness.[1]

[1] Quoted in Gilbert E. Roe's *Our Judicial Oligarchy*, p. 51. The Viking Press, B. W. Huebsch, Inc., New York, 1912.

The Supreme Court and workmen's compensation

In factories and on railroads many people were injured, sometimes through their own carelessness, but often because of defects in machinery or through neglect on the part of employers.

During this period workers aided by reformers began to insist that employers should exercise due care in making working conditions safe. In particular they demanded that employers should bear the costs of injuries which were not the fault of the workers.

In 1906 Congress so far yielded to this demand as to pass a law making the railroads engaged in interstate business liable for injuries to their employees. The Supreme Court declared the law unconstitutional. (Later the law was altered, and the features to which the court objected were removed.)

These examples illustrate the tendency of the Supreme Court to favor large owners of property during the years previous to the World War.

III. POLITICAL LEADERS PROTECTED THE GROWTH OF THE GREAT CORPORATIONS IN OTHER WAYS

Near the end of the period between the Civil War and the World War, investigating committees of Congress disclosed the close relationship between certain politicians of both the Republican and Democratic parties and the corporations. It was established in one investigation that for many years a leading United States senator was in the employ of the Standard Oil Company. He received from that corporation large sums of money with which he purchased one or more newspapers, influenced public opinion, helped elect certain candidates for office, and secured legislation which would help the large business interests.

On the witness stand the heads of great corporations admitted frankly that they paid salaries to Senators, Representatives, and other government officials, whose job it was to secure legislation and court interpretations in their favor. Furthermore, they said freely that they made use of leaders in both the political parties — the Democratic as well as the Republican.

A United States Senator and national political boss tried to prevent the prosecution of a large corporation by a young attorney-general.

Powerful influence was brought to bear upon the young man. The Senator wrote him a letter, warning him against continuing the suit. "You have," he said, "been in politics long enough to know that no man in public office owes the public anything."

"No man in public office owes the public anything!" That was a common enough attitude in those days after the Civil War, but it was not always stated so clearly and boldly as the Senator put it.

We have had space for only a few illustrations of the way in which leaders of business and industry played a part in American government in the 50 years following the Civil War. Many more illustrations could be given from actual testimony before legislative investigating commissions, from court records, and from printed articles in magazines and books.

A new kind of "invisible" government had developed

A noted leader once spoke of the "invisible" government in the United States. By that he meant that working behind the scenes of Congress, state legislatures, city and town councils, were invisible groups of influential persons. Too often it was these groups that really decided what laws should be passed, which officials appointed, and what taxes levied. In the years of business expansion after the Civil War, it was inevitable that much of that invisible government should be unscrupulous, much of it in the interest of the few.

During these years, however, there was also a growing accumulation of protest from the mass of the people themselves — from the farmers of the nation and from the labor groups. Leaders appeared who organized these scattered forces and who inaugurated a struggle for a more democratic and scientific administration of government. To the story of the conflict between the farmer-and-worker groups, on the one hand, and the ruling industrialists, on the other, we turn in the next chapter.

Fig. 176. Marcus A. Hanna

Fig. 177. Thomas Platt

Fig. 178. Boies Penrose

Fig. 179. Joseph Foraker

FOUR SENATORS WHO WIELDED A POWERFUL INFLUENCE IN GOVERNMENT AND IN BIG BUSINESS

INTERESTING READINGS FROM WHICH YOU CAN GET ADDITIONAL INFORMATION

ADAMS, HENRY. Democracy, an American Novel. Henry Holt and Company, New York. For the best readers. It shows the corruption, scandals, and intrigues in the political society of Washington.

ATHERTON, GERTRUDE. Senator North. Dodd, Mead and Company, New York. Many political problems are discussed.

BEARD, CHARLES A. Contemporary American History, 1877–1913. The Macmillan Company, New York. For the best readers.

CHURCHILL, WINSTON. Coniston. The Macmillan Company, New York. Story of an independent political boss.

CHURCHILL, WINSTON. Mr. Crewe's Career. The Macmillan Company, New York. Sequel to *Coniston*; the corporations in politics.

ELSON, HENRY W. Sidelights on American History, Vol. II, pp. 242–262, 325–352. The Macmillan Company, New York.

FRANC, ALISSA. Use your Government, pp. 252–257, 258–259, 260–263. E. P. Dutton & Co., New York.

HALSEY, FRANCIS W. (Editor). Great Epochs in American History, Vol. IX, pp. 131–134; Vol. X, pp. 27–35, 88–95, 186–192. Funk & Wagnalls Company, New York.

HART, ALBERT B. (Editor). American History told by Contemporaries, Vol. IV, pp. 636–638, 641–644, 521–523. The Macmillan Company, New York. For the best readers.

HOWLAND, HAROLD. Theodore Roosevelt and his Times, Vol. XLVII of The Chronicles of America. Yale University Press, New Haven. For the best readers.

ISHAM, F. S. Black Friday. The Bobbs-Merrill Company, Indianapolis. The corner in gold which led to panic in 1869.

KENT, FRANK. The Great Game of Politics. Doubleday, Page & Company, New York. The political machine; the methods of bosses; candidates and their ways; the primaries.

NORRIS, FRANK. The Octopus. Garden City Publishing Company, Garden City, L. I.

NORRIS, FRANK. The Pit. Garden City Publishing Company, Garden City, L. I.

QUICK, HERBERT. The Hawkeye. The Bobbs-Merrill Company, Indianapolis. Second pioneer generation — era of rapid change and political corruption in Iowa.

CHAPTER XX

THE POLITICAL REVOLT OF FARMERS AND CITY WORKERS

Protests against the control of government by Big Business were heard again and again during the years of the later 1800's. The farmers and the city workers frequently complained against a government which they believed was controlled by a small portion of the people. They demanded a government controlled by a majority of the people themselves. Theirs was the century-long cry for democratic government.

Not until the late 1800's, however, was this protest heard. Let us try to get a picture of the scene at that time.

The condition of political affairs in 1880

This was the period of the "last frontier," and the frontier spirit of individual freedom still ruled in politics and government. The slogan "every man for himself" set the temper of the times. Government was not to interfere with the management of private business enterprises or of private property. The politicians of that day believed, for example, that the government should have nothing to say about what business or industrial leaders paid their employees, how many hours they compelled them to work, or the working conditions which they established. This had always been so throughout American history, and business men and politicians were unwilling to allow government interference. Many people honestly believed that the prosperity of the country depended upon the prosperity of Big Business. Anything that curbed Big Business was hurtful to the American people, they said.

A political revolt was brewing, however — a revolt that was to enlist farmers, skilled and unskilled workers, and many political reformers. Let us go back to some of the chief incidents of the new struggle which was to develop for the control of government.

The Farmers tried to gain More Political Power

Note the following complaint of the farmers during the 1870's:

For the past three or four years . . . while every other industry was being fairly remunerated, we had been steadily going behind, until poverty, if not bankruptcy, stared us in the face. . . . We began to see that the men who did nothing but handle the products of our labor were

Fig. 180. The farmer worked alone, but at the polls he joined with others to vote the "farmer ticket." (From Smith, *Grains for Graingers*)

still better off [than we], and were getting rich while we were growing poor. . . . Through all the branches of trade, professions or productions, we found all getting a fair, and some an exorbitant, profit on their commodities and services with which our own would bear no comparison.[1]

Times were indeed hard for the farmers in those days. The prices of farm products were very low. Then, as you know, in 1873 came a nation-wide financial panic. Business collapsed, prices went still lower, and the farmer was in a worse position than ever. He could not profit enough from the sale of his wheat, corn, and cattle to buy clothes for his family and supplies, such as seed, fertilizer, and tools, to carry on his work.

[1] Adapted from Edward W. Martin's *History of the Grange Movement*, pp. 321-323. A. L. Bancroft and Company, San Francisco, 1874.

REVOLT OF FARMERS AND CITY WORKERS

There were many reasons why it was difficult for the farmers to make a living. In many cases the railroads charged high rates for carrying farm products. Then, too, the middlemen paid low prices to the farmers for their products and charged high prices to the consumers. A farmer from Illinois has told this story:

One forenoon a man went past here with a load of sixty bushels of corn. As he returned in the afternoon, I asked him how much he had got for his load of corn. He held up two pairs of boy's boots, and said that his sixty bushels of corn, and $1 in cash, had just purchased them. It took at least seven days' labor of a man and team to raise that corn, and another long day to haul it to market, to say nothing of interest on the farmer's investment and other expenses.[1]

Whether it was corn, as in this case, or wheat or hogs, the man who bought from the farmer fixed the price. Naturally, he paid just as little as possible, and the farmer often got less than it had actually cost him to raise the products.

As a result of the low prices which he received for his farm goods and the high prices which he had to pay for his needs, the farmer often found himself completely without money. Then he had to go to the local bank and ask for a loan. On this money he had to pay interest, always at the rate of 6 per cent, often more. As security he had to mortgage his farm. If he was unable to pay his debt on time, the farm was liable to be sold and the money used to pay the banker. At one time or another most farmers have had to mortgage their land.

After 1870 the farmers combined to protect their interests

During the 1870's new leaders began to go among the farmers. They said to the farmer, "Combination will beat combination."

The merchants, bankers, and manufacturers had long been united. Even some of the laboring men had formed unions. In *A History of American Civilization* you learned how they did this and also how the farmers began to unite too. An organization called the Patrons of Husbandry or the Grange spread rapidly throughout the country. It penetrated into almost every

---

[1] Edward W. Martin, *History of the Grange Movement*, pp. 364–365. A. L. Bancroft and Company, San Francisco, 1874.

little farming community. At first it was used chiefly for educational and social purposes. In the West, particularly, the Grange became the center of social life for the farmers and their families. Thousands of branches were established. It was really the first organization to bring the farmers of the country together.

As time went on the Grange awakened the farmers to a realization of their condition. It showed them how to work together,

FIG. 181. The Grangers meet to discuss their problems. (From *Leslie's Illustrated Newspaper*, August, 1873)

and as it grew the farmers began to see that if they supported the organization wholeheartedly it might become a real political power. In the Middle West — notably in Illinois, Minnesota, Iowa, and Wisconsin — the Grange got control of the state legislatures. Once in power, the farmers began a struggle with the railroads. They passed laws prohibiting the railroads from raising their freight rates above a certain limit. They required that railroad rates should be the same throughout a state.

In many cases the railroads refused to obey the new laws. They claimed that the legislatures did not have the power to establish railroad rates. At other times, instead of disobeying the laws, the railroads would obey them in such a way as to bring about their repeal. For example, if they were required to charge the same rates all over a state, they would raise the low rates instead of lowering the high rates. The Grangers at last realized that without Federal aid they were at the mercy of the railroads. The battle which had gone on between the farmers and the railroads created nation-wide attention, and in Chapter XXI you will see that as a result of it the government finally created a commission which was intended to protect the interests of the farmers.

As a political group the Grange organization died almost as rapidly as it had grown. Bad management within the order and the disappointment of the farmers because they could not accomplish more were perhaps the chief reasons for its collapse. One important result came from the farmers' efforts, however. In ruling on cases which arose from these laws, the courts decided that legislatures *did* have the power to pass laws setting railroad rates within their own states. At the same time they also decided that the courts had the power to judge these laws and to determine whether or not they were reasonable. These were gains for the mass of the people and especially for the farmers.

The Greenback party sponsored the farmers' cause

The farmers who had been disappointed in the Grange now joined a new political party, which seemed to promise an improvement in their affairs. This was called the Greenback party. The city workers played a small part in forming this organization, but the farmers were its backbone.

The chief demand of the party was that the government issue more "greenbacks" — that is, more paper money. More greenbacks would mean more money in circulation. The value of currency would then go down, and the money which the farmer paid in interest on his loans from the bank would not be so valuable. Moreover, so the Greenbackers said, as the value of money went down, the value of farm products would go up. Thus, according to the Greenbackers, the farmer would pay less interest and receive higher prices for his products.

In 1876 the Greenback candidate polled but 82,000 votes. In the 1880 election the party nominated General James B. Weaver for president. Hopes ran high for the Greenback candidate. He polled only a small vote, however, and after that election the Greenback party lost influence. Perhaps this was largely due to the fact that just then the farmer was better off than he had been for years before. There was a "bumper" crop, which

FIG. 182. Those who owned the railroads blamed the farmers for having brought the railroads under the control of state government. In this cartoon the farmer is saying, "Mr. Wildcat Speculator, what am I to do now?" The railroad owner replies, "Solve your own problems, Mr. Farmer Despot." (From *Harper's Weekly*, November, 1873)

brought good prices. The farmer, for the moment, forgot politics and concentrated on making the best of a good thing while it lasted.

The Populist party

Throughout the 1870's, the farmers had seen the need of coöperation. Throughout the 1880's, with the fall of the Greenback party, many smaller parties sprang up representing the interests of the farmer, but their forces were weak and scattered. After 1885 the prices of grain fell, and again the farmer began to remember the word *coöperation*, which he had learned earlier and had forgotten. Farmers' Alliances now spread throughout the country and gradually drew the farmers together into a national movement which was not very different from the old Grange.

REVOLT OF FARMERS AND CITY WORKERS 403

Leaders of farmers' movements went throughout the country speaking at Farmers' Alliance picnics and other agricultural meetings. Everywhere farmers were urged to join a new group which was called the Populist party. This organization would win their rights.

In July, 1892, the Populist party held a national convention. At last there was a fusion of the forces of the farmer and the city worker. The farmers were in control, however. Their platform stated that wealth belongs to him who creates it and every dollar taken from industry without an equivalent is robbery.... The interests of rural and city laborers are the same.

Fig. 183. This cartoon was published to poke fun at the Greenback party, which is represented by the donkey. Columbia is saying: "What angel wakes me from my flowery bed?... Thou art wise as thou art beautiful."

The platform declared that Populists stood for honesty and economy in government and for an income tax which would make the rich as well as the poor pay for government. Finally, they demanded "free and unlimited coinage of silver and gold."

The difficult problem of silver money

You will remember that before the Civil War had ended, the greenback dollar was worth less than 50 cents in gold or silver. Because of this many leaders thought it best to abolish paper money and use only gold or silver. But by an act of Congress it was settled that greenbacks were to be used and were to be as valuable in exchange as either gold or silver.

Another difficult money problem confronted the government, however. Should *both* gold and silver coins be used or gold alone? For many years the Federal government had been making coins from both gold and silver. At this time an ounce of gold was worth 15 times as much as an ounce of silver; so the ratio 15 to 1 was used when the two metals were coined.[1]

Later it developed that persons who manufactured articles out of silver recognized its value as more than one-fifteenth as much as gold, and frequently melted coins instead of buying silver in bars or other forms. Naturally this reduced the number of silver dollars in circulation.

Then in the 1860's and 1870's came the discovery of vast deposits of silver in the mountain states. As the supply increased the value went down. Finally in 1873 Congress stopped coining silver dollars, using gold as the single standard.

After 1870 the relation between silver and gold in coining money became a political issue. On this problem farmers as usual opposed the business men, favoring the plan of coining silver at the ratio of 16 ounces of silver to 1 of gold. As you have learned in the earlier chapters, it had long been the theory of the farmers that if large amounts of money could be put into circulation the selling price of farm products would increase, while they would have more and cheaper money with which to pay their debts. As usual, the investors, the bankers, the money-lenders,— the whole creditor class,— were opposed to this plan. They maintained that to increase the amount of money in circulation would reduce its value, and that hence they would lose money.

The Populist convention of 1892, representing farmers, laborers, and other poor people, demanded the free coinage of silver at the ratio of 16 to 1. They nominated General Weaver, the former Greenback candidate, as the presidential candidate of the party. In the election the Populist party polled over 1,000,000 votes, and its leaders believed great accomplishments lay ahead of them and that the rule of the Republican party

[1] Later the ratio was changed to 16 to 1.

REVOLT OF FARMERS AND CITY WORKERS

was over. They were sure that a new party, "fresh from the people" (as Andrew Jackson would have said), could take the place of the old ones.

What happened to the Populist movement in 1896

The leaders were mistaken. The Republican party became stronger. It represented the interests of the business classes so successfully that those interests worked to keep it in office. The

FIG. 184. Hanna in conference with the Republican leaders of the presidential campaign of 1896. (From *Harper's Weekly*, October, 1896)

Democratic party, on the other hand, was divided in its support of the business interests. It had its conservative wing, it is true; but it also had its progressive wing. To be progressive in those days was to support free coinage of silver.

In 1896 the progressive wing of the Democratic party was dominated by two men. One was the millionaire governor of Illinois, John Peter Altgeld, and the other was a young Nebraska lawyer-politician, William Jennings Bryan. These two men, more than any others, were responsible for the fact that the Democratic party absorbed the Populist party.

The sturdy Altgeld with close-cropped beard "had worked as a farm hand" and "had brought himself to the top of life from the veriest bottom without losing his sympathies with toilers and strugglers." This millionaire governor, with his knowledge of and sympathy with the working classes, was the man behind the scenes who really controlled the 1896 Democratic convention. For William McKinley, the friend of Big Business, who had been nominated by the Republicans some weeks before, he had nothing good to say.

Fig. 185. William Jennings Bryan

Bryan, who had come to the Democratic convention as a delegate from Nebraska, was almost an unknown man. The party was torn with dissension. There were gold Democrats and silver Democrats. One hot July day shortly after the opening of the session the money question was being debated, and several men prominent in Democratic politics had already spoken. Then Bryan took the floor. A man of striking appearance and with a voice of singular depth and power, he at once captured and held the wavering attention of the convention. As he spoke on, men realized that they were hearing the most remarkable speech they had ever heard at a political convention. Fifteen thousand people were in attendance, yet the great hall was so quiet that it might have been empty of its thousands. The speaker concluded with this defiance to the believers in a gold standard: "Having behind us the producing masses of this nation and the world, supported by the commercial interests, the laboring interests, and the toilers everywhere, we will answer their demands for a gold standard by saying to them: You shall not press down upon the brow of labor this crown of thorns, *you shall not crucify mankind upon a cross of gold.*"

The whole convention went wild. It marched and shouted and cheered in mad approval; and before it adjourned it nominated Bryan as the Democratic candidate for president.

Two nominees now stood opposed to each other: McKinley, on the gold standard, high-tariff Republican platform, and Bryan on the free-silver, low-tariff Democratic platform. What would the Populists do? If the Populist convention should nominate another candidate, he and Bryan would split the farmer and labor free-silver vote, and McKinley, the Republican, would surely win.

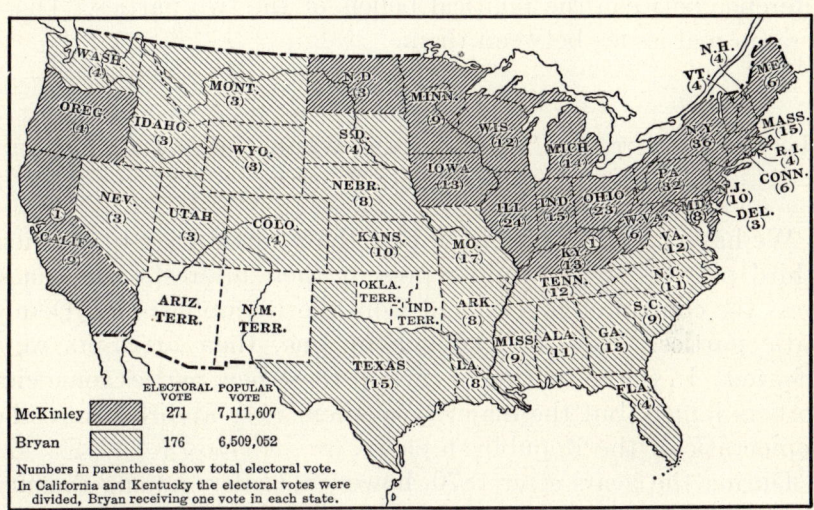

FIG. 186. The presidential election of 1896. Note particularly the *sections* which voted for Bryan and those which voted for McKinley

The Populists decided that the cause for which Bryan fought was similar to their own, and they combined with the Democrats.

What happened in the election of 1896? Even though Populists and Democrats combined, McKinley, the Republican, won. He carried the Northeastern cities and towns, the stronghold of business and industry. Bryan got the farmer votes of the West and South, and many workers' votes in the cities. Although he won a larger territory than McKinley did, the latter won the thickly settled regions, and so the larger number of electoral votes.

The Populist party soon disappeared. The Democratic party, which for this convention had practically adopted the Populist platform, was soon to desert the Populist cause and become conservative. When that happened the farmers and workingmen were left without a party to represent their interests.

After 1896 the political life of the farmer slipped back into the old ruts. There were the Republican and Democratic parties, and between them the farmer and the worker could take their choice. But the Democratic party had now been recaptured by conservatives who were defenders of practically the same policies as the Republicans. Indeed, after 1900, there was very little difference between the political beliefs of the two parties. There were no real issues between them.

IN THE MEANTIME CITY WORKERS WERE ORGANIZING LABOR AND SOCIALIST PARTIES

We have had illustrations of how the farmers tried to organize "third parties" that would represent their interests and would wrest the control of government from the Republican and Democratic parties. Nevertheless, one by one, their attempts were defeated. In the formation of each of these new parties some city workers joined, but the majority of them were absorbed into the Democratic or the Republican party.

During the years after 1870, however, leaders among the city laborers tried to organize political parties of their own. The movement first attracted national attention in 1872, when a small party called *Labor Reformers* nominated a candidate for president. In 1877 another party, known as the Socialist Labor party, was established, but not until 1892 did this party get enough members to nominate a candidate for president. For the next eight years its growth was small, the largest number of votes received by any of its candidates being less than 100,000.

Then in 1900 the Social-Democratic party held a national convention and nominated Eugene V. Debs as its candidate for president. For three succeeding elections after 1900, this party, now known as the Socialist party, increased its vote rapidly. In 1912 the number of votes cast for Debs for president was almost 900,000. In 1917, however, with the coming of the World War and the centering of attention upon international problems, the Socialist vote declined to less than 600,000, and at no time since then has it exceeded about 1,000,000.

What were the political views of the Socialists?

It is difficult to answer that question in a brief statement because there are so many varieties of socialism. There are two extremes: on the one hand, the conservative Socialists and Social Democrats of Germany, France, England, and the United States, and, on the other hand, the radical Communists of Russia. Between these two extreme groups, citizens can be found in almost every country who hold views about government that might be labeled socialistic.

Fig. 187. Eugene V. Debs

The chief question which is raised by socialism is How shall factories, mines, railroads, telephone and telegraph systems, power plants, and like agencies be owned? That is, shall enterprises which *produce and bring* necessities to the people be owned by private individuals or *by all the people* through the government?

In Russia most of these agencies are owned by the government which controls the country — namely, the Communist, the extreme Socialist, party. In most countries today, however, they are owned by private citizens or by private corporations. We call this private capitalism.

Thus almost everywhere all the agencies which produce, distribute, and sell raw materials, foods, and manufactured goods are owned by private citizens or by corporations made up of private citizens. The difference lies between the system of private ownership and the system of public ownership.

The extreme Socialists say that throughout history the chief reason for the misery of the mass of the people has been the division of people into two classes: (1) the capitalists, or owners; (2) the laborers who work for the owners. They maintain that as long as factories, railroads, power plants, and the like are owned privately there will be constant struggle between capitalists and workers, and there will be constant war between competing nations. Hence they believe that every agency that produces, distributes, or sells necessities should be owned in common by all the people. It is important to bear in mind, however, that Socialists (even the Communists of Russia) would not abolish *all* private property. They would permit any private citizen to own land and a house in which he himself lives, clothes, automobiles, horses, and luxuries which he himself uses. They would not permit him, however, to own more of these things than he himself could use. That is an important distinction which we should remember. With this organization they believe it possible to eliminate all class distinctions.

Most Americans, however, oppose socialism. Many of them, it must be confessed, do not understand it and oppose it blindly. On the other hand, some who *do* understand socialism oppose it vigorously. They put forward such arguments as the following:

1. Under the system of private ownership the United States has developed the highest standard of living the world has ever known, and most of our people are living far more comfortable lives than their forefathers of even two generations ago.

2. If under the present system capitalists and workers understood each other's problems and were willing to coöperate, a true democracy could be worked out in America which would give every person his just share of the national income.

3. Each individual should be permitted to own in proportion to his ability. People are not equal in ability. Some are brilliant and others are dull; some have great skill, others have little skill; some are sensitive artists, others are unable to recognize beautiful things; some are strong physically, others are weak. In every respect, these opponents of socialism point out, people are not equal but are very different; hence their rewards should be different, varying in proportion to their abilities.

4. Finally, the opponents of socialism maintain that government enterprises are liable to be inefficient. If the government were to own coal and iron mines, oil wells, power plants, railroads, and factories, the country would not be so well supplied

REVOLT OF FARMERS AND CITY WORKERS 411

with material goods as under the present conditions, and workers would be worse off.

These, then, are the kinds of arguments advanced on the two sides, by friends of socialism and friends of capitalism.

There is one conclusion on which we can agree, however: *The questions raised by the Socialists and their opponents are of the greatest importance.* The whole development of government in the modern world depends upon how they are answered in the years to come. The young people who are now in our schools will be called upon to answer them.

In the meantime these facts are clear: The various Socialist and Labor parties have not enlisted a large per cent of the skilled and unskilled workers. Most of the city laborers, as well as most of the farmers and professional people, have voted within the two leading political parties, the Republican and the Democratic.

Parties and Presidents, 1864–1912

Let us study briefly the parties and the presidential elections during the period which we have been discussing. Look at the chart on page 412.

Lincoln, as you know, was elected by the Republicans in 1860 and re-elected in 1864.

1. *Ulysses S. Grant, Republican, elected in 1868 and in 1872.* At the close of the Civil War, General Grant was regarded as the outstanding national hero. By a large majority of the electoral vote, the Republicans won with him as their candidate in 1868. Four years later, in spite of the national scandals which developed and in spite of the condemnation of the press and leaders generally, he was reëlected, by a fairly large majority.

The race for political control between Republicans and Democrats was close, however. Even as early as 1872 the Republicans kept their control in Congress only by a narrow margin. Indeed, two years later, although Grant had been reëlected, the Democrats elected a majority of the members of the House of Representatives. This was an important sign of the fact that the mass of the people were by no means overwhelmingly Republican. In most of the campaigns between 1870 and 1896 the Democrats won a majority of the seats in the House of Representatives.

2. *Rutherford B. Hayes, Republican.* Then came the close campaign of 1876. So close was the count of the votes that for

POLITICAL PARTIES AND PRESIDENTS, 1864 TO 1928			
Republicans	Year of Election	Democrats	Third Parties
Abraham Lincoln (d. 1865)	1864		
Andrew Johnson			
Ulysses S. Grant	1868		
Ulysses S. Grant	1872		Labor Reform party
Rutherford B. Hayes	1876		Greenback party (Peter Cooper)
James A. Garfield (d. 1881)	1880		National Labor party
Chester A. Arthur			
	1884	Grover Cleveland	Independent Republican "Mugwumps"
Benjamin Harrison	1888		
			Populist party (1891)
	1892	Grover Cleveland	
William McKinley	1896		
William McKinley (d. 1901)	1900		Social-Democratic party (Eugene V. Debs)
Theodore Roosevelt			
Theodore Roosevelt	1904		
William H. Taft	1908		
	1912	Woodrow Wilson	Progressive party (Theodore Roosevelt) split Republican party
	1916	Woodrow Wilson	
Warren G. Harding (d.1923)	1920		
Calvin Coolidge			
Calvin Coolidge	1924		
Herbert C. Hoover	1928		

FIG. 188. Political Parties and Presidents, 1864–1928

some time the result of the election between the Republican, Rutherford B. Hayes of Ohio, and the Democrat, Samuel J. Tilden of New York, was in doubt. Both Republicans and Democrats claimed the election. A commission appointed by Congress finally decided that Hayes had a majority of one electoral vote and he became president. During his administration the two leading parties were almost equally represented in Congress.

3. *James A. Garfield, Republican.* Again, in 1880, the Republicans nominated a Civil War officer and won with a clear margin. Taking office on March 4, 1881, he served only four months, when he was assassinated by a disappointed office-seeker. The vice president, Chester A. Arthur, served for nearly four years, 1881–1885.

4. *Grover Cleveland, Democrat.* In the meantime the Republican party had become somewhat disorganized and, in 1884, the Democrats with Cleveland at their head rode into power for the first time in 28 years. Their stay in office was to last only four years, however.

5. *Benjamin Harrison, Republican.* By 1888 the Republicans were reunited once more, and they selected as their candidate Benjamin Harrison of Indiana, who was also an army officer. Harrison was the grandson of President William H. Harrison. Once more the Republicans won.

6. *Grover Cleveland, Democrat.* In 1892, however, the Democrats elected Grover Cleveland again by a large electoral majority. For four years they remained in power. With the expiration of Cleveland's term they lost control of the presidency for sixteen years.

7. *The Republicans in power from 1897 until 1913 — William McKinley, 1897–1901; Theodore Roosevelt, 1901–1909; William H. Taft, 1909–1913.* Again, in 1896, the Republicans won with another Civil War officer, Major William McKinley of Ohio. In 1900 he was reëlected, but he was assassinated in 1901, about six months after his second inauguration. Colonel Theodore Roosevelt, the vice president, assumed office, served for over three years, and was elected president in 1904 on the Republican ticket by a large majority. He was followed by William H. Taft, who was elected in 1908 and served until 1913.

Thus from 1860 to 1912 — a period of more than 50 years — the Democrats succeeded only twice in electing their candidate for president. Oddly enough on both these occasions they elected the same man, Grover Cleveland. Republican rule, therefore, lasted with but little interruption from 1861, when Lincoln took office, until 1913, the close of Taft's administration. During this period, as was to be expected, most Federal offices were held by Republicans.

The Democrats did control the House of Representatives

It is important to bear in mind the closeness of the race between the Republicans and the Democrats throughout the years between the Civil War and the World War. No better illustration of this fact can be found than that, although the Republicans generally won the presidency and the Senate, the

Fig. 189. Grover Cleveland

Fig. 190. William McKinley

Democrats were often in the majority in the House of Representatives. Between 1872 and 1896 inclusive there were thirteen Congressional elections. In these the Democrats won a majority of the House *eight* times.

Repeatedly after 1789 the national government was divided in its politics. The Senate and the Supreme Court were largely of one party; the House of Representatives was largely of an opposing one.

If the Senate, which was Republican in policy, passed a bill which was opposed by a Democratic House of Representatives, there must necessarily be delay, conflict, and perhaps final compromise before the bill became a law. This meant also that the policy of either party was not based upon a scientific attempt to study the needs of the nation as a whole, but was designed to keep the particular party in power.

Some students regard this "government of checks and balances" as the best way for a democratic government to be organized. It makes for slow changes; hence, for stability. Moreover, it tends to prevent an abuse of power. Other students feel that a government of such complete checks and balances is a bad thing for the country. They maintain that, since life in America is changing rapidly, the government should be organized so as to permit laws to be passed and the Constitution to be amended as the needs of large groups of people require.

All critics agree that the government should be carried on purely and simply in the interests of the people, and not merely to perpetuate the power of one or more political parties.

Your task is to study these matters carefully and to form a thoughtful opinion about them as you grow older. It is, indeed, a very difficult problem — this problem of making the laws and carrying on government in such a vast country as the United States. But it is also a very important one, and one that should engage the minds of all our citizens.

INTERESTING READINGS FROM WHICH YOU CAN GET ADDITIONAL INFORMATION

Buck, Solon J. The Agrarian Crusade, Vol. XLV of The Chronicles of America. Yale University Press, New Haven. See pages 43–59, 99–124, 142–193. For the best readers.

Halsey, Francis W. (Editor). Great Epochs in American History. Funk & Wagnalls Company, New York. See Volume X, pp. 57–63, 96–107, 108–124.

Harris, Frank. The Bomb. Brentano's, New York. For the best readers: the labor riots at Chicago, 1886.

Russell, C. E. The Story of the Nonpartisan League. Harper & Brothers, New York. For the best readers.

CHAPTER XXI

THE COMMON PEOPLE MARCH TOWARD DEMOCRACY

You have learned in the three preceding chapters of the powerful influences which were at work in industry and in government following the Civil War. You have learned how little the feeble protests of small badly organized groups availed to check the unfair use of political position and industrial strength.

In the 1870's and the 1880's, however, the protests were growing louder, and the farmers and city workers were learning that there was power in the vote. In Chapter XX you learned that the farmer and the city worker sometimes combined their demands in one political platform in order to make their voting power more effective. Finally the influence of the new political movements began to be felt, and in 1887 Congress began to act.

1. The Interstate Commerce Act, 1887

By the 1880's the whole country was aroused by the protests of the farmers against the control which the railroads were exerting. Investigation had disclosed that the railroads disobeyed the state laws which were passed to regulate their activities, that they had been giving lower rates to friendly and powerful shippers than they had given to others, and that they were guilty of other unfair practices.

In 1887 Congress passed the *Interstate Commerce Act*. This law established the Interstate Commerce Commission and gave it the power to *investigate* and regulate commerce between the states. The law also forbade the railroads, steamboat companies, and other common carriers to have secret rates and agreements. It did not, however, give the commission the power to fix the rates that the roads could charge.

But the railroads ignored or evaded the law and continued the practice of favoring the big shippers. At the same time the

THE COMMON PEOPLE AND DEMOCRACY

Supreme Court made decisions in their favor. One case after another, tried under the act of 1887, was decided by the United States Supreme Court in such a way that the value of the commission was destroyed. After the commission had been in existence ten years, it declared that its position was intolerable. It had little, if any, real control over the actions of the railroads.

FIG. 191. This cartoon was published in 1887, when the Interstate Commerce Act was passed. Notice in this Wild West show how the "animals" are tearing about. The cowboys (Interstate Commerce Commissioners) are determined to subdue these unruly animals. Uncle Sam is watching to see the outcome of this test of strength.
(By W. A. Rogers, in *Harper's Weekly*, April, 1887)

In President Roosevelt's first message to Congress, he said of the Interstate Commerce Act:

That law was largely an experiment. Experience has shown the wisdom of its purposes, but has also shown, possibly, that some of its requirements are wrong, certainly that the means devised for the enforcement of its provisions are defective.

The act should be amended. The railway is a public servant. Its rates should be just to and open to all shippers alike. . . . At the same time it must not be forgotten that our railways are the arteries through which the commercial life-blood of this Nation flows. Nothing could be more foolish than the enactment of legislation which would unnecessarily interfere with the development and operation of these commercial agencies. The subject is one of great importance and calls for the earnest attention of the Congress.[1]

The people of the country continued to complain of the high rates and unfair practices of the railroads. Finally in 1906 President Roosevelt demanded further action of Congress in the matter of interstate commerce. The result was the Hepburn Act, 1906. This act increased the sphere of the Interstate Commerce Commission, so that it had some supervision over pipe lines, private cars, and connecting lines, and gave it the power to reduce railroad rates upon complaint until such time as the courts might decide the case. Moreover, the Hepburn Act forbade the railroad companies to grant rebates, and it gave the Interstate Commerce Commission power to say how the railroad companies should keep their accounts. President Roosevelt believed this act to be a great step forward. He did not, however, want to go so far in the regulation of interstate commerce as some people desired. The Hepburn Act illustrates clearly the new attitude that was developing, in that it was able to establish a certain amount of governmental control over business. But in spite of the Interstate Commerce Commission, railroad rates continued to be high.

2. The Sherman Anti-Trust Act, 1890

The wave of agitation and legislation against the railroads led to a popular demand for government control over rapidly growing corporations. By buying up smaller companies or by forcing them out of business through unfair competition, certain business organizations had succeeded in gaining control over the supply of oil, coal, sugar, etc. These organizations were commonly known as trusts. In 1890 the *Sherman Anti-Trust Act* was passed by Congress. This forbade the existence of any combination that "restrained" interstate or foreign trade. It attempted to compel the great organizations which held monopolies over business to break up into smaller corporations.

---

[1] Theodore Roosevelt, *Addresses and Presidential Messages, 1902–1904*, pp. 306–307. G. P. Putnam's Sons, New York, 1904.

THE COMMON PEOPLE AND DEMOCRACY 419

Obeying the *letter* of the law, these large corporations "broke up," but in the *spirit* of the law they actually did not. How was this possible? The same capitalists owned the stock of many of the separate companies of a given industry. The directors of one company would also be directors or officers of other companies. These men met secretly and agreed to charge the same prices for their commodities and to do other things in common, just as though they were merely parts of one great "combine," or trust. Thus, although outwardly the trusts had broken up into separate companies, the companies were really acting just as they had before. Can you see how such a system would prevent competition among industries?

3. The Clayton Act, 1914

Twenty-four years later a law was passed which made the Sherman Anti-Trust Act much more effective — namely, the *Clayton Act*, 1914. This law did much more than the earlier one to break up the big trusts into smaller companies. It also forbade unfair competition to drive rival companies out of existence. It stated more clearly what corporations could and could not do. The Sherman Anti-Trust Act of 1890 had not been worded clearly, and the courts had interpreted its meaning in a way which many people did not believe was intended.

The Clayton Act did another very important thing. It stated that the law was *not* to apply to labor unions or agricultural organizations; that is, a labor union or a farmers' alliance, for example, was not to be regarded as "a combination in restraint of trade." This was particularly important to labor people because for 100 years labor unions had been fought by employers, and courts had frequently decided that unions were conspiracies in restraint of trade.

A month before the Clayton Act was passed, the *Federal Trade Commission* had been created. This body was given power to supervise business concerns and to investigate unfair business dealings.

Thus the government was slowly attempting to restrict the powerful agencies that had built up control over it. It was not always successful in doing so, but one important point was established, namely, that the government *could* have authority over Big Business. No longer could any industrial groups manage their affairs in a spirit of defiance. Both by enactments of Congress and by decisions of the Supreme Court, the principle was established that the government could intervene on behalf of the people.

OTHER ATTEMPTS TO MAKE GOVERNMENT MORE DEMOCRATIC

1. The political reformers fought the spoils system

One day when the Civil War was at its height, President Lincoln looked out of the window at a throng of men gathered around the White House. They were the office-seekers waiting to see the President.

"There is something," said Lincoln to the friend who was with him, "which in course of time will become a greater danger to the Republic than the rebellion itself."[1]

You will remember that even during Jackson's administration the spoils system was already well established. As the general population grew the number of employees in the various departments of the government grew also. Upon the election of each new president an ever-increasing horde of office-seekers besieged the Federal offices.

By 1880 every office-seeker, efficient or inefficient, rich or poor, felt that he had the right to demand an office if he had done anything in the campaign for the new president. Thus the spoils system was one of the means by which the party bosses held their organizations together. In return for contributions of money or services, they gave away government positions.

Here and there voices had been heard in both parties opposing the system. After the Civil War George William Curtis and Carl Schurz were the two men who led the earliest fights.

---

[1] William D. Foulke, *Fighting the Spoilsmen*, p. 6. G. P. Putnam's Sons, New York. 1919.

The assassination of a president arouses the country

In 1881 a national tragedy occurred. A man who had been refused a government job by President Garfield assassinated him. Immediately public attention was directed to the need for reform in the selection of people to carry on the work of the government.

Ten years before a law had been passed permitting the president to regulate the Civil Service[1] and to appoint a Civil Service Commission. But the antagonism of the politicians made this law ineffective. The commission could do practically nothing. President Hayes led the fight for civil-service reform with some success.

FIG. 192. The crows represent office-seekers. This cartoon shows what Cleveland thought should be done with them. (From *Puck*, August 11, 1886)

Then Congress refused to grant further appropriations to carry on the work.

In 1883, while people were still aroused by the death of Garfield, the reformers pushed through a bill reëstablishing a Civil Service Commission. The Civil Service Commission was to provide competitive examinations for applicants for such Federal offices as the president should designate. Under this plan an efficient, subordinate government officer could not be removed because he belonged to a rival political party.

Chester A. Arthur, who had succeeded President Garfield, immediately put several thousand government positions on a competitive-examination basis, but the great majority of jobs were still controlled by the spoilsmen-politicians.

---

[1] The Civil Service is the public service other than military and naval. In practice, however, legislative and judicial officers are not regarded as holding Civil Service positions.

Then in 1884 came the election of Cleveland.

Cleveland, of course, was in a difficult position. The politicians of his party had little enough respect for what they called "old-woman reform movements." They were practical men, and they wanted the practical benefits of the spoils system. Cleveland held out against them in certain cases and thereby earned their ill will. Altogether in his two terms he put about 55,000 government jobs on the competitive basis. Nevertheless, his measures were not entirely pleasing to the reformers because he did not go far enough.

In later years it was Theodore Roosevelt who brought the Civil Service Commission and its work into the light more than anyone else had done. President Harrison, who held office between Cleveland's first and second administrations, appointed Roosevelt as Civil Service Commissioner in 1889. For several years Roosevelt kept up an entertaining battle with the opponents of civil-service reform. Steadily more and more jobs were taken away from the spoilsmen and awarded only on the basis of examinations.

Then when Roosevelt himself became president (1901–1909) he put 87,000 additional positions on the Civil Service list. President Wilson added more, and by 1916 over half the 450,000 Federal jobs were out of the control of the spoilsmen. In 1928 there were more than 568,000 jobs, and 75 per cent of them could be secured only by competitive examinations. *The reform which was once so scoffed at had gradually become an accepted practice.*

2. Methods of voting were changed

After the Civil War two great evils in the methods of voting were calling for attention. In the first place, voting was not secret, and, in the second place, political parties furnished their own ballots at elections. Campaign workers for a party could assemble the voters, show them exactly how to vote for their candidate, and make sure that they did. Bribery was frequent, and the party with the most money had a great advantage, which sometimes won the election.

In the 1880's the reformers launched a nation-wide attack

Fig. 193. Theodore Roosevelt

Fig. 194. William H. Taft

Fig. 195. Woodrow Wilson

Fig. 196. Warren G. Harding

THE PRESIDENTS WHO SERVED BETWEEN 1901 AND 1923

424   AMERICAN GOVERNMENT AND CULTURE

against the evils of this open-ballot system of voting. They advocated the method which had already been set up in Australia as the ideal which they should employ. According to this system voting was secret, and ballots were supplied by the government. In 1888 the first skirmish of the battle was won. Massachusetts passed a law adopting the Australian ballot. After that, year by

FIG. 197. By the time Benjamin Harrison became president thousands of jobs were obtained only through competitive examination. But this picture shows that even during Harrison's administration the corridors of the House of Representatives still swarmed with office-seekers awaiting "jobs by appointment." (From *Harper's Weekly*, March, 1891)

year, one or more states adopted it. Before the World War it was in use in all states throughout the country. An important step had been taken in the attempt to make elections fair.

3. Changes in the system of choosing candidates for office

We have discussed many times the great changes which had come in the life of the country during this period. No change has been more important, however, than that of the growing indifference of the mass of the voting public to problems of government. By 1890 little more than a tenth of the eligible voters of a party attended the political meetings (called the party caucuses) at which delegates were selected to the county, state, or national conventions. Hence the professional politicians, the local and state bosses, who were, of course, always on hand at the caucuses, largely chose the delegates who went to the conventions.

By 1900, however, the political reformers had launched a nation-wide campaign to substitute a "direct primary" system of choosing candidates. In the vanguard of this movement was Senator Robert M. La Follette of Wisconsin, an independent who had achieved a great following in his state. His slogan was like Andrew Jackson's: "Go back to the first principles of democracy." In 1903, under the leadership of La Follette, Wisconsin inaugurated the direct-primary system, by which voters in each party went to the polls and cast their votes for the candidates whom they wished to run in the final election. Other states soon adopted this method, and today in all but five states candidates are selected by this direct vote of the people.

4. The initiative, referendum, and recall

During the same years the progressives in both the Republican and the Democratic party achieved three more small steps forward in the march of democracy. They provided several ways by which the people could act upon laws directly rather than through their representatives.

The initiative. By this law a small group of citizens, usually 5 per cent to 8 per cent of the voters, could directly, by means of petition to the legislatures, cause a measure to be voted on by the entire state. If accepted, this became a law. It is clear that in order to do this, the people must be well informed and interested in the problems of government.

The referendum. This law made it possible for a stated number of citizens, by signing a petition, to require that a law passed by the legislature should be submitted to the voters at a general election. Thus reform associations or eagle-eyed independent groups who might be opposed to any law actually passed by the majority of representatives, could bring that law before the whole voting public for their decision. As in the case of the initiative, however, the usefulness of the law depends upon the presence of intelligent, interested groups of citizens watching legislation, keeping it before the voting public, and constantly educating the public to its importance.

The initiative and referendum — the two ideas were generally thought of together — was approved by the independent parties in the early 1890's. The Populists supported it in their campaigns. The Democrats, under the leadership of William J. Bryan, worked for it in 1896. It was not actually passed, however, in any state until 1898, when independent organizations of farmers and laborers in South Dakota passed a state constitutional amendment which established it. Soon it was adopted in Utah; in 1902, in Oregon; and in the next few years, in five more states. Before the United States entered the World War the people in nearly half of the states in the Union had the privilege of initiative and referendum.

President Theodore Roosevelt, a vigorous Progressive Republican, approved the policy. So did Woodrow Wilson, the Democrat. But most leading Congressmen called it "radicalism run wild." Conservatives within the leading parties regarded it as nothing short of political revolution.

The recall. This law provided that if an official did not satisfy the voters they could, on petition, secure the recall of that official; that is, an unsuitable official could be removed from office by the votes of the people of a state. It was used first in the Los Angeles city government in 1903. In eleven states the recall was made a part of the law before the outbreak of the World War.

Thus the forces of reform began to clear away evil practices and made it somewhat easier for the rank and file of the citizens to have a *direct* share in their government. Leaders like President William Howard Taft regarded these as among the most "dangerous changes in our present constitutional form of representative government." These defenders of the old parties predicted that grave harm would come from them. They said America had always had *representative* government. It was dangerous to give up that form and to adopt the more direct methods of letting the people themselves have an immediate voice in legislation.

To these anxious warnings, however, the more liberal groups,

THE COMMON PEOPLE AND DEMOCRACY 427

under such men as La Follette, Roosevelt, and Woodrow Wilson, replied by pointing to the spread of universal education. They had faith that the youth of the nation could be educated to understand the workings of local, state, and national governments. They emphasized the vital importance for all people, young and old, of keeping in touch with their representatives and of reading the newspapers and magazines which reported proposed laws.

Thus, step by step, democracy advanced.

5. The election of United States Senators passed from the hands of state legislatures

For more than a century after the making of the United States Constitution, Senators had been chosen by the legislatures of their respective states. After the Civil War the Senate had constantly been the stronghold of the machine politicians who ruled the Republican and Democratic parties. The leaders in the Senate had succeeded in controlling legislation, in influencing the choice of presidential candidates, in securing the confirmation or rejection of the appointments of Supreme Court judges, and the like.

Most of them had spent the larger part of their professional lives in the Senate, having been reëlected for one six-year term after another. Many of them were bosses in their own state political machines and were elected by legislatures which were under their control. Thus Senators were often able to keep their hands on the controlling positions, not only in the political parties but also in the state and national governments.

Even as early as 1868 President Andrew Johnson had demanded the direct election of United States Senators.

On several occasions the House of Representatives passed the amendment, but the Senate refused to approve it. Meanwhile the legislatures in state after state demanded the reform. Then in 1908 both Republicans and Democrats accepted it as a part of their national policy. Finally in 1911 the *Seventeenth Amendment* to the Constitution was passed by both the House and the Senate, providing that United States Senators should be elected by direct vote of the people. The states soon ratified the amendment, and it became a part of the Constitution in 1913.

6. Votes for women as well as men

An important step in the fight for universal suffrage was still to be taken. More than a century of national history had passed, and in most states women were still deprived of the right to vote.

Even before the Civil War a few women had been working for women's suffrage. In 1869, when the Fifteenth Amendment was under discussion, — the amendment which gave the Negro

© G. V. Buck

FIG. 198. A group of suffragists on the steps of the Capitol bringing Congress their petition for the vote

the vote, — some discussion also arose concerning a proposal to word the amendment so as to include women. But few people were as interested in extending suffrage to women as they were in extending it to Negro men. Indeed, few *women* were then interested in the proposal. As women began to enter the professional and business life of the country their interest grew. Local organizations of women sprang up, advocating suffrage for their sex. For the most part they concentrated their efforts upon securing the right to vote in city, county, and state elections. By 1912 nine states had extended suffrage to women. But almost all these states had been won only after a large number of women had learned to organize and work together. They then applied these lessons of organization and coöperation in a movement to secure an amendment to the Constitution, which would provide for their enfranchisement throughout the nation. On March 17, 1913, shortly after President Wilson's inauguration, a delegation of women waited on the President, hoping to secure his aid. President Wilson stated that the matter was "entirely new" to him and had "never been brought to his attention." From that time on, they constantly kept the question before him. One group of militant suffragists picketed the White House, a number of women standing constantly outside the gate, carrying banners bearing the slogans of their party and messages to the President.

The life of these pickets was by no means an easy one. They were arrested; they were put into prison; they were attacked by mobs. Finally, in January, 1918, in the midst of the World War, President Wilson declared himself in favor of a women's suffrage amendment. The amendment then came before the House and was passed by two votes.

The next problem was to get the Senate's approval. Month after month the women worked, arguing with Senators, appealing to their constituents, bringing all the pressure to bear that they could. But the necessary two-thirds vote was lacking. Twice the amendment came to the vote — but still there were a few less votes than the necessary two thirds.

It was not until June, 1919, that the Senate passed the amendment. Then came the ratification. One state after another approved the amendment, and in 1920 the 36 states necessary for ratification had accepted it. Women voted in the presidential election that year in all the states.

A Growing Danger to Democracy: the Decline in the Proportion of Actual Voters to Possible Voters

Thus the battle for democratic government went on decade after decade. Step by step, vigorous political reformers took away the privileges and some of the powers of the machine politicians, the officeholders, and the financial interests. By the

Australian secret ballot, by the direct-primary selection of candidates, by the initiative, referendum, and recall, by the direct election of United States Senators, and by the passage of the women's suffrage amendment, some of the evils and dangers of representative government were remedied. It cannot be doubted that in the 50 years following 1880, marked gains were thus made for democratic government in America.

But meanwhile our changing civilization was bringing about a serious danger to real democracy. This was the steadily increasing indifference of the mass of the voters to the way in which their government was being managed.

This indifference is proved beyond doubt by the decreasing proportion of eligible voters who cast ballots at succeeding elections.

In 1880, for example, three fourths of the eligible voters in the country cast their ballots for president. Fifty years later, the proportion had dropped to less than half.

What changes have contributed to this decline in the proportion of *actual* to *possible* voters? Undoubtedly there are several, but two important ones stand out above all others: (1) the immigration of many millions of foreign-born people; (2) the rapid growth of towns and cities with the resulting complexity of life.

You know the story of how great numbers of Europeans emigrated to America after 1880. On arrival, most of them knew no English. They crowded together in our Eastern cities and towns in small native European communities. Many, even of those who became naturalized citizens, did not vote, either because they were uninformed or because they were indifferent to American political affairs. But by far the more important cause of this failure to vote is the increasing complexity of American civilization and the growth of towns and cities. So rapidly has our population grown, so swiftly have millions of people concentrated in the cities, that it has become difficult to keep informed of all the laws proposed by city councils, state legislatures, and the national Congress. Thousands of laws are proposed each year, and many are passed. Most of these are never known to more than a small fraction of the population.

THE COMMON PEOPLE AND DEMOCRACY

Then, too, when the voter goes to the polls to choose officers for his government he is confronted by a long ballot. He must choose from a list of names. Unless he has taken pains to inform himself beforehand, many of these names are unknown to him, and he is ignorant of the honesty or ability of the candidates. Under such circumstances undoubtedly many voters, instead of trying, as they should, to learn about the candidates, stay away from the polls.

Thus in spite of the direct primary, the initiative, referendum, and recall, the direct election of Senators, the enfranchisement of women, and other reforms, the proportion of the voting public continues to decline. This fact, more than any other, gives the professional politicians and the industrial and business interests, the organized labor groups, and other small compact minorities an opportunity to run the government.

Is this inevitable? Can it be changed? Will education of the mass of the people help to increase vital interest in matters of government? What do you think? It is a very important problem — one you should think about carefully as you continue your studies of government.

Was government regarded as a profession and as a science during this period?

Throughout our studies of American civilization we have seen repeatedly the way in which men have learned to do things scientifically. Industry, farming, engineering, education,— seemingly every aspect of life,— have been transformed by scientific methods. Has government been scientifically conducted? Have mayors, aldermen, state legislators, representatives, senators, presidents, been trained for their difficult tasks of government?

There are those who believe that they should be so trained, that political officers should not be chosen unless they have studied and practiced the science and art of government. What do you think about this? Do you know arguments on the other side of the question?

CHAPTER XXII

AMERICAN GOVERNMENT EXTENDS ABROAD

In 1783 the Spanish prime minister wrote to his king that although the young American republic had been "born a pygmy," it would become a "giant."

The Spanish minister was correct in his prophecy. In 129 years this republic had expanded from a narrow row of thirteen states on the Atlantic seaboard to a continental nation of 48 states plus nearly 600,000 square miles of territory (Alaska) on the northwest corner of the continent. Then, not content with all this, the United States burst its continental barriers and planted its flag on remote islands of the Pacific Ocean.

The "last frontier" had hardly disappeared before brown-skinned natives in the southwestern Pacific were paying allegiance to the Stars and Stripes. Long before this the United States, like Great Britain, France, Germany, Russia, and Italy, was extending her trade in foreign lands. Then, like the powerful nations of Europe, the United States began to acquire coaling stations and naval bases for her fleets. A tiny empire it was, insignificant in size compared to the empires of Great Britain, France, and Germany, but it was the beginning of empire nevertheless.

Division of opinion among Americans about empire-building

Some Americans contend that our whole history has been one of empire-building. They maintain that the three-century-long conquest of the red man's continent was that. Our European ancestors, they say, came here, conquered the Indian, and forced him to live on reservations.

These people also say that America was building an empire when she took Texas and the Southwest from Mexico. They say she conquered that territory and made Mexicans who were living there American citizens against their will.

On the other hand, some Americans defend empire-building. They maintain that the land of the continent was relatively unsettled in 1600, when the Europeans came. Only about half a million Indians lived here, and they were in a low state of civilization. Their standard of living was poor; health conditions were bad; length of life was short; and customs were barbarous. These defenders of American expansion say that our European forefathers did some things which justified their empire-building — they developed an unused continent, and they built up a higher type of civilization.

There are other arguments of the defenders of empire-building, but the foregoing are typical ones. As you saw in *Changing Civilizations in the Modern World*, the problem is one of very great difficulty. It is also a problem of the greatest importance.

At this point we can get only a brief glimpse of the manner in which lands and peoples outside of continental United States were brought under the American flag.

American Government extended Abroad with the Spread of American Business

In *A History of American Civilization* we learned that American expansion began in the latter half of the 1800's through the extension of American business abroad. In the Samoan Islands, in the Hawaiian Islands, and in the West Indies American business men built up a prosperous trade. Sooner or later they came into conflict either with the native rulers or with European business men who were competing with them. Then, when difficulties arose, the United States government intervened to protect the Americans. Military forces were sent, order was established, and eventually the regions were brought under the government of the United States.

In *A History of American Civilization* we considered the business side of the problem of America's empire-building. Here we shall deal only with its political phases.[1]

[1] At this point you will, no doubt, wish to re-read Chapter XXIV of *A History of American Civilization*.

1. The United States secured one of the Samoan Islands, 1899

During the 1880's the United States, like Great Britain, France, Germany, Russia, and Italy, was building up a navy of steam-driven battleships. Coaling and supply stations were needed at

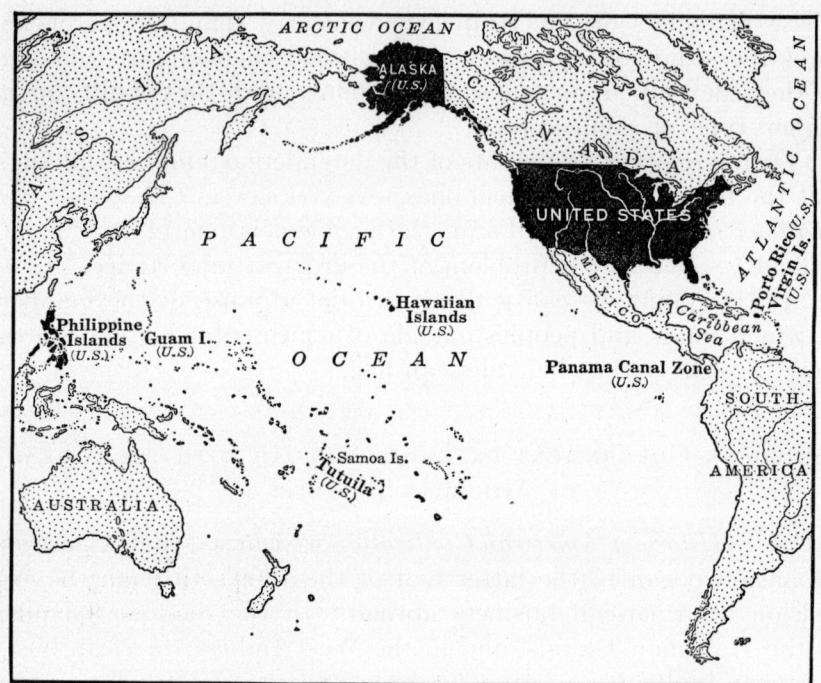

FIG. 199. The most important possessions of the United States

various points on the oceans by all these countries. The Samoan Islands were especially well situated for an American coaling station in the Pacific. In 1872 the Department of State had arranged a treaty with the king of Samoa by which a naval station was granted to the United States in the harbor of Pago Pago on the island of Tutuila. (See figure 199.) At the same time European corporations were building up their foreign trade with the natives of the Samoan Islands.

Then followed a period of trouble because of the claims of rival chiefs to the kingship. In 1889 the disorder was temporarily quieted. The United States, Germany, and Great Britain agreed to manage the affairs of the islands together; that is, they assumed a protectorate over the island group. The joint arrangement was not satisfactory, however. In 1899 Great Britain withdrew from the islands, Tutuila was ceded to the United States, and Germany took the rest of the group, which she held until after the World War, when her share passed under the control of the British Empire. Thus the American government officially acquired Tutuila and embarked on a policy of extension outside the continent of North America.

2. In 1898 the Hawaiian Islands were brought under the American government

As you learned from *A History of American Civilization*, before 1860 American missionaries and traders were living in the Hawaiian Islands. (Note in the map of figure 199 where the islands lie — about five days' steamship journey southwest of San Francisco.) The soil of Hawaii, you remember, was found to be suitable for raising sugar cane. American business men developed great sugar plantations there, became wealthy, and played an increasingly important rôle in the government of the islands. By 1895 native Hawaiians owned less than a third of their former lands and not one twentieth of the manufacturing and trade. Two thirds of the great sugar business was controlled by Americans.

In January, 1893, Americans in Hawaii joined with discontented natives in a revolt against their queen, Liliuokalani. The insurrection was successful, and the Queen was dethroned. Soon troops were landed from American war vessels, and an independent republic was declared. The United States had long held an unofficial protectorate over the Hawaiian Islands.

The new Hawaiian republic now sent representatives to President Benjamin Harrison, asking that Hawaii be annexed to the United States. The matter was referred to the Senate. Before it could be acted upon Grover Cleveland became president for the second time. He was opposed to the annexation of foreign territory and refused to recommend that Hawaii be added to the United States.

436 AMERICAN GOVERNMENT AND CULTURE

In 1897, however, McKinley, the Republican friend of business, became president. Again the Hawaiian representatives asked for annexation. This time the President was willing, and in 1898 Congress declared the islands a part of the country. An American governor was appointed by the President and Senate, and with a native Hawaiian legislature a regular territorial government was organized.

3. In 1898 came the Spanish-American War, and the Philippines, Porto Rico, and Guam became part of the United States

Recall from *A History of American Civilization* the manner in which the natives of Cuba revolted against their Spanish rulers in the 1890's. As a result the United States was drawn into a war with Spain. Spain's navy and armies were weak, and she was soon defeated. Peace was declared in December, 1898. Those who favored the extension of American government and the building of American business abroad were pleased. By the terms of the treaty of peace Spain (1) gave the United States a protectorate over Cuba until such time as Cuba should be in a position to govern itself and (2) ceded outright to the United States the islands of Porto Rico and Guam. Shortly thereafter the Philippine Islands were ceded to the United States upon payment of $20,000,000 to Spain for improvements which she had made in the islands.

The American people were sharply divided over the question of taking the Philippines, Porto Rico, and other islands. Many leaders, especially the progressives of both the leading parties, were outspoken in their opposition to imperialism, as it was called. Other Senators, Representatives, cabinet members, and associates of industry and business, however, advocated extending our government abroad in order to protect and increase American foreign trade.

One writer, who believed that America should take the Philippine Islands, wrote:

We have become a great people. We have a great commerce to take care of. We have to compete with the commercial nations of the world [Great Britain, France, Germany, for example] in far-distant markets. Commerce, not politics, is "King." . . . We are after markets, the greatest markets now existing in the world. Along with these markets will go beneficent institutions; and humanity will bless us.[1]

Another writer, who was opposed to the taking of the Philippines, wrote:

Good order we are trying to give to the Filipinos, but that does not satisfy. The grave is quiet, but it is not freedom. Perhaps it is wrong

FIG. 200. The battle of San Juan Hill in Cuba during the Spanish-American War. (From a painting by Frederic Remington. Courtesy of the Remington Art Association)

for these people to care for freedom, but we once set them the example, as we have to many poor people, to strive for a liberty they have never yet enjoyed.[2]

So the debate over the Philippines has continued from 1898 to the present day. Many American business leaders want to keep them because of their trade. Many students of government advocate giving the Philippines their independence. The latter maintain that the Filipinos are now capable of governing themselves. They point to the fact that their young leaders — engineers, scientists, and educators — have been unusually successful

[1] Morrison I. Swift, *Anti-Imperialism*, pp. 35-36. Public Ownership Review, Los Angeles, 1899.
[2] David S. Jordan, *Imperial Democracy*, p. 74. D. Appleton and Company, New York, 1898.

in acquiring European and American education. They have developed large agricultural enterprises, built railroads and banks, and now conduct their own legislature. In these and other ways, say the opponents of imperialism, the Filipinos are as ready for self-government now as Americans were in 1789.

FIG. 201. When the United States assumed control of the Philippines many people felt that it would be "an elephant" to Uncle Sam. An elephant is a valuable beast indeed, but a burden to anyone who doesn't *need* an elephant. (Courtesy of the New York *Herald*, June 3, 1898)

In the meantime, however, the United States has adopted a constructive and humane policy in the islands. They have built many hundreds of miles of well-paved roads on the thirteen larger islands as well as nearly 1000 miles of railways; they have built sanitary water-supply and sewage systems; they have developed a national school system. Today about a million and a half children go to school, where they are learning to read and write a common language (English), so that later the people of the separate island groups can understand one another and thus build up a unified nation. Physical comfort is much greater than in 1898, and the length of life is much longer. There is no doubt that the policy of development of the Philippine Islands by the American government compares favorably in efficiency and humaneness with that of European nations in Asia and Africa.

Nevertheless, since 1898 the Filipinos have demanded independence. When the Americans first took over the islands from Spain, a native insurrection broke out against them, led by General Aguinaldo. After more than two years of guerrilla warfare

AMERICAN GOVERNMENT EXTENDS ABROAD

in the hills, however, the revolt was subdued, and quiet has reigned generally in the islands since then.

Gradually the United States government has been giving the Filipinos self-government. Since 1913 they have been governed by a native legislature elected by the people of the islands. Many of the government officials are elected by the natives, also. The governor general and the heads of certain bureaus and departments, however, are appointed by the president of the United States.

The act of Congress which provides for the government of the islands declares

that it has always been the purpose of the people of the United States to withdraw their sovereignty over the Philippine Islands and to recognize their independence as soon as a stable government can be established therein.

In a report which was made to President Harding it was recommended

FIG. 202. General Emilio Aguinaldo. (From *Harper's Weekly*, December, 1898)

that the present general status of the Philippine Islands continue until the people have had time to absorb and thoroughly master the powers already in their hands ... that under no circumstances should the American government permit to be established in the Philippine Islands a situation which would leave the United States in a position of responsibility without authority.

Thus the American people confront today the important problem Shall we free the Filipinos? If we do, have we the responsibility of insuring their continued independence? Is there a danger that some other strong country may threaten their independence?

Is our withdrawal from the Philippines a matter which concerns the Philippines and the United States alone?

There is a wide difference of opinion upon these questions, but all thoughtful people realize that the withdrawal of the United States is a serious question and should be considered most carefully.

4. The United States acquired a valuable strip of land in Panama in 1903

From the beginning of American history ships which plied between the Atlantic coast and the Pacific coast had to go all the way around South America. A long, long trip it was. At one point, however, at the Isthmus of Panama, the strip of land between North and South America is very narrow. Here it was that Balboa first saw the shore of the Pacific in 1513.

Since 1550 men had thought of building a canal that would permit vessels to pass from ocean to ocean without taking the long journey around Cape Horn. In 1881 a French company had begun work on a canal at the Isthmus of Panama, but they gave up the enterprise in 1889. By 1903 the machines for digging had rusted in their places.

The trade of the United States was growing, and business men wanted a shorter and less expensive water route from our eastern to our western coast and to the lands of Asia. The government wanted a shorter water route for its navy, so that our fleet might get quickly from one coast to the other in case of need. The demand for a canal grew steadily after the Civil War.

At this time the South American country of Colombia owned the territory called Panama, where the distance was shortest from coast to coast. The Americans saw that the rights of the French company and the consent of Colombia, of which the isthmus was then a part, must be obtained.

The French company was ready to sell its rights and did so for the sum of $40,000,000. Then Colombia put a stumblingblock in the way. A treaty was suggested which provided that the United States should pay $10,000,000 to Colombia immediately and $250,000 each year for the control of a strip six miles wide across the isthmus. The United States Senate approved the

AMERICAN GOVERNMENT EXTENDS ABROAD 441

treaty. The Colombian senate, however, rejected it, saying that $10,000,000 was not enough. Intimations were made that Colombia would accept $25,000,000, but the United States was not willing to pay that amount.

The business men of the province of Panama became disturbed. A canal would bring them prosperity, and they wanted the land sold to the United States. So in 1903 the people of

FIG. 203. A cartoon of the president, Theodore Roosevelt, and the Panama Canal. (Courtesy of the New York *Herald*, November, 1903)

Panama revolted and declared their independence of Colombia. The United States government recognized Panama's independence at once. Then Panama ceded to the United States a zone ten miles wide in exchange for payments equal to those offered to Colombia. Work was commenced on the canal in 1904, and by 1915 it was completed.

In 1921 the United States ratified a treaty with Colombia by which our government agreed to pay Colombia $25,000,000 indemnity, compensating that country for possible loss in Panama. Thus was added a small but very important holding to our territory outside the United States.

5. The purchase of the Virgin Islands

Just east of Porto Rico lies a string of about 100 small islands, called the Virgin Islands. Like the other West Indies, they are on the path of trade along the American coast and across the Caribbean Sea. For more than a half-century American political leaders wanted to bring the largest of the islands under the American government. They were owned by Denmark.

In 1867 negotiations to buy them were begun by the United States government. At that time the Danish parliament agreed to the sale, but just then an earthquake and a hurricane in the Virgin Islands made them seem less desirable, and the United States Senate finally voted against the purchase. Then in 1902 (during Roosevelt's administration) negotiations were opened again. This time the Danes were unwilling. In 1917, however, an agreement concerning the sale was reached, and three of the largest of the Virgin Islands, St. Thomas, St. John, and St. Croix, were sold to the United States for $25,000,000.

Figure 199 shows the most important American possessions. Taken all together the island territory which has been added to the United States is comparatively small. Including the Philippines, Hawaii, Porto Rico, Panama, Guam, American Samoa, and the Virgin Islands, the total land area is 125,856 square miles and the total population is approximately 14,000,000. As compared with the area and population of continental United States and in sharp contrast to the huge empires which have been built by Great Britain and France, the additions are small.

Several important but very difficult problems have been presented to the American government, however, by our island possessions. Perhaps the most important is that of home rule for the natives of each of these regions. Shall they be free to govern themselves? Or shall they be given comparative self-government, remaining under the general protection of the United States? Shall the natives themselves be helped to develop agriculture, industry, and business in their respective regions, or shall American capital be encouraged and helped to develop there?

6. The American sphere of influence extends to Cuba and Haiti

Besides the actual possession of certain territory outside the United States, the American government has extended its control and its protection over territory which it does not possess.

FIG. 204. Officers of the army who took prominent parts in the campaign in Cuba during the Spanish-American War. In the front row are Major General Joseph Wheeler, Colonel Leonard Wood, and Lieutenant Colonel Theodore Roosevelt. (Photograph from Underwood & Underwood)

You remember that after the Spanish-American War Cuba became a protectorate of the United States. Cuba was in a wretched condition. Commerce was at a standstill, plantations were ruined, and there was much disease on the island. Under American control agriculture was resumed, commerce was restored, modern methods of sanitation were taught, and in 1902 the American forces withdrew, leaving Cuba in such a position that it could manage its own affairs.

United States troops have landed in several near-by countries for the purpose of stopping disorder of one kind or another, but such intervention presents troublesome problems. Should we intervene at all? If so, under what conditions? Having taken control of the governments of weaker countries, when should we permit them to resume their responsibilities? All these are questions which raise problems for American government.

The island of Haiti presented such problems to Roosevelt and to every president who has served after him.

a. Dominican Republic

The blue waters of the Caribbean Sea touch on one side the islands of the West Indies and, on the other, Central America. The vessels which carry goods from the Atlantic to the Pacific must cross the Caribbean Sea, and so the islands which border on it are important to the United States. They are valuable as barriers guarding the Gulf of Mexico and the Panama Canal, as markets for American goods, and as regions where tropical crops, such as sugar and coffee, are raised.

The island of Haiti, where Columbus had once been governor, is one of the islands of this group. It is divided into two little countries, the Republic of Haiti and the Dominican Republic. Both the countries had come under French rule late in the 1600's. Both were peopled by a few French and Spanish planters and a horde of Negro slaves. By 1789 and 1803, respectively, the little countries had gained independence from their French masters, but they both continually suffered from revolutions.

The Dominican Republic had the bad fortune to get into debt to citizens of several European nations, notably France, Belgium, and Italy. Some of this debt was the result of bad management on the part of the Dominicans and of the expensive revolutions which occurred so frequently.

In the year 1904 the situation became desperate for the Dominican Republic. The European nations were threatening to come into the country and collect the debts by force. The president of the republic was instructed to appeal to the United States to protect the country from European interference. Roosevelt was president of the United States at the time. He believed in the extension of the power of the United States. Furthermore, he had the American tradition of the Monroe Doctrine to support him.

Roosevelt sent American representatives into the Dominican Republic and took over the control of the customhouse where the import duties were collected. Of the money collected by duties 55 per cent was applied to the Dominican debt, and the country was put on a sound financial basis. Then American bankers took over the loans of the foreign bankers. The Dominican Republic became an American sphere of influence.[1]

In 1916 revolutions again upset the Dominican Republic. Then United States marines were sent to restore order, and military control was established. This control lasted for several years, but gradually it was removed, and the Dominican Republic was allowed to resume control of the government.

b. *The Republic of Haiti*

Most of the story of the Dominican Republic was repeated in the Republic of Haiti. Haiti was heavily in debt to both France and Germany. Much of the Haitian money was being wasted in revolutions. In 1914 after a series of civil wars the European creditors decided that something must be done if their debts were to be collected. Rather than permit European interference, the United States asked the Haitian government to allow the American management of Haiti's financial affairs, as had been done in the case of the Dominican Republic. Upon Haiti's refusal, American troops were landed and the United States assumed financial control. A treaty was signed in 1916 (and renewed in 1926) by which the various departments of the Haitian government were put under American supervision.

This was not accomplished without much protest from the Haitian population. However, under the American administration of Haiti, the people of that country have received some benefits besides a reëstablishment of their credit. Roads have

---

[1] The term *sphere of influence* is used in international law to designate a territory in which the political influence or interests of one nation are acknowledged by all other nations, although the territory is not officially a protectorate of that nation.

been built to improve communication between the principal towns, and a public-school system has been established. Haitians are being trained to run the various departments of their government efficiently. Our treaty with Haiti expires in 1936. Unless it is renewed the American control of the republic will probably be withdrawn, and Haiti will again manage its own affairs. In the meanwhile Haiti remains under the American sphere of influence.

The question of the ownership and control of lands outside the United States presents important problems which you as citizens may be called upon to consider.

INTERESTING READINGS FROM WHICH YOU CAN GET ADDITIONAL INFORMATION

ALEXANDER, M. C. Story of Hawaii. American Book Company, New York.

BEARD, CHARLES A. Contemporary American History, pp. 199–223, 275–279. The Macmillan Company, New York. For the best readers.

BISHOP, JOSEPH B. The Panama Gateway. Charles Scribner's Sons, New York. For the best readers.

DEWEY, GEORGE. Autobiography of George Dewey, Admiral of the Navy. Charles Scribner's Sons, New York. Good reference for the Spanish War and the battle of Manila Bay.

ELSON, HENRY W. Sidelights on American History. The Macmillan Company, New York. See Volume I, pp. 168–194, The Monroe Doctrine — very interesting; and Volume II, pp. 353–401, The Spanish War.

HAGEDORN, HERMANN. The Boys' Life of Theodore Roosevelt. Harper & Brothers, New York.

HALSEY, FRANCIS W. (Editor). Great Epochs in American History. Funk & Wagnalls Company, New York. See Volume V, pp. 133–143; Volume X, pp. 125–131, 132–134, 135–154, 155–158, 169–176.

HART, A. B. (Editor). American History told by Contemporaries, Vol. III, pp. 494–501. The Macmillan Company, New York.

PRIESTLEY, HERBERT I. The Mexican Nation, pp. 375–455. The Macmillan Company, New York. For the best readers.

REED, JOHN. Insurgent Mexico. D. Appleton and Company, New York.

ROOSEVELT, THEODORE. Theodore Roosevelt: an Autobiography. Charles Scribner's Sons, New York. The best readers may be able to use this.

THAYER, WILLIAM R. Theodore Roosevelt. Grossett and Dunlap, New York.

TROWBRIDGE, E. D. Mexico, Today and Tomorrow. The Macmillan Company, New York.

UNIT VIII

THE RED MAN AND THE WHITE MAN'S GOVERNMENT

THE RED MAN AND THE WHITE MAN'S GOVERNMENT

The preceding chapters of the volume have shown you the struggle of the common man for a more democratic government. You learned that as a result of this struggle many more people were given the right to vote. Property and religious restrictions were first removed. Then "color" restrictions were removed, and the Negro was enfranchised. By the Nineteenth Amendment sex restrictions were also removed, and women were granted the right to vote. Thus without regard to class or sex, two races secured representation in the government.

There was a third race — the Indians — whose affairs presented a problem to the American people. You have learned something of their story in A History of American Civilization.

Every president and every Congress from 1790 to 1890 confronted an Indian problem. Throughout that century settlers were taking the Indian's land on the advancing Western frontiers — always with opposition from the Indians who owned it. Hence every president either purchased land for the settlers, conquered tribes, made treaties with chieftains, or established reservations. Every administration confronted the necessity of working out a policy of dealing with the red man.

It is to this aspect of the history of American government that we turn in Chapter XXIII. As you study it, have in mind the following questions:

1. *Were the civilizations of the white man and the red man alike or unlike?*
2. *Did each side have a well-worked-out plan to deal with the other?*
3. *Did the two races understand each other?*
4. *How did the two races compare in numbers and in military power?*
5. *Did each race succeed in keeping its own civilization or was one absorbed by the other?*
6. *Was one side more "right" than the other?*
7. *Would it be possible for two such civilizations to exist side by side on the same continent without one dominating the other?*

CHAPTER XXIII

THE RED MAN AND THE WHITE MAN'S GOVERNMENT

The westward movement of the white man marked the retreat of the Indian[1]

Decade after decade European colonists and, later, American pioneers from eastern territory pushed on in the direction of the setting sun, creating new frontiers as they went. In 1800 the frontier had reached the headwaters of the Ohio; then it advanced to Indiana and Illinois in 1810-1820. In 1830-1840 the frontier had gone forward across the Mississippi River into Missouri, Kansas, and Iowa; and finally it reached over the prairies to the Pacific coast.

At the same time, as the vanguard of hunters, trappers, homesteaders, miners, cattle-raisers, and railroad-builders moved on, they were opposed by the Indians, the original owners of the land. Steadily as the white man marched forward the Indian was obliged to retreat before him. The story is that of a succession of conflicts between the two races.

Government Plans and Indian Treaties

In 1763, during colonial times, King George III proclaimed that the land west of the Appalachians as far as the Mississippi River was to be a large Indian reserve. If the settlers wished to obtain some of this land, they must purchase it from the headmen of all the Indian tribes in council. This was the policy which the colonial governments used in their relations with the Indians from 1763 until the time of the Revolution.

[1] As a background for understanding the story of the relations between the Indian and the white man from 1790 to 1890, review Chapters I, VIII, and IX of *A History of American Civilization*. That will enable you to recall the original friendly relations of the two races, the development of misunderstandings, the continued warfare, and the gradual pushing back of the Indians west of the Appalachians.

At the close of the Revolution, in 1783, a new flood of settlers poured into the Ohio valley, and the American government decided that treaties must be made. In 1785 the first treaty was made, by which Congress agreed to keep settlers from crossing north of the headwaters of the Wabash, the Scioto, and the Miami rivers. Thus the white people were allowed to settle within a territory which is now roughly the southern half of Indiana and Ohio.

The frontiersmen, however, felt that they had had nothing to do with making the treaty. They calmly set aside its provisions and settled wherever they wished. The Indians, finding that the settlers were disregarding the treaty, promptly rallied to the cry "White men shall not plant corn north of the Ohio." Once more there were raids and scalpings along the border.

By 1787 the Second Continental Congress was ready to protect the settlers who had gone beyond the boundaries as defined by the treaty. It provided for surveying the land of the Northwest Territory, dividing it, selling it to settlers, and later bringing into the Union the new states made from it. As you know the Northwest Territory had been acknowledged as part of the United States by the British, but Congress did not provide for buying it from the Indians.

What was the government's Indian problem in 1790?

President Washington planned to continue the policy of the colonial governments by

First, arranging with Indian owners for the taking over of Western land. This involved, decade by decade, purchasing land from the Indians and making new treaties with them.

Second, providing military protection for the Western settlers.

Third, establishing posts for carrying on trade between the white men and the Indians.

As we look back on his plans from the vantage point of a century and a half of history we can see their importance and the difficulty of carrying them out.

The first of Washington's policies assumed that the Americans would continue to take the Western lands of the red men. The second policy recognized that there would be trouble with the Indians as westward settlement advanced, and so provided for the building of forts and the placing of soldiers at strategic points on the frontier. Nevertheless, the government also recognized the

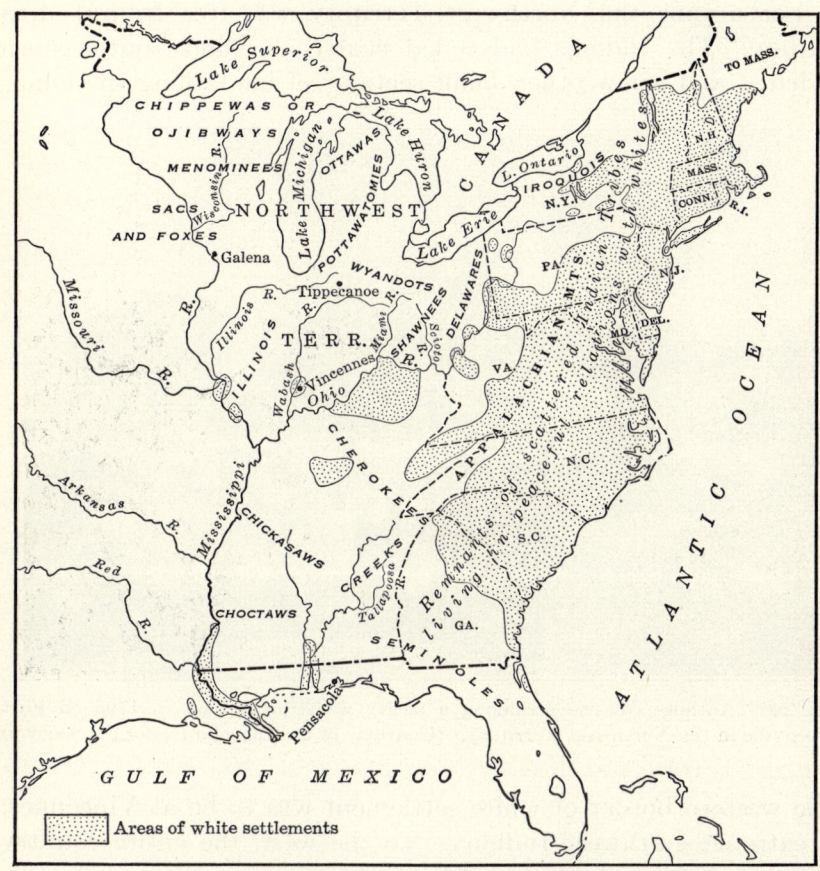

FIG. 205. The Indian tribes in the United States in 1790

Indians' claim to the land and representatives were frequently sent to the tribes to arrange for friendly purchase of land.

By the third policy the Federal government arranged for the development of trade with the Indians. In 1796, at President Washington's suggestion, an act was passed establishing government trading posts in the West. These posts were to exchange white men's products for Indian furs and other goods, and to cultivate the friendship of the red man, so that he would not turn against the Americans. By this time the Indian had begun to depend upon many things which only the white man had — for example, guns and ammunition, implements, and cloth.

For a time the Northwest Territory was free from Indian warfare. The Indians had ceded nearly all Ohio, southeastern Indiana, and a few other small sections of land along the Ohio.

FIG. 206. Anthony Wayne arranging a treaty with the Indians in 1795 on Fort Greenville in the Northwest Territory. (Courtesy of the Chicago Historical Society)

The western border of white settlement was to be at Vincennes, in extreme southwest Indiana. To the west, the entire country was to belong to the Indians.

So rapid was the westward settlement, however, that by 1810 Indiana had become a thriving territory of 25,000 white homesteaders. Most of these homesteaders cared nothing for government treaties. They had endured the hardships of frontier travel and settlement to get this good land, and they were determined to have it. So they helped themselves to land in the Indian hunting grounds. As increasing numbers of settlers arrived the tribes became more and more resentful.

THE RED MAN AND THE GOVERNMENT 453

Just at this time a great Indian leader began to unite his people against the settlers. This was Tecumseh, "the Wild Cat that leaps upon its Prey." Tecumseh was a handsome, intelligent Shawnee, who had hated the whites from childhood. He wished to see the Indians drive out the whites. To aid them, Tecumseh had worked out a clever plan. He planned a great confederation of all the Indians east of the Mississippi. The tribes were to assume joint ownership of all the land which they inhabited. Thus no single chief was to have power to grant land to the United States government.

FIG. 207. Tecumseh, the Indian chief who tried unsuccessfully to unite the Indians east of the Mississippi into a strong confederacy. (Courtesy of the University of Chicago)

In his work Tecumseh was aided by his one-eyed brother, the Prophet, who was an inspired orator. Together they visited the tribes, and when the reasoning of Tecumseh failed the oratory of the Prophet won. Among other things the Prophet urged the Indians to return to their own ways of living — to dress in skins and hunt with bows and arrows. He pleaded with them to reject the gifts of the white man — whisky and weapons. The white man's weapons, however, were too much needed in fighting and food-getting, and so could not be abandoned.

As a meeting place for the united tribesmen, Tecumseh chose a spot in Indiana on Tippecanoe Creek, which was very well located both for communication and for warfare. Many warriors settled there and pretended to be leading quiet lives, farming the land.

By 1809, however, the white frontiersmen became suspicious. General William Henry Harrison, governor of Indiana Territory, called Tecumseh to him for an interview. During the conference Tecumseh firmly stated that if the United States continued to deal with the Indians in separate tribes, he would join forces with Great Britain in the struggle which everyone saw was soon to come. It was impossible for Harrison to agree not to deal with separate tribes, for the Indians were scattered. To secure the consent of *all* the chiefs to a sale of land would have been an almost endless task. So Tecumseh worked untiringly to bring about a powerful Indian federation and also to stop the existing evils among the Indians. He pleaded repeatedly with Governor Harrison not to sell his people whisky. Harrison replied that he would gladly take up the question with the Great White Father in Washington. Tecumseh said that he hoped that the Great Father would keep the white people off the Indians' land. He is reported to have said: "It is true that he is so far off he will not be injured by the war. He may sit still in his town and drink his wine, while you and I will have to fight it out."

FIG. 208. General William Henry Harrison, governor of Indiana Territory, interviewing Tecumseh to try to come to an understanding with the Indian chief. (From a painting by Stanley M. Arthurs)

Then, in 1811, while Tecumseh was away on a mission to unite the Southeastern tribes, a battle took place. Tecumseh's brother attacked Harrison's fort. The Indians finally retreated after a bloody battle.

THE RED MAN AND THE GOVERNMENT 455

Tecumseh returned north to find that many of his people had lost faith in him. He went to Canada to obtain arms and ammunition from the British. While there he was given the rank of brigadier general in the army of His Majesty, the King.

Then came the War of 1812 between Great Britain and the United States, and Tecumseh and his warriors launched their attack. They proved themselves to be excellent soldiers. After months of maneuvering the British and the Indians were defeated by the American soldiers at the battle of the Thames, 1813. Tecumseh was killed on the field.

With the death of this leader, hope for a great Indian confederation was lost. The tribes had made their last stand, and they had failed. From that time for twenty years the whites steadily took over the land between the Ohio, the Mississippi, and the Great Lakes.

More Government Plans and More Treaties

What was the policy of the government after Washington's time?

By the time Thomas Jefferson came into office, a dozen trading posts had been established between the Appalachians and the Mississippi. Jefferson definitely approved and extended Washington's plan for dealing with the Indians. He created a government office, under a Superintendent of Indian Trade, to carry on the building of trading posts. During his administration, also, the War Department, which was then in charge of Indian affairs, sent out exploring parties through the vast region west of the Mississippi. Trails were blazed and information was gathered concerning possibilities of settlement. In *A History of American Civilization* you learned about the most historic of these expeditions, that of Lewis and Clark.

The government decided to make the Great Plains and the mountains a permanent reserve for the Indians

During Monroe's administrations the War Department under Calhoun decided to send out more exploring expeditions to the Far West. One of these, in 1818, under Major Stephen H. Long, resulted in an important government policy concerning the Indians. In his report Long described the great, grassy plains as "almost wholly unfit for cultivation." The government was much influenced by the report.

During Monroe's second administration (1821–1825) Calhoun created a Bureau of Indian Affairs, but the army was to continue to make treaties with the Indian tribes for pieces of land east of the Mississippi. In return for the land the Federal government was to pay the Indians annually a certain sum of money. Government agents were to be located at various outposts on the Indian frontier to pay the tribes their annual installments, to provide them with farming implements, tools, and other supplies, and to act as go-betweens for the settlers and the Indians.

Since the land described by Major Long was reported unfit for white settlement, it could be used as a permanent reserve for the Indians. Thereupon plans were made to buy all the Indian lands east of the Mississippi and move the tribes to the Great Plains, where they were to be allowed to remain "forever." They were excellent plans, to be sure, but no one as yet had seen the difficulty first of persuading the Eastern tribes to move, and then of inducing the Western tribes to welcome them.

As a result of the work of Calhoun and Monroe, government agents were sent among the Indian tribes west of the Mississippi to make treaties to insure peace in the future. In 1825 more than 100 chiefs met government agents on the banks of the Mississippi and signed a treaty promising friendship and continued peace. No definite agreements were reached about land, however; difficulties always stood in the way. The two races understood the ownership of land in different ways. The white settler wanted to buy the land outright, to live upon it permanently, and at his death to pass it on to his children. He regarded it as private property. The Indian had no such idea of private property. He conceived the land as belonging to the whole tribe. It was land to be used for hunting and fishing, not to be held permanently. Only a few tribes — the Cherokees, for one — understood the white man's idea of ownership. Furthermore, the Indians were loath to fix boundaries for their tribes. The idea of confining the rovings of a tribe to one area was distasteful to them.

THE RED MAN AND THE GOVERNMENT

The government plan drawn up by Calhoun also provided for an attempt to teach the Indians how to read and write and how to live according to the settled occupations of the white man.

Schools were established and missions were encouraged by government appropriations. The missionaries succeeded in putting some of the Indian languages into writing. For years they went among the Indians and helped to maintain friendly rela-

FIG. 209. To carry out Calhoun's plan schools were established on the Indian lands and the Indians were taught to read and to write

tions. Frequently they succeeded in opposing the attempts of the government to force the tribes off the land and farther into the Western wilderness.

In earlier times some of the white men had believed that the two peoples could live peaceably side by side if they had a common language and if they both lived more or less according to the same customs. By this time, however, few Americans held this idea. The Americans vastly outnumbered the Indians, and it was evident that they would acquire whatever land they wished. Many Indian leaders feared that the whites would absorb the Indians into their civilization.

In 1832 a Commissioner of Indian Affairs was appointed. Laws were passed, requiring Indian traders to have government licenses, regulating the sale of whisky to the tribes, and forbidding the white men to trespass upon Indian lands.

The history of the period proves clearly that in various administrations the Federal government in Washington made attempts to obtain the Indians' Western lands by purchase and by treaty. It is true, of course, that the government of the white man was infinitely stronger than that of the red man, and the Indian was finally forced to agree to the white man's terms. Nevertheless, the government frequently did try to compensate the Indians, to arrange matters by legal treaties, and to help them in other ways.

The frontier settlers themselves saw the matter in an entirely different light. They had endured the hardships of travel and settlement in the wilderness, and they knew only one thing — there was rich land ready for the taking and they were going to take it. Hence, through decade after decade of the westward movement, from the Appalachians to the Pacific coast, there was constant conflict between the settlers and the Indians. Intervals of peace were broken by attacks upon white communities, destruction of Indian villages, and finally the sending of government troops to protect the settlers and conquer the Indians.

After each important conflict a new treaty was signed, money was paid by the Federal government to the Indian chiefs, and solemn promises were made that *this* treaty was to be permanent. Then within a short time would come more friction, more murders and raids, and more organized warfare. The result was always the defeat of the Indians, the signing of another treaty, and the removal of the Indians to land farther west.

The efforts of the Cherokees to keep their lands

After 1832 peace reigned in the Northwest Territory. In the South the struggle between the white men and the Indians lasted until 1842, when the long war against the Seminoles of Florida ended. But before that time many tragic events had occurred.

THE RED MAN AND THE GOVERNMENT 459

Of all the stories of the Indian tribes there is perhaps none more tragic than that of the Cherokees, and the story is given to show that the Indians of the East were sometimes no more welcome to the Indians of the West than they were to the white people of the East.

The Cherokees were the most civilized of all the Southeastern tribes. They raised many agricultural crops, owned live stock,

Fig. 210. The Cherokees were not the only Southern Indians who led settled lives, as this picture of a Creek house shows. (Courtesy of the Smithsonian Institution)

wove cotton and linen cloth, and carried on many handicrafts — for example, metal-working. They kept inns, built roads, and worked out a way of writing their own language. They taught their young people to read and were in every respect good, quiet citizens. As the tide of settlement surrounded them, they modeled their government more or less on our national government and lived peacefully and quietly.

At the close of the Revolution the United States government bought from them a small amount of land. A treaty was signed, which read, in part:

If any citizen of the United States shall attempt to settle on any of the [Cherokee] lands ... or having already settled, and will not remove from the same within six months after the ratification of this treaty, such person shall forfeit the protection of the United States and the Indians may punish him or not as they please.

In spite of this, settlers came from the East and moved into Cherokee lands. The chiefs protested to the Great White Father at Washington. A new treaty was made, but that, too, was speedily broken. Another protest was sent, but no heed was given it. The Cherokees then decided to use their right to punish settlers themselves, as provided in the treaty, but the Washington government promptly sent out troops to discipline the Indians.

After peace had been made settlement began again. The whites of the South were determined to have the land for their cotton. Soon they outnumbered the Indians. Again history repeated itself, and trouble arose. In 1815, after the Cherokees had been subdued, their chief signed an agreement that gave 1,000,000 acres of Cherokee land to the government in exchange for a sum of money and lands beyond the Mississippi.

Many of the individual tribesmen and warriors had not been consulted, however, and on learning of the treaty those people refused to move. Argument would not change them. The chiefs were powerless to force the dissenting tribesmen to move.

At length, however, one tribe left Tennessee and crossed the Mississippi. Slowly others of the people followed. But the Georgia Cherokees refused to move. They were later given the harsh choice of moving west or of living settled lives under the state laws of Georgia.

The Cherokees who went west were constantly at war with other earlier residents of the plains, among whom were the Osages, the Pawnees, and the Comanches, who refused to share their hunting grounds. Then, too, they found themselves in a strange land, among tribes who lived by hunting. They were not accustomed to the wild, roving life and missed sadly their little farms and gardens. The chiefs, who felt that they had been cheated, journeyed to Washington to lay their case before the President. They were courteously treated and showered with gifts, but they returned to the West with nothing accomplished. At the same time, white people had begun to invade the new territory west of the Mississippi, and Indian agents frequently failed to make the annual payments due to the tribe.

The Indians who had remained in Georgia saw that there was little hope for them since both the national and the state governments opposed them. Their only hope seemed to be to appeal to the United States Supreme Court. Accordingly the Cherokee Nation sued the state of Georgia, asking that the Georgia law be set aside and that the Georgia officials be prohibited from interfering with their lands. The Supreme Court, however, refused, in 1831, to recognize that the Cherokee Nation was a "sovereign state" and denied even the right of the Indians to sue the state of Georgia.

The Situation from 1850 until 1890

By 1850 most of the Indians had either been killed or had moved west of the Mississippi River. Scattered tribes still existed on reservations in the midst of the white men, where they lived peaceful lives.

Most of those who remained in the East — probably 130,000 — had given up their nomadic life and had begun to take on many of the ways of the white man. A few maintained well-developed farms, but most of them lived squalid lives, partly supported by the government but greatly demoralized by whisky and disease. Already there had been much intermarriage between Indians and Negroes and some between Indians and white people. In a number of localities there were small half-breed populations. By 1850 there were almost no remains of the earlier Indian life except occasional Indian reservations and the Indian names which had been given to towns, counties, rivers, streets, and societies.

West of the Mississippi to the north there were the Chippewa (Ojibwa), Sac, Fox, and the various Illinois tribes. Somewhat south of them were the Potawatami, Delaware, and Miami tribes. Still farther south were the Creek, Choctaw, Chickasaw, Cherokee, and Seminole tribes.

Then there were also the original Indians of the Western plains — such as the Shawnees, Peorias, Ottawas, Kickapoos, Missouris,

Omahas, Iowas, and Osages. These tribes had roamed the plains for no one knows how long, but reluctantly they accepted the coming of the Eastern tribes.

During the 1850's the whites of the North and the South were engaged in their struggle for the control of Missouri, Kansas, and Nebraska. The territory was filling up with white people. Tens of thousands of homesteaders were settling on the land and were quarreling with one another over the question of whether it should be slave territory or free territory. Although the tribes that had been moved west into this region did not understand the question, they were constantly harassed by the raiding of the whites upon one another. It was clear that the Indians would soon be driven forth again.

In 1855 the tribesmen began their final migration. Men, women, and children packed up their simple belongings and with their horses and dogs wound their way across the prairies. This time the migration included the Shawnees, Delawares, Iowas, Sacs, Foxes, Kickapoos, Miamis, Wyandots, and members of other small tribes. Indian Territory, now included in the state of Oklahoma, became the home of the remnants of most of the Eastern tribes.

The last stand of the Indians on the Great Plains

In the 1820's, you remember, the Federal government had solemnly promised the Indians that the entire territory west of the Mississippi was to be reserved to them forever.

But even in the 1830's wagon trains of hardy pioneers lumbered their way across the prairies, the mountains, and the deserts to the rich valleys of Oregon and California. Then came the discovery of gold and silver in the West. Soon thousands of miners and, with them, thousands of merchants and traders rushed westward. After them followed ranchers and homesteaders in large numbers.

The path was not clear to the land-and-gold-seeking adventurers, however. West of the Mississippi, on the Great Plains, were large and warlike tribes — the Sioux, the Shoshones, the Cheyennes, the Blackfeet, the Crows, the Comanches, and the

THE RED MAN AND THE GOVERNMENT 463

Arapahoes, to mention only a few of the most important ones. Altogether it is estimated that there were about 300,000 Indians west of the Mississippi, about 225,000 on the plains and foothills of the Rockies, and about 50,000 on the Pacific coast.

As the white people advanced, the Indians began to realize that their last hunting ground would be taken. Immediately the old friction between the white frontiersmen and the Indians developed. Emigrant trains were attacked and sometimes wiped out. Ranch houses were harried; families were murdered. In self-defense settlers began to combine against the Indians.

The government now made new treaties with the Indian tribes, promising them money for their lands and offering them farming implements if they would move on to new reservations which were being created for them. But the plains Indians were not accustomed to the settled life of farming. Indeed, most of them believed that the soil was sacred and must not be touched. Their lives were spent in roaming the vast level land, hunting buffaloes and breeding the half-wild Spanish ponies which they used for hunting and warfare. They could not understand the white man's desire to mark off sections of the earth and live quietly on the land.

Meanwhile the government had built more army posts, and companies of soldiers were installed at various locations on the Western plains. There were rumors in Iowa and Nebraska that railroads would soon be built across the continent. The Indians on hearing these rumors grew restless and fearful, for they knew the great iron road would bring more settlers and end the open range of the buffaloes. Their reservations were steadily being reduced in size. In their few contracts with the traders they had often been cheated and tricked. Would they not have been less than men if they had not rebelled against the coming of the settlers?

But the homesteaders, miners, and ranchers west of the Mississippi believed as had the early frontiersmen that the Indians must be got out of the way. By the end of the Civil War many felt that the best way to deal with the Indians was to kill them without mercy. General Halleck of the United States army wrote in 1866, "They must be hunted and exterminated."

In 1869 the government took the management of Indian affairs out of the hands of the Department of War

For a half-century the army, under the Department of War, had handled many of the Indian problems. But during that time a Bureau of Indian Affairs had been built up in the Department of the Interior. The two departments were jealous of each other, and there was friction. The agents of the bureau accused officers in the Department of War of brutal treatment of the Indians. The officers replied that the agents were inefficient and were dishonest in handling the Indian funds.

It is true that in dealing with the tribes on the reservations, the government agents were often careless and occasionally dishonest. There were times when government payments due to various Indian tribes were not made regularly. For example, in the winter of 1862 the Utah Indians were reduced to a sad state of wretchedness, hunger, and cold because they had not received their government money at the appointed time. The Indians on the reservations were almost altogether dependent upon the white man's money for food, clothing, and other necessities. In 1869 a Board of Indian Commissioners was appointed. This board, together with the Bureau of Indian Affairs, was to handle Indian funds. Thereafter corruption among the agents lessened, although it did not entirely disappear. By 1871 the white man's frontier on the Great Plains appeared to be quieting down.

Custer and the Sioux

This state of affairs was not to last long, however. One powerful group of Indians, the Sioux, stood in the way of the settlement of the "last frontier."

As you have already learned, the building of the transcontinental railroad was begun during the Civil War. At the close of the war construction was carried on rapidly. Across Nebraska and Wyoming, across California, Nevada, and Utah steadily moved the working crews of the Union Pacific and the Central Pacific railroads. Then in 1874 came the discovery of gold in the Black Hills of Dakota Territory and soon afterward the beginning of construction on the Northern Pacific Railway. Thousands of white men advanced west from Minnesota through what is now North Dakota and South Dakota.

Fearfully the Indians of the Western plains watched the white men taking away their land, killing off their buffaloes, ruining their hunting grounds, and driving them ever back and back. They decided to oppose their advance. There were raids, murders,

FIG. 211. The Sioux Indians and representatives of the United States government met in 1868 and signed a treaty. The Sioux agreed to live on a reservation, but insisted upon the right to hunt for buffaloes outside the reservation so long as there were enough buffaloes "to justify the chase." (Courtesy of the United States Signal Corps)

and scalpings. Federal soldiers were sent out to guard the railway work gangs. White settlers and miners coöperated in protecting the army of railroad-builders against the Indians.

By the middle of the 1870's the Sioux, under Sitting Bull, massed to resist the new invasion of the white man. With Sitting Bull, a man of influence, were the well-armed and well-mounted warriors of some 2000 lodges (family groups), led by such daring chiefs as Rain-in-the-Face, Crazy-Horse, and Young-Man-Afraid-of-Horses. It is estimated that they had some 12,000 fighting men.

Seeing that there was to be a real struggle in the Northwest, the Department of War ordered a strong contingent of soldiers to be sent out under Marcus A. Reno and George A. Custer. For months the Indians successfully evaded the soldiers, leading them through mountain passes and fighting in ambush.

Then, in 1876, General Terry was sent out with another body of soldiers to trap the Indians, who were reported to be in Montana near the Yellowstone and the Little Big Horn rivers. Custer and Reno and their troops joined Terry. At length Custer and Reno, annoyed by the constant failure of the army to catch the Indians, took eight companies of the men and plunged into the wilderness alone, cutting themselves off from the rest of the army.

FIG. 212. Sitting Bull. (Courtesy of the Museum of the American Indian)

The main body of troops under Terry slowly advanced, with the Indians always just out of reach and constantly harassing them. More and more difficult grew the problem, as the little army pushed on into the mountain country. They were in constant danger, sometimes crowded together in deep ravines, at other times stretched out in long, thin lines, the men in the rear fearing to lose sight of those in front. At length Terry's men came within a few miles of the Little Big Horn River and halted for the night in a grassy valley.

The next morning the troops started on at daybreak without breakfast. Six friendly Crow scouts went ahead to investigate some smoke which might be that of a Sioux encampment. Suddenly the white troops heard a great wailing from the Indian scouts. One of the guides explained that it was a mourning for

THE RED MAN AND THE GOVERNMENT

the dead. The scouts came rushing back with the terrible news that Custer and his men had all been massacred at the Little Big Horn.

Onward hurried Terry's little army and finally came upon the battlefield where Custer had made his last stand. At the top of a ridge lay Custer himself, surrounded by a narrow circle of dead horses and men. Every officer and man had been killed, except a young Crow scout, who had escaped. Custer had been surrounded while Reno with three companies had been separated from him by only a short distance. Upon the body of a trooper lying at the edge of the field was found a bloodstained message, which Custer had tried to send to Reno.

This was the last important victory of the Indians, however. The Sioux crossed over into Canada, where the Canadian Crows made them welcome. Terry resigned his command, and General Nelson Miles was given the task of making peace along the northwest border.

The task of rounding up the other scattered tribes slowly continued. Finally in 1890 Sitting Bull, the last great leader of the Indians, was killed. The resistance of the Indians was completely broken. By that time nearly all had been brought to live on reservations.

From Wards of the United States to American Citizens

After a century of conquest most of the surviving red men were living on scattered reservations, most of which were west of the Mississippi. The largest was Indian Territory, later to be included in the state of Oklahoma. The Indian people numbered less than 250,000.

As more and more tribes settled peacefully in the reservations there was a change in the attitude of the American government toward the Indians. They were no longer enemies to be exterminated, but wards to be protected. Helpless now, they must be helped. No longer free to roam at will, they must be taught how to live settled lives. They must be educated according to American standards, and American standards of living must be made possible for them. So in the years between 1890 and 1925 the work of the Office of Indian Affairs, which had superseded the earlier Bureau, expanded greatly. By 1925 the government was spending annually through this office $15,000,000 for education, roads, bridges, irrigation and drainage projects, health service, etc. on the Indian reservations.

On some reservations the *tribes* still owned the land. On others a separate gift of land was made to each Indian who applied for it.

The area of all the Indian reservations covered only as much territory as the New England states and the state of New York combined. This land, as you know, had originally been considered undesirable for white settlement. In the years after 1890 coal, oil, lead, zinc, and other minerals were discovered on the reservations. Unscrupulous people then took advantage of the Indian's ignorance of the value of his holdings. Lands were leased from him at a fraction of their worth. Finally laws were passed by Congress for the protection of the Indian. These laws provided that contracts made between Indians on the reservations and those who wished to lease Indian land must receive the approval of the Secretary of the Department of the Interior. The laws stated definitely the cost of rental and the amounts to be received by Indians for all products taken from mines or oil wells. Through these provisions Indians who were fortunate enough to hold mineral-bearing land have attained wealth. In 1925 each Indian of the Osage tribe in Oklahoma, for example, received approximately $13,200. In addition to the discoveries made on the reservation in Oklahoma, oil has also been discovered on Indian lands in Michigan, Arizona, New Mexico, Montana, and Wyoming.

But there are still many Indian reservations on which it is almost impossible for the Indian to live. The land yields no minerals, and the soil is too poor for profitable agriculture. In 1929 approximately 10,000 Indians had to be helped by the government in order to live at all.

The government recently revised its policy again with regard to the Indian. In the words of the Secretary of the Department of the Interior, "The Indian shall no longer be viewed as a ward

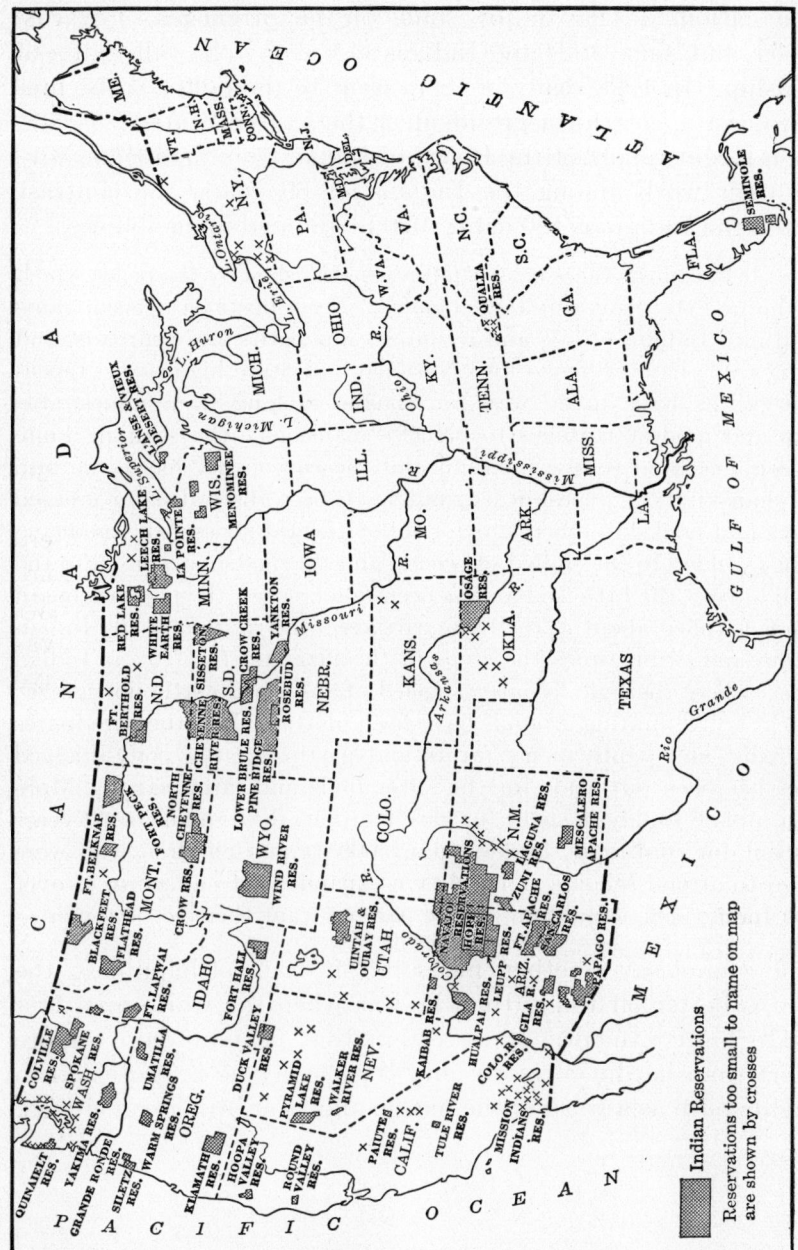

Fig. 213. The important Indian reservations in the United States today

of the nation." They enjoy some of the privileges of wards, however, but since 1924 the Indians also enjoy the full rights of citizenship. In 1928 many of them went to the polls for the first time to cast a vote for a president of the United States.

In a recent report of the Board of Indian Commissioners, covering their work among the Indians for 60 years, the contrast between the Indian of 1869 and 1920 is summed up as follows:

> War between the races has been forever abolished by the peace which is the normal status of a united citizenry; Army posts have been transformed into Indian schools and hospitals, war paths into railroads, and hunting trails have widened into National and State highways; tepees and wigwams have made way for houses, ranging from undesirable shacks and modest cottages to $50,000 mansions; the scalping knife has been relegated to the museum and the can-opener has come into the Indian kitchen; doeskin leggings have been discarded for creased trousers and buckskin moccasins for rubber-heeled shoes; the medicine man has yielded to the skilled physician and the medicine woman to the trained nurse; the little Indian has been taken out of the papoose board and now is rolled about in the baby carriage; the rhythm of the Indian tom-tom and drum times the steps in the jazz and fox trot at Indian dances; where the buffalo once ranged Indian-owned cattle now graze; the great tribal hunting grounds have been plotted off by the wire fences of Indians' and white men's farms and pastures; the pony-dragged travois has been put aside for the automobile and farm wagon. More Indian money to-day is spent for gasoline than the Indians of 60 years ago spent for rum, and the less than 5000 Indian children who were induced to attend schools in 1869 have expanded into an army of over 70,000 Indian school children, whose parents want them to be taught.

One cannot say whether, measured in terms of happiness, the Indian is better off today than he was when the white man first came to his continent. It is certain that he now enjoys more comfort than he did formerly and that today he is protected in his rights both as a ward of the nation and as an American citizen.

UNIT IX

THE CHANGING CULTURE OF THE AMERICAN PEOPLE

THE CHANGING CULTURE OF THE AMERICAN PEOPLE

We have now completed our brief study of American government up to the time of the World War. What do you think was the social life of the people during the half-century before that war? What did life mean to the individual men, women, boys, and girls of the changing America? How did the farmers, the mechanics, the teachers, the doctors, the lawyers, and the well-to-do captains of industry spend their time? Hours of labor became fewer as the century wore on, and time for leisure increased for many people. How did the Americans use their leisure? How did they play?

We have now reached the point where we can bring together our knowledge of the developing culture of the American people; that is, what they thought and talked about, what they liked and disliked, how they played — their songs and their dances, their music and their games, their reading and their theaters. Did all the people have these things, or were most of them concerned only with getting a living, bringing up children, and making money? These are the problems which we shall consider in Chapters XXIV to XXVII inclusive.

In Chapter XXIV we shall consider the way in which the spread of education among the people paralleled America's march toward democracy and the advance of her culture. In Chapter XXV we shall see the changing social life of this period of great industrial expansion.

In Chapters XXVI and XXVII we shall learn how the transformation of our economic civilization brought corresponding changes in the amusements of the common man.

Thus the scenes of the changing culture of America will pass before our eyes.

CHAPTER XXIV

POPULAR EDUCATION AND THE MARCH TOWARD DEMOCRACY

Everything about you has a history. The houses in which you live have advanced by painful stages of growth from times long ago when men lived in caves. The clothes you wear have come to be what they are through periods of constant change. Even the food you eat has been developed by patient toil from the wild life which at one time filled the earth. It is the same with ways of living. Trades, industries, and professions were not always what they are today. Agriculture, amusements, and sports have taken on new forms. Democracy is growing, society is different, government is changing. Everything has its history.

It is so with education. Today every boy and girl goes to school as a matter of course. Do you suppose this was always true? Today we see fine school buildings with large playgrounds about them. The money to run most of the schools is raised by taxes which, by one means or another, all the people pay. The teachers in these schools have spent years in training for their work. Do you think your grandparents and your great grandparents went to schools like these?

Education, a great public enterprise

Education is now the largest public enterprise in America. More money is invested in it than in any other; it costs more annually than any other; and more persons are connected with it than with any other enterprise or business in the United States.

Here are a few important facts about our country's schools and colleges today: (1) approximately 29,000,000 pupils are enrolled in them; (2) approximately 1,000,000 teachers work in them; (3) public-school property is worth $7,000,000,000; (4) in 1928 more than $3,000,000,000 was spent for the maintenance of schools; (5) between one third and one half of all public money is spent for education; (6) altogether, *more than a fourth of all persons in the United States are connected in one way or another with education* — as administrators, teachers, trustees, pupils, etc. It is indeed the largest public enterprise in our country.

Have Americans always been so greatly interested in education? No; the present widespread interest in public education — that is, in education at public expense — is a recent matter,

Fig. 214. A modern high school, part of the " great public enterprise "

chiefly a development of the past fifty years. The entire history of the public-school system covers barely a hundred years.

In 1800, for example, the average American citizen received *in his entire lifetime* less than a hundred days of schooling. What a contrast to the condition today! In a single year most boys and girls now attend school from 160 to 180 days. Some attend more than 225 days. Thus the young people of today receive more schooling in one year than the citizen of 1800 received in his entire lifetime.

Furthermore, conditions improved very slowly during the next half-century. In 1840 the average citizen received in his lifetime little more than a present year's schooling. In the 1840's and 1850's schools developed somewhat more rapidly. But even in 1860 an American received, according to present standards, less than three years' schooling, and in 1880 less than four years' schooling. Decade by decade, however, public education continued to spread. Today it is safe to say that the average is equal to a full elementary schooling of eight years. Speaking in general, an American citizen now attends school more than fifteen times as long as did his forefathers of 1800.

To understand America's march toward democracy, therefore, we must study next the history of this astonishing development in education since 1800.

Education in 1800

The condition of education was distressing, indeed — at least it was distressing according to our present ways of thinking. Most grown-up people could neither read nor write. For that matter, most of them thought reading and writing unnecessary. They were engaged in farming or in some skilled or unskilled manual occupation.

As for the education of children, it was in an even less satisfactory condition. In the larger cities and towns there were elementary schools in which a small proportion of the children learned to "read, write, and reckon." These schools, however, were open only a few weeks in the year. Most of the American children were hard at work. Even the young children worked long hours each day, either on the farms or in the growing factories.

Furthermore, the rank and file of the American people did not believe in "public" education; that is, in supporting schools for *all* children at public expense. From colonial times most people believed that parents should pay for the education of their children. School expenses were paid, therefore, either by the parents of the school children or by philanthropic societies. Each parent contributed a certain amount for each child whom he sent to school. But the idea that the town or city, the county or state, should levy taxes upon *all* the people to pay for the education of *all* the children was not generally accepted.

The children of many well-to-do people either had tutors — private teachers — or were sent to "private and select payschools." But the masses of the people could not afford this.

As for the national government, it played little part in education during the first fifty years of our national life. The Constitution of the United States said nothing about education. Even in the long debates in the Constitutional Convention there were very few references to it. Education, the delegates felt, was to be left to the separate states, to their counties and local communities. From that day to our own it has never been regarded in America as the *responsibility* of the national government.

This does not mean that the national government, even at that time, did not aid the states in providing for education. In the famous Northwest Ordinance, 1787, Congress had set aside one square mile of land in every township, stating that the money obtained from the sale of this land should be used to aid the establishment of public schools. In later periods of American history Congress made additional grants for educational purposes.

In the first half of the 1800's pioneer leaders aroused the people to the need for free public education

In the first decades of the 1800's important changes were coming about which affected education. During these decades the right to vote was gradually being extended to all male citizens twenty-one years of age and over, and the common man was securing a larger control over government. After 1800, great improvements were also made in methods of printing, and printed matter increased in volume and decreased in cost.

These changes brought about a desire as well as an opportunity for additional education. With the growth of industry more money was available for the support of schools and more people could afford to send their children to school. The increased participation of people in the affairs of government pointed to the need for more intelligent action and therefore for better educational opportunities, while the appearance of cheaper and more abundant printed matter offered a chance to a greater number of people to enjoy the benefits of education. A few leaders rose to awaken the people to action. Chief among these were Horace Mann of Massachusetts, Henry Barnard of Connecticut and Rhode Island, Caleb Mills of Indiana, Calvin E. Stowe of Ohio, and other leaders in the central states.

1. *The work of Horace Mann in Massachusetts.* Horace Mann was originally a lawyer and for a while president of the state senate of Massachusetts. Although he was regarded as a "coming" man in law and politics, he gave up his promising career (1837) to serve in the newly created position of Secretary of the State Board of Education. This position made him really the first State Superintendent of Public Education in America.

For twelve years Mann worked to arouse the people of Massachusetts to the need for popular education at public expense. He organized a great campaign in which he sent lawyers, teachers, members of the legislature, and professors all over the state urging the people to ask their legislators for a bigger endowment for the public schools. He secured increases in the amount of taxes levied for schools. He increased the salaries of teachers.

Fig. 215. Horace Mann

He extended the length of the school term one month. He established the first normal schools in the country. He worked constantly to have the state build up and support a great public educational system. No name is better known in the early educational history of America than his.

2. *The work of Henry Barnard in Connecticut and Rhode Island.* Meanwhile Henry Barnard was arousing the people of Connecticut and Rhode Island to the need for better public schools. There he held positions similar to that which Horace Mann held in Massachusetts. He, too, campaigned for public education. In his *Connecticut Common School Journal* also he pleaded for the extension and improvement of public education. He founded the famous *American Journal of Education.* From 1867 to 1870 he served as the first United States Commissioner of Education. Thus Henry Barnard also deserves an important place in American history.

3. *Leaders in the Middle West.* Inspired partly by Mann and Barnard, several pioneer educators were active in the Middle West. Perhaps the best-known of these were the Reverend Calvin E. Stowe of Cincinnati, Ohio; Caleb Mills, president of Wabash College in Indiana; Samuel Lewis and Samuel Galloway of Ohio; Ninian W. Edwards of Illinois; John D. Pierce of Michigan; and Robert J. Breckenridge of Kentucky. These men were descendants of pioneer Eastern families. In the new Middle Western states they helped to organize state systems of public elementary schools. They succeeded in increasing the number of teachers and in having them more adequately paid. They prolonged the school term and added new subjects of study to the curriculum. They also improved the schoolhouses and through their efforts new and better-constructed ones were erected.

Thus, largely as a result of the work of these pioneer leaders in education, even before the Civil War the idea of a public-school system in every American community, paid for by the tax money of all the people and open to all children, was well established throughout the Middle West. By their efforts the existing public-school systems were much improved.

These leaders recognized that democratic government depended upon the education of all the people. They agreed with the signers of the Declaration of Independence that governments obtain "their just powers from the consent of the governed." But, in order to "consent" to acts of government, the people must first "understand" the problems of government, business, and social life; that is, *all of the people must be educated.*

Of course, the aristocrats in the government, such as Alexander Hamilton and John Adams, honestly believed that the common people did not have the ability to understand matters of government. But a few political leaders and most educational leaders believed that they did. The people had sufficient intelligence to govern themselves, but to do so they must be educated. They must learn to read and write and to understand the history and geography of their country. They must be made aware of the ideals of America, and they must understand its economic, political, and social problems.

This became particularly important after 1840, because tens of thousands of foreign immigrants were pouring in from Europe. Most of those who came from Germany and other regions outside the British Isles could not even understand English and knew nothing of the ideals or customs of the American people.

It was a difficult task indeed that confronted Mann, Barnard, and the other leaders. They faced indifference on the part of the people generally and a great opposition from the churches. Until about 1800, young people were taught to read principally that they might be able to read the Bible, the catechism, and other religious books.

Largely as the result of the work of the leaders in American education an increasing number of people became convinced that schools should be supported and conducted by the community as a whole and not by the churches.

In 1818 Connecticut stopped taxing the people for the support of churches and church schools. Fifteen years later Massachusetts followed her lead, and after prolonged contests New Hampshire, Maryland, and Kentucky did likewise.

Nevertheless, many years passed before most of the people willingly paid taxes to carry on free public schools. "Why should I pay for the education of the children of others? I have no children myself in school." This was the common argument heard for many years while the struggle for free public education was going on. As the years went by, however, the protest was heard less and less frequently.

Although education is something more than a means of getting a better job, it is nevertheless true that without an education one can scarcely hope to succeed in the industrial society of today. In the time of which we are speaking, thousands of poor boys succeeded through education to responsible public positions and to easier and better jobs. Eventually, therefore, the rank and file of Americans became enthusiastic over free public education. Even before the Civil War most of the states had adopted, so far as *elementary schools* were concerned, the policy of free public education.

The long battle to establish the free public high school

As the demand for free public schools grew the leaders of educational reform also pleaded for the establishment of high schools. The first one — the English High School in Boston — was built in 1821. Boston's lead was soon followed by other cities in Massachusetts, Maine, Connecticut, and New York. Before many years had passed, cities in the growing Middle West extended their public-school system to include the high school.

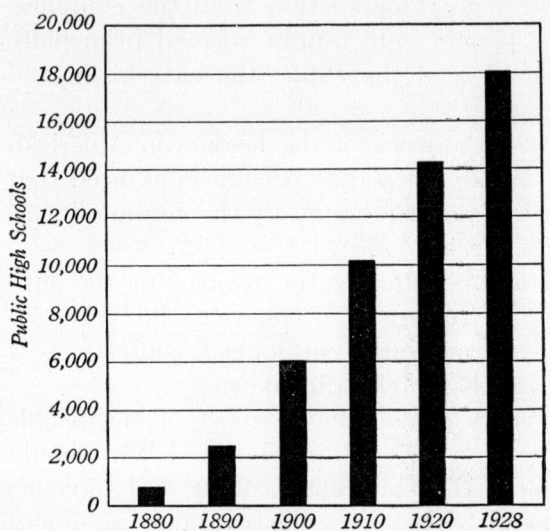

FIG. 216. Growth in the number of public high schools, 1880–1928

There was as much opposition to the free high schools as there had been to free elementary schools, and much the same argument was used in protest. Many citizens believed that higher education should be given only to those whose parents could afford to pay for it. At first, therefore, new high schools were built very infrequently. Through the 1840's and 1850's, however, the number increased until at the outbreak of the Civil War there were 321 free public high schools in the United States. Half of these were in Massachusetts, New York, and Ohio, the states then leading in education.

After the Civil War the increase became still more rapid, and during the thirty years following 1870 free public high schools became firmly established. By 1900 there were 6000 of them. But even then the growth of this type of school had no more than begun.

About this time the junior high school began to come into existence. The public school to which boys and girls went after they had been graduated from the junior high school was known as the senior high school. All these high schools — the four-year high schools and the combined junior and senior high schools — are known as secondary schools. In 1928 there were more than 18,000 free public secondary schools.

The development of the American college

Those who desired a great national system of public education for America were not content with merely elementary and secondary schools. They desired kindergartens[1] and colleges for the people as well. The educational ladder — the ladder of opportunity — must extend from the kindergarten to the college, they said. (See figure 218.)

As in the case of free high schools, the idea of free colleges, too, was revolutionary. Other countries had not adopted it. In England, Germany, and France, for example, colleges were open only to children of parents of high social and political position or of great wealth. America, however, was trying a new experiment in democracy. To succeed in that experiment it must have leaders, and to train leaders easy admission to colleges and universities was demanded.

Would not the old private colleges which had been established before the Revolution fill the need? No, said the leaders of the new democratic education. These old colleges were primarily religious training schools. Those which had been founded in early colonial days had been organized with that idea in mind. Although great changes had taken place after 1750, nevertheless their presidents and many of their professors were ministers of the churches, and their chief aim was to prepare young men for the ministry. Even as late as 1800, instruction in Harvard, for example, was devoted largely to Hebrew, Greek, and Latin.

But as the new industrial section began to form after 1800 in the northeastern part of the country, interest in science and in the problems of industry and of community and national life grew rapidly. In the Middle West especially, there was a spread-

[1] The kindergarten, as most of you know, is a school for children who are not yet old enough to attend the first grade of the elementary school. The early kindergartens in this country were private schools, and parents paid for the teaching of their children. Later, the public-school system was extended downward to include the kindergarten, just as it was extended upward to include the high school.

ing sentiment that a more democratic and more practical kind of higher education should be supplied to the intelligent and well-to-do youth who could afford to go to college.

After 1800, various churches also built new colleges. It is now difficult to say exactly how many colleges were started, so rapidly

FIG. 217. The first class at King's College, New York, in 1754. From this modest beginning Columbia University grew. (From *Harper's New Monthly Magazine*, October, 1884)

did they come into being and so quickly did some of them come to an end. Their number grew nevertheless—24 colleges in America in 1800, 232 in 1860! Then between 1860 and 1900 came an even greater development—the establishment of 262 new colleges.

Of the 232 colleges in existence prior to 1860, however, only seventeen were owned and operated by the state, while 215 were private, most of them under the control of one or another of the church denominations. But a new attitude was growing among the people as the leaders of education in the various states preached democracy and demanded a complete educational system open from lowest to highest years to all the people.

Thus the very idea of democracy meant to the leaders "equal opportunity for all." It was recognized, of course, that the children of the well-to-do would find it easier to continue through high school and college than would the children of the poor. Nevertheless, it was increasingly believed that in a true democracy the entire system of education should be free to every person, irrespective of his race or of his religious, political, economic, or social beliefs.

After 1820, therefore, one state after another established a state university, and by 1860 there were seventeen of them in the thirty-three states then in the Union. To these any child of any citizen could go with the payment of a merely nominal fee (for many years not more than $10 to $25 per year).

Then another advance was made when Congress passed the Morrill, or Land Grant, Act in 1862. This provided aid for the states in the establishment of agricultural and mechanic-arts colleges. As you know, the United States government still owned a vast amount of public land. By the provisions of the Morrill Act each member of Congress was allowed for his state 30,000 acres of this public land. This land might be sold and the money received from its sale used to establish agricultural and mechanic-arts colleges. Altogether more than 11,000,000 acres of public land was given to the states. The results from the sale of the land proved to be very disappointing. It was sold in some states for a few cents an acre; in others from a dollar to six dollars per acre. In only a few cases did the states receive really large sums of money.

Nevertheless, the passage of the bill greatly encouraged those who were trying to arouse the state legislatures to support state universities. In the years after the Civil War all the states in the Union either established or enlarged state universities or state colleges of agriculture and mechanic arts. Today every state and three of the territories (Hawaii, Alaska, and Porto Rico) receive small grants of money annually from the Federal government to aid them in support of agricultural and mechanic-arts colleges.

Another new development: colleges open to women

In 1800 not a college in the United States was open to women. Today hundreds of higher institutions are attended by them.

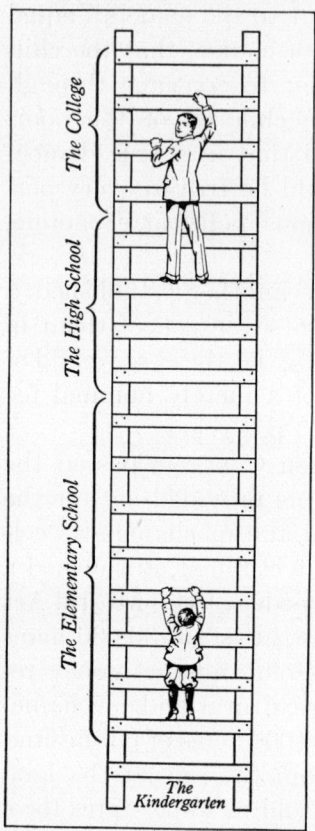

Fig. 218. The American educational ladder. Each rung in the ladder represents a year of education

The change began in the second quarter of the nineteenth century. In 1821 Emma Willard, a pioneer in women's education, established a girls' seminary at Troy, New York. In 1837 Mary Lyon, another educational leader, founded Mount Holyoke Seminary in Massachusetts. After that date seminaries for girls were established rapidly. By 1860 there were more than sixty seminaries for girls in the country. Later at least half of them became colleges for women.

Beyond the Mississippi River the spirit of democracy soon opened the state universities to women. In later years the Eastern state institutions also have admitted them. A large proportion of all the colleges of America today enroll women as well as men.

By 1860 a complete national system of education had been established. A great stride had been taken in America's march toward democracy.

The spirit of democracy, the idea of equal opportunity to all, the belief of leaders that every citizen in America should be educated to the limit of his abilities — all these had contributed to the building of a complete educational ladder. The defenders of democracy had won their battle to establish schools supported by taxation levied upon all the people. The ladder of opportunity, for every American child, now reached from the elementary school through the university.

The Civil War retarded education from 1860 to 1880 both in the South and in the North

Then the development of this national system of public education was held back by the terrible War between the States.

Throughout the South schools were closed and the boys went to work. For nearly fifteen years after the close of the war the energies of the Southern people were devoted to restoring the land and to building up their industries. Naturally, there was little money or energy left to be devoted to schools.

Conditions in the North following the Civil War were better, and many schools managed to continue their work. Nevertheless, there too education was much hampered through the loss of teachers and through the limiting of school funds. Thus two decades passed with little advance in public education.

American Education in 1880

From 1880 dates the modern development of the American school system. The Reconstruction period in the South was practically over, and the sharp industrial changes in the North were beginning to show themselves. In 1880 the great industrial expansion was well under way.

What then was the condition of education? As compared with education in 1800, the school system of 1880 was a thing of great pride. As compared with that of today, it was weak.

Note a few outstanding facts:

1. There were 16,000,000 children of school age in America.
2. About 10,000,000 were enrolled in school, but only about 5,000,000 were actually in attendance in school. Thus certainly 10,000,000 were not really being educated.
3. There were approximately 10,000,000 voters in America. About one fourth of them could not read at all, and nearly half of them were unable to read the daily newspapers and magazines well enough to obtain information about economic, political, or social life.

Clearly much remained to be done in education.

The schools of 1880 and what the pupils studied in them

In 1880 the pupils sat in rows before desks screwed to the floor, reading from a few textbooks and reciting facts which had been memorized. Few elementary schools had auditoriums in which the children could assemble for school lectures etc. They learned

FIG. 219. A "modern" school assembly room of 1863. (From the *New York Illustrated News*, April 4, 1863)

to read, to write, to spell, to compute, and to solve abstract problems in arithmetic. In the high schools science courses had been introduced, and there were some schools which had science laboratories; French and German were also studied, as well as Latin and Greek. But for most of the pupils reading, writing, and reciting took up the hours of the day.

For one reason or another a large proportion of the children left school at the end of the fourth, fifth, or sixth grade. Very few indeed continued into the high school, and only a fraction of 1 per cent of those who entered the high school in the first grade ever went on to take the college course. This was the condition fifty years ago.

THEN, AFTER 1880, THE CHANGING INDUSTRIAL CIVILIZATION BROUGHT STARTLING CHANGES IN EDUCATION

You have already studied the transformation in living conditions that occurred after the Civil War. By 1880 this movement was in full swing. Every aspect of life in America was changing rapidly — ways of producing power, food manufacturing, buying and selling goods, and means of transportation and communication. The keynote became *mass production*. Life was becoming more intense. As people crowded into cities their houses changed from one-family and two-family wooden structures to great many-storied brick or concrete-and-steel apartment houses. Thus in our largest cosmopolitan cities a single city block might come to be the home of several thousand people.

These changes in economic and social life profoundly altered education. As people crowded into cities more and more schools had to be built. The school buildings were no longer large enough, and new rooms were added to them. Today in the large cities elementary schools of thirty rooms are common; some are even larger. The number of children attending school increased. Pupils remained in school through the higher grades, and increasing numbers stayed on through the high school. School buildings became more and more sanitary and attractive, and happier places in which to live and work. Teachers were better trained and better paid.

Increase in attendance

Enrollment increased rapidly after 1880 until in 1928 it was estimated that there were 29,000,000 pupils in the schools and colleges of America.

But it was in the growth of the high school that the most astonishing development came. More than seventeen times as many boys and girls attended high school in 1928 as in 1890 — so rapid was the development of our secondary schools in this period. Furthermore, although in 1890 there were only 2526 free public high schools and 9120 teachers, in 1928 there were 18,116 high schools and 182,637 teachers.

One of the most astonishing changes of all, however, was in

the colleges. Their growth in number of students was rather slow until after 1900. Then the attendance increased steadily year after year. At the beginning of the World War the universities and colleges had changed from little institutions of from two hundred to five hundred students to large, complicated institutions with enrollments of several thousand. At that time several state universities had more than 5000 students in attendance each year. After the World War they grew even more rapidly. Young men and women flocked into the higher institutions. Even during the early 1920's in several universities more than 10,000 students were regularly enrolled each year. More thousands attended during the short summer sessions. Still more thousands went to evening classes and enrolled in correspondence, or home-study, courses. There are today several universities in which the annual enrollment of students of all kinds exceeds 30,000.

An educational revolution indeed! Mass production in education as in industry!

School Studies slowly changed to fit the Changing Civilization

The interest in practical studies was increased by the Centennial Exposition — held in Philadelphia in 1876 in honor of the hundredth anniversary of our national independence. This exposition was attended by people from all over the country. Americans saw exhibited there the products of the practical schools of Germany, France, Switzerland, Austria, and the Scandinavian countries. Especially were our educational leaders impressed by the work of German youth in the manual arts.

As a result courses in manual training and in drawing were soon introduced into city high schools. In St. Louis, in 1880, Calvin Woodward established the first manual-training high school. Manual training began to spread over the entire country. By the 1890's hundreds of high schools included manual-training and drawing courses in their curriculums.

Thus an entering wedge of the practical was driven into the old classical course of study in the high school. Courses in household arts for girls were also introduced. Business courses were offered, which trained young people for clerical and other business occupations. An agricultural high school was established in the University of Minnesota in 1888, and ten years later there were ten others in the country. By 1909 there were sixty independent agricultural high schools, and in 350 other schools some agricultural instruction was offered. So rapid has been the growth since that day that today more than 2000 high schools offer agricultural work. A trade-and-industrial school was established in New York City in 1881, and during the next twenty years many others were started in different parts of the country.

Immediately after the beginning of the twentieth century the interest in vocational education became even more widespread. Manufacturers' associations and commissions of state legislatures as well as of the national government made investigations of vocational education in Europe and of the needs for developing similar industrial schools in America.

FIG. 220. A modern "trade school" in New York City, which has developed from the need of preparing youth to earn a living in an industrial civilization. (Photograph by Ewing Galloway)

In 1913 the United States Congress appointed a commission to investigate the need for national aid in industrial education. As a result of the findings of this commission Congress was led to pass the Smith-Hughes Act (1917), which created a Federal Board for Vocational Education and provided a plan by which the national government and state legislatures were to appropriate large sums of money for the development of courses in scientific work, vocational education, agriculture, home economics, industry, and commerce.

After 1900 it was seen that not only must education become more practical, but it must also introduce young people to an understanding of the civilization which develops around them.

New subjects, such as community civics, were introduced into the curriculums of the schools. To political history were added industrial history and commercial history. Courses in geography also included many of the important facts of modern industry and trade.

FIG. 221. John Dewey. (Photograph from Keystone View Co.)

Many leaders have helped to bring about the changes, but two men have contributed more than the others — Colonel Francis W. Parker and Professor John Dewey. Colonel Parker was an outstanding leader in the fight for the improvement of schools from 1875 to 1901. His pioneer work was chiefly done as principal of the Chicago Normal College from 1883 to 1901.

Professor Dewey has been the leading American philosopher during the past twenty-five years and is today honored and revered all over the world. More than all other educational leaders he saw clearly the needs of the schools in a changing civilization. In 1896 Dr. and Mrs. John Dewey established a new kind of "experimental school" at The University of Chicago, a school in which new ways of teaching were worked out. This was in existence for eight years. As a result of their work in the school and of the widespread interest it created, changes were brought about in hundreds of American schools.

In many elementary schools today the classroom has the spirit of a happy home. Children work together animatedly with the teacher. There is much activity; children are free to move about, to make suggestions. They engage in discussions. They have separate libraries in each room, and in addition a general library in the school. They use tools, they paint, they write plays and act them. They write, edit, and print school newspapers and magazines. They play an important part in the government of the school — taking charge of school assemblies, governing their school and their classes by councils. Thus young people are being trained to live in a democracy.

Of course these things also came about because the training of teachers was so greatly improved. Normal schools were built in all the states of the country, and many of these are now developing into four-year teachers' colleges. Each state university has developed a school of education for the training of educational leaders. Tens of thousands of school teachers are studying in these institutions each year. Each year teachers assemble at conventions in the counties and states of the Union and discuss ways and means of improving the education of young people.

Adult education

The education of grown-ups as well as of children! This is also one of the ideas of our modern age. Adult education is sweeping all over the United States. Why is it necessary? First, because there are still many millions of foreign-born who cannot read the English language or write it. Second, there are millions of immigrants who know little about our institutions, our ways of living, and our ways of thinking. To teach them, "evening schools" are conducted in many cities because most of these adults work at their regular occupations in the day time.

Adult education has also spread rapidly in many parts of the country among the farmers. Some states employ agents who spend their time traveling among the farmers, teaching them new and better methods of raising animals, of treating their soil, of planting, cultivating, and harvesting their crops, and of selling their products. The educational revolution is affecting adults as well as children.

Thus education has become America's greatest public enterprise

So, from being almost completely neglected in colonial times, from being a matter of indifference to most citizens in 1800, public education today has become of direct interest and importance to the American people. As we said at the beginning of this chapter, more than one fourth of all the persons of the United States are engaged in getting an education or in educating others, or are in some way directly connected with the school system. Education is now our greatest single public enterprise. Furthermore, it is changing today even more rapidly than in earlier periods of our history. In this respect it resembles industry and business, government and social life.

CHAPTER XXV

THE SOCIAL LIFE OF HOMESTEAD, VILLAGE, AND CITY, 1865–1900

The history of America means something more than the building of great corporations, the struggle of farmers, city workers, business men, and politicians for the control of government or even the struggle for a democratic educational system. The real history lies in the lives of individual Americans — in their desires and interests, loves and hates, happiness and despair. All these emotions have influenced not only the great industrial, political, and educational movements but the manners and customs of the American people as well. Let us study something of these manners and customs in the period between 1865 and 1900.

The Four Principal Classes of American Society

First, we must say that in all respects no one American citizen is exactly like another American citizen. Our millions of people differ greatly. There are differences in race, in color, in physical traits, in intelligence, in skill, in likes and dislikes, in desires, and in needs. Throughout every period of our history the ways of living of Americans differed widely. Some people were rich, but most were poor. Some lived in luxurious homes and traveled a great deal; but most worked from morning till night on prairie farms, in the slums of industrial cities, in mountain mining towns, or in crossroad hamlets. Some had much leisure and concerned themselves only with the next pleasure, but all too many were constantly worried about getting enough food to hold life together. Moreover, even rich people differed from one another, and poor people differed from one another quite as much. Nevertheless certain ways of living were more characteristic of certain groups than of others. For convenience, therefore, in studying the home life, manners, and customs of the American people, we shall divide them into four classes:

1. The farmers.
2. The great American middle class, living in the growing towns and cities.
3. The tenement dwellers of the towns and cities.
4. The leisure class.

These, then, were the chief classes of Americans. Between 1865 and 1900 these classes included the majority of Americans. It is the home life, manners, and customs of the average or typical citizens in each class that we shall study in this chapter.

I. THE FARMERS

In the 1870's and 1880's, at the very moment when many New England farmers and Virginia and Carolina planters were living in substantial brick or frame residences on land that had been cultivated by their families for two centuries, homesteaders from Minnesota to Colorado were clearing virgin ground and trying to keep warm in mud huts and log houses — so great were the differences between the development of the old East and the young West.

Therefore in our brief space we cannot give even glimpses of home life and customs in each of the many kinds of farm homes then in existence. We shall confine our brief picture to the great mass of farmers who were living between the Appalachians and the Rockies. The class we describe comprised altogether many millions of men, women, and children. You will remember that these were the people whose difficulties and grievances were causing them to join the new political parties — the Greenbackers, the Populists, and the progressive Democrats.

Farm life in the Middle West

American farming in this period was hard physical labor. The constant fight to get a living determined what men and women thought about and worried about. In the cultivating and harvesting seasons everyone toiled from sunup to sundown.

There was always work to do — plowing, planting, and harvesting the hay and grain, tending the cattle, and caring for the newborn lambs and calves, the fat round pigs, and the awkward, shaggy-coated colts. Both men and women worked unceasingly.

The never-ending, monotonous round of tasks gave to the life of the women few of the joys of adventure. They were confined to their house or the barns, standing over a kitchen stove, working in the chicken coop, or caring for the cows and calves. All too frequently their youth faded quickly and old age arrived too early.

The farmers, like their wives, led a monotonous and toilsome life. They, at least, had the advantage of working in the open air, but they hardly knew how to glory in the beauty of the sunrise as they forced their unrested bodies to begin another day's labor at four in the morning, or the grandeur of the sunset as they wearily turned home from the fields.

Fig 222. Making butter in the old-fashioned churn like this was a tiresome task for the women on the farm. (From a photograph by Clifton Johnson)

The American farmer was usually harassed by physical needs and worried about the weather, about drought, locusts and other insect pests, prairie fires, and devastating river floods. Yet there was some satisfaction. As the years went by they could see their farms slowly improving. They could look over the fields which they had plowed and sown and see the fruits of their labor, first green and then golden with the heavy harvests. Occasionally they had visions of more comforts, a better house, and the purchase of some of the new farm machines.

There was hope in the breasts of these men and women. It was the hope that a large crop and high prices would cut down the mortgage on the farm, send the children to high school, perhaps even to college, and make it possible for them to have new dresses and suits. There was hope that their sons and daughters would achieve, through education, a better lot than they had — more comforts and pleasures, more leisure time in which to enjoy life.

Fig. 223. The general store, in which the farm population could buy everything from shoe buttons to scythes, was also a sort of community center. Here, during the winter evenings, three or four farmers were usually to be seen, grouped around a glowing stove, talking over farm affairs. (From a photograph by Clifton Johnson)

By the 1880's much of the isolation of homestead life had disappeared. Nearly all farmers of the Middle West were in touch with a community. Roads connected their farms with the nearest towns. Trips to town by wagon were much more frequent. Families — babies and all — were bundled into the buckboards to rumble over bad roads into town, where social life, supplies, mail, and news awaited them. Then there were shrewd bargaining over purchases, gossip concerning neighbors, and inquiries about friends and relatives. Perhaps on the way back one could stop at a neighbor's home for supper. One was always sure to be welcome whenever he might stop, as eating and talking together were the chief social diversions.

Except at the height of the cultivating and harvesting seasons, there were country dances. Then from the scattered farms of the surrounding countryside gathered the farmers with their wives and children. Babies were usually brought along too, for there were seldom servants with whom to leave them. Frequently the dances lasted until the dawn, when tired but happy parents gathered their offspring together and drove home in time to milk the cows before breakfast and begin another long day's work.

In connection with their work, too, there were social meetings in the farming community. During threshing season, for example, the farmers coöperated and, working from farm to farm, threshed the grain of each member of the community in turn. After the strenuous day's work the men would sit down to a "threshing supper" at the farm on which they had worked that day.

The Granges helped to bring the farmers together

The formation of the Granges in the Western states was a boon to the social life of the farming community as well as to its business interests. Women also belonged to the Grange, and they helped to make real social functions of the meetings. The Granges held picnics, concerts, and lectures, and started libraries. Occasionally dances were given at the Grange hall. In some communities business meetings of the Granges were regularly followed by dances and "socials."

The chief social events of the farming community

Chief among the great holidays of the farmers were the Fourth of July, the Farmers' Picnic, the Grange picnic, the circus, and the county fair. In some communities where the Grange did not flourish, Old Settlers' Day might take the place of the Grange picnic.

On the Fourth of July the farming families drove to the nearest village to celebrate. There were games and contests, such as wrestling, catching the greased pig, and pitching horseshoes. In the evening a supper of fried chicken, watermelon, and ice cream might be served out of doors beneath shady trees. Usually someone made a speech and often there was a parade.

And the circus! When the circus came to town the work of the farm was sure to be neglected for the day. The family buckboard was driven into town and left in an alley, on a vacant lot, or in some quiet side street, where the horses might not be frightened by the commotion. Then farmers joined the townsmen

Fig. 224. The return from the county fair. (From *Harper's Weekly*, October, 1873)

on both sides of Main Street to watch the parade go by. How the children shrieked with delight at the clowns! How they shivered at the lions roaring in their cages! How everyone tapped impatient feet to the music of the circus band! Then, after a hurried lunch, everyone went to the circus ground to see the side shows before the main show under the "big top" began. The freaks were interesting; but they certainly could not compare with the antics of the clowns and the agility of the acrobats, who rode bareback or poised lightly on one toe atop milk-white horses. The excitement of a circus was almost as tiring as a day's plowing, but there were thrills enough to last a year until it was back again.

CHANGING SOCIAL LIFE

Then late in September or early in October came the county fair, which was held at the county seat. The farmers sent their best live stock for exhibit. Prizes were awarded to the owners of the "blue ribbon" animals and to the wives and daughters who baked the best cake and bread and made the finest preserves and butter. Embroidered and crocheted work was also exhibited, and prizes were awarded for the best work of this kind. Anyone who won a prize was envied.

On Sundays and on special holidays, such as Christmas and Thanksgiving, there was much visiting among relatives and neighbors. Often the church was the social meeting place of the community. In the warm season, before and after services, the people gathered out of doors beneath the trees to chat. Frequently after church friends or relatives were invited to Sunday dinner.

Sundays and holidays, however, were, after all, merely bright spots in the life of the farmer — a life which in the main consisted of hard work and worry. Too often there was no room in his life for the enjoyment of the fine and beautiful, even if fine and beautiful things had been at hand.

II. THE MIDDLE-CLASS AMERICANS OF THE TOWNS AND CITIES

In the small towns and cities of the United States lived the middle class.

Who belonged to this new middle class? It was made up of the small retail storekeepers, the skilled mechanics, the teachers, the clerks, the lesser doctors, lawyers, ministers, and bankers. It was a large and growing group — probably more representative of the new industrial America than any other group. In it were many of the descendants of the colonial American stock. It also included the children of many immigrants, who by this time were active in politics, in the skilled trades, in teaching, and to some extent in the professions.

The lives of the middle-class town and city workers held worries as did those of the farmers. The chief concern of these workers was to make a better living, possess a small home, send the children through high school, get a few comforts, and still stay out of debt. The men rose early, worked long hours, and returned home in the evening tired out. The working day of the women likewise was long, from the preparation of an early breakfast to the putting of children to bed at night.

Most of the small communities of the country in the 1880's and 1890's were marked by industriousness and thrift. If the middle-class man was a wage-earner, he wanted to hold his job and if possible get a better one. If he owned a little business

FIG. 225. This picture illustrates a typical middle-class section of a large town in the early 1880's. (From *Harper's New Monthly Magazine*, 1884)

his ambition was to see it grow. His need, therefore, was to have people respect him and like him. He joined one or more of the lodges of the town and became a member of commercial or labor organizations. Furthermore, he tried to avoid the disapproval of his employer or of his customers and neighbors. Hence in politics the great mass of the men of this class joined either the Republican or the Democratic party. Few could be found who associated themselves with the Socialists or, for that matter, the Greenbackers or the Populists.

Thus there was a substantial and conservative atmosphere

in these growing American communities. The citizens were "boosters" for their towns, each of which aspired to be "bigger and better." Each one had a slogan, such as "The Biggest Little City in the World." Pride in the community was developed by the chambers of commerce and the new social clubs of business men which were just coming into existence.

Life centered in the middle-class home

In the 1880's and 1890's the very center of life for the middle-class American was his home. The towns and small cities were still not too crowded to provide family houses surrounded by small lawns. Most of these houses were small wooden (frame) buildings, although the more well-to-do citizens were beginning to favor brick. Many houses were two-family buildings, that is, part of each house was occupied by the owner and part was rented. By renting part of his building the owner increased the family income. The real owners of most of these houses were the banks, which held mortgages upon them. The typical home consisted of five or six small rooms crowded with furniture and cluttered with ornaments. In most houses heat was provided by iron stoves, although in a few of them hot-air furnaces were being installed in the basements.

Usually in each town there were a few people who had built large two-and-half-story frame structures, profusely adorned with jig-saw scroll and "gingerbread" decorations. The half-story was a low-ceilinged garret, in which the old or surplus household equipment was stored. Although the rooms were larger than those in the two-family houses, they were equally cluttered with things. The floors of all the rooms but the kitchen were covered with carpets ornamented with large floral designs. On the walls might be found an engraving of "Washington crossing the Delaware," mottoes in shells, yarns, or grasses, and sometimes framed samples of stitching. On one wall of the parlor there was almost sure to be a painting or photographic enlargement of the family group.

Stacked on the shelves of "whatnots" (How well they were named!) were souvenir spoons, hand-painted china, Indian moccasins, pink sea shells, and daguerreotypes or tintypes of deceased relatives. The best furniture of the family was in the parlor. It was likely to be a three-piece set. Sofa and chairs were almost invariably adorned with crotcheted, embroidered, or drawn-work "tidies." On the table in the parlor one would be sure to find the photograph album, bound in plush and containing pictures of the entire family.

The parlor was used only on rare occasions. It was kept tightly closed except when "company" came to call or when there was an unusual family event.

There were few bathrooms as yet, and the bedrooms were small, bare, and stuffy. In the winter one sank deep into a soft feather bed and slept heavily behind closed windows.

From New England to Oregon the middle-class housewife seemed to be obsessed with the desire to preserve family heirlooms and to accumulate furnishings and other belongings. The quantity of one's belongings seemed to be a mark of one's social standing.

Women and the middle-class home

Until about 1900 "the place of women was in the home." "Nice" women did not enter business, shops, offices, mills, or the professions. As long as their "men-folks" were alive and could support them the "women-folks" remained with their families. Most young men grew up with this point of view; so it behooved a girl to avoid a career if she wanted to marry.

In the homes of the mechanics, clerks, teachers, and many others of the middle class, the daughters of the family spent their time in doing the housework, making clothes, and the like. Those of the professional and more well-to-do families of the middle class had a less back-breaking but hardly more thrilling life in the home. They helped their mothers with the simpler tasks of the household, they read, crocheted, embroidered, knitted, and painted china.

Amusements of the middle-class town and city dwellers

The New England idea of the Puritan still prevailed in 1865; therefore amusements in the growing towns of the Middle West were quiet affairs. Sunday, for example, was a day for religious observance, rest, and quiet. On Sunday mornings church attendance was expected of young as well as old. In the afternoons one could sit on the porch and read or talk, or have a quiet stroll in the woods and fields. If the family were prosperous enough one might take a buggy ride.

Slowly after 1870 the Puritan attitude concerning Sunday began to disappear. In the growing cities the laboring people, who

FIG. 226. Fourth of July among the middle class of the town and city dwellers was a day for assembly, speech-making, and good times. (From *Harper's Weekly*, July, 1867)

had worked long hours for six days in the week, demanded relaxation and sports on Sunday. Baseball slowly became popular, and clubs were formed in many towns to play on the only day which was free from work. Soon amusement parks were permitted to remain open, and concerts were given.

In most small towns secret or fraternal organizations supplied much of the social life of the middle class. For the men there were lodges for every economic and social group. Business men always joined some lodge; it helped business and kept one in touch with the leading men of the community. Women too had their lodges — usually auxiliary branches of the men's organizations.

There is no doubt that the lodges brought new interests into the social life of the small town.

Saturday night was the gayest night of the week. Then it was that stores remained open until ten o'clock, and almost everyone went "down street" to buy supplies for Sunday or for the coming week. It was a national custom, indeed, followed alike in New England, in the South, in the Middle West, and in the Far West. Farmers drove into town, their carriages and wagons standing wheel to wheel around the town square. Friends walked up one side of Main Street and down the other. Little social groups gathered together on the sidewalks.

The barber shops were also real social centers. While waiting their turn men sat there smoking, reading the newspapers, or talking. There the older retired men of the community and the unemployed often passed much of their time. Indeed, for many of them it was a sort of town meeting place or club. Many a bargain for houses, land, machines, what not, was made at the barber shop.

Annual events, such as political elections and the arrival of the circus, provided stimulating social contacts. For weeks before the annual elections the members of the Republican and Democratic clubs dressed themselves up in startling uniforms and, armed with torches, paraded the town. Campaign songs were sung and speeches were made in the public halls. Bonfires were built to which young and old contributed barrels, discarded furniture, and old lumber. Vehement arguments were held on street corners, in barber shops, in lodge meetings, and in kitchen and parlor.

Like the farmers, once each year the town and city people thrilled in anticipation of a circus. When P. T. Barnum's Great Moral Show arrived, small boys and many of their elders crept from bed long before daylight to watch the circus train unload. In the morning the parade took place, and in the afternoon and evening the show itself. Circus day was a day to look forward to and to remember, like Christmas, the Fourth of July, and Labor Day.

Then there were the Lyceum and the Chautauqua lectures. In many towns for a week in the summer there was the Chautauqua offering music, short plays, and "instructive lectures" on all kinds of subjects. The Chautauquas were well attended. They were one of the means which the small-town middle-class American had of keeping up with cultural development.

In 1870 came the invention of the bicycle, and by the 1890's cycling became a popular pastime in towns and cities. The first bicycles were clumsy and rather dangerous. The balance was so unsure and so many riders were thrown off and injured that few people used them. In 1889, however, the "safety bicycle" was perfected. Almost at once its speed and safety appealed to the people. So widespread did the cycling craze become in the 1890's that many manufacturers of sewing machines and weapons began to manufacture bicycles also. With the addition of a "skirt guard" and the removal of the crossbar, women could ride even with the long skirts of the nineties. Young girls and even old ladies could be seen pedaling along country roads and city boulevards on week days and Sunday afternoons. Physicians recommended bicycle-riding as an excellent exercise.

The effect of town-and-city living upon dress

As you have already seen, the place of women prior to 1900 was for the most part in the home. With the turn of the century, however, women began to enter in ever greater numbers into business and professional life. Perhaps owing to this fact and to the greater participation of women in active outdoor life, styles in dress gradually changed to simpler forms. Skirts became somewhat shorter. Tiny waists went out of fashion. Hair was worn more smoothly and simply. In short, as women began to require more freedom of movement for their participation in sports and in gainful occupations styles were altered to meet their needs.

We must be content with this brief glimpse of the changing social life of America's middle class. A broad and varied group of people it certainly was, including both the moderately well-to-do and the wage-earning class of the industrial and business occupations. Like the farmers, the vast majority of these town people were concerned primarily with making a living. Certainly, however, they lived a much more social life than the farmers. They had a greater variety of interests — an increasing variety as the twentieth century was ushered in. Life began to speed up, and recreations and social life changed. Then automobiles came, and an even greater transformation in the social life of the middle-class American was launched.

III. THE TENEMENT DWELLERS OF THE TOWNS AND CITIES

During this period both towns and cities were growing rapidly. Shops, factories, stores, and public utilities were multiplying, and people were crowding from the country into the towns, from the towns into the cities. As this happened the lowest-paid laborers filled to overflowing the tenements of the towns and cities.

FIG. 227. The early bicycles were awkward to mount and dangerous to ride. (Courtesy of the New York Public Library)

Into the larger cities ever-increasing hordes of immigrants were pouring. Steadily the proportion of the Anglo-Saxon population decreased as tens of thousands of immigrants settled in Boston, New York, Philadelphia, and Baltimore, and as thousands made their way out to the lake cities — Buffalo, Cleveland, Detroit, and Chicago.

Inevitably the culture of the cities changed too. In Boston the aristocratic, intellectual culture of the days of Emerson and the Transcendentalists was slowly passing.

Chicago was a thriving city. Its industries were booming and attracting cheap unskilled labor. Naturally the new immigrants cliqued together in little native colonies. Each large city, from Boston to San Francisco, was developing such sections as Little Italy, Chinatown, Little Russia, etc.

Hotels and handsome business buildings were rising in New York and the other large cities. Concrete sidewalks and cobblestone or wood-block pavements were becoming common; street gas lamps, public water systems, and sewage systems were being installed. Yet with all these improvements, with all these signs of a rising standard of living, one would encounter almost in the same city block the palaces of the rich and the rickety and insanitary tenements of the poor.

The homes of the tenement dwellers of our cities

By 1870 the slum had already become a terrible institution in large cities — New York, Boston, and others. These slums were made up of unsafe and insanitary wooden shacks built by miserly, wealthy landlords. The buildings were unheated, and most of them had no sanitary provisions. Most of the individual rentings consisted of one or two rooms, into which families of from five to seven were crowded. In order to pay the rent, most families took in boarders or roomers, who added to the already overcrowded condition.

FIG. 228. The tenement section of a great city in 1896. Most cities had sections like this until after 1900. (Reproduced by permission of Judge Publishing Co., Inc.)

In the crowded districts the surroundings were as disreputable as the tenements themselves. Some streets became so clogged with refuse that traffic was almost impossible. In Philadelphia conditions were so bad in 1870 that a clean-up campaign required two and a half months to remove the garbage from the streets, the crew taking away a thousand loads a day.

In Boston the slum district was not so large as that of New York, but it was no better. An official report of the Massachusetts Board of Health for 1872 describes a Boston tenement thus:

> The room was unspeakably filthy; the furniture, two or three old chairs and an old dirty table. No fire, and the room damp, dark, and cold. It was the only room the family occupied except a little dark box in the corner with no window in it — a part of the room itself partitioned off for a bedroom. And such a bed! The oldest children were dirty and ragged and leaning against the window on the other side of the room. The youngest . . . child was pinched with the cold.[1]

Throughout the other cities of New England and the Atlantic seaboard where industry was flourishing, conditions were equally bad. Of course deaths among tenement dwellers were frequent. Scarlet fever, smallpox, and many other diseases raged in the unhealthful districts.

The work of the tenement dwellers

For the most part the slum dwellers were poor immigrants who had come to this country to improve their fortunes. They were uneducated, unskilled, and unaccustomed to American ways and were forced to take whatever work they could find. In many cases they could not earn enough to make even a bare living.

The lot of the tenement women was distressing, indeed. The wives of most of the workers were forced to help out either in their homes or in the factories. Perhaps they added to the family income by making garments in their homes. Their earnings totaled no more than $2 to $4 a week. These women workers had no legal protection, and they were not organized into unions as were many of the women workers employed in factories.

---

[1] F. W. Draper, "The Homes of the Poor in our Cities," Massachusetts State Board of Health, Fourth Annual Report for 1872, Massachusetts Public Documents, Vol. IV, No. 31, pp. 396–441.

Thus the poorest workers of the cities were in the most tragic situation of any class of people in the country. They were never free from worries. They could never quite make ends meet. Of course they could afford no luxuries; they lacked even the bare necessities of life. Some of them turned to crime and vice as a possible means of securing more money or of forgetting their lot.

Social workers and reformers tried to help the poorest city workers

A few public-spirited citizens in the larger towns and cities recognized the terrible conditions in which slum dwellers lived. Wishing to better these conditions, they organized charity associations.

Citizens and politicians also tried to secure relief for the tenement dwellers through the city and state governments. Progress was slow, but eventually they secured laws abolishing child labor, improving the conditions under which women worked, and otherwise protecting public health. By 1900 the worst tenements were being condemned and torn down. As a result of the efforts of the early city-reformers came public-health commissions, city housing commissions, and city-planning.

The work of the reformers, however, developed very slowly, indeed. In the meantime vice and crime flourished in the slums. In 1880 the census showed that among the 492 cities of 5000 inhabitants or more there were some 100,000 saloons and other drinking places. Gambling dens were common.

The amusements of the poor

Although the poor people of the cities had little or no time and money to spend in amusing themselves, there were certain inexpensive pleasures which they did enjoy. There were the beer gardens, — made popular by the coming of German immigrants, — where one might listen to music and enjoy an opportunity to sit and talk undisturbed.

The "concert saloon," which made its appearance shortly after the Civil War, became a favorite resort for the poor. It offered such kinds of entertainment as short skits in pantomime called "illuminated transparencies." In these the room was darkened and a light behind a sheet threw the outlines of actors into sharp relief. At the same time amusement parks came into popularity. Even the tenement dwellers could occasionally go to these. At Coney Island near New York City and in amusement parks close by other cities there were side shows and sidewalk attractions. At these places outdoor walks and beaches offered rest to tired city workers. Rides on the horse cars were a cheap and popular means of getting out into the open air. Dime museums and circuses attracted as many of the poorest people as could afford to go. The theater was popular with the American people, and seats could be had in the galleries varying in price, according to the city, from 10 to 25 cents each.

Thus in towns and cities, especially in the larger cities, the unskilled workers of America struggled to find a little recreation. But even more than was the case with the farmers and the middle-class people of the towns, their lives were concerned with food and shelter. As we look back upon them from a distance of 50 years we may think that they had one slight advantage over the farmer. At least they were not lonely; they had other human beings around them all the time. They were *compelled* to live a "social" life. But what a meager, monotonous, unhealthful social life it was!

IV. The Social Life of the Leisure Class

In this class were a few cultured persons of the older well-to-do families, living in quiet seclusion; a few students and scientists; a handful of scholarly statesmen and world travelers. They were the exceptions, however. They were rich in something better than money. In fact, some of them had little of the world's goods and belonged to the leisure class because they were content with inexpensive pleasures.

The leisure class, however, was made up, for the most part, of people of a different sort.

In the 1870's, 1880's, and 1890's in every large city of America there was a small growing class of newly rich. Some had worked hard, honestly, and intelligently for their money. Others had gambled and profiteered to get it. Many of them were the people who had found their wealth in oil in Pennsylvania, gold or silver in the Rockies, iron in Minnesota and Wisconsin, or lumber in Michigan or Oregon. Others were the families of those who had bought land for a song and held it for a great rise in value. Still others were the people who had secured franchises for railroads or other transportation systems and had profiteered at the expense of the municipal, state, or national government.

FIG. 229. New Year's Day was important socially until about 1900. It was sometimes spoken of as "calling day." Formal calls were made by wealthy young men upon all the ladies of their acquaintance

In 1861 there were only three millionaires in the United States. In 1900 there were 3800. It was generally agreed that at that time *one tenth of the American people owned nine tenths of the wealth.* By 1900 this tenth of the people (probably fewer than that) set the standards of the new "society" which was evolving in the United States.

In contrast to the lack of display in the lives of these aristocrats many of the newly rich plunged into a glittering display of wealth.

In building their mansions in the seventies, eighties, and nineties the newly rich copied European styles. Their houses, gloomy piles of stone and brick, were a jumble of towers, turrets, gables, balconies, stone lacework, minarets, and Moorish arches. On one fashionable thoroughfare alone there were Persian mansions, Italian and Spanish villas, medieval English castles, Greek temples, and many other styles.

In these houses in the seventies and eighties went on an endless round of luncheons, teas, and dinners, interspersed with driving in the park, theaters, and week-ends at fashionable resorts.

FIG. 230. A scene portraying a game of croquet in the year when it became "epidemic." (From *Harper's Weekly*, September, 1866)

In the late sixties and early seventies horse racing was fashionable among the wealthy people of the cities. This became the favorite sport of the wealthy after 1855, when the American Jockey Club was opened. At this opening the sale of liquor was forbidden, and ladies were invited. General Grant, soon to be president, attended, and the grand stand was filled to its capacity of 8000 people. Shortly after that James Gordon Bennett, Jr., son of the editor of the *New York Herald*, introduced polo at the fashionable summer resort of Newport, Rhode Island. Since that time it has become the leading sport of the very wealthy.

Among the seacoast towns from New Jersey to Maine popular summer resorts sprang up — Newport, Rhode Island, Long Branch, New Jersey, and others. During Grant's administration the President made Long Branch fashionable by spending vacations there. Yachting, swimming, tennis, and golf became popular sports among the rich.

In the summer of 1866 the *Nation* (New York) reported: "Of all the epidemics that have swept our land, the swiftest and most infectious is croquet." From East to Middle West spacious lawns were dotted with croquet wickets. Young ladies in hoop skirts and young gentlemen in long coats and tight trousers spent hours gayly batting wooden balls through the wickets.

In spring, summer, and autumn more and more wealthy Americans turned away from the cities. The well-to-do hunted in the White Mountains or in Maine. During the seventies and eighties, as the danger from Indian attacks disappeared, they flocked to the Rocky Mountains. It was then regarded as very smart to spend a summer at Colorado Springs at the foot of Pikes Peak or to hunt buffaloes on the plains under the guidance of hardy frontiersmen.

Thus a large, new, wealthy leisure class emerged in America. It was by no means confined to the bigger Eastern cities. Each thriving town of the West and the Middle West also had its aristocracy — a group of its "best people." Everywhere within the new society social lines were carefully drawn. The pinnacle was New York's Four Hundred, named from those who were invited to Mrs. William Astor's balls. (Her ballroom would hold only 400; hence the mystic number of the socially elect.) Ranged along the social ladder below this small group of social leaders were many wealthy little cliques. Before 1900 each large city could boast of a well-organized "best society."

Thus the leisure class of America was developing. Many of its members were extravagant, pompous, and wasteful. Yet gradually the tastes of the newly rich were improving. Steadily a more cultured, quieter social group developed, not only in the Eastern cities but throughout the other sections of the country.

Summing up

We must summarize briefly our glimpses of the social and cultural life which emerged in the new America between 1865 and 1900. We have seen how utterly differently the four classes of Americans lived — the farmers, the middle-class town and city people, the poverty-stricken tenement dwellers, and the well-to-do. The lives of all but the small leisure class, however, centered about "work and worry," and even in this class, because of the American tradition of work, the men spent most of their waking hours at their office desks. The goal of almost every ambitious young American was a bigger wage or salary, a better house, better clothes, vacations, and luxuries.

Recreation to the great mass of tired and worried Americans merely provided an opportunity to forget their worries about the future and their fatigue. Social life, like work life, therefore, became increasingly active. People thought more about "going somewhere," buying something new, seeing something new, getting a new thrill, playing a new game, than they did about intellectual or artistic enjoyment. An atmosphere of hurry and restlessness was spreading in America by 1900.

Does that mean that all Americans were concerned with piling up more dollars, building larger houses, and owning more and costlier things? No; here and there lived small groups of cultured people who were possessed by other ambitions than those of wealth. In every section of the country there were moderately wealthy and sometimes even poor people who were cultured and whose energies were not altogether consumed by the race for the dollar. The more well-to-do among them patronized the opera, the symphony orchestras, chamber concerts, and encouraged art of every kind. They attended the more worth-while things in the theater. They arranged informal gatherings in their homes where interesting people could meet one another. They encouraged the work of young artists, writers, and scientists. They devoted time and money to charity.

In the meantime the young artists, writers, and scientists whom they helped were laying the foundation of a new cultural life in America. They too were learning how to enjoy life richly without extravagance or display.

By 1910, however, important changes were beginning to take place even in the culture of the common man. As you know from your study of *An Introduction to American Civilization*, hours of labor were being reduced, and many of the middle class were obtaining increasing amounts of leisure. Correspondingly, recreations were changing. Sport — baseball, tennis, football, boxing, and the like — was becoming the great American pastime.

INTERESTING READINGS FROM WHICH YOU CAN GET ADDITIONAL INFORMATION

CATHER, WILLA. My Antonia. Houghton Mifflin Company, Boston. The story of an immigrant family who struggled to make a living from a farm in Nebraska.

CATHER, WILLA. O Pioneers! Houghton Mifflin Company, Boston. A novel of Middle-Western farm life.

FERBER, EDNA. Cimarron. Doubleday, Doran & Company, Garden City, New York. The opening of Oklahoma, and the life of the last frontier community.

FERBER, EDNA. So Big. Doubleday, Doran & Company, Garden City, New York, How a heroic woman won a living for herself and her son on a truck farm of the Middle West.

GALE, ZONA. Miss Lulu Bett. D. Appleton and Company. Life in a small Middle-Western village, centering about a very charming character.

HERGESHEIMER, JOSEPH. The Three Black Pennies. Alfred A. Knopf, New York.

HOWELLS, WILLIAM DEAN. The Rise of Silas Lapham. Houghton Mifflin Company, Boston. The romance of a business man.

OSTENSO, MARTHA. Wild Geese. Dodd, Mead and Company, New York.

QUICK, HERBERT. The Hawkeye. The Bobbs-Merrill Company, Indianapolis, Indiana. A novel of farm life in Iowa.

QUICK, HERBERT. Vandemark's Folly. The Bobbs-Merrill Company, Indianapolis, Indiana. A romance of Middle-Western farm life.

ROLVAAG, OLE EDVART. Giants in the Earth and Peder Victorious. Harper & Brothers, New York and London. Two sequel novels of the lives of Scandinavian immigrant farmers in North Dakota.

TWAIN, MARK. Life on the Mississippi. Harper & Brothers. A novel of life along the Mississippi.

TWAIN, MARK. The Gilded Age. Harper & Brothers. Small-town life in Missouri after the Civil War.

WHARTON, EDITH. The Age of Innocence. D. Appleton and Company, New York. A novel of New York society.

WHARTON, EDITH. The Custom of the Country. Charles Scribner's Sons, New York. The story of a newly rich Middle-Western family and its invasion of New York society.

CHAPTER XXVI

AMERICAN SPORTS

Henry Courtney, junior partner in Courtney & Son, turned to his father with an inquiring look. "Where are we going in athletics in this country? Everything is size, money, attendance, professionalism. Now just look at these headlines:

MORE THAN 2,000,000 PEOPLE SEE 10 MAJOR FOOTBALL GAMES

80,000 See Yale Beat Harvard

Record Crowd of 87,000 at California-Stanford

MICHIGAN BEATS CHICAGO BEFORE 79,000

Colleges take in $5,000,000 in One Afternoon

"Yes," replied Courtney, Senior, reminiscently, "athletics, like everything else, has become Big Business. Not much like my youth. I remember seeing the first baseball game between the old Cincinnati Red Socks and the Chicago White Stockings in 1870. It was a great game, played hard, but what a different setting. A tiny crowd, no cement-and-steel stadium . . . only a few wooden bleachers . . . rickety old thing, too . . . part of it fell down in the excitement of 'Pop' Anson's home run in the fourth. No $70,000 salaries, no big corporations, no 'ballyhoo' in the newspapers."

"The *purpose* of sport seems to have changed in the last twenty-five years," continued Courtney, Senior, thoughtfully. "I am at as great a loss as you to know where we are going in athletic sports. But we ought to know where we want to go. What *is* the purpose of sports like baseball, anyway?"

Such queries are being made and discussed by *thoughtful* Americans. People are beginning to question the *trend* in American sports, to ask seriously whether we are getting the right thing out of athletics and outdoor games.

They are asking such questions as these:

1. What is now the real purpose of American sports? What ought the purpose to be, that is, what is true success in athletics?
2. Is it possible to bring young people to accept this true purpose and not the false ones?
3. How can it be done?

Our next problem in this book is to learn something about American sports and about the change that has come to pass in them. Through understanding the history of baseball, football, and tennis, perhaps we can begin to see more clearly the purposes of sports.

I. Baseball: from Barn Ball to Big Leagues

There are various theories regarding the origin of baseball. One is that it began as a game called barn ball, played by schoolboys in England and Scotland a century or more ago.

Another theory is that baseball began as a game called by various names — rounders, round ball, or town ball. Because it was somewhat similar to our game of baseball some regard it as the beginning of the modern game. The ball was pitched toward the batter. He batted it and ran toward a base. If he was hit or touched by the ball thrown from the hand of one of the players, he was "out." As played at Harvard and other places in the 1820's there was no definite number of players, and the field had no definite shape. About 1840 a "diamond" with bases began to be used, the number of players was reduced to eleven, and the game began to be known as baseball.

In the 1840's and 1850's the game was played very generally throughout the villages and towns of the eastern half of the United States. Schools and colleges had teams, and many village and town lots were the scenes of exciting games on afternoons and week-ends. By 1858 the game was definitely known as baseball and was played as it is today by nine men. Professional as well as amateur clubs had been formed in many towns and cities. In the East the National Association of Baseball Players was formed, to which several hundred ball teams belonged. These teams arranged regular schedules and charged small admission fees. Probably this marks the beginning of commercialized and professionalized sports.

Then during the Civil War came the necessity of providing for the recreation of thousands of soldiers. Interest in baseball developed greatly among soldiers and also among prisoners in prison camps. By the close of the war baseball began to be recognized as the national game of America. Professional clubs were organized, and in annual conventions of the National Association hundreds of baseball teams were represented. As early as 1867 this organization of clubs included teams from as far west as the Mississippi River.

Even before 1870 competition for the best players developed, and in the larger cities clubs offered their players well-paid business positions in order to keep them in the city and eligible for their local team. In 1869 the Red Stockings of Cincinnati organized themselves as a professional team. Their example was followed in Chicago with the organization of the White Stockings, in Philadelphia, of the Athletics, and in Washington, of the Nationals. By 1871 there were ten clubs, playing regular series of games each season. Then in 1876 the National League of Professional Players was formed. The league took a firm stand against betting, against breaking contracts, and against "throwing" games for bribes.

So during the eighties and nineties baseball spread over the country both as an amateur and as a professional game. Children of eight and ten years played it. Almost every small town had its amateur "nines." Every small-town neighborhood boasted its juvenile Phœnix Athletic Club, its Myrtle Avenue Sluggers, or its West Enders. By the 1890's nearly every small-town high school had its baseball team. From these juvenile clubs developed an increasing host of skilled players.

Naturally, as the game grew older it became much more efficient and specialized. Some youths were found to be best in pitching, some in catching, some in the field. The cleverer ones invented new ways of pitching — the incurve, the outcurve, the cross fire, the fade-away, and others. Catching became an art, and playing first base, second, third, shortstop, or any infield or outfield position became a highly specialized job. The young players trained themselves carefully and thoroughly in the art of batting.

FIG. 231. Baseball as played today by a team in one of the leagues. (Photograph from Keystone View Co.)

In the meantime clever business men saw that there was much money to be made in baseball, and they increasingly put business methods into the game. By 1890 the National League estimated its investment at over $500,000. Each club became a strong corporation. The capitalization of each club increased, and more and more the stock of these corporations passed into the hands of successful business men who had made money in one industry or another.

The "plants" of the clubs were enlarged and improved. Larger and larger grand stands were built in place of the old wooden bleachers. By 1915 Big League teams had hundreds of thousands invested in their stadiums and diamonds. Larger and larger became the seating capacity, until finally in 1923 the Yankee Stadium of the New York American League team was built, seating approximately 62,000 people. Diamonds were tenderly cared for by expert crews. Players' salaries mounted after 1910. Admission prices steadily rose also; "fans" who had once paid 25 cents to sit in the bleachers later paid $2 or $3 to sit perhaps an eighth of a mile away from the diamond.

"High-powered" salesmanship entered the Big Business of baseball. Newspapers, some of them in close coöperation with owners of baseball clubs, developed extensive sporting departments. Professional baseball writers, some of whom had formerly been players, developed special columns and departments, and their writings were sold daily among national syndicates of newspapers. They too received large salaries. Not only were the various games reported in detail each day and announced through every daily newspaper of the country, but special articles were written regularly on some aspect of the sport or upon the star players.

By 1900 competition among the growing clubs brought about the reorganization of various leagues. It was finally agreed that the two major leagues should be the National League and the American League, each consisting of eight teams. Of somewhat lesser importance were the American Association, the Pacific Coast League, the International League, the Three I League, the Southern Association, and a host of smaller ones. Thus the national game became organized into levels of regional importance. The players of unusual skill in the minor leagues were promoted to positions and big salaries in the major leagues. As major-league players became "old" (that is, over 30 or 35) they were "retired" into the minor leagues and finally found employment possibly as coaches of school or college teams, as writers on sports, or as managers of lesser professional teams.

It is true that boys still play ball in the sand lots and that school and college games are played without a thought of salaries for the players. Nevertheless, it is also true, as was not true in the early days of the sport, that baseball has entered the field of Big Business. In the meantime, from active participation in the game millions of men have become onlookers. To a certain extent there is no help for this. Great audiences who witness professional games live in cities, where it would be impossible to provide for even an inconsiderable part of them to play the game themselves. This, however, does not dispose of the question. A vast number of young men who are getting their thrills on the bleachers could also be playing ball even in the meager space available in a big city. Moreover, there are other kinds of athletics than baseball — games which permit the participation of greater numbers than are on the field in a baseball game. It still remains true that many who might well be participants in amateur games of baseball now sit still and watch a few trained experts play the game. It is estimated that each year more than 40,000,000 people now pay a dollar or more each to watch the games of the two major leagues alone. Large profits are made by the stockholders of the clubs. Thrills, excitement, and variety our baseball fans certainly get. They are taken out of doors by the lure of competitive baseball. These are certainly gains for leisure.

II. School and College Football becomes a Highly Organized Sport

Football developed as an amateur sport earlier than baseball. It is difficult to find the origin of football. Some historians say that it really started hundreds of years ago in the rough kicking games of young English plowboys on public holidays.

Even in the early American colonies a game similar to the football of today was played. In colonial days, however, the game consisted more of throwing and kicking the ball than of rough-and-tumble fighting.

After the American Revolution, the rough-and-tumble game provided a good means of letting the rival classes in colleges fight it out. So dangerous and disorderly did the games become, however, that by 1860 the faculties of both Harvard and Yale forbade the students to play.

During the 1860's, while the Civil War was going on, football teams were organized. The game was still almost without rules, however.

AMERICAN GOVERNMENT AND CULTURE

From an account of one of the first intercollegiate football games (1869) — that between Rutgers and Princeton — we learn how undeveloped the game was, even at that time. There were 25 men on each side; the players did not wear uniforms; the ball could be passed in any way the players thought best — by kicking, batting, dribbling, or throwing.

Then in the 1870's and 1880's American football began to shape itself into our modern game. In 1874 the students of

FIG. 232. As football was played by the college teams in 1857. Compare it with figure 233, page 523, which shows how football is played today. (From *Harper's Weekly*, August, 1857)

McGill University (Montreal, Canada) introduced from England the improved game of Rugby, which had probably developed from the sport of the plowboys' kicking games. In Rugby the ball is kicked more than it is carried by the players. American universities and colleges soon adopted the game; but under the leadership of Walter Camp of Yale and other coaches it gradually changed into the American form. The number of players was reduced to eleven; rough-and-tumble fighting was eliminated; rules were developed, and the work of each player was specialized. Coaches like Camp made a scientific study of tackling and "interference." Special plays, such as the famous "guards back" of Pennsylvania and the "flying wedge" of Princeton, were worked out by the various teams, and their opponents were trained to meet them. Coach Alonzo A. Stagg of the University of Chicago led in the improvement, specialization, and standardization of the game in the Middle West as Camp was leading in the East.

In 1906 the colleges of the country formed the American Football Rules Committee. The committee reorganized the game, revised its rules, and in various ways tried to eliminate unfair practices. They barred freshmen from intercollegiate contests. In various ways they made football less brutal and more spectacular

Fig. 233. A modern game of football. (Photograph from Underwood & Underwood)

to watch. In place of the old "mass" plays, which were dangerous and not easy for spectators to follow, there came the open, forward-passing, long-run game.

By 1910 football, like baseball, revealed many of the characteristics of American civilization. It was highly organized; nearly every college and high school had a team which played regular schedules of games. Great intercollegiate and interscholastic rivalry developed. By every means known to business, these institutions organized their sports to win. Professional coaches and trainers were employed and given regular positions on faculties. Year by year their salaries grew larger and larger until the directors of athletics received larger salaries than leading professors of world reputation. Millions were spent upon the erection of great stadiums, some of which seated as many as 100,000 spectators.

Some educators and investigators have recently recommended the abolition of intercollegiate athletics. Others desire to reduce the number of games played each year. They wish to confine football, baseball, and other sports to games between groups within the colleges instead of sending the teams on long journeys to play at rival institutions. They would like to dispense with the high-salaried coaches and athletic directors, training tables, and publicity departments.

Essentially they are seeking to abolish the emphasis upon the money-making side of sport, upon winning at all costs. In place of this emphasis they desire to develop in their young men and women an interest in the art of sport. They aim at developing the joy of playing and appreciation of fine skill, irrespective of the side to which a player belongs. These leaders are interested in the truly cultural development of each individual young man and woman.

Year by year colleges and schools are confronting the increasingly difficult problem of group sports. They are asking, How can college and school sports be carried on so as to provide interesting physical exercise for all, enjoyable recreation for all, and at the same time avoid the evils of commercialization of leisure time?

III. Tennis and Golf: from Leisure-Class Sports to the Games of the Common Man

In the late 1870's lawn tennis was regarded as a game only for women. Few men played it, and among the women it was not a very active game. Women had to struggle against the handicap of long, tight-fitting dresses. Little skill was developed, and there was no attempt to "organize" the game.

By 1880, however, men had begun to see that the game had competitive possibilities. As college students began to play it, regular matches were arranged, and tennis teams from one institution competed with those from another. The size of courts was standardized, rackets and balls were improved, and rules were developed.

As in football and baseball, tennis experts soon appeared who devised special kinds of strokes. Players learned how to "lob," how to "serve" with great speed, or how to "volley" skillfully. Interest in the game spread, but much time was required for practice and for tournaments, and few working people had the leisure time on the tennis courts in which to become proficient.

FIG. 234. This picture presents an amusing contrast to the sights we see on the tennis courts of our day. (From *Harper's Weekly*, October, 1883)

Gradually, however, high-school as well as college youth adopted the game. By 1910 thousands of both sexes were playing it.

In 1900 Dwight F. Davis, a prominent Harvard player, offered a silver cup, to be held each year by the international singles and doubles champions. Since that time the Davis Cup matches have become the chief interest of tennis teams in a dozen countries of the world. Each year an increasing host of young aspirants for tennis honors look forward to the three great championship tournaments. These are for the American singles and doubles championships, the British singles and doubles championships (at Wimbledon, England), and the Davis Cup matches. The Davis Cup match is always held in the country which has won the championship the previous year.

New champions have come and gone. Every few years a new group of young players appears to take the laurels from the older men.

At the same time that tennis was becoming a man's sport, it continued to be a popular woman's sport. As the fashions for women's clothing changed and became freer and looser, the players were able to adopt the flashing technique which men were perfecting. During the last few years the women who played in the international tennis matches have proved themselves to be formidable players.

Tennis has come to be a popular sport in the United States. Year by year tennis is being played by greater numbers of American people. Indeed, tennis has become an international sport. In the United States Lawn Tennis Association and the affiliated clubs there were enrolled more than 1,000,000 members by 1921. More than 50 nations play it, 34 of which send their representatives to play in the leading tournaments. These international tennis matches are important from another point of view: since common likes help to promote mutual understanding, they offer one possibility for developing more friendly relations among nations.

In the meantime golf has steadily increased in popularity. It was introduced into America from Scotland and was played in the early days of our country's history, but not until the late 1880's was it taken up by any considerable number of people. Even then it increased in popularity very slowly. Golf links were expensive to make and to maintain, and at first only people of wealth were able to play the game. In the early 1900's, however, greater numbers of golf courses were built. Outside of every large city several country clubs were established, each with its golf links. Gradually even the smaller towns began to have clubs, and in some cities public parks had their links as well. In California alone, where the weather is favorable so many months in the year for outdoor sports, a score of golf clubs were established in the early 1900's, and from California came some of the early champions.

By the outbreak of the World War the golf courses had produced skilled young players, many of whom had begun as caddies on the links. Today a vastly greater number of American people are interested in and participate in the game.

In sharp contrast to baseball and football, tennis and golf have not been commercialized. It is true that there are many professional players, most of whom make a living by teaching beginners how to play. A few professionals earn large incomes

FIG. 235. Enthusiasts of golf cannot follow the details of the game very well from stadium or galleries; so they follow the trail of the players as this picture shows

at the game. In the main, however, these two sports increasingly attract larger and larger numbers of people. They are important social diversions as well as excellent forms of outdoor exercise. By them more people than formerly are enabled to engage in games for their health's sake and for the joy of playing.

IV. THE GROWTH OF OTHER OUTDOOR AND INDOOR SPORTS

While some of the more spectacular sports have become large business enterprises, others continue to supply the rank and file of Americans with interesting diversions and with the means of preserving their health — such sports as hiking, swimming, hunting, fishing, camping, and the like. Millions of Americans engage in them. In the larger coast cities, on Saturdays, Sundays, and holidays, crowds throng the beaches, refreshing themselves in the water and on the sands. More thousands are fishing along the ocean shores, and in creeks and rivers, lakes and ponds. A large number of sportsmen are hunting wild animals in the woods during the seasons in which it is permitted by law. Recently an increasing interest has developed in archery and in rifle and pistol shooting.

During the winter season many people enjoy tobogganing, snowshoeing, and skiing. In certain Northern centers — for example, at Hanover, New Hampshire, at Montreal and other Canadian centers, and in the regions of the northwestern and north-central states — regular winter carnivals are held. Thus sports which used to be popular only among the Indians and among northern people like the Canadians and the Scandinavians are being taken up more generally by Americans of the leisure class.

Indoor sports have also grown in popularity. The business workers of the urban middle class have turned more and more to gymnasiums. Increasing numbers of clerks, business executives, and other office workers fill the Y.M.C.A. and the Y.W.C.A. gymnasiums in the evenings. There they not only take setting-up exercises, but they play basket ball, handball, squash, and volley ball. In this connection it should be noted that in many small towns a great enthusiasm has recently developed for basket ball. In the Middle West, during the closed-in winter months, whole communities have their main interest in the success of their town high-school basket-ball teams. The attendance at the games, which has grown tremendously, is made up of older men and women as well as of young people. Gymnasiums and public halls have been enlarged. State and national tournaments are played, and all kinds of "championships" are decided each year. In this game coaches are hired, large sums are taken in at the box office, and the commercial spirit has entered as in baseball and football.

V. THE CHIEF OUTDOOR RECREATION

Let us close this brief sketch of the development of sports in America with a recreation that can scarcely be called a sport, but that has become one of the most common ways of spending leisure time — namely, *riding in automobiles*.

In 1890 nearly everybody in America walked. Then, after 1910, came the standardization of machines, installment buying, and the rapid reduction in prices of small cars. Today as a result we have about 25,000,000 automobiles in America; practically all but the very poorest can ride.

By this means Americans travel more than ever before. We can surely say that their "radius of understanding" has been enlarged and that the variety of their lives has been increased.

But there are difficult questions which, as students of American civilization, we must study. For example, what is the significance of this craze for movement that is so typically American? As motors have become more powerful, cars are traveling at much greater speeds. People are driving faster than ever. Apparently they are much more interested in the number of miles that they cover than they are in the beauties of the country through which they are driving.

A modern writer has told how the American automobilist longs for speed and motion:

> Somewhere a slow-mover is holding up the line. He creeps along, deaf, dumb, and blind; rebellion in his rear. More sirens blare; clutches shift; brakes bite. What is the matter up there, anyway? Somebody must be looking at the scenery! Doesn't that fellow know that if the rest of us don't get to Jamesport at 2:30, we won't reach Creston until after three? — and if we don't reach Creston until after three? — well, then we won't reach Smithtown by 3:45.... Not that there is anything special for us to do, at Smithtown.[1]

Thus the craze for riding in automobiles reflects more conspicuously than any other sport the growing restlessness of our modern life, the tendency to "get somewhere," do something, achieve something, acquire something. Those who are anxious

---
[1] Charles Merz, *The Great American Bandwagon*, p. 13. The John Day Company, New York, 1928.

about the development of such tendencies ask if it is not possible to educate the next generation to value more highly "being somebody."

What, then, is the Result of the American Development of Sport and Outdoor Recreation?

Our brief outline has shown us how closely the rise of organized sports has paralleled the development of other aspects of American civilization since 1865. One is impressed with the similarity in steps of advance. Like the production of food, shelter, and clothing, some of them have become business enterprises. Large property interests have been built up in each one. Tens of millions of dollars are invested in plants, equipment, salaries, and expenses. A money premium has been placed upon physical skill in athletics exactly as it has been on skill in occupational life. Millions of people crowd stadiums, race tracks, playing fields, and arenas, watching a few highly trained experts perform. Is there a danger that the American people will give up nearly altogether active participation in sports and become instead observers of the play of a few professionals? Millions are taken out of doors by these sports, to watch if not to engage in them.

Much of the brutality and vulgarity of earlier days has disappeared. Wholesome entertainment and variety of recreations are provided for the rank and file of the people. Millions of young people are acquiring physical skill hitherto unknown even to professionals.

How do the advantages and disadvantages balance? What do you think?

CHAPTER XXVII

THE "LIVELY ARTS"

Mr. and Mrs. Thurston sat in the living room of their home in "Middletown." It was Saturday evening. Now and then Mr. Thurston glanced at his watch uneasily. Mrs. Thurston, in a rocking-chair, was trying with no great success to read the newspaper. From the dining room at the end of the hall, the rat-a-tat of a drum keeping time to a radio jazz orchestra drifted into the living room.

The telephone rang in the hall, and Henry, the elder of the Thurston sons, rushed down the stairs to answer it. After a moment of hurried conversation he dashed into the living room.

"O Dad," he said, "may I go to the 'movies'? Helen and George are going."

Before Mr. Thurston could reply, the doorbell rang. Mr. Thurston arose. "I'm going to tell Bobby that he's got to take his drum elsewhere," he said, and continued somewhat apologetically, "That's Sam Wilson at the door, and he and I want to listen to Hoover's radio speech on the tariff. It's about due. Bobby has now been practicing on his drum for an hour, and it's time for him to go to bed, anyway."

Pauline, who had answered Mr. Wilson's ring at the door, now brought him into the living room. After greetings had been exchanged Mr. Wilson smilingly said: "I have a message for Pauline. Some young people dropped in to dance to the radio this evening, and my family think their party will not be complete without your daughter." Having delivered his message, Mr. Wilson disappeared down the hall to join Mr. Thurston. The sounds of the jazz orchestra had now been replaced by the words of Mr. Hoover's speech, but they floated into the living room unheeded by Mrs. Thurston. In her hands had been left the decision as to her children's Saturday-evening amusements.

Almost any evening in the 1930's in "Middletown"—indeed, in any town in America—such scenes take place. Millions of the great middle class of America, well-to-do business people, professional and skilled workers, unskilled laborers, share alike in the new "lively arts"[1]—technicolor-motion-talking pictures, vaudeville, musical-comedy, revue, tabloids, comic strips, Sunday rotogravure. What a contrast these recreations of the American people are to the social life of only a generation ago!

Our recreations are as expressive of American civilization as are our industry and business, and our other forms of social life.

Let us have a glimpse at the astonishing development of some of these "lively arts," in the short space of one generation.

I. THE POPULAR AMERICAN THEATER

From the "nickelodeon" to the "cathedral" of the motion pictures

Nothing less than a Cinderella-like transformation is the rise of the motion-picture theater, which had its beginning in "kinetoscope parlors" and "nickelodeons." In 1895 a few thousand Americans were paying 5 cents admission to peep at 50 feet of crude, flickering moving pictures showing dancers, acrobats, strong men, or fighters. Today approximately 50,000,000 Americans pay from 15 cents to $3 a seat to see motion pictures.

In them the whole world is brought before our eyes. We are taken into the jungles of Africa and sit unharmed within 50 feet of lions, tigers, and elephants. We watch the herds of giraffes speed across the plains with ungainly gait. Thousands of miles from Africa, we hear the speech of her people and the voices of her animal kingdom. The "News of the World" permits us to witness in quick succession a battle in China, a disaster in Haiti, a bullfight in Madrid, and a parade in Boston. We both see and hear the tumultuous welcome to Admiral Byrd first at Melbourne, Australia, and later at the Canal Zone. Later still we ride with him through the cheering throngs of Broadway in New York, etc. Night after night the American people, well-to-do and poor alike,

---

[1] *The Seven Lively Arts* is what Gilbert Seldes so aptly named his interesting book on the same subjects that are included in this chapter.

THE "LIVELY ARTS"

resort to their popular theater for romance, for world news, for opera, for tragedy and for comedy, for laughs and for thrills.

Yet it has not always been so with the "movies." Forty years ago there was no Universal City, no Hollywood, no R K O, no technicolor talkies — there was nothing but Edison's kinetoscope.

How pictures were made to move

The motion pictures of today were made possible by the invention in 1829 of the photographic process by M. Daguerre, a Frenchman. No sooner could "still pictures" be taken, however, than people began to demand pictures of objects in motion. By the time of the Civil War, inventors were trying out various kinds of devices. One experimenter as early as 1860 fastened single pictures taken at various stages of motion to a wheel and turned the wheel rapidly to give the observer the impression of movement.

Fig. 236. A modern "cathedral" motion-picture building. (From Paramount Publix Corporation)

With such a device, however, the movement was not continuous; it was merely a series of jerks.

Then in 1872 ex-Governor Leland Stanford of California engaged a photographer to photograph a horse in action. After long experimentation, the photographer produced the effect of motion by arranging a battery of 24 cameras so that each camera snapped a picture as a horse ran in front of it. Then the pictures were projected in rapid succession. This did give the effect of motion, but there was one serious defect. The horse seemed to be standing in one spot, kicking the landscape past him.

Then Thomas A. Edison, the "electrical wizard," about whom we have read in other volumes of this series, tried to record motion as well as sound. After some years of trial, however, he gave up the experiment temporarily. At the time it was regarded as a failure. Nevertheless, nearly 40 years later, the "sound picture" proved that his general theory was approximately correct.

In 1889 George Eastman was manufacturing kodaks and, in connection with his experiments, had perfected a thin, flexible film. Edison studied this film and concluded that by using it a motion-picture machine could be made. He turned part of the work over to William K. L. Dickson, one of his assistants. Dickson succeeded in perfecting a moving film contained in a little black box. A hole in the side of the box permitted one observer at a time to peer at the film. The assistant also perfected a motion-picture camera and a machine for projecting a picture on a large screen. When Edison saw the work of his assistant he rejected the projecting machine and improved and patented the peephole machine. It was known as the kinetoscope.

The "kinetoscope parlors" of that day were well patronized. Sometimes fairly long lines of people stood waiting to get a chance to view the latest showing. The novelty of the kinetoscope gave it some success as a business venture, but it was hampered by the fact that only one person at a time could peer at its meager 50 feet of film. When Edison took out his patents on the kinetoscope he did not think it worth while to patent the machine in Europe. Thus it was possible for European inventors to work upon motion-picture problems without the interference of patents, and important improvements were soon made in France and England. In America experiments were also continued.

In 1893 Edison and his assistants fitted up the first motion-picture studio and called it the "Black Maria." Pictures were taken in the open in daylight. There was no scenery whatever, and the films photographed were the simplest sort of pictures of dancers, wrestlers, picturesque figures like Buffalo Bill, and Sandow the strong man. Occasionally short skits from popular plays were photographed.

In the same year Woodville Latham and his sons, Otway and Grey Latham, a Virginia family, experimented with the projection of pictures upon a screen, so that crowds could view the same picture. The year 1894 was the first year in which motion pictures were exhibited publicly. In June, 1895, Thomas Armat perfected a projector that made satisfactory motion pictures possible.

As a result of the increased experimentation on both sides of the Atlantic, motion-picture theaters were opened in the 1890's, and regular showings were made in London, Paris, New York, and even in much smaller cities. It was not long before the idea of projecting the picture on a screen had entirely replaced the kinetoscope. In 1896 the first motion-picture corporation — the American Biograph Company — was formed. It was soon followed by rival companies, and competition among them became very keen.

By 1900 the development of "the silent art" was well under way. Regular actors were being employed, and drama was given. Wild West "thrillers" were especially popular. It is interesting to note that persons prominent in public life also appeared on the screen. Even as early as 1896 William McKinley was filmed during his campaign for election to the presidency.

By the early 1900's the kinetoscope parlor had given way to the "nickelodeon," which was a small moving-picture theater to which the price of admission was a nickel. Immigrants, who could not understand English, received with enthusiasm the picture plays given in these theaters, and soon in the poorer quarters of cities there was an epidemic of "nickelodeons."

At that time the actors that were employed did more than act. They were handy men around the studio, making scenery, costumes, and doing odd jobs, for which the best of them received only $5 a day. In 1906 Maurice Costello asserted the dignity of the actor, saying, "I am an actor and I will act, but I will not build sets and paint scenery."

Perhaps one might call this the beginning of the "star" system, because more and more after this time the pictures developed around prominent stars and producers. Between 1905 and 1910 people with stage experience began to engage in screen work.

In 1910 the location of the motion-picture industry was changed. From New York, which had been its center, it was moved to Los Angeles, California. Three years before that time a pioneer producer had filmed *The Count of Monte Cristo* near Los Angeles. It was then recognized that the succession of clear, dry days which were then needed for the photographic work could be counted on in southern California. The nearness to mountains, deserts, plains, valleys, and ocean beaches gave that location many other advantages over New York, and in 1910 a small group of successful motion-picture actors established a little studio on a vacant lot in Los Angeles.

Then followed rapid development. In 1915 the first "spectacle" picture, *The Birth of a Nation*, was staged by the new producer Griffith. This was a most ambitious portrayal of events connected with the Civil War. It marked the beginning of great spectacles featuring masses of people in action.

In the following years also many changes were occurring in the organization of the motion-picture industry. Intense competition brought about mergers among companies. As with the businesses of railroads, steel, oil, agricultural machinery, shoe machinery, and the like, the motion-picture business became concentrated largely in the hands of a few men.

About 1926 came another change; the silent drama began to talk. Although the "talkies" were received with great skepticism at first, within five years they became a pronounced success. Many of the earlier defects in the mechanical reproduction of speech have been eliminated. Not only has sound been added to the silent film, but color has also been successfully introduced.

Recently the motion-picture industry has attracted to it some of the finest actors and musicians from the theater and the opera. Artists and poets have begun to contribute their bit to the creation of real art in the popular American theater.

Less spectacular motion pictures have been developed in Germany, Russia, and other European centers. These films since 1925 have set for the American films a high standard of artistry.

Thus the common man has been given a theater which he enjoys and through which he lives with the whole world. But most pictures even today have little of permanent value. They do not make Americans think or meditate. They give them thrills, laughs, and sobs, out of all proportion to the real meanings in life.

The motion picture is still in the experimental stage, of course, and new and startling developments are promised for the near future. Methods of making films, machines and instruments for producing them, projecting apparatus — everything seems to be changing and improving. Creative artists, authors, poets, and actors of the legitimate stage are adopting the motion-picture theater as a proper place for the display of their work.

Nothing which America has done illustrates better the development of a new cultural life than the motion picture.

II. From the Variety Show to Vaudeville and the Musical Revue

1. The vaudeville

During the 1870's and 1880's the only theater of the workingmen of the larger cities was the vulgar variety show and burlesque. The variety show was a series of acts of slap-stick, rough-and-tumble comedy, vulgar jokes, and poor dancing and singing.

In the 1890's, however, the variety show was being rivaled by the so-called vaudeville theater. The financial and business leader in this new development was B. F. Keith of Boston, who opened his first theater in 1883.

What was this "refined and continuous vaudeville"? It was essentially a series of short acts, ranging from eight minutes to half an hour. Each act was given by a different performer or group of performers. A program three hours long would perhaps include short plays, and "turns" by skilled acrobats, jugglers, trained animals, dancers, and singers. Often there was a highly dramatic one-act play with shooting, murder, and detectives. Sometimes a magician pulled rabbits out of silk hats, named cards the faces of which he could not see, and did disappearing tricks. Admission prices were low. To attract still larger numbers of people, prominent actors, actresses, and singers were employed.

538   AMERICAN GOVERNMENT AND CULTURE

Thus the vaudeville theater began to expand as you have already seen that sports and motion pictures expanded. It too began to reflect the characteristics of corporate growth. The chain vaudeville theaters developed as did the chains of five-and-ten-cent stores, department stores, banks, and other industrial and financial enterprises during the same years. Finally in 1928 the Keith, the Orpheum, and other circuits of vaudeville theaters

FIG. 237. A variety theater of 1900

joined hands with the Radio Corporation of America and established a huge, nation-wide chain of hundreds of vaudeville theaters. Thus we see the influence of capital and the corporation in the theater as in all other aspects of American civilization.

Important gains were achieved for the developing vaudeville theater. The increasing capital of the larger chains made it possible for them to employ better performers — the world's best acrobats, jazz orchestras, concert singers, musical-comedy stars, and dancers. Admission prices increased, but attendance continued to grow. Somehow the common man managed to afford the money to see his favorite vaudeville.

With the development of vaudeville it has been repeatedly

proved that audiences appreciate the more artistic offerings. The old variety show is gone. Among the vaudeville performers the truer artists draw the popular crowds. The audiences are made up not only of the poorer people but of the wealthier people as well.

What do these audiences like best? You may be sure that many keen minds have studied this question. The history of the last fifteen years shows that the audiences applaud most heartily (1) perfection of skill, (2) strength and endurance, (3) speed, (4) comedy, and (5) originality. Skill, endurance, speed, and originality — typical American standards, are they not?

Thus in vaudeville we see another kind of popular American theater. Another "lively art" has developed.

2. The rise of the revue: the colorful theatrical spectacle

From the old variety show also came the modern revue. It too began in the theaters of poorer sections of our larger cities. Like the vaudeville the early revues lacked continuous plots. They were merely short acts — a dialogue between the principals, dancing and singing by a "star" performer supported by a chorus. The chorus, which was also known in the variety theater, was usually larger and better trained for the revue. In the selection of the revue chorus more attention was paid to beauty, and gradually better singing voices and greater skill in dancing were demanded.

After 1910 the revue also began to adopt the varied acts of the vaudeville. Its scenes began to include acrobats, short one-act skits, expert song-and-dance men, monologists, magicians, and professional "introducers." In this respect the modern revue differs little from the modern vaudeville. In other respects, however, it stands by itself — namely, in magnificence of costumes and settings, in electrical devices for lighting the stage, and in greatly enlarged orchestras.

It was the corporation also that did these things. Producers, backed by great wealth, spent hundreds of thousands of dollars in staging single productions. Popular-song-writers, famous jazz-composers, and noted writers coöperated with expert designers. The most skillful dancers were employed.

Advertising, especially in the form of billboard and newspaper publicity, was lavishly employed to draw in the crowds. Admission prices were raised from $1 to $3 at the outbreak of the World War, and to $3, $5, and $6 after 1920. By this time the revue was no longer the theater of the common people.

The contribution of the revue to the development of the "lively arts" in America was the amazingly successful use of color in costuming, the elaborate design of stage sets, and the use of electric lights.

3. The operetta and the musical comedy

During 1878 and 1879 the more cultured and well-to-do theatergoers of America attended with great enthusiasm several operettas written by two Englishmen, William S. Gilbert and Arthur Sullivan — *H.M.S. Pinafore*,[1] *The Pirates of Penzance*, *The Mikado*, and *Iolanthe*. The "catchy" airs and rhythms of Sullivan's music, the clever and subtle humor of Gilbert's lines (poking fun as they did at prominent world characters), secured for these plays an immediate vogue in America.

This was the beginning of the operetta and of the musical comedy of today. Throughout the eighties Gilbert and Sullivan were indeed kings of the better sort of light musical entertainment. Gradually these operettas were introduced to the less prosperous audiences. During the late 1890's and early 1900's many a popular outdoor amusement park filled its theater, afternoons and evenings, with audiences of the common people by offering the Gilbert and Sullivan operettas.

From 1895 to 1905 Viennese musical comedies were played in the American theaters, and American composers, such as Victor Herbert, began to write music for the American stage. Waltz songs had been included in the Viennese operettas and had become so popular that American composers frequently included them in their musical comedies.

After 1910, however, the waltz songs began to give way to a new kind of song the music of which we call jazz. Jazz entered into the musical comedy and also into vaudeville and the revue.

---

[1] "H. M. S." is the abbreviation of "His Majesty's ship."

By the end of the World War, therefore, the operetta of the Gilbert and Sullivan, Viennese, and Victor Herbert type had given way to the semi-revue jazz type of musical comedy.

After 1915 business captured musical comedy as it did everything else in the "lively arts." The size of the chorus was increased, there was more dancing, songs by popular-song-writers were inserted, and stage settings and costumes became more spectacular. As this happened, the lines spoken by the actors and the plot were given less and less attention until finally there was almost no plot at all. Today even the rank and file of musical-comedy audiences make fun of the absurdity of the lines spoken by the actors. There are, of course, important exceptions. In these exceptions there is a more connected plot and an opportunity for singers to exhibit fine voices and to give performances which require skill.

Most musical comedies today, however, have become mere spectacles of sight and sound. Admission prices are high, sometimes as high as those of the revues; and as the prices mount, fewer of the poorer people are able to attend.

III. Jazz: from Negro Dance Hall to Symphony

In the 1890's — the story goes — a tramp Negro entertainer by the name of Jazbo Brown frequently made the rounds of levee restaurants and dance halls along the lower Mississippi, playing weird syncopated rhythms on fiddle, guitar, or piano. This itinerant hobo played and sang "for his supper." Legend has it also that out of the enthusiastic demands of the black audiences for "mo' Jaz" came the name of the most popular music of the common man in America — jazz. Another story of the origin of jazz is that in 1895 a blind newsboy of New Orleans who was called "Stale Bread" got together a Negro street band. This was known as "Stale Bread's Spasm Band." Its swift syncopated rhythms found great popularity among the roustabouts on the levees and streets of New Orleans. About the same time similar crude native music was known in Cuba, Haiti, and in other islands of the West Indies. These are interesting stories, but probably neither is a true explanation of the origin of the word "jazz."

We really do not know where the word came from, but we do know that the peculiar syncopated rhythm of jazz is very old, even in the Old World. As early as the 1500's composers used syncopation. But in a sense, jazz is an original American combination of time beat, accent, and rhythm. By applying syncopation and the steady fox-trot time beat to the melody almost any musical composition can be made over into jazz. Indeed, some popular-song-writers have taken classical melodies and have made jazz pieces out of them. For example, the song "I'm always chasing Rainbows" is a more or less jazzed version of Chopin's "Fantaisie Impromptue."

Whatever may be the origin of jazz we know that similar music and dancing is more than a generation old. As long ago as 1880 some of the Negro spirituals and other songs of Negro origin had rhythms that resembled the jazz of today. Thus one thing is clear about the history of American jazz: its origin is certainly to be found among the Negroes of the West Indies and the South. Since 1915, however, white composers, singers, and players have modified it and popularized it all over the United States and in many centers of Europe. So American jazz is partly Negro and partly white.

By 1915 jazz had moved north. It was then being introduced in Chicago and was developing independently in Los Angeles. Young leaders were experimenting with new combinations of instruments. In Los Angeles in 1915, for example, a jazz band consisted of a piano, trombone, violin, banjo, two saxophones, a set of drums, and a cornet, almost exactly the same instruments regularly used today in jazz orchestras.

Once these young band men got started there began a decade of experimentation with time beat, orchestration, and new ways of playing instruments. Experimenting leaders encouraged the individual players of their orchestras to invent new sounds and combinations of tones. The saxophonist learned to imitate human conversation and animal noises, such as the whinny of a horse; he learned to imitate the playing of a fine stringed instrument. The trombone, cornet, and trumpet players softened and muted their tones with derby hats, "wa-was," and "kazoos." The drummer learned to produce seductive time beats by brushing a fly-swatter across a snare drum. Every player has become in a sense a composer.

By 1920 Paul Whiteman had developed jazz to the point of using full written orchestration. The various instruments had definite parts written for them. Thus the music became more unified and harmonious. It became less noise and more music.

FIG. 238. A modern cabaret jazz band. (Photograph from Underwood & Underwood)

In February, 1924, Whiteman's orchestra, which previously had not aspired to better places than cabarets, gave a concert in Æolian Hall, New York. It was regarded as an epoch-making event and was attended by many patrons of classical music. Some were perplexed by its novelty, while others hailed it as an example of original American music. The chief composition played in this concert was George Gershwin's[1] "Rhapsody in Blue." This was the first "classical" jazz composition for orchestra.

[1] Gershwin first attracted notice as a young untrained musical prodigy of Brooklyn, New York. From the time he was seventeen he had been playing the piano for vaudeville and revue actors and writing sheet music. That he has real musical genius, however, is indicated by the fact that his symphony "An American in Paris" was played in 1929 by the New York Philharmonic Symphony Orchestra, an orchestra devoted to the rendition of classical music.

544   AMERICAN GOVERNMENT AND CULTURE

Jazz became increasingly popular in Europe as original American music. Jazz orchestras appeared in the hotels and restaurants of London, Paris, and other European cities. Students of American life are recognizing that jazz is already a unique American contribution. One may dislike it, but one cannot deny its

FIG. 239. Radio performers and the studio from which their programs are broadcast. (Photograph from Underwood & Underwood)

force, its vitality, its power to set people singing and dancing. There has been much poor, noisy, discordant jazz, which is not art at all, but already there is jazz which reveals true art.

The popularity of jazz has been aided by the radio and the phonograph

In the meantime jazz had completely ousted the popular dance music of 1900 — the waltz, two-step, and schottish. After 1910 the one-step, the fox trot, and certain exaggerated forms of dancing to jazz were adopted in public dance halls and elsewhere. As phonographs were improved and radios were introduced into homes, more and more people began to dance. Here was a "lively art" in which Americans could actually *participate* and not act merely as observers.

It is estimated that each night not less than 20,000,000 Americans listen to the radio and that several millions more listen to the phonograph. What do they hear through these new avenues of music? A symphony concert? Lectures on science and art? Political speeches? Literary readings? No! Most of them listen to jazz.

It is well known that the broadcasting stations try to supply the public with what they like rather than what the stations think they ought to have. From the daily programs we see that jazz forms the major demand of radio audiences. It appeals to people because of its primitive, rhythmic qualities. Its audiences are found among the cultured and the uncultured alike. This new American music is still in the experimental stage. What it will produce eventually we can scarcely predict.

This must conclude our all-too-brief study of the arts of the common man. Well named they are — the "lively arts." Lively are their rhythms, their vocabularies, their intense speed. And arts they are already beginning to be. Is it not an astonishing advance which has been made in a single generation? Within less than 40 years new machines, new techniques, new rhythms, new combinations of tone and melody, light and shade, have been originated. Wealth has backed the originators, and a whole new range of arts have been produced — the motion picture, high-grade vaudeville, the operetta, the tuneful musical comedy, the dazzling revue, and jazz.

Inevitably these arts of the common man reflect the characteristics of Americans and American life — bigness, speed, money success. Naturally they appeal to the emotional side of human nature rather than to the intellectual side. Like the entire civilization of America they are new and they are experimental. No one can predict the outcome of their development during the next generation.

UNIT X

THE UNITED STATES AFTER 1914:
CURRENT PROBLEMS

THE UNITED STATES AFTER 1914: CURRENT PROBLEMS

We now turn from the cultural life of the American people to the stirring events of the World War and the problems which it brought to America. In earlier volumes we have seen how the industrial nations of Europe engaged in a long, destructive struggle and how even distant America was finally drawn in. References have already been made to America's participation in the war and the important changes brought about in her position in the modern world. The story of the part played by American government in the war itself, however, and the important political developments following the armistice have not been told. To those important events we turn in the two chapters of this concluding unit.

In Chapter XXVIII we shall see the rôle of our national government in the war itself.

In Chapter XXIX we shall trace some of the important happenings of the past decade. These are so near to us that they can hardly be regarded as "history." Rather they are "current events." In Chapter XXIX we shall also sketch the economic and political problems which the people of the United States have yet to solve. Some of these problems are new to the American people; some are as old as American history.

Thus the concluding unit of our history will serve both as a summary of America's march toward democracy and as a summary of the problems which her citizens confront and may be called upon to solve in the immediate future.

CHAPTER XXVIII

AMERICA AND THE WORLD WAR

We have already studied the story of American government to the outbreak of the World War, 1914. Most of it has dealt with happenings on the North American continent.

Steadily throughout the 1800's American history was becoming more closely interwoven with the history of other countries. Foreign trade was increasing, larger amounts of money were being invested abroad, and American-made goods were being sold in every continent of the world. After 1900 these contacts of the United States with the rest of the world increased rapidly.

In spite of the participation of America in the business affairs of the world, however, our government kept itself comparatively free from political alliances with other countries. While Great Britain, France, Russia, Germany, Austria, and other European nations were making secret treaties of alliance, especially after 1890, our government carried on its affairs quite independent of them all. Thus, for about 100 years after the War of 1812, the United States kept almost aloof from the political problems of European countries.

Then came 1914 and the outbreak of the great World War. By 1914, as you learned in *Changing Civilizations in the Modern World,* two groups of nations comprising six of the greatest powers in Europe were allied by secret treaties. In the Triple Alliance were Germany, Austria-Hungary, and Italy. In the Triple Entente were France, Great Britain, and Russia. Various other treaties bound many of the smaller countries to one or another of these six great powers. You have learned that Italy withdrew from the alliance with Germany and joined forces with Great Britain and her allies. You also know that early in 1917 the Russian Revolution took place and that Russia withdrew from the war. Great Britain, France, and the countries which aided them in the World War became known as the Allies. Germany led the second group, known as the Central Powers.

The war raged for more than four years. In spite of itself our government was drawn into the terrible conflict. The nations of the world had become so interdependent for raw materials, manufactured goods, and capital that no large or powerful nation could remain indifferent to a world war. From that day to this the affairs of our country have been brought ever more closely into touch with those of other countries.

For Nearly Three Years (1914–1917) European Nations tried to draw the United States into the War

No sooner had the war begun than each group involved — the Allies and the Central Powers — hoped to draw the United States into the war on its side. To do this the nations at war spread propaganda among the American people; that is, the Allies circulated stories among them about the Central Powers, and vice versa. Most of these stories were false, as later events proved. Each side was endeavoring to injure its enemies by prejudicing the American people against them.

What were these stories to which the American people listened?

First, both sides spread stories of atrocities committed by enemy troops. Both Great Britain and Germany circulated such accounts throughout the United States by means of newspapers and magazines and by means of lectures in public halls, churches, schools and colleges, and at rallies in public squares. Few of these accounts proved to be true.

It was not difficult to spread propaganda in the United States. The American people were descended chiefly from Europeans. Millions were of Anglo-Saxon or Latin blood, millions of others traced their ancestry to German, Irish, Austrian, or Slavic people. The war had hardly started when many of the descendants of these Europeans began to sympathize with one side or the other, and as the propaganda of both sides spread, the stories were believed by tens of millions of Americans.

Second, at the same time each side sent out official documents which claimed to prove that its enemies had caused the war.

Third, at the very beginning of the war, you will recall, Germany marched her armies swiftly across Belgium in the attempt to capture Paris before the French could arm themselves to defend it. Belgium was a neutral country, and Germany's "violation of neutrality" was contrary to international law. So in their propaganda Great Britain, France, and Italy used this German deed to influence the American people against Germany and Austria-Hungary. In their published documents it was insisted that the Germans were outlaws in the international world and could not claim the friendship of other nations.

Fourth, the later propaganda of the Allies made much of the German submarine warfare. Some of the German submarines ruthlessly attacked merchant vessels and killed women and children and other noncombatants without warning. These deeds, said the Allies, also proved that the Germans were outlaws among the nations. The Germans and Austrians replied that Great Britain was also violating international law in seizing and confiscating food, clothing, medical supplies, and other nonmilitary necessities on the way to the Central Powers.

Thus it was that the enemy countries carried on propaganda in the United States. Thus it was that each side — the Allies and the Central Powers — tried to "educate" our people to side with them.

President Wilson's Long Conflict with Both Sides over Attacks upon Neutrals

Great Britain and Germany each tried to cut off the trade of the other

A modern war depends upon supplies. In the end the victor is almost sure to be the one who has the largest supply of men, food, and munitions to draw upon. England and Germany both knew this fact; therefore each wanted to cut off supplies sent to the enemy by other countries, particularly by the United States.

Great Britain was able to act first. Long mistress of the seas, she had a navy strong enough to shut in that of Germany, so that it could not get out on the high seas. With the German navy bottled up German merchant ships were unable to go abroad and bring goods home. Nor could merchant ships from neutral countries carry goods into German ports unless the British vessels blockading Germany permitted. At first Great Britain declared that she would seize and hold only those vessels going into German ports with munitions on board. Later she included also cotton, copper, and rubber in the list of products she would not allow to pass her blockade. Still later she included all foodstuffs. The British believed that they could succeed in starving the Germans into submission. Ever tighter became Great Britain's blockade.

FIG. 240. A cartoon showing Uncle Sam handing his notes of protest to England and Germany, and saying, "Now, Gentlemen —" (Courtesy of *Review of Reviews*, New York, March, 1915)

What did Germany do? She made use of a comparatively new invention — submarine boats. Traveling under water, the submarines could evade the ever watchful British navy. So Germany tried to establish a *submarine blockade* around the British Isles. One German proclamation read:

The waters surrounding Great Britain and Ireland, including the whole of the English channel, are hereby declared to be a war zone. On and after the 18th of February, 1915, every enemy merchant ship found in the said war zone will be destroyed without its being always possible to avert the dangers threatening the crews and passengers on that account.

Even neutral ships are exposed to danger in the war zone.

Between the blockades established by the two countries the trade of the United States would suffer seriously.

Therefore the American government began to address notes of protest to both sides, asking them to respect the rights of neutral trade. At first, as a result of these protests, the governments of Great Britain and of Germany made concessions. Soon after, however, both countries continued their policy of trying to prevent supplies from reaching the enemy country.

Great Britain's blockade was effective; most of the American trade was with the Allies

The British largely succeeded in keeping the German ships fastened up in their ports. But the submarine blockade which Germany tried to set up around the British Isles was not at first successful. It is true that many ships were sunk, but many others managed to escape and carry goods into British ports. Therefore, as time went on, the trade of American merchantmen was chiefly with the Allies.

At first the Allies paid for these goods with gold, but as the months of heavy expenditures passed their gold supply ran low. Then the Allies had to borrow money from the United States to pay the companies which sold munitions, fuel, food, and other products. In this way, as you know, Great Britain, France, and the other Allies became debtors of the United States.

From 1914 to 1917 the war dragged on in an indecisive way. Now the balance went in favor of the Central Powers, now in favor of the Allies. The bankers and manufacturers to whom the Allies owed money grew more nervous whenever there was an Allied defeat. If the Central Powers should win the war, the Allies would probably not be able to pay their debts. Thus sentiment in favor of helping the Allies grew among American business men.

Gradually the sentiment of the American people as a whole came to favor the Allies. There were various reasons, but among them the effect of the German submarine blockade was most important. The nature of submarine warfare does not permit a submarine to notify a ship when it is to be torpedoed, because the submarine might then be located and destroyed. The attack must be sudden and unexpected. Therefore the crews and passengers of merchant ships going to England were always in danger. During the first year of the war merchantmen were torpedoed without warning.

Then came a great tragedy of which the American government had to take notice.

On Saturday, May 1, 1915, a British steamship, the *Lusitania*, sailed from the port of New York. Her sailing might have been like the sailing of any other steamship if it had not been for certain warning signs.

It was known that the *Lusitania* carried munitions and that she was therefore subject to attack by German submarines. The newspaper which carried the announcement of her sailing also carried a warning from the German embassy advising Americans not to sail on her. Nevertheless many people, among them Americans, sailed on the *Lusitania* on that fateful Saturday.

Seven days later, as the ship entered the submarine zone, it was torpedoed. Many of the passengers were drowned. Over 100 of those who lost their lives were Americans. A storm of protest arose in the United States. American newspapers were bitter in their denunciation of Germany. Many people who had remained neutral in their feelings up to this time now wanted the United States to enter the war against the Central Powers.

Although many Americans demanded that we go to war on the side of the Allies, President Wilson continued to try to gain his ends by diplomacy. At once he protested vigorously against the sinking of the *Lusitania*. He demanded a different submarine policy, and Germany a little later did limit her submarine warfare. She agreed that merchant ships should not be sunk without warning and neutral lives and property should be protected.

Early in 1917 unlimited submarine warfare was resumed by Germany

On January 31, 1917, the German ambassador handed to the American Secretary of State a note withdrawing the earlier promise that submarine warfare should be limited. The war party in Germany was launching the final attempt to win the war. Week after week the number of merchantmen torpedoed increased. As a result England found herself in a desperate condition. The American ambassador to England wrote President Wilson three months later:

> There is reason for the greatest alarm about the issue of the war caused by the increasing success of the German submarines. I have it from official sources that during the week ending 22nd April, 88 ships of 237,000 tons, allied and neutral, were lost. The number of vessels successfully attacked indicated a great increase in the number of submarines in action.
>
> This means practically a million tons lost every month till the shorter days of autumn come. By that time the sea will be about clear of shipping.
>
> The British transport of troops and supplies is already strained to the utmost, and the maintenance of the armies in the field is threatened. There is food enough here to last the civil population not more than six weeks or two months.[1]

Things were going badly with the Allies. Early in 1917 the Central Powers seemed to be winning. Voices in the United States spoke more loudly than ever for war against Germany. Newspapers condemned the peace policy of the President. Even the mass of the people, who had for so long been opposed to our entrance into the war, were coming to accept it as necessary.

Finally, the government acted. The German ambassador was dismissed. Merchant ships going into the submarine zone were armed. On April 2 President Wilson called upon the Congress of the United States to declare war upon Germany. Four days later the United States had entered the war.

The gigantic task of arming a nation unprepared for war

The United States was unprepared to take part in a great world war. In April, 1917, millions of seasoned European soldiers were fighting on the battle front. At that moment, however, the regular army of the United States totaled 128,000 men and the navy 75,000!

A gigantic task, indeed, confronted the officials of our government — a gigantic task involving hundreds of problems.

---

[1] Burton J. Hendrick, *The Life and Letters of Walter H. Page*, Vol. II, pp. 278–279. Houghton Mifflin Company, Boston, 1922.

The national government, faced by the crisis, took over dictatorial power

Only the Federal government was big enough to do the job of concentrating the resources of the nation and of sending the fullest possible aid to the Allies. To do so the President, as chief executive of the nation, must have unlimited power to act quickly and effectively.

Accordingly, President Wilson asked the Congress to grant him the power to conscript troops and to requisition raw materials, food, goods, military and civilian supplies, railroads, ships, telegraphs — anything needed in the great crisis. And although in times of peace a majority of Congress was solidly opposed to Wilson, now in a great war they calmly voted him these powers. Within a few months after our entrance into the war, he was virtually the dictator of America.

Recruiting and training a huge army. Voluntary enlistment does not usually provide enough men to carry on a modern war. Men must be had, not by the thousands, but by the millions. Nations, therefore, turn to conscription, the draft — that is, to forced service in the army or navy or both. The European countries had done it; the United States now did it. The steps in drafting and preparing the men for service were as follows:

1. All men between the ages of 21 and 30 were registered. (Before the war closed the age limits were 18 and 45.)
2. These men were classified according to their fitness for warfare and according to their usefulness in other government service.
3. Men to the number of 500,000 were first drawn by lot from the classified lists. (As the war went on successive drafts brought the total of American soldiers to nearly 4,000,000.)
4. These men were sent to camps where they received preliminary training for service in battle.
5. After months of hard training regiments and brigades were sent to France, where they went through final training for actual engagement in warfare.

While the men were being drafted for service, great training camps were rapidly built in various parts of the country. Land was bought, buildings were erected, and water supplies and sanitary systems were provided. Soon the recruits arrived. Even before uniforms had been received from the factories men were being drilled day and night by officers from the regular army. Thus not many months passed before whole brigades of raw recruits were transformed into trained soldiers.

Getting the money to pay for the war. But such tremendous enterprises required vast sums of money. Billions of dollars had

FIG. 241. During the World War training camps were established in various parts of the United States. Here men, used to civil life, were trained for war

to be raised immediately. Where could it be obtained? Only from the American people themselves. How? By taxes? Partly. Heavy taxes (see *Appendix*, Sixteenth Amendment to the Constitution) were laid on personal incomes, on the profits of business enterprises, and on inheritances. But these were far from sufficient to raise the money needed. Only huge loans would do that. No help could be expected from the Allies, who were already heavily in debt. So to carry on the World War the United States government turned to the American people for help.

In 1917 and 1918 the Federal government carried on five great bond-selling campaigns. Liberty Bonds were sold to the people in every community of the country. Never before had Americans witnessed such a selling campaign. A great nation-wide organization was created. From the stages of theaters, the pulpits of churches, and the platforms of schoolhouse auditoriums speakers lectured on the necessity for buying bonds. Placards confronted the people in store windows and on the trains and cars. Posters covered the billboards, denouncing the Germans and pleading for money.

FIG. 242. One of our World War loan posters

Everybody was urged to "Buy until it Hurts." And buy the people did. Wage-earners, tens of thousands of them, bought at least a $50 bond each. Many of the poorer people lent their meager savings to the government to finance the war. In every little town there was a committee. In every factory and store the workers were urged to buy bonds. One drive after another poured the people's money into the government's coffers.

In the nineteen months during which the United States participated in the World War the five loan drives brought in the gigantic sum of $21,448,120,300. This was approximately the total cost of the war to the United States. Mostly in addition to this vast sum about half as much more (about $11,000,000,000) was lent by the government to the Allies.

The government controlled industry through the War Industries Board. Business men were told that the needs of the government had the first claim on all raw materials, manufactured goods, food, and the like. Peace-time manufacturing must stand aside until the war needs were satisfied. To control industry the War Industries Board was created. This board was given power to decide which industries should have the first claim on raw materials, to control prices, etc. It began its work giving factories which manufactured supplies needed for the war the first claim on iron, steel, rubber, cotton, and so on.

The government also took control of the railroads. During the early months of the war the railroads were very inefficient in handling freight. Being under the control of different companies, the various railroads did not coöperate well. Neither did they coöperate efficiently with the steamship companies which had to carry from the ports the freight brought there by the railroads.

The government solved these problems by taking over the management of the railroads and putting them under the United States Railroad Administration. Mr. William G. McAdoo was made director general and ran all the lines as one system. He and his officials decided which kinds of goods were most important, and these were carried first. Thus the railroads of the country were unified into one great system, and the vast freight of the nation was handled quickly and efficiently.

The American people, accustomed to peace, were educated to support war

Thus a people who had struggled for nearly 300 years for democracy, voluntarily gave up much of their liberty and many of their rights. Business men, clerks, mechanics, professional people, wealthy and poor alike, took orders from and obeyed the government.

How could such a change in attitude come about in a democratic country in which the rights and the liberty of the individual citizen were most sacred things? It came about because the government conducted a great campaign of education to convince the people that our country confronted a great crisis and that *while the war continued* the government must be given complete power. So with the understanding that it should be only *while the war continued* the people submitted and gave the government dictatorial power over their very lives.

But what a campaign was conducted to bring the people to this conclusion! A nation-wide organization was created under the Committee on Public Information.

Back of the firing line, back of armies and navies, back of the great supply-depots, another struggle was waged with the same intensity and with almost equal significance attaching to its victories and defeats. It was the fight for the *minds* of men, for the "conquest of their convictions," and the battle line ran through every home in every county.[1]

The great machine of publicity which the government built up in order to gain the support of the people was felt in every community. The Committee on Public Information printed pamphlets and distributed them by the millions. It sent out information and appeals to newspapers and magazines. It used advertising space everywhere. It gathered artists and writers to make posters and write books. It made moving-picture films. It used churches, clubs, chambers of commerce, and labor unions to win the support of the population for the war. Its publicity flooded the country in English, German, Italian, Yiddish, Polish, and the other tongues we hear on the streets of our towns and cities.

The Espionage Act (1917) and the Sedition Act (1918). In its endeavor to win the war the government did some things which many leaders, then and later, condemned. For example, in June, 1917, it passed the Espionage Act and in May, 1918, the Sedition Act. The Sedition Act was such a severe intrusion on personal liberty that one fourth of the members of the United States Senate refused to approve it. However, by May, 1918, public opinion helped to force its passage. These acts gave the government control over the spoken opinions as well as the acts of the people, in that they authorized the government to fine or imprison persons who were disloyal to the United States, who interfered with the work of the government in any way, even those who used "abusive language about the government or institutions of the country." Under these acts a vast organization of spies was developed by the Federal departments of State,

---

[1] George Creel, *How We Advertised America*, p. 3. Harper & Brothers, New York, 1920. Mr. Creel was Chairman of the Committee on Public Information.

War, the Navy, and the Post Office. Government watchers listened in on conversations in trains, in restaurants, and other public places. Neighbors spied upon neighbors, employers upon employees. Detectives trailed many people. Statements made in personal conversation were sent to Washington. Information about thousands of citizens was collected, much of it utterly false. College professors and teachers who protested were discharged. The Sedition Act of 1918 has been described as an even more severe attack on personal liberty than the Sedition Act of 1798. Thus in many ways freedom of speech was done away with.

President Wilson's plan to end war: the Fourteen Points

In two famous addresses before the United States Congress (January, 1917, and January, 1918) President Wilson set forth to the world the aims which it was hoped might be attained by the war. These aims embodied principles of international relations in a democratic world and are known as the Fourteen Points. The following are the most important:

No private understandings. Open covenants of peace, openly arrived at, after which there shall be no private international understandings of any kind, but diplomacy shall proceed always frankly and in the public view.

Freedom of the seas. Absolute freedom of navigation upon the seas outside territorial waters, alike in peace and in war, except as the seas may be closed in whole or in part by international action for the enforcement of international covenants.

No economic barriers. The removal, so far as possible, of all economic barriers and the establishment of an equality of trade conditions among all the nations consenting to the peace and associating themselves for its maintenance.

Reduction of national armaments. Adequate guaranties given and taken that national armaments will be reduced to the lowest point consistent with domestic safety.

A League of Nations. A great league to be set up to bind together the peoples of the earth and to exert a force to prevent future wars.

The last point was probably the most important of all, for it meant a new international system whereby disputes between nations might be settled not by war but on their merits.

The American Army and Navy in the World War

Service rendered by the American navy

Within a month after the United States declared war, its navy was actively helping the Allied navies. While new ships were being built in great haste in the growing shipyards of the country, battleships, cruisers, submarine-chasers, and torpedo boats went

Fig. 243. American soldiers embarking for France during the World War

speedily into action. Two kinds of service were rendered by the American navy: First, its cruisers, torpedo boats, and other swift war vessels joined the British and French fleets in the war zone, hunting down German submarines. These, as you know, were destroying many Allied merchantmen. Month after month the search for the submarines went on, and month after month the destruction of supply ships was reduced.

A second indispensable service was that of protecting the waters about the United States from German submarines and in convoying hundreds of troop ships to Europe. During the nineteen months in which the United States took part in the war nearly 2,000,000 American soldiers were transported to Europe. Each fleet of transports was protected by naval vessels.

What the American army did in France

In the meantime a great army was being recruited and trained. Within three months after our declaration of war, troops from our regular army were in France. On arrival there they were first sent to French training camps, where they were taught the new kinds of warfare that the World War had developed. After several months of such training they were sent up to the trenches on the battle line.

After October, 1917, boatload after boatload of new troops trained in the 50 cantonments and camps of the United States arrived in French harbors. There they were sent to training camps and prepared for the terrible warfare which they would soon share. All through the winter of 1917-1918 the training of American soldiers went on. As a result, by August, 1918, the United States had 1,200,000 trained soldiers in France.

May-July, 1918 — the battles at Cantigny, Belleau Wood, and Château-Thierry. Even in the spring of 1918 General John J. Pershing, commander of the American troops, had thrown his men in with the French to hold the Germans back in their last great drive on Paris. In May the Americans aided in opposing the advance of the Germans at *Cantigny*. In June they took their part in a terrible struggle in *Belleau Wood*. Inch by inch the Germans pressed forward, with the French and Americans slowly retreating before them. In July came the crisis of the great German offensive. At times it seemed as though the Germans would break through and capture Paris. All along the Marne River the battle raged. At *Château-Thierry* another bloody battle was fought, in which Americans played an important part. At last the French, with the help of the fresh American troops, held their ground. It was the last of the great German drives.

August-November, 1918 — St. Mihiel and the Meuse-Argonne drive. By August, 1918, the American army was so large and so well trained and equipped that it could begin an offensive campaign of its own. On September 12 a great battle opened at *St. Mihiel*. The German lines were attacked by 550,000 American troops and about 180,000 French troops. Slowly the Americans and French advanced; slowly the Germans fell back. The result was an important victory for the Allies, with the recovery of a great deal of territory from the Germans and the capture of 16,000 prisoners and much equipment.

From that time on the American troops were in action almost constantly in the *Meuse-Argonne* section. The last great German offensive had been defeated, and now the tired Allies, supported

FIG. 244. American soldiers at St. Mihiel

by a large fresh American army and with increased supplies and equipment, were driving the Germans back. The city of *Sedan* was captured, and a deep wedge was driven into the German line.

NEGOTIATIONS FOR PEACE

Recognizing that they were defeated, the German leaders began to negotiate for peace. As early as August, 1918, the Kaiser had been informed by the commander of his army that Germany and her allies were then practically defeated. From that moment the German government began negotiations to secure the best peace terms obtainable from the victorious Allies. They reorganized their government and placed at the head of it the somewhat more democratic Prince Max of Baden.

By September Bulgaria, one of the allies of Germany, had surrendered. Late in October this news was followed by the announcement of the complete defeat of the Austrians by the Italians and the request of Austria for peace.

Before that time the German government had asked President Wilson to negotiate a peace. For another month, however, the war went on. Day by day the British, French, and American troops steadily drove the Germans back. Surrounded on land by advancing armies, tightly blockaded on the sea, Germany and Austria were starving to death. Provisions of food, raw materials, and manufactured goods were very low; nothing could be brought in from outside nations.

Finally, on November 11, 1918, an armistice was signed, and fighting ceased. The greatest war of history was over.

The Allied victory was decisive. It was not the "peace without victory" for which President Wilson had hoped. His own soldiers had helped to put Germany at the mercy of the victorious Allies. Now that they had won would they decide the peace on Wilson's great principles — the Fourteen Points?

The Peace Conference and the Treaty of Versailles

On December 4 President Wilson sailed to the Peace Conference on the steamship *George Washington*. In Europe the mass of the people received the President as they had never received an American before — as, indeed, few men have ever been received. They were tired of war. They had suffered enough. Workingmen and peasants believed that this man, who had come to Europe with more power than a king, would make a new and better world.

And then the conference began at Versailles. It was a big conference, composed of the foremost men of many countries. But there were four men who counted more than any others, for they represented the four greatest powers on the winning side. They were Georges Clemenceau (called "the Tiger"), the premier of France; David Lloyd George, the prime minister of England; Vittorio Orlando, the premier of Italy; and Woodrow Wilson, the president of the United States.

But Wilson had not realized how hard it would be to secure a settlement which would start Europe toward permanent peace. It seemed to many as though the leaders of the victorious countries were more anxious to get all they could out of Germany than to establish a lasting peace. England wanted the German colonies. France wanted German coal regions. Italy wanted Austrian territory. Japan wanted Germany's rights in China.

Fig. 245. President Wilson at the Peace Conference

All of them wanted money. All except the United States asked for spoils. Secret treaties came to light in which the various Allies had promised each other certain territories in case of victory.

Thus the American president seemed alone in his desire for a fair peace.

At the crisis of his fortunes the President was a lonely man. Caught up in the toils of the Old World, he stood in great need of sympathy, of moral support, of the enthusiasm of masses. But buried in the Conference . . . no echo reached him from the outer world, and no throb of passion, sympathy, or encouragement from his silent constituents in all countries.[1]

[1] John Maynard Keynes, *The Economic Consequences of the Peace*, pp. 48–49. Harcourt, Brace and Company, New York, 1920.

Through long months the Peace Conference dragged on. Some of the suggestions contained in the Fourteen Points were carried out. Alsace-Lorraine was given back to France. The independence of several smaller nations — formerly parts of Germany, Austria, Hungary, or Russia — was recognized. These smaller nations are Poland, Czechoslovakia, Finland, Yugoslavia, Lithuania, Latvia, and Estonia. President Wilson did get his desire for the establishment of a League of Nations, but it was not so democratic a league as he and many other people had hoped for. It was in the control of the great Allied powers. Germany was not included. It was very doubtful whether the League would have the power to prevent war. Still, said many people, it was the beginning of better things.

Other suggestions contained in the Fourteen Points were ignored. Even if the President had been a better diplomat, one man could not have stood against the powerful influences brought to bear on him from his own and other countries. Much territory was taken away from Germany, including all her colonies. The Austro-Hungarian monarchy was split up into the two states of Austria and Hungary, and their territory was greatly reduced by the formation of the new states of Czechoslovakia and Yugoslavia. Japan was given the former German claims in China (Shantung). Germany and her allies were compelled to pay huge "reparations" (compensation given for a wrong done).

Thus the peace could hardly be called a "peace without victory." On the contrary, it was about as harsh as the harshest could have desired.

The League of Nations and the Treaty of Versailles were rejected by the American Senate

The President came back from Europe with the Treaty of Versailles and the Covenant of the League of Nations. They must go together, he said. One could not be accepted without the other. Since the Senate of the United States has to ratify all treaties, the League and the treaty were laid before the Senators.

The Senate, after long discussion, refused to ratify the treaty which Wilson had signed. Their opposition to the League of

Nations caused them to reject the entire treaty. Many Senators were not ready to admit that the United States was now bound up politically with the rest of the world. They overlooked the fact that the United States had become a world power during the war and that her economic life was bound up with every continent of the world.

For the first time in the history of the United States, American troops fought in Europe. For the first time in its national history the American government entered deeply into "entangling alliances" with other countries. Was the policy of standing aloof from the political affairs of Europe to be definitely changed? In Chapter XXIX we shall see.

We learned how propaganda can be spread among a people; how newspapers and magazines, pamphlets and books, etc., can be used to create opinions. We have learned that these agencies of communication were indispensable in uniting our people in the support of the war once our government had entered it. Not only are such things effective in binding the people together; there are also grave dangers that they will be used to cause dissension and misunderstanding.

We also learned that in a great crisis even a democratic government may have to become an autocracy. So it is in all times of crisis — times of earthquake, great fires, or floods. When communities are imperiled great power must be given to one man and a few assistants. But that dictatorial power is retained only for the duration of the great crisis. When it has passed, the democratic government must again be reëstablished.

Finally, we learned of the difference between the aims of the American government and those of the governments of the European countries. Whereas our government asked for no spoils of war, the other Allied governments demanded colonies, land, concessions, money. We must remember that this was not the demand of all the people of those countries; it was the demand of the political leaders.

Thus we recognize the difficult problem of developing a true spirit of international understanding and coöperation, and we see America's great opportunity and great obligation for leadership.

CHAPTER XXIX

THE UNITED STATES SINCE THE WORLD WAR: FACING THE PROBLEMS OF DEMOCRACY

In our brief study of American history we have now reached the most difficult task of all, namely, that of understanding the events of the decade following the World War, a period when every nation was faced with new and troublesome problems.

To understand these events is especially difficult because they have happened so recently that it is hard to estimate their importance. They are reported to us by magazines and books, and we cannot be sure of their accuracy. They have not yet been judged by historians. The problems which they illustrate are complicated and difficult. Nevertheless, as American citizens we ought to try to understand them.

We now have one important aid at our command. We can see current problems as the result of great movements of history. Some of them have been problems to our people ever since they began their experiment in living together on the continent of North America. At this point, therefore, you should review carefully the great movements of earlier times, especially of the half-century between the Civil War and the World War.

In bringing this history of American government and culture to a close, we shall divide our study into two parts:

First, we shall consider the history of America's relations with other countries since 1918 and the problems which these relations present. These we shall call *international problems*.

Second, we shall consider what has occurred within the boundaries of the United States since 1918 and the problems developing among our own people. These we shall call *domestic problems*.

Then we shall note a few of the problems of economic and cultural life for which there is an urgent need of solution.

I. International Problems of the American Government

Should the United States join the League of Nations?

At the close of the war one great problem confronted the peoples of the world: How could a permanent world peace be established? That is to say, how could war be outlawed?

No nation occupied a more favorable position than the United States to help solve that problem. Our country had become "the rich man of the earth." Our material resources were enormous, our industries huge, our farmers prosperous. Our business men traded with every continent, and our people, descended from every nation, were bound by inheritance to the other peoples of the world. In 1919, therefore, other peoples looked to us to take the leadership in the building up of a friendly world of nations.

It cannot be doubted that the sentiment of the American people themselves was overwhelmingly against war. If the United States were to join the League of Nations, would its influence prove to be strong enough to insure continued world peace, or would its membership in the League merely draw the American people into European quarrels? On that question both the American people and their leaders were divided. Some favored joining the League as the next step in bringing about permanent world peace. Others opposed it, saying that to do so would entangle us in "Europe's private quarrels."

The American Senate, as you know, voted (1919) to stay out of the League. Many people believed that "politics" and not real conviction had led the Senate to do that. Wilson, a Democrat, had favored the League. The Senate was controlled by the Republicans. Hence, the argument ran, the Republican Senate defeated the Democratic proposal to join the League.

The presidential election of 1920

A year later the question of joining the League of Nations was presented to the American people themselves in the presidential campaign of 1920. It was made an important issue between the Republican and Democratic parties. The Democrats generally were supposed to favor joining the League; the Republicans were supposed to be generally opposed to it. The candidates of both parties, however, favored "some kind of world association." The Republican candidate, Senator Warren Gamaliel Harding, said in a campaign address: "I am in favor of a world association — call it what you will, the name is of slight consequence — that will discourage or tend to prevent war." The Democratic candidate, Governor James M. Cox of Ohio, definitely favored joining the League itself.

The Republicans won the election with a majority of more than 7,000,000 votes, and in 1921 Senator Harding became the twenty-ninth president of the United States. The Republicans claimed that this meant that *the American people* had voted against joining the League of Nations. Really, however, it was difficult to be sure of this, for other important factors helped to decide the way people voted. Nevertheless, the Senate continued to stand aloof from the League.

Accordingly, when the delegates of 41 nations assembled at Geneva, Switzerland, on November 15, 1920, for the first session of the Assembly of the League of Nations, the United States was not represented. From that day to this, our government has not been officially represented in the League.

Furthermore, for three years after Harding's election the United States declined to take official part in the European conferences called to revise the financial terms of the Treaty of Versailles. The leading European powers held several international conferences of great importance to consider the debt situation between the nations and to revise the amount of reparations that Germany and her allies should pay. It is true that "observers" were sent by the United States to some of these conferences, who informally gave advice and reported to our government. But no delegates who could speak officially in the name of the United States government were present.

Relations with Russia

The United States government took the same position in its relations with the revolutionary government of Russia. For several years that new government, known as the Union of Socialist Soviet Republics, was not approved by any of the Allied powers. Most of the leaders recognized, however, that the trade of the countries of Europe — indeed, of Asia and the other continents — was bound up closely with that of Russia. The world had become interdependent. Hence the leading governments of the world began to send ambassadors to Russia and to permit Russian representatives to establish embassies and consulates within their borders. That is, they resumed diplomatic as well as trade relations with the radical Soviet government. In spite of the fact that American business men had begun to exchange goods with the Russians, the American government refused to recognize the new Russian government, and to the present day has not established official relations with it.

What part did America take in other world affairs?

Although our government remained officially outside of the League of Nations and refused to recognize Russia, it did participate in other ways in world affairs. Let us note several examples:

1. *A separate treaty of peace with Germany in 1921*

The first step was to sign a separate treaty of peace with Germany. For more than two years and a half after the signing of the armistice, the United States was officially at war with Germany, although actually at peace. As you know, the United States Senate had refused to ratify the Treaty of Versailles. In August, 1921, this unusual situation was adjusted by President Harding's government, which signed a separate treaty of peace with Germany.

2. *The difficult problems caused by international debts*

During the war Americans had lent more than $11,000,000,000 to their European allies. Most of this great debt was owed to us by Great Britain and France. Hence an important question had to be met by our government: How should this huge debt be paid? Some Europeans, as well as some Americans, maintained that it should be canceled — either altogether or in large part. These persons maintained that Great Britain and France had had to carry the chief burden of the long war against Germany. The United States was not officially in the war until 1917, and not until 1918 did she have any considerable number of troops engaged in it. So these so-called internationalists said, "Our allies have done their part; let us do ours by canceling the war debts."

But this argument had little effect upon our government. During the administration of President Harding and that of his successor, President Coolidge, the government said, "The Europeans borrowed the money; let them repay it." What proportion of the American people took the same attitude it is impossible to know. It was probably a large proportion.

In 1923 the British government arranged for the payment of its debt to the United States. It was the first of the European governments to do so. The plan provided that annual interest payments should be made together with a portion of the principal of the debt itself, so that at the end of a very long term of years the entire debt would be paid. Gradually the other European governments made similar arrangements. In nearly all cases, though in varying degrees, the American government reduced the principal and accepted a low rate of interest.

3. *What reparations should Germany pay?*

In January, 1924, the United States government took a long step toward resuming its leadership in international politics. It joined with the British government in sending into Germany a commission of financial and business experts to find out what Germany's financial condition really was and to determine how much she could and ought to pay to the Allies in reparation. European trade was in an unsatisfactory condition, and it was recognized that one reason for this was the uncertainty concerning the reparations Germany could pay and still carry on her domestic and foreign trade.

One of the American commissioners was the Chicago banker Charles G. Dawes, afterwards vice president of the United States, and his name was given to the plan which was finally drawn up.

The Dawes plan fixed the amount of the German reparations. It also provided that to help Germany resume its trade British and American bankers should lend her money. The plan was accepted by Germany and eventually confirmed by Great Britain and the United States.

4. *The Washington Conference on the limitation of armaments*

Other events occurred which showed that, although our government refused to become entangled in Europe's quarrels, it was actively participating in the study of important world problems.

One group of these had to do with the conflicting claims of various powers to lands bordering on the Pacific. Another group of problems, in many ways related to the conflicting interests in the Far East, was concerned with the limitation of naval armaments. Some of the nations had built up powerful navies before the World War; but numbers of their vessels had been sunk or captured. Immediately following the war some of these nations again began to reëstablish their navies. Many people believed that these navies threatened war again; at any rate, the recovery of the world from the last war was being delayed because of the enormous expenditure of public money for naval establishments.

President Harding and his advisers saw that to settle these difficult problems peaceably the American government must coöperate with the other leading powers of the world. Hence, in November, 1921, at his suggestion a conference was held in Washington to consider the reduction of naval armaments and to arbitrate other differences. Representatives from Great Britain, France, Japan, China, Italy, Belgium, Portugal, and the Netherlands met with those of the United States. It was at this meeting that the American Secretary of State, Charles Evans Hughes, startled the entire world by announcing the readiness of the United States to destroy certain battleships already in service and others under construction provided the other nations would do likewise. Within a few hours telegraph wires around the world hummed with the epoch-making proposal. Hope spread among the common peoples of the world that their governments would this time take an important step toward permanent world peace.

After weeks of discussion four of the nations — Great Britain, the United States, France, and Japan — made a Four-Power Treaty. Four of its provisions were important:

First, a partial "naval holiday" was declared. The building of battleships was to be stopped until 1931. Certain other ships were to be destroyed, and for ten years smaller ships alone were to be built, and those only in stated amounts, so that the navies of the United States, Great Britain, and Japan should be maintained at certain proportions satisfactory to all of them and sufficient to protect their interests.

Second, each country agreed to recognize and respect the territories of the others in the Pacific. This meant, for example, that Great Britain, France, and Japan would respect the American control of the Philippine Islands and that the other powers would respect the possessions of Great Britain in China, in the Malay States, and in other British possessions bordering on the Pacific Ocean.

Third, the United States agreed not to build fortifications in the Philippines, and Japan and England each agreed not to fortify their island possessions.

Fourth, the four powers agreed that in all trade relations they would maintain the "open door" in China. This meant that all countries should have an equal opportunity to build up trade with China. No country was to demand more concessions or privileges than another.

Other important provisions were contained in the treaty. As a result of one of them Japan returned to China the rich industrial peninsula of Shantung, which she had received when Germany's colonial empire was divided at the close of the war.

5. *The Briand-Kellogg Peace Pact*

In 1927 the French minister of foreign affairs, Aristide Briand, suggested to the United States that France and the United States sign a pact denouncing war and agreeing to arbitrate differences that might arise. Frank B. Kellogg, the American Secretary of State, suggested a similar pact to Great Britain, Germany, Italy, and Japan, all of which countries approved it. On August 27,

1928, these six countries together with nine others signed what is known as the Briand-Kellogg Peace Pact. Since then 59 nations — practically the entire civilized world — either have signed or have agreed to sign the pact.

6. *Should the United States take part in the World Court?*

Twice before the World War the leading powers had met in peace conferences at the Hague in Holland to discuss international problems. Then in 1921 a World Court was established at the Hague by the League of Nations. The United States government was urged to participate in it. President Harding, and after him President Coolidge, recommended that the United States Senate officially permit such participation. But the Senate refused. In 1926 it was the subject of long debate by the Senate. Finally, the entrance of the United States into the World Court was approved, but with many cautious reservations as to the responsibilities and rights of our government. When presented to them, however, the European governments would not accept the reservations, and officially the United States did not join the Court.

Nevertheless, influential American citizens continued to play an active part in it. As early as 1920 Elihu Root had served on the committee of the League of Nations which organized the World Court, and John Bassett Moore, another prominent international lawyer, was one of the elected judges. In 1928 Charles Evans Hughes was elected a judge of the Court, and upon his appointment as Chief Justice of the United States Supreme Court in 1930, Frank B. Kellogg, former Secretary of State, was elected to succeed him.

7. *More naval conferences: Geneva, 1927, and London, 1930*

In 1927 President Coolidge invited Great Britain, France, Italy, and Japan to hold another conference on the limitation of armaments. Although France and Italy declined to send representatives, those of Great Britain, Japan, and the United States held a prolonged conference at Geneva, Switzerland. The Washington Conference had been restricted to the question of battleships. At the Geneva conference the governments considered the reduction of submarines, cruisers, and other smaller ships. After long discussion of the matter, however, no definite agreement was reached.

Three years later, in January, 1930, the great powers met again in another conference on limitation of armaments. This time Great Britain, the United States, France, Italy, and Japan sent their most prominent leaders of foreign affairs to a meeting in London. This conference lasted three months, and during this time the delegates discussed again the cessation of battleship-building and also the reduction of the building of cruisers, submarines, and other smaller ships. Although they did not agree to as large reductions as many citizens of their countries desired, nevertheless important advances were made in the limitation of navies. Fairly large sums of money were saved by the agreement not to build battleships until 1936 and also to scrap certain ships already in existence. The hope was expressed that "battleships will in due time disappear altogether." Agreements were also reached concerning the respective numbers of smaller ships which each country was to build. Proposals were made by Great Britain and the United States to abolish all submarines. This, however, was not agreed to by France and Japan. On the whole, the conference was regarded as having achieved another slight step in the direction of the gradual disarmament of the nations.

Though America remained outside the League of Nations, the League did an important work

In the meantime, although American Senators would have nothing to do with it, the League of Nations carried on a most important work. On January 10, 1920, the League formally came into existence. At the first meeting of the Assembly there were 41 member nations. Today there are 54.[1] Twenty-seven countries now belonging to it lie outside of Europe. These 54 countries carry on the entire work of the League for an annual

---

[1] The number at one time was 56, but Brazil and Costa Rica afterwards withdrew, making 54 members. In 1926 Germany was admitted to full membership in the League. The countries which do not belong to the League are the United States, Russia, Mexico, Brazil, Costa Rica, Turkey, Afghanistan, Ecuador, Egypt, Yemen, Muscat, Hejaz, and Nejd.

expenditure of not more than the cost of a single submarine, namely, about $5,000,000. This comparatively small sum of money supports not only the work of the League itself but also that of the World Court and of the International Labor Office.[1]

The directive work is carried on by the *League Assembly*, which consists of three representatives from each member country, and by the *League Council*, which now has fourteen members, five of which are permanent — the British Empire, France, Italy, Germany, and Japan. The League is not to be regarded as a great world state. Its actions do not bind the governments of the member countries without their approval. It is simply a vast organization designed for closer coöperation and greater understanding among the nations of the world.

At the headquarters of the League at Geneva, Switzerland, there are approximately 600 officials doing a work of great world importance. Let us note a few examples of what has been done by the League during its short existence.

During the ten years that have passed since its first session the League has established bodies of experts called Technical Organizations. There are three of these: (1) the organization for *Communication and Transit*, which aims to facilitate travel among nations; (2) the *Health Organization*, which conducts investigations and plans methods of stamping out disease — as a result of its work great advances have been made in eliminating contagious diseases and preventing their spread from one country to another; (3) the *Economic and Financial Organization* — under this body the League has arranged for loans to be made to Austria, Hungary, Greece, and other needy countries.

Other expert advisory commissions have been established; for example, that for the regulation and elimination of the opium traffic, that on mandates (which supervises the governing of some 18,000,000 peoples formerly ruled by Turkey and Germany), and that on the protection of women and children in industry. There is still another one, which governs the region of the Saar valley.

[1] Although the International Labor Organization, of which the Office is a subdivision, is not a definite part of the League of Nations, it is closely related to the League and is supported by it. This body also has its headquarters at Geneva, where a large staff of labor experts conduct conferences, draft international agreements, and in various ways aim to improve labor conditions all over the world.

Although the League of Nations lacks the power to enforce its decisions, nevertheless it has already succeeded in preventing wars by settling a number of international disputes through arbitration. For example, in 1925, when war was threatened between Greece and Bulgaria, the League Council intervened between the two countries. It requested Greece and Bulgaria to withdraw their troops within their own frontiers and urged them to arbitrate their differences. This was done. The two countries accepted the League's recommendations, and war was prevented.

Thus the hope grows around the world that the establishment of the League of Nations will increasingly bind the nations peaceably together.[1] It is regarded by many people as the corner stone of a world community which will be built in the future. These people regret the fact that the American government stands aloof, refusing to take part.

Summing up the gains of the past decade

Thus in the years that have passed since the signing of the armistice these important gains have been achieved:

1. The League of Nations has been established, and through it marked progress has been achieved in international coöperation.

2. Countries in every continent have expressed their desire to arbitrate international disputes, that war may be abolished.

3. For the first time the great powers have definitely agreed to limitation of naval armaments.

4. The attention of students of world affairs has been directed to the "sore spots" of the Far East, the Near East, etc. Public discussion of these and the activities of the League are helping to solve by peaceful means the problems arising in these regions.

5. Governing officials increasingly take the people into their confidence and tend to seek popular opinion in support of their acts. Although it is doubtful whether the people yet receive full and unbiased reports of international relations, nevertheless there is an increasing tendency to carry on world affairs in the open.

[1] Most of the Latin-American countries are members of the League of Nations. There is a separate body — the Pan-American Congress — which has met from time to time since 1901 and which is a sort of separate league. The idea originated in the United States, and the sixth conference of this body was held in 1928, at which it was agreed that international disputes between American countries should be settled by arbitration. These congresses too may be regarded as a contribution of the United States to world peace.

6. Undoubtedly, secret treaties are still being made between the armed powers. A number of these have been revealed since the close of the war. How many secretly made treaties are now in force in Europe we have no means of knowing. Because of the greater force of public opinion, however, and the growing influence and independence of the press, it is probable that there are fewer war-breeding secret agreements in existence than there were before the World War.

7. The Permanent Court of International Justice (the World Court) has been established and is giving important aid in settling international difficulties through reason and judgment instead of by war.

Are the fundamental problems of international relations being solved?

In spite of the sure gains in international coöperation serious dangers confront the nations of the world. Insistent problems remain. In the few remaining pages in this book we can merely state some of these problems briefly.

First, how shall the nations peaceably agree on the fair distribution and use of the great undeveloped natural resources and trade of nonindustrial regions? Vast amounts of basic minerals and fertile land are still undeveloped. The business corporations of the industrial nations are competing furiously for these and for the trade of the changing agricultural regions. Although some progress is being made in forming international corporations, great dangers to world peace lie in the race between rival corporations of various nations for trade in oil, steel, chemicals, textiles, and food.

Thoughtful students of international relations have long urged that an important step be taken; namely, that some central world body be created to control and distribute, in the interests of all the people of the earth, the world's basic minerals, like coal and oil, and other raw products which are sources of international friction. The whole problem is not yet clearly understood even by the experts. But many are coming to believe that some advance must be made toward international ownership and control of basic resources if war is to be permanently outlawed.

Second, how shall trade be carried on among the nations with fair prices to the business men and fair wages to the workers of all countries? This centers attention on many difficult questions, chief among which are (1) the tariffs on goods imported into one country from another; (2) the sharp differences between wages, prices, costs of production, and standards of living generally in different countries; (3) the demands of business men in each country that their industries be adequately protected; etc. Can you see the danger to the peace of the world in this tendency to exclude the goods and raw materials of other countries? Do you see a relation between it and our dependence upon other countries for raw materials, for certain kinds of food, and for manufactured goods?

Third, another critical problem which the people of America and other industrial countries confront is that of the changing agricultural countries. As they adopt industrial ways of living, generally they too enter into competition with the already established industrial nations, and their imports from these countries decline. As they build up nationalistic points of view, following the example of European nations, international friction increases. Thus world problems become more and more complicated, and international coöperation becomes increasingly more important.

Fourth, another serious problem is that of national armies and navies. Is it sufficient to limit the sizes of armies and navies? Are the conferences on limitation of armaments removing the real dangers of future wars? Many experts are confident that they are not. They maintain with much force that armaments of any size merely exaggerate the possibilities of war. They recommend the almost complete abolition of all armies and navies. They would keep in existence only enough naval vessels to police the seas (this means very few ships indeed) and enough soldiers to keep order within the various countries.

On the other hand, advocates of preparedness maintain that large standing armies and navies are the only sure guaranty against aggression by strong nations and against war.

But the real problem still confronts the nations. How can international understanding be developed?

On one matter, however, there is universal agreement. Every possible step shall be taken to build up among each people understanding of the others. True understanding is the basis of enduring friendship.

We have stated only a few of the most pressing problems of our changing world. All these problems you will perhaps study in your later school years. But little space remains, and we must pass on to a brief review of the problems which the American people confront within their own boundaries.

II. Domestic Problems

Changing business from war time to peace time

In 1919 the country's first problem was to readjust itself to peace-time conditions.

For nearly two years the American people had toiled at the business of war. It dominated their work, their conversation, their thought. By November, 1918, the whole country had become adjusted to war. Then came the armistice, and all at once these American people had to rearrange their ways of living. With the coming of peace there came also difficult problems of reorganizing the industries and business of the country. For two years industries, mines, farms, railroads, stores, and banks had worked mainly at carrying on a war. Suddenly these gigantic enterprises had to be changed over to peace-time work. Thousands of factories which had been making guns, munitions, uniforms, shoes, hats, and military and office supplies had to be readjusted to the production of very different things. Thousands of machines had to be scrapped; other thousands had to be altered. Vast quantities of goods on hand had to be disposed of, and new supplies for peace-time use produced. Millions of workmen who had learned how to run special war machines now had to be taken over into regular peace-time occupations. Thus the months immediately following the signing of the armistice were times of great difficulty for business men and for skilled and unskilled workers, as well as for farmers and professional people.

1. *The problem of taking the soldiers back into occupational life*

More than 4,000,000 soldiers had been taken out of industry, business, agriculture, and the professions. Work had to be supplied to all. Some of the soldiers were taken back immediately

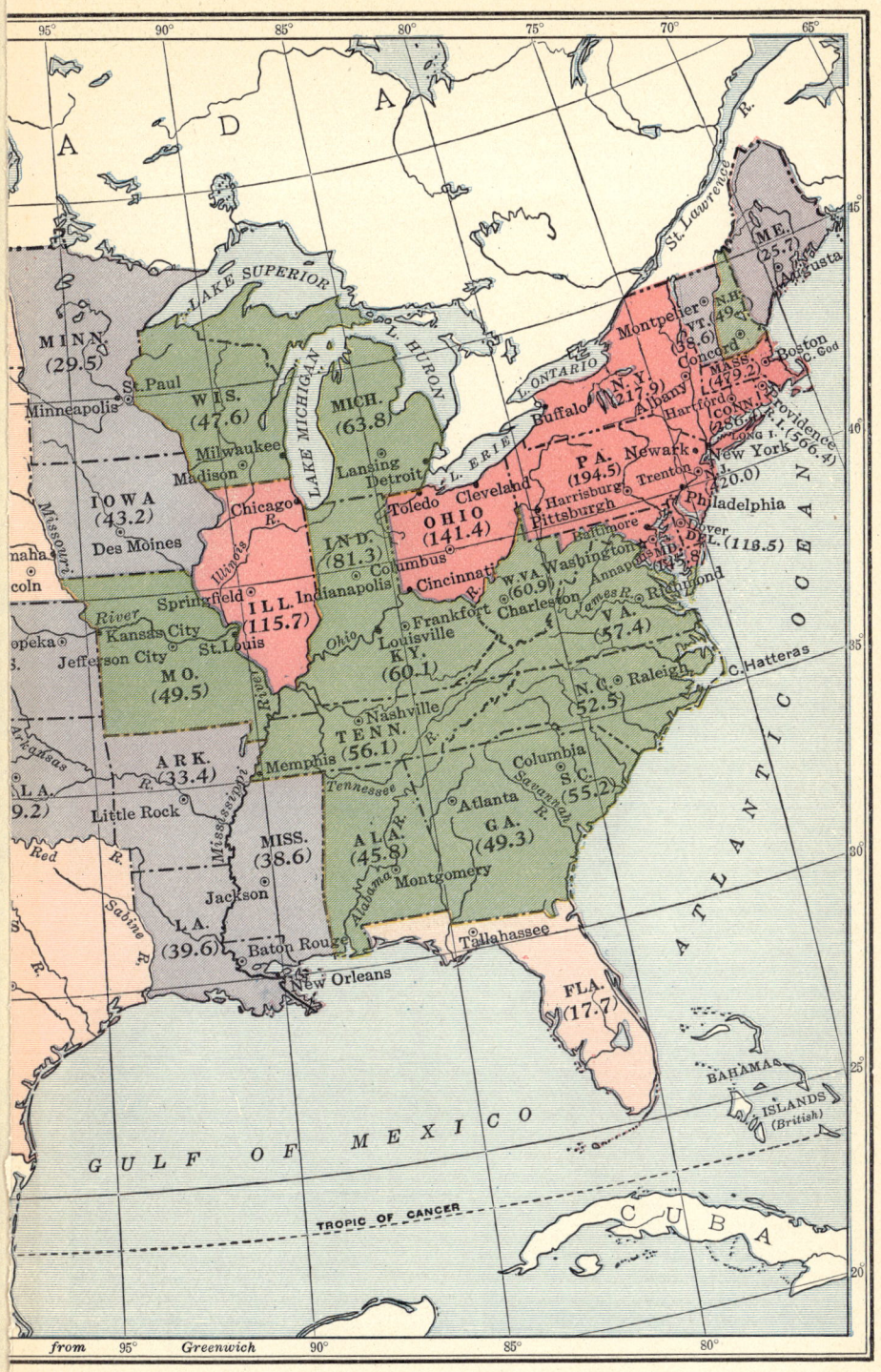

into their former positions in factories, mills, mines, offices, schools, or stores. Others, for one reason or another, were unable to get their old jobs back. It was, indeed, a period of great strain and anxiety, of poverty and worry, for many of the American people. As the months of 1919 and 1920 passed, however, most of the huge number of men mustered for war were slowly absorbed into the peace-time occupations of the country.

2. *The government's problem of rewarding and protecting the soldiers*

Almost at once arose the question of rewards for the returned soldiers. Many people, including Representatives in the Congress, felt that the soldiers should be given pensions or bonuses or life-insurance policies for their service to their country. It was pointed out that many of them had given up profitable work to enter the war and that they had received small pay while they were in the service — at least, small in comparison with the high wages paid to civilians in industry and in government work and with the huge profits that had been made by business men during the war. Thus the demand rose from many quarters that the soldiers should be given something in the way of a bonus. Bills granting them aid were presented in Congress, and several were passed only to be vetoed by President Harding and later by President Coolidge.

Pressure upon Congressmen steadily increased, however, and in 1924 they passed a bill over the veto of President Coolidge, giving each American soldier a paid-up life-insurance policy. Thus the wives, children, and other dependents of the soldiers were given some degree of protection for the future.

3. *The problem of government ownership of railways and other public utilities*

The return of peace raised another important problem of government: What should be done with the railways and other public utilities? These had been operated by the government during the war. For the first time in our history, all the transportation of the country had been woven together into a unified system. Many people came to the conclusion that as the government had efficiently handled this great utility during the last year of the war it proved that the American people as a whole should own and operate railroads, telegraphs, telephones, power plants, and other basic utilities upon which the lives of the people depended. They pointed out that the public owned and operated most of the water-supply systems of the country. Why should not these other necessary utilities be carried on in the same way?

Public opinion, however, was greatly divided on the question. The private owners of the utilities naturally were opposed to giving up their property to the government. Business men generally were against public ownership. Although much was said in favor of it, by 1920 it was clear that the majority of our representatives in the government were in favor of private ownership. In that year Congress passed the Transportation Act, which dissolved the United States Railroad Administration and returned the transportation system to its private owners.

4. *Should the government own and operate a merchant marine?*

Congress faced similar questions with respect to the merchant marine which had been built up during the war by the government. Should the national government continue to own and operate merchant ships? Should it aid private shipowners? For many years these questions had been answered in the negative. The United States had never adopted the European policies of owning and operating merchant ships or of aiding private citizens in doing so. Partly because of this, American merchant fleets had long been much smaller than those of Great Britain and other European nations. For many years, therefore, attempts had been made to persuade the government to pay subsidies (grants of money) to American shippers engaged in the ocean-carrying trade. Those who proposed such subsidies defended them on the ground that they would provide experienced American sailors who could be employed in our navy in the event of war.

The question of government ownership and operation of the merchant marine was eventually settled by the Jones Act of 1920, which directed the Shipping Board to sell all these government-owned vessels to private corporations "as soon as practicable."

Thus once more the American business interests through Congress declared themselves in favor of private ownership and operation of public utilities.

Nevertheless, the question remains to be faced in the future: *Under which system of ownership and operation of basic public utilities — public or private — will the security and advantage of all the people be better conserved?*

5. *The difficult problems of American farmers*

No group of Americans faced more serious problems of getting a living at the close of the war than did the farmers. During the war itself they had become more prosperous than at any previous time in American history. From 1914 to 1920 European countries had purchased from them stupendous quantities of wheat, corn, oats, rye, potatoes, and other agricultural products. Prices of these products rose, and American farmers made large profits. Their lands increased astonishingly in value, especially in the great grain regions of the Middle West. Land which had formerly been valued at, say, $200 an acre was sold and resold during the last years of the war at $300, $400, even $600 an acre. The farmers were indeed very well off until 1920.

By the end of 1920, however, the people of Europe had reëntered the peace-time occupations and were producing most of their own food. Hence they bought decreasing amounts of American farm products, and soon our farmers found themselves in serious straits. Prices of products as well as of land fell rapidly. Thousands of farmers lost money, sold their farm land, and went to live in cities. Others eked out a living as best they could on their farms.

As a result there arose a widespread demand that the government do something to help the farmer. Most students of economic life were convinced that laws would help the farmer little. They felt that a long study of the whole problem of producing and selling food to the people of the world should be made by the best experts. Nevertheless, Congress tried to relieve the farmers temporarily by passing laws to aid them in forming coöperative associations and in borrowing money from banks. Other proposals were made, among them bills to fix prices on farm products. One such bill, the McNary-Haugen Bill, was passed by Congress in 1927, but was vetoed by President Coolidge. To the present time neither agricultural experts, economists, nor government officials have been able to work out satisfactory plans for aiding the farmers to carry on their farms profitably. Thus we have another difficult problem which the American people now confront: *How can matters be arranged so that the farmers shall receive a fair share of the national income?*

6. *With the return of peace business men demanded a still higher tariff on imports*

In 1921, as you know, the Republicans once more secured control through the presidency and Congress. They drew up a new tariff law. Although American industries were now among the most powerful enterprises in the world, the owners were demanding still more protection. Furthermore, new industries had grown up during the war,— the manufacture of dyestuffs, for example,— and the owners of these businesses demanded a tariff high enough to keep out European-made goods. In 1922 the Fordney-McCumber Act was signed by President Harding. This law raised the tariffs so high on a long list of raw materials, farm products, and manufactured goods that many European products could no longer be sold in the United States.

This tariff law and its successor, the Hawley-Smoot Act, are having serious international results. Other countries are setting up similar tariffs against foreign-made goods, including those of the United States. Here we have another economic problem of tremendous importance to the American people as a whole.

7. *Problems of immigration*

During the years immediately preceding 1914 nearly 1,000,000 foreign people were being received into the United States each year. The vast majority of these were from Italy, Russia, Poland, and other southern and eastern European regions. Then the World War stopped this flood of European immigrants into American ports.

At the close of the war immigration began again. In the meantime public opinion in the United States had grown strongly in favor of restricting it. Laboring men demanded restriction on the ground that the incoming immigrants worked for small wages and thereby reduced the wages of native citizens. Many careful students of immigration also urged that immigration be restricted in order that the millions of foreign-born already in America could learn our language and be assimilated into our national life.

Congress responded to the pressure brought to bear by various groups of people and in 1921 passed the first law which limited the number of immigrants that were to enter the country. This law permitted to enter each year only 3 per cent of the number of foreign-born persons of any one nationality who were living in the United States in 1910. It greatly reduced the flood of immigration. Nevertheless, many native citizens maintained that it still permitted too many southern and eastern Europeans to enter and not enough northwestern Europeans. Hence in 1924 Congress passed another law, which permitted only 2 per cent of any one nationality to enter in any one year and based the computation upon the number of that nationality living in the United States in 1890 instead of 1910. It also forbade the immigration of all Japanese, and provided that after July 1, 1927, the total number of immigrants who could enter in any one year be reduced to 150,000. Thus, many students think, the country will be given more time to assimilate the foreign-born who are already here.

These events remind us, therefore, of another important problem before our people: *How shall scores of nationalities and races be assimilated into one unified nation?*

8. *The problem of increasing the efficiency and economy of government*

At the close of the war our government found itself saddled with a gigantic national debt. The annual interest alone on this debt was approximately as large as the entire annual expenditures of the government just before the war, that is, $1,000,000,000. Each of the three Republican presidents — Harding, Coolidge, and Hoover — who have held office since the war have faced the problem of reducing this debt. All three adopted the slogan of "economy and efficiency" and attempted to set up plans to carry it out.

In President Harding's administration an important step was taken to reduce waste in government, namely, the establishment of a national budget. In 1922 the Bureau of the Budget was set up in Washington, which was given charge of estimating the financial needs of the government. Charles G. Dawes, the same banker who served as head of the German Reparations Commission and as vice president under President Coolidge, was the first director of this bureau. The operation of the national government became still more businesslike. Appropriations made by Congress for the carrying on of various kinds of government work were based upon carefully estimated needs.

Under this plan and because of other economies set up by President Harding and President Coolidge, waste in government was reduced and efficiency increased. Each year the Department of the Treasury, under Secretary Andrew Mellon, reported a large surplus and a considerable reduction of the war debt. As government expenses were reduced and the national debt was cut down, taxes were also lowered. Special war taxes were repealed, and year by year income taxes declined. Thus the eight years of the Harding and Coolidge administrations (1921–1929) came to be regarded as an era of great national prosperity.

9. *Problems of the relation between employers and employees*

During the war the demand for workers to satisfy the war needs was so great that the labor unions were able to secure higher wages and shorter hours than ever before in the history of the country. In 1916 Congress passed the Adamson Act, giving railway employees an eight-hour day and extra pay for overtime. In most occupations the eight-hour day was established by 1920.

In the business depression that followed the war employers insisted that wages be reduced. To this workingmen would not consent, and wherever wage reductions were made strikes occurred. Great industrial unrest developed throughout the country. In a single year (1919) there were more than 3000 strikes in the nation's industries. Some of these were local, but two were of nation-wide scope — the steel strike and the coal strike. In the former 200,000 men left their jobs, and in the latter twice that number refused to work.

Such examples of industrial unrest show us the continued seriousness of problems of labor in the great basic industries.

10. *Problems caused by illegal powers*

In every epoch of America's march toward democracy powerful groups of private citizens have played a dominant rôle in carrying on the government.

We have learned that unscrupulous individuals stole land, forests, mines, and other natural resources and privileges from the government. Particularly did that happen whenever our government went to war. It was so at the close of the Civil War, and history repeated itself at the close of the World War.

Scandals in national government. It was not until after the death of President Harding in 1923 that it was discovered that a ring of national politicians was robbing the government of huge sums of money by leasing government oil lands. Valuable government oil reserves at Elk Hills, California, and Teapot Dome, Wyoming, had been set aside for the use of the navy. It was later discovered that in 1922 President Harding's Secretary of the Interior, Albert B. Fall, had leased these oil fields to private oil speculators, one of whom openly said he could make $100,000,000 out of his share. An investigation revealed that there had been secret illegal relations between government officials and the oil corporations. After long controversy the United States Supreme Court ordered that the lands be returned to the control of the national government.

The startling spread of crime in our larger cities. An even more difficult problem of illegal power which you will probably consider in your later studies is the outlaw rule of criminal gangs in our metropolitan centers. In several of the larger cities gangs of criminals have organized what are called "rackets" in more than 60 different kinds of businesses. In each of these businesses criminal gangsters are obtaining regular tribute from the owners under threat to murder them or bomb their buildings if the money is not paid.

Nearly all the larger cities are influenced to some extent by these illegal groups. In spite of efforts made by citizens little progress is being made in controlling the increasing crime wave. Here, therefore, is another of our difficult and important problems of government.

11. *Problems of improving government by political parties*

The presidential election of 1924. Some people believed that a solution could be found for some of these problems by a new political party representing the mass of the people. For many years Senator Robert M. La Follette, for example, was an ardent advocate of such a new party. In 1924 he was a candidate for the presidency on a platform designed to unite the Republican and Democratic "progressives."

Trouble had long been brewing in both the old parties because there were many people who believed that the party organizations were too largely controlled by the big business interests. The progressive wings of the two parties were largely made up of groups of farmers and workingmen and, here and there, business and professional men. They demanded in general lower tariffs, higher taxes on big incomes, more control by the government over the railroads and industry, and other measures intended to benefit the mass of the people. The conservatives, on the other hand, rather openly favored the business interests. They favored a "hands off" business policy and high protective tariffs. These were not issues which divided the two parties from each other. They were issues which revealed differences of opinion within the parties.

The election of 1924, therefore, was a three-cornered fight. Calvin Coolidge, who as vice president had become president when President Harding died, was the candidate on the Republican ticket. John W. Davis was the Democratic candidate, and Senator La Follette led an independent Progressive party.

Although the progressives of all parties were joined in the

support of La Follette, they polled less than 5,000,000 votes out of nearly 29,000,000. The Republicans swept the country and elected Calvin Coolidge.

The presidential election of 1928. Then came four years of great prosperity under the presidency of Calvin Coolidge. In 1928, therefore, many Republicans urged that he be nominated again. Coolidge declined, and the party nominated Herbert

© Underwood & Underwood, N.Y.
Fig. 246. Calvin Coolidge

© Harris and Ewing
Fig. 247. Herbert C. Hoover

Hoover, Secretary of Commerce under Coolidge. Hoover had been a successful mining engineer, and during the course of the World War and afterwards he had attained world renown for his efficient organizing of European relief work. The Democrats nominated Alfred E. Smith, who was then completing his fourth term as governor of New York State. Although several other parties presented candidates, the real struggle in this election also took place between the two old parties. After a strenuous campaign the Republicans won, overwhelmingly electing Mr. Hoover as the thirty-first president of the United States.

Today, as formerly, the American experiment in democracy is based on the selection of officials by popular election and through political parties. Most of the voters of the country continue to vote within one of the two major parties. It is clear that all recent attempts to establish political control through a new party have failed. In 60 years no issue has been advocated by new parties which has been strong enough to attract a majority of the eligible voters from the old parties.

Some leaders are suggesting radical changes in government, even the abolition of political parties. Government, say these experimenters, should be carried on scientifically by trained and experienced people. It should not be conducted by private organized interests and unscrupulous politicians who exploit the government for their own gain.

In the meantime fewer people are going to the polls. The American people as a whole are taking less and less interest in political affairs.

Thus we have another problem: *How can the American people be aroused to participate in political affairs?*

12. *How far shall the majority of the people control the minority?*

The American experiment in democracy is based upon the belief that the decision of the majority should rule. If public opinion were sharply divided, this might mean that 51 per cent of a group could control the other 49. To be sure, in practice the division is rarely so close, perhaps never, but such is the principle. Partly to relieve a large minority from the rule of a small majority, certain important matters require more than a bare majority. For example, Congress cannot propose an amendment to the Constitution except by a vote of two thirds of both Houses. Many laws, however, are passed by narrow majorities, both in the Federal Congress and in state legislatures. Whether the majorities are large or small, controversies often arise because a minority attempts to repeal laws of which it does not approve.

An example: national prohibition. The difficulties of majority rule have been revealed in the case of the Eighteenth Amendment (see Appendix), which prohibits the manufacture, sale, and distribution of intoxicating liquor. There was no question in this case about the size of the majority in favor of the amendment.

The vote by Congress exceeded three to one, and the amendment, required to be ratified by 36 states, was in fact ratified by 46.

For more than 50 years sentiment had accumulated against the use of strong drink. As early as 1872 the Prohibition party was formed and presented a candidate for the presidency. In 1874, under the leadership of Frances E. Willard, the Woman's Christian Temperance Union was organized. In 1895 the Anti-Saloon League was established. By 1919, 26 states had adopted state-wide prohibition.

Meanwhile in December, 1917, Congress proposed the Eighteenth Amendment. It was ratified by the states in 1919 and came into force in 1920.

For a number of years the minority has made increasing attempts to repeal or revise the amendment and the laws based upon it. Thus prohibition has frequently been made a political issue in state and national elections.

Both in the early development of sentiment in favor of prohibition and in the immediate problem with respect to repeal or revision of the Eighteenth Amendment, we have an admirable illustration of majority rule and minority protest.

Conclusion: Insistent Problems of American Life

As you have studied the history of America's march toward democracy, you have realized that difficult problems have always confronted the people. This is true today as it has been true in the past. Some of the problems of the moment are old problems in new forms. Some of them are peculiar to the period in which we are living. Each year in the immediate future will bring forward new plans and experiments, new attempts to solve these problems, as well as new problems. As Americans you are in duty bound to study these problems carefully to become informed concerning them and, whenever possible, to contribute to their solution.

We shall bring this chapter to a close by stating, without an attempt at discussion, a few of the insistent problems of American life. For the most part these problems may be thought of as either economic or cultural.

1. Difficult problems of economic life

First, the economic problems:

1. *The increasing difficulty of finding work.* Today, in the industrial nations of the world, not less than 12,000,000 workers are out of work; the lives of not less than 50,000,000 people are thereby affected. The invention of new machines and the lack of careful planning in production of goods and food are throwing people out of work more rapidly than new jobs can be created for them.

2. *The rapid multiplication of human wants.* "High power" advertising and the increase in the number of attractive things surrounding our people constantly cause them to buy more than they can afford. More and more people are living on credit, making the future pay for the present.

3. *The unequal division of the national income among the people.* We have learned of the low standard of living of the masses as compared with the wasteful and extravagant mode of living of a small wealthy class. How can government help produce a fairer division of our enormous wealth and rapidly increasing national income?

4. *The difficulty of the farmers in their efforts to secure a fair share of the national income.* No problem of the distribution of the national wealth and income is more important than that which deals with the share of the farmer. Can government help to arrange matters so that the farmers can get a fair return for their labor?

2. Equally difficult problems of cultural life

Paralleling these problems of economic life are equally difficult questions of social and cultural life.

What shall the rank and file of the people do with their leisure time? Up to the present it is being spent in restless entertainment. Our people rush about over the countryside in automobiles. Millions crowd the football, baseball, and prize-fight amphitheaters. Millions more watch the "movies" each night in the week. Still other millions listen to the radio or read the sensational newspapers and magazines.

Noting these tendencies, thoughtful students of American culture are raising important questions. Here we cannot discuss them; we can merely state them briefly.

1. *How can more people be persuaded to take more active part in physical recreation?*
2. *How can more Americans be brought to participate actively in the arts?*
3. *How can the craft spirit be cultivated in our people?*
4. *How, with the increasing growth of manufacturing and trading cities, can country home life be secured that will permit people generally to enjoy natural beauty?*
5. *How can the increasing restlessness of the people be reduced?*
6. *How can we offset the growing dangers to American homes?*

Government agencies, commissions of expert economists, and bureaus of economic research are collecting information about the economic problems, and sociologists, welfare workers, and publicists are studying the cultural problems. But all these will fail unless the people are able to appreciate and to apply the results of their findings. The most far reaching, therefore, of all the plans proposed by thoughtful students for coping intelligently with the insistent problems of American life is the development of the finest possible education for our people. This will involve (in fact it already involves) childhood education, the education of youth, and the continuing education of adults. As our national wealth increases, our best investment of it will be in education. As the leisure time of adults increases, the best expenditure of that time will be in education.

Thus a great opportunity and a great obligation confront the youth of the country — the opportunity and obligation to help build up the finest possible system of education. One of the purposes of this system should be broader tolerance, wider understanding, and a more genuine goodwill among all our people. Thus may America continue her onward march toward democracy.

APPENDIX A

DECLARATION OF INDEPENDENCE[1]

IN CONGRESS, JULY 4, 1776

A DECLARATION BY THE REPRESENTATIVES OF THE UNITED STATES OF AMERICA, IN CONGRESS ASSEMBLED

WHEN, in the course of human events, it becomes necessary for one people to dissolve the political bands which have connected them with another, and to assume, among the powers of the earth, the separate and equal station to which the laws of nature and of nature's God entitle them, a decent respect to the opinions of mankind requires that they should declare the causes which impel them to the separation.

We hold these truths to be self-evident: — That all men are created equal; that they are endowed by their Creator with certain unalienable rights; that among these are life, liberty, and the pursuit of happiness. That, to secure these rights, governments are instituted among men, deriving their just powers from the consent of the governed; that, whenever any form of government becomes destructive of these ends, it is the right of the people to alter or to abolish it, and to institute a new government, laying its foundation on such principles, and organizing its powers in such form, as to them shall seem most likely to effect their safety and happiness. Prudence, indeed, will dictate, that governments long established should not be changed for light and transient causes; and accordingly all experience hath shown that mankind are more disposed to suffer while evils are sufferable, than to right themselves by abolishing the forms to which they are accustomed. But when a long train of abuses and usurpations, pursuing invariably the same object, evinces a design to reduce them under absolute despotism, it is their right, it is their duty, to throw off such government, and to provide new guards for their future security. Such has been the patient sufferance of these colonies; and such is now the necessity which constrains them to alter their former systems of government. The history of the present King of Great Britain is a history of repeated injuries and usurpations, all having in direct object the establishment of an absolute tyranny over these states. To prove this, let facts be submitted to a candid world.

He has refused his assent to laws the most wholesome and necessary for the public good.

---

[1] The original copy of the Declaration of Independence is kept in the Department of State in Washington. The Declaration was adopted July 4, 1776, and was signed by the members representing the thirteen states August 2, 1776. John Hancock, whose name appears first among the signers, was president of the Congress.

He has forbidden his governors to pass laws of immediate and pressing importance, unless suspended in their operation till his assent should be obtained; and when so suspended, he has utterly neglected to attend to them.

He has refused to pass other laws for the accommodation of large districts of people, unless those people would relinquish the right of representation in the legislature — a right inestimable to them, and formidable to tyrants only.

He has called together legislative bodies at places unusual, uncomfortable, and distant from the depository of their public records, for the sole purpose of fatiguing them into compliance with his measure.

He has dissolved representative houses repeatedly, for opposing, with manly firmness, his invasions on the rights of the people.

He has refused, for a long time after such dissolutions, to cause others to be elected, whereby the legislative powers, incapable of annihilation, have returned to the people at large for their exercise; the State remaining, in the mean time, exposed to all the dangers of invasions from without, and convulsions within.

He has endeavored to prevent the population of these States; for that purpose obstructing the laws for the naturalization of foreigners; refusing to pass others to encourage their migration hither, and raising the conditions of new appropriations of lands.

He has obstructed the administration of justice, by refusing his assent to laws for establishing judiciary powers.

He has made judges dependent on his will alone for the tenure of their offices, and the amount and payment of their salaries.

He has erected a multitude of new offices, and sent hither swarms of officers to harass our people and eat out their substance.

He has kept among us in times of peace, standing armies, without the consent of our legislatures.

He has affected to render the military independent of, and superior to, the civil power.

He has combined with others to subject us to a jurisdiction foreign to our constitutions, and unacknowledged by our laws; giving his assent to their acts of pretended legislation:

For quartering large bodies of armed troops among us;

For protecting them, by a mock trial, from punishment for any murders which they should commit on the inhabitants of these States;

For cutting off our trade with all parts of the world;

For imposing taxes on us without our consent;

For depriving us, in many cases, of the benefits of trial by jury;

For transporting us beyond seas, to be tried for pretended offences;

For abolishing the free system of English laws in a neighboring province, establishing therein an arbitrary government, and enlarging its boundaries, so as to render it at once an example and fit instrument for introducing the same absolute rule into these colonies;

For taking away our charters, abolishing our most valuable laws, and altering, fundamentally, the forms of our governments;

For suspending our own legislatures, and declaring themselves invested with power to legislate for us in all cases whatsoever.

He has abdicated government here, by declaring us out of his protection, and waging war against us.

He has plundered our seas, ravaged our coasts, burned our towns, and destroyed the lives of our people.

He is at this time transporting large armies of foreign mercenaries to complete the works of death, desolation and tyranny, already begun with circumstances of cruelty and perfidy scarcely paralleled in the most barbarous ages, and totally unworthy the head of a civilized nation.

He has constrained our fellow-citizens, taken captive on the high seas, to bear arms against their country, to become the executioners of their friends and brethren, or to fall themselves by their hands.

He has excited domestic insurrection among us, and has endeavored to bring on the inhabitants of our frontiers the merciless Indian savages, whose known rule of warfare is an undistinguished destruction of all ages, sexes, and conditions.

In every stage of these oppressions we have petitioned for redress in the most humble terms; our repeated petitions have been answered only by repeated injury. A prince whose character is thus marked by every act which may define a tyrant, is unfit to be the ruler of a free people.

Nor have we been wanting in our attentions to our British brethren. We have warned them, from time to time, of attempts by their legislature to extend an unwarrantable jurisdiction over us. We have reminded them of the circumstances of our emigration and settlement here. We have appealed to their native justice and magnanimity; and we have conjured them, by the ties of our common kindred, to disavow these usurpations, which would inevitably interrupt our connections and correspondence. They, too, have been deaf to the voice of justice and consanguinity. We must, therefore, acquiesce in the necessity which denounces our separation, and hold them, as we hold the rest of mankind, enemies in war, in peace friends.

We, therefore, the Representatives of the United States of America, in General Congress assembled, appealing to the Supreme Judge of the world for the rectitude of our intentions, do, in the name and by the authority of the good people of these colonies, solemnly publish and declare, That these united Colonies are, and of right ought to be, free and independent states; that they are absolved from all allegiance to the British crown, and that all political connection between them and the state of Great Britain is, and ought to be, totally dissolved; and that, as free and independent states, they have full power to levy war, conclude peace, contract alliances, establish commerce, and do all other acts and things which independent states may of right do. And, for the support of this declaration, with a firm reliance on the protection of Divine Providence, we mutually pledge to each other our lives, our fortunes, and our sacred honor.

The foregoing Declaration was, by order of Congress, engrossed, and signed by the following members:

JOHN HANCOCK

NEW HAMPSHIRE
JOSIAH BARTLETT
WILLIAM WHIPPLE
MATTHEW THORNTON

MASSACHUSETTS BAY
SAMUEL ADAMS
JOHN ADAMS
ROBERT TREAT PAINE
ELBRIDGE GERRY

RHODE ISLAND
STEPHEN HOPKINS
WILLIAM ELLERY

CONNECTICUT
ROGER SHERMAN
SAMUEL HUNTINGTON
WILLIAM WILLIAMS
OLIVER WOLCOTT

NEW YORK
WILLIAM FLOYD
PHILIP LIVINGSTON
FRANCIS LEWIS
LEWIS MORRIS

NEW JERSEY
RICHARD STOCKTON
JOHN WITHERSPOON
FRANCIS HOPKINSON
JOHN HART
ABRAHAM CLARK

PENNSYLVANIA
ROBERT MORRIS
BENJAMIN RUSH
BENJAMIN FRANKLIN
JOHN MORTON
GEORGE CLYMER
JAMES SMITH
GEORGE TAYLOR
JAMES WILSON
GEORGE ROSS

DELAWARE
CÆSAR RODNEY
GEORGE READ
THOMAS M'KEAN

MARYLAND
SAMUEL CHASE
WILLIAM PACA
THOMAS STONE

CHARLES CARROLL, of Carrollton

VIRGINIA
GEORGE WYTHE
RICHARD HENRY LEE
THOMAS JEFFERSON
BENJAMIN HARRISON
THOMAS NELSON, JR.
FRANCIS LIGHTFOOT LEE
CARTER BRAXTON

NORTH CAROLINA
WILLIAM HOOPER
JOSEPH HEWES
JOHN PENN

SOUTH CAROLINA
EDWARD RUTLEDGE
THOMAS HAYWARD
THOMAS LYNCH, JR.
ARTHUR MIDDLETON

GEORGIA
BUTTON GWINNETT
LYMAN HALL
GEORGE WALTON

Resolved, That copies of the Declaration be sent to the several assemblies, conventions, and committees, or councils of safety, and to the several commanding officers of the continental troops; that it be proclaimed in each of the United States, at the head of the army.

APPENDIX B

CONSTITUTION OF THE UNITED STATES

Preamble

WE, THE people of the United States, in order to form a more perfect union, establish justice, insure domestic tranquillity, provide for the common defense, promote the general welfare, and secure the blessings of liberty to ourselves and our posterity, do ordain and establish this CONSTITUTION for the United States of America.

ARTICLE I. LEGISLATIVE DEPARTMENT

SECTION 1. CONGRESS

All legislative powers herein granted shall be vested in a Congress of the United States, which shall consist of a Senate and House of Representatives.[1]

SECTION 2. HOUSE OF REPRESENTATIVES

Election of Members. The House of Representatives shall be composed of members chosen every second year by the people of the several States, and the electors in each State shall have the qualifications requisite for electors of the most numerous branch of the State Legislature.

Qualifications. No person shall be a representative who shall not have attained to the age of twenty-five years, and been seven years a citizen of the United States, and who shall not, when elected, be an inhabitant of that State in which he shall be chosen.

Apportionment. Representatives and direct taxes shall be apportioned among the several States which may be included within this Union, according to their respective numbers,[2] which shall be determined by adding to the whole number of free persons, including those bound to service for a term of years, and excluding Indians not taxed, three-fifths of all other persons.[3] The actual enumeration shall be made within three years after the first meeting of the

---

[1] The term of each Congress is two years. It assembles on the first Monday in December and "expires at noon of the fourth of March next succeeding the beginning of its second regular session, when a new Congress begins."

[2] The apportionment under the census of 1910 is one representative for every 212,407 persons.

[3] The word "persons" refers to slaves. The word "slave" nowhere appears in the Constitution. This paragraph has been amended (Amendments XIII and XIV) and is no longer in force.

Congress of the United States, and within every subsequent term of ten years, in such manner as they shall by law direct. The number of representatives shall not exceed one for every thirty thousand, but each State shall have at least one representative: and until such enumeration shall be made, the State of New Hampshire shall be entitled to choose three; Massachusetts, eight; Rhode Island and Providence Plantations, one; Connecticut, five; New York, six; New Jersey, four; Pennsylvania, eight; Delaware, one; Maryland, six; Virginia, ten; North Carolina, five; South Carolina, five; and Georgia, three.

Vacancies. When vacancies happen in the representation from any State, the executive authority [1] thereof shall issue writs of election to fill such vacancies.

Officers. Impeachment. The House of Representatives shall choose their Speaker [2] and other officers; and shall have the sole power of impeachment.

Section 3. Senate

Number of Senators: Election. The Senate of the United States shall be composed of two senators from each State, chosen by the Legislature thereof, for six years; and each senator shall have one vote. [Repealed in 1913 by Amendment XVII.]

Classification. Immediately after they shall be assembled in consequence of the first election, they shall be divided as equally as may be into three classes. The seats of the senators of the first class shall be vacated at the expiration of the second year; of the second class, at the expiration of the fourth year; of the third class, at the expiration of the sixth year, so that one-third may be chosen every second year; and if vacancies happen by resignation, or otherwise, during the recess of the Legislature of any State, the executive [1] thereof may make temporary appointments until the next meeting of the Legislature, which shall then fill such vacancies. [Modified by Amendment XVII.]

Qualifications. No person shall be a senator who shall not have attained to the age of thirty years, and been nine years a citizen of the United States, and who shall not, when elected, be an inhabitant of that State for which he shall be chosen.

President of Senate. The Vice-President of the United States shall be president of the Senate, but shall have no vote, unless they be equally divided.

Officers. The Senate shall choose their other officers, and also a president *pro tempore*, in the absence of the Vice-President, or when he shall exercise the office of President of the United States.

Trials of Impeachment. The Senate shall have the sole power to try all impeachments: When sitting for that purpose, they shall be on oath or affirmation. When the President of the United States is tried, the Chief-Justice shall preside: and no person shall be convicted without the concurrence of two-thirds of the members present.

---

[1] Governor.

[2] The Speaker, who presides, is one of the representatives; the other officers — clerk, sergeant-at-arms, postmaster, chaplain, doorkeeper, etc.— are not.

APPENDIX B

Judgment in Case of Conviction. Judgment in cases of impeachment shall not extend further than to removal from office, and disqualification to hold and enjoy any office of honor, trust, or profit under the United States; but the party convicted shall nevertheless be liable and subject to indictment, trial, judgment, and punishment, according to law.

Section 4. Both Houses

Manner of electing Members. The times, places, and manner of holding elections for senators and representatives shall be prescribed in each State by the Legislature thereof; but the Congress may at any time, by law, make or alter such regulations, except as to the places of choosing senators.[1]

Meetings of Congress. The Congress shall assemble at least once in every year, and such meeting shall be on the first Monday in December, unless they shall by law appoint a different day.

Section 5. The Houses separately

Organization. Each house shall be the judge of the elections, returns, and qualifications of its own members, and a majority of each shall constitute a quorum to do business; but a smaller number may adjourn from day to day, and may be authorized to compel the attendance of absent members, in such manner, and under such penalties, as each house may provide.

Rules. Each house may determine the rules of its proceedings, punish its members for disorderly behavior, and, with the concurrence of two-thirds, expel a member.

Journal. Each house shall keep a journal of its proceedings, and from time to time publish the same, excepting such parts as may in their judgment require secrecy, and the yeas and nays of the members of either house on any question shall, at the desire of one-fifth of those present, be entered on the journal.

Adjournment. Neither house, during the session of Congress, shall, without the consent of the other, adjourn for more than three days, nor to any other place than that in which the two houses shall be sitting.

Section 6. Privileges and Disabilities of Members

Pay and Privileges of Members. The senators and representatives shall receive a compensation for their services, to be ascertained by law, and paid out of the treasury of the United States. They shall in all cases, except treason, felony, and breach of the peace, be privileged from arrest during their attendance at the session of their respective houses, and in going to and returning from the same; and for any speech or debate in either house, they shall not be questioned in any other place.

Prohibitions on Members. No senator or representative shall, during the time for which he was elected, be appointed to any civil office under the au-

---

[1] This is to prevent Congress from fixing the places of meeting of the state legislatures.

thority of the United States, which shall have been created, or the emoluments whereof shall have been increased, during such time; and no person holding any office under the United States shall be a member of either house during his continuance in office.

Section 7. Method of passing Laws

Revenue Bills. All bills for raising revenue shall originate in the House of Representatives; but the Senate may propose or concur with amendments as on other bills.

How Bills become Laws. Every bill which shall have passed the House of Representatives and the Senate shall, before it become a law, be presented to the President of the United States; if he approve, he shall sign it, but if not, he shall return it, with his objections, to that house in which it shall have originated, who shall enter the objections at large on their journal, and proceed to reconsider it. If after such reconsideration, two-thirds of that house shall agree to pass the bill, it shall be sent, together with the objections, to the other house, by which it shall likewise be reconsidered, and if approved by two-thirds of that house, it shall become a law. But in all such cases the votes of both houses shall be determined by yeas and nays, and the names of the persons voting for and against the bill shall be entered on the journal of each house respectively. If any bill shall not be returned by the President within ten days (Sundays excepted) after it shall have been presented to him, the same shall be a law, in like manner as if he had signed it, unless the Congress by their adjournment prevent its return, in which case it shall not be a law.

Resolutions, etc. Every order, resolution, or vote to which the concurrence of the Senate and House of Representatives may be necessary (except on a question of adjournment) shall be presented to the President of the United States; and before the same shall take effect, shall be approved by him, or being disapproved by him, shall be repassed by two-thirds of the Senate and House of Representatives, according to the rules and limitations prescribed in the case of a bill.

Section 8. Powers granted to Congress

Powers of Congress. The Congress shall have power:

To lay and collect taxes, duties, imposts, and excises, to pay the debts and provide for the common defense and general welfare of the United States; but all duties, imposts, and excises shall be uniform throughout the United States;

To borrow money on the credit of the United States;

To regulate commerce with foreign nations, and among the several States, and with the Indian tribes;

To establish a uniform rule of naturalization, and uniform laws on the subject of bankruptcies throughout the United States;

To coin money, regulate the value thereof, and of foreign coin, and fix the standard of weights and measures;

To provide for the punishment of counterfeiting the securities and current coin of the United States;

To establish post-offices and post-roads;

To promote the progress of science and useful arts, by securing, for limited times, to authors and inventors the exclusive right to their respective writings and discoveries;

To constitute tribunals inferior to the Supreme Court;

To define and punish piracies and felonies committed on the high seas, and offenses against the law of nations;

To declare war, grant letters of marque and reprisal,[1] and make rules concerning captures on land and water;

To raise and support armies, but no appropriation of money to that use shall be for a longer term than two years;

To provide and maintain a navy;

To make rules for the government and regulation of the land and naval forces;

To provide for calling forth the militia to execute the laws of the Union, suppress insurrections and repel invasions;

To provide for organizing, arming, and disciplining the militia, and for governing such part of them as may be employed in the service of the United States, reserving to the States respectively the appointment of the officers, and the authority of training the militia according to the discipline prescribed by Congress;

To exercise exclusive legislation in all cases whatsoever over such district (not exceeding ten miles square) as may, by cession of particular States, and the acceptance of Congress, become the seat of the government of the United States,[2] and to exercise like authority over all places purchased by the consent of the Legislature of the State in which the same shall be, for the erection of forts, magazines, arsenals, dockyards, and other needful buildings; — And

Implied Powers. To make all laws which shall be necessary and proper for carrying into execution the foregoing powers, and all other powers vested by this Constitution in the government of the United States, or in any department or officer thereof.[3]

Section 9. Powers forbidden to the United States

Absolute Prohibitions on Congress. The migration or importation of such persons as any of the States now existing shall think proper to admit, shall not be prohibited by the Congress prior to the year one thousand eight hundred and eight, but a tax or duty may be imposed on such importation, not exceeding ten dollars for each person.[4]

---

[1] Letters granted by the government to private citizens in time of war, authorizing them, under certain conditions, to capture the ships of the enemy.

[2] The District of Columbia.

[3] This is the famous elastic clause of the Constitution.

[4] This refers to the foreign slave trade. "Persons" means "slaves." In 1808 Congress prohibited the importation of slaves. This clause is, of course, no longer in force.

The privilege of the writ of habeas corpus [1] shall not be suspended, unless when in cases of rebellion or invasion the public safety may require it.

No bill of attainder [2] or ex-post-facto law [3] shall be passed.

No capitation or other direct tax shall be laid, unless in proportion to the census or enumeration hereinbefore directed to be taken. [Extended by Amendment XVI.]

No tax or duty shall be laid on articles exported from any State.

No preference shall be given by any regulation of commerce or revenue to the ports of one State over those of another; nor shall vessels bound to, or from, one State, be obliged to enter, clear, or pay duties in another.

No money shall be drawn from the treasury but in consequence of appropriations made by law; and a regular statement and account of the receipts and expenditures of all public money shall be published from time to time.

No title of nobility shall be granted by the United States: And no person holding any office of profit or trust under them, shall, without the consent of the Congress, accept of any present, emolument, office, or title, of any kind whatever, from any king, prince, or foreign state.

Section 10. Powers forbidden to the States

Absolute Prohibitions on the States. No State shall enter into any treaty, alliance, or confederation; grant letters of marque and reprisal; coin money; emit bills of credit; make anything but gold and silver coin a tender in payment of debts; pass any bill of attainder, ex-post-facto law, or law impairing the obligation of contracts, or grant any title of nobility.

Conditional Prohibitions on the States. No State shall, without the consent of the Congress, lay any imposts or duties on imports or exports, except what may be absolutely necessary for executing its inspection laws; and the net produce of all duties and imposts, laid by any State on imports or exports, shall be for the use of the treasury of the United States; and all such laws shall be subject to the revision and control of the Congress.

No State shall, without the consent of Congress, lay any duty of tonnage, keep troops, or ships-of-war, in time of peace, enter into any agreement or compact with another State, or with a foreign power, or engage in war, unless actually invaded, or in such imminent danger as will not admit of delay.

---

[1] An official document requiring an accused person who is in prison awaiting trial to be brought into court to inquire whether he may be legally held.

[2] A special legislative act by which a person may be condemned to death or to outlawry or banishment without the opportunity of defending himself which he would have in a court of law.

[3] A law relating to the punishment of acts committed before the law was passed.

ARTICLE II. EXECUTIVE DEPARTMENT

SECTION 1. PRESIDENT AND VICE-PRESIDENT

Term. The executive power shall be vested in a President of the United States of America. He shall hold his office during the term of four years, and, together with the Vice-President, chosen for the same term, be elected, as follows:

Electors. Each State shall appoint, in such manner as the Legislature thereof may direct, a number of electors, equal to the whole number of senators and representatives to which the State may be entitled in the Congress: but no senator or representative, or person holding an office of trust or profit under the United States, shall be appointed an elector.

Proceedings of Electors and of Congress. [¹ The electors shall meet in their respective States, and vote by ballot for two persons, of whom one at least shall not be an inhabitant of the same State with themselves. And they shall make a list of all the persons voted for, and of the number of votes for each; which list they shall sign and certify and transmit sealed to the seat of the government of the United States, directed to the president of the Senate. The president of the Senate shall, in the presence of the Senate and House of Representatives, open all the certificates, and the votes shall then be counted. The person having the greatest number of votes shall be the President, if such number be a majority of the whole number of electors appointed; and if there be more than one who have such majority, and have an equal number of votes, then the House of Representatives shall immediately choose by ballot one of them for President; and if no person have a majority, then from the five highest on the list the said house shall, in like manner, choose the President. But in choosing the President, the votes shall be taken by States, the representation from each State having one vote; a quorum for this purpose shall consist of a member or members from two-thirds of the States, and a majority of all the States shall be necessary to a choice. In every case, after the choice of the President, the person having the greatest number of votes of the electors shall be the Vice-President. But if there should remain two or more who have equal votes, the Senate shall choose from them by ballot the Vice-President.]

Time of choosing Electors. The Congress may determine the time of choosing the electors, and the day on which they shall give their votes; which day shall be the same throughout the United States.²

Qualifications of President. No person except a natural born citizen, or a citizen of the United States at the time of the adoption of this Constitution, shall be eligible to the office of President; neither shall any person be eligible

---

¹ This paragraph in brackets has been superseded by the Twelfth Amendment.

² The electors are chosen on the Tuesday next after the first Monday in November, preceding the expiration of a presidential term. They vote (by Act of Congress of February 3, 1887) on the second Monday in January for President and Vice-President. The votes are counted, and declared in Congress on the second Wednesday of the following February.

to that office who shall not have attained to the age of thirty-five years, and been fourteen years resident within the United States.

Vacancy. In case of the removal of the President from office, or of his death, resignation, or inability to discharge the powers and duties of the said office, the same shall devolve on the Vice-President, and the Congress may by law provide for the case of removal, death, resignation, or inability, both of the President and Vice-President, declaring what officer shall then act as President; and such officer shall act accordingly until the disability be removed, or a President shall be elected.[1]

Salary. The President shall, at stated times, receive for his services a compensation which shall neither be increased nor diminished during the period for which he shall have been elected, and he shall not receive within that period any other emolument from the United States, or any of them.

Oath. Before he enter on the execution of his office, he shall take the following oath or affirmation: — "I do solemnly swear (or affirm) that I will faithfully execute the office of President of the United States, and will, to the best of my ability, preserve, protect, and defend the Constitution of the United States."

Section 2. Powers of the President

Military Powers; Reprieves and Pardons. The President shall be commander-in-chief of the army and navy of the United States, and of the militia of the several States, when called into the actual service of the United States; he may require the opinion, in writing, of the principal officer in each of the executive departments, upon any subject relating to the duties of their respective offices; and he shall have power to grant reprieves and pardons for offenses against the United States, except in cases of impeachment.

Treaties; Appointments. He shall have power, by and with the advice and consent of the Senate, to make treaties, provided two-thirds of the senators present concur; and he shall nominate, and by and with the advice and consent of the Senate shall appoint ambassadors, other public ministers and consuls, judges of the Supreme Court, and all other officers of the United States, whose appointments are not herein otherwise provided for, and which shall be established by law: but the Congress may by law vest the appointment of such inferior officers, as they think proper, in the President alone, in the courts of law, or in the heads of the departments.

Filling of Vacancies. The President shall have power to fill up all vacancies that may happen during the recess of the Senate, by granting commissions which shall expire at the end of their next session.

---

[1] This has now been provided for by the Presidential Succession Act of 1886.

APPENDIX B

Section 3. Duties of the President

Message; Convening of Congress. He shall from time to time give to the Congress information[1] of the state of the Union, and recommend to their consideration such measures as he shall judge necessary and expedient; he may, on extraordinary occasions, convene both houses, or either of them, and in case of disagreement between them with respect to the time of adjournment, he may adjourn them to such time as he shall think proper; he shall receive ambassadors and other public ministers; he shall take care that the laws be faithfully executed, and shall commission all the officers of the United States.

Section 4. Impeachment

Removal of Officers. The President, Vice-President, and all civil officers of the United States, shall be removed from office on impeachment for, and conviction of, treason, bribery, or other high crimes and misdemeanors.

ARTICLE III. JUDICIAL DEPARTMENT

Section 1. United States Courts

Courts established; Judges. The judicial power of the United States shall be vested in one Supreme Court, and in such inferior courts as the Congress may from time to time ordain and establish. The judges, both of the Supreme and inferior courts, shall hold their offices during good behavior, and shall, at stated times, receive for their services a compensation which shall not be diminished during their continuance in office.

Section 2. Jurisdiction of United States Courts

Federal Courts in General. The judicial power shall extend to all cases, in law and equity, arising under this Constitution, the laws of the United States, and treaties made, or which shall be made, under their authority; — to all cases affecting ambassadors, other public ministers, and consuls; — to all cases of admiralty and maritime jurisdiction; — to controversies to which the United States shall be a party; — to controversies between two or more States; — between a State and citizens of another State;[2] — between citizens of different States; — between citizens of the same State claiming lands under grants of different States, and between a State, or the citizens thereof, and foreign states, citizens or subjects.

Supreme Court. In all cases affecting ambassadors, other public ministers and consuls, and those in which a State shall be party, the Supreme Court

---

[1] The president gives this information through a message to Congress at the opening of each session. Washington and John Adams read their messages in person to Congress. Jefferson, however, sent a written message to Congress. This method has been followed by all succeeding presidents except President Wilson, who returned to the earlier custom.

[2] This has been modified by the Eleventh Amendment.

shall have original jurisdiction. In all other cases before mentioned, the Supreme Court shall have appellate jurisdiction, both as to law and fact, with such exceptions and under such regulations as the Congress shall make.

Trials. The trial of all crimes, except in cases of impeachment, shall be by jury; and such trial shall be held in the State where the said crimes shall have been committed; but when not committed within any State, the trial shall be at such place or places as the Congress may by law have directed.

Section 3. Treason

Treason defined. Treason against the United States shall consist only in levying war against them, or in adhering to their enemies, giving them aid and comfort.

No person shall be convicted of treason unless on the testimony of two witnesses to the same overt act, or on confession in open court.

Punishment. The Congress shall have power to declare the punishment of treason, but no attainder of treason shall work corruption of blood, or forfeiture, except during the life of the person attainted.

ARTICLE IV. RELATIONS OF THE STATES TO EACH OTHER

Section 1. Official Acts

Full faith and credit shall be given in each State to the public acts, records, and judicial proceedings of every other State. And the Congress may by general laws, prescribe the manner in which such acts, records, and proceedings shall be proved, and the effect thereof.

Section 2. Privileges of Citizens

The citizens of each State shall be entitled to all privileges and immunities of citizens in the several States.

Fugitives from Justice. A person charged in any State with treason, felony, or other crime, who shall flee from justice, and be found in another State, shall, on demand of the executive authority of the State from which he fled, be delivered up, to be removed to the State having jurisdiction of the crime.

Fugitive Slaves. No person [1] held to service or labor in one State, under the laws thereof, escaping into another, shall, in consequence of any law or regulation therein, be discharged from such service or labor, but shall be delivered up on claim of the party to whom such service or labor may be due.

---

[1] "Person" here includes slave. This was the basis of the Fugitive Slave Laws of 1793 and 1850. It is now superseded by the Thirteenth Amendment, by which slavery is prohibited.

Section 3. New States and Territories

Admission of States. New States may be admitted by the Congress into this Union; but no new State shall be formed or erected within the jurisdiction of any other State; nor any State be formed by the junction of two or more States, or parts of States, without the consent of the Legislatures of the States concerned as well as of the Congress.

Territory and Property of United States. The Congress shall have power to dispose of and make all needful rules and regulations respecting the territory or other property belonging to the United States; and nothing in this Constitution shall be so construed as to prejudice any claims of the United States, or of any particular State.

Section 4. Protection of the States

The United States shall guarantee to every State in this Union a republican form of government, and shall protect each of them against invasion, and on application of the Legislature, or of the Executive (when the Legislature cannot be convened) against domestic violence.

ARTICLE V. AMENDMENTS

How proposed; how ratified. The Congress, whenever two-thirds of both houses shall deem it necessary, shall propose amendments to this Constitution, or, on the application of the Legislatures of two-thirds of the several States, shall call a convention for proposing amendments, which, in either case, shall be valid to all intents and purposes, as part of this Constitution, when ratified by the Legislatures of three-fourths of the several States, or by conventions in three-fourths thereof, as the one or the other mode of ratification may be proposed by the Congress; provided that no amendment which may be made prior to the year one thousand eight hundred and eight shall in any manner affect the first and fourth clauses in the ninth section of the first article; and that no State, without its consent, shall be deprived of its equal suffrage in the Senate.

ARTICLE VI. GENERAL PROVISIONS

Public Debt. All debts contracted, and engagements entered into, before the adoption of this Constitution, shall be as valid against the United States under this Constitution, as under the Confederation.

Supremacy of Constitution. This Constitution, and the laws of the United States which shall be made in pursuance thereof; and all treaties made, or which shall be made, under the authority of the United States, shall be the supreme law of the land; and the judges in every State shall be bound thereby, anything in the Constitution or laws of any State to the contrary notwithstanding.

Official Oath; Religious Test. The senators and representatives before mentioned, and the members of the several State Legislatures, and all executive and judicial officers, both of the United States and of the several States, shall be bound by oath or affirmation to support this Constitution; but no religious test shall ever be required as a qualification to any office or public trust under the United States.

ARTICLE VII. RATIFICATION OF THE CONSTITUTION

Ratification. The ratification of the Conventions of nine States shall be sufficient for the establishment of this Constitution between the States so ratifying the same.

Done in convention, by the unanimous consent of the States present, the seventeenth day of September, in the year of our Lord one thousand seven hundred and eighty-seven, and of the independence of the United States of America the twelfth.

In witness whereof, we have hereunto subscribed our names.[1]

GEORGE WASHINGTON,
President, and Deputy from Virginia

NEW HAMPSHIRE
JOHN LANGDON
NICHOLAS GILMAN

MASSACHUSETTS
NATHANIEL GORHAM
RUFUS KING

CONNECTICUT
WILLIAM SAMUEL JOHNSON
ROGER SHERMAN

NEW YORK
ALEXANDER HAMILTON

NEW JERSEY
WILLIAM LIVINGSTON
DAVID BREARLEY
WILLIAM PATERSON
JONATHAN DAYTON

PENNSYLVANIA
BENJAMIN FRANKLIN
THOMAS MIFFLIN
ROBERT MORRIS
GEORGE CLYMER
THOMAS FITZSIMONS
JARED INGERSOLL
JAMES WILSON
GOUVERNEUR MORRIS

DELAWARE
GEORGE READ
GUNNING BEDFORD, JR.
JOHN DICKINSON
RICHARD BASSETT
JACOB BROOM

MARYLAND
JAMES M'HENRY
DANIEL OF ST. THOMAS JENIFER
DANIEL CARROLL

VIRGINIA
JOHN BLAIR
JAMES MADISON, JR.

NORTH CAROLINA
WILLIAM BLOUNT
RICHARD DOBBS SPAIGHT
HUGH WILLIAMSON

SOUTH CAROLINA
JOHN RUTLEDGE
CHARLES C. PINCKNEY
CHARLES PINCKNEY
PIERCE BUTLER

GEORGIA
WILLIAM FEW
ABRAHAM BALDWIN

Attest: WILLIAM JACKSON, *Secretary*

---

[1] There were sixty-five delegates chosen to the convention: ten did not attend; sixteen declined or failed to sign; thirty-nine signed. Rhode Island sent no delegates.

AMENDMENTS

Religion, Speech, Press, Assembly, Petition. ARTICLE I.[1] Congress shall make no law respecting an establishment of religion, or prohibiting the free exercise thereof; or abridging the freedom of speech, or of the press; or the right of the people peaceably to assemble, and to petition the government for redress of grievances.

Militia. ARTICLE II. A well-regulated militia being necessary to the security of a free State the right of the people to keep and bear arms shall not be infringed.

Soldiers. ARTICLE III. No soldier shall, in time of peace, be quartered in any house, without the consent of the owner; nor in time of war but in a manner to be prescribed by law.

Unreasonable Searches. ARTICLE IV. The right of the people to be secure in their persons, houses, papers, and effects, against unreasonable searches and seizures, shall not be violated, and no warrants shall issue, but upon probable cause, supported by oath or affirmation, and particularly describing the place to be searched, and the persons or things to be seized.

Criminal Prosecutions. ARTICLE V. No person shall be held to answer for a capital, or otherwise infamous crime, unless on a presentment or indictment of a grand jury, except in cases arising in the land or naval forces, or in the militia, when in actual service in time of war and public danger; nor shall any person be subject for the same offense to be twice put in jeopardy of life or limb; nor shall be compelled in any criminal case to be a witness against himself, nor to be deprived of life, liberty, or property, without due process of law; nor shall private property be taken for public use, without just compensation.

ARTICLE VI. In all criminal prosecutions, the accused shall enjoy the right to a speedy and public trial, by an impartial jury of the State and district wherein the crime shall have been committed, which district shall have been previously ascertained by law, and to be informed of the nature and cause of the accusation; to be confronted with the witnesses against him; to have compulsory process for obtaining witnesses in his favor, and to have the assistance of counsel for his defense.

Suits at Common Law. ARTICLE VII. In suits at common law, where the value in controversy shall exceed twenty dollars, the right of trial by jury shall be preserved, and no fact tried by a jury shall be otherwise reëxamined in any court of the United States than according to the rules of common law.

Bail, Punishments. ARTICLE VIII. Excessive bail shall not be required, nor excessive fines imposed, nor cruel and unusual punishments inflicted.

Reserved Rights and Powers. ARTICLE IX. The enumeration in the Constitution of certain rights shall not be construed to deny or disparage others retained by the people.

[1] These amendments were proposed by Congress and ratified by the legislatures of the several states, pursuant to the fifth article of the Constitution. The first ten were offered in 1789 and adopted before the close of 1791.

ARTICLE X. The powers not delegated to the United States by the Constitution, nor prohibited by it to the States, are reserved to the States respectively, or to the people.

Suits against States. ARTICLE XI.[1] The judicial power of the United States shall not be construed to extend to any suit in law or equity, commenced or prosecuted against any of the United States by citizens of another State, or by citizens or subjects of any foreign state.

Method of electing President and Vice-President. ARTICLE XII.[2] The electors shall meet in their respective States, and vote by ballot for President and Vice-President, one of whom, at least, shall not be an inhabitant of the same State with themselves; they shall name in their ballots the person voted for as President, and in distinct ballots the person voted for as Vice-President; and they shall make distinct lists of all persons voted for as President, and of all persons voted for as Vice-President, and of the number of votes for each, which list they shall sign and certify, and transmit sealed to the seat of the government of the United States, directed to the president of the Senate; — the president of the Senate shall, in the presence of the Senate and House of Representatives, open all the certificates, and the votes shall then be counted; — the person having the greatest number of votes for President — shall be the President, if such number be a majority of the whole number of electors appointed; and if no person have such majority, then from the persons having the highest numbers not exceeding three on the list of those voted for as President, the House of Representatives shall choose immediately, by ballot, the President. But in choosing the President, the votes shall be taken by States, the representation from each State having one vote; a quorum for this purpose shall consist of a member or members from two-thirds of the States, and a majority of all the States shall be necessary to a choice. And if the House of Representatives shall not choose a President whenever the right of choice shall devolve upon them, before the fourth day of March next following, then the Vice-President shall act as President, as in the case of the death or other constitutional disability of the President. The person having the greatest number of votes as Vice-President, shall be the Vice-President, if such number be a majority of the whole number of electors appointed; and if no person have a majority, then from the two highest numbers on the list, the Senate shall choose the Vice-President; a quorum for the purpose shall consist of two-thirds of the whole number of senators, and a majority of the whole number shall be necessary to a choice. But no person constitutionally ineligible to the office of President shall be eligible to that of Vice-President of the United States.

Slavery abolished. ARTICLE XIII.[3] *Section 1.* Neither slavery nor involuntary servitude, except as a punishment for crime, whereof the party shall have been duly convicted, shall exist within the United States, or any place subject to their jurisdiction.

[1] Proposed in 1794; adopted in 1798.   [2] Adopted in 1804.   [3] Adopted in 1865.

Section 2. Congress shall have power to enforce this article by appropriate legislation.

Negroes made Citizens. ARTICLE XIV.[1] *Section 1.* All persons born or naturalized in the United States, and subject to the jurisdiction thereof, are citizens of the United States and of the State wherein they reside. No State shall make or enforce any law which shall abridge the privileges or immunities of citizens of the United States; nor shall any State deprive any person of life, liberty, or property, without due process of law, nor deny to any person within its jurisdiction the equal protection of the laws.

Section 2. Representatives shall be apportioned among the several States according to their respective numbers, counting the whole number of persons in each State, excluding Indians not taxed. But when the right to vote at any election for the choice of electors for President and Vice-President of the United States, representatives in Congress, the executive or judicial officers of a State, or the members of the Legislature thereof, is denied to any of the male inhabitants of such State, being twenty-one years of age, and citizens of the United States, or in any way abridged, except for participation in rebellion or other crime, the basis of representation therein shall be reduced in the proportion which the number of such male citizens shall bear to the whole number of male citizens twenty-one years of age in such State.

Section 3. No person shall be a senator or representative in Congress, or elector of President or Vice-President, or hold any office, civil or military, under the United States, or under any State, who having previously taken an oath as a member of Congress, or as an officer of the United States, or as a member of any State Legislature, or as an executive or judicial officer of any State, to support the Constitution of the United States, shall have engaged in insurrection or rebellion against the same, or given aid or comfort to the enemies thereof. But Congress may, by a vote of two-thirds of each house, remove such disability.

Section 4. The validity of the public debt of the United States, authorized by law, including debts incurred for payment of pensions and bounties for services in suppressing insurrection or rebellion, shall not be questioned. But neither the United States nor any State shall assume or pay any debt or obligation incurred in aid of insurrection or rebellion against the United States, or any claim for the loss or emancipation of any slave; but all such debts, obligations, and claims shall be held illegal and void.

Section 5. The Congress shall have power to enforce, by appropriate legislation, the provisions of this article.

Negroes made Voters. ARTICLE XV.[2] *Section 1.* The rights of citizens of the United States to vote shall not be denied or abridged by the United States, or by any State, on account of race, color, or previous condition of servitude.

Section 2. The Congress shall have power to enforce this article by appropriate legislation.

[1] Adopted in 1868.   [2] Adopted in 1870.

Income Tax. ARTICLE XVI.[1] The Congress shall have power to lay and collect taxes on incomes from whatever source derived, without apportionment among the several States, and without regard to any census or enumeration.

ARTICLE XVII.[1] The Senate of the United States shall be composed of two Senators from each State, elected by the people thereof for six years; and each Senator shall have one vote. The electors in each State shall have the qualifications requisite for electors of the most numerous branch of the State Legislatures.

Direct Election of Senators. When vacancies happen in the representation of any State in the Senate, the executive authority of such State shall issue writs of election to fill such vacancies: Provided, that the Legislature of any State may empower the Executive thereof to make temporary appointments until the people fill the vacancies by election as the Legislature may direct.

This amendment shall not be so construed as to affect the election or term of any Senator chosen before it becomes valid as part of the Constitution.

National Prohibition. ARTICLE XVIII.[2] *Section 1.* After one year from the ratification of this article the manufacture, sale, or transportation of intoxicating liquors within, the importation thereof into, or the exportation thereof from the United States and all territory subject to the jurisdiction thereof for beverage purposes is hereby prohibited.

Section 2. The Congress and the several States shall have concurrent power to enforce this article by appropriate legislation.

Section 3. This article shall be inoperative unless it shall have been ratified as an amendment to the Constitution by the Legislatures of the several States, as provided in the Constitution, within seven years from the date of the submission hereof to the States by the Congress.

Woman Suffrage. ARTICLE XIX.[3] *Section 1.* The right of citizens of the United States to vote shall not be denied or abridged by the United States or by any State on account of sex.

Section 2. Congress shall have power to enforce this article by appropriate legislation.

[1] Ratified in 1913.   [2] Ratified in 1919. In force in 1920.   [3] Ratified in 1920.

APPENDIX C

THE STATES OF THE UNION

No.	State	Date of Admission	Population, 1930	Area
1	Delaware	*Original States*	238,380	2,307
2	Pennsylvania		9,640,802	45,126
3	New Jersey		4,028,027	8,222
4	Georgia		2,902,443	59,265
5	Connecticut		1,604,711	4,965
6	Massachusetts		4,253,646	8,266
7	Maryland		1,629,321	12,327
8	South Carolina		1,732,567	30,989
9	New Hampshire		465,293	9,341
10	Virginia		2,419,471	42,627
11	New York		12,619,503	49,204
12	North Carolina		3,170,287	52,426
13	Rhode Island		687,232	1,248
14	Vermont	1791	359,092	9,564
15	Kentucky	1792	2,623,668	40,598
16	Tennessee	1796	2,608,759	42,022
17	Ohio	1803	6,639,837	41,040
18	Louisiana	1812	2,094,496	48,506
19	Indiana	1816	3,225,600	36,354
20	Mississippi	1817	2,007,979	46,865
21	Illinois	1818	7,607,684	56,665
22	Alabama	1819	2,645,297	51,998
23	Maine	1820	800,056	33,040
24	Missouri	1821	3,620,961	69,420
25	Arkansas	1836	1,853,981	53,335
26	Michigan	1837	4,842,280	57,980
27	Florida	1845	1,466,625	58,666
28	Texas	1845	5,821,272	265,896
29	Iowa	1846	2,467,900	56,147
30	Wisconsin	1848	2,930,282	56,066
31	California	1850	5,672,009	158,297
32	Minnesota	1858	2,566,445	84,682
33	Oregon	1859	952,691	96,699
34	Kansas	1861	1,879,946	82,158
35	West Virginia	1863	1,728,510	24,170
36	Nevada	1864	90,981	110,690
37	Nebraska	1867	1,378,900	77,520
38	Colorado	1876	1,035,043	103,948
39	North Dakota	1889	682,448	70,837
40	South Dakota	1889	690,755	77,615
41	Montana	1889	536,332	146,997
42	Washington	1889	1,561,967	69,127
43	Idaho	1890	445,837	83,888
44	Wyoming	1890	224,597	91,914
45	Utah	1896	502,582	84,990
46	Oklahoma	1907	2,391,777	70,057
47	New Mexico	1912	427,216	122,634
48	Arizona	1912	435,833	113,956

APPENDIX D

THE PRESIDENTS

No.	Terms	Presidents	Born	Died	State
1	1789–1793	George Washington	1732	1799	Virginia
	1793–1797	George Washington			
2	1797–1801	John Adams	1735	1826	Massachusetts
3	1801–1805	Thomas Jefferson	1743	1826	Virginia
	1805–1809	Thomas Jefferson			
4	1809–1813	James Madison	1751	1836	Virginia
	1813–1817	James Madison			
5	1817–1821	James Monroe	1758	1831	Virginia
	1821–1825	James Monroe			
6	1825–1829	John Quincy Adams	1767	1848	Massachusetts
7	1829–1833	Andrew Jackson	1767	1845	Tennessee
	1833–1837	Andrew Jackson			
8	1837–1841	Martin Van Buren	1782	1862	New York
9	1841–1845	William H. Harrison	1773	1841	Ohio
10		John Tyler	1790	1862	Virginia
11	1845–1849	James K. Polk	1795	1849	Tennessee
12	1849–1853	Zachary Taylor	1784	1850	Louisiana
13		Millard Fillmore	1800	1874	New York
14	1853–1857	Franklin Pierce	1804	1869	New Hampshire
15	1857–1861	James Buchanan	1701	1868	Pennsylvania
16	1861–1865	Abraham Lincoln	1809	1865	Illinois
17	1865–1869	Abraham Lincoln			
		Andrew Johnson	1808	1875	Tennessee
18	1869–1873	Ulysses S. Grant	1822	1885	Illinois
	1873–1877	Ulysses S. Grant			
19	1877–1881	Rutherford B. Hayes	1822	1893	Ohio
20	1881–1885	James A. Garfield	1831	1881	Ohio
21		Chester A. Arthur	1830	1886	New York
22	1885–1889	Grover Cleveland	1837	1908	New York
23	1889–1893	Benjamin Harrison	1833	1901	Indiana
24	1893–1897	Grover Cleveland	1837	1908	New York
25	1897–1901	William McKinley	1843	1901	Ohio
26	1901–1905	William McKinley			
		Theodore Roosevelt	1858	1919	New York
	1905–1909	Theodore Roosevelt			
27	1909–1913	William H. Taft	1857	1930	Ohio
28	1913–1917	Woodrow Wilson	1856	1924	New Jersey
	1917–1921	Woodrow Wilson			
29	1921–1925	Warren G. Harding	1865	1923	Ohio
30		Calvin Coolidge	1872	—	Massachusetts
	1925–1929	Calvin Coolidge			
31	1929–	Herbert Hoover	1874	—	California

INDEX

Page numbers in italics refer to maps

Abolitionists, 259, 301–304, 313, 316, 325, 359
Adams, Abigail, 210, 214, 215
Adams, John, 67–68, 79, 84, 90, 91, 130, 228; sent to Holland, 97; sent to confer with Howe, 105; at peace conference, 115, 116; elected vice president, 154; denounces French Revolution, 165, 168; as president, 169, 170, 172, 309; defeated in presidential election, 173–174
Adams, John Quincy, in Congress, 196; as probable co-author of Monroe Doctrine, 201; elected president, 227–228, 309; opposes annexation of Texas, 288; on secession, 295; as leader of National Republicans, 307
Adams, Samuel, 87, 228; asks colonies to unite, 74; and the tea tax, 78; at First Continental Congress, 79; escapes arrest, 82–83; at Second Continental Congress, 90; absent from Constitutional Convention, 130; opposed to ratification of Constitution, 143
Adamson Act, 588
Adult education, 491
Agricultural high schools, 489
Aguinaldo, Emilio, 438
Alabama, admitted as a slave state, 286; secedes from Union, 322; readmitted to Union, 363–364
Alabama, the, 333–334
Alaska, 432, *434*
Aldrich, Nelson W., 389
Alien Act, 170–171, 173, 192
Allen, Ethan, 103
Alsace-Lorraine returned to France, 567
Amendments to the Constitution: first ten (Bill of Rights), 157; First, 171; Twelfth, 180; Tenth, 234; Nineteenth, 260, 428–429, 448; denial of part of First, 304; proposed amendment on slavery, 326; Thirteenth, 355, 361; Fourteenth, 362–363, 391–392; Fifteenth, 368; Seventeenth, 427; Sixteenth, 557; Eighteenth, 592–593
American Antislavery Society, 302, 303
American Revolutionary War, events leading to the, 51–81; beginning of the, 81–92; contrasting resources of Great Britain and America in the, 93–101; campaigns in New England and Canada during the, 101–104, *103*; campaigns in the middle states during the, 104–110, *105*, *108*; France aids America in the, 111–112; capture of Northwest Territory during the, 112; campaigns in South during the, 112–114, *113*; Treaty of Paris concluding the, 114–116, *115*
Amnesty Act of 1872, 369–370
Anderson, Major Robert, 326–327
Andros, Sir Edmund, 58–59
Anthony, Susan B., 259
Antietam Creek, *339*; battle at, 340
Antifederalist party, 207, 309; origin, policies, and groups composing, 142; opposed to ratification of Constitution, 142–146; becomes Republican party, 164
Anti-Masonic Party, 309
Anti-Saloon League, 593
Appomattox Court House, *352*; Lee's surrender at, 352–353
Arapaho Indians, 463
Arizona admitted to United States, 293
Arkansas, admitted as a slave state, 287, 294; joins Confederacy, 327; sets up government after war, 358; readmitted to Union, 363–364
Arkwright, Sir Richard, 94
Armaments, limitation of naval, 574–575, 576–577

619

620 AMERICAN GOVERNMENT AND CULTURE

Armat, Thomas, 535
Armored ships, first use of, 334–335
Arnold, General Benedict, 100, 103–104
Arthur, Chester A., 412, 413, 421
Articles of Confederation, ratification of the, 120; weaknesses of the, 128; convention called to revise the, 129; discarding of the, 132; plan for representation under the, 134
Assumption Bill, 160–161
Astor, Mrs. William, 513
Atlanta captured during Civil War, 351
Australian ballot adopted, 424
Automobiling as a national recreation, 529–530

Bacon, Nathaniel, 40–42
Bacon's Rebellion, 39–42
Baldwin, Joseph, 280
Baltimore, Lord, 21
Barnard, Henry, 476, 479
Barnum, P. T., 253–254, 504
Baseball, history of, 517–521
Beauregard, General P. G. T., 336; seizes Fort Sumter, 326–327; succeeds Johnston, 342
Beecher, Henry Ward, 325
Belknap, William W., 384
Bell, John C., 319
Belleau Wood, battle of, 563
Bennett, James Gordon, Jr., 512
Berkeley, Governor, 39–42, 51, 56
Bernard, John, 213
Bicycle, invention and use of the, 505
Biddle, Nicholas, 240
Bill of Rights, early Virginian, 24; Constitutional, 157, 304
Bingham, Mr. and Mrs. William, 209–210
Birney, James G., 301, 302, 313
Birth of a Nation, The, 536
Blackfeet Indians, 462
Blanchard, Jean, 218
Bloomer, Amelia Jenks, 259, 260
Bonus, military, 583
Booth, John Wilkes, 353–354
Boston, Dickens' description of, 250. *See also* American Revolutionary War, Boston Massacre, Boston Tea Party, Massachusetts, Massachusetts Bay Colony
Boston Massacre, 74

Boston Tea Party, tax leading to the, 74; events of the, 77–79
Bragg, General Braxton, 350
Brandywine, *105*; battle of, 107
Breckenridge, Robert J., 478
Breckinridge, John C., 319, 320
Briand, Aristide, 575
Briand-Kellogg Peace Pact, 575–576
Brook Farm, 256–258
Brooklyn Heights, *105*; battle of, 104
Brown, David, 172
Brown, John, raid of, 305–306
Bryan, William Jennings, as leader of Democratic party, 405; runs for president, 406, *407*; works for initiative and referendum, 426
Bryant, William Cullen, 264, 266
Buchanan, James, 311; nominated by Democrats, 316–317; election and administration of, 309, 317, 323
Bull Run, *339*; first battle of, 335–336; second battle of, 338–339
Bunker Hill, *103*; battle of, 101–102
Bureau of the Budget, the, 588
Burgoyne, General John, 107, 108
Burlesque, 537
Burnside, General Ambrose E., 336; placed in command of Army of the Potomac, 340; attacks Lee at Fredericksburg, 340
Burr, Aaron, 173, 174, 205

Calhoun, John C., 186, 196, 270, 273; proposes second National Bank, 197; supports protective tariff, 198–199; opposes Jackson, 233; defends slavery, 305; in charge of Indian affairs, 455–456
California, acquisition of, 292; controversy over admission of, 295, 296
Camp, Walter, 522
Canada, 202; Revolutionary campaign in, 103–104; campaigns of War of 1812 in, 188–190; settlement of Oregon claims in, 293–294; Sioux Indians migrate to, 467
Cantigny, battle of, 563
Carpetbaggers, 365–366, 369
Caucus method of nomination, the, 226–227
Chancellorsville, *349*; battle of, 348
Charles I of England, 16

INDEX 621

Charleston, life in, 271–273; surrender of Fort Sumter at, 326–327
Château-Thierry, battle of, 563
Chattanooga, capture of, 350
Chautauqua lectures, 504–505
Cherokee Indians, 456, 459–461
Cheyenne Indians, 462
Chicago, development of, 247
Chickamauga, battle of, 350
Chickasaw Indians, 461
China, Japan returns Shantung to, 575
Chippewa Indians, 461
Choctaw Indians, 461
Cincinnati, growth of, 248
City Gazetteer and Daily Advertiser, 179
Civil Rights Bill, 362–363
Civil Service, 421–422
Civil War: beginning, 326–327; resources of North and South, 328; how financed in the South, 328–330; how financed in the North, 330–331; armies of each side, 331–332; blockades, 332–333, *332*; early eastern campaigns, 335–341, *339*; western campaigns, 341–344, *342*; Emancipation Proclamation, 345–346; opposition of parties in North and South, 347–348; later campaigns, 348–351, *349*; final campaigns, 351–352, *352*; end, 353; effects, 354, 355, 485; cost, 355
Clark, George Rogers, 112, 223
Clay, Henry, 186, 196–197, 270; as presidential candidate, 227, 308, 312–313; made Secretary of State, 228; as co-author of Compromise of 1850, 296; as leader of National Republicans, 307
Clayton Act, 419
Clemenceau, Georges, 565
Cleveland, Grover, elected president, 388, 390, 413; urges tariff reduction, 388; refuses to sign Wilson-Gorman Bill, 390; promotes civil-service reform, 422; opposed to annexation of Hawaii, 435
Clinton, General Henry, 110, 113
Colleges, founding of, 261; development of, 481–484, 487–488
Colombia and the Panama Canal, 440–441
Columbia, District of, 214 (note); slave trade prohibited in, 296

Comanche Indians, 460, 462
Committees of Correspondence, 76–77, 78
Common Sense, 87–89, 130
Compromise of 1850, 296, 297, 315
Concord, battle of, 81–83
Coney Island, 510
Confederate States of America, formation of the, 322; North Carolina, Tennessee, Arkansas, and Virginia join the, 327; economic resources of the, 328; refused readmission to Union, 361; refuse to ratify Fourteenth Amendment, 363; readmitted to Union, 363–364. *See also* Civil War
Confederation, Articles of. *See* Articles of Confederation
Congregational church, political power of the, 33–38
Congress, conflicts over organization and powers of, 134–136; powers granted to, 138–140; Senators elected by direct vote to, 427, 430
Congress, the, 334
Connecticut, founding of, 36–37; Constitution ratified by, 143; and the Assumption Bill, 161; and education, 477, 479
Conscription. *See* Draft
Constitution of the United States, Convention meets to make the, 129–132; conflicts in making the, 134–136; compromises in making the, 136–137; checks and balances of power as set by the, 138–141; attitude of people toward the, 141–142; ratification of, 142–146; difficulty of changing the, 146; purposes of government as set forth by the, 151; dispute over powers given by the, 234–238. *See also* Amendments to the Constitution
Constitution, the, frigate, 190
Constitutional Convention, 129–141
Constitutional Union Party, 309, 319
Continental Congress, meeting of the First, 79–80, 81; meeting of the Second, 83; Declaration of Independence proclaimed by the Second, 90–92; lack of power of the Second, 110, 128; Ordinance of the Northwest Territory passed by the Second, 285
Continental paper money. *See* Paper money

Cooke, Jay, 331, 384
Coolidge, Calvin, 412, 573, 576, 583, 586, 587–588, 590, 591
Cooper, James Fenimore, 266
Cornwallis, Lord Charles, 112–114
Cosby, William, 59–61
Costello, Maurice, 535
Cotton gin, slavery affected by the, 284
Cotton kingdom, life in the, 268–280; location of the, *275*
Country gentlemen, life of, 212–214, 268–274
Crawford, William, 227
Crédit Mobilier, 380–381
Creek Indians, 461
Crown Point, Fort, 102, *103, 108*
Cuba becomes protectorate of United States, 436, 443
Cumberland, the, 334
Cumberland Road, 182
Curtis, George William, 420
Custer, George A., 464–467
Czechoslovakia made independent, 567

Daguerre, Louis Jacques Mandé, 533
Daily Advertiser, the, 207
Dale, Sir Thomas, 22
Davis, Dwight F., 525
Davis, Jefferson, elected president of Confederate States of America, 322; orders Beauregard to take Fort Sumter, 326; tries to arrange peace terms 352
Davis, John W., 590
Davis Cup, 525–526
Dawes, Charles G., 573–574, 588
Dawes, William, 82
Deane, Silas, 97
Debs, Eugene V., as candidate of Social-Democratic party, 408
Declaration of Independence, 152; writing and signing of the, 90–92; effects of the, 97; rescue of original copy of the, 191; comparison of attitude on slavery in original and final drafts of the, 283–284
Delaware, ratifies Constitution, 143; remains within Union, 327–328
Delaware Indians, 461, 462
Democracy, background of American, 8–10; beginnings of, 23–25; development of, 25–46, 224–233, 249–250, 397, 448; Constitution guards against excess of, 137–141; Jefferson's policies do not further, 180; education and, 261–262, 476, 478, 484; hindrances to greater, 374. *See also* Suffrage
Democratic party, 309, 411–414; origin of the, 307; Jackson the leader of the, 308; Whigs defeat the, 312, 315; contests between Republican party and the, 321, 411–414; groups composing the, 377–378; tariff and the, 378, 388–389, 390, 391; Populist party absorbed by the, 405–407; Bryan nominated by the, 406; League favored by the, 570–571. *See also* Jackson, Andrew, *and* Democrats, government under control of
Democratic Republican party, 307, 309. *See also* Jackson, Andrew, *and* Democratic party
Democrats, government under control of: 309, 411–415; Van Buren's election and administration, 308; Polk's election and administration, 313–314; attitude toward slavery, 315; Pierce's election, 315; Buchanan's election and administration, 317–325; control of South, 369; Cleveland's elections and administrations, 388, 390, 413; Wilson's administration, 422, 426, 427, 429, 551–556, 561, 565–567. *See also* Jackson, Andrew, *and* Democratic party
Detroit, growth of, 248
Dew, Thomas R., 279, 305
Dewey, John, 490
Dial, the, 257, 259, 263
Dickson, William K. L., 534
Dingley Tariff Bill, 391
"Direct primary" system, 425
Dominican Republic becomes American sphere of influence, 444–446
Donelson, Fort, 341, *342*
Dorcas Society, 250
Dorr, Thomas, 225, 226
Dorr's Rebellion, 226
Douglas, Stephen A., and the Kansas-Nebraska Bill, 297–298; in debates with Lincoln, 317–318; nominated for presidency, 319, 320
Draft, during the Civil War, 347–348: during the World War, 556

INDEX

Dred Scott Decision, 300–301, 317, 318
Dudley, Thomas, 28

Early, General Jubal, 351
East India Company, 74
Eastman, George, 534
Edison, Thomas A., 534
Education, spread of, 261–262, 473–492; Southern, 279; necessity for, 374, 476, 595; relation of national government to, 476, 489; leaders in, 476–478; effect of Civil War on, 485; effect of changing industrial civilization on, 487–488; recent changes in, 488–491; adult, 491
Edwards, Ninian W., 478
Eighteenth Amendment, 592–593
Elementary schools, development of public, 476–479, 487
Emancipation Proclamation, 345–346
Embargo Act, 183–185, 186, 193
Emerson, Ralph Waldo, 256, 257, 258, 263, 264, 296
Empire-building, arguments for and against, 432–433, 436–437
England. *See* Great Britain
"Era of good feeling," 196–197
Ericsson, John, 335
Espionage Act, 560
Estonia made independent, 567

Fall, Albert B., 589
Farmers, unfavorable economic position of, 398–399, 585–586, 594; Grange formed by, 399–401; Greenback party joined by, 401–402; Populist party organized by, 402–403; no political party representing, 408; Clayton Act not applicable to alliances of, 419; life among, 245–247, 274–276, 494–499. *See also* Cotton kingdom *and* Country gentlemen
Farmers' Alliance, 402–403
Farragut, Admiral David Glasgow, 332, 342–343
Fathers of the Constitution, 129–130, 137–138, 139, 140, 141
Federal Board for Vocational Education, 489
Federal government. *See* National government
Federal Trade Commission, 419

Federalist, The, 143
Federalist party, 207, 210, 307, 309; origin and early policies, 142; groups composing, 164; elects John Adams president, 169; falls from power, 173–175, 194. *See also* Federalists, government under control of
Federalists, government under control of: 151–175, 309; ratification of Constitution, 142–146; foreign policies, 165–169; Alien and Sedition Acts, 170–171
Fenno, John, 173, 206
Fifteenth Amendment, 368
Filipinos. *See* Philippines
Fillmore, Millard, 309, 315, 316
Finland becomes independent, 567
Fire-Eaters, 319
First Amendment, 171
Fisk, James, Jr., 382–383
Fitch, John, 212
Florida, admitted to Union, 295; secedes from Union, 322; readmitted to Union, 363–364
Foraker, Joseph, 393
Football, history of, 521–524
Foote, Commodore Andrew H., 341
Fordney-McCumber Act, 586
Forts: Crown Point, 102, *103, 108*; Ticonderoga, 102, *103, 108*; McHenry, *189*, 191; Leavenworth, 290, *291*; Sumter, 326–327; Monroe, 338, *339*; Henry, 341, *342*; Donelson, 341, *342*
Foster, Stephen, 254
Four-Power Treaty, provisions of the, 575
Fourteen Points, Wilson announces the, 561; Peace Conference carries out some of the, 567
Fourteenth Amendment, 362–363, 391–392
Fox Indians, 461, 462
France, colonies seek aid from, 89–90; colonies aided by, 97, 111–112; peace conference attended by representatives of, 114–116; debt owed to, 157; American attitude toward revolution in, 165–166; purchase of Louisiana from, 180–181; popularity of fashions from, 218; World War debt owed United States by, 572; Four-Power Treaty signed by, 575;

refusal to abolish submarines by, 577. *See also* French and Indian War, War of 1812, *and* World War

Franklin, Benjamin, 125–126; representing colonies in England, 72; representing colonies in France, 97; at peace conference, 115, 116; at Constitutional Convention, 129; as head of postal system, 156

Fredericksburg, *339*; battle of, 340

Free Soil party, 309, 314, 315

Freedom of speech, fight for, 59–61; guarantee of, 157, 171; attempts to suppress, 171–172, 303–304, 560–561

Frémont, John C., 290, 316

French and Indian War, effect on English colonies of the, 64–65

French Revolution influences American politics, 165–166

Frontier life, 218–220, 249–250; effect on democracy of, 223, 224–225. *See also* Indians

Fugitive Slave Law, 296; Northern opposition to the, 296–297; Dred Scott and the interpretation of the, 300–301

Fuller, Margaret, 256, 257, 259

Funding Bill, 158–160

Fur trading, restrictions on, 65

Gadsden, James, 292 (note)

Gadsden Purchase, *291*, 292 (note)

"Gag resolution," 304

Gage, General, 81, 101, 103

Gallatin, Albert, 170–171, 182, 194

Galloway, Samuel, 478

Gang rule, 589–590

Garfield, James A., 412, 413, 421

Garrison, William Lloyd, 301, 303–304

Gates, General Horatio, 100, 108, 112

General Court of Massachusetts Bay Colony, 25, 26, 28, 29

Genêt, Edmond, 168

Geneva Conference. *See* Naval conferences

Geographic influences on government, 12, 187–188, 285, 374

George III, 64, 79, 87, 88, 98

Georgia, ratifies the Constitution, 143; secedes from the Union, 322; readmitted to the Union, 363–364

German colonists in Pennsylvania, 43

Germantown, *105*; battle of, 107

Germany, how the United States was brought into the war against, 549–555; final campaigns against, 563–564; negotiations for peace with, 564–565; post-war settlements with, 566–567; United States signs peace treaty with, 572; Dawes plan fixes reparations to be paid by, 573–574

Gerry, Elbridge, 137

Gershwin, George, 543

Gettysburg, battle of, 349

Gilbert, William S., 540

Golf, 526–527

Gould, Jay, 382–383

Grand Army of the Republic, 377

Grange, the, 399–401, 497

Grant, Ulysses S., in Civil War, 341–342, 343–344, 350–353; as president, 379, 411–412; and national scandals following Civil War, 379–386

Great Britain, government of, in colonial times, 16–19, 53; American colonies of, *88*; friendship between United States and, 202; settlement of Oregon claims with, 293–294; American Civil War and, 345–346; payment to United States of World War debt of, 572–573; limitation of armaments agreed to by, 574–575. *See also* American Revolutionary War, War of 1812, World War, Massachusetts Bay Colony, Virginia Colony, etc.

"Great Pacificator," the. *See* Clay, Henry

Greeley, Horace, 259, 335, 346

"Green Mountain Boys," 102

Greenback party, the, 401–402, 412

Greene, Major General Nathanael, 100, 113

Grimké, Angelina, 301, 302

Grimké, Sarah, 301, 302

Griswold, Roger, 170

Guam, *434*; acquisition of, 436

Guerrière, the, 190

Haiti becomes American sphere of influence, 444–446

Hamilton, Alexander, 205, 209; at the Constitutional Convention, 129; favors rule by aristocrats, 138; defends the Constitution, 143, 144; as Secre-

INDEX

tary of Treasury, 155, 156, 157; proposes the Funding Bill, 158, 159; proposes the Assumption Bill, 160–161; establishes the National Bank, 162–163; as leader of the Federalist party, 164; opposed to the French Revolution, 165, 168; disapproves of the Sedition Act, 171; loses power, 173; helps to elect Jefferson, 174

Hamilton, Andrew, 60, 61

Hancock, John, attempted arrest and escape of, 81–83; Constitution opposed by, 143

Hanna, Marcus A., 390–391

Harding, Warren G., 412, 571, 572, 583, 586, 587–588, 589, 590

Hargreaves, James, 94

Harpers Ferry, John Brown's raid at, 305–306

Harrison, Benjamin, 389, 412, 413, 422

Harrison, William Henry, in War of 1812, 190; as president, 308, 309, 310, 312; dies, 312; as governor of Indiana Territory, 453–454

Hartford Convention, 194

Haswell, Anthony, 172

Hawaiian Islands, *434*; acquisition of, 433, 435–436

Hawley-Smoot Act, 586

Hawthorne, Nathaniel, 257, 264

Hayes, Rutherford B., 412, 421

Hayne, Robert Y., 236–237, 270, 273

Henry, Fort, 341, *342*

Henry, Mrs., 207

Henry, Patrick, proposes resolutions, 68–70; at First Continental Congress, 79; speaks before Virginia Convention, 80; at Second Continental Congress, 90; calls for volunteers, 112; absent from Constitutional Convention, 130; opposed to Constitution, 143, 144

Hepburn Act, 418

Herbert, Victor, 540, 541

Hessians, 98, 100, 106

High schools, development of public, 480–481, 487

Holmes, Oliver Wendell, 264

Homestead Act of 1862, 377

Hooker, General Joseph, succeeds Burnside, 340; defeated at Chancellorsville, 348; replaced by General Meade, 349

Hooker, Thomas, 35, 36–37

Hooper, Johnson Jones, 280

Hoover, Herbert C., 412, 588, 591

House of Commons, 17, 18, 19, 53. *See also* Parliament

House of Lords, 17

House of Representatives, conflicts over organization and powers of, 134–136; powers granted to, 138–140; balance of political power in, 411–415, 570

Houston, General Sam, 287

Howe, Admiral Lord, 104–105

Howe, General, 86, 103, 107, 108, 109, 110

Howe, Julia Ward, 259

Hudson, Port, *342*, 344

Hudson River School of painters, 266

Hughes, Charles Evans, 574, 576

Hutchinson, Anne, 35, 37–38

Illinois admitted as a free state, 286

Immigrants, 374; life of, in cities, 506–508; laws limiting admission, 586–587

Imperialism. *See* Empire-building

Income tax, declared unconstitutional, 392; laid to meet war expenses, 557; lowered, 588; demand for raising of, 590

Independence, Declaration of. *See* Declaration of Independence

Independent Republican party (Mugwumps), 412

Independent Treasury Act, 242–243

Indian Affairs, Bureau of, 456, 464, 468

Indian Territory, 462

Indiana, admitted as a free state, 286; settled, 452

Indians, 36, 39–40, 43, 218, 219, 235; government's problem with, 448; policy of colonial governments toward, 449; treaties with, 450, 456; Washington's policy toward, 450–452; Tecumseh's attempt to unite, 453–455; Jefferson's policy toward, 455; Monroe's policy toward, 456; schools established for, 457; westward migration of, 458–462; last stand of, 462–467; government protection of, 467–468; citizenship given to, 470; reservations of, *451*, *469*. *See also* Arapaho Indians, Kickapoo Indians, Sioux Indians, etc.

Industrial Revolution, 146
Industry, after the Revolution, 126; after 1800, 224
Initiative, the, 425–426, 430, 431
International Labor Organization, 578 (note)
Interstate Commerce Act, 416–417; supplemented by Hepburn Act, 418
Interstate Commerce Commission. *See* Interstate Commerce Act
Intolerable Acts, 79
Iolanthe, 540
Iowa admitted as a free state, 294
Iowa Indians, 462
Irving, Washington, 266

Jackson, Andrew, 249, 276; defeats British at New Orleans, 192; defeated in presidential election, 227–228; elected president, 228, 308, 309; holds democratic beliefs, 230–231; and the spoils system, 231–232; and states-rights issue, 234–238; abolishes National Bank, 238–241; and the gag resolution, 304; as the leader of the Democratic Republicans, 307; defeats Clay, 308
Jackson, General T. J. ("Stonewall"), 336, 348
James I of England, 16
Jamestown, founding of, 19
Japan, agrees to limitation of naval armaments, 575; returns Shantung to China, 575; refuses to abolish submarines, 577
Jay, John, sent to Spain, 97; at peace conference, 115, 116; favors closer union among states, 129; defends Constitution, 143; as Chief Justice, 156; makes treaty with England, 168–169
Jay Treaty, 168–169
Jazz, 541–545
Jefferson, Thomas, 87, 176, 205, 207, 209, 211, 215–216, 309; as author of Declaration of Independence, 90–91; absent from Constitutional Convention, 130; made Secretary of State, 155; opposes Funding Bill, 160; and Assumption Bill, 161; opposed to National Bank, 163; as leader of the Republicans, 164; in sympathy with French, 167; elected vice president, 169; attacked by Federalists, 170; author of Kentucky Resolutions, 172; elected president, 174; as president, 177–185; advised Monroe, 201; and Indian question, 455
Johnson, Andrew, 276, 412; Lincoln succeeded by, 359–360; administration of, 360–365; attempt to impeach, 364–365; direct election of senators demanded by, 427
Johnston, General Albert S., 336, 342
Johnston, General Joseph E., 336, 352, 353
Jones Act, 584

Kansas, 295 (note); and Kansas-Nebraska Bill, 297–300; remains within Union, 327–328
Kansas-Nebraska Bill, 297–300, *299*, 316
Kearney, Colonel Stephen W., 290
Kearsarge, the, 334
Keith, B. F., 537
Keith circuit, 538
Kellogg, Frank B., 575
Kendall, Amos, 304
Kentucky, 127, 219; passes nullification resolutions, 172–173; joins Union as slave state, 285; remains within Union, 327–328; and education, 479
Kentucky Resolutions, 172–173
Key, Francis Scott, 191
Kickapoo Indians, 461, 462
Kinetoscope, 534
King, Rufus, 130, 131, 170
Know-Nothing Party, 309, 314–315
Knox, General Henry, 155, 157, 206
Ku-Klux Klan, 367–368

Labor Reformers, 408, 412
Labor Unions, and the Clayton Act, 419; in post-war depression, 588–589
Lafayette, Marquis de, 111, 113, 165
La Follette, Robert M., urges direct-primary system, 425; approves reforms, 427; as candidate of Progressive party, 590–591
Lake Erie, *189*; battle of, 189–190
Latham, Woodville, Otway, and Grey, 535
Latvia made independent, 567
League of Nations, Wilson proposes organization of, 561; establishment of,

INDEX

567; rejection by American Senate of, 567, 570; United States remains outside of, 570–571; World Court established by, 576; nations belonging to, 577 (note); organization and work of, 577–579

Leavenworth, Fort, 290, *291*

Leaves of Grass, 264

Lee, Arthur, 97

Lee, Richard Henry, 90, 143, 144

Lee, Robert E., 336; at Harpers Ferry, 306; invades Maryland, 339–340; attacked at Fredericksburg, 340; defeats Hooker at Chancellorsville, 348; marches into Pennsylvania, 348; at the battle of Gettysburg, 349; surrenders to Grant, 352–353

Legaré, Hugh, 272–273

Leisure, problem of use of, 594–595

Leisure class, life of, 203–217, 269–274, 510–513

Lewis, Meriwether, 223

Lewis, Samuel, 478

Lexington, battle at, 81–82

Liberator, The, 303

Liberty Bonds, 557–558

Liberty party, the, 309, 313, 314

Liliuokalani, Queen, 435

Lincoln, Abraham, 412; as leader of Republicans, 317; in debates with Douglas, 317–318; nominated for president, 319; elected president, *320*, 321; and slavery, 317–318, 319, 320, 325; makes inaugural speech, 325; calls for volunteers, 327; issues Emancipation Proclamation, 345–346; appoints Grant head of Union armies, 350; assassinated, 353–354; makes speech on news of Confederate surrender, 357; and reconstruction of the South, 358; and the spoils system, 420

Lind, Jenny, 253

Lithuania made independent, 567

Livingston, Edward, 171

Livingston, Robert, 212

Lloyd George, David, 565

"Lobby," definition of, 198

Local government, responsibilities of, 10

"Locofoco" Democrats, 309

London Company, 19, 20, 21, 23

London Conference. *See* Naval conferences

Long, Stephen H., 455–456

Longfellow, Henry Wadsworth, 264

Longstreet, A. B., 280

Lookout Mountain, battle of, 350

Louisiana, admitted as a slave state, 285–286, 294; secedes from the Union, 322; sets up government after the Civil War, 358; readmitted to the Union, 363–364

Louisiana Purchase, 180–181

Lowell, James Russell, 264

Lundy, Benjamin, 301, 302

Lusitania, sinking of the, 554

Lyceum lectures, 504

Lyon, Mary, 484

Lyon, Matthew, 170, 171–172

Lyon, General Nathaniel, 343

McAdoo, William G., 559

McClellan, General George B., made commander of Northern armies, 336; besieges Yorktown, 338; in Seven Days' Battle, 338; fails to take Richmond, 338; removed from command, 340

McDonald, John, 383

MacDonough, Lieutenant Thomas, 190

McDowell, General Irvin, 336

McHenry, Fort, *189*, 191

McKinley, William, 412, 535; in debate with Mills, 388; carries a high tariff bill, 389; elected president, 390–391, 407, 413; assassinated, 413; favors annexation of Hawaii, 436

McLoughlin, John, 293–294

McNary-Haugen Bill, 586

Madison, Dolly, 216

Madison, James, at Constitutional Convention, 129–130, 131, 135; in defense of rights of minority, 137; in defense of Constitution, 143, 144; opposition to the Funding Bill, 160; in opposition to National Bank, 163; in opposition to Hamilton, 164; as leader of Republican party, 169; elected to presidency, 185; as president, 185–195, 309; advises Monroe, 201

Maine admitted as a free state, 286

Manassas Junction, *339*; battle of, 335–336

Mann, Horace, 476, 477, 479

Mardi gras, 274
Marshall, John, in sympathy with French Revolution, 165; as Secretary of State, 173; as Chief Justice of Supreme Court, 175, 199-200; increases power of national government, 199-200; declares Georgia law void, 235
Maryland, ratifies Constitution, 144; remains within Union, 327-328; Lee invades, 339-340; stops taxation for churches and church schools, 479
Maryland Colony, government of, 21
Mason and Dixon's line, 285, *287*
Mass production, 487
Massachusetts, 135; ratifies Constitution, 144; opposed to Assumption Bill, 160-161; opposed to War of 1812, 192-194; and education, 477, 479, 480. See also Massachusetts Bay Colony, and American Revolutionary War
Massachusetts Bay Colony, founding of, 19; government of, 20-21, 25-29, 33-38, 56-59; religious intolerance in, 25-26, 33-38, 56-59; taxation in, 27; resistance to navigation and trade laws in, 56-59; charter taken away from, 62; resistance to Writs of Assistance in, 67-68. See also Boston Massacre, Boston Tea Party, Massachusetts
Mather, Increase, 59
Meade, George G., 349
Mechanics' Free Press, 261
Mellon, Andrew, 588
Merchant marine, 584-585
Merry, Anthony, 177
Meuse-Argonne drive, 563-564
Mexican War, *289, 291*; causes of, 287-289; campaigns of, 289-291; treaty concluding, 292-293
Miami Indians, 461, 462
Michigan admitted as a free state, 287
Middle class, life of, 217-218, 250-256, 274-276, 499-506
Middle West, development of democratic spirit in, 223-224; culture of, 244-250, 494-499
"Midnight judges," 175
Mikado, The, 540
Miles, General Nelson, 467

Miller, William, 255
Mills, Caleb, 476
Mills, Roger Q., 388
Mills Bill, 389
Milwaukee, early days of, 248
Minnesota Rate Case, 392
Missionary Ridge, battle of, 350
Mississippi, admitted as a slave state, 286; secedes from Union, 322; readmitted to Union, 364
Missouri, admitted as a slave state, 286, 294; remains with Union, 327-328
Missouri Compromise, 286, *287*, 296; repeal of, 298
Missouri Indians, 461
Money. See Paper money, *and* Silver, free coinage of
Monitor, the, 334, 335
Monroe, Fort, 338, *339*
Monroe, James, 180-181; administration of, 196-202; election of, 307, 309; Indian policy of, 455-456
Monroe Doctrine, 200-202
Montgomery, General Richard, 103-104
Monticello, 212
Moore, John Bassett, 576
Mormons settle Utah, 292-293
Morrill Act, 483
Morris, Gouverneur, 130, 214
Morris, Robert, 98, 130, 165, 206
Motion pictures, development of, 533-537
Mott, Lucretia, 259
Mount Holyoke Seminary, 484
Mount Vernon, 205
"Movies." See Motion pictures
"Mugwumps." See Independent Republican party
Musical comedy, 540-541
My Old Kentucky Home, 254

Napoleon Bonaparte, 167
Narraganset Indians, 36
Nashoba colony, 302-303
National Association of Baseball Players, 518
National Bank, establishment of first, 162-163; Republicans defeat attempts to renew charter of first, 195; establishment of second, 197; abolishment of second, 238-243
National Gazette, 169
National Government, 10, 11; powers

granted by Constitution to, 137; departments of, 155; disputes over the powers of, 172–173, 192–194, 234–238; Marshall adds to powers of, 199–200; dictatorial powers assumed by, 556. *See also* Senate, House of Representatives, etc.

National Labor party, 412

National League of Professional Players, 518, 519, 520

National Republicans, 307, 309. *See also* Adams, John Quincy

National Treasury, 242–243, 588

National Women's Rights Convention, 260

Native Americans. *See* Know-Nothing Party

Naval conferences: at Washington, 574–575; at Geneva, 576; at London, 577

Navigation Acts, 54–55; colonial resistance to, 55–63; enforcement of, 65

Nebraska, 295 (note); and Kansas-Nebraska Bill, 297–300

Negroes, sold in New York, 207; as slaves in South, 269, 276–278; and Emancipation Proclamation, 345–346; given freedom by Thirteenth Amendment, 355; in post-war South, 355, 359, 361, 366, 368–369; protected by Civil Rights Bill, 362; made citizens by Fourteenth and Fifteenth Amendments, 362–363, 368–369; and Republican party, 377. *See also* Slavery

Neutrality Proclamation, 168

New England Antislavery Society, 303

New England Emigrant Aid Society, 298

New Hampshire, 144, 479

New Jersey, 143. *See also* American Revolutionary War

New Mexico, ceded to United States, 293; and popular sovereignty, 296

New Orleans, battle of, 192; life in, 273–274; Union forces take, 338, 342–343, *342*

New York, Zenger trial in, 59–61; Washington inaugurated in, 154–155, 203; national capital at, 204–209; growth of, 250–251

New York state, 144, 480. *See also* American Revolutionary War

New York Tribune, 325, 335, 346

Nickelodeons, 532, 535

Nineteenth Amendment, 260, 428–429, 448

Nonintercourse Act, 185, 186, 193

Normal schools, 477

North, in conflict with South over making of Constitution, 135–136; in conflict with South over National Bank, 162–163; loses political power to South, 178; in conflict with South over states rights, 234–238. *See also* Civil War

North Carolina, ratifies Constitution, 145; resists taxation, 161; joins Confederacy, 327; readmitted to Union, 363–364

North Dakota, 295 (note)

Northwest Ordinance. *See* Ordinance of the Northwest Territory

Northwest Territory, capture of, 112; emigration to, 127; Ordinance of, 285, 476; Indian problem in, 450, 452; peace in, 458

Nullification of national laws, by Kentucky and Virginia, 172–173; by New England, 192–194; by Maryland, 234; by Georgia, 235; by the South, 235–236; by South Carolina, 237–238. *See also* Secession

Ogden, Reverend John, 172

Ohio, 219; joins Union as free state, 285; establishes free public high schools, 480

Ojibwa Indians, 461

Oklahoma, 295 (note)

Old Ironsides, 190

Old South Church, 78

Omaha Indians, 462

Open-ballot system of voting, 422, 424

Operetta, development of the, 540

Ordinance of the Northwest Territory, 285, 476

Ordinance of Nullification, 237–238

Ordinance of Secession, 322 (note)

Oregon admitted as a state, 294 (note)

Oregon territory, acquired by the United States, 293–294; as issue in presidential election of 1844, 313–314

Orlando, Vittorio, 565

Orpheum circuit, 538

Osage Indians, 462

Otis, James, 67-68
Ottawa Indians, 461

Pago Pago, 434
Paine, Thomas, 88-89, 130, 165
Pakenham, General Edward, 192
Panama Canal Zone, *434*; acquisition of, 440-441
Pan-American Congress, 579 (note)
Panic, of 1837, 241-243; of 1873, 384
Paper money, colonial, 61-62; continental, 96-98, 122-125, 126-127; during Civil War, 329-331
Parker, Captain, 81
Parker, Francis W., 490
Parliament, 17, 53, 54, 73, 74. *See also* House of Commons; Pitt, William; Townshend, Charles; etc.
Patrons of Husbandry. *See* Grange
Pawnee Indians, 460
Pea Ridge, battle of, 343
Pemberton, General J. C., 344
Pennsylvania, 62; founding of, 43; Scotch-Irish colonists in, 43; German colonists in, 43; Quakers in, 43, 44; struggle for democratic government in, 43-44; ratification of Constitution by, 143-144; the Assumption Bill and, 161
Pension system, after Civil War, 377; after World War, 583
Peoria Indians, 461
Perry, Commodore Oliver Hazard, 189-190
Pershing, General John J., 563
Petersburg, siege of, 352
Philadelphia, Second Continental Congress meets at, 83; British capture, 107; national capital at, 209-211; life in, 250
Philanthropist, The, 302
Philippines, *434*; acquisition of, 436-437; question of giving independence to, 437-438; problems concerning government of, 439-440; powers agree to respect American control of, 575; United States agrees not to fortify, 575
Pickering, Timothy, 127
Pickett, General, 349
Pierce, Franklin, 309, 315
Pierce, John D., 478
Pierce, William, 156

Pinafore, H. M. S., 540
Pinckney, Charles, 130
Pinckney, Charles Cotesworth, 130
Pioneers. *See* Frontier life
Pirates of Penzance, The, 540
Pitcairn, Major, 82
Pitt, William, 72
Pittsburg Landing. *See* Shiloh, battle of
Plymouth Colony, founding of, 19, 34, 59
Poland made independent, 567
Political parties, 309, 412; beginning of, 163-164; organization of, 375-376. *See also* Democrats, Federalists, National Republicans, Republicans, Republicans (Antifederalists), Social Democrats, Whigs, etc.
Polk, James K., 288, 309, 313
Poor Soldier, The, 206
Pope, General John, 338, 339
Popular education. *See* Public education
Popular sovereignty, *299*; provided by the Compromise of 1850, 296; as issue in election of 1860, 319
Population, comparison of British and American colonial, 93-94
Populist party, 402-407, 412, 426
Port Bill, 79
Porto Rico, *434*; acquisition of, 436
Potawatami Indians, 461
Prescott, Colonel, 101
Price, General Sterling, 343
Primary system. *See* Direct-primary system
Princeton, battle of, *105*, 106-107
Private ownership of utilities. *See* Public ownership of utilities versus private ownership
Progressive party, 590
Prohibition party, 592
Prohibition question, 592-593
Propaganda, 550-551
Prophet, the, 453, 454
Public education, development of, 477-485; effect of changing industrial civilization on, 487-488; curriculum changes in, 488-491
Public Information, Committee on, 560
Public lands, speculation in, 126-127. *See also* Homestead Act, *and* Crédit Mobilier
Public ownership of utilities versus private ownership: arguments, 409-411;

railroads placed under control of government, 559; railroads returned to private ownership, 583–584; merchant marine returned to private ownership, 584–585
Puritans, 19, 20, 26, 33–38
Putnam, General Israel, 100, 101

Quakers, in Massachusetts, 34, 57; in Pennsylvania, 43–44; in antislavery crusade, 301
Quartering Act, 79

Railroads, *329*; building of, 380–381, *380*; struggle of Grange with, 400–401; power of legislatures to fix rates of, 401; Interstate Commerce Act passed to restrain, 416; Hepburn Act passed to restrain, 418; United States Railroad Administration placed in control of, 559; returned to private owners, 584–585; Adamson Act and employees of, 588; demand for government control of, 590
Randolph, Edmund, 130, 137, 144, 156, 157, 163
Recall, the, 426, 430, 431
Reconstruction of the South, 357–370, *364*
Reconstruction Act, 363–364, 365
Referendum, the, 425–426, 430, 431
Reform movement, social, 256–263
Regulators, 45–46
"Reign of Terror" in America, 171–173
Religious intolerance in Massachusetts Bay Colony, 25, 33–38, 56–59
Reno, Marcus A., 466
Reparations, question of German, 573–574
Representative government, in Virginia, 23–25, 39–42; in Massachusetts, 25–29, 56–59; in Connecticut, 36–37; in Pennsylvania, 43–44; in North Carolina, 45–46; in New York and New Jersey, 58–59; demanded by Virginia Resolutions, 68–71. *See also* Suffrage, Congress, House of Representatives, Senate, etc.
Republican (Antifederalist) party, 309; origin of, and groups composing, 164; attitude toward France of, 166, 167–168; Jefferson and the, 169, 173–174; opposition to Alien and Sedition Laws by, 170–171. *See also* Republicans (Antifederalists), government under control of
Republican party, 309, 411–415; origin of, and groups composing, 316; Lincoln nominated by, 319; Lincoln elected by, 321; negro support sought by, 366; Ku-Klux Klan attempts to break power of, 367–368; control of South lost by, 369; political power held by, 374–375; groups composing, 376–377; McKinley nominated and elected by, 390–391, 406–407; Democratic party and the, 411–414
Republicans (Antifederalists), government under control of: 309, 176–202; reforms, 178–179; Louisiana Purchase, 180–181; internal improvements, 181–182; the Embargo and Nonintercourse Acts, 183–185; War of 1812, 185–195; second National Bank, 197; protective tariff, 197–199. *See also* Republican (Antifederalist) party
Republicans, government under control of: 309, 411–415; election and administration of Lincoln, 322–356; reconstruction policies, 357–370; "the Dreadful Decade," 379–386; McKinley tariff, 389; McKinley's administration, 390–391, 406, 407, 413; Dingley Tariff Bill, 391; Supreme Court decisions, 391–393; opposition of farmer and labor parties, 397–411; reforms, 416–429; foreign policies, 432–446, 570–582; domestic policies, 582–592. *See also* Republican party; Grant, Ulysses S.; Coolidge, Calvin; etc.
Reservations, Indian, *451, 469*
Revere, Paul, 82
Revue, development of, 539–540
Rhett, Robert, 305
Rhode Island, founding of, 35–36; paper money in, 122–123; Constitution accepted by, 145–146; education in, 477
Richmond, Confederate capital at, 322 (note); campaigns to capture, 338, 351–352
Ripley, George, 257

632 AMERICAN GOVERNMENT AND CULTURE

Rochambeau, General, 114
Roosevelt, Theodore, 412; as president, 413; recommends amending Interstate Commerce Act, 417–418; promotes civil-service reform, 422; approves initiative and referendum, 426, 427
Root, Elihu, 576
Rosecrans, General W. S., 350
Rumsey, James, 212
Russia, 409; United States refuses to recognize government of, 571–572

Sac Indians, 461, 462
St. Croix, *434*; purchase of, 442
St. John, *434*; purchase of, 442
St. Mihiel, battle of, 563
St. Thomas, *434*; purchase of, 442
Samoan Islands, *434*; acquisition of Tutuila in, 434–435
Saratoga, *108*; battle of, 107
Savannah, capture of, 351
Scalawags, 365–366, 367
School for Scandal, The, 206
Schurz, Carl, 420
Schuyler, General Philip, 100
Scotch-Irish colonists, 43
Scott, General Winfield, in Mexican War, 290; runs for president, 315; in Civil War, 335–336
Secession, New England threatens, 192–194; the South threatens, 295, 320; Lincoln opposed to, 317–318; South Carolina votes for, 322; Ordinance of, 322 (note); Mississippi, Florida, Alabama, Georgia, Louisiana, and Texas vote for, 322; Southern leaders defend, 323; division of United States over question of, *324*
Secondary schools. *See* High schools
Sedan, capture of, 564
Sedition Act (1798), 171, 172, 173, 192
Sedition Act (1918), 560–561
Self-government. *See* Representative government
Seminole Indians, 458, 461
Senate, conflicts over organization and powers of, 134–136; powers granted to, 138–140
Senators elected by direct vote of people, 427, 430. *See also* Senate
Seventeenth Amendment, 427
Seward, W. H., 360

Shantung returned to China, 575
Shawnee Indians, 461
Shays's Rebellion, 123–125
Sheridan, General P. H., 352
Sherman, General W. T., captures Atlanta and marches to the sea, 351; receives Johnston's surrender, 353
Sherman, Roger, 130, 203
Sherman Anti-Trust Act, passed, 418; evaded by corporations, 419; strengthened by Clayton Act, 419–420
Shiloh, battle of, 342
Shoshone Indians, 462
Silver, free coinage of, 403–408
Simms, William Gilmore, 280; defends slavery, 305
Sioux Indians, 462, 464–467
Sitting Bull, 465, 467
Slavery, 207, *324*; controversy during Constitutional Convention over, 136; attitude of Washington and Jefferson toward, 213; Missouri Compromise and, 286–287, *287*; the Compromise of 1850 and, 295–296; the Fugitive Slave Law and, 296–297; the Kansas-Nebraska Bill and, 297–300, *299*; the Dred Scott Decision and, 300–301; abolitionists crusade against, 301–304; leading Southerners defend, 305; split in Whig party over, 313; politics based on issue of, 315–321; proposed amendment protecting, 326; Emancipation Proclamation and, 345–346; Thirteenth Amendment abolishes, 355
Sloat, Commander, 290
Smith, Alfred E., 591
Smith-Hughes Act, 489
Social classes, in colonies, 30–31; in states following War for Independence, 121–127; political division of, 164; in the South (1830–1860), 268–269; in American society, 493–494
Social-Democratic party, 412; Debs nominated by, 408; political views of, 409–410; arguments against views of, 410–411
Society of Friends. *See* Quakers
Sons of Liberty, 70, 71, 72, 73, 78
South, in conflict with North over making of Constitution, 135–136; in conflict with North over National Bank, 162–163; comes into political power

INDEX 633

with Jefferson, 178; in conflict with North over states rights, 234–238; social life in, 269–274; life of poorer class in, 274–276; life of slaves in, 276–278; culture of, 279–280; postwar conditions in, 354–355; Reconstruction Period in, 357–370. *See also* Civil War

South Carolina, ratifies Constitution, 144; secedes from Union, 322; readmitted to Union, 363–364

South Dakota, 295 (note)

Soviet Republics, Union of Socialist. *See* Russia

Spanish-American War, 436

Specie, definition of, 241

Sphere of influence, definition of, 445 (note). *See* Haiti

Spoils system, beginning of, 231–233; Lincoln's opinion about, 420; growth of, 420; Civil Service Commission appointed to check, 421–422; gradual decline of, 422

Sports: baseball, 517–521; football, 521–524; tennis and golf, 524–527; miscellaneous, 527–528

"Squatter" sovereignty. *See* Popular sovereignty

Stagg, Alonzo A., 522

Stamp Act, 66; effect on English colonies of, 68; resistance to, 70–72; repeal of, 72

Stamp Act Congress, 70

Standish, Captain Miles, 34

Stanford, Leland, 533

Stanton, Edwin M., 364

Stanton, Elizabeth Cady, 259

"Star-Spangled Banner, The," 191

State government, responsibilities of, 10; powers granted by Constitution to, 136–137. *See also* Georgia, Massachusetts, Virginia, etc.

States rights, 172–173, 192–194, 234–238

Stevens, Thaddeus, 361

Stockton, Commander R. F., 290

Stone, Lucy, 259, 260

Stowe, Calvin E., 476

Strong, Caleb, 206

Submarine blockade by Germany, beginning of, 552–553; effects of, 554–555; American navy and, 562

Suffrage, in colonial Massachusetts, 25, 32, 33, 57, 58; in colonial Connecticut, 36–37; Jefferson's attitude toward, 180; struggle to secure more general, 224–226. *See also* Fourteenth Amendment, Nineteenth Amendment, Representative government, Voting

Sugar Act, 65–66

Sullivan, Arthur, 540

Sumter, Fort, 326–327

Supreme Court, 138, 140, 156; Adams appoints John Marshall to, 175; adds power to national government, 199–200; interprets Fugitive Slave Law in Dred Scott case, 300–301; favors Big Business, 391; reinterprets Fourteenth Amendment, 391–392; declares income tax unconstitutional, 392; declares workmen's compensation law unconstitutional, 393; makes decisions in favor of railroads, 416–417; denies Cherokees' right to sue Georgia, 461; orders oil lands to be returned to government, 589. *See also* Marshall, John

Swanee River, 254

Symposium Club, 256–258, 263

Taft, William H., 412; reforms opposed by, 426

Tammany Society, 173, 384

Tariff, 197–199, 581; Republicans in favor of, 377; Democrats opposed to, 378; maintained at high level (1860–1884), 388; Democrats fail in attempt to lower, 388–389; McKinley Bill raises, 389; Wilson-Gorman Bill fails to lower, 390; Dingley Tariff Bill raises, 391; Payne-Aldrich Bill reduces, 391; Underwood Tariff Bill reduces, 391; Fordney-McCumber Act and Hawley-Smoot Act raise, 586; differences within the political parties over, 590

Taxation, in colonial Virginia, 24; in colonial Massachusetts, 27; in later colonial Virginia, 40; in North Carolina, 45; under new Federal government, 161–162, 163; under Jefferson's Republican administration, 178–179; for education, 475, 477, 479; lowered, 588. *See also* Income tax

Taylor, Zachary, 288, 289, 309, 314, 315

Tecumseh, 453–455
Temperance movement, 259, 592–593
Tenement-dwellers, life of, 506–510
Tennessee, joins Union as slave state, 285; joins Confederacy, 327; reconstruction begins in, 358; readmitted to Union, 363
Tennis, 524–526
Tenth Amendment, 234
Tenure of Office Act, 364
Terry, General, 466, 467
Texas, Mexican control of, 287; Republic of, 288; admitted as slave state, 288; Mexican War over, 288–293, *289, 291*; secession from Union of, 322; readmission to Union of, 364
Textile machines, effect on slavery of invention of, 284
Theater, growing popularity of, 206–207, 253. *See also* Motion pictures, Vaudeville theater, Revue, Operetta, Musical comedy
Thirteenth Amendment, 355, 361
Thompson, William Tappan, 280
Thoreau, Henry, 256, 263–264
Ticonderoga, Fort, 102, *103, 108*
Tilden, Samuel J., 412
Tippecanoe Creek, 453; battle of, 454. *See also* Harrison, William H.
Tobacco-growing in South, 23
Tories, 77, 79, 84, 86, 94, 103, 110, 112
Town meeting, 29; restriction on, 79
Townshend, Charles, 73
Townshend Acts, 73; partial repeal of, 74
Trade, growth of, 53, 55, 62–63; international problems connected with, 580–581
Trade and industrial schools, 489
Trade laws, 54–55; colonial resistance to, 55–63; enforcement of, 65, 73
Trading companies, 19–20, 21, 25, 26, 51
Transcendentalists, 256–258
Treaty of Paris, 114–116
Trenton, *105*; American victory at, 106
Trial by jury, 28, 157; denial of rights to, 300, 461
"Triangular trade," 283
Triple Alliance, 549
Triple Entente, 549
Trusts, definition of, 418; attempts to break, 418–420
Tryon, Governor, 44

Turner, Nat, 303
Tutuila, *434*; acquisition of, 434–435
Tweed, William Marcy, 385
Tweed Ring, 384–386
Twelfth Amendment, 180
Tyler, John, 225, 233, 288, 309, 312

"Underground railroad," 297
Underwood Tariff, 391
Union Humane Society, 302
Union League Club, the, 366
Union Pacific Railroad scandal, 380–381
United States Gazette, 169, 173, 206
United States Lawn Tennis Association, 526
United States Railroad Administration, 559
Utah, *291*; settled by Mormons, 292; ceded by Mexico to United States, 293; made a territory, 293; and popular sovereignty, 296

Valley Forge, *105*; American army at, 109
Van Buren, Martin, 242; elected president, 308, 309; fails of reëlection, 312
Variety show, 537
Vaudeville theater, 537–539
Vera Cruz, American army lands at, 290
Vermont, 102, 103, 171, 172, 285
Vermont Gazette, 172
Versailles, Treaty of: terms, 567; rejection by Senate, 567–568; United States declines to take part in revision, 571
Versailles Peace Conference, 565–567
Veto, president's power of, 140
Vice president, method of electing, 153–154, 169
Vicksburg, *342*; fall of, 343–344
Virgin Islands, *434*; purchase of, 442
Virginia, ratifies Constitution, 144; opposes Assumption Bill, 160–161; joins Confederacy, 327; reconstruction in, 358; readmitted to Union, 364
Virginia, the, 333, 334
Virginia, University of, 212, 279
Virginia Colony, government of, 20, 21–25, 39–42; taxation in, 24, 40; resistance to navigation and trade laws in, 55–56; resolutions passed in assembly of, 69–70
Virginia Company, 19, 21, 23

INDEX

Virginia Resolutions, 172–173
Voting, reform in methods of, 422, 424. *See also* Suffrage

Walden, 264
Walker, Mary, 259, 260
Wall Street, New York, 206
War of 1812, causes of, 167–169, 183–186; groups in favor of, 187–188; campaigns of, 188–192; opposition to, 192–194; outcomes of, 194–195; Indians in, 455
War Hawks, 186, 187
War Industries Board, 558–559
Warner, Seth, 102
Washington admitted as a state, 294 (note)
Washington (capital), national capital established in, 177, 214; social life in, 177–178, 214–217; British capture of, 190–191; Jackson's inauguration at, 230–231; Confederate attempt to take, 351; scandal in connection with improving, 383
Washington, George, at First Continental Congress, 79; as commander in chief, 83–86, 100, 102–104, 106–111, 114, 115; working for strong central government, 128, 129, 131, 134; as president, 153–155, 156, 157, 162, 164, 165, 168, 203, 204, 212, 309; and Indians, 450–452
Washington, Martha, 205
Washington Conference. *See* Naval conferences
Watkins, Tobias, 233
Watt, James, 94
Weaver, James B., 401–402, 404
Webster, Daniel, 270; opposes second National Bank, 197; opposes protective tariff, 199; in debate with Hayne, 236–237; as co-author with Clay of Compromise of 1850, 296
Welles, Gideon, 360
West Virginia becomes separate state, 295 (note), 327
Whigs, 240, 309; origin and policies of, 307; Tyler opposes, 312; campaigns of, 312–315
Whisky Ring, 383
Whisky tax, 161–162
White House, the, 214, 230–231

Whiteman, Paul, 543
Whitman, Walt, 263, 264
Whittier, John Greenleaf, 264
Willard, Emma, 484
Willard, Frances E., 592–593
William and Mary College, 176
Williams, Roger, 35–36
Wilson, Woodrow, 412; promotes civil-service reform, 422; approves initiative and referendum, 426, 427; in favor of women's suffrage, 429; attempts to keep America out of World War, 551–555; calls for declaration of war, 555; becomes virtual dictator during war, 556; sets forth Fourteen Points, 561; at the Peace Conference, 565–567
Wilson's Creek, battle of, 343
Wilson-Gorman Bill, 390
Winthrop, John, 26, 27–28, **34–35**, 38
Wisconsin, 295
Women's Christian **Temperance Union**, 592–593
Women's suffrage, early movement for, 258–260; passage of amendment for, 428–429, 430
Woodward, Calvin, 488
Worden, Captain John L., 335
World Court, 576, 580
World War, outbreak of, 549; Allies in, 549–550; Central Powers in, 550; attempts to draw United States into, 550–551; events which brought United States into, 551–555; United States enters, 555–561; American navy in, 562; American army in, 563–564; close of, 564–565; making of peace treaty concluding, 565–567; Senate rejects treaty concluding, 567–568; conclusions from study of, 568; domestic economic problems following, 582–595
Wright, Frances, 258, 301, 302
Writs of Assistance, 66, 67, 68
Wyandot Indians, 462

Yancey, William L., 305
Yankee Stadium, 520
Yeardley, Sir George, 23
Yorktown, *113*; battle of, 114
Yugoslavia made independent, 567

Zenger trial, 59–61